ILLUMINATED
MANUSCRIPTS

GARLAND REFERENCE LIBRARY
OF THE HUMANITIES
(VOL. 89)

Plate I

ILLUMINATED MANUSCRIPTS
An Index to Selected Bodleian Library Color Reproductions

compiled and edited by
Thomas H. Ohlgren
Associate Professor of English
Purdue University

GARLAND PUBLISHING, INC. • NEW YORK & LONDON
1977

Library of Congress Cataloging in Publication Data

Oxford. University. Bodleian Library.
  Illuminated manuscripts.

    (Garland reference library of the humanities ; v. 89)
    1. Illumination of books and manuscripts, Medieval--
Catalogs. 2. Illumination of books and manuscripts,
Medieval--Indexes. 3. Illumination of books and manuscripts,
--Slides--Indexes. 4. Illumination of books and manu-
scripts--England--Oxford--Catalogs. 5. Illumination
of books and manuscripts--England--Oxford--Indexes.
6. Oxford. University. Bodleian Library. I. Ohlgren,
Thomas H., 1941-   II. Title.
ND2920.09 1977   016.7456'7'07402574   76-52689
ISBN 0-8240-9884-6

PRINTED IN THE UNITED STATES OF AMERICA

CONTENTS

v

ILLUSTRATIONS

All illustrations are from the slide sets listed in this volume. The SM (Slides Medieval) numbers refer to Purdue's shelving scheme; the first number denotes the abstract/ slide set number while the second indicates the frame/ slide number. The photographs are published with the kind permission of the Bodleian Library.

Plate I. *Frontispiece*
MS. Douce 296, f. 40 (SM 3-23), English, 11th, Psalter. Christ treading on the beasts.

Plate II. *facing page 1*
a. Abstract 9, MS. Canon. Liturg. 376 (SM 9-30), Italian/ Milan, 15th/ before 1402, Gospel Lectionary. Christ with book.
b. Abstract 46, MS. Douce 176 (SM 46-6), French/ Chelles, 9th/ c. 800, Gospel Lectionary. Zoomorphic capitals.
c. Abstract 414, MS. Canon. Misc. 248, f. 42 (SM 414-4), French, 14th/ 3rd quarter, Treatise on astronomy and the calendar. Zodiacal man.
d. Abstract 491, MS. Douce 213, f. 1 (SM 491-14), French/ Anjou (?), 15th/ before 1467, Boccaccio's *Decameron*. Garden with people listening to poet; Boccaccio sits outside garden listening and writing.

Plate III. *facing page 242*
a. Surgery, MS. e Mus. 19, f. 162 (SM 109-9), Italian, 14th/ 3rd quarter, Surgical tracts. Surgeon stands between operating table and naked patient fettered to table.
b. Medieval English Polyphony, MS. Rawl. C. 892, f. 67ᵛ-68 (SM 29-2), Irish, 12th, Gradual. Dicant nunc.
c. Hell, MS. Douce 134, f. 87 (SM 499-2), French, 15th/ c. 1450-70, *Livre de la Vigne nostre Seigneur*. Pool of fire and brimstone.

b. English/ Middle English, MS. Douce 104, f. 33 (SM 97-11), English, 15th/ 1427, *Piers Plowman* (C Text) by William Langland. Pilgrim with typical hat, staff bound with cloth, bell and scrip slung at his side.

c. French, MS. Digby 223, f. 77 (SM 201-7), French/ North (?), 13th, *Romance of Lancelot du Lac.* Lancelot exhorted by the hermit.

d. Italian, MS. Canon. Ital. 108, f. 41ᵛ-42 (SM 93-3), Italian/ South, 14th, Dante's *Divine Comedy.* Oderisi, the proud angel of humiliation.

Plate X. *facing page 346*

a. Matthew Paris (d. 1259), MS. Ashmole 304, f. 42, (SM 335-23), English/ St. Albans, 13th, Fortune Telling Tracts. Pythagoras writing.

b. Limbourg brothers, MS. Douce 144, f. 129 (SM 24-31), French/ Paris, 15th/ 1407, Book of Hours. St. Michael.

c. Herman Scheere, MS. Lat. liturg. f. 2, f. 146ᵛ (SM 84-22), Flemish/ English, 15th/ c. 1405-13, Book of Hours. Martyrdom of Archbishop Richard le Scrope.

d. Master of Mary of Burgundy, MSS. Douce 219-220, f. 186ᵛ (SM 14-42), Flemish, 15th/ c. 1480-90, Book of Hours. David and Goliath.

Plate XI. *facing page 348*

a. Bede, MS. Univ. Coll. 165, f. 26 (SM 253-18), English/ Durham, 12th, *Life of St. Cuthbert.* Angel serves heavenly bread.

b. Boethius, MS. Auct. F. 6. 5., f. viiᵛ (SM 253-1), English/ Winchester or Hereford (?), 12th, *de consolatione philosophiae.* Capital C frames Boethius, seated, writing book.

c. Chaucer, MS. Rawl. Poet 223, f. 183 (SM 132-7), English, 15th/ c. 1450-60, *The Canterbury Tales.* Beginning of the Tale of Melibeus.

d. Petrarch, MS. Canon. Ital. 69, f. 1 (SM 93-7), Italian/ Lombardy, 15th/ c. 1420-30, *Il Canzoniere.* Crowning of the poet.

PREFACE

W. O. Hassall

M.A., D.Phil., F.S.A., F.R.Hist. Soc.
Senior Assistant Librarian of the Bodleian Library
Librarian of the Earls of Leicester at Holkham

Custodians of great collections of manuscripts and early-printed books have the contradictory problem of preserving treasures for posterity while also making them accessible for scholarship. They can never exhibit more than a fraction of these treasures, and books exhibited can be displayed to reveal only a single opening of two facing pages.

While centuries must elapse before any high proportion of the contents of the manuscripts can be reproduced in color, on paper, the Bodleian Library has made many, many pages available by less conventional means, such as 35mm. color microfilm.

This work has proceeded for some fifteen years.* What has been produced on film can be used as separate slides. Many of the chief pages in the chief manuscripts are now thus accessible, although the proportion of what has been reproduced, compared with what could be reproduced, is not high. The quantity reproduced is, however, sufficiently great to present problems of retrieval, especially to those who are unfamiliar with the originals and who are physically far away from them.

Among those who have sought a solution to this problem, Professor Thomas Ohlgren has completed a remarkable work. Each of the Bodleian films is normally accompanied by a brief handlist that gives information about the source and nature of its contents. After six years' work, Professor Ohlgren has produced a computer-generated catalogue with indices of five hundred of the

*See "Colour Slides," *Bodleian Library Record*, July 1973.

xiii

Bodleian color microfilms. With its aid, scholars and teachers can find many references to visual materials both in the original manuscripts and in the large collection of slides, mounted from Bodleian Library films, at Purdue University. The original manuscripts are mostly in the Bodleian Library at Oxford. The Bodleian reproductions can be available in any library of the world that chooses to buy any of them, always provided that this is not prevented by the Customs and Imports regulations of its government.

The Bodleian Library welcomes this opportunity of explaining a number of important points:

The references in Professor Ohlgren's *Illuminated Manuscripts: An Index to Selected Bodleian Library Color Reproductions* are, of course, intended primarily as a key to the holdings at Purdue University. They are useful for identifying themes, styles, types of manuscripts, and Bodleian shelfmarks. When scholars use them for ordering material direct from the Bodleian Library, it is important to note that the "abstract" numbers in the index are not the same as the Bodleian Library roll numbers. The correct Bodleian roll numbers are listed in the abstracts under the heading **Negative Reference.** As there may be occasional ambiguities in the numbering of slides, those ordering individual slides should include the subject as well as the Bodleian reference number of each slide.

The Bodleian Library issues a printed price list of films, arranged by roll number. For historical reasons, some films record all the illuminations in one manuscript; others contain a selection of pictures with a common factor, such as subject or provenance, taken from one or more manuscripts. Often the original selections were made to meet the requirements of a particular scholar. Recently the Bodleian has produced a series of "Miscellany" filmstrips, which include omissions from earlier filmstrips together with material ordered by customers wanting only one or two slides that could not in themselves form an entire roll. Details of the earliest "Miscellany" films are available on the latest price list. It is hoped that more will be made available soon.

The Bodleian Library makes a great effort to keep a stock of every item listed. The earliest negatives, because of their age, may occasionally have faults. It is not practical, however, to rephotograph them, and the library has decided to continue to sell the originals even with such blemishes rather than to delete them from the series. The Bodleian cannot unfortunately undertake to lend, hire, or send any of its transparencies on approval.

The Bodleian Library's success in making tens of thousands of reproductions available to the world is mainly due to the assistance of a group of devoted, unpaid volunteers. As it is impossible to thank all by name, it seems invidious to name any of them. However, it would be unjust not to mention Mrs. G. Spriggs, Mrs. Stone, Mrs. L. Valentine, and the Hon. Mrs. Wilson among those who did much of the work of producing descriptions of the separate illuminations in some thousands of manuscripts. Other volunteers have made it possible for visitors to the Bodleian to have access to two series of mounted slides, from every existing roll. From these they may purchase anything required. One series is arranged in numerical order according to the handlist, the other under various broad topics. Apart from the series of slides available for sale, others are available in the Bodleian Library for consultation. One complete set is arranged by library shelfmark and page or folio number. Other select sets are arranged by date and locality of production, and by Biblical or other topic.

An obvious defect in the treasury of pictorial source material as yet available lies in the piecemeal nature of the coverage of some important manuscripts. It is hoped that this will be remedied by the production of color microfiches.

A defect of the handlists is that they have to be very brief indeed and contain inconsistencies. More leisurely and detailed descriptions of three dozen of the chief manuscripts, with some discussion of the styles, types of manuscripts, and the donors of the great collections from which they come, are assembled with reproductions in color, often of the original size, in A. G. and W. O. Hassall, *Treasures from the Bodleian Library* (Gordon Fraser, 1976).

It is important, also, to observe that no reproductions may be made from slides without prior permission from the Bodleian Library. Although all the photographs, with a few exceptions, are copyrighted by the Bodleian Library, the copyright of some of the originals belongs elsewhere.

The bulk of the reproductions are from Bodleian Western Manuscripts, but some printed material, notably of the John Johnson collection of printed ephemera, is included. Some of the manuscripts photographed belong to Oxford College Libraries and even to libraries outside Oxford, notably that at Holkham. The project, however, excludes all Oriental manuscripts in the Bodleian.

The vast accumulation of material now available presents a difficult problem of retrieval even to those familiar with it, and with the originals that it reproduces. Thomas Ohlgren has attacked this problem with great success. *Illuminated Manuscripts: An Index to Selected Bodleian Library Color Reproductions* is a valuable and useful contribution to medieval and Renaissance studies. Lecturers and research workers have now a means of finding what this corpus of visual information consists of that is relevant to their immediate needs, even though they have never before seen either the slides or the original manuscripts. Many will derive benefit from Professor Ohlgren's labors without realizing their debt to his index. For many, illustrated manuscripts and books will give a truer image of the past, thanks to the tool that Professor Ohlgren has provided for medieval research.

GENERAL INTRODUCTION
Thomas H. Ohlgren

The moment one enters the Duke Humphrey's Library in the Bodleian, a magnificent fifteenth-century chest, called the Chest of the Three Philosophies and the Seven Liberal Arts, comes into view. The chest once contained all the manuscripts pertaining to the study of the seven liberal arts—the *trivium* and the *quadrivium*—and the three philosophies (natural, moral, and metaphysical) given to Oxford University by Humphrey, Duke of Gloucester, the youngest brother of King Henry V. This great chest was founded for the benefit of students, and masters of arts, lecturing in these subjects, borrowed from it. Today, over five hundred years later, students and scholars around the world still have access to these and many other manuscripts in the form of color microfilms. The keeper of this chest of over nine hundred films is Dr. W. O. Hassall, Senior Assistant Librarian in the Department of Western Manuscripts. The transparencies reproduce with amazing clarity the illuminations and partial texts from the chief Western manuscripts and early-printed books, dating in the main from the ninth through the sixteenth centuries, in the Bodleian, several Oxford College libraries, and several other libraries.

The Bodleian Library microfilms, which are more faithful in coloration to the original illuminated folios than are reproductions on paper, are available to teachers and scholars at the surprisingly low cost of about ten cents per unmounted transparency. Largely because of the low price and high quality of these microfilms, Purdue University in West Lafayette, Indiana, has purchased, mounted as slide sets, and catalogued a large portion of the Bodleian collection. The holdings in the Medieval Photographic Archive at Purdue consist of over 750 mounted slide sets.

xvii

According to John Ruskin, "Great nations write their autobiographies in three manuscripts: the book of their deeds, the book of their words, and the book of their art. Not one of these books can be understood unless we read the two others." The book of deeds (history), the book of words (literature), and the book of art (manuscript and book illustration) are all richly represented in the Bodleian Library's vast collection of transparencies, and *Illuminated Manuscripts: An Index to Selected Bodleian Library Color Reproductions* is the key that unlocks this beautiful repository of knowledge about the ascent of Western man. This reference tool provides intellectual access to five hundred of the Bodleian slide sets containing some 20,000 color transparencies from over 1,100 manuscripts and books. This volume mainly contains descriptions of the illuminations and texts from the chief medieval manuscripts and Renaissance books in the Bodleian collection. A supplement, now in preparation, will provide access to an additional 250 Bodleian rolls. Some of the thousands of topics illustrated by the slides include: alchemy, allegory, architecture and castle life, arms and armor, astronomy and astrology, Biblical iconography, botanical and zoological illustration, calendars, Church history, Classical texts, costume, domestic life, drama, engineering, furniture, gardens, heraldry, maps, mathematical texts, medicine, military science, music, paleography, philosophy, poetry, romance, saints, tournaments, and typology.

This volume should appeal to a variety of users. For teachers, it provides means to illustrate historical periods once called dark. With the resurgence of interest in medieval and Renaissance studies, teachers at all levels will find its contents invaluable. Some teachers of early periods have discovered that academic subjects, such as history, literature, art history, and philosophy, can best be taught by employing a broad cultural approach. Such courses strive to demonstrate cultural correlatives and interrelations among the arts. This volume will facilitate the location of apposite photographic materials for teaching. For scholars and archivists, *Illuminated Manuscripts* constitutes a reference guide to the chief illuminated manuscripts and books in the Bodleian Library. Access to these documents is, of course, possible through other reference tools, but this volume is unique in giving descriptions of the iconography of each illuminated folio or page. Since each descriptor is followed by a frame number, individual slide retrieval is possible. For library scientists and literary historians, this volume provides access to documents that represent the history of the book from roll to codex. Many of the documents, in addition, are literary in nature. In the development of the book arts in the Western world, we must remember that only one-third of the book's history has been typographic. From the Egyptian papyrus rolls to the late medieval codex, the book was a scribal product. The inspiration to illustrate written texts is almost as old as writing itself. Illustrations in the form of diagrams and scenic drawings were incorporated into written texts to improve the reader's understanding by helping him remember important ideas and concepts in the text. Many illustrations were not mere decorative embellishments but had a didactic purpose: to describe and to explain through pictorial language the written word.

Each slide set is represented in this volume by a structured abstract. Each abstract is divided into a maximum of fourteen fields of information. The **Library** field contains the name of the library possessing the manuscript or book. The **Slide Set Title** field indicates the title assigned to the slide set by the Bodleian. The **Negative Reference** field contains the roll number assigned to each filmstrip by the Bodleian; when ordering rolls from the Bodleian Library, the purchaser must cite this number. The **Rental Fee** field contains the fee for renting the slide set from Purdue University; for specific information on how to place a rental order, see the instructions for users at the end of the introduction. The **Comments** field contains a natural-language description of the slide set. The **Title of Manuscript** field indicates the name, other than the shelfmark, assigned to the manuscript or book by the Bodleian. The **Shelfmark** field indicates the cataloguing scheme employed by the Bodleian in shelving the original manuscript or book. The **Provenance** field contains the country and, if known, the city in which the document originated.

The **Date Executed** field indicates the century and, if known, the year in which the manuscript or book was produced. The **Language** field indicates the language of the text. The **Artist/ School** field indicates the name of the artist or scribe or the school of illumination. Similarly, the **Author** field permits access to the works of specific authors whose texts may or may not be illustrated. The **Type of Manuscript** field classifies each manuscript according to dominant generic type, e.g., bestiary, chronicle, herbal, or psalter. The **Contents** field, finally, consists of a keyphrase description of the contents of each slide in the set. Each keyphrase is followed immediately by a numerical code: the number before the slash indicates the specific set in Purdue's collection; the number after the slash indicates the specific slide within the set. The index generated from the **Contents** field permits individual slide retrieval.

The index comprises eleven separate indices, one for each field of information in the five hundred abstracts, except for the **Library**, **Rental Fee**, and **Comments** fields, which were not indexed. To locate specific slide sets or even specific slides within the collection, users have a number of avenues of access, depending upon their areas of interest or specialization. If you are interested in bestiaries, for instance, you should probably turn first to the **Type of Manuscript** index, where you will find two types of listings: (1) the term *bestiary*, followed by a list of thirteen abstract numbers in the right-hand column; these numbers indicate that there are at least thirteen slide sets devoted to bestiary illumination; (2) beneath the main entry are sixteen listings with double numerical codes, such as 177/5-6; this indicates that only part—slides 5 and 6—of set 177 contains bestiary illuminations. You should also refer to the term *bestiary* in the **Contents** index. Here you will find some seventeen entries, including 263/55-93, which is not cross-listed under **Type of Manuscript**. Thus, it is wise to check a number of indices to make sure you have located all of the examples in the collection.

All indices lead users to the appropriate abstracts, which, in turn, lead you to (a) the desired slide sets at Purdue; (b) the unmounted rolls at the Bodleian Library; or (c) the original manuscripts themselves in Oxford. For some scholars no verbal description or even a photographic reproduction will suffice. To permit direct access to the manuscripts, Bodleian shelfmarks have been provided, although folio numbers by necessity have been omitted.

To place a rental order from Purdue University, supply the abstract number, the title of the slide set, the desired date of use, the shipping address, and the billing address. The fee listed under the **Rental Fee** field in each abstract is for two days of use. Shipping time is not charged. For each additional day of use, the cost is one-fifth of the base rate. In addition, you will be charged for shipping costs. Return all shipments to Purdue by the same carrier that was used to ship the slide set to you. For reservations, cancellations, changes, corrections, or extensions, call the Audio-Visual Center at 1-317-749-6188 or write Purdue University, Audio-Visual Center, Stewart Center, West Lafayette, Indiana 47907.

Scholars are also welcome to use the Bodleian collection at Purdue University. Facilities for viewing the slides as well as for study and research are available in the Audio-Visual Center. For reservations, write or call the Audio-Visual Center.

It is important to note that the *unmounted* rolls of transparencies can be purchased directly from the Bodleian at a cost comparable to renting the mounted slide set from Purdue University. Once mounted, of course, the purchased slides become part of your institution's permanent collection.

This volume is the result of six years's labor and support by many individuals here and abroad. I am indebted to Dr. W. O. Hassall, who encouraged this project from its inception in 1969; to John Leyerle, former Chairman of the Mediaeval Academy's Standing Committee on Centers and Regional Associations (CARA), who provided me with several opportunities to present papers on this project at scholarly conferences; to the National Endowment for the Humanities for a Younger Humanist Fellowship in 1973-1974 that permitted me to complete the data gathering in England; to Robert L. Ringel, Dean of the School of Humanities, Social

Sciences, and Education at Purdue, who provided funds to acquire over 750 rolls of Bodleian filmstrips; to Jacob H. Adler, Head of the Department of English at Purdue, who provided funds to mount the collection of slides; to David Moses, Carl Snow, and Roberta Kovac, who coordinated the massive job of filing the collection in Purdue's Audio-Visual Center; to Sarah Rawlings, Linda Carmody, and Nancy Shah, who aided in the keypunching of over one million characters of text; to Chaim Weissmann, who tirelessly coded the five hundred abstracts and provided the *Coder's Introduction*; to Gary C. Lelvis, former Team Manager of General Systems at Purdue, who provided invaluable technical assistance; and finally to Peter L. Jobusch, Senior Systems Analyst, who patiently solved the many technical problems that would have prevented the successful completion of the project.

CODER'S INTRODUCTION
Chaim B. Weissmann

In the Summer of 1973, while a graduate student in English at Purdue University, I was given the opportunity by Professor Thomas Ohlgren to begin coding the abstracts for *Illuminated Manuscripts: An Index to Selected Bodleian Library Color Reproductions*. Four years and some 20,000 slides later, my work is finally completed. An awareness of the coding problems faced, the solutions developed, and the final methodology evolved should help the user to better utilize this index as a pedagogical and scholarly reference work.

The initial limitation was one of time. Because of the large amount of data, it was impossible to check each slide against the Bodleian handlists that accompany each set. Consequently, the handlists were our main source of information. The lists, however, had been compiled over a long period of time by many hands. The quantity and quality of the data varied greatly. Whenever possible, we consulted Pächt and Alexander's *Illuminated Manuscripts in the Bodleian Library* (Clarendon Press, 1966-1973), particularly as a check on details of dating, origin, and artist and school. We accepted Pächt and Alexander's data as definitive, even when it contradicted information in the handlists. We were unable, however, to verify the accuracy of information in every abstract, particularly those containing illustrations from a large number of different manuscripts. In addition, it was not possible to verify data about manuscripts not included in Pächt and Alexander. The verification effort was greatly helped by Dr. Hassall and his staff, who provided us with a large number of corrections.

Coding operations were further complicated because the Bodleian filmstrips lack a uniform principle of selection. Some sets represent the sequential filming of the illuminations of a single manuscript text, such as Bodleian roll 131A (Abstract 21), containing 144 illustrations from a twelfth-century English manuscript of Terence's *Comedies*. Others contain the illuminations from a number of different manuscripts based upon a common topic, motif, or person, such as Bodleian roll 132 (Abstract 22), "Treasures of Corpus Christi College," containing sixty-eight slides from nine manuscripts of the twelfth to the sixteenth centuries. Still others contain only text and no illustrations, such as Bodleian roll 129 (Abstract 19), "History of Printing." In the latter case, the **Contents** field was left blank and the descriptions of each text were placed in the bibliographic fields. It was left to the coder to translate this diverse and complex material into a structure suitable for computer processing.

In the *Programmer's Introduction*, Gary Lelvis lists certain shortcomings in the computer programs. Of these, the restrictions on the length of phrases and the use of internal punctuation, such as commas, forced us to compose highly compressed descriptions, especially in the **Contents** field. The syntax of some of the indexed phrases is by necessity paratactic, that is, lacking coordinating elements. Users should consult the abstract entries, where they will find the terms in each phrase separated by slashes.

Additional coding problems concern the **Negative Reference** field. The numbers assigned by the Bodleian to each roll of unmounted transparencies consist of a roll number plus a part number, as in rolls 79A, 101B, and 113E. The Bodleian employed the alphabetic code for the parts up through roll 212K, after which they switched to a numeric code for the parts, as in rolls 213.1, 218.11, and 260.4. To maintain consistency, we adhered to the earlier scheme throughout. As a result, rolls 213.1, 218.11, and 260.4 are listed as 213A, 218J, and 260D in this volume.

As outlined in the *General Introduction*, each of the five hundred abstracts contains up to fourteen fields of information. With the exception of the **Contents** field, the coding of the fields was relatively straightforward. The **Contents** field, however, presented several problems. First, since the index consists of alphabetically arranged keyphrases, we had to anticipate what initial keyword in each phrase would be the most useful for users. When coding Biblical scenes, the choice of the initial keyword was relatively simple. We adhered to standard classification schemes for Christian art. Thus, common terms such as "Agony in the Garden," "Annunciation," "Ascension," "Baptism," "Crucifixion," "Deposition," "Entombment," etc., were used as the initial terms in phrases describing events in the life of Christ. Problems arose, however, when describing secular iconography, particularly when the persons in the scenes are not identifiable by name. Consequently, we had to employ generic nouns, such as "knight," "lady," "man," "woman," and "peasant," as the initial terms in many keyphrases. Second, time and space prohibited a complete listing of every iconographic motif in each slide. In a typical illumination from the *Romance of Alexander*, for instance, the major motif is "Alexander exhorting his troops." In the same scene, however, are ships, castles, armored knights, plumed horses, and war machines. Since space prohibited the separate listing of each motif, we assume that users will know to look for these details in abstracts of romances, chronicles, and histories. In addition, if a topic, such as "astrolabe," appears frequently in a set, we did not necessarily list it in the initial position every time. We listed items in as many different ways as possible, in order to increase the avenues of access. As a general rule, then, users should always consult the abstract in question, where they may find additional examples of the desired motif. Third, contrarieties in spelling were a constant problem. Some of the variety of forms were due to differences between British and American spelling, such as "ploughing" and "plowing." Other irregularities were due to the deliberate inclusion of manuscript spellings, and no attempt was made to normalize them. Finally, because of the large quantity of Bodleian handlists, many of which contain data in a multitude of foreign languages, we were unable to verify the correct spelling of every term. In addition, it was not possible to include accents or diacritical marks.

PROGRAMMER'S INTRODUCTION
Gary C. Lelvis

The following comments are intended for humanists interested in computer applications in the humanities. Manual methods of indexing scholarly material, which have been used for centuries, are effective only up to a point, after which the volume and complexity of the material can overwhelm the most carefully planned research effort. With the cost of manual labor rising and the cost of computer operations falling, common sense would seem to dictate considering the computer as an essentially clerical aid, to store, manipulate, and retrieve the data created by the researcher.

A recent article by Stanley Klein points out rather well the contrast between the traditional and computational approaches to indexing. The article, "Homer, Plato, and Aristotle Meet the Minicomputer" (*Mini-Micro Systems*, January 1977, pp. 22, 26), describes a Latin thesaurus project, started in Munich in 1894, which to date is completed to letter "N." The data base consists of nine million words, handwritten on file cards stored in thousands of shoe boxes. The projected completion date is 2025 A.D. By contrast, Klein also describes a more recent project at the University of California at Irvine where a Greek thesaurus is being developed with the aid of a computer. The ninety-million-word project has already generated eighteen million words of data in only a few years time.

We wish to make clear, however, that the computer is no panacea to problems of data storage, manipulation, and retrieval. The use of computers in humanistic research may not be as routine as it seems. It is, of course, a myth that indices, concordances, and thesauri magically appear by powering-up your local IBM 370 and pushing the button. The preparation of the information for this volume consumed about three years of manual labor before the abstracts were keypunched. We have learned that: (1) a computational approach in the humanities is a very complex matter, involving human, political, and technical considerations; (2) good organization and planning from the beginning are essential to the success of the computer-aided project; and (3) resource and policy limitations can seriously restrict the range of choices available and, indeed, directly affect the final results.

Before embarking on such a project, the researcher would be well advised to consult the standard journals in the field, such as *Computers and the Humanities* (CHum), *Computer Studies in the Humanities and Verbal Behavior*, and *Computers and Medieval Data Processing* (CAMDAP). Both CHum and CAMDAP list research projects in progress. For a survey of computer applications in medieval studies, readers should consult "Computers and the Medievalist" by Vern Bullough, Serge Lusignan, and Thomas Ohlgren (*Speculum* 49, April 1974, pp. 392-402) as well as David Herlily's "Computer-Assisted Analysis of the Statistical Documents of Medieval Society," *Medieval Studies: An Introduction*, pp. 185-211 (Syracuse University Press, 1976).

A review of the projects completed, in progress, and especially those aborted will help potential users to make the basic decisions that will directly affect the results to be obtained. What follows are some questions that might be considered before undertaking a computer-assisted approach. First, what is the form of the raw data? Is it convertible to machine-readable form or must it be generated anew? We must remember David Vance's warning that a commitment to complete, verify, or update records before input would probably exclude forever the very information the computer's data file is intended to make available. If just ten minutes were spent creating, verifying, or updating each of the descriptions of the 20,000 transparencies in the Bodleian collection, it would take one researcher over 3,000 hours to prepare the data prior to input. The first step, then, is to determine the nature and quality of the existing data. Even if some of our data is incomplete or even inaccurate, we would maintain that the purpose of this volume is to guide researchers to documents they can study and, if necessary, reclassify for themselves. Other questions include: In what machine-readable format is the data to be recorded for the most efficient and accurate conversion? What conversion devices are to be used? What facilities and procedures are needed for editing and updating the converted data to insure maximum accuracy consistent with cost? What facilities are required to store and to retrieve the converted data? What are the limitations of the hardware and software? How is the data to be published? All of these questions must be answered at the beginning of the project.

Considering the charges for professional programming time today, the cost of development of an in-house information system was considered prohibitive. Our solution was to obtain a commercially available, generalized package of indexing programs. Fortunately, the BIRS (Basic Information Retrieval Systems) package, offered by the Information Systems Laboratory at Michigan State University, came to our attention. Its purpose is to offer a variety of facilities through which customized information systems can be constructed by educators with a minimum of data-processing experience.

The package of programs provides six functions: (1) storage of converted data; (2) ability to update the stored data; (3) printing of the abstracts; (4) printing of KWIC and KWOC indices based on individual words or phrases; (5) printing of KWOC indices with accompanying abstracts; and (6) retrieval of applicable abstracts and printing of reports in response to specific questions posed by users. We have employed the first five functions to develop this volume; the sixth has not yet been fully exploited.

Although BIRS has proved both economical to purchase and adaptable to our general needs, the program package contained limitations that shaped the format and structure of the contents of this volume. Because of economic and other considerations, we were unable to rectify the flaws by reprogramming the system. The first shortcoming was that keyphrases were restricted to no more than ten terms or sixty-five characters, including the numerical code. As a result, some of the keyphrases are highly compressed. When ten terms were not enough to describe adequately the contents of each slide, a second or even a third entry was added. Second, since we generated keyphrase KWOC indices, each phrase had to begin with the most important term in the phrase. Consequently, the syntax of some of the phrases is awkward if not ungrammatical. However, had we generated an alphabetical listing of every term in every keyphrase, we would have produced over 2,500 pages of data. Third, the use of internal punctuation, such as commas, semicolons, and periods, which would have clarified syntactic relations among terms, was prohibited by the programs. The restriction on internal commas forced us to use slashes as delimiters within keyphrases, such as:

FEMALE ALLEGORICAL FIGURES/TRUTH/PURITY/HUMILITY/POVERTY 13-111.

Although the slashes appear correctly in the abstracts, they were deleted from the indices. In addition, apostrophes mysteriously disappeared from the indices and were replaced by slashes. Fourth, numerical terms were sorted in the indices out of numerical sequence: the term 3-20 sorted before the term 3-2. Also, a term such as 5-5 was truncated and printed as 5.

Whenever the decision is made to acquire a package of programs for a particular purpose, limitations will be encountered. The program designers, too, must work under technical and economic restrictions and thus make some hard choices. As users, we must find the best possible liaison between our needs and the available facilities.

From a technical point of view, this project has been successful. A usable package of programs was purchased at a reasonable price, installed, and operated to produce the contents of this volume. Future developments may include the ability to update and to retrieve data through the use of remote terminals. A growing problem that could preclude such developments is the limited amount of computer time available. The Bodleian Library data base now contains over one million characters of data. To process this data takes about three hours of central processing time on a shared computer facility. Allowing access to the data through a terminal during regular working hours would have a severe impact on other terminal users.

For additional technical information about this project, readers should consult "Medieval and Renaissance Photographic Information Retrieval" by Thomas Ohlgren (*Computer Studies in the Humanities and Verbal Behavior*, November 1972, pp. 228-230) and "The Digital Scriptorium: Computer Indexing of Medieval Manuscript Illuminations" by Thomas Ohlgren and Gary Lelvis (*Art and Archaeology Research Papers*, December 1973, pp. 149-157).

TECHNICAL NOTE
Peter L. Jobusch

Computer processing to produce this volume required three hours of central processing time on an IBM 370 model 145 computer with an OS/VS1 operating system. The following table summarizes the tasks performed, the time required, and the storage needed:

Task	CPU Time	Partition size
1. to prepare abstract listings		
a. card preprocessing	23 minutes	64K
b. non-BIRS text formatting	37 minutes	120K
2. to generate information file	30 minutes	120K
3. to prepare contents index	45 minutes	150K
4. to prepare other indices	47 minutes	150K

Fifteen thousand punched cards were required to contain the one million characters of information entered into the system.

To overcome format limitations of BIRS, the abstract listings were processed by TEXT-360. This approach required the additional reprocessing of the punched cards to put them into a format acceptable by TEXT-360.

The printouts were produced on an IBM 1403-N1 lineprinter equipped with a TN print chain. This volume was photographically reproduced from the output.

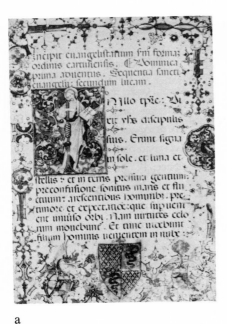

a

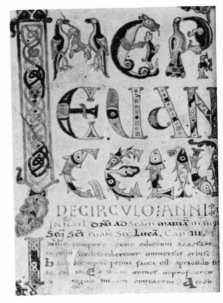

b

c

d

Plate II

```
*$ABSTRACT 1
 *LIBRARY BOD
 *SLIDE SET TITLE ROMANCE OF ALEXANDER
 *NEGATIVE REFERENCE ROLL 79
 *RENTAL FEE SM 001 $8.05
 *TITLE OF MANUSCRIPT ROMANCE OF ALEXANDER
 *SHELFMARK MS BODLEY 264
 *PROVENANCE FLEMISH
 *DATE EXECUTED 14TH/1338-1344
 *LANGUAGE FRENCH
 *ARTIST/ SCHOOL JEHAN DE GRISE
 *TYPE OF MANUSCRIPT ROMANCE
 *CONTENTS ALEXANDER/ ROMANCE  1/1-105, ROMANCE OF ALEXANDER
  1/1-105, ALEXANDER IN TENT 1-1, FORT ON BOATS 1-1, ALEXANDER
 IN TENT 1-2, GREEKS ATTACKED BY GAZAITES 1-2, GREEKS FORAGING
 IN THE VAL DE JESAFAILLE 1-2, ALEXANDER UNINFORMED OF BATTLE
 1-2, ALEXANDER AT JERUSALEM  1-3, ALEXANDER RECEIVES LETTER
 FROM DARIUS 1-3, ALEXANDER CONFRONTS PERSIANS 1-3, ALEXANDER
 CONFRONTS PORUS AND ASSAULTS HIS CITY 1-4, BUCEPHALUS   1-5,
 ALEXANDER   RELEASES  DEVIL  1-5,  DEVIL  AND  ALEXANDER  1-5,
 ALEXANDER'S HOST WITH CART 1-5, ALEXANDER RECEIVES LETTER 1-6,
 CROSSBOWS 1-6, MELCHIS EPISODE 1-7, ALEXANDER AND MELCHIS 1-8,
 HORSE-SHOEING  1-8,  CASSAMUS  WITH  YOUTHS  AND  LADIES  1-9,
 MUSICIANS  1-9, FRONTISPIECE TO RESTOR DU PAON 1-10, ALEXANDER
 AND KNIGHTS AT GATEWAY 1-10, ALEXANDER'S DEATH PRESAGED BY
 MONSTER  1-11,  MONSTER  1-11,  FEAST  1-11,  AVENGING OF ALEXANDER
 1-12, CAPTURE OF GADRES  1-13,  ALEXANDER  APPROACHES  ASCALEN
 1-13, BARREL IN CART 1-13, ALEXANDER WITH ELEPHANT AND CASTLE
 CONFRONT PORUS 1-14, DRUMMER BOY  1-14,  ALEXANDER  AND  PORUS
 1-15, MORRIS BOARD 1-15, WELL HEAD  1-16, LADIES ON MOUNT
 RECEIVE MESSAGE 1-16, DOG TAUGHT TO BEG  1-16, DIVINUS PATER
 AND ANTIPATER WORRIED BY LETTER 1-17, LOVERS 1-17, ALEXANDER
 RECEIVES MESSAGE VIA CANDALUS  1-18,  DOMINICAN  SERMON  1-18,
 ALEXANDER'S  ASCENT  1-19, ALEXANDER'S ASCENT  1-20, ADMIRAL
 PREPARES BABYLON AGAINST ALEXANDER 1-21, BABYLON AND ALEXANDER
 1-21, QUINTAIN 1-21, SOLDIER HAMMERS PEG 1-22, TURN SPIT 1-22,
 SALTIRE 1-22, CAVALRY FIGHT 1-23, GAME ON SIX-LEGGED TABLE
 1-23, ADMIRAL AND KING GALIGOR IN COUNCIL 1-24, TWIRLING BASIN
 ON STICK  1-24, THOLOMER DEMANDS FIRST BLOW IN BATTLE 1-25,
 COCK ON STILTS 1-25, ALEXANDER ARMS AGAINST ADMIRAL  1-26,
 HUNTSMAN 1-26, ADMIRAL'S RICH TOMB 1-27, BOYS IN ORCHARD 1-27,
 QUEEN  OF  FEMINIE ASLEEP 1-28, QUEEN SENDS TO MAKE PEACE WITH
 ALEXANDER  1-29,  QUEEN'S  MAIDEN  MESSENGERS  APPROACH  1-30,
 MONKEYS IN BARROW 1-30, ALEXANDER'S FEAST  1-31, FEAST OF
 ALEXANDER 1-31, BALANCING 1-31, ALEXANDER WATCHES FIGHT BY
 MAGIC MEN 1-32, DONKEY-CART 1-32, ESCHEVIE 1-33, GAMBLERS
 1-33, CASSAMUS AND LADIES  1-34, GAME OF MORELLES 1-34,
 CASSAMUS TALKING  1-35, YOUTH AND LADY 1-35, ALEXANDER AND
 GADIFER AND CASSAMUS ACCEPT SWORDS OF EMENIDUS 1-36, GAME OF
 LADLE AND CAULDRON 1-36, CASSAMUS AGAINST MARCIENS 1-37,
 JUGGLER TWIRLING BASIN 1-37, PORUS ATTACKED 1-38, BUTTERFLIES
 1-38, MARCIENS AND CASSAMUS TALK 1-39, HOSTAGES 1-39, CLARUS
 ENCOURAGES HIS MEN BEFORE  BATTLE  1-40, SHIP OF KING WITH
 RUDDER/ BOWSPRIT AND FORECASTLE 1-40, ALEXANDER BEFORE BATTLE
 1-41, MUSICIANS 1-41, ALEXANDER TAKING GENTLY 1-42, ALEXANDER/
 ZONIE/ PORUS/ EDEUS/ YDORIA/ BAUDRAIN/ MARCIENS FEAST 1-43,
 MUSICIANS 1-43, ALEXANDER ARRANGES HIS HOST 1-44, MUSICIANS
 1-44, BAUDRAIN GRASPS ALEXANDER'S SWORD 1-45, SWORD OF
 ALEXANDER 1-45, CARTLOAD 1-45, PORUS WOUNDED 1-46, KING GETS
 LETTER 1-47, MESSENGERS WITH JAVELINS 1-47, ELIOS TALKS WISELY
 1-48, LADY WITH HAWK  1-48, MUSICIANS  1-48, MOURNERS  1-49,
 ALEXANDER ENCAMPED 1-50, ALEXANDER GOES TO CITY OF PORUS 1-50,
 ALEXANDER AT WAR WITH ADMIRAL 1-51, ALEXANDER WARNED IN LETTER
 BY MOTHER OLIMPIAS 1-52, EMERIDIUS TAKES THE CITY 1-53, NEWS
 OF ALEXANDER 1-53, BAUDRIAN CAPTURED 1-54, CLAP-NET AND HAWKS
 1-54, FISHING ON DRAWBRIDGE 1-55, PORUS AND PLORIDUS JOUST
 1-55, ROBBER BEHEADED 1-56, AYMES SHEATHES SWORD AND WALKS
 WITH DAMSEL 1-56, AYMES SHOWS CHEST 1-57, YOUTH WITH BOUND
 HANDS 1-57, DAMSEL KNEELS 1-57, LADY LIFTED OFF HORSE  1-58,
 KING BETWEEN BRIDE AND BRIDEGROOM 1-59, FEAST 1-59, EDEA
 BEHIND TABLE WITH PEACOCK  1-60, PORUS LEADS HORSE 1-60,
 BAUDRAIN AND SWORD 1-60, MARCIENS AND HAWK 1-60, GADIFER AND
```

1

BANNER 1-60, CAULUS AND HELMET 1-60, REVEL OF ELIOS AND
EMENIDUS 1-61, ALEXANDER ASKS NEWS OF STRANGER 1-62, ALEXANDER
TALKS TO THOLOMER 1-63, YOUTH HOLDS UP APPLE 1-64, ALEXANDER
SPEAKS TO EMENIDUS 1-64, SCYTHE AND HOOK 1-65, SAWYERS 1-66,
JUMPING THROUGH HOOP 1-67, CAPE TO BREAK FALL 1-67, BLIND MEN
MISLED 1-68, BATHROOMS/ TWO 1-69, LADIES SPORT 1-70, LURE/ TWO
WINGS ON A CORD 1-70, BLIND MAN AND DOG 1-71, POT-RACK 1-72,
FORGE 1-72, ALEXANDER BESIEGES THE ADMIRAL 1-73, FORGE WITH
BELLOWS 1-73, MONKEYS CAROUSING AND IN CLASS 1-74, QUEEN OF
FEMINIE AND ALEXANDER 1-75, COCKS FIGHTING 1-75, BAGGAGE TRAIN
1-76, TILTING 1-77, POLISHING AND GRINDING A SWORD 1-78,
SWORD/ POLISHING AND GRINDING 1-78, TILTING 1-79, STAG-HUNTING
1-80, FOWLERS 1-81, FALCONERS WITH PERCHES AND AND LURES 1-82,
FIRE WITH ANDIRONS AND STORK'S NEST 1-82, VINTNERS 1-83,
BUTTERFLIES 1-84, KNIGHT WITH ATTENDANTS 1-85, KNIGHT WITH
ATTENDANTS 1-86, RIDERS 1-87, KNIGHTS WITHOUT HORSES 1-88,
KNIGHTS WITHOUT HORSES 1-89, LONGBOWS AND CROSSBOWS 1-90,
PORRUS STABS ALEXANDER'S HORSE 1-91, DRINK AT SALTIRE 1-91,
KNIGHTS AND HORSES 1-92, PAGES AND HORSES 1-93, COOKING 1-94,
CATAPULT AND BALISTA 1-95, VICTUALLERS 1-96, WINDMILL 1-97,
MAID GIVES HEART TO YOUTH 1-99, GRAVEDIGGERS 1-99, WINDMILL
1-100, BAGGAGE CART 1-101, CRIPPLES FIGHT 1-102, SCHOLARS
1-103, TWINS 1-104, SMITHS 1-105

*$ABSTRACT 2
  *LIBRARY BOD
  *SLIDE SET TITLE SIGNS OF JUDGMENT
  *NEGATIVE REFERENCE ROLL 89
  *RENTAL FEE SM 002 $2.70
  *TITLE OF MANUSCRIPT LA VIGNE NOTRE SEIGNEUR
  *SHELFMARK MS DOUCE 134
  *PROVENANCE FRENCH
  *DATE EXECUTED 15TH/C1450-70
  *LANGUAGE FRENCH
  *ARTIST/ SCHOOL RELATED TO CHANTILLY/ MUSEE CONDE
  *TYPE OF MANUSCRIPT LIFE OF CHRIST/VINEYARD OF OUR LORD
  *CONTENTS APOCALYPSE/ SIGNS OF JUDGMENT 2/1-18, SIGNS OF
JUDGMENT 2/1-18, JUDGMENT SIGNS 2/1-18, JUDGMENT/ 1ST SIGN
2-1, SEA RISES TO MOUNTAIN TOPS 2-1, JUDGMENT/ 2ND SIGN 2/2,
SEA DESCENDS OUT OF SIGHT 2/2, JUDGMENT/ 3RD SIGN 2-3,
GATHERING TOGETHER OF FISH AND SEA MONSTERS 2-3, JUDGMENT/ 4TH
SIGN 2-4, WATERS BURN 2-4, JUDGMENT/ 5TH SIGN 2-5, TREES AND
PLANTS SWEAT BLOOD 2-5, JUDGMENT/ 6TH SIGN 2-6, BUILDINGS AND
TOWNS FALL TO THE GROUND 2-6, JUDGMENT/ 7TH SIGN 2-7, STONES
FIGHT WITH EACH OTHER 2-7, JUDGMENT/ 8TH SIGN 2-8, EARTH
QUAKES 2-8, JUDGMENT/ 9TH SIGN 2-9, EARTH MADE FLAT 2-9,
JUDGMENT/ 10TH SIGN 2-10, PEOPLE EMERGE SPEECHLESS FROM HIDING
PLACES 2-10, JUDGMENT/ 11TH SIGN 2-11, DEAD RISE FROM THEIR
TOMBS 2-11, JUDGMENT/ 12TH SIGN 2-12, STARS FALL 2-12,
JUDGMENT/ 13TH SIGN 2-13, LIVING DIE IN ORDER TO RISE AGAIN
2-13, JUDGMENT/ 14TH SIGN 2-14, EARTH AND SKY CONSUMED BY FIRE
2-14, JUDGMENT/ 15TH SIGN 2-15, SUN AND MOON AWAIT COMING OF
CHRIST 2-15, JUDGMENT/ LAST 2-16, DAMNED DEVOURED BY WORMS
2-17, LUCIFER AND LESSER DEVILS 2-18

*$ABSTRACT 3
  *LIBRARY BOD
  *SLIDE SET TITLE LIFE OF CHRIST
  *NEGATIVE REFERENCE ROLL 101A
  *RENTAL FEE SM 003 $3.20
  *COMMENTS A COMPANION PUBLICATION TO BODLEIAN PICTURE BOOK 5
  *SHELFMARK MS ASHMOLE 1511 3-1, MS DOUCE 79 3/2-3, MS CANON
LITURG 198 3-4, MS BODLEY 264 3-5, MS GOUGH LITURG 2 3-6, MS
DOUCE 293 3-7, MS GOUGH LITURG 2 3/8-9, MS DOUCE 366 3-10, MS
GOUGH LITURG 2 3-11, MS AUCT D 2 6 3-12, MS AUCT D 4 4 3-13,
MS DOUCE 293 3-14, MS RAWL LITURG D 1 3-15, MS BARLOW 22
3/16-17, MS DIGBY 227 3-18, MS GOUGH LITURG 8 3-19, MS DIGBY
227 3-20, MS GOUGH LITURG 8 3-21, MS GOUGH LITURG 2 3-22, MS

2

DOUCE 296 3-23, MS DOUCE 366 3-24,
*PROVENANCE ENGLISH/ ALL EXCEPT 3-5, FLEMISH 3-5
*DATE EXECUTED 11TH 3-23, 12TH 3/7 AND 14 AND 12, 13TH 3-1,
13TH/C1200 3/6 AND 8-9 AND 11 AND 22, 14TH3/16-17 AND 19 AND
21, 14TH/C1370-80 3-13, 14TH/1338- 44 3-5, 15TH/C1420 3/18 AND
20
*ARTIST/ SCHOOL MASTER OF THE QUEEN MARY PSALTER 3/2-3, JEHAN
DE GRISE 3-5, WILLIAM ABELL 3/18 AND 20
*AUTHOR JEHAN DE GRISE 3-5, ANSELM OF CANTERBURY 3-12
*TYPE OF MANUSCRIPT BESTIARY 3-1, LIVES OF ADAM AND EVE 3/2-3,
ROMANCE 3-5, PRAYERS AND MEDITATIONS 3-12, BOOK OF HOURS 3-15,
MISSAL 3/18 AND 20, PSALTER/ ALL OTHERS
*CONTENTS CHRIST/ LIFE OF 3/1-24, LIFE OF CHRIST 3/1-24,
CHRIST/ CREATOR OF STARS 3-1, ANNUNCIATION 3-2, NATIVITY 3/3,
JESSE TREE 3-4, WISE MEN 3-5, SHEPHERDS HEAR OF CHRIST'S BIRTH
3-6, PRESENTATION IN THE TEMPLE 3-7, FLIGHT INTO EGYPT 3-8,
BAPTISM OF CHRIST 3-9, TEMPTATION OF CHRIST 3-10, MARRIAGE AT
CANA 3-11, ST PETER ENTRUSTED WITH THE KEYS 3-12, LAZARUS
RAISED 3-13, CHRIST WASHING PETER'S FEET 3-14, LAST SUPPER
3-14, CHRIST'S AGONY IN THE GARDEN 3-15, CHRIST TEACHING 3-16,
CHRIST'S BETRAYAL 3-16, CHRIST'S SCOURGING 3-16, CHRIST
CARRYING CROSS 3-16, CHRIST'S DEATH 3-17, CHRIST'S DEPOSITION
3-17, CHRIST'S ENTOMBMENT 3-17, CHRIST'S RESURRECTION 3-17,
CRUCIFIXION 3-18, HERALDRIC ARMS OF ABINGDON ABBEY 3-18,
CHRIST'S DESCENT INTO HELL 3-19, RESURRECTION 3-20, THOMAS'S
INCREDULITY 3-21, ASCENSION 3-22, CHRIST TRIUMPHANT 3-23,
CHRIST ON RIGHT HAND OF GOD 3-24

*$ABSTRACT 4
*LIBRARY BOD
*SLIDE SET TITLE ENGLISH ILLUMINATION OF THE 13TH-14TH
CENTURIES
*NEGATIVE REFERENCE ROLL 101B
*RENTAL FEE SM 004 $4.00
*COMMENTS A COMPANION PUBLICATION TO BODLEIAN PICTURE BOOK 10
*SHELFMARK MS ASHMOLE 1511 4-1, MS BODLEY 764 4-2, MS ASHMOLE
304 4-3, MS RAWL A384 4-4, MS AUCT D 4 17 4-5, MS LAUD LAT 5
4/6-7, MS DOUCE 50 4-8, MS GOUGH LITURG 18 4/9-10, MS AUCT D 3
2 4/12-14, MS AUCT D 3 4 4-15, MS AUCT D 4 8 4/16-17, MS ENG
POET A L 4-18, MS AUCT D 3 2 4-19, MS DOUCE 180 4/20-21, MS
TANNER 184 4-22, MS CANON BIBL LAT 62 4-23, MS DOUCE 79 4-24,
MS GOUGH LITURG 8 4-25, MS DOUCE 231 4-26, MS BARLOW 22
4/27-28, MS DOUCE 366 4-29, MS ASHMOLE 1523 4-30, MS AUCT D 4
4 4/31-32, MS DOUCE 131 4/33-34, MS LAUD MISC 188 4-35, MS
RAWL G 185 4-36, MS BODLEY 581 4/37-40, MS AUCT D 3 2 4-41
*PROVENANCE ENGLISH
*DATE EXECUTED 13TH-14TH
*CONTENTS ENGLISH ILLUMINATION/ 13TH-14TH 4/1-41, PEACOCK 4-1,
UNICORN 4-2, SOCRATES WRITING 4-3, PLATO STANDING 4-3,
CONSANGUINITY TABLE 4/4, ST JOHN'S LIFE 4-5, VIRGIN AND CHILD
4-6, CRUCIFIXION 4-7, PENTECOST 4-8, CRUCIFIXION 4-9, VIRGIN
AND CHILD 4-10, MONK PRAYING 4-10, SAUL ANOINTED 4-11, DAVID
4-12, VIRGIN AND CHILD 4-12, FRIAR/ AUGUSTINIAN 4-12, ADAM AND
EVE/ TEMPTATION 4-13, EZEKIEL'S VISION 4-14, INITIAL TO
GENESIS 4-15, ST MATTHEW WRITING 4-16, ST PAUL BEING SCOURGED
4-17, NATIVITY 4-18, ST FRANCIS PREACHING TO BIRDS 4-19, ANGEL
MEASURES CITY 4-20, VINEPRESS 4-21, ANGEL CHAINING DRAGON
4/22-23, VIRGIN'S CORONATION 4-24, FLAGELLATION 4-25, VIRGIN
AND ST ANNE 4-26, INITIAL TO PSALM 68 4-27, JONAH AND WHALE
4-27, CORONATION/ DEATH AND ASSUMPTION OF VIRGIN 4-28,
VIRGIN'S DEATH 4-28, ASSUMPTION OF VIRGIN 4-28, INITIAL TO
PSALM 51 4-29, DOEG KILLING THE PRIESTS 4-29, PSALM 80 4-30,
CHRIST WITH ANGELS AND MUSICIANS 4-30, ADAM AND EVE/ SCENES OF
LIFE 4-31, VIRGIN SAVES WOMAN FROM DROWNING 4-32, VIRGIN AND
CHILD WITH KNEELING LADY 4-33, KNIGHT RESCUING MAN 4-34, GIANT
4-34, NATIVITY 4-35, ST JOSEPH AND ANGELS 4-35, MUSICAL
INSTRUMENTS 4-35, JESSE TREE 4-36, GEOMANTIC FIGURES 4/37-40,
DAVID AND GOLIATH 4-41

3

*$ABSTRACT 5
  *LIBRARY BOD
  *SLIDE SET TITLE ENGLISH ROMANESQUE ILLUMINATION
  *NEGATIVE REFERENCE ROLL 101C
  *RENTAL FEE SM 005 $3.45
  *COMMENTS A COMPANION PUBLICATION TO BODLEIAN PICTURE BOOK 1
  *SHELFMARK MS DIGBY 20 5-1, MS AUCT F 6 5 5-2, MS BODLEY 14?
    5-3, MS BODLEY 717 5-4, MS BODLEY 269 5-5, MS UNIVERSITY
    COLLEGE 165 5/6-7, MS LAUD MISC 247 5/8-9, MS BODLEY 614 5-10,
    MS AUCT F 2 13 5-11, MS BODLEY 614 5-12, MS DIGBY 83 5-13, MS
    AUCT E INF 2 5-14, MS AUCT D 2 8 5-15, MS AUCT D 2 15 5-16, MS
    AUCT D 2 6 5/17-18, MS AUCT D 1 13 5-19, MS AUCT E INF 1
    5/20-21, MS LAUD MISC 752 5/22-24, MS AUCT E INF 6 5-25, MS
    LAUD MISC 752 5-26, MS GOUGH LITURG 2 5-27, MS DOUCE 293 5-28,
    MS ASHMOLE 1511 5-29
  *PROVENANCE ENGLISH
  *CONTENTS ENGLISH ROMANESQUE ILLUMINATION 5/1-29, BEDE WRITING
    5-1, BOETHIUS WRITING 5-2, LION HUNT 5-3, VIRGIN BETWEEN
    ISAIAH AND JEROME 5-4, PAULA'S BURIAL 5-4, VIRGIN AND CHILD
    5/5, ST CUTHBERT AS PILGRIM 5-6, ALFRED/ KING 5-6, ST
    CUTHBERT'S LEG HEALED BY ANGEL 5-7, AMOS AND HIS GOATS 5-8,
    HUNTING BEAVER 5-9, ORION 5-10, TERENCE 5-11, HEDGE PRUNING
    5-12, PEGASUS 5-13, ST JEROME WRITING 5-14, DAVID WITH HARP
    5-14, INITIAL WITH HARES 5-15, ZACHARIUS AND ANGEL 5-16, ST
    MARY MAGDALENE ANOINTING CHRIST'S HEAD 5-17, CHRIST IN GARDEN
    5-17, DRUSIANA CARRIED TO BURIAL 5-18, ST JOHN RAISES DRUSIANA
    FROM DEAD 5-18, ST PAUL'S LIFE 5-19, INITIAL TO DANIEL 5-20,
    INITIAL TO OBADIAH 5-21, ST MARK 5-22, INITIAL OF MURDER OF
    EGLON 5-23, SOLOMON ANOINTED 5-24, DAVID BURIED 5-24, INITIAL
    FROM PSALTER OF HERBERT OF BOSHAM 5-25, INITIAL P FROM BIBLE
    5-26, NATIVITY 5-27, NATIVITY 5-29, WHALE 5-29

*$ABSTRACT 6
  *LIBRARY BOD
  *SLIDE SET TITLE BYZANTINE ILLUMINATION
  *NEGATIVE REFERENCE ROLL 101D
  *RENTAL FEE SM 006 $3.90
  *COMMENTS A COMPANION PUBLICATION TO BODLEIAN PICTURE BOOK 8
  *SHELFMARK MS BARROCCI 230 6-1, MS CROMWELL 16 6-2, MS CROMWELL ?
    INF 1 10 6-3, MS AUCT B 511 6-4, MS CANON GR 110 6/5-6, MS
    CROMWELL 16 6-7, MS CANON GR 103 6-8, MS AUCT T INF 1 10 6-9,
    MS CANON GR 110 6/10-11, MS AUCT T INF 2 7 6/12-13, MS E
    CLARKE 6 6-14, MS NEW COLLEGE 44 6/15-16, MS AUCT T INF 1 10
    6-17, MS CANON GR 36 6-18, MS SELDEN SUPRA 6 6-21, MS GR TH
    L 6/22-23, MS AUCT T INF 1 10 6-24, MS E D CLARKE 10 6-25, MS
    BAROCCI 230 6-27, MS BAROCCI 15 6-27, MS LINCOLN COLLEGE GR 3?
    6/28-29, MS ROE 6 6-30, MS GR TH F L 6/31-32, MS CANON GR 10?
    6/33-34, MS AUCT T INF 2 7 6-35, MS AUCT T 5 34 6-36, MS CANON
    GR 103 6-37, MS AUCT F 3 25 6-38
  *PROVENANCE BYZANTINE
  *DATE EXECUTED 10TH-15TH
  *CONTENTS BYZANTINE ILLUMINATION/ 10TH-15TH 6/1-28, MENOLOGION
    6-1, CANON TABLES 6/2-3, ST MARK 6-4, ST PAUL 6-5, ST JOHN
    6/6, ST MATTHEW 6-7, ST GREGORY OF NAZIANZUS 6-8, ST LUKE AND
    THEOPHILUS 6-9, ASCENSION 6-9, ST PETER 6-10, ST PETER 6-11,
    ST MATTHEW 6-12, ST JOHN 6-13, ST MATTHEW 6-14, MIOAH 6-15,
    JEREMIAH 6-16, ST JOHN DICTATING BIBLE TO PROCHROS 6-17,
    HARROWING OF HELL 6-17, ST MARK 6-18, ST MATTHEW/ SYMBOL 6-19,
    ST JOHN 6/20-21, CHRIST'S PRESENTATION IN THE TEMPLE 6-22,
    CHRIST'S BAPTISM 6-23, ST PAUL'S CONVERSION 6-24, FLIGHT INTO
    EGYPT 6-25, MENOLOGION FOR SEPTEMBER 6-26, RED SEA CROSSED
    6-27, LADY OF GOOD HOPE 6-28, THEODORUS COMENNOS 6-29, PUDOCIA
    6-29, NATIVITY 6-30, ST MICHAEL/ MIRACLE IN CHONAE 6-31, ST
    SOZON 6-31, TRANSFIGURATION 6-32, ST GREGORY PREACHING AT
    FUNERAL OF ST BASIL 6-33, INITIAL T 6/34-35, INITIAL
    ZOOMORPHIC 6-36, INITIAL A 6-37, HARROWING OF HELL 6-37,
    ZODIAC SIGNS 6-28

4

```
*$ABSTRACT 7
 *LIBRARY BOD
 *SLIDE SET TITLE BYZANTINE ILLUMINATION II
 *NEGATIVE REFERENCE ROLL 103A
 *RENTAL FEE SM 007 $5.25
 *COMMENTS 65 SLIDES FROM 4 MSS OF 10TH-14TH CENTURIES
 *SHELFMARK MS AUCT T INF 110 7/1-30, MS CANON GR 110  7/31-41,
  MS E D CLARKE 10 7/42-52, MS LINCOLN GREEK 35 7/53-65
 *PROVENANCE CONSTANTINOPLE
 *DATE  EXECUTED  12TH 7/1-30, 10TH 7/31-41, 12TH/C1100 7/42-52,
  14TH/C1310 7/53-65
 *TYPE OF MANUSCRIPT NEW TESTAMENT  7/1-30,  ACTS  AND  EPISTLES
  7/31-41, GOSPELS 7/42-52, TYPICON 7/53-65
 *CONTENTS BYZANTINE ILLUMINATION/ 10TH-14TH 7/1-65, SAINTS 7-1,
  CANON TABLES 7/2-11, ST MATTHEW 7-12, NATIVITY 7-12, HEADPIECE
  TO  GOSPEL  OF  ST MARK 7-15, ST LUKE 7-16, ANNUNCIATION 7-16,
  HEADPIECE TO GOSPEL OF ST JOHN 7-17, ST JOHN 7-18, HARROWING
  OF  HELL  7-18,  HEADPIECE FOR GOSPEL OF ST LUKE 7-19, ST LUKE
  AND THEOPHILUS 7-20, ASCENSION 7-20, HEADPIECE TO ACTS  7-21,
  ST  JAMES  7-22, ST PETER 7-23, ST JOHN 7-24, SHIP 7-24,
  HEADPIECE 7-25, ST JUDE 7-26, ST PAUL 7-27, HEADPIECE 7/28-30,
  ST LUKE 7-31, DECORATIVE HEADPIECE 7-32, INITIAL T 7-32, ST
  JAMES  7-33,  DECORATIVE  HEADPIECE  7-34,  ST PETER 7-35,
  DECORATIVE HEADPIECE 7-36, ST JOHN 7-37, ST JUDE 7-38, ST PAUL
  7-39, DECORATIVE HEADPIECE  7/40-41,  HEADPIECE  7-42,  CHRIST
  BETWEEN  THE  FOUR  EVANGELISTS  7-43,  CANON  TABLES 7-44, ST
  MATTHEW 7-45, HEADPIECE FOR GOSPEL OF ST MATTHEW 7-46, FLIGHT
  INTO EGYPT 7-46, ST MARK 7-47, HEADPIECE FOR GOSPEL OF ST MARK
  7-48,  FIG  TREE/  BARREN  7-48,  ST  LUKE 7-49, HEADPIECE FOR
  GOSPEL OF ST LUKE 7-50, NATIVITY 7-50, ST JOHN 7-51, HEADPIECE
  FOR GOSPEL OF ST JOHN 7-52, HARROWING OF HELL 7-52, PORTRAIT
  OF  FOUNDRESS  OF  NUNNERY  OF  OUR  LADY  7-53, PORTRAIT  OF
  FOUNDRESS WITH HUSBAND 7-53, VIRGIN AND CHILD 7-53, PORTRAIT
  OF  PARENTS  OF  THE  FOUNDRESS  7-54,  VIRGIN AND CHILD 7-54,
  PORTRAIT OF HUSBAND AND WIFE 7-55, CHRIST BLESSING 7/55-57,
  PORTRAIT  OF  HUSBAND  AND  WIFE 7/56-57, CONSTANTINOS COMNENOS
  AND EUPHROSYNE 7-58, CHRIST CHILD BLESSING 7-58, PORTRAIT OF
  TWO  WOMEN WITH CHILD 7-59, VIRGIN AND CHILD 7-59, PORTRAIT OF
  SON OF FOUNDER AND HIS  WIFE  7-60,  VIRGIN  AND  CHILD  7-60,
  PORTRAIT  7-61,  CHRIST CHILD 7-61, VIRGIN AND CHILD 7-62, LADY
  OF GOOD HOPE 7-62, FOUNDRESS AND DAUGHTER AS NUNS 7-63,
  COMMUNITY OF NUNS 7-64, HEADPIECE 7-65


*$ABSTRACT 8
 *LIBRARY BOD
 *SLIDE SET TITLE BYZANTINE ILLUMINATION III
 *NEGATIVE REFERENCE ROLL 103B
 *RENTAL FEE SM 008 $3.25
 *COMMENTS 25 SLIDES FROM 3 MSS OF THE 10TH-11TH CENTURIES
 *SHELFMARK  MS  CANON GR 103 8/1-12, MS SELDEN SUPRA 6 8/13-20,
  MS AUCT E 5 11 8/21-25
 *PROVENANCE BYZANTINE
 *DATE EXECUTED  12TH/C1100  8/1-12,  14TH/C1300  8/13-20,  10TH
  8/21-25
 *AUTHOR GREGORY OF NAZIANUS 8/1-12
 *TYPE OF MANUSCRIPT SERMONS 8/1-12, GOSPELS 8/13-25
 *CONTENTS  BYZANTINE  ILLUMINATION/  10TH-11TH  8/1-25, GREGORY
  PORTRAIT 8-1, DECORATIVE HEADPIECE 8-2, HARROWING OF HELL 8-2,
  PENTECOST/ HEADPIECE 8-3, INITIAL T 8-4, CHRIST/ ELEAZAR  AND
  MOTHER  OF  MACCABEES  8-4,  INITIAL  M 8-5, ST GREGORY AND ST
  CYPRIAN 8-5, INITIAL T 8-6, ST GREGORY WRITING TO JULIAN  8-6,
  INITIAL  8-7,  SHEPHERD'S  JOURNEY  8-7,  NATIVITY 8-7, CHRIST
  CHILD WASHED 8-7,  INITIAL  E  8/8,  ST  GREGORY'S  SERMON  AT
  FUNERAL  OF ST BASIL 8/8, DECORATIVE HEADPIECE 8-9, BAPTISM OF
  CHRIST 8-9, INITIAL 8-10, ST GREGORY AND BROTHER OF  ST  BASIL
  8-10,  INITIAL  A  8-11,  ST  GREGORY  AND ST ATHANASIUS 8-11,
  INITIAL T 8-12, ST GREGORY PREACHING  AND  SUPPLIANT  CITIZENS
  8-12,  ST  MATTHEW  8-13,  HEADPIECE  FOR GOSPEL OF ST MATTHEW
  8-14, ST MARK 8-15, HEADPIECE FOR GOSPEL OF ST MARK  8-16,  ST
  LUKE 8-17, HEADPIECE FOR GOSPEL OF ST LUKE 8-18, ST JOHN 8-19,
```

HEADPIECE FOR GOSPEL OF ST JOHN 8-20, CANON TABLES 8-21, ST MATTHEW 8-22, ST MARK 8-23, ST LUKE 8-24, ST JOHN 8-25

*$ABSTRACT 9
  *LIBRARY BOD
  *SLIDE SET TITLE NORTHERN ITALIAN ILLUMINATION
  *NEGATIVE REFERENCE ROLL 108
  *RENTAL FEE SM 009 $4.60
  *COMMENTS 52 SLIDES FROM 7 MSS FROM 15TH-16TH CENTURIES
  *SHELFMARK MS DOUCE 14 9/1-24, MS RAWL G 98 9/25-28, MS CANON ITAL 69 9-29, MS CANON LITURG 376 9-30, MS CANON CLASS LAT 86 9/31-38, MS CANON LITURG 378 9/39-42, MS CANON LITURG 388 9/43-52
  *PROVENANCE ITALIAN MILAN 9/1-28, ITALIAN LOMBARDY 9-29, ITALIAN MILAN 9-30, ITALIAN LOMBARDY OR VERONA 9/31-38, ITALIAN MILAN 9/39-42, ITALIAN LOMBARDY 9/43-52
  *DATE EXECUTED 16TH/1500-1505 9/1-24, 15TH 9/25-28, 15TH/C1420-30 9-29, 15TH/C1402 9-30, 15TH 9/31-42, 15TH/C1460 9/43-52
  *AUTHOR MASTER OF THE ARCIMBOLDO MISSAL 9/1-24, VIRGIL/ GEORGICS 9/25-28, PETRARCH 9-29, SENECA 9/31-38, MASTER OF THE MAINARDI MISSAL 9/43-52
  *LANGUAGE LATIN
  *TYPE OF MANUSCRIPT BOOK OF HOURS 9/1-24, VIRGIL GEORGICS 9/25-28, PETRARCH SONNETS 9-29, SENECA TRAGEDIES 9/31-38, GOSPEL BOOK 9-30, PSALTER 9/39-42, BREVIARY 9/43-52
  *CONTENTS ITALIAN ILLUMINATION/ 15TH-16TH 9/1-52, OFFICE OF THE VIRGIN 9-1, ANNUNCIATION 9-1, ST JOHN 9-2, INITIAL 9/3-4, RESURRECTION OF LAZARUS 9-5, ST JEROME 9-6, ST FRANCIS 9-7, BETRAYAL OF CHRIST 9-8, ST AUGUSTINE WITH BOOK 9/9, SCOURGING OF CHRIST 9-10, SAINT 9-11, BEAR EATING DUCK 9-11, CHRIST BEFORE PILATE 9-12, OFFICE OF THE CROSS 9-13, MAN OF SORROWS 9-13, OFFICE OF THE HOLY GHOST 9-14, ST PETER 9-14, RESURRECTION 9-15, MASS OF THE VIRGIN 9-16, VIRGIN AND CHILD 9-16, ASCENSION 9-17, PENITENTIAL PSALMS 9-18, DAVID IN PRAYER 9-18, ROAD TO CALVARY 9-19, LITANY 9-20, ST GREGORY THE GREAT 9-20, CRUCIFIXION 9-21, OFFICE OF THE DEAD 9-22, ST SEBASTIAN 9-22, PENTECOST 9-23, ST CATHERINE 9-24, PLOUGHING AND SOWING 9-25, VIRGIL WRITING 9-25, TENDING VINES 9-26, VIRGIL WRITING 9/26-28, SHEPHERD AND SHEEP 9-27, COWHERD AND COWS 9-27, BEEKEEPING AND BEEHIVES 9-28, PETRARCH CROWNED WITH LAURELS 9-29, HUNTING SCENE 9-29, CHRIST WITH BOOK 9-30, VISCONTI ARMS 9-30, DRAMA/ SENECA TRAGEDIES 9/31-38, HERCULES FURENS 9-31, THERSITES 9-32, THEBAS OEDIPUS 9-33, ANTIGONE 9-33, HIPPOLYTUS WITH HORSEMEN 9-34, MONSTER 9-34, HORSEMEN 9-34, MEDEA 9-35, DRAGON/ WINGED 9-35, AGAMEMNON 9-36, OCTAVIA 9-37, HERCULES@ DEATH 9-38, PSALM 1 9-39, DAVID WITH PSALTERY 9-39, PSALM 32 9-40, BELLS 9-40, PSALM 105 9-41, CARTHUSIAN KNEELING 9-41, PSALM 109 9-42, TRINITY 9-42, TEMPORALE 9-43, ST PAUL 9-43, CHRIST 9-43, ST AUGUSTINE 9-43, PSALM 1 9-44, DAVID WITH PSALTERY 9-44, CROWD 9-44, HARP 9-44, DULCIMER 9-44, PSALM 38 9-45, DAVID 9-45, PSALM 80 9-46, DAVID 9-46, MONK READING 9-46, PSALM 97 9-47, MONKS SINGING 9-47, PSALM 109 9-48, DAVID WITH CROWN OR REBEC 9-48, SANCTORALE 9-49, ST SATURNIUS 9-49, ST ANDREW 9-49, TOBIAS 9-49, VISITATION 9-50, VIRGIN'S BIRTH 9-51, SAINTS/ ALL 9-52, ANGELS WITH PIPES 9-52

*$ABSTRACT 10
  *LIBRARY HEREFORD CATHEDRAL LIBRARY
  *SLIDE SET TITLE ENGLISH ILLUMINATION OF THE 12TH CENTURY
  *NEGATIVE REFERENCE ROLL 115
  *RENTAL FEE SM 010 $2.30
  *SHELFMARK MS HEREFORD CATHEDRAL LIBRARY O I VIII
  *PROVENANCE ENGLISH
  *DATE EXECUTED 12TH
  *LANGUAGE LATIN
  *ARTIST/ SCHOOL MASTER OF THE ALBANI PSALTER
  *TYPE OF MANUSCRIPT GOSPELS

*CONTENTS ENGLISH ILLUMINATION 10/1-5, INITIAL FOR ST MATTHEW'S
GOSPEL 10-1, ST MARK SYMBOL 10-2, ST MARK SYMBOL 10-3, INITIAL
FOR ST MARK'S GOSPEL 10-4, INITIAL FOR ST LUKE'S GOSPEL 10-5,
INITIAL WITH ST JOHN 10-5

*$ABSTRACT 11
*LIBRARY BOD
*SLIDE SET TITLE DUTCH ILLUMINATION
*NEGATIVE REFERENCE ROLL 116
*RENTAL FEE SM 011 $2.60
*COMMENTS 12 SLIDES FROM 5 MSS OF 15TH CENTURY
*SHELFMARK MS AUCT D INF 2 13 11/1-3, MS BODLEY 283 11/4-5, MS
DOUCE 30 11/6-8, MS DOUCE 93 11/9-11, MS DOUCE 248 11-12
*PROVENANCE DUTCH 11/1-3, ENGLISH 11/4-5, DUTCH UTRECHT 11/6-12
*DATE   EXECUTED   15TH/C1470   11/1-3,   15TH   11/4-8,
15TH/C1460-5-11/9-11, 15TH 11-12
*LANGUAGE LATIN 11/1-3, ENGLISH 11/4-5, LATIN 11/6-8, LATIN AND
FRENCH 11/9-11, DUTCH 11-12
*ARTIST/ SCHOOL MASTER OF GIJSBRECHT VAN BREDERODE 11/1-3,
MASTER OF GIJSBRECHT VAN BREDERODE 11/9-11
*TYPE OF MANUSCRIPT BOOK OF HOURS 11/1-3, MIROIR DE MONDE
11/4-5, BOOK OF HOURS 11/6-12
*CONTENTS DUTCH ILLUMINATION/ 15TH 11/1-12, CRUCIFIXION 11-1,
ENTOMBMENT 11-2, OFFICE OF THE DEAD 11-3, MOSES RECEIVES THE
TABLETS 11-4, ISRAELITES ADORING THE GOLDEN CALF 11-4, LAST
JUDGMENT 11-5, OFFICE OF THE VIRGIN 11-6, VIRGIN AND CHILD
11-6, NATIVITY AND ADORATION 11-6, ANNUNCIATION 11-6, OFFICE
OF THE CROSS 11-7, CRUCIFIXION 11-7, OFFICE OF THE DEAD 11-8,
BURIAL IN CHURCH 11-8, LAST JUDGMENT 11-9, OFFICE OF THE DEAD
11-10, COFFIN IN CRYPT 11-10, KINGS 11-10, CRUCIFIXION 11/11,
TOURNAMENT 11/11, OFFICE OF THE VIRGIN 11-12, CIRCUMCISION OF
CHRIST 11-12

*$ABSTRACT 12
*LIBRARY BOD
*SLIDE SET TITLE DALMATIAN ILLUMINATION
*NEGATIVE REFERENCE ROLL 117
*RENTAL FEE SM 012 $3.20
*COMMENTS FRAMES 1-20 ARE FROM A MASS LECTIONARY IN BENEVENTAN
SCRIPT MADE FOR BENEDICTINE NUNS OF ST MARY'S ZARA DALMATIA,
FRAMES 21-24 ARE FROM A BOOK OF HOURS FROM ST MARY'S ZARA
DALMATIA
*SHELFMARK MS CANON BIBL LAT 61 12/1-20, MS CANON LITURG 277
12/21-24
*PROVENANCE DALMATIA/ZARA
*DATE EXECUTED 11TH/1081-6 12/1-20, 11TH 12/21-24
*LANGUAGE LATIN
*ARTIST/ SCHOOL BARI
*TYPE OF MANUSCRIPT GOSPEL LECTIONARY 12/1-20, BOOK OF HOURS
12/21-24
*CONTENTS DALMATIAN ILLUMINATION/ 11TH 12/1-24, INITIAL 12-1,
EAGLE WITH BOOK 12-2, ST MATTHEW 12-3, INITIAL 12-4, WINGED OX
12-5, ST MATTHEW 12-6, ST MATTHEW 12-7, ST JOHN 12-8, ST JOHN
12-9, EAGLE 12-10, EAGLE 12-11, EAGLE-PEACOCK 12/12, INITIAL
12-13, INITIAL 12-14, AGNUS DEI 12-15, INITIAL 12-16, APOSTLE
12-17, EAGLE-PEACOCK 12/18-19, LION 12-20, EAGLE-PEACOCK
12-21, INITIALS 12-22, EAGLE-PEACOCK 12-23, INITIALS 12-24

*$ABSTRACT 13
*LIBRARY BOD
*SLIDE SET TITLE FLEMISH ILLUMINATION 1
*NEGATIVE REFERENCE ROLL 119A
*RENTAL FEE SM 013 $8.40
*COMMENTS 128 SLIDES FROM 5 MSS OF THE 14TH-15TH CENTURIES
*SHELFMARK MS DOUCE 374 13/1-73, MS DOUCE 208 13/74-84, MS
CANON LITURG 92 13/85-109, MS DOUCE 365 13/110-114, MS DOUCE

7

```
223 13/115-128
*PROVENANCE FLEMISH
*DATE EXECUTED 15TH/1467-77 13/1-73, 15TH 13/74-84, 15TH/C1400
13/85-109, 15TH 1475 13/110-114, 15TH/C1480 13/115-128
*LANGUAGE FRENCH 13/1-84, LATIN AND FRENCH 13/85-109, FRENCH
13/110-114, LATIN 13/115-128
*ARTIST/ SCHOOL JEAN TAVERNIER 13/1-73, MASTER OF EDWARD IV
13/74-84, MASTER OF MARY OF BURGUNDY 13/110-128
*AUTHOR TRANSLATED BY JEAN MIELOT 13/1-73, TRANSLATED BY JEAN
DU QUESNE 13/74-84, DAVID AUBERT FOR MARGARET OF YORK
13/110-114
*TYPE OF MANUSCRIPT MIRACLES OF THE VIRGIN 13/1-73,
COMMENTARIES OF CAESAR 13/74-84, HOURS OF OUR LADY 13/85-109,
MORAL AND RELIGIOUS TREATISES 13/110-114, BOOK OF HOURS
13/115-128
*CONTENTS FLEMISH ILLUMINATION/ 14TH-15TH 13/1-128, PHILIP THE
GOOD OR CHARLES BOLD PRESENTED TO VIRGIN 13-1, ST ANDREW 13-1,
NORMANS ROUTED BY BISHOP OF CHARTES 13-2, BATTLE AND TENTS
13-2, VIRGIN RESCUES LADY FROM DEVIL 13-3, VISION OF JUDGMENT
13-4, VIRGIN RESCUES MAN FROM DEVIL 13-4, DEVILS TAKE SOUL OF
EBROIN TO HELL 13-5, MONKS 13-5, HOLY MAN ADVISES WOMAN TO
INVOKE VIRGIN 13-6, VISION OF VIRGIN AND PRIESTS CELEBRATING
MASS 13-7, LILY WITH AVA MARIA GROWING FROM MONK'S TOMB 13-8,
HOLY MAN FORCES MAN TO CONFESS HE IS DEVIL 13-9, VIRGIN
SUMMONS DYING GOOD MAN TO HEAVEN 13-10, MONK OF PAVIA HAS
VISION OF SKELETON DESCRIBING PARADISE 13-11, CLERK CONFESSES
FAULT BEFORE CONGREGATION 13-12, LADY WELCOMES KING AND
RETINUE 13/13, TOLEDO 13-14, JEWS DESECRATION OF TOLEDO 13-14,
SLAUGHTER OF JEWS BY CHRISTIANS 13-14, VISION OF VIRGIN BY
WRONGED WIFE 13-15, ADULTRESS PENITENT 13-15, JEW WHO
DESECRATED PICTURE OF VIRGIN PUT TO DEATH 13-16, CHRISTIAN
RESTORES PICTURE AND KNEELS BEFORE VIRGIN 13-16, DEATH AND
BURIAL OF PIOUS MONK 13-17, HELL SEEN IN MOUTH OF MONSTER
13-18, NUN KNEELING 13-18, PROCESSION AT CHURCH AT LE PUY/
AUVERGNE 13-19, BRIDEGROOM LEAVES FEAST 13-20, VIRGIN 13-20,
GIRL IN BED AWAITING CALL OF VIRGIN 13-21, MONK'S LIFE 13-22,
MONK PRAYS TO VIRGIN TO RESCUE BOY FROM DEVIL 13-23, BOY
CROUCHES NEAR MONK 13-23, CHURCH INTERIOR 13-24, PENITENT
KNEELS FOR ABSOLUTION 13-24, DANCING AT WEDDING OF CLERK
13-25, VIRGIN 13-25, ANGEL CLOTHES BISHOP IN VESTMENT GIVEN BY
VIRGIN 13-26, VIRGIN AND ANGELS RESCUE SOUL OF KNIGHT FROM
DEVILS 13-27, CHILD OFFERS BREAD TO IMAGE OF JESUS 13-28, LADY
IMPRISONS BROTHER IN LAW IN TOWER 13-29, VIRGIN PROTECTS
PILGRIMS ON WAY TO MONT ST MICHEL 13-30, MOTHER OF DEAD CHILD
PRAYS IN ABBEY 13-31, ST DUNSTAN SEES VISION OF VIRGIN AND
ANGELS 13-32, PILGRIMS DROWNED AS SHIP FOUNDERS 13-33, JEW WHO
DEFRAUDS CHRISTIAN IS PUNISHED 13-34, VISION OF JUDGMENT
13-35, MAN RESCUED FROM HELL BY VIRGIN 13-35, SACRISTAN OF
ABBEY FOUND DROWNED IN RIVER 13-36, SACRISTAN'S BODY RECOVERED
BY MAN IN BOAT 13-37, VIRGIN APPEARS TO KNIGHT IN CHAPEL
13-38, DEVIL OFFERS MAN MONEY TO DENY GOD AND SAINTS 13-39,
MAN REFUSES BRIBE 13-39, WOMAN GIVES CHILD APPLE AS REWARD FOR
DILIGENCE 13-40, DIVINE PUNISHMENT FOR MAN WHO WORKS ON
SAINT'S DAY 13-41, CRIPPLE HEALED IN ENGLISH CHURCH 13-42, MAN
MUTILATED AFTER FALSE ACCUSATION 13-43, VIRGIN HEALS MAN
13-43, NUN KNEELS BEFORE VIRGIN 13-44, MONK ON TRIP STOPS TO
SAY AVES 13-45, MONK/ DISSOLUTE RESPECTS GIRL NAMED MARY
13-46, MONK REDEEMED FOR ACTION 13-46, WOMAN'S SOUL SURROUNDED
BY DEVILS 13-47, WOMAN SAVED BY VIRGIN AND SENT TO PURGATORY
13-47, ROBBER MORTALLY WOUNDED RECEIVES LAST SACRAMENT 13-48,
WOMAN KILLS CHILD OF INCESTUOUS UNION 13-49, WOMAN SAVED BY
VIRGIN 13-49, ABBESS PARDONED BY VIRGIN 13-50, HEALING OF MANY
PEOPLE AT SOISSONS 13-51, VIRGIN CALLS TO PARADISE A BEGGAR
WHO GAVE ALMS 13-52, DEVIL 13-53, VIRGIN SAVES MAN AFTER HE
BREAKS NECK 13-54, ROBBER RECEIVES LAST SACRAMENTS 13-55,
BATTLE ON HORSEBACK 13-55, VISION OF VIRGIN BY DYING CHILD
13-56, CHILD CARRIED TO PARADISE 13-56, ST FRANCIS HAS VISION
13-57, ANGEL EXPOUNDS VISION TO ST FRANCIS 13-57, DISSOLUTE
PRIEST HAS VISION OF VIRGIN 13-58, CHILD SAVED BY VIRGIN
13-59, BLIND WOMAN HEALED 13-60, PLOUGHING 13-61, PLOUGHMAN
RECEIVED BY VIRGIN 13-62, CONDEMNED MURDERER RECEIVED BY
VIRGIN 13-63, DEVIL BEGS PAINTING MONKS TO REPRESENT HIM AS
```

8

HANDSOME 13-64, VIRGIN RESTORES AMPUTATED FOOT 13-65, DEATHBED
AND EXHUMATION 13-66, DISSOLUTE BUT PENITENT SCHOLAR'S SKIN
CHANGED BY VIRGIN 13-67, VIRGIN WITH LADY AND LOVER 13-68,
REPENTANT NUN KNEELS BEFORE VIRGIN 13-69, SICK PEOPLE HEALED
13-69, ABBESS ACCUSED OF UNCHASTITY 13-70, KNIGHTS GIVE HER
SON TO HERMITS 13-70, HERMIT KNEELS BEFORE PROVOST OF AQUILEIA
13-71, KNIGHT KNEELS BEFORE HERMIT 13-72, WORLDLY CLERK HAS
VISION OF JUDGMENT 13-73, VIRGIN SAVES CLERK 13-73, BOOKSHOP
13-74, CAESAR ADDRESSING SCRIBE AT DESK 13-74, CAESAR'S BIRTH
13-75, SURGEON AND NURSE 13-75, BOOK 2 13-76, CAESAR RIDES
WITH ARMY BY RIVER 13-76, BOOK 3 13-77, BELGIAN BURGHERS
SURRENDER KEYS OF CITY 13-77, BOOK 4 13-78, BARGE LOADED BY
WATER GATE 13-78, BOOK 5 13-79, GERMANS CROSSING RHINE 13-79,
BOOK 6 13-80, CAESAR PREPARES FOR THE INVASION OF BRITAIN
13-80, SHIPS 13-80, BOOK 7 13-81, CAESAR GIVES LETTER TO
MESSENGER 13-81, BOOK 8 13-82, GALLIC REBELLION 13-82,
SOLDIERS KILLING CIVILIANS 13-82, BOOK 9 13-83, SUPPLIANT
CIVILIANS KNEEL TO CAESAR 13-83, BOOK 10 13-84, MURDER OF
CAESAR 13-84, ST JOHN WITH EAGLE 13-85, ST MATTHEW WRITING
GOSPEL 13-86, ST MARK WITH LION 13-87, HOLY GHOST BLOWS DOVE
TOWARD VIRGIN 13-88, ANGEL HOLDING SCROLL 13-88, VISITATION
13-89, GOD BLESSING VIRGIN AND ST ELIZABETH 13-89, NATIVITY
13-90, SHEPHERDS RECEIVE TIDINGS FROM TWO ANGELS 13-91, MAGI
PRESENTING MYRRH TO CHRIST 13-92, SLAUGHTER OF THE INNOCENTS
13-93, FLIGHT INTO EGYPT 13-94, CORONATION OF VIRGIN 13-95,
LAST JUDGMENT 13-96, CRUCIFIXION 13-97, PENTECOST 13-98,
VIRGIN AND CHILD SEATED IN GARDEN 13-99, TRINITY 13-100,
OFFICE OF THE DEAD 13-101, ST ANTHONY 13-102, PRAYER FOR ALL
ANGELS 13-103, ST MICHAEL 13-103, INITIAL WITH VIRGIN AND
CHILD 13-104, VIRGIN WITH CHILD 13-105, ST SEBASTIAN 13-106,
ST CHRISTOPHER 13-107, ST CATHERINE 13-108, ST NICHOLAS
13-109, MARGARET OF YORK AT PRAYER 13-110, FEMALE ALLEGORICAL
FIGURES TRUTH/ PURITY/ HUMILITY/ POVERTY 13-111, PETER OF
LUXEMBOURG AND NUN IN CELL 13-112, CLOISTER 13-112, MARGARET
OF YORK AT PRAYER 13-113, SENECA PRESENTING BOOK TO CALYO
13-114, CALYO PRESENTING BOOK TO PHILIP OF BURGUNDY 13-114, ST
VERONICA WITH HANDKERCHIEF 13-115, PRAYER IN MEMORY OF ST
VERONICA 13-116, ST ANTHONY AND ST PAUL IN DESERT 13-117, ST
CATHERINE OF ALEXANDRIA 13-118, ST BARBARA 13-119, ST
APPOLLONIA 13-120, PENTECOST 13-121, JEWELED BORDER AGAINST
GOLD BACKGROUND 13-122, NATIVITY 13-123, BORDER WITH ERASED
COAT OF ARMS 13-124, ASSUMPTION OF VIRGIN 13-125, PENITENTIAL
PSALMS 13-126, DAVID KNEELING 13-126, DEATH VIGIL WITH NUNS
AND MONKS IN CHOIR 13-127, PRAYER BEFORE CRUCIFIX 13-128,
PEACOCK BORDER 13-128

*$ABSTRACT 14
 *LIBRARY BOD
 *SLIDE SET TITLE FLEMISH ILLUMINATION II
 *NEGATIVE REFERENCE ROLL 119B
 *RENTAL FEE SM 014 $4.35
 *COMMENTS MADE FOR ENGELBERT OF NASSAU, LIEUTENANT OF THE REALM
  UNDER PHILIP THE FAIR
 *SHELFMARK MS DOUCE 219-220
 *PROVENANCE FLEMISH
 *DATE EXECUTED 15TH/1480-90
 *LANGUAGE LATIN
 *ARTIST/ SCHOOL MASTER OF MARY OF BURGUNDY
 *TYPE OF MANUSCRIPT BOOK OF HOURS/ DOMINICAN
 *CONTENTS FLEMISH ILLUMINATION/ 15TH 14/1-47, ST VERONICA'S
  HANDKERCHIEF 14-1, VIRGIN AND CHILD HOLDING FLOWER 14-2,
  FLOWERS AND INSECTS IN STREW PATTERN 14-3, ST SEBASTIAN
  EXECUTED BY ARCHERS 14-4, ST ANTHONY SEATED ON A ROCK 14-5,
  FLOWERS AND INSECTS IN STREW PATTERN 14-6, ST CHRISTOPHER
  STANDING BY ROADSIDE CROSS 14-7, ST CATHERINE OF ALEXANDRIA
  KNEELING BEFORE MONK 14-8, ST BARBARA READING 14-9, AGONY IN
  GARDEN 14-10, BETRAYAL 14-11, FLOWERS AND INSECTS IN STREW
  PATTERN 14/12-13, CHRIST LED BEFORE HEROD 14/14, FLOWERS/
  BERRIES/ INSECTS IN BLUE BORDER 14-15, CHRIST CROWNED WITH
  THORNS AND MOCKED 14-16, CHRIST NAILED TO CROSS 14-17,

9

CRUCIFIXION 14-18, ARABESQUES WITH SNAILS/ FLOWERS/ INSECTS ON
GOLD BORDER 14-19, DESCENT FROM CROSS 14-20, FLOWERS AND
INSECTS IN STREW PATTERN 14-21, ENTOMBMENT 14-22, ANNUNCIATION
14-23, VISITATION/ VIRGIN GOES TO ST ELIZABETH 14-24,
VISITATION/ ST ELIZABETH KNEELS BEFORE VIRGIN 14-25, MARY AND
JOSEPH REFUSED ADMISSION TO INN 14-26, TOURNAMENT BETWEEN
MONKEYS AND WILD MEN 14-27, MINIATURE/ FULL PAGE 14-28,
NATIVITY 14-28, CIRCUMCISION OF CHRIST 14-29, ADORATION OF THE
MAGI 14-30, MAGI RIDE HOME WITH ATTENDANTS 14-31, PRESENTATION
IN THE TEMPLE 14-32, JOSEPH RECEIVES WARNING FROM ANGEL 14-33,
LION WEARING HELMET 14-34, UNICORN 14-34, MONKEY RIDING
PILLION 14-34, LEGEND OF THE GROWING CORN 14-35, FLIGHT INTO
EGYPT 14-36, VIRGIN'S DEATH 14-37, CORONATION OF VIRGIN 14-38,
LAST JUDGMENT 14-39, DAVID AND DOG DEFEND FLOCK FROM BEAR
14-40, DAVID ATTACKS LION 14-41, DAVID AND GOLIATH 14-42,
DAVID BRINGS HEAD OF GOLIATH ON PIKE 14-43, DAVID PLAYS HARP
BEFORE TWO LADIES 14-44, DAVID LIES ASLEEP IN TENT 14-45,
DAVID KNEELS BEFORE VISION OF ANGEL 14-46, BURIAL OF THE DEAD
14-47

*$ABSTRACT 15
  *LIBRARY BOD
  *SLIDE SET TITLE FLEMISH ILLUMINATION III
  *NEGATIVE REFERENCE ROLL 119C
  *RENTAL FEE SM 015 $4.75
  *COMMENTS DEDICATED TO THE DUKE OF BEDFORD 1435
  *TITLE OF MANUSCRIPT LE PELERINAGE DE L/AME
  *SHELFMARK MS DOUCE 305
  *PROVENANCE FLEMISH/ LILLE
  *DATE EXECUTED 15TH/1435
  *LANGUAGE FRENCH
  *AUTHOR GALLOPEZ/ JEAN
  *TYPE OF MANUSCRIPT PILGRIMAGE OF THE SOUL
  *CONTENTS FLEMISH ILLUMINATION/ 15TH 15/1-55, AUTHOR PRESENTS
VOLUME TO DUKE OF BEDFORD 15-1, SCRIBE AT WORK 15-2, SCRIBE IN
BED NEAR DESK 15-3, ANGEL AND DEVIL STRUGGLE FOR SOUL 15-4,
PILGRIM ME MEETS DEVILS 15-5, ANGEL INTERPOSES BETWEEN PILGRIM
AND DEVILS 15-6, DEVIL TRYING TO HOOK SOUL FROM ANGEL 15-7,
CHRIST SEATED WITH KNEELING ANGELS AND MEN 15-8, CHRIST
WEIGHING SOULS IN SCALES 15-9, GOD WITH CHRIST ON CROSS 15-10,
ST MICHAEL 15-10, GOD SEATED WITH PILGRIM AND ANGEL ON LEFT
15-11, GOD SEATED WITH WOMEN / DEVIL/ MONSTER/ PILGRIM/
ANGELS/ MEN 15-12, GOD WITH PILGRIM/ ANGEL/ WOMAN/ DEVIL/
MONSTER 15-13, DEVIL PRESENTS SCROLL TO THREE WOMEN 15-14, GOD
FLANKED BY ANGEL/ WOMAN/ PILGRIM AND SAINT 15-14, GOD/ WOMEN/
SAINT/ DEVIL/ PILGRIM 15/15, GOD/ WOMEN/ SAINT/ DEVIL/ PILGRIM
15-16, GOD/ WOMEN/ DEVIL/ SAINT/ ANGEL/ PILGRIM 15-17, GOD/
SAINTS/ BISHOP/ WOMEN/ PILGRIM/ ANGEL 15-18, PARADISE 15-19,
GOD ENTHRONED WITH CHRIST ON CROSS 15-20, ANGEL PUSHES
PILGRIMS IN HELL HOUTH 15-21, HELL MOUTH IN FLAMES 15-21, PIT
IN FLAMES WITH GOAT-HEADED DEVIL 15-22, HELL AS FIERY PIT WITH
2 PILGRIMS 15-23, HELL AS FIERY PIT WITH 3 PILGRIMS AND ANGELS
15-24, LANDSCAPE/ SKY WITH CONCENTRIC CIRCLES 15-25, LANDSCAPE
WITH CONCENTRIC RINGS WITH HELL'S MOUTH IN CENTER 15-26, HELL
MOUTH 15-26, ANGEL GUIDING PILGRIM TO BUILDING 15-27, ANGEL
AND PILGRIM SEE PENITENT ADMONISHED 15-28, CADAVER WITH ANGELS
AND PILGRIM 15-29, CONCENTRIC CIRCLES DEPICTING HELL'S MOUTH
15-30, ANGEL AND PILGRIM 15-30, FIERY PIT WITH DEVILS AND
FEMALE FIGURES 15-31, FIERY PIT WITH 6 DEVILS/ ANGEL/ PILGRIM
15-32, GALLOWS WITH FIGURE OVER FIERY PIT/ ANGEL/ PILGRIM
15-33, FIERY PIT WITH MEN FIGHTING WITH SWORDS/ ANGEL/ PILGRIM
15-34, TOWER/ WHEEL/ 2 FIGURES 15-35, FIERY PIT WITH 3 FIGURES
DEVOURED BY WOLVES 15-36, FIERY PIT WITH DEVILS/ ANGEL/
PILGRIM 15-37, WHEEL WITH PILGRIMS TURNED BY DEVILS 15-38,
FIERY PIT WITH DEVILS TORMENTING BOUND FIGURES 15-39, FIERY
PIT WITH 5 FIGURES 15-41, FIERY PIT WITH PRAYING COUPLES
15-40, MEN BETWEEN TREES 15-42, TREES WITH GIRL AND ROBED
FIGURE 15-43, GOD WITH ANGELS AND CHRIST 15-43, ANGEL AND
PILGRIM 15/43-53, CHRIST IN TREE 15-44, FIGURES ROBED 15-44,
LANDSCAPE WITH TREES AND TWO FIGURES 15-45, BATTLEMENTS WITH

MOUNTED KNIGHT AND OTHER FIGURES 15-46, PORTICO WITH CROWNED
FIGURE AND MEN 15-47, PORTICO WITH CROWNED FIGURE AND
ATTENDANTS 15-48, CROWNED FIGURE IN RAISED BOX WITH ATTENDANTS
15-49, KNIGHT AND GIRL BELOW 15-49, LANDSCAPE WITH DEVILS/
PILGRIMS/ SAINTS 15-50, LANDSCAPE/ 6 DOVES WITH SCROLLS 15-51,
CONCENTRIC COLORED RINGS WITH FACE IN CENTER 15-52, SAINTS
KNEELING AND LOOKING UP TO GOD ENTHRONED 15-53, PRIEST
CELEBRATING MASS 15-54, VIRGIN AND CHILD SEATED 15-55, ST
AGNES 15-55, ST JOHN BAPTIST 15-55, ST CHRISTOPHER 15-55

*$ABSTRACT 16
  *LIBRARY BOD
  *SLIDE SET TITLE BRETON ILLUMINATION
  *NEGATIVE REFERENCE ROLL 120
  *RENTAL FEE SM 016 $2.25
  *COMMENTS GIVEN TO EXETER BY LEOFRIC
  *SHELFMARK MS AUCT D 2 16
  *PROVENANCE FRENCH/ LANDEVENNEC/ BRITTANY
  *DATE EXECUTED 10TH
  *TYPE OF MANUSCRIPT GOSPEL LIST
  *CONTENTS BRETON ILLUMINATION/ 10TH 16/1-5, ST MATTHEW 16-1, ST
  MARK 16-2, ST MARK 16-3, ST LUKE 16-4, ST JOHN 16-5

*$ABSTRACT 17
  *LIBRARY BOD
  *SLIDE SET TITLE HOVEDEN MAP OF WHEATLEY
  *NEGATIVE REFERENCE ROLL 121B
  *RENTAL FEE SM 017 $2.40
  *COMMENTS MAPS SHOWING ARABLE STRIPS AND WOODLAND AT WHEATLEY
  1583-4
  *SHELFMARK HOVEDEN ATLAS
  *PROVENANCE ENGLISH
  *DATE EXECUTED 16TH/1583-4
  *LANGUAGE ENGLISH
  *TYPE OF MANUSCRIPT ATLAS
  *CONTENTS MAP/ ARABLE STRIPS 17/1-8, WEST FIELD 17-1, QUARRIES
  17-1, DETAIL OF FRAME 1 17-2, QUARRY IN WEST FIELD CALLED
  CEORLA GRAF 17-3, OLD WHEATLEY/ LOST VILLAGE 17-4, COOMBE WOOD
  17- 4, EAST END OF HIGH STREET 17-5, LYE FIELD/ UPPER FIELD/
  COOMBE WOOD 17-6, ROMAN VILLA 17-6, SAXON GRAVEYARD 17-6,
  WHEATLEY BRIDGE 17-6, ENCLOSURES AT SITE OF OLD WHEATLEY 17-7,
  UPPER FIELD 17-8, ENCLOSED GROUND BETWEEN RIVER AND UPPERFIELD
  NOT SHOWN 17-8

*$ABSTRACT 18
  *LIBRARY BOD
  *SLIDE SET TITLE BESTIARY ILLUMINATION I
  *NEGATIVE REFERENCE ROLL 126
  *RENTAL FEE SM 018 $2.90
  *SHELFMARK MS BODLEY 764 18/1-9, MS BODLEY 602 17/10-17, MS
  DOUCE 167 17-18
  *PROVENANCE ENGLISH
  *DATE EXECUTED 13TH
  *LANGUAGE LATIN
  *ARTIST/ SCHOOL SCHOOL OF MATTHEW PARIS 17/10-17
  *TYPE OF MANUSCRIPT BESTIARY
  *CONTENTS BESTIARY 18/1-18, TIGER DECEIVED BY OWN IMAGE IN
  GLASS BALL 18-1, HUNTSMAN CARRIES OFF TIGER CUB 18-1, UNICORN
  WITH HEAD IN VIRGIN'S LAP SPEARED BY HUNTER 18-2, ELEPHANT
  CARRYING TOWER OF WARRIORS FIGHTING FOOT SOLDIERS 18-3, HYENA
  EATING CORPSE 18-4, CATHEDRAL 18-4, FOX FEIGNING DEATH TO
  ATTRACT BIRDS 18-5, FOX CARRYING OFF CAPTURED BIRD 18-5, EAGLE
  FLYING TOWARD SUN 18-6, EAGLE PLUNGING INTO WATER 18-6, EAGLE
  RISING FROM WATER WITH FISH 18-6, MERMAIDS/ SIRENS PUTTING
  SAILORS TO SLEEP WITH SONG 18-7, ASP CHARMED WITH EAR STOPPED
  WITH TAIL AND OTHER 18-8, SHIP GROUNDED ON BACK OF WHALE 18-9,

WHALE WITH BUSHES ON BACK AND SAILOR FANS FIRE 18-9, LION
CHASED BY HUNTSMEN 18-10, LION AND LIONESS WITH CUBS 18-10,
LIONS SLEEPING WITH EYES OPEN 18-10, SIRENS WITH MUSICAL
INSTRUMENTS 18-11, CENTAURS FIGHTING 18-11, SIMIA/ BABOON AND
FEMALE WITH BABIES 18-12, PANTHER BELCHING SWEET SCENT AND 6
OTHER ANIMALS 18-13, SALAMANDERS/ ONE PUTTING OUT FLAMES
18-14, OYSTER/ PEARL WITH VIRGIN AND CHILD 18-15, VIRGIN AND
CHILD 18-15, TEREBOLEM/ FIRESTONES SHOWN AS MALE AND FEMALE
18-16, FIRESTONES 18-16, OSTRICH WITH 2 EGGS 18-17, UNICORN
CAPTURED 18/18

*$ABSTRACT 19
 *LIBRARY BOD
 *SLIDE SET TITLE HISTORY OF PRINTING
 *NEGATIVE REFERENCE ROLL 129
 *RENTAL FEE SM 019 $2.90
 *COMMENTS 18 SLIDES INCLUDING ILLUSTRATIONS FROM 18 MSS AND
 PRINTED BOOKS OF THE 15TH-20TH CENTURIES
 *TITLE OF MANUSCRIPT IL FILOCOLO 19-1, BIBLIA PAUPERAM 19-2,
 42-LINE BIBLE 19-3, MAINZ PSALTER 19-4, BREVIARY 19-5,
 COMMENTARIA GRAMMATICA 19-6, HYPNOROTOMACHIA 19/7-8,
 SCHOLEMASTER 19-9, BUCOLICA 19-10, OPERA 19-11, HISTORY OF THE
 HOLY WAR 19-12, HISTORY OF GODFREY OF BOULOGNE 19-13, DOVES
 PRESS BIBLE 19-14, FUGITIVE PIECES 19-15, JEROME 19-16, GAME
 AND PLAY OF CHESSE 19-17, PICTAS UNIVERSITATIS 19-18
 *PROVENANCE ITALIAN 19-1, GERMAN MAINZ 19-4, ITALIAN VENICE
 19-5, ENGLISH 19/9-10, ENGLISH 19/12-15, SWISS BASLE 19-16,
 ENGLISH 19/17-18
 *DATE EXECUTED 15TH/1460-80 19-1, 15TH/C1450 19/2-3, 15TH/1462
 19-4, 15TH/C1480 19-5, 15TH/1471 19-6, 15TH/1499 19/7-8,
 16TH/1570 19-9, 18TH/1757 19-10, 18TH/1791 19-11, 19TH/1840
 19-12, 19TH/1893 19-13, 20TH/1903-5 19-14, 18TH/1758 19-15,
 16TH/1516 19-16, 15TH/C1481, 18TH/C1702 19-18
 *LANGUAGE ITALIAN 19-1, LATIN 19/2-8, ENGLISH 19-9, LATIN
 19/10-11, ENGLISH 19/12-15, LATIN 19-16, ENGLISH 19/17-18
 *ARTIST/ SCHOOL HOLBEIN 19-16
 *AUTHOR BOCCACCIO 19-1, VALLA/ LAURENTIUS 19-6, ASCHAM 19-9,
 VIRGIL 19-10, HORACE 19-11, FULLER/ THOMAS 19-12, WALPOLE/
 HORACE 19-15, ERASMUS 19-16
 *TYPE OF MANUSCRIPT BIBLE 19/2-3, BREVIARY 19-4, HISTORY
 19/12-13, BIBLE 19-14
 *CONTENTS PRINTING/ HISTORY OF 19/1-18

*$ABSTRACT 20
 *LIBRARY BOD
 *SLIDE SET TITLE GOSPELS
 *NEGATIVE REFERENCE ROLL 130C
 *RENTAL FEE SM 020 $2.85
 *COMMENTS WRITTEN IN RANSHOFEN IN UPPER AUSTRIA UNDER ABBOT
 ADELHARD AND LIUTOLD THESAURARIUS
 *SHELFMARK MS CANON BIBL LAT 60
 *PROVENANCE BAVARIA/ RANSHOVEN
 *DATE EXECUTED 12TH/1178
 *LANGUAGE LATIN
 *TYPE OF MANUSCRIPT GOSPELS
 *CONTENTS GOSPELS 20/1-17, CANON TABLES 20/1-8, ST MATTHEW AT
 DESK 20-9, ANGEL 20-9, INITIAL L 20-10, ST MARK AT DESK 20-11,
 LION 20-11, INITIAL I 20-12, ST LUKE AT DESK 20-13, BULL
 20-13, INITIAL Q 20-14, ST JOHN AT DESK 20-15, EAGLE SYMBOL
 20-15, INITIAL I 20-16, CRUCIFIXION 20-17

*$ABSTRACT 21
 *LIBRARY BOD
 *SLIDE SET TITLE TERENCE COMEDIES
 *NEGATIVE REFERENCE ROLL 131A
 *RENTAL FEE SM 021 $9.20

*COMMENTS COPIED IN MID 12TH CENTURY PROBABLY AT ST ALBANS FROM
A CAROLINGIAN VERSION OF A LATE ROMAN MS
*TITLE OF MANUSCRIPT TERENCE COMEDIES
*SHELFMARK MS AUCT F 2 13
*PROVENANCE ENGLISH/ ST ALBANS
*DATE EXECUTED 12TH
*LANGUAGE LATIN
*AUTHOR TERENCE
*TYPE OF MANUSCRIPT PLAYS
*CONTENTS DRAMA/ TERENCE COMEDIES 21/1-144, LITERATURE/ TERENCE
COMEDIES 21/1-144, MASKED PLAYERS POINTING TO PORTRAIT OF
TERENCE 21-1, PLAYER'S MASKS ON SHELVES 21-2, ANDRIA 21/3-27,
PROLOGUS POINTS TO TEXT 21-3, SYMO AND SOSIA 21-4, SYMO AND
DAVUS 21-5, MYSIS AND MIDWIFE 21-6, PAMPHILUS SPEAKS TO MYSIS
21-7, CHARINUS/BYRRIA/PAMPHILUS 21-8, DAVUS/PAMPHILUS/CHARINUS
21-9, SYMO/ DAVUS/ PAMPHILUS 21-10, BYRRIA/ SYMO LISTEN TO
PAMPHILUS 21-11, PLAYERS MASKED 21-12, PLAYERS TALKING
CONFIDENTIALLY 21-13, FRAME 14 IS DUPLICATE OF FRAME 11, FRAME
15 IS DUPLICATE OF FRAME 12, SYMO GESTURES TOWARD CHREMES
21-16, DAVUS RUNS TOWARDS SYMO AND CHREMES 21-17, PAMPHILUS
SPEAKS TO DAVUS 21-18, CHARINUS REPROVES PAMPHILUS AND DAVUS
LISTENS 21-19, MYSIS/ PAMPHILUS/ CHARINUS/ DAVUS 21-20, DAVUS
HANDS INFANT TO MYSIS 21/21, CRITO SPEAKS TO MYSIS AND DAVUS
LISTENS 21-22, CHREMES SPEAKS TO SIMO 21-23, DAVUS/ CHREMES/
SYMO/ DROMO 21-24, PAMPHILUS/ SYMO/ CHREMES 21-25, PAMPHILUS/
CRITO/ CHREMES/ SYMO 21-26, CHARINUS LISTENS TO PAMPHILUS AND
DAVUS TO RIGHT 21-27, EUNUCHUS 21/28-54, PHAEDRIA LISTENS TO
PARMENO 21-28, THAIS/ PHAEDRIA PARMENO 21-29, PHAEDRIA
GESTURES TOWARDS PARMENO 21-28, PHAEDRIA LED BY GNATHO AND
PARMENO AT RIGHT 21-31, CHAEREA GESTURES TOWARDS PARMENO
21-32, LACHES LISTENS TO GNATHO AND PARMENO AT RIGHT 21-33,
GNATHO/ THRASO/ THAIS/ EUNUCH/ PARMENO/ PYTHIAS/ WOMAN
21/34-35, ANTIPHO COMES TO SEE CHAEREA 21-36, ANTIPHO TALKS TO
CHAEREA 21-37, DORIAS 21-38, PHAEDRIA 21-39, PYTHIAS SPEAKS TO
PHAEDRIA AND DORIAS 21-40, DORUS/ PYTHIAS/ DORIASIN 21-41,
CHREMES AND PYTHIAS 21-42, THAIS/ CHREMES/ PYTHIAS 21-43,
THRASO/ THAIS AND FOLLOWERS STUGGLE 21-44, THAIS AND PYTHIAS
21-45, CHAEREA/ THAIS/ PYTHIAS 21-46, PYTHIAS/ CHREMES/
SOPHRONA 21-47, PARMENO AND PYTHIAS 21-48, PARMENO SPEAKS TO
PYTHIAS 21-49, LACHES LISTENS TO PARMENO 21-50, PYTHIAS SPEAKS
TO PARMENO 21-51, GNATHO LISTENS TO THRASO 21-52, CHAEREA/
PARMENO/ THRASO/ GNATHO 21-53, PHAEDRIA/ CHAEREA/ GNATHO/
THRASO 21-54, HEAUTONTIMORUMENOS 21/55-76, PROLOGUS 21-55,
CHREMES SPEAKS TO MENEDEMUS 21-56, CLITIPHO LISTENS TO CHREMES
21-57, CLITIPHO 21-58, CLINIA LISTENS TO CLITIPHO 21-59, SYRUS
SPEAKS AS DROMO/ CLINIA/ CLITIPHO LISTEN 21-60, ANTIPHILA/
CLINIA/ BACCHIS/ CLITIPHO/ SYRUS 21-61, CHREMES SPEAKS TO
MENEDEMUS 21-62, SYRUS LISTENS TO CHREMES 21-63, CHREMES/
SYRUS/ CLITIPHO 21-64, SOSTRATA/ NURSE/ CHREMES/ SYRUS 21-65,
SYRUS 21-66, CLINIA LISTENS TO SYRUS 21-67, CLINIA/ BACCHIS/
PHRYGIA/ DROMO/ SYRUS 21-68, CHREMES LISTENS TO SYRUS 21-69,
CLITIPHO LISTENS TO SYRUS 21-70, CHREMES/ CLITIPHO/ CYRUS
21-71, MENEDEMUS LISTENS TO CHREMES 21-72, MENEDEMUS/ CHREMES/
CLITIPHO/ SYRUS 21-73, SOSTRATA CHIDES CHREMES 21-74,
CLITIPHO/ SOSTRATA AND CHREMES 21-75, MENEDEMUS/ CHREMES/
SOSTRATA/ CLITIPHO 21-76, PROLOGUS 21-77, ADELPHOE 21/77-103,
MICIO 21-78, DEMEA REBUKES MICIO 21-79, PARMENO STRIKES SANNIO
AND AESCHINUS 21-80, SYRUS TO SANNIO 21-81, CTESIPHO AND SYRUS
21-82, AESCHINUS/ CTESIPHO/ SYRUS/ SANNIO 21-83, SOSTRATA
SPEAKS TO CANTHARA 21-84, GETA/ SOSTRATA/ CANTHARA 21-85,
DEMEA 21-86, SNAKES 21-87, HEGIO/ GETA/ DEMA 21-88, CTESIPHO
LISTENS TO SYRUS 21-89, DEMEA/ SYRUS/ CTESIPHO 21-90, MICIO
AND HEGIO 21-91, AESCHINUS 21-92, MICIO LISTENS TO AESCHINUS
21-93, DEMEA 21-94, MICIO SPEAKS TO DEMEA 21-95, SYRUS LISTENS
TO DEMEA 21-96, DROMO/ SYRUS AND DEMEA 21-97, MICIO SPEAKS TO
DEMEA 21-98, DEMEA SPEAKS TO SYRUS 21-99, GETA LISTENS TO
DEMEA 21-100, AESCHINUS LISTENS TO DEMEA 21-101, MICIO AND
AESCHINUS LISTEN TO DEMEA 21-102, SYRUS/ DEMEA/ AESCHINUS/
MICIO 21-103, PROLOGUS 21-104, HECYRA 21/104-122, PHILOTIS
LISTENS TO SYRA 21-105, PARMENO SPEAKS TO PHILOTIS AND SYRA
21-106, LACHES SPEAKS TO SOSTRATA 21-107, PHIDIPPUS SPEAKS TO
LACHES AND SOSTRATA LISTENS 21-108, PAMPHILUS LISTENS TO

13

PARMENO 21-110, SOSTRATA 21-109, SOSTRATA AND PARMENO LISTEN
TO PAMPHILUS 21-111, PAMPHILUS 21-112, PARMENO/ SOSIA/
PAMPHILUS/ MASKED PLAYER 21-113, LACHES/ PHIDIPPUS/ PAMPHILUS
21-114, MYRRINA LISTENS TO PHIDIPPUS 21-115, SOSTRATA/
PAMPHILUS/ LACHES 21-116, LAHES/ SOSTRATA/ PAMPHILUS 21-117,
PHIDIPPUS/ PAMPHILUS/ LACHES 21-118, BACCHIS LISTENS TO LACHES
21-119, NURSE/ PHIDIPPUS/ LACHES/ BACCHIS 21-120, PARMENO
SPEAKS TO BACCHIS 21-121, PAMPHILUS/ PARMENO/ BACCHIS 21-122,
PHORMIO 21/123-144, PROLOGUE 21-123, DAVUS 21-124, GETA SPEAKS
TO DAVUS 21-125, ANTIPHO AND PHAEDRIA 21-126, DEMIPHO SPEAKS
TO PHAEDRIA AND GETA 21-127, DEMIPHO SPEAKS TO ANTIPHO AND
PHAEDRIA 21-128, PHORMIO SPEAKS TO GETA 21-129, DEMIPHO/ GETA/
PHORMIO/ HEGIO/ CRATINUS/ CRITO 21-130, PHAEDRIA/ ANTIPHO/
DORIO/ GETA 21-131, PHAEDRIA AND ANTIPHO LISTEN TO GETA
21-132, DEMIPHO SPEAKS TO CHREMES 21-133, GETA 21-134,
ANTIPHO/ GETA/ DEMIPHO/ CHREMES 21-135, ANTIPHO LISTENS TO
GETA 21-136, CHREMES/ DEMIPHO/ GETA 21-137, SOPHRONIA 21-138,
DEMIPHO AND GETA 21-139, PLAYERS 21-140, ANTIPHO 21/141-142,
PHORMIO SPEAKS TO ANTIPHO 21-143, GEAT/ ANTIPHO/ PHORMIO
21-144

*$ABSTRACT 22
 *LIBRARY BOD
 *SLIDE SET TITLE TREASURES OF CORPUS CHRISTI COLLEGE
 *NEGATIVE REFERENCE ROLL 132
 *RENTAL FEE SM 022 $5.40
 *COMMENTS 68 SLIDES FROM 9 MSS OF THE 12TH-16TH CENTURIES
 *SHELFMARK MS C C C 2 ASTERISK 22/1-2, MS C C C 13 22/3-6, MS C
  C C 14 22/7-10, MS C C C 30 22/11-12, MS C C C 157 22/13, MS C
  C C 385 22/15-21, MS C C C 386 22/22-30, MS C C C 387
  22/31-51, MS C C C 385A 22/52-68
 *PROVENANCE ENGLISH 22/1-2, FLEMISH 22/3-10, BYZANTINE
  22/11-12, ENGLISH 22/13-14, FRENCH 22/15-51, ITALIAN 22/52-68
 *DATE EXECUTED 13TH 22/1-2, 16TH/1514-20 22/3-10, 12TH/C1118-40
  22-13, 16TH/C1515 22/15-30, 15TH 22/31-51, 13TH 22/52-68
 *ARTIST/ SCHOOL MATTHEW PARIS 22-2
 *TYPE OF MANUSCRIPT NEW TESTAMENT 22/3-10, CHRONICLE 22/13-14,
  BIBLE 22/15-30, CALENDAR AND BOOK OF HOURS 22/31-51, LIBER
  FIGURARUM 22/52-68
 *CONTENTS DEPOSITION 22-1, MARYS AT SEPULCHRE 22-1, MAP OF
  PALESTINE BY MATTHEW PARIS 22-2, ST MATTHEW AT DESK 22-3, ST
  MARK AT DESK WITH LION 22-4, ST LUKE AT DESK WITH OX 22-5, ST
  JOHN WITH EAGLE 22-6, INITIAL I 22-7, ST PAUL WITH PEN AND
  INKWELL 22-8, INITIAL P 22-9, INITIAL Q 22-10, ST MARK 22-11,
  ST LUKE 22-12, PEASANTS AND BARONS 22-13, PEASANTS/ THREE
  STAND BY SLEEPING KING 22-14, ADAM/ EVE AND GOD 22-15, EXODUS
  22-16, MOSES FOUND BY PHARAOH'S DAUGHTER 22-16, SLAUGHTER OF
  THE EGYPTIANS 22-16, BURNING BUSH 22-16, LEVITICUS 22-17,
  AARON CONSECRATED 22-17, NUMBERS 22-18, MOSES AND AARON COUNT
  CHILDREN OF ISRAEL 22-18, SPIES RETURN EITH GRAPES 22-18,
  DEUTERONOMY 22-19, JACOB DYING 22-19, JOSHUA 22-20, JUDGES
  22-21, GIDEON WITH DEW ON FLEECE 22-21, DAVID BEFORE SAUL
  22/22, CHRONICLES 22-23, ADAM AND EVE WITH CAIN AND ABEL
  22-23, ESDRAS 22-24, CYRUS GIVING ESDRAS LEAVE TO BUILD TEMPLE
  22-24, ESDRAS 22-25, JOB WITH MESSENGER POINTING AT HIS HOUSE
  22-26, TOBIT/ TOBIAS HEALS FATHER TOBIT 22-27, JUDITH/ PUTTING
  HEAD OF HOLOFERNES IN BAG 22-28, ZEROBABEL BEGS DARIUS TO
  ALLOW TEMPLE 22-29, ESTHER/ OFFERED CROWN BY AHASUERUS 22-30,
  ANNUNCIATION WITH VIRGIN READING 22-31, ANGELS 22-32,
  CRUCIFIXION 22-33, VIRGIN SURROUNDED BY APOSTLES 22-34, PIETA
  22-35, ST BARBARA EXECUTED 22-36, NATIVITY 22-37, ANNUNCIATION
  OF SHEPHERDS 22-38, ADORATION OF THE MAGI 22-39, PRESENTATION
  IN TEMPLE 22-40, FLIGHT INTO EGYPT 22-41, CORONATION OF VIRGIN
  22-42, DAVID PLAYING HARP 22-43, GOD AND HELL 22-44, JOB ON
  DUNGHILL WITH COMFORTERS 22-45, CHRIST PRAYS IN GARDEN WITH
  DISCIPLES ASLEEP 22-46, CHRIST WASHING DISCIPLES FEET 22-47,
  LAST SUPPER 22-48, CHRIST BEFORE PILATE 22-49, ST JOHN WITH
  EAGLE 22-50, VIRGIN AND CHILD 22-50, ST MATTHEW WITH ANGEL
  22-51, JOACHIM OF FIORE/ LIBER FIGURARUM 22/52-68

*$ABSTRACT 23
  *LIBRARY BOD
  *SLIDE SET TITLE IRISH AND ANGLO-SAXON ILLUMINATION
  *NEGATIVE REFERENCE ROLL 135A
  *RENTAL FEE SM 023 $2.80
  *COMMENTS 16 SLIDES FROM 4 MSS OF THE 9TH-11TH CENTURIES
  *TITLE OF MANUSCRIPT MACREGOL OR RUSHWORTH GOSPELS 23/1-7, ST
  MARGARET'S GOSPELS 23/8-12, CAEDMON MANUSCRIPT 23/13-15, ST
  DUNSTAN/S CLASSBOOK 23-16
  *SHELFMARK MS AUCT D 2 19 23/1-7, MS LAT LITURG F 5 23/8-12, MS
  JUNIUS 11 23/13-15, MS AUCT F 4 32 23-16
  *PROVENANCE IRISH/ ENGLISH
  *DATE EXECUTED 09TH 23/1-7, 11TH 23/8-15
  * TYPE OF MANUSCRIPT GOSPELS 23/1-12
  *CONTENTS ENGLISH AND IRISH ILLUMINATION/ 9TH-11TH 23/1-16,
  ORNAMENTED PAGE 23-1, ST MARK 23-2, ORNAMENTED PAGE 23-3, ST
  LUKE 23-4, ORNAMENTED PAGE 23-5, ST JOHN 23-6, ORNAMENTED PAGE
  23-7, ST MATTHEW 23-8, INITIAL ORNAMENTED 23-9, ST MARK 23-10,
  ST LUKE 23-11, ST JOHN 23-12, LUCIFER@S PRESUMPTION AND FALL
  23-13, ARK 23-14, NIMROD'S PROGRESS 23-15, ST DUNSTAN AT FEET
  OF CHRIST 23-16

*$ABSTRACT 24
  *LIBRARY BOD
  *SLIDE SET TITLE BOOK OF HOURS
  *NEGATIVE REFERENCE ROLL 135B
  *RENTAL FEE SM 024 $4.10
  *TITLE OF MANUSCRIPT BOOK OF HOURS
  *SHELFMARK MS DOUCE 144
  *PROVENANCE FRENCH/ PARIS
  *DATE EXECUTED 15TH/1407
  *LANGUAGE LATIN AND FRENCH
  *ARTIST/ SCHOOL MASTER OF ETIENNE LOYPEAU 24/4-15, BOUCICAUT,
  BEDFORD MASTERS, LIMBOURG BROTHER
  *TYPE OF MANUSCRIPT BOOK OF HOURS
  *CONTENTS BOOK OF HOURS/ FRENCH 24/1-42, ST JOHN 24-1, ST LUKE
  24-2, ST MARK 24-3, CALENDAR FOR JANUARY 24-4, FIRESIDE 24-4,
  CALENDAR FOR FEBRUARY 24-5, WOODING 24-5, CALENDAR FOR MARCH
  24-6, DIGGING 24-6, CALENDAR FOR APRIL 24-7, TREE PLANTING
  24-7, CALENDAR FOR MAY 24-8, HAWKING 24-8, CALENDAR FOR JUNE
  24-9, SCYTHING 24-9, CALENDAR FOR JUNE 24-10, REAPING 24-10,
  CALENDAR FOR AUGUST 24-11, THRESHING 24-11, CALENDAR FOR
  SEPTEMBER 24-12, WINE PRESSING 24-12, CALENDAR FOR OCTOBER
  24-13, SOWING 24-13, CALENDAR FOR NOVEMBER 24-14, KNOCKING
  DOWN ACORNS FOR SWINE 24-14, CALENDAR FOR DECEMBER 24-15, PIG
  KILLING 24-15, VIRGIN WEAVING 24-16, VIRGIN AND CHILD 24-17,
  ANNUNCIATION 24-18, VISITATION 24-19, NATIVITY AND ADORATION
  24-20, ANGELS AND SHEPHERDS 24-21, ADORATION OF THE MAGI
  24-22, PRESENTATION IN THE TEMPLE 24-23, FLIGHT INTO EGYPT
  24/24, PROCESSION OF LITANIES 24-25, PROCESSION FOR
  TRANSFERENCE OF RELICS 24-26, PROCESSION OF FLAGELLANTS 24-27,
  CRUCIFIXION 24-28, VIRGIN AND CHILD 24-29, LAST JUDGMENT
  24-30, ST MICHAEL 24-31, ST PETER 24-32, ST PAUL 24-33, ST
  ANDREW 24-34, ST JOHN THE EVANGELIST 24-35, ST STEPHEN 24-36,
  ST DENIS 24-37, ST NICHOLAS 24-38, ST MARTIN OF TOURS 24-39,
  ST ANTHONY 24-40, ST MARY MAGDALENE 24-41, ST CATHERINE 24-42

*$ABSTRACT 25
  *LIBRARY BOD
  *SLIDE SET TITLE BESTIARY ILLUMINATION I
  *NEGATIVE REFERENCE ROLL 136A
  *RENTAL FEE SM 025 $3.80
  *SHELFMARK MS BODLEY 764
  *PROVENANCE ENGLISH
  *DATE EXECUTED 13TH
  *TYPE OF MANUSCRIPT BESTIARY
  *CONTENTS BESTIARY/ ENGLISH 25/1-36, LION/ SICK EATING MONKEY
  AS CURE 25-1, LION REFRAINS FROM EATING 3 PROSTRATE MEN 25-1,

LION AFRAID OF COCK 25-1, TIGER DECIVED BY OWN IMAGE IN GLASS
BALL 25-2, TIGER CUB TAKEN BY HUNTSMAN 25-2, PANTHER'S BREATH
ATTRACTS OTHER ANIMALS 25-3, LEOPARD 25-4, UNICORN WITH VIRGIN
SPEARED BY HUNTSMAN 25-5, GRIFFIN FIGHTING WITH HORSE 25-6,
ELEPHANT CARRYING TOWER OF WARRIORS 25-7, BEAVER CASTRATES
SELF BEFORE HUNTERS 25-8, IBEX HUNTED AND FALLS FROM MOUNTAIN
25-9, HYENA EATING CORPSE 25-10, BONNACON SPEARED BY HUNTSMEN
25-11, MONKEY/ FEMALE WITH BABIES CHASED BY HUNTERS 25-12,
STAG AND DOE WITH YOUNG 25-13, GOATS NIBBLING AT TREES 25-14,
MONOCEROS/ UNICORN HEAD AND PAWS WITH HORSE'S BODY 25-15, BEAR
SHAPING NEWBORN CUBS WITH TONGUE 25-16, CROCODILE WITH MAN
WITH AXE 25-17, CROCODILE EATING FISHES 25-17, MANTICORE/
HUMAN HEADED LION WITH SCORPION TAIL 25-18, GARAMANTES RESCUED
BY HOUNDS 25-19, HYRCUS/ HE GOAT 25-20, BOAR/ WILD WITH DOG
BALANCED ON SPEAR 25-21, ASINUS/ DONKEY 25-22, HORSES IN TEAM
25-23, BADGERS PULLING A THIRD ALONG WITH A STICK 25-24, CATS/
THREE 25/25, HEDGEHOGS AND GRAPEVINE 25-26, SALAMANDERS IN
FLAMES 25-27, EAGLES FLYING/ PLUNGING INTO WATER/ LIFTING
MOUSE 25-28, GEESE/ BARNACLE HANGING FROM TREE 25-29,
CALADRIUS/ MYTHICAL BIRD 25-30, OSTRICHES LOOKING AT PLEIADES
AND TURNING OVER EGGS 25-31, PHOENIX ON FUNERAL PYRE 25-32,
EAGLE OWL BUBO WITH MAGPIE AND BIRDS 25-33, SIRENS/ MERMAIDS
PUTTING SAILORS TO SLEEP 25-34, ASP ENCHANTED BY SNAKE CHARMER
25-35, WHALE WITH SHIP ON BACK AND SAILORS 25-36

*$ABSTRACT 26
 *LIBRARY BOD
 *SLIDE SET TITLE IVORY AND ENAMEL BOOK COVERS OF THE 10TH-15TH
  CENTURIES
 *NEGATIVE REFERENCE ROLL 136C
 *RENTAL FEE SM 026 $2.30
 *COMMENTS 6 SLIDES FROM 5 MSS
 *SHELFMARK MS AUCT D 120 26-1, MS DOUCE 176 26-2, MS DOUCE 292
  26-3, MS AUCT T INF 1 10 26-4, MS AUCT D 4 2 26/5-6
 *PROVENANCE ITALIAN 26-1, FRENCH 26-2, LIEGE REGUM 26-3,
  BYZANTINE 26-4, FRENCH 26/5-6
 *DATE EXECUTED 14TH 26-1, 09TH 26-2, 11TH 26-3, 10TH 26-4,
  15TH/C1400 26/5-6
 *ARTIST/ SCHOOL COURT SCHOOL OF CHARLEMAGNE 26-2
 *CONTENTS MANUSCRIPT AND BOOK COVERS 26/1-6, IVORY BOOK COVERS
  22/1-6, TRIPTYCH 26-1, VIRGIN AND CHILD 26-1, ST VINCENT OF
  SARAGOSSA 26-1, OLD TESTAMENT PROPHET 26-1, ST LAWRENCE AND
  VIRGIN 26-1, LIFE OF CHRIST 26-2, CHRIST WITH EVANGELIST
  SYMBOLS 26-4, IVORY CARVING 26-3, CORONATION OF VIRGIN 26-5,
  ENAMEL COVER 26-5, ANNUNCIATION 26-6

*$ABSTRACT 27
 *LIBRARY BOD
 *SLIDE SET TITLE MUSICAL INSTRUMENTS
 *NEGATIVE REFERENCE ROLL 137
 *RENTAL FEE SM 027 $3.20
 *COMMENTS 24 SLIDES FROM 4 MSS DEPICTING MUSICAL INSTRUMENTS
 *SHELFMARK MS BODLEY 264 27/1-14, MS ASHMOLE 1523 26-15, MS
  LITURG 198 26-16, MS DOUCE 144 26/17-21, MS BODLEY 264
  27/22-24
 *PROVENANCE FLEMISH 26/1-14, ENGLISH 26/15-16, FRENCH 26/17-21,
  FLEMISH 26/22-24
 *DATE EXECUTED 14TH 27/1-15, 14TH-15TH 27-16, 15TH/1407
  27/17-21, 14TH 27/22-24
 *CONTENTS MUSICAL INSTRUMENTS 27/1-24, FLUTE 27-1, SHAWM 27-2,
  TRUMPET 27-2, ORGAN/ PORTATIVE 27-2, FIDDLE/ OVAL 27-2,
  MANDORA 27-2, PSALTERY 27-2, GITTERN 27-3, ORGAN/ PORTATIVE
  27-4, TRUMPET 27-4, FIDDLE/ OVAL 27-4, CITTERN LIKE
  FINGERBOARD INSTRUMENT 27-5, ORGAN/ PORTATIVE 27-6, FLUTE/
  TRANSVERSE 27-7, NAKERS 27-7, BAGPIPES 27-7, TIMBREL 27-8,
  HAND BELLS 27-8, FLUTE 27-8, TIMBREL 27-9, ORGAN/ PORTATIVE
  27-9, NAKERS 27/9-10, HAND BELLS 27-9, TRUMPETS 27-10,
  BAGPIPES 27-10, SHAWM 27-10, FIDDLE/ OVAL 27-10, HARP 27-10,

16

FIDDLE/ GUITAR 27-11, CYMBALS 27-11, HANDBELLS 27-11, PSALTERY
WITH QUILL PLECTRA 27-11, FIDDLE 27/12-13, NAKERS 27/12-13,
ORGAN/ PORTATIVE 27/12-13, CAROLE 27-12, BAGPIPES 27-13, TABOR
27-13, CYMBALS 27-13, HAND BELLS 27-13, TRUMPET 27-13,
PSALTERY 27-13, MANDORA 27-13, FLUTE 27-14, HAND BELLS 27-14,
DRUM WITH SNARE 27-14, SHAWMS 27-14, HARP 27-14, BAGPIPES
27-14, TABOR 27-14, PIPE 27-15, TABOR 27-15, PSALTERY 27-15,
FIDDLE/ OVAL 27/15-18, TRUMPET 27-15, SINGERS 27-16, ORGAN/
PORTATIVE 27-17, PSALTERY 27-18, ORGAN/ PORTATIVE 27-18, HARP
27-18, REBEC WITH MANDORA PEG BOX 27-19, ORGAN/ PORTATIVE
27-20, CORNET 27-21, ORGAN/ PORTATIVE 27-22, MANDORA 27-23,
TRUMPETS WITH SLIDING MOUTHPIECES 27-24

*$ABSTRACT 28
  *LIBRARY BOD
  *SLIDE SET TITLE ENGLISH SCRIPT FROM WINCHESTER
  *NEGATIVE REFERENCE ROLL 138B
  *RENTAL FEE SM 028 $2.45
  *COMMENTS 9 SLIDES FROM 4 MSS OF THE 10TH-11TH CENTURIES
  *TITLE OF MANUSCRIPT JUNIUS PSALTER 28/1-3
  *SHELFMARK MS JUNIUS 27 28/1-3, MS BODLEY 775 28/4-7, MS DOUCE
   125 28-8, MS BODLEY 49 28-9
  *PROVENANCE ENGLISH
  *DATE EXECUTED 10TH-11TH
  *LANGUAGE LATIN 28/1-9, OLD ENGLISH GLOSS 28/1-3
  *AUTHOR PSEUDO BOETHIUS 28-8, ALDHELM/ DE LAUDE VIRGINITATIS
   28-9
  *TYPE OF MANUSCRIPT PSALTER 28/1-3, TROPER 28/4-7, PHILOSOPHY
   28-8
  *CONTENTS PALEOGRAPHY/ ENGLISH 28/1-9, SCRIBAL WRITING/ ENGLISH
   28/1-9, CALENDAR 28-1, PSALM 46 28-2, PSALM 56 28-3,
   WINCHESTER TROPER 28/4-7, BOETHIUS GEOMETRIA 28-8, ALDHELM DE
   LAUDE VIRGINITATIS 28-9

*$ABSTRACT 29
  *LIBRARY BOD
  *SLIDE SET TITLE MEDIEVAL ENGLISH POLYPHONY
  *NEGATIVE REFERENCE ROLL 139A
  *RENTAL FEE SM 029 $4.80
  *COMMENTS 57 SLIDES FROM 15 MSS
  *SHELFMARK MS BODLEY 572 29-1, MS RAWL C 892 29-2, WOOD 591
   29/3-6, MS DOUCE 139 29/7-8, MS C C C 489 29/9-12, MS C C C 59
   29-13, MS BODLEY 257 29/14-15, MS LAT LITURG D 20 29/16-20, MS
   LAT LITURG D 3 29/21-22, MS E MUSAEO 7 29/23-26, MS HATTON 81
   29/27-32, MS E MUSAEO D 143 29-33, MS LAUD LAT 95 29/34-35, MS
   ARCH SELD B 26 29/36-55, MS LAT LITURG A 9 29/56-57
  *PROVENANCE ENGLISH
  *CONTENTS MUSIC/ POLYPHONY/ ENGLISH 29/1-57, UT TUO PROPITIATUS
   29-1, DICANT NUNC 29-2, O LAUDANDA VIRGINITAS 29/3-4, SALVE
   ROSA 29/5-6, FOWELES IN THE FRITH 29-7, DANCES 29-8, FLOS
   REGALIS 29/9-10, VIRGO ROSA 29/11-12, EDI BEO THU 29-13, GAUDE
   PER QUAM 29/14-15, INCIPITS 29/1-57, DULCIFLUA TUA MEMORIA
   29-16, INVIOLATA 29/17-18, IN TUIS LAUDIBIS 29-19, MATER ORA
   FILIUM 29-20, VIRGO PUDICICIE 29-21, SALVE VIRGO 29-22, AVE
   MILES 29/23-24, DEUS CREATOR 29/25-26, OVET MUNDUS 29-27,
   SALVE IUBAR 29-28, IUSA CUM SILENTIO 29/29, OVET MUNDUS 29-30,
   HOSTIS HERODES 29/31-32, HIC EST VERE 29-32, ALLELUYA/ HIC EST
   VERE 29-33, CONDITOR ALME 29/34-35, MATER ORA FILIUM 29-36,
   SANCTA MARIA 29/37-38, BEATA AMTER 29-39, MILES CHRISTI
   29/40-41, ALLELUYA PRO VIRGINE 29-42, ALLELUYA 29-43, AVE
   REGINA 29-44, DEO GRATIAS 29-45, AS I LAY 29-46, NESCIENS
   MATER 29-47, SANCTA MARIA 29-48, NOVUS SOL 29-49, NESCIENS
   MATER 29-50, ECCE QUOD 29-51, LAUS HONOR 29-52, BLESSID BE
   29-51, SPECIOSA 29-54-55, MAGNIFICAT 29/56-57

17

```
*$ABSTRACT 30
 *LIBRARY BOD
 *SLIDE SET TITLE ENGLISH ILLUMINATION
 *NEGATIVE REFERENCE ROLL 139B
 *RENTAL FEE SM 030 $3.80
 *TITLE OF MANUSCRIPT BOHUN PSALTER
 *SHELFMARK MS AUCT D 4 4
 *PROVENANCE ENGLISH
 *DATE EXECUTED 14TH/1370-80
 *LANGUAGE LATIN
 *TYPE OF MANUSCRIPT PSALTER
 *CONTENTS ENGLISH ILLUMINATION/ 14TH 30/1-36, CRUCIFIXION 30-1,
  VIRGIN AND CHILD 30-2, MARY BOHUN IN PRAYER 30-2, CRUCIFIXION
  30-3, SAINTS 30-4, LAZARUS RAISED 30-5, CREATION 30-6,
  TEMPTATION 30-7, EXPULSION 30-7, DIXI CUSTODIAM 30-8, ARK
  30-9, DIXIT INSIPIENS 30-10, SALVUM ME FAC 30-11, EXULTATE DEO
  30-12, LOT'S WIFE 30-13, CANTATO DOMINO 30-14, DOMINE EXAUDI
  30-15, DIXIT DOMINUS 30-16, AD DOMINUM 30-17, JACOB'S LADDER
  30-18, ANNUNCIATION 30-19, VISITATION 30-20, NATIVITY 30-21,
  MIRACLE 30-22, ADORATION OF THE MAGI 30-23, PRESENTATION IN
  THE TEMPLE 30-24, CRUCIFIXION 30-25, RESURRECTION 30-26,
  CORONATION OF VIRGIN 30-27, LAST JUDGMENT 30-28, OFFICE OF THE
  DEAD 30/29-30, PRAYERS TO HOLY SPIRIT AND TRINITY 30-31,
  INITIALS OF SAINTS BARTHOLOMEW/ MATTHEW/ SIMON 30-32, ST
  MARK'S LION 30-33, ST MATTHEW'S EAGLE 30-34, ST LUKE'S OX
  30-35, ST JOHN'S EAGLE 30-36


*$ABSTRACT 31
 *LIBRARY BOD
 *SLIDE SET TITLE DEVELOPMENT OF CHILDREN'S BOOKS
 *NEGATIVE REFERENCE ROLL 140A
 *RENTAL FEE SM 031 $3.95
 *SHELFMARK MS ASHMOLE 1504 31/4-7
 *COMMENTS 40 SLIDES FROM 29 BOOKS AND MANUSCRIPTS
 *TITLE OF MANUSCRIPT FABLES 31/1A-3, HERBAL AND BESTIARY
  31/4-7, DIVES PRAGMATICUS 31/8-9, BOOK FOR BOYS AND GIRLS
  31/10-11, DIVINE SONGS 31-12, FABLES IN VERSE FOR THE
  IMPROVEMENT OF YOUNG AND OLD 31/13-14, LITTLE GOODY TWO SHOES
  31-15, BUTTERFLY/S BALL 31-16, LIFE AND DEATH OF AN APPLE PIE
  31-17, TOM THUMB/S ALPHABET 31-18, ORIGINAL MOTHER GOOSE
  MELODY 31-19, GERMAN POPULAR STORIES 31/20-21, WONDERFUL
  STORIES FOR CHILDREN 31-22, VILLAGE SCHOOL 31-23, LITTLE LORD
  FAUNTLEROY 31-24, JACKANAPES 31-25, STORY OF THE TREASURE
  SEEKERS 31-26, JACK HARKAWAY AT OXFORD 31-27, PETER PARLEY/S
  ANNUAL 31-28, WALLYPUG OF WHY 31-29, ROSE AND THE RING 31-30,
  SLEEPING BEAUTY AND BLUEBEARD 31/31, JOHN GILPIN 31-32, BABY/S
  OWN AESOP 31-33, BOOK OF NONSENSE 31-34, A APPLE PIE 31-35,
  ALPHABET 31-36, STRUWELPETER 31-37, HISTORY OF THE FAIRCHILD
  FAMILY 31/38-39
 *PROVENANCE ENGLISH
 *DATE EXECUTED 15TH/1483 31/1A-3, 16TH/1504 31/4-7, 16TH/1563
  31/8-9, 17TH/1686 31/10-11, 18TH/1735 31-12, 18TH/1765
  31/13-14, 18TH/1766 31-15, 19TH/1807 31-16, 19TH/1892 31-19,
  19TH/1823-6 31/20-21, 19TH/1846 31-22, 19TH/1800 31-23,
  19TH/1887 31-24, 19TH/1884 31-25, 19TH/1899 31-26, 19TH/1880
  31-27, 19TH/1847 31-28, 19TH/1895 31-29, 19TH/1855 31-30,
  20TH/1914 31-31 , 19TH/1892 31-32, 19TH/1887 31-33, 19TH/1862
  31-34, 19TH/1886 31-35, 19TH/1877 31-36, 20TH/1904 31-37,
  19TH/1876 31/38-39
 *LANGUAGE ENGLISH
 *AUTHOR AESOP 31/1A-3, NEWBERRY/ T 31/8-9, BUNYAN/ J 31/10-11,
  WATTS/ I 31-12, AESOP/ ABRAHAM JR 31/13-14, ROSCOE/ W 31-16,
  PERRAULT/ C 31-19, GRIMM/ J L C 31/10-21, ANDERSEN/ H C 31-22,
  KILNER/ D 31-23, BURNETT/ F H 31-24, EWING/ J H 31-25, NESBIT/
  E 31-26, HEMYNG/ S B 31-27, FARROW/ G E 31-29, THACKERAY/ W M
  31-30, CRANE/ W 31/31, COWPER/ W 31-32, CRANE/ W 31-33, LEAR/
  E 31-34, GREENAWAY/ K 31-35, HOFFMAN/ H 31-37, SHERWOOD/ M M
  31-38
 *TYPE OF MANUSCRIPT CHILDREN/S BOOKS 31/1A-39
 *CONTENTS CHILDREN'S BOOKS/ DEVELOPMENT OF 31/1-40, LITERATURE/
```

CHILDREN'S 31/1-40, APPLE TREE 31-4, OAK TREE 31-5, COCKATRICE
31-6, HORSE 31-7

*$ABSTRACT 32
  *LIBRARY BOD
  *SLIDE SET TITLE IRISH ILLUMINATION OF THE 12TH CENTURY
  *NEGATIVE REFERENCE ROLL 140D
  *RENTAL FEE SM 032 $3.20
  *COMMENTS 24 SLIDES FROM 4 MSS OF THE 12TH CENTURY
  *SHELFMARK MS RAWL B502 32/1-10, MS AUCT D 2 4 32-11, MS C C C
  122 32/12-18, MS C C C 282 32/19-24
  *PROVENANCE IRISH
  *DATE EXECUTED 12TH
  *LANGUAGE LATIN
  *CONTENTS   IRISH ILLUMINATION/ 12TH 32/1-24, BIRD 32-1, INITIAL
  32/2-6, DESIGN 32-7, INITIAL 32/8-9, FISH 32-10, INITIAL D
  32-11, CANON TABLES 32-12, CANON TABLES WITH STATIONS OF THE
  CROSS 32-13, LIBER GENERATIONIS 32-14, XRI AUTEM 32-15, MARK
  I/ INITIUM EVANGELII 32-16, LUKE I/ QUONIAM QUIDEM 32-17,
  INITIAL H/ ZOOMORPHIC HIC EST 32-18, MASS OF THE HOLY GHOST
  32-19, JOHN V 24 32-20, CHRISTMAS DAY 32-21, PALM SUNDAY
  32-22, O/ DIAMOND SHAPED 32-23, ST JOHN'S DAY/ INITIAL 32-24

*$ABSTRACT 33
  *LIBRARY BOD
  *SLIDE SET TITLE RED BOOK OF HENGEST
  *NEGATIVE REFERENCE ROLL 142
  *RENTAL FEE SM 033 $3.10
  *TITLE OF MANUSCRIPT RED BOOK OF HENGEST
  *SHELFMARK MS JESUS COLLEGE 111
  *PROVENANCE WELSH
  *DATE EXECUTED 14TH-15TH
  *TYPE OF MANUSCRIPT COLLECTION OF PROSE AND POETRY
  *CONTENTS WELSH LITERATURE 33/1-22, LITERATURE/ RED BOOK OF
  HENGEST 33/1-22, RED BOOK OF HENGEST 33/1-22, BINDING 33-1,
  ASCENDERS AND PATCHES IN MS 33-2, CATCHWORDS/ DECORATIVE AND
  GROTESQUES 33/3-9, GEOFFREY OF MONMOUTH'S HISTORY OF BRITAIN
  33-10, CHRONICLE OF THE PRINCES 33-11, ROMANCE OF CULHWCH AND
  OLWEN 33/12-13, SIR BEVIS OF HAMPTON 33-14, RISSERDYN'S POETRY
  33-15, GRIFFITH AP MEREDITH'S POETRY 33-16, HOWEL YSTORYM'S
  POETRY 33-16, IUSTUS LLWYT'S POETRY AND ANON WRITERS 33-17,
  EINION WAN/ MADOG DWYGRAIG/ IOLO GOCH'S POETRY 33-18, ARTHUR
  AND DEATH OF UTHER PENDRAGON 33-19, HISTORY OF BRITAIN'S END
  33-20, CHRONICLE OF WELSH PRINCES/ BEGINNING 33-20, MEDICAL
  TEXT 33-21, MYDDFAI PHYSICIANS 32-21, GRIFFITH AP MEREDITH/
  ODE TO OWEN AP THOMAS 33-22

*$ABSTRACT 34
  *LIBRARY BOD
  *SLIDE SET TITLE HUMANISTIC SCRIPT OF THE 15TH-16TH CENTURIES
  *NEGATIVE REFERENCE ROLL 144
  *RENTAL FEE SM 034 $3.35
  *COMMENTS 27 SLIDES FROM 22 MSS OF THE 15TH-16TH CENTURIES
  *TITLE OF MANUSCRIPT PHYSIOLOGUS 34-1, DIALOGUES 34-2, ORATOR
  34-3, HISTORIES 34-4, COMEDIES 34-5, HECYRA/ ARGUMENT 34-5,
  ELEGIES 34-6, EPITOME 34-7, EPIGRAMS 34-8, CATILINE 34-9,
  EPIGRAMS 34-10, COOKERY BOOK 34-11, MARTYROLOGY 34-12, PSALTER
  34-13, HOURS OF THE VIRGIN 34-14, EXPOSITIO IN PSALM XXX
  34-15, CHEMIN DE PARADIS 34-16, SPECIMEN BOOK 34/17-18,
  SUPERSTITIONE 34-19, LATIN EXERCISE BOOK 34/21-24, LETTER FROM
  ELIZABETH TO SOMERSET 34-25, LETTER FROM LADY STUART TO
  BURGHLEY 34-26, ODES OF HORACE 34-27
  *SHELFMARK MS AUCT T 2 23 34-1, MS CANON PAT LAT 105 34-2, MS
  LAT CLASS D 37 34-3, MS DIGBY 224 34-4, MS E D CLARKE 28 34-5,
  MS CANON CLASS LAT 31 34-6, MS CANON CLASS LAT 138 34-7, MS
  CANON CLASS LAT 85 34-8, MS RAWL G 42 34-9, MS AUCT F 4 33

19

34-10, MS CANON CLASS LAT 168 34-11, MS CANON LITURG 301
34-12, MS MONTAGUE E 9 34-13, MS DOUCE 29 34-14, MS UNIVERSITY
COLLEGE 40 34-15, MS BODLEY 883 34-16, MS CANON ITAL 196
34/17-18, MS UNIVERSITY COLLEGE 17 34-19, MS RAWL D 1317
34-20, MS AUTOGR E 2 34/21-24, MS ASHMOLE 1729 34/25-26, MS
LAT CLASS E 38 34-27
*PROVENANCE FRENCH 34-1, ITALIAN 34/2-14, DUTCH 34-15, FRENCH
34-16, ITALIAN 34/17-18, ENGLISH 34/19-27
*DATE EXECUTED 09TH 34-1, 12TH 34-2, 15TH/1412 34-3, 15TH/1430
34-4, 15TH/1466 34-5, 15TH/1480 34-6, 15TH 34/7-10, 15TH/1490
34-11, 15TH/1481-89 34-12, 16TH/C1516 34-13, 16TH/C1530-40
34-14, 16TH/1514-17 34-15, 16TH/C1540 34/16-18, 16TH/1544-6
34-19, 16TH/1542 34-20, 16TH/1548 34/21-24, 16TH/1549 34-25,
17TH/1603 34-26, 19TH/ 1875-6 34-27
*AUTHOR GREGORY THE GREAT 34-2, CICERO 34-3, LIVY 34-4, TERENCE
34-5, PROPERTIUS 34-6, JUSTIN 34-7, MARTIAL 34-8, APICIUS
34-11, PIERANTONIO SALLANDO OF REGGIO 34-12, PETER MEGHEN OF
HERTOGENBOSCH IN BRABANT 34-15, JEAN MALLARD 34-16,
GIOVANBATTISTA PALATINO 34/17-18, JOHN CHEKE 34-19, ROGER
ASCHAM 34-20, ELIZABETH 34-25, ARABELLA STUART 34-26, WILLIAM
MORRIS 34-27
*CONTENTS SCRIPT/ HUMANISTIC 34/1-27, PALEOGRAPHY/ ENGLISH
34/1-27

*$ABSTRACT 35
*LIBRARY BOD
*SLIDE SET TITLE BOCCACCIO IL FILOCOLO
*NEGATIVE REFERENCE ROLL 145B
*RENTAL FEE SM 035 $2.50
*TITLE OF MANUSCRIPT IL FILOCOLO
*SHELFMARK MS CANON ITAL 85
*PROVENANCE ITALIAN/ MANTUA OR FERRARA
*DATE EXECUTED 15TH/C1463-4
*LANGUAGE ITALIAN
*ARTIST/ SCHOOL RELATED TO SCHOOL OF COSSA IN THE SCHIFANOIA
PALACE FERRARA
*AUTHOR BOCCACCIO
*TYPE OF MANUSCRIPT PROSE
*CONTENTS LITERATURE/ IL FILOCOLO 35/1-10, IL FILOCOLO 35/1-10,
ITALIAN LITERATURE/ IL FILOCOLO 35/1-10, JUNO IN CHARIOT DRAWN
BY PEACOCK 35-1, POPE AND CARDINAL IN COURTYARD 35-1, JUNO IN
CHARIOT DRAWN BY PEACOCKS 35-2, ALTAR/FLAMING WITH GONZAGA
ARMS 35-3, VENUS INSTRUCTS AMOR 35-3, DETAIL OF VENUS AND AMOR
35-4, COURTIERS IN COURTYARD 35/5-6, RIDERS WITH HORSES IN
CITY SQUARE 35/7-8, WATERFRONT SCENE 35/9-10

*$ABSTRACT 36
*LIBRARY BOD
*SLIDE SET TITLE MEDIEVAL FOOD AND FEASTING
*NEGATIVE REFERENCE ROLL 145C
*RENTAL FEE SM 036 $2.75
*COMMENTS 15 SLIDES FROM 10 MSS OF THE 14TH-16TH CENTURIES
*SHELFMARK MS DOUCE 178 36-1, MS DOUCE 5 36/2-3, MS BODLEY 264
36/4-6, MS GOUGH LITURG 7 36-7, MS DOUCE 374 36-8, MS DOUCE
308 36-9, MS RAWL LITURG E 36 36/10-11, MS DOUCE 276 36-12, MS
CANON LITURG 99 36-13, MS AUCT D INF 2 11 36/14-15
*PROVENANCE ITALIAN 36-1, FLEMISH 36/2-8, FRENCH 36/9-15
*DATE EXECUTED 14TH 36/1-3, 14TH/1339-44 36/4-6, 16TH 36/7-8,
14TH 36-9, 15TH 36/10-13, 15TH/1430-40 36/14-15
*TYPE OF MANUSCRIPT LANCELOT CYCLE 36-1, PSALTER 36/2-3,
ROMANCE 36/4-6, PRIVATE PRAYERS 36-7, MIRACLES OF THE VIRGIN
36-8, ROMANCES 36-9, BOOK OF HOURS 36/10-15
*CONTENTS FOOD AND FEASTING 36/1-15, FEAST 36-1, BUTCHER'S SHOP
36-2, BAKING 36-3, FEAST 36/4-5, COOKING 36-6, OPEN AIR STALLS
IN MARKET 36-7, FEAST 36/8-9, BAKER AT OVEN 36-10, FEAST
36-11, COOKING 36-12, BAKING 36-13, FEASTING 36-14,
SLAUGHTERING 36-15

```
*$ABSTRACT 37
  *LIBRARY BOD
  *SLIDE SET TITLE BIBICAL ICONOGRAPHY
  *NEGATIVE REFERENCE ROLL 145D
  *RENTAL FEE SM 037 $2.85
  *COMMENTS 17 SLIDES FROM 10 MSS OF THE 12-16TH CENTURIES
  *SHELFMARK MS BODLEY 270 B 37/1-5, MS AUCT D 5 17 37-6, MS
   DOUCE 313 37/7-8, MS CANON LITURG 99 37-9, MS LAUD MISC 752
   37/10-12, MS SELDEN SUPRA 38 37-13, MS BODLEY 283 37-14, MS
   DOUCE 29 37-15, MS DOUCE 14 37-16, MS DOUCE 9 37-17
  *PROVENANCE FRENCH 37/1-9, ENGLISH 37/10-13, DUTCH 37-14,
   ITALIAN 37/15-17
  *DATE EXECUTED 13TH 37/1-6, 14TH/C1319 37/7-8, 15TH 37-9, 12TH
   37/10-11, 14TH/1300 37-13, 15TH 37-14, 16TH/1530-40 37-15,
   16TH/1500-5 37-16, 16TH/1507 37-17
  *LANGUAGE LATIN
  *TYPE OF MANUSCRIPT BIBLE
  *CONTENTS ICONOGRAPHY/ BIBLICAL 37/1-17, MOSES RECEIVES LAW
   37-1, GOLDEN CALF WORSHIPPED 37-2, EARTH SWALLOWING KORAH
   37-3, AGAG EXECUTED 37-4, ELIJAH FED BY RAVENS 37-5, MOSES
   WITH THE TABLETS 37-6, GOLDEN CALF WORSHIPPED 37-7, JONAH
   BEFORE GATEHOUSE OF NINEVEH 37-8, CURE AT CAPERNAUM 37-9,
   KORAH SWALLOWED BY EARTH 37-10, ELIJAH AND ELISHA 37-11, JONAH
   UNDER THE GOURD 37-12, CURE AT CAPERNAUM 37-13, MOSES WITH
   TABLETS 37-14, GOLDEN CALF WORSHIPPED 37-14, ELIJAH AND ELISHA
   37-15, LAZARUS RAISED 37/16-17


*$ABSTRACT 38
  *LIBRARY BOD
  *SLIDE SET TITLE BIBLE
  *NEGATIVE REFERENCE ROLL 146A
  *RENTAL FEE SM 038 $4.80
  *SHELFMARK MS AUCT E INF 1
  *PROVENANCE ENGLISH/ WINCHESTER
  *DATE EXECUTED 12TH
  *LANGUAGE LATIN
  *TYPE OF MANUSCRIPT BIBLE
  *CONTENTS BIBLE INITIALS/ 12TH/ ENGLISH 38/1-56, INITIAL F
   38-1, INITIAL O 38-2, INITIAL I 38-3, INITIAL D 38-4, INITIAL
   H 38-5, INITIAL V 38-6, INITIAL R 38-7, INITIAL L 38-8,
   INITIAL V 38-9, INITIAL H 38-10, INITIAL P 38-11, INITIAL T
   38-12, INITIAL P 38-13, INITIAL L 38-14, INITIAL V 38-15,
   INITIAL D 38/16-20, INITIAL F 38-21, INITIAL N 38-22, INITIAL
   F 38-23, INITIAL S 38-24, INITIAL E 38-25, INITIAL R 38-26,
   INITIAL C 38-27, INITIAL N 38-28, INITIAL V 38-29, INITIAL C
   38-30, INITIAL O AND S 38-31, INITIAL V 38-32, INITIAL J
   38-33, INITIAL E 38/34-35, INITIAL D 38-36, INITIAL A 38-37,
   INITIAL N 38/38, INITIAL V 38/39-42, INITIAL E 38-43, INITIAL
   V 38-44, INITIAL O 38/45-46, INITIAL V 38-47, INITIAL I 38-48,
   INITIAL I 38-50, INITIAL O 38-51, INITIAL S 38-52, INITIAL H
   38-53, INITIAL C 38-54, INITIAL D 38-55, INITIAL V 38-56


*$ABSTRACT 39
  *LIBRARY BOD
  *SLIDE SET TITLE JEROME COMMENTARY ON ISAIAH
  *NEGATIVE REFERENCE ROLL 146C
  *RENTAL FEE SM 039 $3.15
  *COMMENTS EX LIBRIS OF EXETER CATHEDRAL
  *TITLE OF MANUSCRIPT COMMENTARY ON ISAIAH
  *SHELFMARK MS BODLEY 717
  *PROVENANCE FRENCH/ NORMANDY
  *DATE EXECUTED 11TH
  *LANGUAGE LATIN
  *ARTIST/ SCHOOL HUGO PICTOR
  *AUTHOR ST JEROME/ COMMENTARY ON ISAIAH
  *TYPE OF MANUSCRIPT BIBLE COMMENTARY
  *CONTENTS COMMENTARY ON ISAIAH 39/1-24, TITLE 39-1, ISAIAH
   SEATED UNDER ARCH 39-2, CITY WITH CHURCH TOWERS 39-2, ST
```

21

JEROME AND ST EUSTACHIA AND ABBESS 39-3, INITIAL E 39-4,
VIRGIN ENTHRONED BETWEEN ISAIAH AND ST JEROME 39-4, ST PAULA'S
BURIAL 39-4, INITIAL V WITH CHRIST ENTHRONED 39-5, INITIAL P
39-6, INITIAL S 39-7, INITIAL I 39-8, INITIAL P 39-9, DRAGON/
WINGED 39-9, INITIAL Q 39-10, INITIAL S 39/11-12, BEAST
CROWNED AND WINGED WITH ITS YOUNG 39-12, INITIAL V 39-13,
CARYATID/ GROTESQUE 39-13, INITIAL D 39-14, INITIAL D 39-15,
INITIAL N 39-16, INITIAL M 39-17, INITIAL D 39-18, FINIALS OF
MEN'S HEADS 39-18, INITIAL E 39/19-20, MONSTER HYDRA HEADED
39-20, MONKEY/ GREEN 39- 20, INITIAL Q 39-21, INITIAL D 39-22,
MONK 39-23, HUGO PICTOR INSCRIBED ON PICTURE 39/23-24

*$ABSTRACT 40
 *LIBRARY BOD
 *SLIDE SET TITLE PSALTER CODEX VOSSIANUS
 *NEGATIVE REFERENCE ROLL 146D
 *RENTAL FEE SM 040 $9.65
 *TITLE OF MANUSCRIPT PSALTERIUM ROMANUM/ CODEX VOSSIANUS
 *SHELFMARK MS JUNIUS 27
 *PROVENANCE ENGLISH/ WINCHESTER
 *DATE EXECUTED 10TH
 *LANGUAGE LATIN WITH ANGLO-SAXON GLOSS
 *TYPE OF MANUSCRIPT PSALTER
 *CONTENTS PSALTER CALENDAR AND INITIALS 40/1-153, CALENDAR
40/1-10, CALENDAR FOR JANUARY 40-1, CALENDAR FOR MARCH 40-2,
CALENDAR FOR APRIL 40-3, CALENDAR FOR MAY 40-4, CALENDAR FOR
JUNE 40-5, CALENDAR FOR JULY 40-6, CALENDAR FOR AUGUST 40-7,
CALENDAR FOR SEPTEMBER 40-8, CALENDAR FOR NOVEMBER 40-9,
CALENDAR FOR DECEMBER 40-10, INITIAL D/ DOMINE QUID
MULTIPLICASTI/ PSALM 3 40-11, INITIAL C/ CUM INVOCAREM/ PSALM
4 40-12, INITIAL V/ VERBA MEA AURIBUS / PSALM 5 40-13, INITIAL
D/ DOMINE NE IN FURORE / PSALM 6 40-14, INITIAL D/ DOMINE DEUS
MEUS/ PSALM 7 40-15, INITIAL D/ DOMINE DOMINUS NOSTER/ PSALM 8
40-16, INITIAL C/ CONFITEBOR TIBI DOMINE/ PSALM 9 40-17,
INITIAL I/ IN DOMINO CONFIDO/ PSALM 10 40-18, INITIAL S/
SALVUM ME FAC/ PSALM 11 40-19, INITIAL U/ USQUEQUO DOMINE/
PSALM 12 40-20, INITIAL D/ DIXIT INSIPIENS/ PSALM 13 40-21,
INITIAL D/ DOMINE QUIS HABITABIT/ PSALM 14 40-22, INITIAL C/
CONSERVA ME DOMINE/ PSALM 15 40-23, INITIAL E/ EXAUDI DOMINI
IUSTITIAM/ PSALM 16 40-24, INITIAL D/ DILIGAM TE DOMINE/ PSALM
17 40-25, INITIAL C/ COELI ENARRANT/ PSALM 18 40-26, INITIAL
E/ EXAUDIAT TE DOMINUS/ PSALM 19 40-27, INITIAL D/ DOMINE IN
VIRTUTE/ PSALM 20 40-28, INITIAL D/ DEUS DEUS MEUS/ PSALM 21
40-29, INITIAL D/ DOMINUS REGIT ME/ PSALM 22 40-30, INITIAL D/
DOMINI EST TERRA/ PSALM 23 40-31, INITIAL A/ AD TE DOMINE
LEVAVI/ PSALM 24 40-32, INITIAL I/ IUDICA ME DOMINE/ PSALM 25
40-33, INITIAL D/ DOMINUS ILLUMINATIO MEA/ PSALM 26 40-34,
INITIAL A/ AD TE DOMINE CLAMABO/ PSALM 27 40-35, INITIAL E/
EXALTABO TE DOMINE/ PSALM 29 40-36, INITIAL I/ IN TE DOMINE
SPERAVI/ PSALM 30 40-37, INITIAL B/ BEATI QUORUM/ PSALM 31
40-38, INITIAL G/ GAUDETE IUSTI/ PSALM 32 40-39, INITIAL B/
BENEDICAM DOMINUM/ PSALM 33 40/40, INITIAL I/ IUDICA DOMINE
NOCENTES ME/ PSALM 34 40-41, INITIAL D/ DIXIT INIUSTUS/ PSALM
35 40-42, INITIAL N/ NOLI AEMULARI/ PSALM 36 40-43, INITIAL D/
DOMINE NE IN IRA TUA/ PSALM 37 40-44, INITIAL D/ DIXI
CUSTODIAM/ PSALM 38 40-45, INITIAL B/ BEATUS QUI INTELLIGIT/
PSALM 40 40-46, INITIAL S/ SICUT CERVUS/ PSALM 41 40-47,
INITIAL I/ IUDICA ME DEUS/ PSALM 42 40-48, INITIAL D/ DEUS
AURIBUS NOSTRIS/ PSALM 43 40-49, INITIAL D/ DEUS NOSTER
REFUGIUM/ PSALM 45 40-50, INITIAL O/ OMNES GENTES PLAUDITE/
PSALM 46 40-51, INITIAL M/ MAGNUS DOMINUS/ PSALM 47 40-52,
INITIAL A/ AUDITE HAEC OMNES GENTES/ PSALM 48 40-53, INITIAL
D/ DEUS DEORUM/ PSALM 49 40-54, INITIAL D/ DIXIT INSIPIENS/
PSALM 52 40-55, INITIAL D/ DEUS IN NOMINE TUO/ PSALM 53 40-56,
INITIAL E/ EXAUDI DEUS/ PSALM 54 40-57, INITIAL M/ MISERERE
MEI DEUS/ PSALM 55 40-58, INITIAL M/ MISERERE MEI DEUS/ PSALM
56 40-59, INITIAL S/ SI VERE UTIQUE/ PSALM 57 40-60, INITIAL
E/ ERIPE ME/ PSALM 58 40-61, INITIAL D/ DEUS REPULISTI NOS/
PSALM 59 40-62, INITIAL E/ EXAUDI DEUS / PSALM 60 40-63,
INITIAL N/ NONNE DEO / PSALM 61 40-64, INITIAL D/ DEUS DEUS

MEUS AD TE/ PSALM 62 40-65, INITIAL E/ EXAUDI DEUS ORATIONEM/
PSALM 63 40-66, INITIAL T/ TE DECET/ PSALM 64 40-67, INITIAL
I/ IUBILATE DEO/ PSALM 65 40-68, INITIAL D/ DEUS MISEREATUR /
PSALM 66 40-69, INITIAL E/ EXURGAT DEUS/ PSALM 67 40-70,
INITIAL D/ DOMINE DEUS IN ADUITORIUM/ PSALM 69 40-71, INITIAL
D/ DEUS IN TE SPERAVI/ PSALM 70 40-72, INITIAL D/ DEUS
IUDICIUM TUUM/ PSALM 71 40-73, INITIAL Q/ QUAM BONUS DEUS
ISRAEL / PSALM 72 40-74, INITIAL U/ UT QUID REPULISTI NOS
DEUS/ PSALM 73 40-75, INITIAL D/ CONFITEBIMUR TIBI/ PSALM 74
40-76, INITIAL N/ NOTUS IN JUDAEA/ PSALM 75 40-77, INITIAL V/
VOCE MEA/ PSALM 76 40-78, INITIAL D/ DEUS VENERUNT GENTES/
PSALM 78 40-79, INITIAL Q/ QUI REGIS ISRAEL/ PSALM 79 40-80,
INITIAL D/ DEUS STETIT/ PSALM 81 40-81, INITIAL D/ DEUS QUIS
SIMILIS/ PSALM 82 40-82, INITIAL Q/ QUAM DILECTA/ PSALM 83
40-83, INITIAL B/ BENEDIXISTI DOMINE/ PSALM 84 40-84, INITIAL
I/ INCLINA DOMINE/ PSALM 85 40-85, INITIAL F/ FUNDAMENTA EIUS/
PSALM 86 40-86, INITIAL D/ DOMINE DEUS SALUTIS/ PSALM 87
40-87, INITIAL M/ MISERICORDIAS TUAS DOMINE/ PSALM 88 40-88,
INITIAL D/ DOMINE REFUGIUM/ PSALM 89 40-89, INITIAL Q/ QUI
HABITAT/ PSALM 90 40-90, INITIAL B/ BONUM EST CONFITERI/ PSALM
91 40-91, INITIAL D/ DOMINUS REGNAVIT / PSALM 92 40-92,
INITIAL D/ DEUS ULTIONUM/ PSALM 93 40-93, INITIAL V/ VENITE
EXULTEMUS/ PSALM 94 40-94, INITIAL C/ CANTATE DOMINE/ PSALM 95
40-95, INITIAL D/ DOMINUS REGNAVIT/ PSALM 96 40-96, INITIAL C/
CANTATE DOMINO/ PSALM 97 40-97, INITIAL D/ DOMINUS REGNAVIT/
PSALM 98 40-98, INITIAL I/ IUBILATE DEO/ PSALM 99 40-99,
INITIAL M/ MISERICORDIAM ET IUDICIUM/ PSALM 100 40-100,
INITIAL D/ DOMINE EXAUDI/ PSALM 101 40-101, INITIAL B/ BENEDIC
ANIMA/ PSALM 102 40-102, INITIAL B/ BENEDIC ANIMA/ PSALM 103
40-103, INITIAL C/ CONFITEMINI DOMINO/ PSALM 104 40-104,
INITIAL C/ CONFITEMINI DOMINO/ PSALM 105 40-105, INITIAL C/
CONFITEMINI DOMINO/ PSALM 106 40-106, INITIAL P/ PARATUM COR
MEUM/ PSALM 107 40-107, INITIAL D/ DEUS LAUDEM MEAM/ PSALM 108
40-108, INITIAL D/ DIXIT DOMINUS/ PSALM 109 40-109, INITIAL C/
CONFITEBOR TIBI DOMINE/ PSALM 110 40-110, INITIAL B/ BEATUS
VIR/ PSALM 111 40-111, INITIAL L/ LAUDATE PUERI/ PSALM 112
40-112, INITIAL I/ IN EXITU ISRAEL/ PSALM 113 40-113, INITIAL
D/ DILEXI/ PSALM 114 40-114, INITIAL C/ CREDIDI/ PSALM 115
40-115, INITIAL L/ LAUDATE DOMINUM/ PSALM 116 40-116, INITIAL
C/ CONFITEMINI DOMINO/ PSALM 117 40-117, INITIAL B/ BEATI
IMMACULATI/ PSALM 118 40-118, INITIAL R/ RETRIBUE SERVO TUO/
PSALM 118 40-119, INITIAL L/ LEGEM PONE MIHI DOMINE/ PSALM 118
40-120, INITIAL M/ MEMENTO VERBI TUI/ PSALM 118 40-121,
INITIAL B/ BONITATEM FECISTI/ PSALM 118 40-122, INITIAL D/
DEFECIT IN SALUTARI TUO/ PSALM 118 40-123, INITIAL Q/ QUOMODO
DILEXI LEGEM TUAM/ PSALM 118 40-124, INITIAL I/ INIQUOS ODIO
HABUI / PSALM 118 40-125, INITIAL M/ MIRABILIA TESTIMONIA TUA/
PSALM 118 40-126, INITIAL C/ CLAMAVI IN TOTO CORDE MEO/ PSALM
118 40-127, INITIAL P/ PRINCIPES PERSECUTI SUNT ME/ PSALM 118
40-128, INITIAL A/ AD DOMINUM/ PSALM 119 40-129, INITIAL L/
LEVAVI OCULOS/ PSALM 120 40-130, INITIAL L/ LETATUS SUM/ PSALM
121 40-131, INITIAL A/ AD TE LEVAVI/ PSALM 122 40-132, INITIAL
N/ NISI QUOD DOMINUS/ PSALM 123 40-133, INITIAL Q/ QUI
CONFIDUNT/ PSALM 124 40-134, INITIAL I/ IN CONVERTENDO/ PSALM
125 40-135, INITIAL N/ NISI DOMINUS/ PSALM 126 40-136, INITIAL
B/ BEATI OMNES/ PSALM 127 40-137, INITIAL S/ SEPE
EXPUGNAVERUNT/ PSALM 128 40-138, INITIAL D/ DE PROFUNDIS/
PSALM 129 40-139, INITIAL D/ DOMINE NON EST/ PSALM 130 40-140,
INITIAL M/ MEMENTO DOMINE/ PSALM 131 40-141, INITIAL E/ ECCE
QUAM BONUM/ PSALM 132 40-142, INITIAL E/ ECCE NUNC BENEDICITE/
PSALM 133 40-143, INITIAL L/ LAUDATE NOMEN DOMINI/ PSALM 134
40-144, INITIAL C/ CONFITEMINI DOMINO/ PSALM 135 40-145,
INITIAL S/ SUPER FLUMINA/ PSALM 136 40-146, INITIAL C/
CONFITEBOR TIBI/ PSALM 137 40-147, INITIAL D/ DOMINE PROBASTI/
PSALM 138 40-148, INITIAL E/ ERIPE ME DOMINE/ PSALM 139
40-149, INITIAL V/ VOCE MEA/ PSALM 141 40-150, INITIAL D/
DOMINE EXAUDI/ PSALM 142 40-151, INITIAL B/ BENEDICTUS
DOMINUS/ PSALM 143 40-152, INITIAL E/ EXALTABO TE DEUS/ PSALM
144 40-153

*$ABSTRACT 41
  *LIBRARY BOD
  *SLIDE SET TITLE GOSPELS OF SS MATTHEW AND MARK
  *NEGATIVE REFERENCE ROLL 146E
  *RENTAL FEE SM 041 $2.75
  *COMMENTS PROBABLY MADE FOR A GERMAN KING OR EMPEROR WHO IS
  PORTRAYED ON THE BINDING
  *SHELFMARK MS DOUCE 292
  *PROVENANCE FRENCH/ LIEGE
  *DATE EXECUTED 11TH/C1050
  *LANGUAGE LATIN
  *TYPE OF MANUSCRIPT GOSPELS
  *CONTENTS GOSPELS/ 11TH/ FRENCH 41/1-15, FRONT COVER 41/1-2,
  CANON TABLES 41/3-10, ST MATTHEW AT LECTERN AT SCROLL 41-11,
  INCIPIT FOR ST MATTHEW'S GOSPEL 41-12, ST MATTHEW'S GOSPEL/
  BEGINNING 41-13, ST MARK SEATED WITH BOOK 41-14, INCIPIT FOR
  ST MARK'S GOSPEL 41-15

*$ABSTRACT 42
  *LIBRARY BOD
  *SLIDE SET TITLE ASTRONOMY AND ASTROLOGY
  *NEGATIVE REFERENCE ROLL 150A
  *RENTAL FEE SM 042 $4.25
  *COMMENTS 45 SLIDES SELECTED FROM 15 MSS FROM THE 12TH-16TH
  CENTURIES
  *SHELFMARK MS MEX D 1 42-1, MS ARCH SELD A 1 42/2-4, MS MEX D 1
  42/5-6, MS RAWL D 1220 42/7-13, MS AUCT F 2 20 42-14, MS AUCT
  D 2 6 42/15-19, MS BODLEY 266 42-20, MS ASHMOLE 304 42/21-22,
  MS DIGBY 46 42/23-24, MS DOUCE 276 42-25, MS DOUCE 6 42-26, MS
  BALLIOL 238 42-27, MS RAWL C 117 42-28, MS LAUD MISC 644
  42-29, MS DIGBY 107 42-30, MS BODLEY 614 42/31-34, MS BODLEY
  270 42-35, MS TANNER 192 42-36, MS C C C 144 42-37, MS LAUD
  MISC 657 42-38, MS ASHMOLE 1522 42-39, MS BODLEY 68 42-40, MS
  DIGBY 17 42-41, MS ASHMOLE 191 42/42, MS BODLEY 68 42-43, MS
  ASHMOLE 370 42-44, MS SAVILE 100 42-45
  *PROVENANCE MEXICAN 42/1-6, ENGLISH 42/7-13, FRENCH 42-14,
  ENGLISH 42/15-19, ITALIAN 42-20, ENGLISH 42/21-24, FRENCH
  42/25-26, ENGLISH 42/27-34, FRENCH 42-35, ENGLISH 42/36-45
  *DATE EXECUTED 15TH 42/7-13, 13TH 42-14, 12TH/1140-58 42/15-19,
  15TH/C1450 42-20, 13TH 42/21-22, 14TH 42/23-24, 15TH 42-25,
  14TH/C1300 42-26, 15TH/1445-8 42-27, 15TH/C1400 42-28,
  13TH/1270 42/29-30, 12TH 42/31-34, 13TH 42-35, 13TH/ 1288-1301
  42-36, 14TH/1326 42-37, 15TH 42-38, 15TH/C1400 42-40,
  14TH/1301 42-41, 15TH 42-42, 15TH/C1400 42-43, 15TH/C4124
  42-44, 16TH/1552 42-45
  *CONTENTS ASTRONOMY 42/1-45, ASTROLOGY 42/1-45, CROSSED STICK
  LOOKED THROUGH BY OBSERVER 42-1, ECLIPSE OF THE SUN 42/2-3,
  PRIESTS TAKING THEIR TIME FROM THE STARS 42-4, EYE IN NOTCH OF
  CROSSED STICKS IN TEMPLE DOORWAY 42-5, STAR DESCENDING INTO
  NOTCH OF CROSSED STICKS 43-6, SATURN 42-7, JUPITER 42-8, MARS
  42-9, SUN 42-10, VENUS 42-11, MERCURY 42-12, MOON 42-13,
  ZODIAC SIGNS AND CIRCLES WITH PLANETS 42-14, JANUARY-APRIL
  CALENDAR 42-15, WATERBEARER AND BULL 42-15, TWINS AND CRAB
  42-16, MAY-JULY CALENDAR 42-16, JULY-AUGUST CALENDAR 42-17,
  LION AND VIRGIN 42-17, SEPTEMBER NOVEMBER CALENDAR 42-18,
  SCALES AND SCORPION 42-18, NOVEMBER DECEMBER CALENDAR 42-19,
  ARCHER AND GOAT 42-20, SUN IN CHARIOT 42-21, EUCLID HOLDING
  SPHERE AND DIOPTRA 42-21, HERMANNUS HOLDING ASTROLABE 42-21,
  TOWERS OF THE SEVEN PLANETS 42-22, BERNARDUS SILVESTRIS 42-23,
  EUCLID WITH SPHERE AND DIOPTRA 42-23, HERMANNUS WITH ASTROLABE
  42-23, TOWERS OF THE SEVEN PLANETS 42-24, TUBE APPLIED TO EAR
  OF ASTRONOMER 42-25, QUADRANT 42-26, PYTHAGORAS WITH DIOPTRA
  42-27, SOCRATES WITH DIVIDERS 42-27, TABLE OF STAR'S POSITIONS
  42-28, CETUS AND ORION 42-28, ECLIPSES AND OTHER DIAGRAMS
  42-30, BEDE'S SIGNS OF HEAVEN 42-29, SUN AND MOON IN CHARIOTS
  42-31, PLANETS 42-32, ASTRONOMER WITH ASTROLABE 42-33,
  ERIDANUS POURING OUT GREEN WATER 42-34, ASTRONOMER'S AND
  PHILOSOPHER'S VAINGLORY AT NOUGHT 42-35, QUADRANT 42-36,
  RECTANGULUS OF RICHARD OF WALLINGFORD 42/37-38, TORQUETUM
  42-39, SUNDIAL 42-40, ASTROLABE AND QUADRANT 42-41, QUADRANT/

HORARY 42/42, QUADRANT/ SINECAL 42-43, LUNAR VOLVELLE 42-44,
EQUATORIUM 42-45

*$ABSTRACT 43
 *LIBRARY BOD
 *SLIDE SET TITLE VERNON MANUSCRIPT
 *NEGATIVE REFERENCE ROLL 150B
 *RENTAL FEE SM 043 $2.90
 *TITLE OF MANUSCRIPT VERNON MS
 *SHELFMARK MS ENG POET A 1
 *PROVENANCE ENGLISH/ WEST MIDLANDS
 *DATE EXECUTED 14TH/ AFTER 1382
 *LANGUAGE ENGLISH / MIDDLE ENGLISH AND ANGLO-NORMAN
 *TYPE OF MANUSCRIPT LIFE OF CHRIST AND MIRACLES OF THE VIRGIN
 *CONTENTS LIFE OF CHRIST 43/1-18, MIRACLES OF THE VIRGIN
 43/1-18, VIRGIN AND ELIZABETH GREET EACH OTHER 43-1,
 ANNUNCIATION 43-2, ANGEL APPEARS TO ZACARIAS 43-3, NATIVITY
 43-4, JOSEPH REASSURED BY ANGEL ABOUT MARYƏS CHILD 43-5, ST
 JOHN BAPTIST'S BIRTH 43-6, ZACHARIAS WRITING NAME ON TABLET
 43-6, ANGEL APPEARING TO SHEPHERDS IN FIELDS 43-7, CROTEY/
 CITY BESEIGED BY ROLLO RELIEVED 43-8, CHILD RESTORED TO LIFE
 AFTER KILLED BY JEW 43-9, HARLOT CONVERTED BY EXHORTATIONS OF
 HERMIT 43-10, JEW WHO THREW CHILD IN OVEN FOR ENTERING CHURCH
 43-11, VIRGIN HEALS AMPUTATED FOOT 43-12, CONSTANTINOPLE
 MERCHANT WHO BORROWED MONEY FROM JEW 43-13, PRIEST WHO LAY
 WITH NUN 43-14, MONK/ INCONTINENT DROWNED 43-15, VIRGIN GIVING
 HER MILK TO MONK 43-16, PATER NOSTER/ ILLUMINATED 43-17, GOD
 THE FATHER AND CHRIST ON CROSS 43-18

*$ABSTRACT 44
 *LIBRARY BOD
 *SLIDE SET TITLE OCCUPATIONS OF THE MONTHS I
 *NEGATIVE REFERENCE ROLL 151A
 *RENTAL FEE SM 044 $3.20
 *COMMENTS 24 SLIDES FROM 2 MSS SHOWING MONTHLY AGRICULTURAL
 OCCUPATIONS
 *SHELFMARK MS C C C 285 44/1-12, MS RAWL D 939 44/13-24
 *PROVENANCE ENGLISH
 *DATE EXECUTED 13TH/1280 44/1-12, 14TH/C1370 44/13-24
 *CONTENTS OCCUPATIONS OF THE MONTHS 44/1-24, LABORS OF THE
 MONTH 44/1-24, CALENDAR 44/1-24, JANUARY 44-1, JANUS FEASTING
 44-1, FEBRUARY 44-2, MAN COOKING AND WARMING FEET BY FIRE
 44-2, MARCH 44-3, PRUNING 44-3, APRIL 44-4, TREE PLANTING
 44-4, MAY 44-5, FLOWER PICKING 44-5, JUNE 44-6, MOWER WITH
 SCYTHE 44-6, JULY 44-7, REAPER WITH HOOK 44-7, AUGUST 44-8,
 THRESHER WITH FLAIL 44-8, SEPTEMBER 44-9, TREADING GRAPES
 44-9, OCTOBER 44-10, SOWING 44-10, NOVEMBER 44-11, ACORNS
 KNOCKED DOWN FOR SWINE 44-11, DECEMBER 44-12, SLAUGHTERING
 WITH AXE 44-12, JANUARY 44-13, MAN COOKING AND WARMING FEET IN
 FRONT OF FIRE 44-13, FEBRUARY 44-14, DITCHING WITH IRON SPADE
 AND PITCHER 44-14, MARCH 44-15, PRUNING 44-15, APRIL 44-16,
 TREE PLANTING 44-16, MAY 44-17, HAWKING 44-17, JUNE 44-18,
 THISTLES BEING CUT 44-18, JULY 44-19, MOWER WITH SCYTHE 44-19,
 AUGUST 44-20, REAPER WITH HOOK 44-21, SEPTEMBER 44-22, SOWING
 44-22, NOVEMBER 44-23, SLAUGHTERING WITH AXE 44-23, DECEMBER
 44-23, FEASTING 44-24

*$ABSTRACT 45
 *LIBRARY BOD
 *SLIDE SET TITLE ILLUSTRATING THE OLD TESTAMENT TO THE END OF
 PSALMS
 *NEGATIVE REFERENCE ROLL 152A
 *RENTAL FEE SM 045 $7.50
 *TITLE OF MANUSCRIPT BIBLE HISTORIALE
 *SHELFMARK MS DOUCE 211
 *PROVENANCE FRENCH

*DATE EXECUTED 14TH
*LANGUAGE FRENCH
*ARTIST/ SCHOOL STYLE OF JEAN DE PAPELEU
*AUTHOR DESMOULINS/ GUYART
*TYPE OF MANUSCRIPT BIBLE HISTORIALE
*CONTENTS ICONOGRAPHY/ OLD TESTAMENT 45/1-110, PETRUS COMESTOR
HANDS BOOK TO MESSENGER 45-1, WILLIAM/ ARCHBISHOP OF SENS
RECEIVES BOOK 45-1, CREATION 45/2-5, GOD CREATING WORLD 45-2,
GOD CREATING FIRMAMENT 45-3, GOD CREATING EARTH 45-4, GOD
DIVIDING DAY FROM NIGHT 45-5, ADAM AND EVE EXPELLED FROM
PARADISE 45-6, CAIN AND ABEL OFFER SACRIFICE 45-7, CAIN
KILLING ABEL 45-8, ENOCH BORN 45-9, SETH BORN 45-10, MOSES
WRITING 45-11, NOAH BUILDING ARK 45-12, GOD TELLS NOAH OF
COMING FLOOD 45-13, NOAH SENDS OUT DOVE 45-14, NOAH
SACRIFICING AFTER FLOOD 45-15, ORIGIN OF IDOLS 45-16, GOD
SENDS ABRAHAM TO SEEK NEW LAND 45-17, ABRAHAM HEARS THAT SEED
WILL BE LIKE STARS 45-18, GOD MAKES COVENANT WITH ABRAHAM
45-19, ANGELS APPEAR TO ABRAHAM 45-20, LOT AND HIS FAMILY FLEE
FROM SODOM 45-21, SARAH RESTORED TO ABRAHAM 45-22, SACRIFICE
OF ISAAC 45-23, ESAU AND JACOB BORN 45-24, ISAAC BEFORE
ABIMELECH 45-25, JACOB'S LADDER 45-26, LABAN'S FLOCK SEPARATED
45-27, JACOB WRESTLES WITH ANGEL 45-28, JOSEPH AND BROTHERS
FEEDING SHEEP 45-29, JOSEPH EXPLAINS DREAMS OF PHARAOH'S
SERVANTS 45-30, JOSEPH'S BROTHERS COME TO BUY CORN IN EGYPT
45-31, JOSEPH PRESENTS JACOB TO PHARAOH 45-32, TWELVE TRIBES
OF ISRAEL 45-33, MOSES AND BURNING BUSH 45-34, AARON AND MOSES
MEETING 45-35, GOD SPEAKS TO MOSES BEFORE FIRST PLAGUE 45-36,
GOD SPEAKS TO MOSES BEFORE SECOND PLAGUE 45-37, CHILDREN OF
ISRAEL LEAVE EGYPT 45-38, CHILDREN OF ISRAEL FOLLOW PILLAR OF
CLOUD 45-39, CHILDREN OF ISRAEL LED BY MOSES 45-40, MOSES AND
AARON PROMISE ISRAEL GOD WILL FEED THEM 45-41, CHILDREN OF
ISRAEL IN WILDERNESS 45-42, JETHRO BRINGS MOSES' FAMILY WITH
HIM 45-43, GOD SPEAKS TO MOSES AND AARON ON MT SINAI 45-44,
LAW/MAN DISMISSES MAIDSERVANT 45/45, GOD SPEAKS TO MOSES AND
ISRAEL 45-46, GOD INSTRUCTS MOSES TO BUILD TABERNACLE 45-47,
MOSES OVERSEES BUILDING OF GOLDEN ARK 45-48, ARK COMPLETED
45-49, LOAVES OF PROPOSITION ON TABLE 45-50, CANDLESTICK/
GOLDEN WITH FOUR BRANCHES 45-51, TABERNACLE COMPLETED WITH ARK
INSIDE 45-52, AARON STANDS BEFORE TABERNACLE 45-53, TABERNACLE
SHOWING ARK 45-54, ALTAR OF BRASS 45-55, CHILDREN OF ISRAEL
WORSHIPPING GOLDEN CALF 45-56, GOD DICTATES LAW TO MOSES ON MT
SINAI 45-57, SHEEP BEING SACRIFICED 45-58, GOD SPEAKS TO MOSES
ABOUT LAWS OF SACRIFICE 45-59, PRIEST OFFERS CALF ON ALTAR
45-60, GOD TELLS MOSES CONSECRATE AARON AND SONS 45-61, NADAB
AND ABIHU BENEATH FLAMING CLOUD 45-62, GOD TELLS MOSES ABOUT
AARON ENTERING SANCTUARY 45-63, MOSES COUNTS MEN FIT FOR WAR
45-64, TABERNACLE DEDICATED 45-65, GOD TELLS MOSES ABOUT USE
OF SILVER TRUMPETS 45-66, CHILDREN OF ISRAEL STONE MAN WHO
GATHERED STICKS SABBATH 45-67, MOSES STRIKES WATER FROM ROCK
45-68, SHEEP BEING SACRIFICED 45-69, SHEEP SACRIFICED AND
PRIESTS BLOW TRUMPETS 45-70, MOSES WRITING 45-71, GOD TELLS
JOSHUA TO LEAD PEOPLE ACROSS JORDAN 45-72, JUDAH FIGHTING
AGAINST CANAANITES 45-73, ANGEL FORETELLS BIRTH OF SAMSON
45-74, SAMSON KILLING LION 45-75, SAMSON KILLING PHILISTINES
WITH JAWBONE 45-76, MICAH AND MOTHER ADMIRE SILVER STATUE
45-77, ELIMELECH/ NAOMI AND SONS GOING TO MOAB 45-78, ELKANAH
AND TWO WIVES 45-79, NAAS/ AMMONITE BEFORE TOWN OF JEBESH
GILEAD 45-80, DAVID AND GOLIATH 45-81, DAVID ORDERS EXECUTION
OF SAUL'S MURDERER 45-82, DAVID ANOINTED 45-83, ABSALOM'S
DEATH 45-84, SOLOMON CROWNED BY ZADOR AND NATHAN 45-85,
DAVID'S DEATH 45-86, SOLOMON'S DEATH 45-87, QUEEN OF SHEBA
COMES TO SOLOMON 45-88, REBOAM/ SOLOMON'S SON ADDRESSED BY OLD
MAN 45-89, DUPLICATE OF FRAME 88 45-90, ZEDEKIAH LED CAPTIVE
TO BABYLON 45-91, JOB HEARS OF DESTRUCTION OF HIS FLOCKS
45-92, TOBIT PRAYING 45-93, TOBIAS ATTACKED BY HUGE FISH
45-94, JEWS WARN GEDALIAH OF ATTEMPT ON LIFE 45-95, EZEKIEL
PROPHESYSING TO JEWS IN BABYLON 45-96, NEBUCHADNEZZAR
ADDRESSING DANIEL/ SHADRACH/ MESHAK/ ABEDNEGO 45-97, SUSANNAH
AND THE ELDERS 45-98, DANIEL AND NEBUCHADNEZZAR BEFORE IDOL
BEL 45-99, NEBUCHADNEZZAR GIVES ORDERS TO HOLOFERNES 45-100,
DARIUS REMINDED OF VOW TO REBUILD JERUSALEM 45-101, AHASEURUS
AND ESTHER WITH GUESTS 45-102, DARIUS AND ALEXANDER BATTLE

26

45-103, PSALM 1 45-104, DAVID WITH HARP 45-104, PSALM 52
45-105, CHRIST TOUCHES DAVID'S EYES 45-105, PSALM 38 45-106,
DAVID POINTS TO MOUTH 45-106, PSALM 52 45-107, FOOL WITH BALL
AND BAUBLE 45-107, PSALM 68 45-108, DAVID IN THE WATERS
45-108, PSALM 80 45-109, DAVID WITH BELLS 45-109, PSALM 97
45-110, PRIESTS/ TWO SINGING 45-110, PSALM 109 45-111, TRINITY
45-111

*$ABSTRACT 46
 *LIBRARY BOD
 *SLIDE SET TITLE MEROVINGIAN INITIALS
 *NEGATIVE REFERENCE ROLL 153B
 *RENTAL FEE SM 046 $2.45
 *SHELFMARK MS LAUD MISC 126 46/1-7, MS DOUCE 176 46/8-9
 *PROVENANCE FRENCH
 *DATE EXECUTED 09TH
 *LANGUAGE LATIN
 *ARTIST/ SCHOOL ADA SCHOOL 46/8-9
 *TYPE OF MANUSCRIPT TREATISE 46/1-7, GOSPEL BOOK 46/8-9
 *CONTENTS INITIALS/ MEROVINGIAN 46/1-9, INITIAL D 46-1, FISHES
 46-1, INITIAL L 46-2, INITIAL H 46-3, INITIAL Q 46-4, INITIAL
 I 46-5, INITIAL H 46-6, LETTERS 46-7, ZOOMORPHIC CAPITAL
 46/8-9

*$ABSTRACT 47
 *LIBRARY BOD
 *SLIDE SET TITLE BIBLE MORALISEE
 *NEGATIVE REFERENCE ROLL 155
 *RENTAL FEE SM 047 $4.20
 *TITLE OF MANUSCRIPT BIBLE MORALISEE PART I
 *SHELFMARK MS BODLEY 270B
 *PROVENANCE FRENCH
 *DATE EXECUTED 13TH
 *LANGUAGE LATIN
 *TYPE OF MANUSCRIPT BIBLE
 *CONTENTS ICONOGRAPHY/ OLD TESTAMENT 47/1-44, CREATION 47/1-5,
 GOD MAKES FIRMAMENT IN WATERS 47-1, TREE BEARING FRUIT 47-2,
 GOD MAKES SUN/MOON/STARS 47-3, GOD CREATES BIRDS AND REPTILES
 47-4, GOD CREATES ALL LAND ANIMALS 47-5, NOAH SENDS OUT RAVEN
 47-6, TOWER OF BABEL BUILT 47-7, LOT AND FAMILY GUIDED FROM
 SODOM BY ANGELS 47-8, ABRAHAM LEADING ISAAC TO SACRIFICE 47-9,
 ESAU AND JACOB BORN TO REBEKAH 47-10, ISAAC BLESSES JACOB
 47-11, ESAU OFFERS VENISON TO FATHER FOR BLESSING 47-12, JACOB
 COMPLAINS TO RACHEL AND LEAH ABOUT LABAN 47-13, LABAN PURSUES
 THEM FOR SEVEN DAYS 47-14, LABAN OVERTAKES THEM BUT GOD IN
 DREAM STOPS HIM 47-15, LABAN SEARCHES RACHEL'S TENT FOR IMAGES
 47-16, GOD PROMISES JACOB POWER AND NAME ISRAEL 47-17, MOSES
 PLEADS WITH PHARAOH FOR RELEASE OF JEWS 47-18, PLAGUE OF FLIES
 47-18, PRIEST PREPARES OBLATION IN BAKING PAN 47-19, MOSES
 TELLS PEOPLE WHICH BIRDS NOT TO EAT 47-20, GOD IN CLOUD WITH
 TWO FINGERS POINTED AT MOSES 47-20, MOSES SAYS WINGED CREEPING
 THINGS NOT TO BE EATEN 47-21, WINGED CREATURE WITH HEAD OF
 MONK 47-21, MOSES AND AARON REJECT PEOPLE WITH NOSES IMPERFECT
 47-22, MOSES WITH POOR YOUNG MAN KNEELING BEFORE HIM 47-23,
 MOSES WATCHING MEN WITH MUZZLED OXEN 47-24, JOSHUA KEEPS
 VIRGIN DAUGHTERS OF FIVE CONQUERED KINGS 47-25, JOSHUA
 DIRECTED BY GOD TO DIVIDE LAND AMONG ISRAELITES 47-26, GIDEON
 DELIVERS PRINCES INTO HANDS OF EPHRAIM 47-27, GIDEON SPEAKS TO
 MEN OF SUCCOTH ABOUT THEIR BREAD 47-28, GIDEON ASKS HELP OF
 MAN OF PENUEL 47-29, TREES OFFERED CROWN AND WARNED OF FIRE
 47-30, ISRAELITES GO AGAINST GIBEAH AND DESTROY BENJAMITES
 47-31, BENJAMITES FLEE TO ROCK OF RIMMON 47-32, RUTH REAPING
 AND GREETED BY NAOMI AT CITY 47-33, ELI'S SONS TAKE WOMEN AT
 TABERNACLE 47-34, AHIMELECH GIVES DAVID SHOWBREAD 47-35, DAVID
 LEARNS FROM MEN OF NABAL'S REFUSAL 47-36, DAVID SMITES
 AMALEKITES AND RESCUES TWO WIVES 47-37, NATHAN COMES TO DAVID
 WITH PARABLE 47-38, TEMPLE COMPLETED WITH FOUNTAIN SHOWN
 47-39, ELISHA FEEDS SONS OF PROPHETS AND GEHAZI WITH POTTAGE

47-40, LEPERS WHO PLUNDER CAMP BECAUSE OF HUNGER 47-41, JUDITH
HAS GATES OPENED FOR SHE AND MAID 47-42, ISRAELITES PUT UP
HOLOFERNES' HEAD AND CHASE ASSYRIANS 47-43, ROUNDELS ON WHOLE
PAGE 47-44

*$ABSTRACT 48
  *LIBRARY BOD
  *SLIDE SET TITLE ROMANCE OF THE ROSE
  *NEGATIVE REFERENCE ROLL 157A
  *RENTAL FEE SM 048 $8.40
  *COMMENTS BELONGED TO LOUISE OF SAVOY, WIFE OF CHARLES OF
  ORLEANS, COUNT OF ANGOULEME, AND MOTHER OF FRANCIS I
  *TITLE OF MANUSCRIPT ROMANCE OF THE ROSE
  *SHELFMARK MS DOUCE 195
  *PROVENANCE FRENCH
  *DATE EXECUTED 15TH/1487-1495
  *LANGUAGE FRENCH
  *ARTIST/ SCHOOL ROBINET TESTARD
  *AUTHOR GUILLAUME DE LORRIS AND JEAN DE MEUNG
  *TYPE OF MANUSCRIPT ROMANCE
  *CONTENTS ROMANCE OF THE ROSE 48/1-128, LITERATURE/ ROMANCE OF
  THE ROSE 48/1-128, MAN SEATED READING BY WINDOW 48-1, POET
  DREAMING CALLS ROMANCE OF ROSE TO HONOR LADY 48-2, LOVER
  WALKING NEAR CASTLE 48-3, LOVER KNEELING BESIDE STREAM 48-4,
  LOVER APPROACHES GARDEN OF PLEASURE 48-5, HATRED 48-6,
  VILLAINY 48-7, COVETOUSNESS 48-8, AVARICE 48-9, ENVY 48-10,
  SADNESS 48-11, OLD AGE 48-12, HYPOCRISY 48-13, POVERTY 48-14,
  IDLENESS 48-15, LOVER ENTERS GARDEN 48-16, COURTIERS PERFORM
  ROUND DANCE 48-17, GOD OF LOVE PURSUES LOVER 48-18, LOVER
  COMES TO FOUNTAIN 48-19, NARCISSUS STORY 48-20, GOD OF LOVE
  SEES LOVER SURPRISED BY ROSE 48-21, GOD OF LOVE STRIKES LOVER
  48-22, LOVER KNEELS TO GOD OF LOVE 48-23, GOD OF LOVE EMBRACES
  LOVER 48-24, LOVER AND BEL ACQUEIL APPROACH GARDEN 48-25,
  DANGIER ATTACKS LOVER AND BEL ACQUEIL 48-26, LOVER STANDS
  BEFORE LADY 48-27, LOVER ADRESSED BY AMI 48-28, LOVER SPEAKS
  TO DANGIER 48-29, LOVER THANKS AMI 48-30, FRANKNESS AND PITY
  SPEAK TO DANGIER 48-31, WOMEN SPEAK TO BEL ACQUEIL 48-32,
  FRANCHISE SENDS BEL ACQUEIL TO LOVER 48-33, VENUS COMES TO
  LOVER 48-34, LOVER KISSES ROSE 48-35, MALEBOUCHE SPEAKS BADLY
  OF LOVER 48-36, MODESTY SPEAKS TO DANGIER 48-37, CASTLE OF
  JEALOUSY 48-38, REASON COMES TO LOVER 48-39, MARTYRDOM OF
  VIRGINIA 48-40, LOVER FACES FORTUNE 48-41, NERO'S MURDER OF
  HIS MOTHER 48-42, NERO'S MURDER OF SENECA 48-43, KING CROESUS
  OF LYDIA AT FEAST 48-45, NERO FLEES TO GARDEN 48-44, BATTLE OF
  BENEVENTO 48-46, REASON LECTURES LOVER 48-47, LOVER CONSULTS
  AMI 48/48, LOVERS OF LONG AGO 48-49, CRUEL HUSBAND 48-50, RAPE
  OF LUCRECE 48-51, BEAUTY AND UGLINESS ASSAIL CHASTITY 48-52,
  HERCULES FIGHTS MONSTER 48-53, SUSPICIOUS HUSBAND MALTREATS
  WIFE 48-54, HOUSE WHERE HUSBAND AND WIFE AGREE 48-55, LOVER
  RIDES FROM CASTLE 48-56, LOVER ASKS RICHESSE THE WAY 48-57,
  RICHESSE DISMISSES LOVER 48-58, GOD OF LOVE APPEARS TO LOVER
  48-59, BARONS OF LOVE ARRIVE 48-60, JUPITER CASTRATES SATURN
  48-61, WOMAN PLAYING BAGPIPES AT FEAST 48-62, GOD OF LOVE
  SPEAKS TO FAUX SEMBLANT 48-63, GOD OF LOVE BESIEGES CASTLE
  48-64, FAUX SEMBLANT AND ABSTINENCE DRESSED AS PILGRIMS 48-65,
  FAUX SEMBLANT AND ABSTINENCE AT HOUSE OF MALEBOUCHE 48-66,
  FAUX SEMBLANT STRANGLES MALEBOUCHE 48-67, FAUX SEMBLANT AND
  ABSTINENCE GO TO CASTLE 48-68, WOMAN JAILER GOES TO BEL
  ACQUEIL 48-69, QUEEN DIDO'S DEATH 48-70, JASON AND GOLDEN
  FLEECE 48-71, LOVE OF VENUS AND MARS 48-72, WOMAN TELLS LOVER
  HOW TO GET BEL ACQUEIL 48-73, DOUX REGARD SHOWS BEL ACQUEIL TO
  LOVER 48-74, DANGIER AND OTHERS SEIZE LOVER 48-75, LOVER
  WISHES TO BE IN STOCKS/ NOT BEL ACQUEIL 48-76, BATTLE IN FRONT
  OF CASTLE 48-77, LOVER TEACHES SERVANTS TO CATCH RABBITS
  48-78, FRANCHISE ATTACKS DANGIER 48-79, PITY COMES TO AID OF
  FRANCHISE 48-80, SHAME REPROVES DANGIER 48-81, PITY OVERCOMES
  DANGIER 48-82, DELIGHT COMES TO DEFEND DANGIER AGAINST SHAME
  48-83, BIEN CELER ATTACKS SHAME 48-84, FORTITUDE AND FEAR
  FIGHT BEFORE GOD OF LOVE 48-85, ARRIVAL AT HILL OF CYTHERON
  48-86, VENUS AND ADONIS 48-87, ADONIS' DEATH 48-88, VENUS

28

RIDES IN CHARIOT 48-89, CASTLE BESIEGED 48-90, NATURE FORGES
BIRDS AND ANIMALS 48-91, ART KNEELS BEFORE NATURE 48-92,
SUPREMACY OF NATURE SHOWN BY FIVE VIRGINS 48-93, NATURE
CONFESSES SIN BEFORE GENIUS 48-94, WIFE TRYS TO LEARN
HUSBAND'S SECRET 48-95, DELILAH CUTS SAMSON'S HAIR 48-96,
GENIUS LISTENS TO NATURE 48-97, EMPEDOCLES' DEATH 48-98,
THEMIS ADVISES PYRRHA AND DEUCALION 48-99, DREAMER 48-100,
ALEXANDER THE GREAT AND TWO COUNSELLORS 48-101, WORD OF GOD
QUOTED BY PLATO 48-102, CHRIST IN MAJESTY IN CRESCENT MOON
48-103, ALBUMASAR WITH CHRIST CHILD 48-104, CHRIST SPEAKS TO
KNEELING MAN 48-105, GENIUS CHANGES HIS CLOTHES 48-106, GENIUS
APPEARS BEFORE CUPID 48-107, GOD OF LOVE ATTIRES GENIUS AS
BISHOP 48-108, GENIUS PREACHES TO FAUX SEMBLANT AND OTHERS
48-109, RAVAGES OF ATROPOS 48-110, JUPITER CREATING THE ARTS
SHOWN AS SOWER 48-111, GOOD SHEPHERD VIGILANT 48-112, FOUNTAIN
OF LIFE 48-113, VENUS BEGINS ASSAULT ON TOWER 48-114, VENUS
PREPARES TO SHOOT ARROW AT SILVER STATUE 48-115, THREE PEOPLE
ADMIRE SILVER STATUE 48-116, PYGMALION CARVING STATUE 48-117,
PYGMALION ADMIRING FINISHED STATUE 48-118, PYGMALION DRESSING
STATUE 48-120, PYGMALION SINGING AND PLAYING ORGAN BEFORE
STATUE 48-121, PYGMALION KNEELS BEFORE STATUE 48-119,
PYGMALION EMBRACES STATUE 48-122, PYGMALION MAKES REQUEST TO
VENUS 48-123, PYGMALION'S STATUE COMES TO LIFE 48-124,
PYGMALION AND GALATES GIVE THANKS 48-125, VENUS SETS CASTLE OF
JEALOUSY ON FIRE 48-126, LOVER APPROACHES SANCTUARY 48-127,
LOVER EMBRACES THE ROSE 48-128

*$ABSTRACT 49
*LIBRARY BOD
*SLIDE SET TITLE OCCUPATIONS OF THE MONTHS II
*NEGATIVE REFERENCE ROLL 157B
*RENTAL FEE SM 049 $3.10
*SHELFMARK MS AUCT D 2 6 49/1-10, MS DOUCE 118 49/11-22
*PROVENANCE ENGLISH 49/1-10, FRENCH 49/11-22
*DATE EXECUTED 12TH/1140-1158 49/1-10, 14TH/C1302 49/11-22
*LANGUAGE LATIN
*TYPE OF MANUSCRIPT CALENDAR 49/1-10, PSALTER AND CALENDAR
49/11-22
*CONTENTS OCCUPATIONS OF THE MONTHS 49/1-22, CALENDAR 49/1-22,
JANUARY FEBRUARY 49-1, JANUS FEASTING 49-1, APRIL-MAY 49-2,
PRUNING AND PLANTING TREES 49-2, MAY-JUNE 49-3, TRAINING HAWKS
49-3, JUNE-JULY 49-4, SHEEP SHEARING 49-4, JULY-AUGUST 49-5,
SETTING OUT WITH SCYTHE 49-5, AUGUST SEPTEMBER 49-6, CARRYING
SHEAVES 49-6, SEPTEMBER OCTOBER 49-7, PICKING GRAPES 49-7,
OCTOBER NOVEMBER 49-8, KNOCKING DOWN ACORNS FOR SWINE 49-8,
NOVEMBER DECEMBER 49-9, SLAUGHTERING 49-9, DECEMBER JANUARY
49-10, JANUARY 49-11, JANUS FEASTING 49-11, FEBRUARY 49-12,
WARMING HANDS IN CHIMNEY CORNER 49-12, MARCH 49-13, PRUNING
TREES 49-13, APRIL 49-14, PLANTING TREES 49-14, MAY 49-15,
HAWKING 49-15, JUNE 49-16, SCYTHING 49-16, JULY 49-17, CUTTING
CORN 49-17, AUGUST 49-18, THRESHING 49-18, SEPTEMBER 49-19,
BRINGING GRAPES FROM VINEYARD AND MAKING WINE 49-19, OCTOBER
49-20, SOWING 49-20, NOVEMBER 49-21, KNOCKING DOWN ACORNS FOR
SWINE 49-21, DECEMBER 49-22, SLAUGHTERING 49-22

*$ABSTRACT 50
*LIBRARY BOD
*SLIDE SET TITLE BOOK OF HOURS
*NEGATIVE REFERENCE ROLL 157C
*RENTAL FEE SM 050 $3.50
*TITLE OF MANUSCRIPT BOOK OF HOURS/USE OF ROME
*SHELFMARK MS DOUCE 20
*PROVENANCE FLEMISH
*DATE EXECUTED 16TH
*LANGUAGE LATIN
*ARTIST/ SCHOOL ATELIER OF THE MASTER OF THE PRAYER BOOKS
*TYPE OF MANUSCRIPT BOOK OF HOURS
*CONTENTS BOOK OF HOURS/ FLEMISH/ 16TH 50/1-28,DEVOTION TO THE

HOLY FACE 50-1, CRUCIFIXION/ OFFICE OF THE CROSS/ MATINS 50-2,
PENTECOST/ OFFICE OF HOLY GHOST/ MATINS 50-3, JESSE TREE/
OFFICE OF VIRGIN / MATINS 50-4, VISITATION/ OFFICE OF THE
VIRGIN/ PRIME 50-5, NATIVITY/ OFFICE OF VIRGIN/ PRIME 50-6,
SHEPHERDS AND ANGEL/OFFICE OF VIRGIN/TERCE 50-7, ADORATION OF
MAGI/OFFICE OF VIRGIN/SEXT 50-8, PRESENTATION IN TEMPLE/OFFICE
OF VIRGIN/NONES 50-9, MASSACRE OF INNOCENTS OFFICE OF
VIRGIN/VESPERS 50-10, FLIGHT INTO EGYPT/OFFICE OF VIRGIN/
COMPLINE 50-11, TRINITY AND VIRGIN/OFFICE OF VIRGIN/VESPERS
50-12, DAVID IN PRAYER 50-13, THREE LIVING AND THREE DEAD
KINGS/OFFICE OF DEAD 50-14, PIETA 50-15, ST MICHAEL 50-16, ST
JOHN THE BAPTIST 50-17, SS PETER AND PAUL 50-18, ST JAMES THE
ELDER 50-19, ST ANTHONY 50-20, ST JEROME 50-21, ST NICHOLAS
50-22, ST MARY MAGDALENE 50-23, ST CATHERINE 50-24, ST BARBARA
50-25, ST SUSANNAH 50-26, ST MARGARET 50-27, SAINTS ALL 50-28

*$ABSTRACT 51
  *LIBRARY BOD
  *SLIDE SET TITLE FRANCISCAN MISSAL
  *NEGATIVE REFERENCE ROLL 158B
  *RENTAL FEE SM 051 $9.00
  *COMMENTS ILLUMINATED IN GRISAILLE WITH COLOURED TINTS
  *TITLE OF MANUSCRIPT FRANCISCAN MISSAL
  *SHELFMARK MS DOUCE 313
  *PROVENANCE FRENCH/ PARIS
  *DATE EXECUTED 14TH/ MID
  *LANGUAGE LATIN
  *ARTIST/ SCHOOL FOLLOWER OF JEAN PUCELLE
  *TYPE OF MANUSCRIPT MISSAL
  *CONTENTS MISSAL/ FRENCH/ 13TH 51/1-140, CHRIST ON RAINBOW
  BETWEEN SYMBOLS OF EVANGELISTS 51/1-3, CRUCIFIXION 51/1-3, DEW
  AND RAIN WITH CHRIST AND VIRGIN 51-4, LORD'S HOUSE ESTABLISHED
  ON TOP OF MOUNTAINS 51-5, LORD SPOKE TO ACHEZ 51-6,
  ANNUNCIATION 51-7, JESSE WITH ROD AND VIRGIN ON IT 51-8,
  VISITATION 51-9, ANGEL COMES TO THREE CHILDREN IN FURNACE
  51-10, ST JOHN BAPTIST PREACHING BY RIVER 51-11, ST PAUL TO
  THE CORINTHIANS 51-12, ANGEL POINTS OUT OLD JOSEPH ASLEEP TO
  VIRGIN 51-13, VALLEY OF DEATH WITH PEOPLE SEEING GREAT LIGHT
  51-14, NATIVITY AND ANGELS APPEAR TO SHEPHERDS 51-15, ST JOHN
  BAPTIST TELLING OF NATIVITY TO PEOPLE 51-16, ST STEPHEN STONED
  51-17, MASSACRE OF INNOCENTS 51-18, FLIGHT INTO EGYPT 51-19,
  MARTYRDOM OF ST THOMAS OF CANTERBURY 51-20, CHRIST THE GOOD
  SHEPHERD 51-21, CHRIST WITH LAMP AND SPEAKING TO EVANGELISTS
  51-22, CIRCUMCISION 51-23, ST PAUL TO TITUS WITH EPISTLE
  51-24, GOD SPEAKING FROM CLOUD TO SAINTS WITH JOSEPH/HEROD
  51-25, ST PETER WITH SCROLL 51-26, ISAIAH BEFORE JERUSALEM
  51-26, ISAIAH BEFORE JERUSALEM 51-27, HEROD WITH RULERS AND
  PRIESTS 51-28, MAGI WITH GIFTS/HOLY FAMILY IN STABLE 51-29,
  HOLY FAMILY IN STABLE AND MAGI 51-30, MAGI WARNED BY ANGEL
  51-31, GOD WITH SERAPHIM AND TWENTY FOUR ANGELS 51-32, BAPTISM
  OF CHRIST 51-33, MARRIAGE AT CANA 51-34, CHRIST ASLEEP ON BOAT
  DURING STORM ON GALILEE 51-35, MAN ON BED WITH GOD ABOVE AND
  HELL BELOW 51-36, HELL 51-36, PARABLE OF WORKERS IN VINEYARD
  51-37, PARABLE OF THE SOWER 51-38, CHRIST HEALS BLIND MAN
  OUTSIDE JERICHO 51-39, CHRIST BLESSES PARALYSED SERVANT OF
  CENTURION 51-40, OLD MAN RECEIVES NEEDY WANDERER INTO HOUSE
  51-41, CHRIST WALKING ON WATERS 51-42, TEMPTATIONS OF CHRIST
  51-43, CHRIST IN MAJESTY SEPARATES PEOPLES 51-44, CHRIST
  OVERTURNS TABLES OF MONEYCHANGERS IN TEMPLE 51-45, MOSES TELLS
  OF GOD'S GLORY ON MOUNT SINAI 51-46, ELIAS BROUGHT BREAD AND
  WATER BY ANGEL 51-47, SCRIBE AND PHARISEE REFUSED SIGN BY
  JESUS 51-48, PRIEST LAYS HAND ON KNEELING PENITENT 51-49,
  CHRIST TALKS TO CRIPPLE AT POOL OF BETHESDA 51-50, SOLDIERS
  APPROACH ALTAR WHERE HALOED FIGURE SACRIFICES 51/51,
  TRANSFIGURATION 51-52, ELIJAH AND THE WIDOW'S CURSE 51-53,
  PARABLE OF DIVES AND LAZARUS 51-54, JOSEPH TELLS HIS BRETHERN
  HIS DREAM 51-55, PARABLE OF THE VINEYARD 51-56, REBECCA BRINGS
  JACOB TO RECEIVE FATHER'S BLESSING 51-57, PARABLE OF THE
  PRODIGAL SON 51-58, CHRIST CASTING OUT WINGED DEVIL FROM DUMB
  MAN 51-59, NAAMAN THE LEPER BEING WASHED SEVEN TIMES IN JORDAN

51-60, ELISHA WATCHES WIDOW POUR OUT OIL 51-61, CHRIST
BLESSING SIMON PETER'S MOTHER IN LAW 51-62, MOSES STRIKES
WATER FROM ROCK 51-63, CHRIST AND WOMAN OF SAMARIA 51-64,
SUSANNA AND THE STONING OF THE LYING ELDERS 51-65, CHRIST AND
THE WOMAN TAKEN IN ADULTERY 51-66, FEEDING OF THE MULTITUDE
51-67, SOLOMON'S WISDOM 51-68, PURGING OF THE TEMPLE 51-69,
ISAIAH PREACHING 51-70, CHRIST HEALING THE MAN BLIND FROM
BIRTH 51-71, CHRIST RAISING THE SON OF THE WIDOW OF NAIN
51-72, ELIJAH RAISES SON OF WIDOW OF ZAREPHATH 51-73, CHRIST
RAISING LAZARUS FROM THE DEAD 51-74, CHRIST CALLING THE
THIRSTY TO THE WATER OF LIFE 51-75, JONAH BEFORE THE GATES OF
NINEVEH 51-76, DANIEL IN LION'S DEN 51-77, CHRIST IN GALILEE
WITH DISCIPLES 51-78, CHRIST IN SOLOMON'S PORCH TO TEMPLE
51-79, MOSES AT ELIM BEFORE WELLS AND PALMS 51-80, CHRIST'S
ENTRY INTO JERUSALEM 51-81, CHRIST AT SUPPER IN HOUSE OF MARY
AND MARTHA 51-82, FAITHFUL KNEELING BEFORE GOD WITH CHRIST AT
RIGHT 51-83, JUDAS RECEIVING BAG OF SILVER FROM CHIEF PRIESTS
51-84, CHRIST WASHES DISCIPLES FEET 51-85, PRIEST AT ALTAR
CELEBRATING MASS 51-86, PRIEST READS MISSAL FOR EMPEROR 51-87,
PRIEST BAPTIZING MEN 51-88, PRIEST WITH ATTENDANT AT
ALTAR/FIGURES AND BOAT 51-89, PRIESTS PRAY AT ALTAR 51-90,
SYNAGOGUE AND JEWISH ELDER REPRESENTED BY FIGURES 51-91,
PAGANS KNEEL BEFORE ALTAR 51-92, CREATION 51-93, ARK 51-94,
SACRIFICE OF ISAAC 51-95, EGYPTIANS' CAMP 51-96, PASSING OF
RED SEA 51-97, NEBUCHADNEZZAR SEATED BESIDE GOLDEN IMAGE
51-98, MESSENGER WITH LETTER SPEAKING TO CORINTIAN 51-99,
MARYS AND SALOME AT SEPULCHRE 51-100, ROAD TO EMMAUS 51-101,
CHRIST APPEARS BY SEA OF TIBERIAS 51-102, MOSES LEADING
CHILDREN THROUGH RED SEA 51-103, CHRIST MANIFESTING HIMSELF TO
APOSTLES NEAR GALILEE 51-104, CHRIST LOOKS DOWN ON MEN AND
WOMEN DANCING 51-105, SS PETER/ MARY/JOHN AT SEPULCHRE 51-106,
ST THOMAS PUTS FINGER IN CHRIST'S WOUND 51-107, MERCY/ANGELS
WITH PRISONERS 51-108, CHRIST THE GOOD SHEPHERD 51-109, MEN
PRAISING GOD ON MUSICAL INSTRUMENTS 51-110, DAVID WITH HARP
AND MONKS SINGING 51-111, QUOTE FROM LUKE 51-112, ASCENSION
51-113, CHRIST AND DISCIPLES IN UPPER ROOM 51-114, CHRIST
APPEARS TO DISCIPLES AT TABLE 51-115, MESSENGER WITH SCROLL
FROM SAMARIA 51-116, CHRIST POINTS AT KING MOUNTING LADDER
TOWARD HEAVEN 51-117, ST PETER ADDRESSES THE ELEVEN DISCIPLES
51-118, CHRIST HEALS MAN WITH PALSY 51-119, ANGEL COMES TO
SHADRACH/ MESHACH AND ABENDEGO IN FURNACE 51-120, SHADRACH/
MESHACH AND ABENDEGO 51-120, CHRIST HEALS SIMON PETER'S MOTHER
IN LAW OF FEVER 51-121, CHRIST PROTECTOR WITH CLOAK AROUND
SUPPLIANT 51-122, PARABLE OF GREAT SUPPER 51-123, CHRIST
EATING WITH SINNERS 51-124, ST LUKE'S WINGED OX 51-125,
MIRACULOUS DRAFT OF FISHES 51-126, FEEDING OF THE MULTITUDE
51-127, CHRIST'S TEARS OVER DESTRUCTION OF JERUSALEM 51-128,
CHRIST HEALS DEAF MAN BY SEA OF GALILEE 51-129, PARABLE OF
GOOD SAMARITAN 51-130, LEPERS HEALED 51-131, DAVID PLAYING
HARP WITH MEN WITH MUSICAL INSTRUMENTS 51-132, EZRA READING
THE LAW OF MOSES 51-133, MARY MAGDALENE ANOINTING CHRIST'S
FEET 51-134, CHRIST IN BOAT WITH APOSTLES AND HEALED MAN
51-135, CHRIST HEALING NOBLEMAN'S SON BY CAPERNAUM 51-136,
PARABLE OF THE KING WHO TOOK ACCOUNT OF SERVANTS 51-137,
PHARISEES QUESTION CHRIST ABOUT MONEY 51-138, CHRIST
APPROACHED BY RULER ASKING HELP FOR DAUGHTER 51-139, WOMAN
WITH BLOOD ISSUE TOUCHES CHRIST'S GARMENT 51-139, SECOND
COMING WITH CHRIST 51-140

*$ABSTRACT 52
*LIBRARY BOD
*SLIDE SET TITLE NOTITIA DIGNITATUM
*NEGATIVE REFERENCE ROLL 159B
*RENTAL FEE SM 052 $7.35
*COMMENTS MADE FOR PIETRO DONATO, BISHOP OF PADUA
*TITLE OF MANUSCRIPT NOTITIA DIGNITATUM
*SHELFMARK MS CANON MISC 378
*PROVENANCE FRENCH
*DATE EXECUTED 15TH/1436
*LANGUAGE LATIN

31

*$ABSTRACT 53
  *LIBRARY BOD 53/4-20, HOLKHAM 53/1-3
  *SLIDE SET TITLE MIRACLES OF CHRIST
  *NEGATIVE REFERENCE ROLL 159C
  *RENTAL FEE SM 053 $3.00
  *COMMENTS 20 SLIDES SELECTED FROM 6 MSS OF THE 12TH-15TH
  CENTURIES
  *SHELFMARK MS HOLKHAM 3 53/1-3, MS DOUCE 313 53/4-10, MS SELDEN
  SUPRA 38 53/11-16, MS AUCT D 4 4 53-17, MS BODLEY 270B
  53/18-19, MS DOUCE 266 53-20
  *PROVENANCE BYZANTINE 53/1-3, FRENCH 53/4-10 AND 18-19, DUTCH
  53-20
  *DATE EXECUTED 12TH 53/1-3, 14TH 53/4-10, 13TH 53/18-19, 15TH
  53-20
  *LANGUAGE LATIN 53/1-19, LATIN AND DUTCH 53-20
  *ARTIST/ SCHOOL FOLLOWER OF JEAN PUCELLE 53/4-10
  *TYPE OF MANUSCRIPT GOSPELS 53/1-3, MISSAL 53/4-10, BIBLE
  MORALISEE 53/18-19, BOOK OF HOURS 53-20
  *CONTENTS CHRIST/ MIRACLES 53/1-20, MIRACLES OF CHRIST 53/1-20,
  CHRIST HEALS LEPER 53-1, MAN WASHES IN POOL OF SILOAM 53-1,
  CHRIST HEALS BLIND MAN 53-1, CHRIST BIDS PARLYTIC TO PICK UP
  BED 53-1, CHRIST AND ZACCHEUS 53-1, BAPTISM OF CHRIST 53-2,
  TRANSFIGURATION 53-2, MIRACLE OF THE LOAVES 53-2, MARY
  MAGDALENE WASHES FEET OF CHRIST 53-2, RAISING OF LAZARUS 53-3,
  CHRIST'S ENTRY INTO JERUSALEM 53-3, CHRIST RAISING DEAD MAKING
  LAME WALK AND BLIND SEE 53-4, MARRIAGE AT CANA 53-5, CHRIST
  BLESSES THE CENTURION'S SERVANT 53-6, FEEDING OF THE MULTITUDE
  53-7, RAISING OF LAZARUS 53-8, LAZARUS RISING FROM THE TOMB
  53-9, FEEDING OF THE MULTITUDE 53-10, JESUS HEALS BROTHER
  JAMES 53-11, CHRIST MARY AND GUESTS AT FEAST 53-11, JESUS WITH
  ELDERS IN TEMPLE 53-12, MARRIAGE AT CANA WITH CHRIST AT FEAST
  53-13, CHRIST CHANGES WATER TO WINE 53-14, MARRIAGE AT CANA
  TEXT 53-15, JESUS EMBRACING MOTHER 53-16, RAISING OF LAZARUS
  53-17, ELISHA RAISES SON OF SHUNAMITE WOMAN 53-18, ELISHA
  FEEDS SONS OF PROPHETS 53-18, GEHAZI PUTS MEAL IN POT 53-18,
  GEHAZI AND ELISHA FEED STARVING PEOPLE 53-18, SARA RETREATS TO
  ROOM 53-19, TOBIT CALLS SON TO HIM 53-19, TOBIT FINDS ANGEL TO
  GO WITH HIM 53-19, ANGEL PROMISES TOBIT TO BRING BACK TOBIAS
  53-19, RAISING OF LAZARUS 53-20

*$ABSTRACT 54
  *LIBRARY EXETER COLLEGE OXFORD
  *SLIDE SET TITLE EXETER COLLEGE BOHUN PSALTER
  *NEGATIVE REFERENCE ROLL 160
  *RENTAL FEE SM 054 $11.80
  *COMMENTS WRITTEN FOR HUMPHREY DE BOHUN/ EARL OF HEREFORD
  *TITLE OF MANUSCRIPT BOHUN PSALTER
  *SHELFMARK EXETER COLLEGE 47
  *PROVENANCE ENGLISH
  *DATE EXECUTED 14TH/C1370
  *LANGUAGE LATIN
  *TYPE OF MANUSCRIPT PSALTER
  *CONTENTS PSALTER/ ENGLISH/ 14TH 54/1-197, OCCUPATIONS OF THE
  MONTHS 54/1-12, CALENDAR 54/1-12, JANUARY 54-1, JANUS CROWNED
  HOLDING SCEPTRE AND CUP 54-1, FEBRUARY 54-2, MAN WARMING HANDS
  BY FIRE 54-2, MARCH 54-3, PRUNING TREES 54-3, APRIL 54-4,
  HAWKING 54-4, MAY 54-5, WOMAN HOLDING FLOWERING BRANCHES 54-5,
  JUNE 54-6, CUTTING HAY AND THISTLES 54-6, JULY 54-7, SCYTHING
  54-7, AUGUST 54-8, GLEANING 54-8, SEPTEMBER 54-9, TREADING
  GRAPES 54-9, OCTOBER 54-10, SCATTERING SEEDS 54-10, NOVEMBER
  54-11, FEEDING HOGS 54-11, DECEMBER 54-12, SLAUGHTERING HOGS
  54-12, PSALM 3 54-13, CAIN AND ENOCH AND BUILDING OF CITY
  54-13, PSALM 4 54-14, CAIN INVENTS WEIGHTS AND MEASURES 54-14,
  PSALM 5 54-15, NOAH BUILDS ARK 54-15, PSALM 6 54-16, NOAH'S
  ARK/ ANIMALS ENTER 54-16, PSALM 7 54-17, NOAH'S ARK/ GOD
  BLESSES 54-17, PSALM 8 54-18, NOAH SENDS OUT DOVE 54-18, PSALM
  9 54-19, NOAH'S ARK/ DOVE WITH BRANCH RETURNS 54-19, PSALM 10
  54-20, NOAH AND FAMILY COME TO DRY LAND 54-20, PSALM 11 54-21,
  NOAH PLANTING VINE 54-21, PSALM 12 54-22, NOAH'S SHAME 54-22,
  PSALM 27 54-23, ABRAHAM'S SERVANT SEES REBECCA AT WELL 54-23,

WITH BISHOP'S REGALIA 54-190, ST MARY MAGDALENE WITH COVER
CUP 54-191, INITIAL O 54-192, ST URSULA 54-193, ST MARK/ ANGE
AND LION 54-194, ST MATTHEW/ ANGEL AND TRUMPETER 54-195,
LUKE/ ANGEL AND OX 54-196, ST JOHN/ ANGEL AND EAGLE 54-197

*$ABSTRACT 55
  *LIBRARY BOD
  *SLIDE SET TITLE VENETIAN PORTOLANO
  *NEGATIVE REFERENCE ROLL 161A
  *RENTAL FEE SM 055 $3.00
  *COMMENTS 20 SLIDES WITH MAPS OF COUNTRIES BORDERING ON T
   MEDITERRANEAN
  *SHELFMARK MS DOUCE 390
  *PROVENANCE ITALIAN
  *DATE EXECUTED 15TH/C1400
  *LANGUAGE LATIN
  *ARTIST/ SCHOOL RELATED TO STYLE OF MASTER OF THE URSULA PANE
  *TYPE OF MANUSCRIPT PORTOLANO OF MAPS
  *CONTENTS MAPS/ ITALIAN/ 15TH 55/1-20, FRONT COVER/ IVORY INL
   AND COLORED WOODS 55-1, GABRIEL 55-2, VIRGIN MARY 55-3, BLAC
   SEA/ EASTERN PART 55-4, BLACK SEA/ WESTERN PART 55-5, EASTER
   MEDITERRANEAN/ CYPRUS AND NILE 55-6, CRETE AND GREEK ISLANE
   55-7, CENTRAL MEDITERRANEAN/ CRETE AND SOUTHERN GREECE 55-8
   CENTRAL MEDITERRANEAN/ SICILY/ SOUTHERN ITALY 55-9, ADRIATIC
   DALMATIAN ISLANDS/ EASTERN ITALY 55-10, ADRIATIC WITH SICI
   AND SOUTHERN ITALY 55-11, WESTERN MEDITERRANEAN WITH ITALY AN
   SICILY 55-12, WESTERN MEDITERRANEAN WITH CORSICA/ SARDINIA
   BALERICS 55-13, SPAIN'S EAST COAST AND BALERICS 55-14, IBERIA
   PENINSULA AND STRAITS OF GIBRALTER 55-15, EUROPE/ WEST COAS
   WITH FRISIA TO SPAIN 55-16, ENGLAND AND IRELAND 55-17, ST MAR
   55-18, ST PAUL 55-19, LEATHER CASE 55-20

*$ABSTRACT 56
  *LIBRARY BOD
  *SLIDE SET TITLE DANTE DIVINE COMEDY
  *NEGATIVE REFERENCE ROLL 161B
  *RENTAL FEE SM 056 $4.55
  *TITLE OF MANUSCRIPT DIVINE COMEDY
  *SHELFMARK MS CANON ITAL 108
  *PROVENANCE ITALIAN
  *DATE EXECUTED 14TH
  *LANGUAGE ITALIAN
  *AUTHOR DANTE
  *TYPE OF MANUSCRIPT LITERATURE
  *CONTENTS LITERATURE/ DIVINE COMEDY 56/1-51, ITALIA
   LITERATURE/ DIVINE COMEDY 56/1-51, DANTE AND VIRGIL 56-1
   DANTE AND VIRGIL COME TO DARK WOOD 56-2, DANTE AND VIRGIL MEE
   BEATRICE 56-3, DANTE AND VIRGIL COME TO GATE OF HELL 56-4
   HELL GATE 56-4, CHARON'S BOAT 56-5, MINOS AND A GROUP OF SOUL
   ENTER HOLE 56-6, DANTE AND VIRGIL WATCH CARNAL SINNERS 56-7
   PAOLO AND FRANCESCA 56-8, DEVIL THREATENS SOULS WITH CLU
   56-9, CERBERUS/ SOULS FLY TO 56-9, PLUTO 56-10, CROWD OF TH
   WRATHFUL FIGHTING 56-11, DANTE AND VIRGIL COME TO TOWER WIT
   BEACONS 56-12, DANTE AND VIRGIL SEE SOULS INSIDE MOUNTAI
   56-13, DEVILS WITH SEVEN HORNS GUARD CITY OF DIS 56-14, CIT
   OF DIS 56-14, VIRGIL REASONS WITH A DEVIL 56-15, DEVIL AN
   VIRGIL 56-15, FURIES/ THREE 56-16, DANTE AND VIRGIL AND SOUL
   BEFORE GATE OF DIS 56-17, POETS SPEAK TO FARINATA WHO LEAVE
   HERETICS TOMB 56-18, POETS MEET OLD MAN OF CRETE ON MOUNTAI
   56-19, VIRGIL HOLDS THE LEOPARD OF LUZURIA 56-20, POETS FLY O
   GERYON'S BACK PAST BURNING SINNERS 56-21, DEVILS WITH HORN
   SCOURGE NAKED SINNERS 56-22, BARRATORS BEING STEEPED IN PITC
   IN CAULDRON 56-23, DEVILS ACCOST DANTE AND VIRGIL 56-23
   CALCABINA DIVES INTO PITCH AFTER SINNER 56-24, BEGINNING O
   PURGATORIO 56-25, DANTE AND VIRGIL IN SAILING SHIP 56-25
   MANFRED SHOWS POETS THE WAY 56-26, ANGEL AND DEVIL FIGHT FO
   SOUL OF BUONCONTE 56-27, DEVIL AND ANGEL FIGHT FOR SOUL 56-27
   POETS APPROACH MOUNTAIN WHERE SORDELLO'S SOUL SITS 56-28

SORDELLO SHOWS POETS THE SOULS OF NEGLIGENT RULERS 56-29,
ANGELS GUARD PURGATORY FROM THE SERPENT 56-30, SORDELLO SHOWS
POETS THE SERPENT 56-31, SERPENT 56-31, SEVEN STARS
REPRESENTING MORAL AND THEOLOGICAL VIRTUES 56-31, SERPENT
LICKS BACK WHEN ROUTED BY ANGELS 56-32, ANGEL WHO GUARDS THREE
STEPS CHALLENGES THE POETS 56-33, TRAJAN AND HIS FOLLOWERS
56-34, PROUD SOULS BENT UNDER MOUNTAINS OF STONE 56-35, ANGEL
OF HUMILITY SHOWS STEPS TO SECOND TERRACE 56-36, ENVIOUS SOULS
FLY TOWARDS THE POETS 56-37, ANGEL OF MERCY SHOWS A LESS STEEP
ASCENT 56-38, VIRGIN MARY IN TEMPLE TO SHOW GENTLENESS 56-39,
ST STEPHEN STONED 56-40, SOULS OF ONCE WRATHFUL SPIRITS CHANT
AGNUS DEI 56-40, VIRGIL AND DANTE DREAM 56-41, HAMAN DIES ON
CROSS 56-41, AHASUERUS/ ESTHER AND MORDECAI TALK 56-41, DANTE
DREAMS OF THE SIREN 56-42, SUN APPEARS FROM BEHIND MOUNTAIN
56-43, SOULS OF THE AVARICIOUS AND PRODIGAL 56-43, ANGEL OF
CHASTITY DESCENDS FROM SUN TO POETS 56-44, SOULS OF LUSTFUL
APPROACH GLOWING FIRE 56-44, SPIRIT FLIES DOWN TO POETS AT
NIGHT 56-45, POETS SLEEP IN GARDEN OF EDEN 56-46, EDEN 56-46
LEAH GATHERS FLOWERS 56-46, POETS REACH SUMMIT OF PURGATORY
56-46, POETS SPEAK TO MATILDA ACROSS STREAM 56-47, DIVINE
PAGEANT 56-48, MATILDA AND POETS SEE 24 ELDERS 56-48, CHURCH
TRIUMPHANT AS CHARIOT 56-49, SYMBOLISM/ CHURCH AS CHARIOT
56-49, DIVINE PAGEANT 56/50-51

*$ABSTRACT 57
 *LIBRARY BOD
 *SLIDE SET TITLE MARCO POLO LES LIVRES DU GRAUNT CAAM
 *NEGATIVE REFERENCE ROLL 161C
 *RENTAL FEE SM 057 $3.90
 *TITLE OF MANUSCRIPT LES LIVRES DU GRAUNT CAAM
 *SHELFMARK MS BODLEY 264/ FOL 218 TO END
 *PROVENANCE ENGLISH
 *DATE EXECUTED 15TH/C1400
 *LANGUAGE FRENCH
 *ARTIST/ SCHOOL JOHANNES AND HIS SCHOOL
 *AUTHOR MARCO POLO
 *TYPE OF MANUSCRIPT TRAVELOGUE
 *CONTENTS TRAVEL LITERATURE/ MARCO POLO 57/1-38, MARCO POLO
57/1-38, MARCO POLO'S FATHER AND UNCLE 57-1, KHAN PRESENTS
GOLDEN BOOK TO NICCOLO AND MAFFEO POLO 57-2, PAPAL LETTERS
PRESENTED TO KHAN BY POLOS 57-3, CAPTURE OF BAGHDAD 57-4,
CHRISTIANS ALARMED AT WORDS OF CALIPH OF BAGHDAD 57-5, MARCO
POLO HEARS OF THREE KINGS IN PERSIA 57-6, CITY OF KAMADIN
57-7, GARDEN LIKE PARADISE 57-8, RIVER BALACIAN IN PROVINCE OF
BADASHAN 57-9, CITY OF KAMPION 57-10, BATTLE OF GHENGIS KHAN
AND PRESTER JOHN 57-11, GOD OF THE TARTARS 57-12, HAWKING
OUTSIDE CITY OF CIANDU OR SHANG-TU 57-13, INCENSE AND MUSIC
BEFORE ALTAR 57-14, BATTLE BETWEEN KAHN AND NAIAN THE TRAITOR
PREPARED 57-15, KHAN CONDEMNS NAIAN TO DEATH AND REWARDS OWN
OFFICERS 57-16, KHAN REWARDS HIS OFFICERS 57-17, KHAN'S
BIRTHDAY PARTY 57-18, KHAN HUNTING DEER/ BOAR AND BEAR 57-19,
HUNTING SCENE 57-19, BARONS ESTABLISHED TO MANAGE KHAN'S
PROPERTY 57-20, KHAN GIVING ALMS TO POOR IN CAMBALUC OR PEKIN
57-21, SHIPPING ON RIVER KARACORAN 57-22, BRIDGE OF SINDUFU IN
TIBET 57-23, MARCO POLO JOURNEYS TOWARDS TIBET 57-23, TRENCHES
FOR CATCHING SERPENTS 57-24, BUTCHER'S SHOP 57-24, SICK BED
AND DINING TABLE 57-25, TOWERS OF ROYAL COMB AT MIEN IN BURMA
57-26, CORPSE BURNED IN CITY OF CHANGLU IN CHINA 57-27, BOATS
IN FRONT OF CITY 57-28, KHAN'S SOLDIERS ATTACKING
SIANG-YANG-FU IN PROVINCE MANZI 57-29, KANZAI/ CAPITAL OF
PROVINCE OF MANZI 57-30, CHESS IN CASTLE GARDEN 57-31, INDIAN
SHIPS ARRIVING AT CARCAN 57-32, MARVELS OF INDIA 57-33,
WONDERS OF CIANDA 57-34, KINGS BEFORE GOLDEN IDOL 57-35, PEARL
FISHING IN HARBOR OF MAABAR 57-36, PILGRIMS IN SLAVINS BEFORE
SHRINE OF ST THOMAS 57-37, ST THOMAS/ SHRINE IN MAABAR 57-37,
MEETING OF SIX KINGS 57-38

*$ABSTRACT 58
  *LIBRARY BOD
  *SLIDE SET TITLE SAINT ANNE
  *NEGATIVE REFERENCE ROLL 161D
  *RENTAL FEE SM 058 $3.00
  *COMMENTS 20 SLIDES FROM 19 MSS OF THE 14TH-16TH CENTURIES
  *SHELFMARK MS DIGBY 227 58-1, MS LAUD MISC 302 58-2, MS LAU
  MISC 93 58-3, MS CANON LITURG 388 58-4, MS AUBREY 31 58-5, M
  DOUCE 112 58-6, MS DOUCE 231 58-7, MS AUCT D INF 2 11 58-8, M
  RAWL LITURG D L 58-9, MS ADD A 185 58-10, MS BUCHANAN E
  58-11, MS LAT LITURG F 2 58-12, MS AUCT D INF 2 13 58-13, M
  DOUCE 93 58/14-15, MS DOUCE 51 58-16, MS LAT LITURG G
  58-17, MS DOUCE 112 58-18, MS DOUCE 19 58-19, MS RAWL A 41
  58-20
  *PROVENANCE ENGLISH/ ABINGDON ABBEY 58-1, ENGLISH 58/2 AND
  AND 7 AND 9 AND 12, ENGLISH 58-17, FRENCH 58/3 AND 8 AND 10-1
  AND 20, ITALIAN 58/4 AND 19, FLEMISH 58/6 AND 13 AND 16 AN
  18, DUTCH 58/14-15
  *DATE EXECUTED 15TH/1461 58-1, 15TH 58/2-5 AND 8-17 AND 20
  14TH 58-7, 16TH 58-6 AND 18-19
  *LANGUAGE LATIN
  *TYPE OF MANUSCRIPT RELIGIOUS TEXTS 58/1-20, MISSAL 58/1-2
  BOOK OF HOURS 58/5 AND 7 AND 9 AND 12, OFFICE OF THE HOL
  GHOST 58-17
  *CONTENTS ST ANNE 58/1-20, BED 58-1, BED AND TWO ATTENDANT
  58-2, VIRGIN AS INFANT BEING WASHED 58-3, VIRGIN WASHED 58-4
  JOACHIM HOLDING INFANT VIRGIN 58-5, PRESENTATION OF CHRIST I
  TEMPLE 58-6, VIRGIN SHELTERED BY ANNE 58-7, HOLDING BOOK I
  GARDEN WITH VIRGIN 58-8, TEACHING CHILD VIRGIN TO READ 58-9
  TEACHING VIRGIN TO READ 58/10-12, CHRIST AS INFANT WITH VIRGI
  58-13, INITIAL 58-14, VIRGIN AND CHILD WITH ST ANNE 58/15-19
  OFFICE OF THE HOLY GHOST 58-17, ST ANNE WITH FAMILY 58-20

*$ABSTRACT 59
  *LIBRARY BOD
  *SLIDE SET TITLE BAPTISM
  *NEGATIVE REFERENCE ROLL 161E
  *RENTAL FEE SM 059 $4.30
  *COMMENTS 48 SLIDES SELECTED FROM 19 MSS OF THE 14-16T
  CENTURIES
  *SHELFMARK MS AUCT D INF 1 10 59-1, MS ROE 6 59-2, MS E
  CLARKE 6 59-3, MS GR F 1 59/4-5, MS C C C 410 59/6-7, MS CANO
  ITAL 280 59-8, MS CANON LITURG 388 59-9, MS DOUCE 14 59-10, M
  BODLEY 270B 59/11-30, MS DOUCE 118 59-31, MS DOUCE 31
  59/32-33, MS AUCT D INF 2 11 59-34, MS LITURG 41 59-35, M
  DOUCE 135 59-36, MS DOUCE 204 59/37-39, MS LITURG 396 59-40
  MS GOUGH LITURG 2 58-41, MS AUCT D 3 4 59-42, MS AUCT D 3
  59-43, MS AUCT D 4 8 59-44, MS GOUGH LITURG 8 59-45, MS C C
  161 59/46-48
  *PROVENANCE BYZANTINE 59/1-5, ITALIAN 59/6-10 AND 37-39, FRENC
  59/11-36, FLEMISH 59-40, ENGLISH 59/41-48
  *DATE EXECUTED 12TH 59/1 AND 41, 13TH 59/2 AND 11-30 AND 40 AN
  42-44, 14TH 59/4-7 AND 32-33, 15TH 59/34-35 AND 37-39 AN
  46-48
  *LANGUAGE LATIN
  *TYPE OF MANUSCRIPT RELIGIOUS TEXTS
  *CONTENTS BAPTISM 59/1-48, BAPTISM 59-1, BAPTISM OF CHRIS
  59-2, BAPTISM 59-3, BAPTISM WITH CHRIST IMMERSED TO SHOULDER
  59-4, BAPTISM OF CHRIST 59-5, CHRIST SEES JOHN BAPTISING 59-6
  ANGELS HOLD CHRIST'S CLOTHES 59-7, ANGELS WITH TOWEL AND THRE
  WITNESSES 59-8, FONT OF SILVER AND VIRGIN WASHED 59-9, BAPTIS
  59-10, CONVERSION OF PAUL 59-11, FLOWERS ON CANDLESTICK AN
  LILY 59-12, WASHING OF AARON 59-13, BAPTISMAL WATERS FRE
  CONVERTED INFIDEL 59-14, LEPERS CLEANSED 59-15, CHILD BAPTISE
  59-16, WATERS OF JORDAN RAISED BEFORE ISRAELITES 59-17
  CONVERTS BAPTISED IN TUB 59-18, CHRIST TAKES SIN AWAY B
  PENANCE 59-19, MAN AS MONK AND ONE WITH MONEYBAGS AFTE
  BAPTISM 59-20, CHRIST'S DISCIPLES BAPTISE MANY SONS 59-21
  PRIEST PERFORMING BAPTISM 59-22, BAPTISM 59-23, OIL OF DAVI
  IS BAPTISM 59-24, NAKED FIGURES BAPTISED 59-25, SYNAGOGU

FREED OF DEVIL BY WATER OF BAPTISM 59-26, APOSTLES TRANSMIT
BAPTISM 59-27, GENTILES WITH JOY ACCEPT BAPTISM 59-28, MAN WHO
HEARS VOICE ONE WHO GETS SACRAMENTS 59-29, WATER OF BAPTISM
59-30, FONT OF MARBLE 59-31, MAN BAPTISED 59-32, NAKED MEN
BAPTISED FROM JUG 59-33, CHRIST BAPTISED WAIST-DEEP IN WATER
59-34, PETER PERFORMS BAPTISM 59-35, BAPTISM 59/36-37, LAVER
OF BRONZE 59-38, NAAMAN WASHES IN JORDAN 59-39, CHRIST
BAPTISED 59-40, CHRIST BAPTISED 59-41, ST JOHN BAPTIST
BAPTISES CHRIST 59-42, ST PAUL BAPTISED 59-43, BAPTISM OF
CHRIST 59/44-46, LAVER OF BRONZE 59-47, NAAMAN WASHES IN
JORDAN 59-48

*$ABSTRACT 60
 *LIBRARY BOD
 *SLIDE SET TITLE GOUGH MAP
 *NEGATIVE REFERENCE ROLL 161G
 *RENTAL FEE SM 060 $2.40
 *COMMENTS THE EARLIEST ROAD MAP OF GREAT BRITAIN
 *TITLE OF MANUSCRIPT GOUGH MAP
 *SHELFMARK MS GOUGH GEN TOP 16
 *PROVENANCE ENGLISH
 *DATE EXECUTED 14TH/C1360
 *LANGUAGE ENGLISH
 *TYPE OF MANUSCRIPT MAP
 *CONTENTS MAP/ ENGLISH/ 14TH 60/1-10, GOUGH MAP 60/1-10,
 ENGLAND AND WALES 60-1, IRELAND/ EAST COAST 60-1, NORTHERN
 ENGLAND AND SCOTLAND 60-2, HADRIAN'S WALL 60-2, WALES AND THE
 SEVERN 60-3, BRISTOL CHANNEL 60-3, MIDLANDS AND SOUTH-EAST
 ENGLAND 60-4, LONDON TO SEVERN ROAD 60-5, YORK AND HUMBER
 ROADS 60-6, LONDON ROADS 60-7, WINDSOR CASTLE SHOWN AND VALE
 OF WHITE HORSE 60-7, IRISH SEA AND HUMBER ROADS 60-8,
 SCOTLAND'S NORTH WITH ORKNEYS AND ISLES 60-9, SOUTHERN ENGLAND
 AND WALES 60-10, ISLE OF WIGHT AND CHANNEL ISLANDS 60-10

*$ABSTRACT 61
 *LIBRARY BOD
 *SLIDE SET TITLE DANTE INITIALS 61/1-4, SECRETA FIDELIUM CRUCIS
 61/5-36, CARTHUSIAN BREVIARY 61/37-68
 *NEGATIVE REFERENCE ROLL 162A%1-3<
 *RENTAL FEE SM 061 $5.40
 *TITLE OF MANUSCRIPT PARADISIO 61/1-2, INFERNO 61/3-4, SECRETA
 FIDELIUM CRUCIS 61/5-36, CARTHUSIAN BREVIARY 61/37-68
 *SHELFMARK MS CANON ITAL 105-107 61/1-4, MS TANNER 190 61/5-36,
 MS CANON LITURG 410 61/37-68
 *PROVENANCE ITALIAN
 *DATE EXECUTED 15TH 61/1-4, 14TH 61/5-36, 15TH/1480 61/37-68
 *LANGUAGE ITALIAN 61/1-4, LATIN 61/5-68
 *ARTIST/ SCHOOL CHRISTOPHORUS CONTEXA 61/1-4, JACOMETTO
 VENEZIANO 61/37-68
 *AUTHOR DANTE 61/1-4, MARINUS SANTUTUS/ KNOWN AS TORSELLUS
 61/5-36,
 *TYPE OF MANUSCRIPT LITERATURE 61/1-4, CRUSADER'S HANDBOOK
 61/5-36, BREVIARY 61/37-68
 *CONTENTS INITIAL A 61-1, DANTE KNEELING AND GAZING AT BEATRICE
 61-1, INITIAL L 61-2, GOD ENTHRONED IN MAJESTY 61-2, INITIAL N
 61-3, DANTE AND VIRGIL 61-4, INITIAL S 61-5, CLERIC LASSOES
 ANIMAL ALSO SHOT BY SARACEN 61-6, INITIAL I WITH CHRIST
 WALKING ON WATERS 61-7, INITIAL Q 61-7, NEGROES WITH TURBANS
 61-7, INITIAL P 61-8, GALLEY WITH ROWERS AND OARS VISIBLE
 61-9, CHRIST IN MAJESTY 61-10, INITIAL D 61-10, CHRIST IN BLUE
 MANDORLA 61-11, INITIAL Q 61-12, INITIAL A 61-13, INITIAL T
 61-14, NOAH TO ABRAHAM'S PEDIGREE 61-15, INITIAL F 61-16,
 INITIAL I 61-17, INITIAL P 61-18, INITIAL C 61-19, INITIAL P
 61-20, GODFREY OF JERUSALEM 61-20, INITIAL I 61-21, INITIAL T
 61-22, INITIAL O 61-23, SALADIN BRANDISHING SWORD AT
 CHRISTIANS 61-23, INITIAL C 61-24, INITIAL P 61-25, INITIAL I
 61-26, ST LOUIS WITH FLEUR-DE-LYS 61-26, INITIAL C 61-27, MAP
 OF HOLY LAND 61-28, MILITARY TRAINING DEPICTED 61-29, JOUSTING

39

61-30, MAP OF THE WORLD IN CIRCLE 61-31, MAP OF MIDDLE EAS
61-32, MAP OF PALESTINE 61-33, MAP OF JERUSALEM 61-34, MAP C
ACRE 61-35, CHRONOLOGICAL TABLE OF RULERS IN TEXT 61-36, DAVI
AS ORIENTAL WRITING PSALMS 61-37, INITIAL E 61-38, INITIAL
61-39, INITIAL D/ DOMINUS ILLUMINATIO 61-40, KING POINTS T
HIS EYE 61-40, INITIAL E/ EXULTATE 61-41, HARPIST SEATE
61-41, INITIAL D WITH JEWEL 61-42, INITIAL D/ DIXI CUSTODIA
61-43, OLD MAN POINTS TO LIPS 61-43, INITIAL D WITH PEAR
61-44, INITIAL D/ DIXIT INSIPIENS 61-45, FOOL WITH STAF
61-45, INITIAL D WITH PEARL 61-46, INITIAL S/ SALVUM ME FA
61-47, MAN/NAKED IN WATER PRAYING 61-47, INITIAL D WITH PEAR
61-48, INITIAL Q WITH URN AND FOLIAGE 61-49, INITIAL I WIT
ARCHITECTURAL MOTIF 61-50, INITIAL C/ BEARDED FIGURE WITH HAR
61-51, INITIAL D/ BEARDED MAN PRAYING 61-52, INITIAL C WIT
HEAD 61-53, INITIAL D WITH ARCHITECTURAL BACKGROUND 61-54
INITIAL I 61-55, INITIAL C WITH PEARL 61-56, INITIAL E WIT
PEARLS/ DECORATED PAGE 61-57, INITIAL D/ VIRGIN AND CHIL
61-58, VIRGIN AND CHILD 61-58, HOLES PAINTED ON PARCHMEN
61/54 AND 58, INITIAL S WITH PEARLS 61-59, INITIAL S WIT
PEARLS 61-60, INITIAL D/ SAINT WITH BANNER 61-61, INITIAL
WITH JEWELS 61-62, INITIAL O WITH MONSTRANCE 61-63, INITIAL
61-64, INITIAL P WITH MITRED BISHOP 61-65, SILENUS DRAGGED E
ROPE AND BIRCHED BY PUTTI 61-65, INITIAL D WITH PEARLS 61-66
INITIAL D WITH JEWEL 61-67, INITIAL S/ SAINT WITH PALM AN
BOOK 62-68, PUTTI RIDING RAM AND GOAT 61-68

*$ABSTRACT 62
 *LIBRARY BOD
 *SLIDE SET TITLE FOOLS
 *NEGATIVE REFERENCE ROLL 162C
 *RENTAL FEE SM 062 $3.00
 *COMMENTS 20 SLIDES SELECTED FROM 12 MSS OF THE 13TH-15T
 CENTURIES
 *SHELFMARK MS CANON BIBL LAT 11 62-1, MS RAWL G 126 62-2, M
 AUCT D 2 2 62-3, MS ASHMOLE 1523 62-4, MS RAWL G 185 62-5, M
 DOUCE 18 62-6, MS HATTON 10 61-7, MS BODLEY 953 62-8, MS C C
 17 62-9, MS LAUD LAT 114 62-10, MS DOUCE 118 62/11-12, M
 DOUCE 211 62-13, MS LITURG 60 62-14, MS DOUCE 80 62-15, M
 DOUCE 135 62-16, MS LAUD LAT 84 62-17, MS CANON LITURG 37
 62-18, MS DOUCE 272 62-19, MS DOUCE 314 62-20
 *PROVENANCE ENGLISH 62/1-10, FRENCH 62/11-16, FLEMISH 62-17
 ITALIAN 62/19-20
 *DATE EXECUTED 13TH 62-1, 14TH 62/2-5 AND 11-13, 15TH 62/6-1
 AND 14-15 AND 18-20, 16TH 62-16
 *CONTENTS FOOL NAKED BUT FOR CLOAK WITH CLUB AND LOAF 62-1
 FOOL HALF NAKED WITH CLUB AND LOAF 62-2, FOOL IN JESTER'
 DRESS 62-3, FOOL IN THREE-TAILED HOOD AND BARE LEGS 62-4, FOO
 DISPUTING WITH MONK 62-5, FOOL IN JESTER'S COSTUME 62-6, FOO
 IN JESTER'S CAP AND BELLS WITH DIPPER 62-7, FOOL IN GOWN AN
 HOOD ON STOOL 62-8, FOOL WITH CLUB 62-10, FOOL BALD WITH CLU
 AND STONE 62-11, FOOL WITH BEARD AND CAPE HOOD AND BELL
 62-12, FOOL TONSURED WITH BALL AND FOOLSTICK 62-13, JESTER I
 BLUE AND RED WITH BAUBLE 62-14, MAN FROM BUSHES IN FOOL'
 COSTUME 62-15, PERSON IN FOOL'S COSTUME WITH DEATH 62-16, FOO
 WITH GREEN STAFF AND DEVIL 62-17, FOOL WITH CLUB 62-18, FOO
 WITH BELLS ON HEAD 62-19, FOOL WITH GREEN CLUB AND FLOWERS I
 HAIR 62-20

*$ABSTRACT 63
 *LIBRARY BOD
 *SLIDE SET TITLE DOMESTIC EQUIPMENT
 *NEGATIVE REFERENCE ROLL 162D
 *RENTAL FEE SM 063 $4.40
 *COMMENTS 48 SLIDES SELECTED FROM 10 13TH CENTURY FRENCH MSS
 *SHELFMARK MS DOUCE 48 63/1-7, MS ADD A 46 62/8-10, MS DOUCE 2
 62/11-13, MS DOUCE 49 62/14-17, MS DOUCE 118 62/18-19, MS AUC
 D 4 3 63-20, MS AUCT D 2 6 63-21, MS BODLEY 264 63/22-25, M
 DOUCE 6 63/26-43, MS BODLEY 270B 63/44-48

*PROVENANCE FRENCH
*DATE EXECUTED 13TH
*CONTENTS DOMESTIC EQUIPMENT 63/1-48, JUG WITH MAN POURING
63-1, FIREPLACE AND CHIMNEY WITH MAN WARMING HANDS 63-2,
BILLHOOK USED TO PRUNE TREE 63-3, POT HANGING OVER FIRE 63-4,
BED 63-5, TABLE SETTING 63-6, WAGON 63-7, MAN EATING 63-8,
FRUIT PICKED 63-9, WOMAN WITH FRUIT BASKET AND MAN SOWING
SEEDS   63-10,   LADDER AND MAN 63-11, SCYTHE 63-12, PIG
SLAUGHTERED WITH AXE 63-13, SPADE 63-14, SICKLE 63/15-16,
BAKER AND OVEN 63-17, FISHING 63-18, JESUS WASHED IN TUB
63-19, GRAPES IN BASKET 63-20, TABLE SETTING 63-21, PLOUGH
63-22, FARM TOOLS 63-23, CART WITH TWO WHEELS AND BATTLE
AROUND IT 63-24, MAN AND WOMAN COOKING 63-25, FRUIT PICKED
63-26, BASKET 63-27, BELLOWS 63-28, DEPOSITION 63-29, POTS
63-30, RAKE 63-31, MAN DRINKING 63-32, MAN WITH JAR AND MONKEY
WITH BASKET 63-33, FLAGON BESIDE MAN DRINKING 63-34, FLEECE
CARDED 63-35, BARREL TAPPED AND MAN DRINKING 63-36, BARROW
WITH CLOWN AND APES WHEELING IT 63-37, STORK/ MONKEYS/ PIPER/
POT 63-39, BARREL 63-40, BEDROOM WITH HANGINGS AND STOOL
63-41, OVEN 63-42, WAGON 63-43, JACOB'S WAGON AS EVANGELISTS
63-44,   GENESIS   45   VERSES   16-18/ JACOB'S WAGON 63-44,
TABERNACLE 63-45, EXODUS 25 VERSES 23-29/ TABERNACLE 63-45,
ARCHER 63-46, I KINGS 20 VERSES 20-22/ JONATHAN THE ARCHER
63-46, ISHBOSHETH'S MURDER 63-47, II KINGS 4 VERSE 5/ MURDER
OF ISHBOSHETH 63-47, MURDERER WITH MATTOCK 63-48, JOB 24 VERSE
3/ MURDERER WITH MATTOCK 63-48

*$ABSTRACT 64
*LIBRARY BOD
*SLIDE SET TITLE BOOK PRODUCTION IN THE SOUTHERN LOW COUNTRIES/
NORTHERN LOW COUNTRIES/ ENGLAND AND FRANCE
*NEGATIVE REFERENCE ROLL 163A %1-5<
*RENTAL FEE SM 064 $6.95
*COMMENTS 99 SLIDES SELECTED FROM 63 MSS OF THE 15TH CENTURY
*SHELFMARK MS CANON LITURG 125 64-1, MS RAWL LITURG E 14
64/2-4, MS CANON LITURG 118 64/5-6, MS CANON LITURG 17 64/7-8,
MS CANON LITURG 91 64/9-11, MS CANON LITURG 92 64-12, MS CANON
LITURG 147 64-13, MS CANON LITURG 116 64-14, MS CANON LITURG
276 64-15, MS LAUD MISC 204 64-16, MS RAWL LITURG F 34 64-17,
MS BUCHANAN E 5 64/18-19, MS CANON LITURG 64-20, MS CANON
LITURG 108 64-21, MS CANON LITURG 129 64/22-23, MS CANON
LITURG 175 64-24, MS CANON LITURG 227 64-25, MS CANON LITURG
229 64-26, MS CANON LITURG 252 64-27, MS DOUCE 182 64-28, MS
DOUCE 208 64-29, MS DOUCE 365 64-30, MS DOUCE 374 64/31-32, MS
GOUGH LITURG 15 64/33-34, MS LITURG 58 64-35, MS RAWL 410
64-36, MS RAWL LITURG E 26 64-37, MS DOUCE 256 64/38-39, MS
DOUCE 311 64-40, MS DOUCE 266 64/41-42, MS BUCHANAN F 1 64-43,
MS DOUCE 93 64/44-45, MS DOUCE 381 64/46-48, MS JONES 43
64-49, MS BODLEY 62 64-50, MS DOUCE 18 64/51-52, MS RAWL
LITURG D 1 64-53, MS RAWL E 1 64-54, MS RAWL LITURG E 9 64-55,
MS AUCT D INF 2 13 64/56-58, MS BODLEY 283 64-59, MS GOUGH
LITURG 6 64-60, MS BODLEY 939 64-61, MS AUCT D INF 2 11 64-62,
MS AUBREY 31 64-63, MS DOUCE 381 64-64, MS LITURG 400 64-65,
MS LITURG 401 64-66, MS BARLOW 47 64-67, MS DOUCE 62
64/68-73, MS DOUCE 80 64/74-76, MS RAWL LITURG F 21 64/77-78,
MS RAWL E 12 64-79, MS RAWL E 25 64-80, MS RAWL E LITURG 32
64/81-82, MS RAWL LITURG E 27 64-83, MS RAWL LITURG F 26
64-84, MS CANON LITURG 389 64/85-86, MS LITURG 100 64/87-88,
MS DOUCE 144 64/89-94, MS LITURG 238 64-95, MS CANON LITURG 75
64-96, MS RAWL LITURG E 23 64/97-98, MS LAT LITURG F 2 64-99
*PROVENANCE DUTCH 64/1-48, ENGLISH 64/49-67, FRENCH 64/68-99
*DATE EXECUTED 15TH
*TYPE OF MANUSCRIPT BOOK OF HOURS 64/1-27 AND 33-35 AND 37-50
AND 52-99, COMMENTARIES 64/28-29, TREATISE ON WITCHCRAFT
64-36, PSALTER 64-51
*CONTENTS   VIRGIN AND INITIAL S 64-1, ANNUNCIATION 64-2,
NATIVITY 64-3, TRINITY 64-4, ST CHRISTOPHER 64-5, CRUCIFIXION
64-6, CHRIST BEFORE PILATE 64-7, CRUCIFIXION 64-8, VISITATION
64-9, PRESENTATION 64-10, HOLY INNOCENTS 64-11, FIFTEEN JOYS
64-12, INITIAL O 64-13, ANNUNCIATION 64-14, ROAD TO CALVARY

64-15, ANNUNCIATION 64-16, NATIVITY 64-17, CRUCIFIXION 64-18
FLIGHT INTO EGYPT 64-19, BORDER/ DECORATED 64-20, FLAGELLATIO
64-21, NATIVITY 64-22, ADORATION OF THE MAGI 64-23, OPENING O
BOOK OF HOURS 64-25, ST JOSEPH 64-26, TEXT OF BOOK OF HOUR
64-27, PENTECOST 64-24, TOURNAMENT 64-28, TEXT OF CAESA
COMMENTARIES 64-29, MARGARET OF YORK 64-30, MONT SAINT MICHE
64-31, SACRISTAN DROWNED 64-32, CRUCIFIXION 64-33, BURIA
SCENE 64-34, ADORATION OF THE MAGI 64-35, DEVIL WORSHIP/ MA
DOES HOMAGE 64-36, ANGEL WITH SHEPHERDS 64-37, PENTECOS
64-38, LAZARUS RAISED 64-39, PENTECOST 64-40, PENITENTIA
PSALMS 64-41, LAZARUS RAISED 64-42, PENTECOST 64-43
ANNUNCIATION 64-44, TEXT OF BOOK OF HOURS 64-45, ST ADRIA
64-46, ST BARBARA 64-47, ANNUNCIATION 64-48, BORDER OF BOOK O
HOURS 64-49, TEXT OF BOOK OF HOURS 64-50, ANGELS/ SHEPHERDS
MAGI 64-51, DAVID 64-52, GETHSEMANE 64-53, TEXT OF BOOK O
HOURS 64-54, BORDER OF BOOK OF HOURS 64-55, CHRIST WITH OR
64-56, CHRIST WITH CROSS 64-57, LAST JUDGMENT 64-58
COMMANDMENTS/ TEN 64-59, ENTOMBMENT 64-60, ST DOROTHY 64-61
CHRIST BETRAYED 64-62, DESCENT FROM CROSS 64-63, ST JOH
BAPTIST 64-65, ST JOHN BAPTIST 64-66, TEXT OF BOOK OF HOUR
64-67, VIRGIN AND CHILD 64/64, VIRGIN AND CHILD 64-65
VISITATION 64-69, ADORATION OF THE MAGI 64-70, HELL 64-71
CHRIST BEFORE PILATE 64-72, PREPARATION OF CROSS 64-73, ROA
TO CALVARY 64-74, VIRGIN AND CHILD 64-75, LAST JUDGMENT 64-76
BORDERS OF BOOK OF HOURS 64-77, PENTECOST 64/78-79
ANNUNCIATION 64-80, ANNUNCIATION 64-81, JESSE TREE 64-81, LAS
JUDGMENT 64-82, ANNUNCIATION 64-83, BURIAL 64-84, INITIA
64-85, PENTECOST 64-86, CRUCIFIXION 64-87, TEXT AND BORDER O
BOOK OF HOURS 64-88, PRESENTATION 64-89, PROCESSION O
LITANIES 64-90, LITANIES FOR TRANSFERENCE OF RELICS 64-91
LITANIES FOR FLAGELLANTS 64-92, LITANIES FOR ST TORMENIS AN
ST MICHAEL 64-93, ST ANDREW 64-94, INITIAL 64-95, ANNUNCIATIO
64-96, FLIGHT INTO EGYPT 64-97, OFFICE OF THE DEAD 64-98
PIETA 64-99

*$ABSTRACT 65
 *LIBRARY BOD
 *SLIDE SET TITLE DANCING
 *NEGATIVE REFERENCE ROLL 163B
 *RENTAL FEE SM 065 $3.00
 *COMMENTS 20 SLIDES FROM 17 MSS OF C1150-1728 DEPICTING DANCIN
 *SHELFMARK MS AUCT D 2 6 65-1, MS AUCT D 4 3 65-2, MS AUCT D
 2 65-3, MS BODLEY 264 65-4, MS ADD A 22 65-5, MS DOUCE 19
 65-6, MS E MUSAEO 65 65-7, MS BODLEY 264 65/8-9, MS LAUD MIS
 302 65-10, MS DOUCE 276 65/12-13, MS DOUCE 93 65-14, MS DOUC
 204 65-15, MS DOUCE 195 65-16, MS DOUCE 371 65-17, MS DOUC
 374 65-18, MS DOUCE 135 65-19, MS DOUCE 7 65-20
 *PROVENANCE ENGLISH 65/1 AND 3 AND 10, FLEMISH 65/2 AND 4 AN
 8-9 AND 18, FRENCH 65/5-7 AND 11-13 AND 15-17 AND 19, DUTC
 65-14, GERMAN 65-20
 *DATE EXECUTED 12TH/C1150 65-1, 13TH 65/2-3, 14TH 65/4-9, 15T
 65/10-18, 16TH 65-19, 18TH/1717-28 65-20
 *CONTENTS DANCING 65/1-20, DANCE OF SALOME WITH SWORDS 65-1
 DANCE OF MAN CROWNED WITH LEAVES 65-2, DANCERS MAKING LIVEL
 LEAPS 65-3, COUPLES DANCING 65-4, CAROLE DANCED BY TWO COUPLE
 65-5, DANCERS SURROUND LANCELOT 65-6, DANCERS UNDER TREE WIT
 MUSICIANS 65-7, DANCERS/ 3 WITH ANIMAL MASKS 65-8, DANCERS I
 RING 65-9, DANCE IN RING OF FOXES AND GEESE AROUND OWL 65-10
 DANCE WITH COUPLES AND MUSICIAN 65-11, MORRIS JIG 65-12
 DANCING FARANDOLE TO PIPE AND TABOR 65-13, DANCE IN RING O
 SHEPHERDS AT NATIVITY 65-14, DANCING COURTIERS GREE
 TRIUMPHANT DAVID 65-15, DANCE IN ROUND AS LOVER INVITED T
 JOIN 65-16, DANCERS AT COURT OF MIRTH 65-17, DANCING I
 COURTYARD AT WEDDING 65-18, DANCE OF DEATH 65-19, DANCING A
 INN 65-20

*$ABSTRACT 66
 *LIBRARY BOD

*RENTAL FEE SM 066 $3.00
*SLIDE SET TITLE COSTUME
*NEGATIVE REFERENCE ROLL 163C
*COMMENTS 20 SLIDES SELECTED FROM 15 MSS OF 14TH-16TH CENTURIES
  DEPICTING COSTUMES
*SHELFMARK MS AUCT D 2 2 66-1, MS DOUCE 360 65-2, MS NEW
  COLLEGE 65 66-4, MS DOUCE 300 66/4-5, MS D/ORVILLE 76 66-6, MS
  AUCT D INF 2 11 66/7-8, MS BODLEY 686 66-9, MS DOUCE 204
  66/10-11, MS DOUCE 364 66/12-14, MS DOUCE 353 66-15, MS DOUCE
  276 66-16, MS DOUCE 20 66-17, MS DOUCE 205 66-18, MS ASHMOLE
  1504 66-19, MS FRENCH E 1 66-20
*PROVENANCE ENGLISH 66/1 AND 3 AND 9 AND 19, FRENCH 66/2 AND
  4-5 AND 7-8 AND 12-16 AND 20, ITALIAN 66-6, SPANISH 66/10-11,
  FLEMISH 66/17-18
*DATE EXECUTED 14TH 66/1-3, 15TH 66/4-16, 16TH 66/17-20
*TYPE OF MANUSCRIPT PSALTER 66-1, ROMANCE 66/2 AND 12-15,
  APOCALYPSE 66-3, PILGRIMAGE OF THE SOUL 66/4-5, ORATIONS 66-6,
  BOOK OF HOURS 66/7-8 AND 16-17, CANTERBURY TALES 66-9, HISTORY
  66-18, BESTIARY 66-19, ADDRESS 66-20
*CONTENTS COSTUME 66/1-20, DAVID WITH JESTER 66-1, PEASANT MAN
  AND WOMAN WITH COOK AND FOX 66-2, ARCHER 66-3, CHARITY
  ADDRESSES KNEELING PILGRIMS 66-4, GRACE-DIEU WATCHES
  DISPLEASED AS PILGRIM TAKES OFF ARMOR 66-5, SCHOOLMATER AND
  PUPILS 66-6, MAN RIDING WITH HAWK ON WRIST 66-8, PEASANTS
  WORKING ON VINES 66-7, YOUNG MAN FASHIONABLY DRESSED 66-9, ST
  JOSEPH AND VIRGIN MARY BETROTHED BEFORE HIGH PRIEST 66-10,
  WISE WOMAN OF THECUA SPEAKS TO DAVID 66-11, COURTIERS AND
  MUSICIAN RICHLY-DRESSED 66-12, JEALOUSY/ SHAME AND FEAR AS
  LADIES 66-13, BARONS ARRIVE AT COURT OF GOD OF LOVE 66-14, GOD
  OF LOVE 66-14, HECUBA STONED BY MOB 66-15, CHILDREN PLAYING
  66-16, VIRGIN MARY VISITS SAINT ELIZABETH 66-17, COURT OF HOLY
  ROMAN EMPEROR HENRY VI 66-18, MAN CHOPPING WOOD 66-19,
  ELIZABETH THE QUEEN 66-20

*$ABSTRACT 67
  *LIBRARY BOD
  *SLIDE SET TITLE BOOK OF HOURS
  *NEGATIVE REFERENCE ROLL 163D
  *RENTAL FEE SM 067 $4.65
  *TITLE OF MANUSCRIPT BOOK OF HOURS
  *SHELFMARK MS DOUCE 112
  *PROVENANCE FLEMISH
  *DATE EXECUTED 16TH/C1500
  *LANGUAGE LATIN
  *ARTIST/ SCHOOL MASTER OF THE DAVID SCENES OF THE GRIMANI
  BREVIARY
  *TYPE OF MANUSCRIPT BOOK OF HOURS
  *CONTENTS BOOK OF HOURS/ FLEMISH/ 16TH 67/1-53, SALVATOR MUNDI
  67-1, ST VERONICA'S LIFE 67-1, SALVE SANCTA FACIES 67-2, CITY
  BESIEGED 67-2, MOSES AND BRAZEN SERPENT 67-3, PASSION SCENES
  67-3, PENTECOST WITH DESCENT OF HOLY GHOST 67-4, MOSES
  RECEIVES TABLETS OF LAW 67-5, BUILDING OF THE TEMPLE 67-5,
  VIRGIN AND CHILD 67-6, TOWN LIFE IN FLANDERS 67-6, MASS
  CELEBRATION 67-7, APE CHAINED TO COLONADE 67-8, WORKS OF MERCY
  67-9, STREET SCENES 67-9, ST JOHN ON PATMOS 67-10, ST LUKE AT
  EASEL WITH OX AND VIRGIN 67-11, ST MATTHEW WITH ANGEL 67-12,
  ST MARK WITH WINGED LION 67-13, CHRIST'S AGONY IN GARDEN
  67-14, CITY WITH TURRETS 67-14, PASSION ACCORDING TO ST JOHN
  67-15, TEMPTATION OF ADAM AND EVE 67-16, MAN CARRYING HARE BY
  STREAM 67-17, GIRL IN CONVENT GARDEN 67-18, MOSES PUTS ARK IN
  TEMPLE 67-19, AARON'S ROD FLOWERING 67-20, MARY THE EGYPTIAN'S
  PENITENCE 67-20, MOSES AND BURNING BUSH 67-21, ADORATION OF
  SHEPHERDS 67-21, QUEEN OF SHEBA COMES TO SOLOMON 67-22,
  PRESENTATION OF CHRIST IN TEMPLE 67-23, JOACHIM AND ANNE AT
  PRESENTATION OF VIRGIN 67-23, MICHAL AND DAVID 67-24, QUEEN
  ATHALIAH 67-25, PENITENTIAL PSALMS 67-26, OFFICE OF THE DEAD
  67-27, ST GREGORY'S MASS WITH VISION OF RISEN CHRIST 67-28,
  TRINITY WITH CELESTIAL HOST AND ECCLESIASTICAL PROCESSION
  67-29, OBSECRO TE WITH PIETA 67-30, INITIAL WITH SAINT JOHN
  COMFORTING VIRGIN 67-31, ARCHITECTURAL BORDER 67-31, ST

43

MICHAEL SLAYING DEVIL 67-32, ST JOHN BAPTIST WALKING IN LANDSCAPE WITH AGNUS DEI 67-33, ST JOHN EVANGELIST EXORCISING POISONED CHALICE 67-34, SS PETER AND PAUL IN CHURCH 67-35, TABAITHA RAISED 67-35, ST JAMES THE GREAT AS PILGRIM ON ISLAND 67-36, CASTLE AND SHIP 67-36, ST ANDREW WITH SALTIRE AND EXPELLING DEVIL FROM BANQUET 67-37, ST CHRISTOPHER CARRYING CHRIST ACROSS RIVER 67-38, ST SEBASTIAN'S MARTRYDOM 67-39, ST GEORGE ON HORSEBACK SLAYING DRAGON 67-41, PRINCESS OUTSIDE CASTLE 67-41, ST ADRIAN WITH LION AT FEET 67-40, ST LAWRENCE AS DEACON WITH BOOK AND GRIDIRON 67-42, ST ANTHONY WITH PIG EXPOUNDING SCRIPTURE 67-43, ST NICHOLAS AND LEGENDS OF PICKLING TUB AND JEW 67-44, ST FRANCIS RECEIVES STIGMATA FROM SERAPH 67-45, ST ANTHONY OF PADUA WITH NEWBORN CHILD 67-46, ST ANNE WITH VIRGIN AND CHILD IN GARDEN 67-47, ST MARY MAGDALENE NAKED WITH POT OF OINTMENT 67-48, ST CATHERINE WITH BOOK AND SWORD 67-49, CITY BESIEGED WITH SAINT ON WHEEL 67-49, ST MARGARET EMERGING FROM BACK OF DRAGON 67-51, ST APOLLONIA IN COURTYARD WITH TOOTH IN PINCERS 67-52, SAINTS/ ALL WITH CHRIST AND VIRGIN 67-53, ST BARBARA WITH FOOT ON REJECTED SUITOR 67-50, ANGELS PLAYING HARP AND MANDOLIN 67-53

*$ABSTRACT 68
 *LIBRARY BOD
 *SLIDE SET TITLE MEDIEVAL PROFESSIONS
 *NEGATIVE REFERENCE ROLL 164A
 *RENTAL FEE SM 068 $2.50
 *COMMENTS 10 SLIDES SELECTED FROM 10 MSS OF THE 11TH-16TH
  CENTURIES DEPICTING MEDIEVAL PROFESSIONS
 *SHELFMARK MS JUNIUS 11 68-1, MS C C C OXFORD 157 68-2, MS
  BODLEY 602 68-3, MS ASHMOLE 1462 68-4, MS ASHMOLE 399 68-5, MS
  DOUCE 180 68-6, MS AUCT D 2 2 68-7, MS LITURG 401 68-8, MS NEW
  COLLEGE 288 68-9, MS RAWL D 1220 68-10
 *PROVENANCE ENGLISH
 *DATE EXECUTED 11TH 68-1, 12TH/1118-1140 68-2, 12TH 68-3, 13TH
  68/4-6, 14TH/C1420 68-7, 15TH 68/8-10
 *TYPE OF MANUSCRIPT GENESIS 68-1, CHRONICLE 68-2, BESTIARY
  68-3, SCIENTIFIC TREATISES 68-4, MEDICAL TREATISES 68-5,
  APOCALYSE 68-6, PSALTER 68-7, BOOK OF HOURS 68-8, ASTRONOMICAL
  TREATISE 68-10
 *CONTENTS PROFESSIONS 68/1-10, OCCUPATIONS 68/1-10, SAXON NURSE
  AT BEDSIDE OF ENOCH'S WIFE 68-1, BISHOPS AND ABBOTS 68-2,
  SCRIBE AT LECTERN 68-3, SURGEONS OPERATING ON EYE 68-4,
  PHYSICIAN AND SWOONING LADY 68-5, FRIAR 68-6, MONKS 68-7,
  JUDGE/ PONTIUS PILATE 68-8, MASTER AND SCHOLARS OF NEW COLLEGE
  OXFORD 68-9, ARTISTS AND OTHERS UNDER INFLUENCE OF PLANET
  MERCURY 68-10

*$ABSTRACT 69
 *LIBRARY BOD
 *SLIDE SET TITLE MEDIEVAL TOWN LIFE
 *NEGATIVE REFERENCE ROLL 164B
 *RENTAL FEE SM 069 $2.50
 *COMMENTS 10 SLIDES FROM 7 MSS OF THE 11TH-16TH CENTURIES
 *TITLE OF MANUSCRIPT APOCRYPHAL CHILDHOOD OF CHRIST 69-1,
  APOCALYPSE 69/2-3, PIERS PLOWMAN 69/4-5, ASTRONOMICAL TREATISE
  69/6-7, COMMENTARIES OF CAESAR 69-8, CALENDAR 69/9-10
 *SHELFMARK MS SELDEN SUPRA 38 69-1, MS AUCT D 4 17 69-2, MS
  BODLEY 401 69-3, MS DOUCE 104 69/4-5, MS RAWL D 220 69/6-7, MS
  DOUCE 208 69-8, MS GOUGH LITURG 7 69/9-10
 *PROVENANCE ENGLISH 69/1-7 AND 9-10, FLEMISH 69-8
 *DATE EXECUTED 13TH 69-2, 14TH 69/1 AND 3, 15TH 69/4-8, 16TH
  69/9-10
 *TYPE OF MANUSCRIPT LIFE OF CHRIST 69-1, APOCALYPSE 69/2-3,
  ALLEGORY 69/4-5, ASTRONOMICAL TREATISE 69/6-7, COMMENTARIES
  69-8, CALENDAR 69-10
 *CONTENTS TOWN LIFE 69/1-10, DYER TO WHOM WAS APPRENTICED 69-1,
  CITY WALL 69-2, MERCHANTS WATCHING ARRIVAL OF CARGOES 69-3,
  FRIAR/ FRANCISCAN 69-4, PILGRIM 69-5, CLOCK-MAKER 69-6, BEGGAR

WITH LEG STRAPPED UP 69-7, MAN IN STOCKS 69-7, MIDWIFE AND
BIRTH OF CAESAR 69-8, MARKET WITH CATTLE AUCTION 69-9,
BUTCHER'S SHOP 69-10

*$ABSTRACT 70
  *LIBRARY BOD
  *SLIDE SET TITLE MEDIEVAL SHIPS AND SHIPPING
  *NEGATIVE REFERENCE ROLL 164C
  *RENTAL FEE SM 070 $2.55
  *COMMENTS 11 SLIDES SELECTED FROM 9 MSS OF THE 12TH-16TH
  CENTURIES DEPICTING SHIPS
  *SHELFMARK MS BODLEY 614 70-1, MS C C C OXFORD 157 70-2, MS
  GOUGH LITURG 2 70-3, MS AUCT D 4 17 70-4, MS AUCT E 17 70-5,
  MS DOUCE 88 70-6, MS DOUCE 374 70-7, MS CANON CLASS 374
  70/8-9, MS DOUCE 353 70-10, MS ASHMOLE 1504 70-11
  *PROVENANCE ENGLISH 70/1-6 AND 11, FLEMISH 70-7, ITALIAN
  70/8-9, FRENCH 70-10
  *DATE EXECUTED 12TH 70/1-3, 13TH 70/4-6, 15TH 70/7-10, 16TH
  70-11
  *TYPE OF MANUSCRIPT CALENDAR 70-1, CHRONICLE 70-2, PSALTER
  70-3, APOCALYPSE 70/4-5, BESTIARY 70-6, MIRACLES OF THE VIRGIN
  70-7, MILITARY TEXT 70/8-9, ROMANCE 70-10, HERBAL 70-11
  *CONTENTS SHIPS 70/1-11, SHIP/VIKING STERN WITH FIGUREHEAD AND
  OARS 70-1, SHIP/SAILING WITH EAGLE'S BEAK 70-2, BOAT WITH MEN
  REGULATING SAIL 70-3, SHIP AND SMALL BOAT AT ANCHOR 70-4,
  BOATMEN PUSHING OFF BOAT WITH LONG HOOK 70-5, SHIP/SAILING
  WITH MEN ROWING AND SAILS HOISTED 70-6, SHIPWRECK 70-7, SHIPS
  LINKED 70-8, BOAT BUILDING DIAGRAM SHOWING SECTIONAL
  CONSTRUCTION 70-9, SHIP WITH GANGPLANK 70-10, SHIP LIKE
  GALLEON WITH SMALL BOAT AT ANCHOR 70-11

*$ABSTRACT 71
  *LIBRARY BOD
  *SLIDE SET TITLE MEDIEVAL WARFARE
  *NEGATIVE REFERENCE ROLL 164D
  *RENTAL FEE SM 071 $2.50
  *COMMENTS 10 SLIDES SELECTED FROM 7 MSS OF THE 14TH-15TH
  CENTURIES
  *SHELFMARK MS RAWLINSON Q B 6 71-1, MS E MUSAEO 65 71-2, MS
  DOUCE 217 71/3-5, MS CANON ITAL 136 71-6, MS CANON CLASS LAT
  81 71-7, MS DOUCE 208 71-8, MS DOUCE 383 71/9-10
  *PROVENANCE FRENCH 71/1-5, ITALIAN 71/6-7, FLEMISH 71/8-10
  *DATE EXECUTED 14TH 71/1-2, 15TH 71/3-10
  *TYPE OF MANUSCRIPT ROMANCE 71/1-2 AND 9-10, HISTORY 71/3-6,
  COMMENTARIES 71-8,
  *CONTENTS WARFARE 71/1-10, TOURNAMENT WITH ARTHUR'S KNIGHTS AND
  THE HUNDRED KNIGHTS 71-1, GOD OF LOVE CALLS WARRIORS TOGETHER
  71-2, BATTLE OF CHARLES THE BALD AT FORTENAY 71-3, BATTLE
  BETWEEN MOUNTED SOLDIERS 71-4, SIEGE OF LA ROCHELLE BY LOUIS
  VIII 71-5, BATTLE SCENE 71-6, BATTLE ON LAND 71-7, BELGIAN
  BURGHERS SURRENDER KEYS 71-8, TOURNAMENT BEFORE KING ARTHUR
  71-9, KNIGHTS IN TOURNEY YARD 71-10

*$ABSTRACT 72
  *LIBRARY BOD
  *SLIDE SET TITLE MEDIEVAL TRANSPORT
  *NEGATIVE REFERENCE ROLL 164E
  *RENTAL FEE SM 072 $2.50
  *COMMENTS 10 SLIDES FROM 10 MSS OF THE 13TH-16TH CENTURIES
  *SHELFMARK MS DOUCE 48 72-1, MS RAWLINSON Q B 6 72-2, MS DOUCE
  6 72-3, MS BODLEY 264 72-4, MS DOUCE 276 72-5, MS CANON CLASS
  LAT 185 72-6, MS DOUCE 208 72-7, MS DOUCE 256 72-8, MS DOUCE
  383 72-9, MS GOUGH LITURG 7 72-10
  *PROVENANCE FRENCH 72/1-3 AND 5, ENGLISH 72/4 AND 10, ITALIAN
  72-6, FLEMISH 72/7-9
  *DATE EXECUTED 13TH 72-1, 14TH 72/2-3, 15TH 72/4-9, 16TH 72-10

*TYPE OF MANUSCRIPT PSALTER 72/1 AND 3, ROMANCE 72/1 AND 9,
TRAVEL BOOK 72-4, BOOK OF HOURS 72/5 AND 8, MILITARY TEXT
72-6, CAESAR GALLIC WAR 72-7, CALENDAR 72-10
*CONTENTS TRANSPORTATION 72/1-10, CART 72-1, CART DRAWN BY
HORSE WITH STUDDED WHEELS 72-2, WAGON 72-3, PACKHORSE AND
DRIVER APPROACH INN 72-4, WAGON 72-5, CART DRAWN BY 2 OXEN
WITH MEN CARRYING CROSSBOWS 72-6, BARGE LOADED BY WATER-GATE
72-7, QUAY WITH BOATS MOORED TO IT 72-8, CART WITH KNIGHT IN
IT/ ARMS AND LEGS BOUND 72-9, CART LOADED WITH HAY AND HOIST
FROM LOFT NEARBY 72-10

*$ABSTRACT 73
  *LIBRARY BOD
  *SLIDE SET TITLE MEDIEVAL SYMBOLISM
  *NEGATIVE REFERENCE ROLL 164F
  *RENTAL FEE SM 073 $2.50
  *COMMENTS 10 SLIDES FROM 9 MSS OF THE 13TH-16TH CENTURIES
  *SHELFMARK MS ASHMOLE 1511 73/1-2, MS DOUCE 167 73-3, MS BODLEY
  270B 73-4, MS DOUCE 381 73-5, MS CANON ITAL 108 73-6, MS DOUCE
  313 73-7, MS AUCT D 4 4 73-8, MS ADD A 185 73-9, MS DOUCE 300
  73-10
  *PROVENANCE ENGLISH 73/1-3 AND 5 AND 8, FRENCH 73/4 AND 7 AND
  9-10, ITALIAN 73-6
  *DATE EXECUTED 13TH/C1200 73/1-3, 13TH 73-4, 14TH 73/5-8, 15TH
  73/9-10
  *TYPE OF MANUSCRIPT BESTIARY 73/1-3, BIBLE MORALISEE 73-4,
  MISSAL 73-7, PSALTER 73-8, BOOK OF HOURS 73-9, PILGRIMAGE OF
  LIFE 73-10
  *CONTENTS SYMBOLISM 73/1-10, LION BREATHING LIFE INTO CUBS
  73-1, PHOENIX ON PYRE 73-2, UNICORN CAPTURED BY HUNTERS WITH
  HEAD IN VIRGIN'S LAP 73-3, ROSE/LILY/VIOLET AS MARTYRDOM/
  CHASTITY/ PERSEVERERENCE 73-4, JESSE TREE 73-5, CHARIOT AS
  CHURCH TRIUMPHANT 73-6, GRIFFIN DRAWS CHARIOT 73-6,
  EVANGELISTS IN CHARIOT 73-6, CRUCIFIXION 73-7, EVANGELIST'S
  SIGNS 73-7, PELICAN AT TOP OF CROSS IN PIETY 73-7, LAST
  JUDGMENT 73-8, AGES OF MAN EXEMPLIFIED BY MAGI 73-9, SINS/ 7
  DEADLY ATTACK PILGRIM 73-10

*$ABSTRACT 74
  *LIBRARY BOD
  *SLIDE SET TITLE MEDIEVAL BUILDINGS AND ARCHITECTURE
  *NEGATIVE REFERENCE ROLL 164G
  *RENTAL FEE SM 074 $2.50
  *COMMENTS 10 SLIDES SELECTED FROM 9 MSS OF THE 15TH-16TH
  CENTURIES SHOWING BUILDINGS AND ARCHITECTURE
  *TITLE OF MANUSCRIPT REGISTER IN HONOR OF RICHMOND/ YORKSHIRE
  74-1, CHRONICLE OF FRANCE 74-2, SPECULUM HUMANAE SALVATIONIS
  74-3, MIRACLES OF THE VIRGIN 74-5, ROMANCE OF THE DESTRUCTION
  OF TROY 74-7
  *SHELFMARK MS LYELL 22 74-1, MS DOUCE 217 74-2, MS DOUCE 204
  74-3, MS ADD A 185 74-4, MS DOUCE 374 74-5, MS GOUGH LITURG 15
  74-6, MS DOUCE 353 74-7, MS DOUCE 256 74/8-9, MS DOUCE 112
  74-10
  *PROVENANCE ENGLISH 74-1, FRENCH 74/2 AND 4 AND 7, SPANISH
  74-3, FLEMISH 74/5-6 AND 8-10
  *DATE EXECUTED 15TH/C1410 74-1, 15TH/C1440-1450 74/3-4, 15TH
  74-2, 15TH/1460 74-5, 15TH/C1465 74-6, 15TH/C1460 74-7,
  16TH/C1500 74/8-10
  *TYPE OF MANUSCRIPT REGISTER 74-1, CHRONICLE 74-2, MORAL
  TREATISE 74-3, BOOK OF HOURS 74/4 AND 6 AND 8-10, MIRACLES OF
  THE VIRGIN 74-5, ROMANCE 74-7
  *CONTENTS ARCHITECTURE/ 15TH-16TH 74/1-10, HERALDRY OF RICHMOND
  CASTLE 74-1, BUILDINGS 74/1-10, DAGOBERT SUPERVISING BUILDING
  74-2, PLUMMET AND TRIANGULAR TROWEL 74-2, SOLOMON'S TEMPLE
  BUILT 74-3, PULLEY 74-3, ST MARK 74-4, ROOM INTERIOR WITH
  TILED FLOOR/ WINDOWS/ ORNAMENTAL CEILING 74-4, CHURCH AT
  SOTSSONS 74-5, WORKMEN FORCED BY VIRGIN TO COMPLETE CONTRACT
  ON BUILDING 74-5, PRESENTATION OF CHRIST IN TEMPLE 74-6,

CHURCH INTERIOR WITH VAULTED ROOF 74-6, TROY RECONSTRUCTED 74-7, CRANE AND WORKMEN WITH TOOLS 74-7, DAVID AT PRAYER 74-8, BUILDING WITH GABLED FRONT/ CHIMNEY/ TOWERS/ TURRETS/ BRIDGE 74-8, ST MATTHEW 74-9, COTTAGES WITH THATCHED TIMBERED ROOFS 74-9, BUILDING OF STONE WITH DORMER WINDOW 74-9, MOSES RECEIVES LAW 74-10, TEMPLE BEING BUILT 74-10, WINCH FOR LIFTING BASKET 74-10, WORKMEN WITH ADZE/ CHISEL/ MALLET 74-10

*$ABSTRACT 75
  *LIBRARY BOD
  *SLIDE SET TITLE MEDIEVAL HISTORIOGRAPHY
  *NEGATIVE REFERENCE ROLL 164I
  *RENTAL FEE SM 075 $2.55
  *COMMENTS 11 SLIDES SELECTED FROM 6 MSS SHOWING THE DEVELOPMENT
  OF ANNALS AND CHRONICLES
  *TITLE OF MANUSCRIPT CHRONICLE OF EUSEBIUS 75/1-2, TABLE FOR
  THE RECKONING OF EASTER FOR YEARS 817-832 75-3, ANGLO-SAXON
  CHRONICLE 75-4, FLORENCE OF WORCESTER CHRONICLE 75/5-7, LIBER
  FIGUARUM 75/10-11
  *SHELFMARK MS AUCT T 2 26 75/1-2, MS AUCT F 4 32 75-3, MS LAUD
  MISC 636 75-4, MS BODLEY 297 75/5-7, MS BODLEY 309 75/8-9, MS
  C C C OXFORD 255 75/10-11
  *PROVENANCE ITALIAN 75/1-2 AND 10-11, WELSH 75-3, ENGLISH
  75/4-9
  *DATE EXECUTED 05TH 75/1-2, 09TH/817-832 75-3, 12TH 75/4-7,
  13TH 75/10-11
  *TYPE OF MANUSCRIPT ANNALS AND CHRONICLES AND TABLES
  *CONTENTS HISTORIOGRAPHY 75/1-11, CHRONICLES/ DEVELOPMENT OF
  75/1-11, CHRONOLOGICAL TABLES WITH ANCIENTS/ LATIN KINGS/
  CONSULS 75-1, CHRONOLOGY OF OLYMPIADS/ JEWS/ ROMANS 75-2,
  REIGNS OF EMPERORS NERO TO VITELLIUS 75-2, REIGNS OF VESPASIAN
  TO FALL OF JERUSALEM 75-2, EASTER TABLES FOR 817-832 75-3,
  YEARS 951-959 OF ENGLISH HISTORY 75-4, EXILE OF SAINT DUNSTAN
  75-4, DEATHS OF AELFHEAH/ EADRED/ WULFSTAN 75-4, YEARS 1-38 OF
  ENGLISH HISTORY 75-5, YEARS 532-570 OF ENGLISH HISTORY 75-5,
  YEARS 1064-1102 OF ENGLISH HISTORY 75-5, YEARS 531 AND 1063 OF
  ENGLISH HISTORY 75-6, DEVELOPMENT OF FLORENCE OF WORCESTER
  FROM MARIANUS 75-7, END OF FIRST GREAT CYCLE 75-8, BEGINNING
  OF SECOND GREAT CYCLE 75-8, YEARS 813-851 75-9, TREE OF
  HISTORY 75-10, TREE OF HISTORY ENDING WITH SECOND ADVENT 75-11

*$ABSTRACT 76
  *LIBRARY BOD
  *SLIDE SET TITLE ADAM AND EVE
  *NEGATIVE REFERENCE ROLL 164J
  *RENTAL FEE SM 076 $2.50
  *COMMENTS 10 SLIDES SELECTED FROM 10 MSS OF THE 14TH-16TH
  CENTURIES DEPICTING ADAM AND EVE
  *TITLE OF MANUSCRIPT SPECULUM HUMANAE SALVATIONIS 76/2-3 AND
  10, FALL OF PRINCES 76-6, ROMANCE OF LANCELOT OF THE LAKE
  76-8, BIBLE HISTORIALE 76-9
  *SHELFMARK MS DOUCE 268 76-1, MS C C C OXFORD 161 76-2, MS
  DOUCE 204 76-3, MS DOUCE 72 76-4, MS DOUCE 112 76-5, MS BODLEY
  263 76-6, MS DOUCE 88 76-7, MS DOUCE 215 76-8, MS DOUCE 211
  76-9, MS DOUCE 204 76-10
  *PROVENANCE FRENCH 76/1 AND 4 AND 8-9, ENGLISH 76/2 AND 6-7,
  SPANISH 76/3 AND 10, FLEMISH 76-5
  *DATE EXECUTED 14TH 76/7-9, 15TH 76/2-4 AND 10, 16TH 76/1 AND 5
  *AUTHOR LYDGATE 76-6
  *TYPE OF MANUSCRIPT BOOK OF HOURS 76/1 AND 4-5, MORAL TREATISE
  76/2-3 AND 10, EPIC POETRY 76-6, BESTIARY 76-7, ROMANCE 76-8,
  BIBLE HISTORIALE 76-9
  *CONTENTS ADAM AND EVE 76/1-10, EVE CREATED 76-1, ADAM AND EVE
  FORBIDDEN TO EAT FORBIDDEN FRUIT 76-2, EVE TEMPTED BY SERPENT
  76-3, EVE OFFERS APPLE TO ADAM 76-4, ADAM AND EVE CLOTHED BY
  GOD 76-5, ADAM AND EVE OFFERED APPLE BY SERPENT 76-6, ANGEL
  EXPELLS THEM FROM PARADISE 76/6-9, ADAM DIGGING AND EVE
  SPINNING AFTER THE FALL 76-10

47

*$ABSTRACT 77
  *LIBRARY BOD
  *SLIDE SET TITLE ANGELS
  *NEGATIVE REFERENCE ROLL 164K
  *RENTAL FEE SM 077 $3.00
  *COMMENTS 20 SLIDES FROM 7 MSS OF 13TH-15TH CENTURIES DEPICTING
  ANGELS
  *TITLE OF MANUSCRIPT APOCALPYSE 77/1-10, DIVINE COMEDY
  77/12-13, LE PELERINAGE DE L/AME 77/15-16, SPECULUM HUMANAE
  SALVATIONIS 77/17-18, TREATISE ON ANTI-CHRIST JUDGMENT HEAVEN
  AND HELL 77/19-20
  *SHELFMARK MS TANNER 184 77/1-10, MS DOUCE 77 77-11, MS CANON
  ITAL 108 77/12-13, MS BUCHANAN E 2 77-14, MS DOUCE 305
  77/15-16, MS DOUCE 204 77/17-18, MS DOUCE 134 77/19-20
  *PROVENANCE ENGLISH 77/1-11, ITALIAN 77/12-13, FRENCH 77/14 AND
  19-20, FLEMISH 77/15-16, SPANISH 77/17-18
  *DATE EXECUTED 13TH 77/1-10, 14TH 77/11-14, 15TH 77/15-16 AND
  19-20, 15TH/C14440 77/17-18
  *AUTHOR DANTE 77/12-13
  *TYPE OF MANUSCRIPT APOCALYPSE 77/1-10, LIFE OF THE VIRGIN
  77-11, POETRY 77/12-13, BOOK OF HOURS 77-14, PILGRIMAGE OF THE
  SOUL 77-15, MORAL TREATISE 77/17-18, RELIGIOUS TREATISE
  77/19-20
  *CONTENTS ANGELS 77/1-20, ANGELS STAND AT FOUR CORNERS OF EARTH
  77-1, GOD ENTHRONED WITH LAMB/ MARTYRS/ ELDERS/ ANGELS/ SAINT
  JOHN 77-2, ANGEL SOUNDS TRUMPET AND CASTS FIRE-FILLED CENSER
  TO EARTH 77-3, ANGELS SOUND TRUMPETS AND CATASROPHES ON EARTH
  77-4, ANGEL BRINGS SCROLL OF GOSPEL TO SAINT JOHN 77-5, ANGEL
  RELATES BABYLON IS FALLEN 77-6, ANGEL/ FIRST EMPTIES VIAL ON
  EARTH 77-7, ANGEL DROPS MILLSTONE INTO SEA 77-8, ANGEL/ SIXTH
  SOUNDS TRUMPET AND ANGELS LOOSED ON EUPHRATES 77-9, TEMPLE
  OPENED IN HEAVEN 77-10, CRESCENT MOON WHERE WOMAN RECEIVES
  CHILD 77-10, DRAGON WITH 7 HEADS 77-10, ASSUMPTION OF VIRGIN
  77-11, ANGEL OF GOD AND DEVIL FIGHT FOR BUONCONTE'S SOUL
  77-12, ANGELS/ ARMED GUARD PURGATORY FROM SERPENT 77-13, ANGEL
  APPEARS TO SHEPHERDS 77-14, PARADISE WITH GOD ENTHRONED AND
  CHRIST AND SAINTS AROUND 77-15, ANGEL UNBOLTS DOOR TO LET IN
  PILGRIMS 77-15, GOD ENTHRONED WITH CRUCIFIED CHRIST 77-16,
  ANGEL APPEARS TO BALAAM'S ASS 77-17, JACOB DREAMS OF LADDER
  WITH ANGELS 77-18, VIRGIN ENTHRONED WITH ANGELS PLAYING
  INSTRUMENTS 77-19, CHRIST ENTHRONED WITH ANGELS AND SERAPHS
  SWINGING CENSERS 77-20

*$ABSTRACT 78
  *LIBRARY BOD
  *SLIDE SET TITLE DEVILS
  *NEGATIVE REFERENCE ROLL 164L
  *RENTAL FEE SM 078 $3.00
  *COMMENTS 20 SLIDES SELECTED FROM 6 MSS OF THE 13TH-15TH
  CENTURIES DEPICTING DEVILS
  *TITLE OF MANUSCRIPT APOCALYPSE 78/1-5, DIVINE COMEDY 78-6,
  SPECULUM HUMANAE SALVATIONIS 78/7-10, LIFE OF THE VIRGIN
  78-11, LE PELERINAGE DE L'AME 78-12, TREATISE ON ANTI-CHRIST
  JUDGMENT HEAVEN AND HELL 78/13-20
  *SHELFMARK MS TANNER 184 78/1-5, MS CANON ITAL 108 78-6, MS
  DOUCE F 4 78/7-10, MS CANON ITAL 280 78-11, MS DOUCE 305
  78-12, MS DOUCE 134 78/13-20
  *PROVENANCE ENGLISH 78/1-5 AND 7-10, ITALIAN 78/6 AND 11,
  FLEMISH 78-12, FRENCH 78/13-20
  *DATE EXECUTED 13TH 78/1-5, 14TH 78-6, 15TH 78/7-20
  *AUTHOR DANTE 78-6
  *TYPE OF MANUSCRIPT APOCALYPSE 78/1-5, POETRY 78-6, MORAL
  TREATISE 78/7-10 AND 13-20, LIFE OF THE VIRGIN 78-11,
  PILGRIMAGE OF THE SOUL 78-12
  *CONTENTS DEVILS 78/1-20, SATAN LEADING TROOPS OUT OF HELL
  78-1, ST MICHAEL AND ANGELS FIGHTING 78-2, ANGEL WITH KEY TO
  BOTTOMLESS PIT 78-3, DRAGON WITH GREAT CHAIN 78-3, HELL MOUTH
  WITH DEVIL AND DRAGON 78-4, DEVILS/ HORNED AND ARMED GUARD
  CITY OF DIS 78-6, GOD ENTHRONED JUDGING EVIL-DOERS AND
  REWARDING GOOD 78-5, CHRIST RESCUES SOULS FROM HELL 78-7,

CHRIST SHOWS WOUNDS OF PASSION 78-7, HELL'S 4 REGIONS 78-8,
LIMBO 78-8, INFERNO 78-8, HELL PROPER 78-8, CHRIST FREES SOULS
FROM HELL 78-9, TEMPTATION OF CHRIST BY SHAGGY DEVIL WITH
STONE 78-10, HARROWING OF HELL 78-11, HELL MOUTH WITH OPEN
JAWS 78-12, DEVIL PURSUING 4 TORMENTED SOULS 78-12, LAST
JUDGMENT 78-13, SOULS OF BLESSED GO TO HEAVEN DAMNED TO HELL
78-13, LUCIFER WITH MANY HEADS JUDGED BY CHRIST 78-14, DESCENT
OF THE DAMNED INTO HELL 78-15, HELL MOUTH WITH DAMNED AND
DEVILS 78-16, DEVIL BREAKS SOULS OF PROUD AND VAINGLORIOUS ON
WHEEL 78-17, HELL'S RIVERS THE STYX AND PHLEGETON 78-18,
HELL'S RIVERS THE LETHE AND COCYTUS 78-19, LUCIFER THE PRINCE
OF HELL WITH DEVILS 78-20

*$ABSTRACT 79
  *LIBRARY BOD
  *SLIDE SET TITLE EARLY ORNAMENT
  *NEGATIVE REFERENCE ROLL 165B
  *RENTAL FEE SM 079 $4.20
  *COMMENTS 44 SLIDES SELECTED FROM 5 MSS FROM THE 8TH-11TH
  CENTURIES SHOWING EARLY ORNAMENTATION AND INCLUDING THE
  MACREGOL GOSPELS
  *TITLE OF MANUSCRIPT DE TRINITATE 79/1-12, EXPOSITIO IN JOB
  79/14-15, MACREGOL GOSPELS/ CODEX RUSHWORTHIANS 79/29-44
  *SHELFMARK MS LAUD MISC 126 79/1-12, MS LAT BIBL B 2 79-13, MS
  BODLEY 426 79/14-15, MS CANON PAT LAT 112 79/16-28, MS AUCT D
  2 19 79/29-44
  *PROVENANCE FRENCH/ NEAR PARIS 79/1-12, FRENCH 79/16-28,
  ENGLISH 79/13-15, IRELAND/ BIRR 79/29-44
  *DATE EXECUTED 08TH/MID 79/1-12, 08TH 79/13-15, 10TH 79/29-44,
  11TH 79/16-28
  *AUTHOR ST AUGUSTINE 79/1-12, PHILIPPUS 79/14-15, PSEUDO
  ATHANASIUS 79/16-28
  *TYPE OF MANUSCRIPT RELIGIOUS TREATISES 79/1-12 AND 14-28,
  GOSPELS 79/13 AND 29-44
  *CONTENTS INITIAL D 79-1, FISHES AS LETTERS 79-1, INITIAL D
  79-2, PEACOCK WITH LONG TAIL AND FISH IN CLAW 79-2, INITIAL P
  79-3, FISH 79-3, INITIAL Q 79-4, INITIAL A 79-5, INITIAL H
  79-6, INITIAL I 79-7, INITIAL E 79-8, INITIAL N 79-9, INITIAL
  H 79-10, BIRDS AS LETTERS 79-10, PATTERNED LETTERS 79-11,
  INITIAL A 79-12, INITIAL P 79-13, FULL PAGE 79-14, INITIAL U
  79-15, INITIAL T 79-16, EXPLICIT LIBER 79-17, CAPITAL V/ E/ T
  79-17, HUNC IN LARGE LETTERS 79-18, INITIAL Q 79-19, INITIAL H
  79-20, FULL PAGE 79-21, INITIAL H 79-21, FULL PAGE 79-22,
  INITIAL P 79-23, FULL PAGE 79-23, PATTERNED P 79-23, FULL PAGE
  79/24-29, PATTERNED F 79-24, FLORIATED I 79-25, PATTERNED H
  79-26, PATTERNED P 79-27, FLORIATED T 79-28, BIRD'S HEADS IN
  INTERWOVEN PATTERN OF RED 79-30, INITIAL A 79-31, FULL PAGE
  79/32-34, ST MARK 79-32, LION/WINGED WITH SAINT MARK 79-33,
  INITIAL 79-34, DETAIL OF UPPER HALF 79/35 AND 39 AND 43,
  DETAIL OF LOWER HALF 79/36 AND 40 AND 44, OX/WINGED 79-37, ST
  LUKE'S GOSPEL 79-38, EAGLE/WINGED 79-41, ST JOHN'S GOSPEL
  79-42

*$ABSTRACT 80
  *LIBRARY BOD
  *SLIDE SET TITLE SPECULUM HUMANAE SALVATIONIS
  *NEGATIVE REFERENCE ROLL 165C
  *RENTAL FEE SM 080 $6.50
  *COMMENTS MADE FOR GUILLAUME DE MONTJOIE, BISHOP OF BEZIERS
  *TITLE OF MANUSCRIPT SPECULUM HUMANAE SALVATIONIS
  *SHELFMARK MS DOUCE 204
  *PROVENANCE SPANISH/ CATALONIA/ ROUSSILLON
  *DATE EXECUTED 15TH/C1430-50
  *LANGUAGE LATIN
  *ARTIST/ SCHOOL LAURENTIUS DYAMAS THE SCRIBE AND ILLUMINATOR
  *TYPE OF MANUSCRIPT RELIGIOUS WITH BIBLICAL SCENES
  *CONTENTS TYPOLOGY 80/1-92, FALL OF THE ANGELS 80-1, CREATION
  OF EVE 80-1, PROHIBITION OF THE TREE 80-2, TEMPTATION OF EVE

80-2, TEMPATION OF ADAM BY EVE 80-3, EXPULSION FROM PARADISE 80-3, ADAM/TOIL 80-4, NOAH'S ARK 80-4, ANGEL APPEARS TO JOACHIM 80-5, VISION OF ASTYAGES 80-5, GARDEN/ CLOSED AND SEALED FOUNTAIN 80-6, BALAAM'S ASS AND THE ANGEL 80-6, VIRGIN'S BIRTH 80-7, JESSE TREE 80-7, DOOR/CLOSED SYMBOL OF VIRGIN 80-8, TEMPLE OF SOLOMON 80-8, PRESENTATION OF VIRGIN 80-9, GOLDEN TABLE OF THE SUN/ VIRGIN 80-9, JEPHTHAH'S DAUGHTER SACRIFICED 80-10, QUEEN OF PERSIA CONTEMPLATES KINGDOM FROM HANGING GARDENS 80-10, VIRGIN MARY AND JOSEPH MARRIED 80-11, SARA AND TOBIAS MARRIED 80-11, TOWER BARRIS 80-12, TOWER OF DAVID 80-12, ANNUNCIATION 80-13, BURNING BUSH 80-13, GIDEON'S FLEECE 80-14, REBECCA GIVES DRINK ELIEZER 80-14, NATIVITY 80-15, DREAM OF PHARAOH'S SERVANT 80-15, AARON'S ROD 80-16, OCTAVIAN AND SIBYL/ROMAN 80-16, ADORATION OF THE MAGI 80-17, MAGI SEE THE STAR 80-17, DAVID BROUGHT WATER FROM WELL OF BETHLEHEM 80-18, SHEBA BRINGS GIFTS TO SOLOMON 80-18, PRESENTATION IN THE TEMPLE 80-19, ARK OF THE COVENANT 80-19, SEVEN-BRANCHED CANDLESTICK/ VIRGIN 80-20, SAMUEL BROUGHT AS CHILD TO LORD 80-20, FLIGHT INTO EGYPT 80-21, EGYPTIAN IMAGE OF THE VIRGIN 80-21, MOSES CASTS DOWN PHARAOH'S CROWN 80-22, BAPTISM OF CHRIST 80-23, BRAZEN LAVER 80-23, NAAMAN WASHES IN THE JORDAN 80-24, ARK BORNE OVER DRIED-UP JORDAN 80-24, TEMPTATIONS OF CHRIST 80-25, DANIEL DESTROYS BEL AND THE DRAGON 80-25, DAVID OVERCOMES GOLIATH 80-26, DAVID KILLS LION AND BEAR 80-26, PENITENCE OF MARY MAGDALENE 80-27, PENITENCE OF MANASSEH 80-27, RETURN OF PRODIGAL SON 80-28, DAVID AND NATHAN 80-28, ENTRY INTO JERUSALEM 80-29, JEREMIAH WEEPING OVER JERUSALEM 80-29, TRIUMPH OF DAVID 80-30, HELIODORUS REPULSED FROM TEMPLE 80-30, LAST SUPPER 80-31, MANNA IN THE WILDERNESS 80-31, PASSOVER 80-32, MELCHIZADEK REFUSES BREAD AND WINE FROM ABRAHAM 80-32, JESUS ARRESTED AND SOLDIERS FALL BACKWARDS 80-33, SAMSON KILLS THE PHILISTINES 80-33, SHAMGAR KILLS MEN WITH PLOUGHSHARE 80-34, DAVID KILLS 800 MEN WITH KNOTTED SCOURGE 80-34, BETRAYAL 80-35, JOAB KILLS AMASA 80-35, DAVID PLAYS BEFORE SAUL 80-36, CAIN KILLS ABEL 80-36, JESUS MOCKED 80-37, HUR'S DEATH 80-37, NOAH MOCKED BY HAM 80-38, SAMSON BLINDED BY PHILISTINES 80-38, FLAGELLATION 80-39, ACHIOR BOUND TO TREE 80-39, LAMECH BEATEN BY HIS 2 WIVES 80-40, JOB BEATEN BY HIS WIFE 80-40, JESUS CROWNED BY THORNS 80-41, APAME SMITES KING DARIUS 80-41, SHIMEI CASTS STONES AT DAVID 80-42, HANUM INSULTS DAVID'S SERVANTS 80-42, ROAD TO CALVARY 80-43, ISAAC CARRIES WOOD FOR OWN SACRIFICE 80-43, WICKED HUSBANDMEN KILL HEIR 80-44, SPIES CARRY GRAPES FROM ESHCOL 80-44, CHRIST NAILED TO CROSS 80-45, TUBAL-CAIN SMITES ANVIL 83-45, ISAIAH SAWN IN SUNDER 80-46, MOAH SACRIFICES FIRST-BORN SON 80-46, CRUCIFIXION 80-47, NEBUCHADNEZZAR'S DREAM 80-47, DEATH OF KING CRODUS 80-48, ELEAZAR KILLS ELEPHANT 80-48, CRUCIFIED CHRIST MOCKED BY JEWS 80-49, MICHAL SEES DAVID DANCING BEFORE ARK 80-49, ABSALOM DIES 80-50, ENILMERODAIS CUTS FATHER'S BODY INTO 300 PIECES 80-50, DEPOSITION 80-51, JACOB BEWAILS JOSEPH 80-51, ADAM AND EVE MOURN OVER ABEL 80-52, NAOMI BEWAILS HER HUSBAND AND SON 80-52, ENTOMBMENT 80-53, DAVID BEWAILS ABNER 80-53, JOSEPH IN THE PIT 80-54, JONAH CAST INTO SEA 80-54, REALMS OF THE DEAD 80-55, CHILDREN DELIVERED FROM FURNACE 80-55, DANIEL IN LION'S DEN 80-56, OSTRICH DELIVERS YOUNG 80-56, CHRIST TRAMPLES ON SATAN 80-57, BENAIAH SLAYS LION IN PIT 80-57, SAMSON RENDS LION 80-58, EHUD KILLS EGLON 80-58, VIRGIN OVERCOMES DEVIL 80-59, JUDITH KILLS HOLOFERNES 80-59, JAEL KILLS SISERA 80-60, TOMYRIS KILLS CYRUS 80-60, CHRIST LEADS SOULS OUT OF HADES 80-61, MOSES LEADS ISRAELITES OUT OF EGYPT 80-61, ABRAHAM DELIVERED FROM UR 80-62, LOT ESCAPES FROM SODOM 80-62, RESURRECTION 80-63, SAMSON CARRIES OFF THE GATES OF GAZA 80-63, JONAH CAST UP BY WHALE 80-64, STONE REJECTED BY BUILDER 80-64, ASCENSION 80-65, JACOB'S LADDER 80-65, LOST SHEEP BROUGHT BACK 80-66, TRANSLATION OF ELIJAH 80-66, HOLY GHOST COMES AND GIFT OF TONGUES 80-67, CONFUSION OF TONGUES 80-67, GIVING OF THE LAW 80-68, ELISHA SUPPLIES WIDOW WITH OIL 80-68, VIRGIN RETURNS TO HOLY PLACES 80-69, RETURN OF TOBIAS 80-69, LOST PIECE OF SILVER FOUND 80-70, CORONATION OF VIRGIN 80-71, MICHAL MARRIED TO PHATLIEL 80-70, ARK BROUGHT HOME 80-71, WOMAN CLOTHED WITH THE SUN 80-72, SOLOMON SETS

BATHSHEBA ON RIGHT HAND 80-72, VIRGIN INTERCEDES FOR MANKIND
80-73, ABIGAIL APPEASES DAVID 80-73, WOMAN OF TEKOAH APPEASES
DAVID 80-74, WISE WOMAN OF ABELA CASTS OUT HEAD OF SHEBA
80-74, VIRGIN AS DEFENDER OF MANKIND 80-75, THARBIS DEFENDS
CITY AGAINST MOSES 80-75, ABIMELECH KILLED BY WOMAN OF THEBEZ
80-76, MICHAL HELPS DAVID TO ESCAPE 80-76, CHRIST INTERCEDES
FOR MANKIND 80-77, ANTIPATER SHOWS WOUNDS TO JULIUS CAESAR
80-77, VIRGIN SHOWS BREASTS TO CHRIST 80-78, ESTHER INTERCEDES
FOR HER PEOPLE 80-78, LAST JUDGMENT 80-79, PARABLE OF THE
TALENTS 80-79, PARABLE OF THE WISE AND FOOLISH VIRGINS 80/80,
WRITING ON THE WALL 80/80, PAINS OF HELL 80-81, DAVID PUNISHES
THE MEN OF RABBAH 80-81, GIDEON PUNISHING MEN OF SUCCOTH
80-82, PHARAOH AND HOST DROWNED IN RED SEA 80-82, JOYS OF
HEAVEN 80-83, QUEEN OF SHEBA VISITS SOLOMON 80-83, FEAST OF
AHASUERUS 80-84, JOB FEASTING WITH CHILDREN 80-84, MIRACLE OF
THE PASSION 80-85, LAST SUPPER 80-85, AGONY ON CROSS 80-86,
CHRIST BEFORE PILATE 80-86, ROBE BROUGHT FOR CHRIST 80-87,
FLAGELLATION 80-87, PILATE WASHES HIS HANDS 80-88, PIERCING OF
THE SIDE 80-88, MEDITATIONS ON SUFFERINGS OF CHRIST AND VIRGIN
80-89, PRESENTATION 80-89, FLIGHT INTO EGYPT 80-90, JESUS WITH
DOCTORS IN TEMPLE 80-90, SORROW/FOURTH OF MARY 80-91,
CRUCIFIXION 80-91, DEPOSITION AND ENTOMBMENT 80-92, VIRGIN
REVISITS SCENES OF SORROWS 80-92, DUPLICATE OF FRAME 24 80-93

*$ABSTRACT 81
 *LIBRARY BOD
 *SLIDE SET TITLE MASTER OF GAME
 *NEGATIVE REFERENCE ROLL 165E
 *RENTAL FEE SM 081 $3.95
 *TITLE OF MANUSCRIPT MASTER OF GAME
 *SHELFMARK MS DOUCE 335
 *PROVENANCE ENGLISH
 *DATE EXECUTED 15TH
 *LANGUAGE ENGLISH
 *AUTHOR EDWARD DUKE OF YORK
 *TYPE OF MANUSCRIPT LITERATURE
 *CONTENTS HUNTING SCENES 81/1-39, HUNTSMAN IN GREEN WITH
FINGERS RAISED DIDACTICALLY 81-1, MASTER OF GAME KNEELING AS
HE PRESENTS BOOK 81-2, HARE 81-3, HART 81-4, BUCK 81-5, ROE
81-6, WILD BOAR 81-7, WOLF 81-8, FOX 81-9, GREY 81-10, WILD
CAT 81-11, OTTER 81-12, HOUNDS 81-13, HOUNDS/ SICK 81-14, ALAN
81-15, SPANIEL 81-16, MASTIFFS 81-17, MEN WITH HOUND 81-20,
KENNEL WITH LEASHES ON WALL 81-21, HUNTER'S HORN 81-23, HART'S
FOOTPRINTS 81-24, HART'S DROPPINGS/ FUMES 81-25, HART FRAYING
HEAD AGAINST TREE 81-26, MAN SPEAKING ABOUT OFFICE OF VENERYE
81-27, HART IN A COVERT 81-28, HUNTSMAN WITH BOW AND ARROW
WITH HOUND 81-29, HUNTER WITH SCIMITAR AND PARTISAN FOLLOWS
HOUND 81-30, HUNTER AND HOUND AMONG COPSES 81-31, HUNTER IN
GREAT COVERT 81-32, HUNTER AND PARTISAN WITH HOUND 81-33,
HUNTER IN FOREST LISTENING TO HARTS BELLOWING 81-34, ASSEMBLY
CALLED OFF GATHERING AND GROOMS GIVEN INSTRUCTIONS 81-35, HART
LYING IN FOREST 81-36, HARE IN FIELD 81-37, FOREST FENCE
81-38, FOREST 81-39

*$ABSTRACT 82
 *LIBRARY BOD
 *SLIDE SET TITLE ROMANCE OF TROY
 *NEGATIVE REFERENCE ROLL 165D
 *RENTAL FEE SM 082 $3.50
 *TITLE OF MANUSCRIPT ROMANCE OF TROY
 *SHELFMARK MS DOUCE 353
 *PROVENANCE FRENCH
 *DATE EXECUTED 15TH/C1470
 *LANGUAGE FRENCH
 *ARTIST/ SCHOOL RELATED IN STYLE TO CHANTILLY MUSEE CONDE
 *TYPE OF MANUSCRIPT ROMANCE
 *CONTENTS LITERATURE/ ROMANCE OF TROY 82/1-30, ROMANCE OF TROY
82/1-30, FRENCH LITERATURE/ ROMANCE OF TROY 82/1-30, NYNUS/

51

KING ON THRONE UNDER CANOPY WITH ARMOR AROUND 82-1, NYNUS/
KING ARMED FOR BATTLE BY SERVANTS 82-2, NYNUS/ KING WITH
RETAINERS WATCHING DUEL 82-3, BATTLE BETWEEN 6 ARMED HORSEMEN
82-4, TOWN BESIEGED BY SOLDIERS WITH CANNON 82-5, THEBES IN
RUINS 82-7, HERCULES SLAYS GIANT ANTHEUS 82-8, JASON AT COURT
OF KING PELEUS 82-9, BATTLE OUTSIDE WALLS OF THEBES 82-6,
ARGO EQUIPPED 82-10, CARPENTERS AND COOKS ON QUAY 82-10, JASON
AND HERCULES PLAY CHESS 82-10, CHESS BEING PLAYED 82-10,
ARGONAUTS LAND ON ISLAND OF COLCHOS 82-11, JASON WITH SWORD
AND MAGIC PHIAL STEPS OFF GANGPLANK 82-11, JASON SLAYS
FIRE-BREATHING BULLS 82-12, JASON TAKES GOLDEN FLEECE 82-12,
MEDEA GIVES JASON GOLDEN PHIAL AND FIGURE 82-13, NURSE WITH
JASON'S CHILDREN 82-14, TROY AS WALLED CITY WITH GARDENS
82-15, ILION ON RED SANDSTONE AND HEAD OF LAOMEDON SEEN 82-15,
JASON AND HERCULES LAND IN TROY 82-16, ARGO MOORED IN
BACKGROUND 82-16, PRIAM AND FOLLOWERS SURVEY RUINS OF TROY
82-17, TROY RECONSTRUCTED WITH WORKMEN USING CRANE 82-18,
JUDGMENT OF PARIS 82-19, HECTOR KILLING POLYBETES 82-20,
ACHILLES SPEARING HECTOR IN BATTLE 82-21, ARMIES OPPOSING EACH
OTHER 82-22, PARIS KILLS PALAMEDES 82-22, TROILUS DIES WHEN
ACHILLES STABS HIM 82-23, PARIS KILLS ACHILLES IN TEMPLE OF
APOLLO 82-24, HECTOR AND TROILUS LIE DEAD ON FLOOR 82-24,
PARIS WOUNDS AJAX SHOOTING HIM IN BACK 82-25, AJAX KILLS PARIS
WITH ARROW STILL IN HIM 82-26, PYRRHUS KILLS PENTHESILEA
82-27, PYRRHUS KILLS PRIAM IN TEMPLE OF APOLLO 82-28, PYRRHUS
LANDS FROM SHIP AND KILLS POLYXENA 82-29, HECUBA'S MADNESS
82-30

*$ABSTRACT 83
 *LIBRARY BOD
 *SLIDE SET TITLE GOWER CONFESSIO AMANTIS
 *NEGATIVE REFERENCE ROLL 166B
 *RENTAL FEE SM 083 $2.60
 *COMMENTS 12 SLIDES SELECTED FROM 4 MSS OF GOWER'S CONFESSIO
 AMANTIS
 *TITLE OF MANUSCRIPT CONFESSIO AMANTIS
 *SHELFMARK MS BODLEY 294 83/1-3, MS BODLEY 693 83/4-6, MS
 BODLEY 902 83/7-9, MS C C C 67 83/10-12
 *PROVENANCE ENGLISH
 *DATE EXECUTED 15TH
 *LANGUAGE LATIN
 *ARTIST/ SCHOOL HERMAN SCHEERRE AND JOHANNES
 *AUTHOR JOHN GOWER
 *TYPE OF MANUSCRIPT ROMANCE
 *CONTENTS LITERATURE/ CONFESSIO AMANTIS 83/1-10, CONFESSIO
 AMANTIS 83/1-10, ENGLISH LITERATURE/ CONFESSIO AMANTIS
 83/1-10, NEBUCHADNEZZAR' DREAM 83-1, LOVER AND THE CONFESSOR
 83-2, TEXT OF CONFESSIO AMANTIS 83-3, PRECIOUS METALS IN DREAM
 83-4, LOVER AND THE CONFESSOR 83/5 AND 9 AND 11, TEXT WITH
 BORDER OF CONFESSIO AMANTIS 83/6-8 AND 12, PRECIOUS METALS IN
 DREAM 83-10

*$ABSTRACT 84
 *LIBRARY BOD
 *SLIDE SET TITLE HOURS OF THE VIRGIN MARY
 *NEGATIVE REFERENCE ROLL 166C
 *RENTAL FEE SM 084 $3.10
 *TITLE OF MANUSCRIPT HOURS OF THE VIRGIN MARY/SARUM USE
 *SHELFMARK MS LAT LITURG F 2
 *PROVENANCE ENGLISH
 *DATE EXECUTED 15TH/C1405-1413
 *LANGUAGE LATIN AND FRENCH
 *ARTIST/ SCHOOL HERMAN SCHEERRE AND HIS SCHOOL
 *TYPE OF MANUSCRIPT BOOK OF HOURS/ USE OF SARUM
 *CONTENTS BOOK OF HOURS/ ENGLISH/ 15TH 84/1-22, TRANSFIGURATION
 84-1, DEVOTION TO FIVE WOUNDS OF CHRIST 84-2, CHRIST/ FIVE
 WOUNDS 84-2, ST CHRISTOPHER 84-3, ST GEORGE AND THE DRAGON
 84-4, PIETA 84-5, ST CATHERINE AND ST MARGARET 84-6,

ANNUNCIATION 84-7, ANNUNCIATION INITIAL 84-8, VIRGIN ENTHRONED 84-9, CHRIST BEFORE PONTIUS PILATE 84-10, FULL PAGE OF BOOK OF HOURS 84-11, VIRGIN AND CHILD 84-12, ST JEROME AND WHOLE FACING PAGE 84-13, LAST JUDGMENT 84-14, VIGIL OF THE DEAD 84-15, FULL PAGE 84-16, VIRGIN MARY AND SAINT ANNE 84-17, ST STEPHEN 84-18, MARY MAGDALENE 84-19, ST MICHAEL 84-20, ST GEORGE AND THE DRAGON 84-21, MARTYRDOM OF ARCHBISHOP RICHARD LE SCROPE 84-22

*$ABSTRACT 85
  *LIBRARY BOD
  *SLIDE SET TITLE BOOK OF HOURS / FRENCH/ EARLY 15TH
  *NEGATIVE REFERENCE ROLL 166H
  *RENTAL FEE SM 085 $3.00
  *TITLE OF MANUSCRIPT BOOK OF HOURS
  *SHELFMARK MS DOUCE 62
  *PROVENANCE FRENCH
  *DATE EXECUTED 15TH/C1400
  *LANGUAGE LATIN AND FRENCH
  *ARTIST/ SCHOOL ZENOBI DA FIRENZE, JACQUEMART D'HESDIN, MASTER
  OF ETIENNE LOYPEAU
  *TYPE OF MANUSCRIPT BOOK OF HOURS/ USE OF PARIS
  *CONTENTS BOOK OF HOURS/ FRENCH/ 15TH 85/1-20, ANNUNCIATION
  85-1, VISITATION 85-2, NATIVITY 85-3, ANGEL APPEARS TO
  SHEPHERDS 85-4, ADORATION OF THE MAGI 85-5, PRESENTATION IN
  TEMPLE 85-6, FLIGHT INTO EGYPT 85-7, CORONATION OF VIRGIN
  85-8, PENITENTIAL PSALMS 85-9, HELL'S TORMENTS 85-9, PENTECOST
  85-10, OFFICE OF THE DEAD 85-11, VIRGIN AND CHILD 85-12,
  BETRAYAL 85-13, SCOURGING 85-14, CHRIST BEFORE PILATE 85-15,
  ROAD TO CALVARY 85-16, PREPARATION OF THE CROSS 85-17,
  CRUCIFIXION 85-18, DEPOSITION 85-19, ENTOMBMENT 85-20

*$ABSTRACT 86
  *LIBRARY BOD
  *SLIDE SET TITLE POWELL ROLL OF ARMS
  *NEGATIVE REFERENCE ROLL 166K
  *RENTAL FEE SM 086 $3.45
  *COMMENTS HERALDRY OF THE TIME OF EDWARD 111
  *SHELFMARK MS ASHMOLE 804
  *PROVENANCE ENGLISH
  *DATE EXECUTED 14TH/C1345-1351
  *LANGUAGE ENGLISH
  *TYPE OF MANUSCRIPT HERALDRY
  *CONTENTS ROLL OF ARMS/ ENGLISH/ 14TH 86/1-29, HERALDRIC
  SHIELDS OF TIME OF EDWARD III OF ENGLAND 86/1-29

*$ABSTRACT 87
  *LIBRARY BOD
  *SLIDE SET TITLE RUSHWORTH OR MACREGOL GOSPELS
  *NEGATIVE REFERENCE ROLL 167A
  *RENTAL FEE SM 087 $2.50
  *COMMENTS GLOSSED IN ENGLAND IN 10TH BY OWUN AND FARMON
  *TITLE OF MANUSCRIPT MACREGOL GOSPELS
  *SHELFMARK MS AUCT D 2 19
  *PROVENANCE IRISH
  *DATE EXECUTED 09TH/C800
  *LANGUAGE LATIN
  *ARTIST/ SCHOOL MACREGOL/ ABBOT OF BIRR
  *TYPE OF MANUSCRIPT GOSPEL
  *CONTENTS GOSPELS/ IRISH/ 9TH 87/1-10, DETAIL 87-1, ST MARK
  WITH WINGED LION 87-2, DECORATED BORDER 87-3, BEARDED MAN
  ABOVE TWO MEN 87-3, CENTRAL SECTION OF FOLIO 87-4, BIRDS 87-4,
  ST LUKE SEATED WITH WINGED OX 87-5, FULL PAGE OF SCRIPT 87-6,
  ST JOHN SEATED WITH EAGLE 87-7, HUMAN FIGURE AND BIRDS 87-8,
  MAN/ BEARDED 87-9, BORDER DECORATIONS 87/9-10

*$ABSTRACT 88
  *LIBRARY BOD
  *SLIDE SET TITLE RANSHOVEN GOSPELS
  *NEGATIVE REFERENCE ROLL 167C
  *RENTAL FEE SM 088 $2.50
  *COMMENTS   WRITTEN   IN   UPPER   AUSTRIA UNDER ABBOT ADELHARD AND
  LIUTOLD THESAURARIUS
  *TITLE OF MANUSCRIPT RANSHOFEN GOSPELS
  *SHELFMARK MS CANON BIBL LAT 60
  *PROVENANCE GERMAN/ SALZBURG
  *DATE EXECUTED 12TH/1178
  *LANGUAGE LATIN
  *TYPE OF MANUSCRIPT GOSPELS
  *CONTENTS GOSPELS/ BAVARIA/ 12TH 88/1-9, FULL PAGE 88/1-2 AND
  10, INITIAL M 88-2, ST MATTHEW/ DETAIL OF FACE AND HANDS 88-3,
  INITIAL S 88-4, ST MARK/ DETAIL OF HEAD AND BUST 88-5, ST
  LUKE/ DETAIL OF HEAD AND BUST 88-6, ST LUKE'S HEAD 88-7, ST
  JOHN/ DETAIL OF HEAD AND BUST 88-8, ST JOHN'S HEAD 88-9

*$ABSTRACT 89
  *LIBRARY BOD
  *SLIDE SET TITLE INITIALS FROM ROMANESQUE PAULINE EPISTLES
  *NEGATIVE REFERENCE ROLL 167D
  *RENTAL FEE SM 089 $2.30
  *TITLE OF MANUSCRIPT PAULINE EPISTLES
  *SHELFMARK MS AUCT D 1 13
  *PROVENANCE ENGLISH/ WINCHESTER
  *DATE EXECUTED 12TH
  *LANGUAGE LATIN
  *TYPE OF MANUSCRIPT EPISTLES
  *CONTENTS EPISTLES/ ENGLISH/ 12TH 89/1-6, FULL PAGE 89/1 AND
  5-6, ST PAUL'S LIFE IN ILLUMINATED P 89-1, ST PAUL TEACHING
  89-2, ST PAUL LOWERED IN BASKET 89-3, ST PAUL'S MARTYRDOM
  89-4, INITIAL P/2 DECORATED 89-5, INITIAL M IN GREEN INK 89-6

*$ABSTRACT 90
  *LIBRARY BOD
  *SLIDE SET TITLE BESTIARY
  *NEGATIVE REFERENCE ROLL 167G
  *RENTAL FEE SM 090 $3.45
  *COMMENTS 30 SLIDES SELECTED FROM AN ENGLISH BESTIARY
  *SHELFMARK MS ASHMOLE 1511
  *PROVENANCE ENGLISH/ PETERBOROUGH
  *DATE EXECUTED 13TH/C1200
  *LANGUAGE LATIN
  *TYPE OF MANUSCRIPT BESTIARY
  *CONTENTS BESTIARY/ ENGLISH/ 13TH 90/1-30, FULL PAGE 90/1-2 AND
  6-9 AND 11 AND 16, FULL PAGE 90/26 AND 28, CHRIST 90-1, BEASTS
  90-2, ILLUMINATION ONLY 90/4-5 AND 10 AND 12-15 AND 19-25,
  ILLUMINATION ONLY 90/27 AND 29-30, BEASTS 90-3, BEASTS 90-4,
  MAN 90-5, CHRIST WITH BOOK 90-6, EVANGELISTS SYMBOLS 9-6,
  FIGURE SEATED PREACHING TO BEASTS 9-7, LION DEPICTED IN THREE
  SECTIONS 90/8-9, TIGER 90-10, GRIFFIN AND ELEPHANT 90-11,
  GRIFFIN CARRYING OFF PIG 90-12, ELEPHANT WITH HOWDAH AND
  KNIGHTS ON BACK 90-13, WILD GOATS 90-14, BEAR SHAPING CUBS
  WITH TONGUE 90-15, DOGS/ 3 90-16, TEXT ONLY OF BESTIARY 90-17,
  ONAGER 90-18, HORSE 90-19, VULTURES 90-20, CRANES 90-21, SWAN
  90-22, PEACOCK 90-23, BEES IN 3 ROWS FLYING INTO 3 SKEPS
  90-24, ASP AND SNAKE-CHARMER 90-25, WHALE WITH FISH AND BOAT
  90-26,WHALE SWALLOWING FISH WITH BOAT AND SAILORS 90-27, ST
  ISIDORE 90-28, ST ISIDORE 90-29, FIRESTONES AND HUMAN FIGURES
  90-30

*$ABSTRACT 91
  *LIBRARY BOD
  *SLIDE SET TITLE ARTHURIAN CYCLE ROMANCE OF GUIRON

54

*NEGATIVE REFERENCE ROLL 167K
*RENTAL FEE SM 091 $2.85
*TITLE OF MANUSCRIPT GUIRON LE COURTOIS
*SHELFMARK MS DOUCE 383/ FOLS 1-18
*PROVENANCE FLEMISH
*DATE EXECUTED 16TH/C1500
*LANGUAGE FRENCH
*AUTHOR HELIE DE BORRON
*ARTIST/ SCHOOL MASTER OF THE ROMANCE OF THE ROSE, MASTER OF
 EDWARD IV
*TYPE OF MANUSCRIPT ROMANCE
*CONTENTS LITERATURE/ ROMANCE OF GUIRON 91/1-17, ROMANCE OF
 GUIRON 91/1-17, FRENCH LITERATURE/ ROMANCE OF GUIRON 91/1-17,
 CASTLE LIFE 91/1-17, COURT OF KING DIODICIAS 91-1, HERALDRIC
 ARMS OF NASSAU AND VIANDEN 91-1, NORHAUT OF THE ISLAND AT
 DINNER 91-2, TRISTAN ARRIVES AT ANTEROOM OF CASTLE 91-3,
 MUSICIANS WITH PIPES AND TABORS 91-3, KNIGHT BOUND HAND AND
 FOOT IN CART 91-4, ARTHUR AND COURTIERS WATCH FROM PAVILION
 91-4, KNIGHTS IN COMBAT 91-5, KNIGHTS IN COMBAT BEFORE ARTHUR
 AND COURT 91-6, DANEBRUN SEES ARRIVAL OF KNIGHT AND LADIES
 91-7, KNIGHTS AT CHASTEL DE L'ISLE PERDUE 91-8, GALEHAUT AND
 LANCELOT TALKING TO GROUP IN GARDEN 91-8, GALEHAUT IN SEARCH
 OF KNIGHT OF THE LITTER 91-9, CASTLE OF THE FOUR WAYS 91-9,
 HELYNOR DE BOSCAGES AND ASCANOR LE GRANT BATTLE 91-10, CHASTEL
 AUX ORGUEILLEUX 91-10, KING OF ESCOCE SLAYS KNIGHT WHO SLAYED
 BROTHER 91-11, ARTHUR AND KNIGHTS RETURN TO CAMELOT 91-12,
 CAMELOT 91-12, MEIADUS ATTEMPTS TO REMOUNT IN MIDST OF BATTLE
 91-13, GUIRON TAKES LEAVE OF ARTHUR AND QUEEN 91-14, KNIGHTS
 IN TOURNEY YARD AND LADIES IN PAVILION 91-15, TOURNAMENT
 BEFORE ARTHUR 91-16, MUSICIANS 91-16, RECORDER/ SHAWM/ CLARION
 91-16, COURT OF ARTHUR TO WHICH DAMSEL COMES 91-17

*$ABSTRACT 92
 *LIBRARY BOD
 *SLIDE SET TITLE MEDIEVAL ENGLISH POLYPHONY
 *NEGATIVE REFERENCE ROLL 168A
 *RENTAL FEE SM 092 $3.10
 *COMMENTS 20 SLIDES SELECTED FROM 6 MSS OF THE 14TH-15TH
 CENTURIES
 *SHELFMARK MS ASHMOLE 1393 92/1-3, MS E MUSAEO 7 92/4-7, MS
 DOUCE 381 92/8-10, MS ASHMOLE 191 92/11-17, MS DOUCE 381
 92/18-20, MS DOUCE 139 92-21, MS MUSAEO 143 92-22
 *PROVENANCE ENGLISH
 *DATE EXECUTED 14TH-15TH
 *LANGUAGE LATIN 92/2-6 AND 20 AND 22, ENGLISH 92/1 AND 8 AND
 10-19, FRENCH 92/7 AND 9 AND 21
 *TYPE OF MANUSCRIPT MUSICAL TEXTS
 *CONTENTS MUSIC/ POLYPHONY/ ENGLISH 92/1-22, ENGLISH SONG/ 2
 PART 92-1, LOVE WOLL I 92-1, LATIN CAROL/ 2 PART 92-2, ECCE
 QUOD NATURA MUTAT SUA IURA 92-2, ENGLISH AND LATIN CAROLS
 92-3, ENIXA EST PUERPERA-A LADY THAT WAS SO FEYRE 92-3, GLORIA
 TIBI DOMINE-A LITIL CHILDE THER IS IBORE 92-3, LATIN SACRED
 PIECES 92/4-5, LATIN SACRED POEMS 92-6, FRENCH LOVE SONG
 FOLLOWED BY LATIN LITURGICAL PIECE 92-7, ENGLISH SONG/ 2 PART
 92-8, I HAVE SET MY HERT SO HYE 92-8, FRENCH SONG/ 2 PART
 92-8, LES EUX OUERT 92-8, FRENCH SONG/ 3 PART 92-9, MON CUR
 92-9, ENGLISH SONG/ 2 PART 92-10, MY CARES COMEN EUER ANEW
 92-10, WRYTH AL MY HERTE NOW 92-10, ENGLISH LOVE SONG/ 2 PART
 92-11, NOW WOLDE I FAYNE 92-11, ENGLISH LOVE SONG/ 2 PART
 92/12-13 AND 15-19, O KENDLY CREATURE 92/12-13, ENGLISH LOVE
 SONG/ 3 PART 92-14, GO HERT 92-14, THUS Y COMPLEYNE 92-15,
 ALAS DEPARTYNGE 92-16, LUF WIL WT VARIANCE 92-17, IE HAVE SO
 LONGE KEPE SCHEPE 92-18, I REDE YOU BE 92-19, LATIN RESPOND/ 2
 PART 92-20, FELIX NAMQUE 92-20, FRENCH SONGS WRITTEN IN
 ENGLAND 92-21, LATIN HYMN TO SAINT JAMES FOLLOWED BY AGNUS DEI
 92-22

*$ABSTRACT 93
 *LIBRARY BOD
 *SLIDE SET TITLE PETRARCH AND OTHER ITALIAN POETS
 *NEGATIVE REFERENCE ROLL 168C
 *RENTAL FEE SM 093 $3.05
 *TITLE   OF   MANUSCRIPT   DIVINE   COMEDY 93/1-4,   POEMS   93-6,
 CANZONIERE 93/7-14, SONNETS TRIONFI 93/15-21
 *SHELFMARK MS CANON ITAL 109 93-1, MS CANON ITAL 108 93/2-4, MS
 CANON ITAL 15 93-5, MS D/ORVILLE 517 93-6, MS CANON ITAL 69
 93/7-14, MS CANON ITAL 62 93/15-21
 *PROVENANCE ITALIAN
 *DATE EXECUTED 15TH/C1400 93-1, 14TH 93/2-4, 15TH/C1420-30
 93/7-14, 15TH 93/ 5-6 AND 15-21
 *LANGUAGE ITALIAN
 *ARTIST/ SCHOOL IN THE STYLE OF FRANCESCO D'ANTONIO DEL CHERICO
 93/15-21,
 *AUTHOR DANTE 93/1-4, FELICE FELICIANO DA VERONA 93-5,   ANTONIO
 CORNAZZANO 93-6, PETRARCH 93/7-21
 *TYPE OF MANUSCRIPT POETRY
 *CONTENTS LITERATURE/ ITALIAN POETS 93/1-21, ITALIAN FIGURE
 HOLDING BOOK 93-1, CHERUBIM 93-1, MALACODA AND BARRATIORS
 93-2, ODERISI PROUD ANGEL OF HUMILIATION 93-3, DANTE AND
 VIRGIL DISCUSS LOVE   93-4,   SLOTHFUL   93-4,   FELICIANO'S
 HANDWRITING 93-5, HERALDRIC ARMS OF VISCONTI D@ARAGONA 93-6,
 HUMANISTIC SCRIPT 93-6, PETRARCH CROWNED 93-7, HUNTING SCENE
 93-7, SONNET I 93-7, SONNETS 62-65 93-8, SONNETS 90-92 93-9,
 SONNETS 222 AND 218 AND 219 93-10, SONNETS 277-279 93-11,
 SONNETS 308-311 93-12, SONNETS 349 AND 351-353 93-13, SONNETS
 354 AND 353 AND 366 93-14, PURSUIT AND TRANSFORMATION OF
 DAPHNE 93-15, CUPID ON CART 93-16, UNICORNS DRAWING CART
 93-17, UNICORNS 93-18, ELEPHANTS DRAWING CART 93-19, OLD AGE
 ON CART DRAWN BY 2 DEER 93-20, GOD BETWEEN CHERUBS 93-21

*$ABSTRACT 94
 *LIBRARY BOD
 *SLIDE SET TITLE EARLY BIBLES
 *NEGATIVE REFERENCE ROLL 168D
 *RENTAL FEE SM 094 $2.50
 *COMMENTS EARLY BIBLES
 *TITLE OF MANUSCRIPT SAYINGS OF JESUS/ GOSPEL OF THOMAS 94-1,
 LAUDIAN ACTS 94/2-3, WYCLIF BIBLE 94-4, COVERDALE BIBLE 94-5,
 MATTHEW BIBLE 94-6, GREAT BIBLE 1539 94-7, TAVERNER'S BIBLE
 94-8, BISHOP'S BIBLE 94-9, AUTHORIZED VERSION OF BIBLE 94-10
 *SHELFMARK MS GR TH E 7 94-1, MS LAUD GR 35 F 77 94/2-3, MS
 BODLEY 959 F 288 94-4, MS SELDEN C 9 94-5, MS BIBL ENG 1537 C
 1 A 94-6, MS BIBL ENG 1539 B 1 94-7, MS SELDEN D 36 94-8, MS
 BIBLE ENG 1602 B 1 F 117 94-9, MS BIBLE ENG 1611 6 1 94-10
 *PROVENANCE GREEK 94/1-3, ENGLISH 94/4 AND 7-10, SWISS 94-5,
 FLEMISH 94-6
 *DATE EXECUTED 03RD 94-1, 06TH 94/2-3, 14TH 94-4, 16TH/1535
 94-5,   16TH/1537   94-6,   16TH/1539 94-7, 16TH/1537 94-8,
 17TH/1602 94-9, 16TH/1611 94-10
 *LANGUAGE GREEK 94-1, LATIN AND GREEK 94/2-3, ENGLISH 94/4-10
 *TYPE OF MANUSCRIPT BIBLES
 *CONTENTS BIBLES 94/1-10

*$ABSTRACT 95
 *LIBRARY BOD
 *SLIDE SET TITLE ROMANCE OF THE PILGRIMAGE OF MAN
 *NEGATIVE REFERENCE ROLL 168E
 *RENTAL FEE SM 095 $2.40
 *COMMENTS COMPILED FROM THE ROMANCE OF THE ROSE
 *TITLE OF MANUSCRIPT ROMANCE OF THE PILGRIMAGE OF MAN
 *SHELFMARK MS LAUD MISC 740
 *PROVENANCE ENGLISH
 *DATE EXECUTED 15TH/C1430
 *LANGUAGE ENGLISH/ TRANSLATED FROM FRENCH
 *TYPE OF MANUSCRIPT ROMANCE

*CONTENTS LITERATURE/ ROMANCE OF THE PILGRIMAGE OF MAN 95/1-8,
ROMANCE OF THE PILGRIMAGE OF MAN 95/1-8, ENGLISH LITERATURE/
ROMANCE OF THE PILGRIMAGE OF MAN 95/1-8, REASON PREACHING IN
PULPIT 95-1, PILGRIM BAPTISED AT FONT BY GRACE 95-2, GRACE OF
GOD AS WOMAN HANDS SCROLL TO MOSES 95-3, PILGRIMS BESIDE GRACE
95-3, MOSES IN ROBES BEFORE ALTAR WITH HOST 95-4, GRACE OF GOD
PLACES WALLET AROUND PILGRIM'S NECK 95-5, GRACE OF GOD HOLDS
SWORD OF RIGHTEOUSNESS 95-6, PILGRIM WITH STAFF OF HOPE 95-6,
PRIDE AS UNICORN MEETS PILGRIM 95-7, FLATTERY AS WOMAN WITH
MIRROR 95-7, PILGRIM BY SEA 95-8, SHIP OF RELIGION SAILING ON
SEA 95-8

*$ABSTRACT 96
 *LIBRARY BOD
 *SLIDE SET TITLE BEDE LIFE OF SAINT CUTHBERT
 *NEGATIVE REFERENCE ROLL 167H
 *RENTAL FEE SM 096 $2.55
 *TITLE OF MANUSCRIPT LIFE OF SAINT CUTHBERT
 *SHELFMARK MS UNIVERSITY COLLEGE 165
 *PROVENANCE ENGLISH
 *DATE EXECUTED 12TH/C1150
 *LANGUAGE LATIN
 *AUTHOR BEDE
 *TYPE OF MANUSCRIPT SAINT'S LIFE
 *CONTENTS ST CUTHBERT 96/1-11, BEDE/ LIFE OF ST CUTHBERT
 96/1-11, ST CUTHBERT FALLING AT GAME OF SHINTY 96-1, ANGEL
 CURES KNEE OF SAINT CUTHBERT 96-2, ST CUTHBERT FED BY DIVINE
 INTERVENTION WHILE ON TRIP 96-3, HORSE WITH CLOTH IN MOUTH
 96-3, BOISIL HAILS SAINT CUTHBERT WHILE DISMOUNTING 96-4,
 EAGLE ADMINISTERS TO CUTHBERT 96-5, DETAIL OF CENTRAL FIGURE
 96-6, ST CUTHBERT SEES DESTRUCTION OF EGGFRITH 96-7, ST
 CUTHBERT'S TRIALS IN SICKNESS AND BURIAL INSTRUCTIONS 96-8,
 DETAIL OF FIGURE SEATED ON BENCH 96-9, MONK'S PARALYSIS HEALED
 BY CUTHBERT 96-10, EYE HEALED BY CUTHBERT'S RELICS 96-11

*$ABSTRACT 97
 *LIBRARY BOD
 *SLIDE SET TITLE PIERS PLOWMAN THE C TEXT OF WILLIAM LANGLAND'S
 POEM
 *NEGATIVE REFERENCE ROLL 168I
 *RENTAL FEE SM 097 $2.90
 *TITLE OF MANUSCRIPT PIERS PLOWMAN/C TEXT
 *SHELFMARK MS DOUCE 104
 *PROVENANCE ENGLISH
 *DATE EXECUTED 15TH/1427
 *LANGUAGE ENGLISH
 *AUTHOR LANGLAND/ WILLIAM
 *TYPE OF MANUSCRIPT ALLEGORY
 *CONTENTS LITERATURE/ PIERS PLOWMAN 97/1-18, PIERS PLOWMAN
 97/1-18, ENGLISH LITERATURE/ PIERS PLOWMAN 97/1-18, LADY MEDE
 RIDING TO WESTMINSTER ON SHERIFF'S SHOULDER 97-1, LADY MEDE
 RECEIVING ABSOLUTION FROM DOMINICAN FRIAR 97-2, PRIDE IN
 JESTER'S COSTUME 97-3, PRIDE 97-4, ENVY SHAKING FIST DRESSED
 IN ROUGH CLOTHING 97-5, WRATH WITH ONE LEG RED/ OTHER BLUE AND
 SWORD 97-6, LECHERY KNEELING WITH HANDS RAISED 97-7,
 COVETOUSNESS PURSE AT GIRDLE AND UNSHAVEN 97-8, GLUTTONY
 DRINKING FROM BOWL 97-9, SLOTH ASLEEP 97-10, PILGRIM WITH
 TYPICAL HAT STAFF AND SCRIP 97-11, FIGURE WITH BAG SLEEVES AND
 HOOD STAVE AND PURSE 97-12, HUNGER WITH EMACIATED FACE 97-13,
 FRIAR/ FALSE IN WHITE HABIT 97-14, PRIEST/ TONSURED WITH WHITE
 GOWN HOLDING PARDON 97-15, FORTUNE WITH HER WHEEL 97-16, FRIAR
 AT DINNER 97-17, PATIENCE WITH CLOAK/ STAFF AND BAG 97-18

*$ABSTRACT 98
 *LIBRARY BOD
 *SLIDE SET TITLE PELERINAGE DE LA VIE HUMAINE

*NEGATIVE REFERENCE ROLL 168J
*RENTAL FEE SM 098 $3.65
*TITLE OF MANUSCRIPT PELERINAGE DE LA VIE HUMAINE
*SHELFMARK MS DOUCE 300
*PROVENANCE FRENCH/FLEMISH
*DATE EXECUTED 15TH/C1400
*LANGUAGE FRENCH
*AUTHOR DEGUILLEVILLE/ GUILLAUME DE
*TYPE OF MANUSCRIPT PILGRIMAGE ALLEGORY
*CONTENTS LITERATURE/ PELERINAGE DE LA VIE HUMAINE 98/1-33,
PELERINAGE DE LA VIE HUMAINE 98/1-33, FRENCH LITERATURE/
PELERINAGE DE LA VIE HUMAINE 98/1-33, PREACHER AND
CONGREGATION 98-1, PILGRIM LYING ASLEEP 98-2, GRACE-DIEU TAKES
PILGRIM TO HER CASTLE 98-3, PILGRIM MARKED WITH SIGN OF CROSS
98-4, MASTER OF CASTLE GIVES OINTMENT TO OFFICIAL 98-5, REASON
COMES OUT TO CHURCH 98-6, OFFICIAL MARRIES TWO PILGRIMS 98-7,
MOSES SHAVES MEN AND REASON ADDRESSES THEM 98-8, PILGRIMS
BEFORE MOSES AND GRACE DIEU 98-9, GRACE-DIEU TURNS BREAD AND
WINE INTO FLESH AND BLOOD 98-10, PENANCE AND CHARITY 98-11,
GRACE-DIEU SHOWS PILGRIM ARMOR 98-12, PILGRIM PUTS ON GAMBESON
WHICH IS PATIENCE 98-13, GRACE-DIEU GIVES PILGRIM CHAIN-MAIL
OF FORTITUDE 98-14, GRACE-DIEU SHOWS PILGRIM ALL ARMOR AND HE
IS DISMAYED 98-15, HELMET OF TEMPERANCE/ GORGET OF SOBRIETY
98-16, PILGRIM STRIPS OFF ARMOR AND GRACE-DIEU DISPLEASED
98-17, MEMORY ASKED TO CARRY PILGRIMØS ARMOR 98-18, PILGRIM
READS COMMISSION OF VILLEIN RUDE ENTENDEMENT 98-19, STAFF OF
OBSTINACY 98-19, REASON TAKES PILGRIM'S SOUL 98-20, FORK IN
ROAD WITH LABOUR AND IDLENESS 98-21, SLOTH STRIKES PILGRIM
WITH AXE 98-22, SLOTH AND PILGRIM MEET PRIDE AND FLATTERY
98-23, ENVY WITH DAUGHTERS DETRACTION AND TREASON 98-24,
AVARICE AS HAG MET BY PILGRIM 98-25, AVARICE SHOWS MONASTERY
BROKEN INTO BY KING FOR MONEY 98-26, GLUTTONY MET BY PILGRIM
98-27, LUXURY RIDING ON A SWINE 98-28, GRACE-DIEU SHOWS
PILGRIM ROCK WITH FLOWING WATER 98-29, SATAN MET BY PILGRIM AS
HE FISHES 98-30, YOUTH CARRIES PILGRIM ON HER BACK 98-31, SHIP
OF RELIGION APPEARS TO PENITENT PILGRIM 98-32, FEAR-OF-GOD
ASKED BY PILGRIM FOR PERMISSION TO BOARD SHIP 98-33

*$ABSTRACT 99
*LIBRARY BOD
*SLIDE SET TITLE LANCELOT DU LAC
*NEGATIVE REFERENCE ROLL 169A
*RENTAL FEE SM 099 $7.05
*TITLE OF MANUSCRIPT LANCELOT DU LAC
*SHELFMARK MS RAWLINSON Q B 6
*PROVENANCE FRENCH/ NORTHERN
*DATE EXECUTED 14TH/C1320-30
*LANGUAGE FRENCH
*TYPE OF MANUSCRIPT ROMANCE
*CONTENTS LITERATURE/ LANCELOT DU LAC 99/1-101, ARTHURIAN
ROMANCE 99/1-101, FRENCH LITERATURE/ LANCELOT DU LAC 99/1-101,
KING BAN SEES CASTLE BURNING 99-1, QUEEN ELAINE TAKES REFUGE
IN ABBEY AND WELCOMES SISTER 99-2, LADY OF THE LAKE AND
COMPANIONS CARRY LANCELOT 99-3, LANCELOT LEARNS TO SHOOT 99-4,
LANCELOT SPEARS STAG AND COMPANION SOUNDS HORN 99-5, LANCELOT/
ARMED AND MOUNTED WITH MESSENGERS IN FOREST 99-6, LANCELOT
MEETS LADY WHOSE HUSBAND WAS KILLED 99-7, GAWAIN AND
COMPANIONS INVITED BY BOATMAN TO CASTLE 99-8, LANCELOT/ WHITE
KNIGHT ATTACKS KNIGHTS OF DOLOROUS GUARD 99-9, ARTHUR AND
QUEEN AND KNIGHTS WELCOMED BY MAIDSERVANTS 99-10, LANCELOT AND
SQUIRE RECEIVE MESSAGE FROM QUEEN 99-11, LANCELOT AT FOUNTAIN
ASKED FOR LADY OF NOHAUT 99-12, KNIGHTS TAKING PART IN
TOURNAMENT 99-13, LADY OF NOHAUT RIDES BESIDE LANCELOT 99-14,
LANCELOT TALKS WITH LADY OF NOHAUT 99-15, GAWAIN AND LADIES
ARRIVE AT CASTLE OF NOHAUT 99-16, LANCELOT LEAVES HERMIT
99-17, GAWAIN TELLS ARTHUR AND QUEEN THAT LANCELOT IS VICTOR
99-18, ARTHUR ENTHRONED 99-19, LANCELOT ARRIVES AT MALAHAUT
AFTER ASSEMBLY 99-20, ARTHUR REPROACHED BY GAWAIN FOR BROODING
OVER DEFEAT 99-21, LANCELOT PRISONER OF LADY OF MALAHAUT
99-22, GALEHOT AND LANCELOT ON ROAD TO SORELOIS 99-23, ARTHUR

AND KNIGHTS RETURN TO CAMELOT 99-24, CAMELOT 99-24, GAWAIN
ENTERS LADY'S PAVILION AS GUEST 99-25, LADY OF ROESTOC SEATED
BETWEEN ARTHUR AND GUINEVERE 99-26, QUEEN AND ATTENDANTS
SUCCOR WOUNDED KNIGHT 99-27, LANCELOT LOVE-SICK SPEAKS TO
GALEHOT 99-28, KNIGHTS SET OUT TO RESCUE HECTOR 99-29,
LANCELOT GRIEVES OVER GUINEVERE'S PLIGHT 99-30, ARTHUR
PRISONER OF FALSE QUINEVERE 99-31, GAWAIN CROWNED AS SUCCESSOR
TO ARTHUR 99-32, GALEHOT CONDUCTS QUEEN TO SORELOIS TO RECEIVE
HOMAGE 99-33, GUINEVERE RETURNED TO ARTHUR 99-34, COURT AT
DINNER 99-35, LANCELOT LIFTS WOUNDED KNIGHT FROM LITTER 99-36,
ARTHUR GREETS LANCELOT AND GAWAIN BEFORE PAVILION 99-37,
LANCELOT HEARS MASS 99-38, DUKE OF CLARENCE AND SQUIRE 99-39,
LANCELOT WITH IWAIN AND LADY 99-40, LANCELOT'S COMPANIONS
DISCUSS HIS ABSENCE 99-41, MORGAN LA FEY IMPRISONS LANCELOT
99-42, MORGAN LA FEY PROMISES TO RELEASE LANCELOT 99-43,
GAWAIN AND OTHERS SET OFF AFTER LANCELOT 99-44, MORGAN LA FEY
HAS LANCELOT RELEASED FROM PRISON 99-45, LADY OF LAKE FINDS
LANCELOT MAD AND STARVING 99-46, LANCELOT RIDES IN CART DRIVEN
BY DWARF 99-47, LANCELOT AT PONT DEPEE 99-48, LANCELOT'S
COMPANIONS HEAR MASS 99-49, LANCELOT TAKEN PRISONER IN ERROR
ON PONT PERDUE 99-50, LANCELOT IN PRISON AT GORRE 99-51,
GUINEVERE RECEIVES APOLOGY FROM KNIGHT 99-52, LANCELOT MEETS
WEEPING LADY 99-53, LANCELOT DINES WITH FRIENDS IN PAVILION
99-54, GUINEVERE TAKEN PRISONER BY KNIGHT 99-55, GUINEVERE
MOURNS SUPPOSED DEATH OF LANCELOT 99-56, LANCELOT SAYS
FAREWELL TO OLD LADY WHO HEALED HIM 99-57, LANCELOT SLEEPING
OBSERVED BY LADIES 99-58, LANCELOT RIDES WITH KNIGHT AND LADY
TO CASTLE 99-59, LANCELOT THREATENS TO KILL ELAINE WHO
DECEIVED HIM 99-60, LANCELOT WEARS FATHER'S CROWN 99-61,
LANCELOT AND COMPANIONS REPORT TO ARTHUR AND SET OUT 99-62,
LANCELOT AND COMPANIONS RIDE OUT ON QUEST 99-63, LANCELOT
WOUNDED BY BLACK KNIGHT 99-64, LANCELOT AND COMPANIONS SEE
LIONS WITH STAG 99-65, QUEST COMPANIONS IN COMBAT 99-66,
LANCELOT SEES LADY IN CANDLE-LIT PAVILION 99-67, LANCELOT IN
PRISON TRYS TO PLUCK ROSE 99-68, LANCELOT WITH RESCUED LIONELL
GREETS MONK 99-69, LANCELOT'S COMPANIONS SEEK NEWS OF HOME
99-70, LANCELOT IN FOREST CLEAVES HEAD OFF LION 99-71, QUEEN'S
LETTER CARRIED TO LADY OF THE LAKE 99-72, ARTHUR CALLS QUEST
COMPANION BEFORE HIM 99-73, ARTHUR RECIEVES CALL FOR HELP
99-74, GUINEVERE BANISHES LANCELOT BECAUSE OF ELAINE 99-75,
HECTOR AND PERCEVAL EXHAUST EACH OTHER IN COMBAT 99-76,
LANCELOT WANDERING AND MAD ARRIVES AT PAVILION 99-77,
LANCELOT'S COMPANIONS SEARCH FOR HIM 99-78, GALAHAD IN QUEST
OF GRAIL MEETS BAUDEMAGUS AND YWAIN 99-79, GALAHAD IN FOREST
99-80, HERMIT PREACHES TO LANCELOT AND URGES HIM TO REPENT
99-81, ADAM AND EVE/ STORY OF HOLY GRAIL 99-82, GALAHAD AND
FRIENDS STARE AT GOLDEN-HILTED SWORD 99-83, GALAHAD AND
PERCEVAL IN CHAPEL PRAY FOR BOHORT 99-84, LANCELOT IN PRAYER
FOR SHIP 99-85, GALAHAD VISITS MORDRAIN WHO EMBRACES HIM
99-86, SCRIBE AT LECTERN WRITING BOOK 99-87, LANCELOT IN BED
RECOVERED FROM WOUNDS 99-88, ARTHUR/ QUEEN AND KNIGHT ARRIVE
AT CASTLE OF TAUROE 99-89, LANCELOT DECLARED CURED BY
PHYSICIANS 99-90, ARTHUR AND SUITE BID FAREWELL TO MORGAN LA
FEY 99-91, LANCELOT AND SQUIRE IN FOREST 99-92, TOURNAMENT AT
CAMELOT 99-93, LANCELOT AND BOHORT RESCUE GUINEVERE FROM THE
STAKE 99-94, ARTHUR NAMES NEW KNIGHTS OF THE ROUND TABLE
99-95, LANCELOT AND FRIENDS LEAVE JOYOUS GUARD FOR HOME 99-96,
ARTHUR PREPARES FOR WAR WITH GAUL 99-97, BISHOP GIVES
GUINEVERE FALSE LETTER OF ARTHUR'S DEATH 99-98, ARTHUR
BESIEGES LANCELOT AT GANNES 99/99, MORDRED BESIEGES THE
QUEEN'S TOWER 99-100, MORDRED AND KNIGHTS DEPART FROM TOWER
99-101

*$ABSTRACT 100
  *LIBRARY BOD
  *SLIDE SET TITLE SIR GAWAIN
  *NEGATIVE REFERENCE ROLL 169B
  *RENTAL FEE SM 100 $3.00
  *COMMENTS   SELECTION FROM VARIOUS MSS ILLUSTRATING THE STORY OF
  SIR GAWAIN

*TITLE OF MANUSCRIPT ROMANCE OF LANCELOT DU LAC 100/5 AND 7-8
AND 10, ROMANCE OF LANCELOT DU LAC 100-20, PELERINAGE DE LA
VIE HUMAINE 100/6 AND 15, ROMANCE OF THE ROSE 100/2 AND 11, LE
MIREUR DU MONDE 10/9 AND 13-14 AND 17-19, L/EPITRE D/OTHES A
HECTOR 100-12, ROMANCE OF GUIRON LE COURTOIS 100/1 AND 3-4
*SHELFMARK MS RAWLINSON Q B 6 100/5 AND 7-8 AND 10, MS
RAWLINSON Q B 6 100-20, MS DOUCE 300 10/6 AND 15, MS DOUCE 364
100/2 AND 11, MS DOUCE 336 100/9 AND 13-14 AND 17-19, MS
BODLEY 421 100-12, MS DOUCE 383 100/1 AND 3-4
*PROVENANCE FRENCH 100/2 AND 5-20,FLEMISH 100 AND 3-4
*DATE EXECUTED 14TH/C1320-30 100/5 AND 7-8 AND 10 AND 20
*LANGUAGE FRENCH
*AUTHOR DEGUILLEVILLE/ GUILLAUME DE 100/6 AND 15
*TYPE OF MANUSCRIPT ROMANCE
*CONTENTS LITERATURE/ SIR GAWAIN 100/1-20, FRENCH LITERATURE/
ROMANCES 100/1-20, TOURNAMENT BEFORE ARTHUR 100-1, MIRTH/
GLADNESS/ COURTESY/ AND LOVER DANCE 100-2, COURT OF KING
DIODICIAS 100-3, MORHAUT OF THE ISLAND AND KNIGHTS 100-4,
GAWAIN LEAVES ARTHUR AND GUINEVERE 100-5, GRACE-DIEU
SUPERINTENDS ARMING OF PILGRIM 100-6, GAWAIN RIDES THROUGH
FOREST 100-7, GAWAIN COMES TO MONASTERY 100-8, TARQUIN
EXPELLED BY CITIZENS OF ROME 100-9, SQUIRE HELPS GAWAIN REMOVE
ARMOR 100-10, CONSTRAINTE ABSTINENCE AND FAUX-SEMBLANT 100-11,
PELEUS AND THETIS MARRIED 100-12, HUNTSMEN STALKING STAG
100-13, HUNTING PARTY WATCHES STAG SWIM STREAM 100-14, PILGRIM
ASLEEP IN BED 100-15, HUNTSMEN PREPARING TO BREAK UP DEER
100-16, BOAR HUNTING 100-17, LUCRECE ENTERTAINS TARQUIN
100-18, HERCULES@ LABORS 100-19, GAWAIN WITH ARTHUR AND
GUINEVERE 100-20

*$ABSTRACT 101
*LIBRARY BOD
*SLIDE SET TITLE GOUGH MAP/ LARGE SCALE DETAILS
*NEGATIVE REFERENCE ROLL 169H
*RENTAL FEE SM 101 $2.60
*COMMENTS 12 FRAMES SELECTED FROM EARLIEST ROAD MAP OF ENGLAND
*TITLE OF MANUSCRIPT GOUGH MAP OF ENGLAND
*SHELFMARK MS GOUGH GEN TOP 16
*PROVENANCE ENGLISH
*DATE EXECUTED 14TH/C1360
*LANGUAGE ENGLISH
*TYPE OF MANUSCRIPT MAP
*CONTENTS MAP/ ENGLISH/ 14TH 101/1-12, GOUGH MAP 101/1-12, ISLE
OF WIGHT 101-1, SELSEY 101-1, NEW FOREST 101-1, ARUNDEL 101-1,
WINCHESTER 101-2, BASINGSTOKE 101-2, FARNHAM 101-2, PETWORTH
101-2, WINDSOR 101-2, HUNGERFORD 101-2, SALISBURY 101-2,
COLLINGBOURNE 101-2, BASINGSTOKE 101-3, BAGSHOT 101-3,
WINCHESTER 101-3, COLNBROK 101-3, WHITE HORSE 101-3, WINDSOR
101-3, WHITE HORSE 101-4, AYLESBURY 101-4, THAME 101-4,
DUNSTABLE 101-4, COLNBROK 101-4, ST ALBANS 101-4, READING
101-4, OXFORD 101-4, WHITE HORSE 101-5, WOBURN 101-5, HERTFORD
101-5, ST ALBANS 101-5, STRATFORD 101-5, HIGH WYCOMBE 101-5,
TETSWORTH 101-5, WALLINGFORD 101-5, BUCKINGHAM 101-5, OXFORD
101-5, WOODSTOCK 101-5, WANSFORD 101-6, TURVEY 101-6, BEDFORD
101-6, NORTHHAMPTON 101-6, DAVENTRY 101-6, PETERBOROUGH 101-6,
SHERWOOD FOREST 101-7, KESTEVEN 101-7, WANSFORD 101-7, LINCOLN
101-7, NEWARK 101-7, NOTTINGHAM 101-7, RIVER TRENT 101-7,
LICHFIELD 101-7, TUTBERY 101-7, RIVER DON 101-7, CHESTERFIELD
101-7, NOTTINGHAM 101-8, KESTEVEN 101-8, DERBY 101-8, LINCOLN
101-8, CHESTERFIELD 101-8, SHEFFIELD 101-8, ASHBOURNE 101-8,
TUTBURY 101-8, LINCOLN 101-9, BAKEWELL 101-9, SHEFFIELD 101-9,
YORK 101-10, RIPON 101-10, RICHMOND 101-10, SETTLE 101-10,
RIVER RIBBLE 101-10, SWALE 101-10, GRETA 101-10, EDEN 101-10,
LOW BLAKEY MOOR 101-11, HIGH BLAKEY MOOR 101-11, STAINMORE
101-11, WHITBY 101-11, RIPON 101-11, RICHMOND 101-11, BOLTON
101-11, PENDRAGON 101-11, POCKLINGTON 101-11, RIVER DERWENT
101-11, EDEN 101-11, GRETA 101-11, SWALE 101-11, HARTLEPOOL
101-12, EASINGTON 101-12, CHEATER 101-12, NEW CASTLE 101-12,
PENRITH 101-12, RIVER TEES 101-12, NORTH TYNE 101-12, SOUTH
TYNE 101-12

*$ABSTRACT 102
  *LIBRARY BOD
  *SLIDE SET TITLE COSTUME
  *NEGATIVE REFERENCE ROLL 170A
  *RENTAL FEE SM 102 $2.75
  *COMMENTS 15 SLIDES FROM SPECULUM HUMANAE SALVATIONIS
  *TITLE OF MANUSCRIPT SPECULUM HUMANAE SALVATIONIS
  *SHELFMARK MS C C C 161
  *PROVENANCE ENGLISH
  *DATE EXECUTED 15TH
  *LANGUAGE LATIN
  *TYPE OF MANUSCRIPT RELIGIOUS TREATISE ON SALVATION
  *CONTENTS   COSTUME   102/1-15, ANGEL AND JOACHIM 102-1, BALAAM'S
  PROPHECY OF THE STAR 102-2, ADORATION OF THE MAGI 102-3, DAVID
  SLAYS LION AND BEAR 102-4, DAVID PLAYS TO SAUL 102-5, JOB
  BEATEN BY HIS WIFE 102-6, SHIMEI CASTS STONES AT DAVID 102-7,
  HANUN INSULTS DAVID'S AMBASSADORS 102-8, ROAD TO CALVARY
  102-9,   EHUD KILLS EGLON 102-10, QUEEN OF SHEBA VISITS SOLOMON
  102-12, ESTHER INTERCEEDS FOR HER PEOPLE 102-11, FEAST OF
  AHASUERUS   102-13,   CHRIST BEFORE PILATE 102-14, CHRIST BEFORE
  HEROD 102-15,

*$ABSTRACT 103
  *LIBRARY BOD
  *SLIDE SET TITLE ARMS AND ARMOUR
  *NEGATIVE REFERENCE ROLL 170B
  *RENTAL FEE SM 103 $2.50
  *TITLE OF MANUSCRIPT SPECULUM HUMANAE SALVATIONIS
  *SHELFMARK MS C C C 161
  *PROVENANCE ENGLISH
  *DATE EXECUTED 15TH
  *LANGUAGE LATIN
  *TYPE OF MANUSCRIPT RELIGIOUS TREATISE ON SALVATION
  *CONTENTS ARMS AND ARMOUR 103/1-10, TOWER BARIS 103-1, GIDEON'S
  FLEECE 103-2, KNIGHTS BRING WATER TO DAVID IN BETHLEHEM 103-3,
  DAVID SLAYS GOLIATH 103-4, HELIODORUS REPULSED FROM TEMPLE
  103-5,   HORSEMEN IN FULL ARMOR 103-5, MELCHIZEDEK 103-6, DAVID
  KILLS 800 PHILISTINES 103-7, NEBUCHADNEZZAR'S BODY CUT IN
  PIECES   BY   HIS   SON 103-8, TOMYRUS KILLS CYRUS 103-9, PHARAOH
  AND HIS HOST DROWNED IN THE RED SEA 103-10, SWORDS 103/1-10,
  HELMETS 103/1-10, ARMOUR 103/1-10, SHIELDS 103/1-10

*$ABSTRACT 104
  *LIBRARY BOD
  *SLIDE SET TITLE LIFE AND WORK
  *NEGATIVE REFERENCE ROLL 170C
  *RENTAL FEE SM 104 $2.60
  *TITLE OF MANUSCRIPT SPECULUM HUMANAE SALVATIONIS
  *SHELFMARK MS C C C 161
  *PROVENANCE ENGLISH
  *DATE EXECUTED 15TH
  *LANGUAGE LATIN
  *TYPE OF MANUSCRIPT RELIGIOUS TREATISE ON SALVATION
  *CONTENTS   OCCUPATIONS   104/1-12,   DOMESTIC EQUIPMENT 104/1-12,
  ADAM/TOIL 104-1,   DISTAFF AND SPINDLE 104-1, SPADE 104-1,
  GARDEN OF EDEN CLOSED 104-2, LOCK AND KNOCKER ON WELL COVER
  104-2, GOLDEN TABLE 104-3, FISHERMEN AND FISHES 104-3, REBECCA
  GIVES DRINK TO ELIEZER 104-4, WELL WITH ROPE AND BUCKET 104-4,
  PASSOVER 104-5, SPIES CARRY GRAPES FROM   ESHCOL   104-6,
  TUBAL-CAIN SMITES ANVIL   104-7,   BLACKSMITH'S LEATHER APRON
  104-7, JONAH PUT IN WHALE'S MOUTH 104-8, SHIP'S RIGGING AND
  RUDDER 104-8, STONE REJECTED BY BUILDERS 104-9, MASONS WITH
  TROWEL/ SET- SQUARE/ HAMMER/ LEVEL 104-9, ELISHA SUPPLIES
  WIDOW WITH OIL 104-10, LOST PIECE OF SILVER FOUND 104-11,
  LANTERN 104-11, JOB FEASTING WITH HIS CHILDREN 104-12, FLAGON
  AND DISH OF FOOD 104-12

61

*$ABSTRACT 105
 *LIBRARY BOD
 *SLIDE SET TITLE CASTLES AND FORTIFICATIONS
 *NEGATIVE REFERENCE ROLL 170D
 *RENTAL FEE SM 105 $2.45
 *TITLE OF MANUSCRIPT SPECULUM HUMANAE SALVATIONIS
 *SHELFMARK MS C C C 161
 *PROVENANCE ENGLISH
 *DATE EXECUTED 15TH
 *LANGUAGE LATIN
 *TYPE OF MANUSCRIPT RELIGIOUS TREATISE ON SALVATION
 *CONTENTS ARCHITECTURE 105/1-9, CLOSED DOOR 105-1, GARGOYLES ON
 PENTAGONAL TOWER 105-1, SOLOMON'S TEMPLE 105-2, PERSIAN QUEEN
 IN HANGING GARDEN 105-3, JEREMIAH WEEPS OVER JERUSALEM 105-4,
 KING OF MOAB SACRIFICES FIRST-BORN SON 105-5, ELEPHANT AND
 CASTLE 105-6, ELEAZAR PIERCES ELEPHANT WITH SPEAR 105-6,
 MICHAL DERIDES KING DAVID 105-7, MICHAL HELPS DAVID ESCAPE
 105-8, MIRACLE OF THE PASSION 105-9, TOWERS 105/1-9, CASTLES
 105/1-9, BATTLEMENTS 105/1-9, PORTCULLIS 105/6-7

*$ABSTRACT 106
 *LIBRARY BOD
 *SLIDE SET TITLE GOTHIC SCRIPT
 *NEGATIVE REFERENCE ROLL 170E
 *RENTAL FEE SM 106 $3.25
 *COMMENTS 25 SLIDES SELECTED FROM 6 MSS SHOWING GOTHIC SCRIPT
 *TITLE OF MANUSCRIPT PENTATEUCH 106/1-6, ORMESBY PSALTER
 106/7-9,
 *SHELFMARK MS AUCT E INF 7 106/1-6, MS DOUCE 366 106/7-9, MS
 LAT LITURG E 6 106/10-12, MS LAT LITURG E 37 106-13, MS CANON
 LITURG 192 106/14-15, MS ORIEL COLLEGE 75 106/16-25
 *PROVENANCE ENGLISH 106/1-13 AND 16-25, FRENCH 106/14-15
 *DATE EXECUTED 13TH 106/1-9, 14TH 106/10-15, 15TH 106/16-25
 *LANGUAGE LATIN
 *TYPE OF MANUSCRIPT PENTATEUCH 106/1-9, BIBLE 106/10-15, MISSAL
 106/16-25
 *CONTENTS GOTHIC SCRIPT 106/1-25, PALEOGRAPHY 106/1-25, GENESIS
 14-15 106-1, EXODUS/ BEGINNING OF BOOK 106-2, LEVITICUS/
 BEGINNING OF BOOK 106-3, NUMBERS/ BEGINNING OF BOOK 106-4,
 NUMBERS 7-8 106-5, DEUTERONOMY 106-6, ORMESBY PSALTER/ TYPICAL
 PAGE 106-7, INITIAL D 106-8, RESURRECTED CHRIST WITH BANNER
 106-8, ORMESBY PSALTER/ PAGE IN SECTION 3 106-9, CALENDAR
 106-10, TEXT 106-11, ILLUMINATED INITIALS 106-12, RUBRICS AND
 INITIALS 106-13, CAPITAL B 106-14, DAVID PLAYING HARP 106-14,
 MAGNIFICAT AND AVE MARIA 106-14, DETAIL OF DISC WITH
 MAGNIFICAT AND AVE MARIA 106-15, BLESSING OF HOLY WATER
 106-16, NATIVITY 106-17, BORDERS AND DOUBLE OPENING 106-18, TE
 IGITUR 106-19, ABRAHAM AND ISAAC 106-19, RESURRECTION IN
 INITIAL 106-20, PENTECOST IN INITIAL 106-21, INITIALS AND
 BORDER 106-22, DOUBLE OPENING SHOWING INITIALS 106/23-24,
 INITIALS 106-25

*$ABSTRACT 107
 *LIBRARY BOD
 *SLIDE SET TITLE ORGANS
 *NEGATIVE REFERENCE ROLL 170F
 *RENTAL FEE SM 107 $2.75
 *COMMENTS 15 SLIDES SELECTED FROM 11 MSS DEPICTING ORGANS
 *SHELFMARK MS C NON LITURG 388 F 225 107-1, MS C C C 17 F 99
 107-2, MS DOUCE 6 107/3-4, MS DOUCE 39 107-5, MS DOUCE 62
 107-6, MS DOUCE 77 107/7-8, MS DOUCE 80 107-9, MS DOUCE 266
 107/10-11, MS DOUCE 267 107/12-13, MS GOUGH LITURG 15 107-14,
 MS RAWL LITURG E 24 107-15
 *PROVENANCE ITALIAN 107-1, ENGLISH 107-2, FLEMISH 107/3-4 AND
 10-11 AND 14, FRENCH 107/5-9 AND 12-13 AND 15
 *DATE EXECUTED 14TH 107/3-6 AND 9-11, 15TH 107/2 AND 7-8 AND
 12-14
 *CONTENTS MUSICAL INSTRUMENTS/ ORGANS 107/1-15, ORGANS

107/1-15, PORTATIVE ORGAN 107/1-3 AND 7-9 AND 12-13 AND 15,
PSALTERY 107-5, POSITIVE ORGAN 107/10-11

*$ABSTRACT 108
  *LIBRARY BOD
  *SLIDE SET TITLE INFANCY OF CHRIST
  *NEGATIVE REFERENCE ROLL 170G
  *RENTAL FEE SM 108 $3.10
  *COMMENTS 22 SLIDES SELECTED FROM ACTS OF ST MARY AND JESUS
  *TITLE OF MANUSCRIPT VITA GLORIOSISSIME VIRGINIS MARIAE
  *SHELFMARK MS CANON MISC 476
  *PROVENANCE ITALIAN/ VENICE
  *DATE EXECUTED 14TH
  *LANGUAGE LATIN
  *TYPE OF MANUSCRIPT LIFE OF CHRIST
  *CONTENTS CHRIST/ LIFE OF 108/1-22, ANNUNCIATION WITH MARY AT
  DESK 108-1, NATIVITY WITH HOLY FAMILY/ OX/ ASS / ANGELS
  108-2, MARY PUTS BABY INTO MANGER 108-3, SONG OF JOSEPH 108-3,
  ADORATION OF THE MAGI 108-4, PRESENTATION IN THE TEMPLE 108-5,
  WARNING FOR FLIGHT INTO EGYPT 108-6, FLIGHT INTO EGYPT 108-6,
  MIRACLES ON FLIGHT INTO EGYPT 108/7-22, MIRACLE OF THE DRAGONS
  108-7, MIRACLE OF THE LOAVES OF BREAD 108-8, MIRACLE OF THE
  DEER/ CALVES/ WILD BEASTS 108-8, CLOUDS PROTECT HOLY FAMILY
  FROM HEAT OF SUN 108-9, BIRDS WORSHIP JESUS AND SING TO HOLY
  FAMILY 108-9, FIRST RECOGNITION OF JESUS IN EGYPT 108-10, HOLY
  FAMILY GIVEN LODGING BY BEARDED EGYPTIAN 108-11, JOSEPH WORKS
  AS CARPENTER IN EGYPT 108-11, JESUS AS INFANT LEARNS TO WALK
  108-11, JESUS AT 10 108-12, JESUS AS CHILD RESTORING WATER POT
  108-12, JESUS AS CHILD HEALS SNAKE BITE 108-13, MULTIPLICATION
  OF THE BREAD IN EGYPT 108-13, VIRGIN AS GODDESS AND JESUS AS
  SON OF JUPITER 108-14, JESUS CROWNED BY EGYPTIAN BOYS 108-14,
  ANGEL COMMANDS JOSEPH TO RETURN TO JUDEA 108-14, JOSEPH
  COLLECTS HERBS IN BASKET FOR MOTHER 108-15, JESUS ACCUSED OF
  CASTING PERSON FROM MOUNTAIN 108-16, JESUS SUSPENDS JAR ON
  SUNBEAM OVER WELL 108-17, MARY TAKES JESUS TO SCHOOL 108-17,
  JESUS CREATES FISH-POND 108-18, JESUS MAKES AND CAUSES CLAY
  BIRDS TO FLY 108-19, LIONS ON ROCK ADORE JESUS 108-20, MARY
  FITS TUNIC ON JESUS 108-21, MARY AND JOSEPH TAKE JESUS TO
  JERUSALEM 108-22

*$ABSTRACT 109
  *LIBRARY BOD
  *SLIDE SET TITLE SURGERY
  *NEGATIVE REFERENCE ROLL 170H
  *RENTAL FEE SM 109 $2.50
  *COMMENTS COMPOSITE LATIN SCIENTIFIC MS
  *SHELFMARK MS ASHMOLE 1462 109/1-5, MS E MUSAEO 19 109/6-10
  *PROVENANCE ENGLISH 109/1-5, ITALIAN 109/6-10
  *DATE EXECUTED 13TH 109/1-5, 14TH 109/6-10
  *LANGUAGE LATIN
  *TYPE OF MANUSCRIPT SCIENTIFIC 109/1-5, SURGICAL TRACTS
  109/6-10
  *CONTENTS MEDICAL TRACTS/ SURGERY 109/1-10, SURGERY 109/1-10,
  FIGURES STANDING AND RECUMBENT WITH RED SPOTS 109/1-4, SURGEON
  OPERATING ON EYE 109-3, SURGEON OPERATING ON NOSE 109-4, MAD
  DOG AND BITTEN MAN 109-5, HENNEBANE 109-5, SIMPHONIACA/ OMEN
  OF RECOVERY 109-5, MUSIC DURING OPERATION 109-6, SURGICAL
  INSTRUMENTS IN MARGINAL DRAWINGS 109/7-8, SURGEON BETWEEN
  OPERATING TABLE AND NAKED PATIENT 109-9, DOCTORS/FAMOUS
  CAUTERISING PATIENTS 109-10

*$ABSTRACT 110
  *LIBRARY BOD
  *SLIDE SET TITLE MUSICAL MANUSCRIPT FRAGMENTS
  *NEGATIVE REFERENCE ROLL 170I
  *RENTAL FEE SM 110 $4.00

63

*SHELFMARK MS C C C 59 110/1-3, MS C C C 134 110/4-23,MS C C
 489 110/24-40
*PROVENANCE ENGLISH/ LLANTHONY
*DATE EXECUTED 13TH 110/1-3, 12TH 110/4-23
*LANGUAGE LATIN
*TYPE OF MANUSCRIPT GLOSSES ON PSALMS 110/1-3, MUSICAL TEXT
 110/4-40
*CONTENTS MUSICAL FRAGMENTS FROM 3 CORPUS CHRISTI COLLEGE MS
 110/1-40

*$ABSTRACT 111
 *LIBRARY BOD
 *SLIDE SET TITLE TOURNAMENTS
 *NEGATIVE REFERENCE ROLL 171F
 *RENTAL FEE SM 111 $2.75
 *TITLE OF MANUSCRIPT LES TOURNOIS DE CHAUVENCY
 *SHELFMARK MS DOUCE 308C/ FOL 107D-139V
 *PROVENANCE FRENCH LORRAINE
 *DATE EXECUTED 14TH/C1320
 *LANGUAGE FRENCH
 *AUTHOR JACQUES BRETEL
 *TYPE OF MANUSCRIPT ROMANCE
 *CONTENTS LITERATURE/ LES TOURNOIS DE CHAUVENCY 111/1-15
 ROMANCE/ FRENCH/ 14TH 111/1-15, FRENCH LITERATURE/ LE
 TOURNOIS DE CHAUVENCY 111/1-15, TOURNAMENTS 111/1-15, POET AN
 CONRAD WARNIER 111-1, JOUST BETWEEN FERRI DE CHARDOGNE AN
 SIEUR DE BAZARTIN 111-2, JOUST BETWEEN SIEUR DER FAUCOGNEY AN
 SIEUR DE BERGHEIM 111-3, JOUST BETWEEN MILLET DE TIL AND FERR
 DER SIERCK 111-4, LADY IN RED ROBE DANCES BEFORE KNIGHT
 111-5, JOUST BETWEEN PERART DE GRILLI AND CANON D'OUVIER
 111-6, JOUST BETWEEN HENRY DE BRIEY AND CONRADIN WARNIE
 111-7, JOUST BETWEEN JOFFREY D'ASPREMONT AND SIEUR DE SARCER
 111-8, JOUST BETWEEN HENRI DE BLAMONT AND SIEUR DE GEMIGN
 111-9, JOUST BETWEEN WALERAN DE LIGNY AND WICHART D'AMANC
 111-10, JOUST BETWEEN JOFFROI D'NEUVILLE AND BAUDOI
 D'AUBRECHICOURT 111-11, JOUST BETWEEN RENAUT DE TRIE AN
 GERART DE LOOZ 111-12, ROBARDEL DANCE 111-13, TOURNAMEN
 111-14, MELEE AT TOURNAMENT OF UNIDENTIFIED HORSEMEN 111-15

*$ABSTRACT 112
 *LIBRARY BOD
 *SLIDE SET TITLE VISITATION
 *NEGATIVE REFERENCE ROLL 171G
 *RENTAL FEE SM 112 $2.45
 *COMMENTS 9 SLIDES SELECTED FROM MSS DEPICTING THE VISITATION
 *SHELFMARK MS DOUCE 93 112-1, MS DOUCE 248 112-2, MS BUCHANAN
 13 112-3, MS BUCHANAN E 12 112-4, MS DOUCE 152 112-5, MS DOUC
 135 112-6, MS DOUCE 39 112-7, MS RAWL LITURG E 36 112-8, M
 BUCHANAN E 5 112-9
 *PROVENANCE DUTCH 112/1-2, FRENCH 112/3-8, FLEMISH 112-9
 *DATE EXECUTED 14TH 112/5 AND 7, 15TH 112/2-4, 16TH 112/6 AN
 8-9
 *LANGUAGE LATIN
 *TYPE OF MANUSCRIPT BIBLE
 *CONTENTS VISITATION 112/1-9, INITIAL OF THE VISITATION 112-1
 HUNTING SCENE IN BORDER 112-1, ELISABETH UNDER DOORWAY 112-2
 VIRGIN AND ST ELISABETH BEFORE LANDSCAPE WITH CASTLE 112-3, S
 ELISABETH RUSHES TO MEET VIRGIN 112-4, VIRGIN AND ST ELISABET
 BEFORE CASTLE GATE 112-5, MINIATURE WITH ARCHEITECTURAL BORDE
 112-6, ST ELISABETH WELCOMES VIRGIN 112-7, ST ELISABETH LAYIN
 HAND ON VIRGINØS PREGNANT FORM 112-8, ST ELISABETH AND VIRGI
 IN LANDSCAPE WITH MOATED HOUSE 112-9

*$ABSTRACT 113
 *LIBRARY BOD
 *SLIDE SET TITLE BATHSHEBA

*NEGATIVE REFERENCE ROLL 171I
*RENTAL FEE SM 113 $2.50
*COMMENTS   BATHSHEBA   SELECTION   FROM   9   MSS   OF   THE   13-16TH
CENTURIES
*SHELFMARK   MS   AUCT   D 4 8 113-1, MS CANON LITURG 99 113-2, MS
RAWL LITURG E 33 113-3, MS RAWL LITURG E 21 113-4, MS RAWL
LITURG E 20 113-5, MS NEW COLLEGE 323 113-6, MS RAWL LITURG E
36 113-7, MS DOUCE 135 113/8-9, MS DOUCE 19 113-10
*PROVENANCE ENGLISH 113-1, FRENCH 113/2-5 AND 7-9, FLEMISH
113-6, ITALIAN 113-10
*DATE EXECUTED 13TH 113-1, 15TH 113/2-5, 16TH 113/6-10
*LANGUAGE LATIN
*TYPE OF MANUSCRIPT BIBLE 113-1, BOOK OF HOURS 113/2-3 AND
5-10, HOURS OF THE VIRGIN MARY 113-4
*CONTENTS BATHSHEBA SCENES 113/1-10

*$ABSTRACT 114
*LIBRARY BOD
*SLIDE SET TITLE PSALTER ILLUSTRATIONS
*NEGATIVE REFERENCE ROLL 171J
*RENTAL FEE SM 114 $2.60
*SHELFMARK MS DOUCE 50
*PROVENANCE ENGLISH
*DATE EXECUTED 13TH/1250-1300
*LANGUAGE LATIN
*TYPE OF MANUSCRIPT PSALTER
*CONTENTS PSALTER/ ENGLISH/ 13TH 114/1-12, CHRIST ENTHRONED
114-1, HELL AND DEVILS 114-2, ADORATION OF THE MAGI 114-3,
PRESENTATION IN THE TEMPLE 114-3, ASCENSION 114-4, PENTECOST
114-4, BEATUS VIR 114-5, DAVID SLINGS STONE AT GOLIATH AND
CUTS HEAD 114-5, ANNOINTING OF DAVID 114-6, DIXI CUSTODIAM
114-7, DAVID HOLDS TONGUE AND CHRIST IN ADMONITION 114-7,
DIXIT INSIPIENS 114-8, FOOL BITING STONE AND DAVID OPPOSITE
114-8, SALVUM ME FAC 114-9, DAVID DESPAIRING AND BESEECHING
GOD 114-9, EXULTATE DEO 114-10, DAVID PLAYING HANDBELLS AND
HARP 114-10, CANTATE DOMINO 114-11, MONKS BEFORE LECTERN
114-11, DIXIT DOMINUS 114-12, TRINITY WITH FATHER AND SON AND
CROSS-NIMBED DOVE 114-12

*$ABSTRACT 115
*LIBRARY BOD
*SLIDE SET TITLE PSALTER ILLUSTRATIONS
*NEGATIVE REFERENCE ROLL 172A
*RENTAL FEE SM 115 $2.70
*SHELFMARK MS BARLOW 22
*PROVENANCE ENGLISH/ PETERBOROUGH
*DATE EXECUTED 14TH/C1321-41
*LANGUAGE LATIN
*ARTIST/ SCHOOL EAST ANGLIAN SCHOOL
*TYPE OF MANUSCRIPT PSALTER
*CONTENTS PSALTER/ ENGLISH/ 14TH 115/1-14, ANNUNCIATION 115-1,
NATIVITY 115-1, ADORATION OF THE MAGI 115-1, PRESENTATION
115-1, CHRIST IN MIDST OF THE DOCTORS 115-2, BETRAYAL 115-2,
SCOURGING 115-2, CHRIST BEARING CROSS 115-2, CRUCIFIXION
115-3, DESCENT FROM CROSS 115-3, ENTOMBMENT 115-3,
RESURRECTION 115-3, JESUS APPEARS TO MARY MAGDALENE 115-4,
JESUS APPEARS TO THOMAS 115-4, RESURRECTION 115-4, PENTECOST
115-4, CORONATION OF VIRGIN WITH JOHN/EVANGELIST AND
JOHN/BAPTIST 115-5, VIRGIN'S DEATH 115-5, ASSUMPTION OF VIRGIN
115-5, HISTORIATED PSALM INITIALS 115/6-14, BEATUS VIR 115-6,
JESSE TREE 115-6, DOMINUS ILLUMINATIO MEA 115-7, DAVID POINTS
TO HIS EYES 115-7, DIXI CUSTODIAM 115-8, CHRIST WITH BOOK
BEFORE SEATED KING 115-8, QUID GLORIARIS 115-9, FIGURE PIERCES
SELF WITH SWORD AND JESTER WITH BAUBLE 115-9, DIXIT INSIPIENS
115-10, KING SEATED WITH JESTER 115-10, SALVUM ME FAC 115-11,
JONAH SWALLOWED BY WHALE 115-11, EXULTATE DEO 115-12, DAVID
HAMMERS BELLS AND SMALL BOY WITH PIPES 115-12, CANTATE DOMINO
115-13, MONKS/ONE WITH LYRE 115-13, DIXIT DOMINUS 115-14,
TRINITY 115-14

*$ABSTRACT 116
 *LIBRARY BOD
 *SLIDE SET TITLE BACKGROUND TO CHAUCER
 *NEGATIVE REFERENCE ROLL 172B
 *RENTAL FEE SM 116 $2.75
 *COMMENTS 15 SLIDES FROM THE ROMANCE OF ALEXANDER
 *TITLE OF MANUSCRIPT ROMANCE OF ALEXANDER
 *SHELFMARK MS BODLEY 264
 *PROVENANCE FLEMISH
 *DATE EXECUTED 14TH/1338-1344
 *LANGUAGE FRENCH
 * ARTIST/ SCHOOL JEHAN DE GRISE
 *TYPE OF MANUSCRIPT ROMANCE
 *CONTENTS LITERATURE/ BACKGROUND TO CHAUCER 116/1-15, ROMANC
 OF ALEXANDER 116/1-15, PEASANTS DANCING 116-1, FRIAR PREACHIN
 116-2, ALEXANDER BORNE UP BY GRIFONS 116-3, MEN APPROACHIN
 MILL WITH SACK AND ONE ON HORSEBACK 116-4, MAN PREPARING T
 JOUST WITH TARGET 116-5, HUNTSMEN WITH HOUNDS AND BLOWING HOR
 116-6, CHESS GAME WITH WOMAN BEATING MAN 116-7, MAN LIFT
 WOMAN ON SHOULDERS 116-8, COCK AND HEN TREADING AND ROOSTER
 FIGHT 116-9, PRIEST MARRIES COUPLE IN FRONT OF CHURCH WIT
 WITNESS 116-10, BOYS PLAYING GAME WITH BOARD 116-11, ARMOURER
 POLISHING SWORD AND SHARPENING ON GRINDSTONE 116-12, KITCHE
 SCENE WITH MORTAR AND BASTING CHICKENS 116-13, SMITH PREPARE
 METAL INSTRUMENTS AROUND FORGE 116-14, MUSICAL INSTRUMENT
 NAKER/ FITHELE/ GYTERNE/ HARP 116-15

*$ABSTRACT 117
 *LIBRARY BOD
 *SLIDE SET TITLE MIRACLES FROM THE FRANCISCAN MISSAL
 *NEGATIVE REFERENCE ROLL 172G
 *RENTAL FEE SM 117 $3.20
 *SHELFMARK MS DOUCE 313
 *PROVENANCE FRENCH
 *DATE EXECUTED 14TH/ MIDDLE
 *LANGUAGE LATIN
 *ARTIST/ SCHOOL BY A FOLLOWER OF JEAN PUCELLE
 *TYPE OF MANUSCRIPT MISSAL/ FRANCISCAN
 *CONTENTS MIRACLES OF CHRIST 117/1-24, CHRIST/ MIRACLE
 117/1-24, CHRIST AND THE LEPER 117-1, STORM ON LAKE OF GALILE
 117-2, CHRIST HEALS BLIND MAN 117-3, CHRIST BLESSES PARALYZE
 SERVANT 117-4, CHRIST WALKING ON THE WATERS OF LAKE 117-5
 CHRIST TOLD SERVANTS GET SCRAPS FROM MASTER'S TABLES 117-6
 CHRIST TALKS TO CRIPPLE NEAR POOL OF BETHESDA 117-7, CHRIS
 CASTING OUT WINGED DEVIL FROM DUMB MAN 117-8, CHRIST HEALIN
 MAN BLIND FRON HIS BIRTH 117-9, CHRIST RAISING WIDOW'S SON T
 LIFE IN NAIN 117-10, CHRIST HEALING MAN WITH PALSY 117-11
 CHRIST HEALING SIMON'S MOTHER OF FEVER 117-12, MIRACULOU
 DRAUGHT OF FISHES IN NET WITH WIDE MESHES 117-13, CHRIST HEAL
 DEAF MAN WITH SPEECH IMPEDIMENT 117-14, HEALING OF LEPER
 117-15, RAISING OF WIDOW'S SON AT NAIN 117-16, CHRIST HEAL
 DROPSY 117-17, CHRIST HEALING ONE POSSESSED WITH DUMB SPIRI
 117-18, CHRIST HEALS THE CROOKED WOMAN 117-19, CHRIST HEALIN
 MAN SICK WITH PALSY 117-20, CHRIST HEALING NOBLEMAN'S SON A
 CAPERNAUM 117-21, CHRIST ASKED TO HEAL RULER'S DAUGHTER O
 BLOOD ISSUE 117-22, PETER AND JOHN HEAL LAME MAN AT BEAUTIFU
 GATE 117-23, PETER SAVED FROM PRISON BY ANGEL 117-24

*$ABSTRACT 118
 *LIBRARY BOD
 *SLIDE SET TITLE PARABLES FROM THE FRANCISCAN MISSAL
 *NEGATIVE REFERENCE ROLL 172H
 *RENTAL FEE SM 118 $2.95
 *SHELFMARK MS DOUCE 313
 *PROVENANCE FRENCH
 *DATE EXECUTED 14TH/ MIDDLE
 *LANGUAGE LATIN
 *ARTIST/ SCHOOL BY A FOLLOWER OF JEAN PUCELLE

66

*TYPE OF MANUSCRIPT MISSAL/ FRANCISCAN
*CONTENTS CHRIST/ PARABLES 118/1-19, PARABLES OF CHRIST
 118/1-19, CHRIST TELLING DISCIPLES OF SIGNS IN SUN/ MOON/
 STARS 118-1, CHRIST THE GOOD SHEPHERD 118-2, CHRIST HOLDING
 LAMP 118-3, EVANGELISTS ADJURED TO GIRD THEIR LOINS 118-3,
 PARABLES 118/4-19, SOWER WHO SOWED GOOD SEED 118-4, WORKERS IN
 VINEYARD 118-5, SOWER WHOSE SEED FELL ON VARYING GROUND 118-6,
 DIVES AND LAZARUS 118-7, LAZARUS 118-7, VINEYARD PARABLE
 118-8, PRODIGAL SON 118-9, FEEDING OF THE FIVE THOUSAND
 118-10, UNJUST STEWARD 118-11, PUBLICAN AND THE SINNER 118-12,
 GOOD SAMARITAN 118-13, MARRIAGE OF KING@S SON 118-14, KING
 THAT TOOK ACCOUNT OF HIS SERVANTS 118-15, TALENTS PARABLE
 118-16, POUNDS PARABLE 118-17,TREASURE HIDDEN IN FIELD 118-18,
 WISE AND FOOLISH VIRGINS 118-19

*$ABSTRACT 119
 *LIBRARY BOD
 *SLIDE SET TITLE CLASSICAL TEXTS I GREEK
 *NEGATIVE REFERENCE ROLL 173A
 *RENTAL FEE SM 119 $2.45
 *TITLE OF MANUSCRIPT PECTARUM LESBIORUM FRAGMENTA 119-2,
 HAWARA/ BISHMU/ ARSINAE 119-3, PARMENIDES 119-4, DIALOGUES
 119-4, ELEMENTS 119-5, GREEK PALIMSEST 119-6, OFFICIIS
 119-8,EDITIO PRINCEPS 119-9
 *SHELFMARK MS GR CLASS 119-1, MS GR CLASS O 76/1 119-2, MS GR
 CLASS A L 119-3, MS E D CLARKE 39 119-4, MS D/ORVILLE 301
 119-5, MS BAROCCI 197 119-6, MS AUCT V 1 51 119-7, MS AUCT L 3
 6 119-8, BYW C 6 2 119-9
 *PROVENANCE GREEK
 *DATE EXECUTED 01ST/79 119-1, 02ND 119/2-3, 09TH/895 AND 888
 119/4-5, 14TH/1344 AND 1363-1437 119/6-7, 15TH/1465 AND 1488
 119/8-9
 *LANGUAGE GREEK
 *AUTHOR SAPPHO 119-2, HOMER 119/3 AND 9, PLATO 119-4, EUCLID
 119-5, CICERO 119-8
 *TYPE OF MANUSCRIPT PAPYRUS ROLLS 119-1, EPIC 119/2 AND 7 AND
 9, PHILOSOPHY 119/4 AND 8, MATHEMATICS 119-5, GOSPEL BOOK WITH
 OLD TESTAMENT LESSONS 119-6
 *CONTENTS GREEK CLASSICAL TEXTS 119/1-9

*$ABSTRACT 120
 *LIBRARY BOD
 *SLIDE SET TITLE CALENDAR FROM A BOOK OF HOURS
 *NEGATIVE REFERENCE ROLL 173B
 *RENTAL FEE SM 120 $2.60
 *TITLE OF MANUSCRIPT BOOK OF HOURS
 *SHELFMARK MS AUCT D INF 2 11
 *PROVENANCE FRENCH
 *DATE EXECUTED 15TH/C1440-50
 *LANGUAGE LATIN AND FRENCH
 *ARTIST/ SCHOOL MASTER OF SIR JOHN FASTOLF
 *TYPE OF MANUSCRIPT BOOK OF HOURS/ USE OF SARUM
 *CONTENTS CALENDAR 120/1-12, OCCUPATIONS OF THE MONTHS
 120/1-12, BOOK OF HOURS/ FRENCH/ 15TH 120/1-12, JANUARY 120-1,
 JANUS FEASTING 120-1, AQUARIUS 120-1, FEBRUARY 120-2, FIRESIDE
 SCENE 120-2, PISCES 120-2, MARCH 120-3, VINE TRIMMING 120-3,
 ARIES 120-3, APRIL 120-4, GATHERING GREEN BRANCHES 120-4,
 TAURUS 120-4, MAY 120-5, HAWKING 120-5, GEMINI 120-5, JUNE
 120-6, MOWING 120-6, CANCER 120-6, JULY 120-7, REAPING 130-7,
 LEO 120-7, AUGUST 120-8, THRESHING 120-8, VIRGO 120-8,
 SEPTEMBER 120-9, WINE PRESSING 120-9, LIBRA 120-9, OCTOBER
 120-10, SOWING 120-10, SCORPIO 120-10, NOVEMBER 120-11, PIG
 FEEDING 120-11, SAGITARIUS 120-11, DECEMBER 120-12,
 SLAUGHTERING 120-12,CAPRICORN 120-12

*$ABSTRACT 121
  *LIBRARY BOD
  *SLIDE SET TITLE SAINTS
  *NEGATIVE REFERENCE ROLL 173C
  *RENTAL FEE SM 121 $3.10
  *TITLE OF MANUSCRIPT BOOK OF HOURS
  *SHELFMARK MS AUCT D INF 2 11
  *PROVENANCE FRENCH
  *DATE EXECUTED 15TH/C1440-50
  *LANGUAGE LATIN AND FRENCH
  *ARTIST/ SCHOOL MASTER OF SIR JOHN FASTOLF
  *TYPE OF MANUSCRIPT BOOK OF HOURS/ USE OF SARUM
  *CONTENTS SAINTS 121/1-22, BOOK OF HOURS/ FRENCH/ 15
  121/1-22, ST MICHAEL WITH WINGS AND DRAGON 121-1, ST JOHN T
  BAPTIST WITH LAMB 121-2, ST JOHN EVANGELIST WITH DRAGON IN C
  AND EAGLE 121-3, SS PETER AND PAUL WITH KEY AND SWORD 121-
  ST ANDREW MARTYRED WITH CROSS SALTIRE 121-5, ST STEPHEN
  VESTMENTS BEING STONED 121-6, ST GEORGE WITH RED-CROSS EMBL
  AND DRAGON 121-7, ST LAWRENCE IS GRILLED 121-8, ST EUSTAC
  LOSING HIS SONS AND WIFE 121-9, ST CHRISTOPHER WITH CHI
  121-10, ST SEBASTIAN BEING MARTYRED WITH ARROWS 121-11, S
  NICHOLAS WITH THREE CHILDREN IN PICKLING TUB 121-12, ST AN
  AND THE VIRGIN 121-13, ST MARY MAGDALEN WITH OINTMENT P
  121-14, ST CATHERINE WITH WHEEL 121-15, ST MARGARET WI
  DRAGON 121-16, ST ETHELBURGA 121-17, ST WINIFRED 121-18, A
  SAINTS 121-19, MASS OF ST GREGORY 121-20, ST JEROME WI
  CARDINAL@S HAT AND LION 121-21, CHRIST CROWNED WITH THORN
  121-22

*$ABSTRACT 122
  *LIBRARY BOD
  *SLIDE SET TITLE FIGURES AND GROTESQUES
  *NEGATIVE REFERENCE ROLL 173E
  *RENTAL FEE SM 122 $2.60
  *TITLE OF MANUSCRIPT HISTORIA ALEXANDRI MAGNI
  *SHELFMARK MS LAUD MISC 751
  *PROVENANCE FLEMISH
  *DATE EXECUTED 15TH/C1470-80
  *LANGUAGE FRENCH
  *ARTIST/ SCHOOL MASTER OF THE CHRONICLE OF ENGLAND
  *AUTHOR CURTIUS/ QUINTUS, VASQUE DE LUCENE/ TRANSLATOR
  *TYPE OF MANUSCRIPT ROMANCE
  *CONTENTS LITERATURE/ CHRONICLE OF ALEXANDER 122/1-2
  CHRONICLE OF ALEXANDER 122/1-21, FRENCH LITERATURE/ CHRONICI
  OF ALEXANDER 122/1-22, GROTESQUES AND FIGURES 122/1-2
  GROTESQUE FACES 122-1, HAIRY FIGURE WITH LANCE RIDING ON BE
  122-2, FIGURES SEATED WITH EMPTY CHESSBOARD 122-3, MAN WI
  BILL-HOOK 122-4, MAN ABOUT TO KILL PIG WITH AXE 122-5, M
  WITH FORELEGS OF WHITE HORSE OVER HIS SHOULDERS 122-6 ARCH
  IN RED JERKIN 122-7, MEN GATHER GRAPES INTO BASKET 122-
  NAKED BEARDED FIGURE WITH CROWN ABOUT TO CLUB BIRD 122-
  MOUNTED KNIGHT IN PLATE ARMOUR 122-10, GROTESQUE FIGURE
  CRUTCHES WITH BASKET OF MONKEYS 122-11, MAN WEARING SWORD A
  AIMING CROSS-BOW 122-12, ARCHER DRAWING LONG-BOW 122-13, M
  PUSHING WHEELBARROW WITH WOMAN PLAYING BAGPIPES 122-1
  GROTESQUE WITH HALF ANIMAL BODY HUMAN FACE AND HAT 122-15, M
  IN APRON REVEALS POSTERIOR TO LADY WITH DISTAFF 122-16, M
  WINDING CROSS-BOW 122-17, MAN SPEARING DOG IN MOUTH 122-1
  MAN ATTACKING KNIGHT THOUGH UNARMED 122-19, CITIZEN IN LO
  RED ROBE ON HORSEBACK 122-20, HAIRY MAN RIDING HORSE WI
  SHIELD AND LANCE 122-21

*$ABSTRACT 123
  *LIBRARY BOD
  *SLIDE SET TITLE ARCHITECTURE AND CASTLE LIFE
  *NEGATIVE REFERENCE ROLL 173F
  *RENTAL FEE SM 123 $2.95
  *TITLE OF MANUSCRIPT HISTORIA ALEXANDRI MAGNI

*SHELFMARK MS LAUD MISC 751
*PROVENANCE FLEMISH
*DATE EXECUTED 15TH/C1470-80
*LANGUAGE FRENCH
*ARTIST/ SCHOOL MASTER OF THE CHRONICLE OF ENGLAND
*AUTHOR CURTIUS/ QUINTUS, VASQUE DE LUCENE/ TRANSLATOR
*TYPE OF MANUSCRIPT ROMANCE
*CONTENTS   LITERATURE/   CHRONICLE   OF   ALEXANDER   123/1-19,
CHRONICLE OF ALEXANDER 123/1-19, FRENCH LITERATURE/ CHRONICLE
OF ALEXANDER 123/1-19, ARCHITECTURE 123/1-19, PRESENTATION OF
BOOK   BY   TRANSLATOR   TO   CHARLES   THE   BOLD   123-1,   ARMS   OF
ENGELBERT OF NASSAU 123-1, ALEXANDER THE GREAT'S BIRTH 123-2,
PHILIP AND ALEXANDER AND ARMY OUTSIDE GATES OF ATHENS   123-3,
ALEXANDER   AND   SOLDIERS   KNEELING   BEFORE   GOLD STATUE 123-4,
BATTLE'S END AGAINST DARIUS   123-5,   ALEXANDER   AT   SIDON   AND
ABDOLOMINUS   GIVEN   GOLD   GARMENT 123-6, WATER-CHUTE TO WOODEN
MILL-WHEEL 123-6, ARBELA SURRENDERED AND ALEXANDER ON WHITE
HORSE   123-7,   ALEXANDER'S   COURT   AND   LANDSCAPE   WITH CASTLE
123-8, PHILOTAS BEFORE ALEXANDER AND THREATENED BY SOLDIERS
123-9, CHURCH WITH BELL TOWER AND BELL 123-9, POLEMON PARDONED
123-10, PARMENIO KILLED AS READS LETTER FROM ALEXANDER 123-11,
BESSUS   AND   COBARES   AT   FEAST 123-12, SLAUGHTER OF BRANCIDAE
123-13,   SCYTHIAN   AMBASSADORS   BEFORE   ALEXANDER   123-14,
ALEXANDER'S   ARMY   CROSSING   RIVER   TO FIGHT SCYTHIANS 123-15,
ALEXANDER   FEASTING   TO   CELEBRATE   KILLING   OF   LION   123-16,
MESSENGER   PRESENTS   LETTER   FROM ALEXANDER TO ROXANNA 123-17,
PEACOCK THE SYMBOL OF JUPITER 123-17, ALEXANDER AND OTHER KING
IN BATTLE 123-18, EXECUTION OF CLEANDER/ SITALCES/ AGATHON/
AND HERACON 123-19, ALEXANDER AND OFFICERS WATCH EXECUTION
FROM BALCONY 123-19,

*$ABSTRACT 124
*LIBRARY BOD
*SLIDE SET TITLE ARTIST AT WORK II
*NEGATIVE REFERENCE ROLL 173H
*RENTAL FEE SM 124 $2.65
*COMMENTS 8 SLIDES DEPICTING ILLUMINATIONS IN VARIOUS STAGES OF
COMPLETION
*TITLE OF MANUSCRIPT JUSTIN ABBREVIATION OF TROGUS POMPEIUS
*SHELFMARK MS AUCT F 2 29
*PROVENANCE ITALIAN
*DATE EXECUTED 15TH
*LANGUAGE ITALIAN
*AUTHOR JUSTIN ABBREVIATION OF TROGUS POMPEIUS
*TYPE OF MANUSCRIPT HISTORY
*CONTENTS   ARTIST   AT   WORK   124/1-8,   SOLDIERS   DISEMBARK   BY
GANGPLANK   AND FIGHT 124-1, PTOLEMY/AMBASSADORS PRESENT CROWNS
124-1, ARMY LED BY EUMENES ATTACK CASTLE 124-2, WALLED TOWN
124-2, WALLED TOWN 124-2, EUMENES ATTACKED AND KILLED OUTSIDE
CASTLE WALL   124-2,   ALEXANDER   MEETS   THELESTRIAS/   QUEEN   OF
AMAZONS   124-3, ALEXANDER SLAYS CLITUS 124-3, ARMED MAN RUSHES
OUT OF CASTLE TO MEET SOLDIERS   124-3,   ALEXANDER   SEATED   AT
TABLE   WITH WOMEN 124-3, ALEXANDER/ FUNERAL 124-4, INFANTRYMEN
CHOOSE THEIR NEW LEADER 124-4, ALEXANDER'S SHIP OF WAR LANDS
TO   CONQUER   ATHENS   124-4,   AGATHOCLES' ARMY ATTACKS SYRACUSE
124-5, CITIZENS COME OUT OF TOWN TO MEET THE SOLDIERS   124-5,
SOLDIERS   MARCHING   INTO TOWN 124-5, SOLDIERS FROM INSIDE TOWN
ADVANCE   124-5,   SOLDIERS   MARCH   TO   SHORE   WHERE   EXPEDITION
ANCHORED   124-5,   BOMILCAR   CRUCIFIED   FOR   TREACHERY   124-5,
ALEXANDER KILLS FATHER'S MURDERERS AT HIS FUNERAL 124-6,
ALEXANDER'S   ARMY   MARCHES   ON   THEBES 124-6, ALEXANDER OFFERS
SACRIFICE 124-6, ANTIGONUS SEATED ON THRONE APPROACHED BY
MESSENGERS   124-7, ALEXANDER'S SON HERCULES KILLED BY SOLDIERS
OF CASSANDER 124-7, SANDROCOTTUS AND A LION IN INDIA 124-7,
ANTIPATER STABS MOTHER OF QUEEN THESSILONICA 124-8, CLEARCHUS
KILLED BY CRION AND LEONIDES 124-8

*$ABSTRACT 125
 *LIBRARY BOD
 *SLIDE SET TITLE MUSICIANS IN GROUPS
 *NEGATIVE REFERENCE ROLL 173J
 *RENTAL FEE SM 125 $2.90
 *SHELFMARK MS DOUCE 332 125-1 , MS DOUCE 371 125-2, MS RAWL
  1220 125-3, MS DOUCE 135 125-4, MS DOUCE 62 125-5, MS DOUC
  195 125-6, MS DOUCE 18 125-7, MS BODLEY 421 125-8, MS CANO
  LITURG 126 125-9, MS DOUCE 364 125-10, MS DOUCE 308 125/12-15
  MS DOUCE 383 125/16-17, MS BODLEY 264 125-18
 *PROVENANCE FRENCH 125/1-2 AND 4-6 AND 8-15, ENGLISH 125/3 AN
  7 AND 18, FLEMISH 125/16-17
 *DATE EXECUTED 14TH 125/1 AND 9 AND 11-15, 15TH 125/2-3 AND 7-
  AND 10 AND 16-18, 16TH 125-6
 *CONTENTS MUSICIANS 125/1-18, MUSICAL INSTRUMENTS 125/1-18
  TRUMPET AND BUMBARDE 125-1, WIND INSTRUMENTS 125-2, HARP
  LUTE/ PIPE/ TABOR/ SHAWM/ BUMBARDE/ CLARION 125-3, FIDDLE AN
  SHAWM 125-4, TRUMPET AND TABOR 125-5, PIPE/ TABOR/ FIDDL
  125-6, SINGERS/ TRUMPETS/ PORTATIVE ORGAN 125-7, HORN
  TRUMPET/ PIPE/ TABOR/ HARPIST 125-8, GITTERN/ FIDDLE/ HOR
  125-9, SHAWM AND BAGPIPES 125-10, TRUMPETS 125/11-13, HARP
  125-14, TABOR AND PIPE 125-15, PIPES AND TABORS 125-16, SHAW
  AND CLARION 125-17, CLARION/ HARP/ SHAWM 125-18

*$ABSTRACT 126
 *LIBRARY BOD
 *SLIDE SET TITLE ANCIENT HISTORY
 *NEGATIVE REFERENCE ROLL 173K
 *RENTAL FEE SM 126 $2.65
 *TITLE OF MANUSCRIPT ABBREVIATION OF TROGUS POMPEIUS
 *SHELFMARK MS AUCT F 2 29
 *PROVENANCE FRENCH
 *DATE EXECUTED 15TH
 *LANGUAGE LATIN
 *AUTHOR JUSTINUS
 *TYPE OF MANUSCRIPT HISTORY
 *CONTENTS TOWNS/ INTERIOR AND EXTERIOR OF CASTLES/ BATTL
  SCENES 126/1-13, NINUS KING OF ASSYRIA WITH TROOPS 126-1
  SEMIRAMIS/ NINUS THE YOUNGER AND OTHERS AT NINUS' DEATHBE
  126-1, SEMIRAMIS DRESSES SON NINUS IN CLOTHES OF RULER 126-1
  SEMIRAMIS AND NINUS THE YOUNGER RECEIVE CITIZENS 126-1
  SEMIRAMIS BUILDS BABYLON 126-1, SEMIRAMIS AND NINUS TH
  YOUNGER 126-1, NINUS THE YOUNGER MURDERS SEMIRAMIS 126-1
  SARDANAPALUS ON THRONE WITH WOMAN WHO DESTROYS RICHES 126-1
  ASTYAGES GIVES BABY CYRUS TO HARPAGUS 126-1, TOMYRIS PUTS HEA
  OF CYRUS IN VESSEL OF BLOOD 126-1, OSTANES' DAUGHTER CHECK
  OROPASTES' EARS IN BED 126-1, LYSANDER RECEIVES SURRENDER O
  ATHENS 126-2, ATHENIANS MEET AS CITY BURNS AND BEWAIL FAT
  126-2, DARIUS DIES 126-2, CYRUS FIGHTS WITH ARTAXERXES 126-2
  CORANUS FOLLOWED BY GREEKS TAKES EDESSA 126-3, MACEDONIAN
  WITH BOY-KING PHILIP REBEL AGAINST ILLYRIANS 126-3, AXYATA
  ENTERTAINS DARIUS 126-3, DEPUTIES ABUSE WOMEN AND ARE ATTACKE
  BY MEN 126-3, PHILIP RECEIVES AMBASSADORS FROM ATHENS 126-4
  LYSIMACHUS AND WIFE 126-5, LYSIMACHUS AND SELEUCUS BATTL
  126-5, DIONYSIUS MAKES EXPEDITION TO MAGNA GRAECIA 126-6
  BATTLE OF CROTONIANS AND LOCRIANS 126-6, DIONYSIUS RECEIVE
  EMBASSY FROM GAUL 126-6, DIONYSIUS AND WIFE DIE AT HANDS O
  THEIR SUBJECTS 126-7, BRATTIA ALLOWS LACONIAN MARAUDERS INSID
  CITY 126-7, AGATHOCLES AND WIFE PART IN BEDCHAMBER 126-7
  HIERO'S LIFE INCIDENTS 126-7, HIERO CROWNED GOVERNOR OF SICIL
  126-7, ANTIGONUS RECEIVES AMBASSADORS FROM GAUL 126-8, GAUL
  ATTACK DESERTED TENTS OF ANTIGONUS 126-8, ANTIGONUS AN
  PYRRHUS/ OR PTOLEMY BATTLE 126-8, PYRRHUS ATTACKS ARGUS 126-8
  ARISTOTIMUS' SOLDIERS SEIZE LOOT IN EPEAN CITY 126-9
  HELLANICUS AND SOLDIERS KILL ARISTOTIMUS 126-9, GAULS MURDE
  WIVES AND CHILDREN TO PROPITIATE GODS 126-9, ARSINOE IN BE
  PROTECTS DEMETRIUS 126-9, PTOLEMY FALLS INTO LIFE O
  LICENTIOUS HABIT 126-10, PTOLEMY'S MISTRESS AND MOTHE
  CRUCIFIED TO AVENGE EURYDICE 126-10, EARTHQUAKE APPEARS BEFOR
  THERA AND THERASIA 126-10, HANNIBAL FLEES BY BOAT TO ANTIOCHU

126-11, HANNIBAL'S SOLDIERS ARE DEFEATED BY ROMANS AT SEA
126-11, FIGHT BETWEEN TROOPS OF EUMENES AND ANTIOCHUS 126-11,
ROMAN COMMISSIONERS FIND PTOLEMY REPULSIVE 126-12, COOKS AND
KITCHEN INSTRUMENTS IN ANTIOCHUS' ARMY 126-12, GERIONES AND
HERCULES FIGHT OVER HERDS 126-13

*$ABSTRACT 127
 *LIBRARY BOD
 *SLIDE SET TITLE LEGENDARY OF DOMINICAN NUNS OF REGENSBURG
 *NEGATIVE REFERENCE ROLL 174A
 *RENTAL FEE SM 127 $5.00
 *TITLE OF MANUSCRIPT LEGENDARY OF DOMINICAN NUNS OF REGENSBURG
 *SHELFMARK MS KEBLE COLLEGE 49
 *PROVENANCE GERMAN
 *DATE EXECUTED 13TH/AFTER 1271
 *LANGUAGE LATIN
 *TYPE OF MANUSCRIPT LEGENDARY
 *CONTENTS CHRIST NAILED TO CROSS BY MISERICORDIA/ SAPINTIA/
 OBEDIENTIA 127-1, CHURCH PIERCES CHRIST WITH LANCE AND FIDEI
 CATCHES BLOOD 127-1, SYNAGOGA BLINDFOLDED DRIVEN AWAY 127-1,
 INITIAL P 127/2 AND 24 AND 29, INITIAL T 127/4 AND 11 AND
 27-28, INITIAL T 127/42 AND 56, INITIAL H 127/5-6 AND 14 AND
 23 AND 26 AND 40, INITIAL D 127/7 AND 36 AND 45, INITIAL B
 127/9-10 AND 30 AND 37 AND 39, INITIAL V 127/12 AND 19,
 INITIAL L 127-13, INITIAL G 127-17, INITIAL F 127/18 AND 31
 AND 47, INITIAL M 127/21 AND 44, INITIAL N 127/32 AND 46,
 INITIAL D 127-36, INITIAL I 127-38, INITIAL A 127-43, INITIAL
 S 127-50, INITIAL E 127-54, INITIAL C 127-55, INITIAL F
 127-57, INITIAL R 127-59, ST ANDREW ON LATIN CROSS 127-2, ST
 NICHOLAS GIVES VIRGINS GOLD 127-3, ST THOMAS AND TWO
 EXECUTIONERS 127-4, ST STEPHEN AND CLERIC 127-5, ST JOHN
 BAPTIST WITH CHALICE PREACHES TO HEROD 127-6, SLAUGHTER OF THE
 INNOCENTS 127-7, ST THOMAS BECKET AT ALTAR 127-8, ST PRISCA
 127-9, ST SEBASTIAN 127-10, CHRIST AND ST AGNES 127-11, ST
 VINCENT 127-12, ST PAUL ON ROAD TO DAMASCUS 127-13,
 PRESENTATION IN TEMPLE 127-14, MARTYRDOM OF ST AGATHA 127-15,
 ST MATTHIAS BEHEADED 127-16, ST GREGORY THE GREAT 127-17, ST
 BENEDICT 127-18, ANNUNCIATION 127-19, ST GEORGE MARTYRED ON
 WHEEL 127-20, ST MARK WRITES AT LECTERN 127-21, SS PHILIP AND
 JAMES MARTYRED 127-22, INVENTION OF TRUE CROSS 127-23, JEWS IN
 CONICAL HATS 127-23, ST DOMINIC'S COFFIN TRANSLATED BY BISHOPS
 AND DOMINICANS 127-24, ZACARIAS WRITES ON SCROLL 127-25, JEWS
 WATCH ZACHARIAS 127-25, ST JOHN BAPTIST 127-26, SS JOHN AND
 PAUL 127-27, ST PETER NAILED TO THE CROSS 127-28, ST PAUL
 BEHEADED 127-29, ST MARGARET MARTYRED IN VAT 127-30, ST MARY
 MAGDALEN 127-31, BEHEADING OF ST JAMES THE LESS 127-32, ST
 PANTALEON TIED TO TREE AND BEHEADED 127-33, ST DOMINIC/
 CHRIST/ VIRGIN 127-34, ST LAWRENCE ROASTED ON GRILL 127-35,
 VIRGIN'S DEATH WITH CHRIST HOLDING SOUL 127-36, ST BERNARDUS
 127-37, ST BARTHOLOMEW WITH MODEL OF CHURCH 127-38, DOMINICAN
 FRIARS PRESENT BOOK TO ST AUGUSTINE 127-39, BEHEADING OF ST
 JOHN BAPTIST WITH HEROD/ HERODIAS/ SALOME 127-40, ST ANNE AND
 THE NATIVITY 127-41, EXALTATION OF THE CROSS 127-42, ST
 EUFEMIA 127-43, ST MATTHEW KNEELING AND RUN THROUGH WITH
 SWORDS 127-44, THEBAN LEGION BEHEADED 127-45, ST MAURICIUS
 BLESSED BY ANGEL 127-45, ST MICHAEL AND DRAGONS 127-46,
 STIGMATIZATION OF ST FRANCIS 127-47, ST DENIS BEHEADED 127-48,
 ST LUKE WRITES AT LECTERN AND VIRGIN SITTING 127-49, ST JUDE
 AND ST SIMON BEHEADED 127-50, ALL SAINTS 127-51, ALL SOULS IN
 LAP OF ABRAHAM 127-52, ST MARTIN AND CRIPPLE 127-53, ST
 ELISABETH ON HER DEATHBED WITH NUNS 127-54, ST CECILIA 127-55,
 ST CLEMENT IN FISHING BOAT 127-56, ST CATHERINE OF ALEXANDRIA
 127-57, VIRGIN AND CHILD 127-58, ST PETER MARTYR 127-59, ST
 ERHARD 127-60

*$ABSTRACT 128
 *LIBRARY BOD
 *SLIDE SET TITLE ALLEGORY FROM THE ROMANCE OF THE ROSE

71

*NEGATIVE REFERENCE ROLL 174E
*RENTAL FEE SM 128 $2.75
*TITLE OF MANUSCRIPT ROMANCE OF THE ROSE
*SHELFMARK MS DOUCE 371
*PROVENANCE FRENCH/ PARIS
*DATE EXECUTED 15TH/C1400
*LANGUAGE FRENCH
*AUTHOR GUILLAUME DE LORRIS AND JEAN DE MEUNG
*TYPE OF MANUSCRIPT ROMANCE/ ALLEGORY
*CONTENTS HATE/ FELONY/ VILLAINY/ COVETOUSNESS AS OLD WOME
128-1, AVARICE AND ENVY AS OLD WOMEN 128-2, SADNESS A YOUN
WOMAN 128-3, OLD AGE AS OLD WOMAN ON CRUTCHES 128-4, HYPOCRIS
AND POVERTY 128-5, DREAMER AND IDLENESS 128-6, GOD OF LOVE AN
DREAMER 128-7, GOD OF LOVE FIRING ARROW AT DREAMER 128-8
DANGER WITH CLUB THREATENING LOVER AND BEL ACQUEIL 128-9
LOVER AND REASON 128-10, FORTUNE AND WHEEL WITH HUMAN FIGURE
128-11, LOVER APPROACHES RICHESSE/ YOUNG WOMAN AND MAN 128-12
HUNGER AS SHABBY WOMAN 128-13, FALSE-SEEMING AS MON
APPROACHING MALEBOUCHE 128-14, DUENNA WITH ABSTINENCE
FALSE-SEMMING/ LARGESSE/ COURTESY 128-15

*$ABSTRACT 129
   *LIBRARY BOD
   *SLIDE SET TITLE FRENCH COSTUME
   *NEGATIVE REFERENCE ROLL 174F
   *RENTAL FEE SM 129 $4.15
   *TITLE OF MANUSCRIPT ROMAN DE LA ROSE
   *SHELFMARK MS E MUSAEO 65
   *PROVENANCE FRENCH
   *DATE EXECUTED 14TH/C1390
   *LANGUAGE FRENCH
   *AUTHOR GUILLAUME DE LORRIS AND JEAN DE MEUNG
   *TYPE OF MANUSCRIPT ROMANCE
   *CONTENTS ROMANCE OF THE ROSE 129/1-43, LITERATURE/ ROMANCE O
   THE ROSE 129/1-43, COSTUMES/ FRENCH 14TH CENTURY 129/1-43
   POET SLEEPING 129-1, POET IN GARDEN IN WHITE ROBE 129-2, HAT
   AS WOMAN IN GREY DRESS AND HEADSCARF 129-3, VILLAINY 129-4
   FELONY 129-4, COVETOUSNESS 129-4, AVARICE 129-4, DANCIN
   LADIES IN LONG DRESSES AND MUSICIANS 129-5, GOD OF LOVE WIT
   WINGS AND LONG DRESS 129-6, ENVY AS FEMALE IN GREY DRES
   129-7, SORROW AS FEMALE BEATING HER BREAST 129-8, IDLENESS A
   FEMALE WITH MIRROR AND COMB 129-9, OLD AGE AS OLD WOMAN I
   GOWN AND CLOAK 129-10, HYPOCRISY AS FEMALE IN DRESS AND VEI
   129-11, POVERTY AS BARE- FOOTED FIGURE IN RAGS 129-12
   FRANCHISE AS FEMALE 129-13, COURTESY AS MAN 129-14, MAIDENS I
   WHITE DRESSES IN GARDEN 129-15, NARCISSUS KNEELS BY POOL WIT
   CHARGER NEARBY 129-16, LOVER KNEELING BY POOL 129-17, GOD O
   LOVE 129-17, LOVER KNEELING BEFORE GOD OF LOVE 129-18, GOD O
   LOVE EMBRACING THE LOVER 129-19, GOD OF LOVE WINGED/ CROWNE
   LOCKS LOVER'S HEART 129-20, LOVER AND BEL ACQUEIL IN LON
   ROBES 129-21, DANGIER AS PEASANT AND MALEBOUCHE 129-22, RAISO
   CROWNED 129-23, DANGIER IN HOOD AND SHORT ROBE 129-24
   JEALOUSY WITH LONG SCARF CHIDES BEL ACQUEIL FOR DRESS 129-25
   FEAR TALKING TO SHAME 129-26, SHAME 129-26, DANGIER UNDER TRE
   AND FEAR AND SHAME NEARBY 129-27, JEALOUSY WEARING LONG DRES
   129-28, JEAN DE MEUNG AS CLERK WITH HOOD AND LECTERN 129-29
   RAISON LA BELLE IN LONG SKIRT TALKS WITH LOVER 129-30, REASO
   DISAPPEARS INTO TOWER AND LOVER TALKS WITH FRIEND 129-31, JEA
   DE MEUNG DRESSED LIKE CLERK 129-32, LUCRETIA KILLS HERSEL
   BEFORE RELATIVES 129-33, JEALOUS HUSBAND IN TUNIC TAKES WIF
   BY PLAITS 129-34, LOVER IN TUNIC FINDS WEALTH IN LONG DRES
   129-35, GOD OF LOVE PLACES HAND ON LOVER'S HEAD 129-36, GOD O
   LOVE FACES BARONS DRESSED IN TUNICS 129-37, GOD OF LOVE WIT
   BARONS 129-38, BARONS DRESSED IN HELMETS/ TUNICS/ BATTLE- AX
   SWORD/ SHIELD 129-38, FAUX SEMBLANT IN LONG BLACK CLOA
   129-39, ABSTINENCE IN BLACK HOODED DRESS WITH ROSARY ON AR
   129-39, FAUX SEMBLANT IN BLACK CLOAK KILLS MALEBOUCHE 129-40
   PRISON OF BEL ACQUEIL WITH WOMEN ON TOWER 129-41, BEL ACQUEI
   ADDRESSED BY OLD WOMAN ON PRISON-TOWER 129-42, OLD WOMA
   ADDRESSING BEL ACQUEIL ON GRASS 129-43

*$ABSTRACT 130
 *LIBRARY BOD
 *SLIDE SET TITLE ENGLISH HISTORY/ THE CONQUEROR TO GEORGE V
 *NEGATIVE REFERENCE ROLL 175A
 *RENTAL FEE SM 130 $3.30
 *COMMENTS 26 SLIDES FROM 24 MSS
 *TITLE OF MANUSCRIPT ANGLO-SAXON CHRONICLE 130-1, MAGNA CARTA
 130/2-3, BOOK OF HOURS 130-4, TREATISE ON THE PLAGUE 130-5,
 CANTERBURY TALES/ PROLOGUE 130-6, OLD TESTAMENT/ NICHOLAS OF
 HEREFORD VERSION 130-7, PIERS PLOWMAN 130-8, AGINCOURT SONG
 130-9, LATIN EXERCISE BOOK 130-10
 *SHELFMARK MS LAUD MISC 636 130-1, MS CH GLOUCS 8 130/2-3, MS
 DOUCE 231 130-4, MS ASHMOLE 1444 130-5, MS BODLEY 686 130-6,
 MS DOUCE 369 130-7, MS DOUCE 104 130-8, MS ARCH SELD B 26
 130-9, MS AUTOGR E 2 130-10, MS ASHMOLE 1729 130-11, MS ADD C
 92 130-12, MS ASHMOLE 1729 130-13, MS FRENCH E 1 130-14, MS
 CLARENDON 49 130/15-16, MS CLARENDON PAPERS 91 130-17, MS
 TANNER 60 130-18, MS CLARENDON 100 130-19, MS RAWLINSON A
 130-19, MS RAWLINSON A 139 B 130-20, MS ADD A 191 130-21, MS
 MONTAGUE D 18 130-22, MS ENG LETT C 139 130-23, MS ACLAND D 70
 130-24, MS AUTOGR D 11 130-25, MS ACLAND D 1 130-26
 *PROVENANCE ENGLISH
 *DATE EXECUTED 12TH/C1121 130-1, 13TH/1217 130/2-3, 13TH/C1295
 130-4, 15TH/C1400 130-5, 15TH/C1430-50 130-6, 15TH/C1415
 130-9, 15TH/C1427 130-8, 16TH/FEB 6 1548 130-11, 16TH/C1550
 130-12, 16TH/APRIL 1572 130-13, 16TH/C1686 130-14,
 17TH/NOVEMBER 10 1654 130-16, 17TH/OCTOBER 16 1646 130-17,
 17TH/AUGUST 4 1645 130-18, 17TH/JUNE 14 1698 130-21,
 18TH/OCTOBER 11 1793 130-22, 19TH/MARCH 20 1829 130-23, 19TH/
 JANUARY 30 1867 130-24
 *LANGUAGE ENGLISH
 *AUTHOR JEAN DE BOURGOYNE 130-5, CHAUCER 130-6, NICHOLAS OF
 HEREFORD/ TRANS 130-7, LANGLAND/ WILLIAM 130-8
 *TYPE OF MANUSCRIPT CHRONICLE 130-1, CHARTER 130-2, BOOK OF
 HOURS 130-4, TREATISE 130-5, BIBLE 130-7, LETTERS 130/11-26,
 EXERCISE BOOK 130-10
 *CONTENTS HISTORY/ ENGLISH 130/1-26, LETTERS/ BY BRITISH
 ROYALTY FROM ELIZABETH TO GEORGE V 130/12-26, NORMAN CONQUEST
 DESCRIBED 130-1, ANGLO-SAXON CHRONICLE 130-1, ST GEORGE AND
 EARL OF LANCASTER 130-4, DO-BETTER PREACHING 130-8, ELIZABETH/
 PRINCESS LETTER TO LORD PROTECTOR SOMERSET 130-12, ELIZABETH I
 TO LORD BURGHLEY 130-13, ELIZABETH PORTRAIT FRONTISPIECE TO DE
 LA MOTTHE POEM 130-14, HENRY DUKE OF GLOUCESTER TO BROTHER
 CHARLES II 130-15, CHARLES I TO HENRIETTA MARIA 130/16-17,
 CROMWELL/ OLIVER HOLOGRAPH LETTER OF FIGHT NEAR SHAFTESBURY
 130-18, CHARLES II PROPOSING VISIT TO SISTER 130-19, MONMOUTH
 ACKNOWLEDGING HIS ILLEGITEMACY ON EXECUTION DAY 130-20,
 MARLBOROUGH/ DUKE JOHN CHURCHILL TO BISHOP OF SALISBURY
 130-21, NELSON/ LORD DURING ENGLISH OCCUPATION OF TOULON
 130-22, WELLINGTON/ DUKE ARTHUR WELLESLEY TO BISHOP OF
 SALISBURY 130-23, NIGHTINGALE/ FLORENCE TO HENRY ACLAND ON
 TRAINING OF NURSES 130-24, RHODES/ CECIL WRITTEN IN CIPHER
 DURING SIEGE OF KIMBERLEY 130-25, GEORGE V AS CHILD TO HENRY
 ACLAND 130-26

*$ABSTRACT 131
 *LIBRARY BOD
 *SLIDE SET TITLE CHURCH HISTORY
 *NEGATIVE REFERENCE ROLL 175B
 *RENTAL FEE SM 131 $2.50
 *COMMENTS 10 SLIDE SELECTED FROM 10 MSS DEPICTING CHURCH
 HISTORY
 *TITLE OF MANUSCRIPT RULE OF ST BENDICT 131-1, HUGH OF ST
 VICTOR 131-2, GLOSS ON THE PSALTER/ PETER LOMBARD 131-3,
 FRANCISCAN BREVIARY 131-4, BIBLE MORALISEE 131-5, WYCLIF BIBLE
 131-6, CANTERBURY TALES 131-7, ACTES AND MONUMENTS 131-8, BOOK
 OF MARTYRS 131-8, DISSENTERS/ LIST MADE AT BAMPTON FOR JOHN
 FELL 131-9, NEWMAN/ JOHN HENRY RESIGNATION FROM ST MARY'S
 131-10
 *SHELFMARK MS HATTON 48 131-1, MS BODLEY 345 131-2, MS AUCT E

73

INF 6 131-3, MS DOUCE 245 131-4, MS BODLEY 270B 131-5, M
BODLEY 959 131-6, MS RAWL POET 223 131-7, MS DOUCE F SUBTUS
131-8, MS OXF DIOC PAPERS C 430 131-9, MS OXF DIOC PAPERS
772 131-10
*PROVENANCE ENGLISH 131/1-3 AND 6-10, FRENCH 131/4-5
*DATE EXECUTED 08TH/C700 131-1, 12TH 131-2, 12TH/C1175-8
131-3, 14TH 131-4, 13TH 131-5, 14TH 131-6, 15TH 131-7
16TH/1563 131-8, 17TH/1682 131-9, 19TH/1843 131-10
*LANGUAGE LATIN 131/1-5, ENGLISH 131/6-10
*AUTHOR CHAUCER 131-7
*TYPE OF MANUSCRIPT RULE/ MONASTIC 131-1, PSALTER/ GLOSS 131-3
BREVIARY 131-4, BIBLE MORALISEE 131-5, BIBLE 131-6, LITERATUR
131-7, BOOK OF MARTYRS 131-8, LIST OF DISSENTERS 131-9
*CONTENTS CHURCH HISTORY/ SCENES FROM 131/1-10, FRIAR IN PULPI
131-7, HOOPER/ JOHN BURNED 131-8

*$ABSTRACT 132
*LIBRARY BOD
*SLIDE SET TITLE LANDMARKS OF ENGLISH LITERATURE I MEDIEVAL
*NEGATIVE REFERENCE ROLL 175C
*RENTAL FEE SM 132 $2.80
*COMMENTS 16 SLIDES SELECTED FROM 11 MSS DEPICTING LANDMARKS I
ENGLISH LITERATURE
*TITLE OF MANUSCRIPT ALFRED/S TRANSLATION OF ST GREGORY'
PASTORAL CARE 132-1, ANGLO-SAXON CHRONICLE 132-2, ORMULU
132-3, OWL AND THE NIGHTINGALE 132-4, COMPLAINT OF MARS AN
VENUS 132-5, CANTERBURY TALES 132-6, TALE OF MELIBEUS 132-7
PIERS PLOWMAN/ C TEXT 132/8-9, VERNON MS OF MIDDLE ENGLIS
POETRY 132/10-11, CAXTON'S ADVERTISEMENT OF THE SARUM ORDINA
132-13, CHAUCER'S WORKS 132/14-16
*SHELFMARK MS HATTON 20 132-1, MS LAUD MISC 636 132-2, M
JUNIUS 1 132-3, MS JESUS COLLEGE 29 132-4, MS FAIRFAX 1
132-3, MS JESUS COLLEGE 29 132-4, MS FAIRFAX 16 132-5, MS RAW
POET 223 132/6-7, MS DOUCE 104 132/8-9, MS ENG POET A
132/10-11, MS ARCH SELD B 24 132-12, MS ARCH G E 37 132-13, M
ASHMOLE 1095 132/14-16
*PROVENANCE ENGLISH
*DATE EXECUTED 09TH/C890-7 132-1, 12TH/C1123 132-2, 13T
132/3-4, 15TH/C1450 132-5, 15TH 132/6-7, 15TH/C1427 132/8-9
15TH 132/10-11, 15TH/C1475 132-12, 15TH/1477 132-13 132-13
16TH/C1532 132/14-16
*LANGUAGE ENGLISH
*AUTHOR ST GREGORY/ TRANSLATED BY ALFRED 132-1, ORM 132-3
CHAUCER 132/ 5-7 AND 14-16, LANGLAND/ WILLIAM 132/8-9, JAME
I/ KING 132-12
*TYPE OF MANUSCRIPT TRANSLATION 132-1, CHRONICLE 132-2
HOMILIES 132-3, POETRY/ MIDDLE ENGLISH 132/4-12 AND 14-16
ADVERTISEMENT 132-13
*CONTENTS LITERATURE/ LANDMARKS OF ENGLISH 132/1-16, BATTLE O
BRUNABURGH 132-2, ANGLO-SAXON CHRONICLE 132-2, FRIAR
FLATTERING 132-9, ST HUGH OF LINCOLN 132-10, JEW WHO THRE
CHILD INTO OVEN FOR ENTERING CHURCH 132-11, KINGIS QUAIR/ POE
BY KING JAMES I 132-12

*$ABSTRACT 133
*LIBRARY BOD
*SLIDE SET TITLE LANDMARKS OF ENGLISH LITERATURE I
POSTMEDIEVAL
*NEGATIVE REFERENCE ROLL 175D
*RENTAL FEE SM 133 $2.65
*COMMENTS 13 SLIDES FROM 13 MSS DEPICTING LANDMARKS OF ENGLIS
LITERATURE
*TITLE OF MANUSCRIPT CENTURIES OF MEDITATION 133-1, VENUS AN
ADONIS 133-2, BIATHANOTOS 133-3, ESSAY ON CRITICISM 133/5-6
ODE TO THE WEST WIND 133-8, VOLUME THE FIRST 133-10, HENRY AN
ELIZA 133-10, GARETH AND LYNETTE 133-11, RUBAIYAT 133-12, WIN
IN THE WILLOWS 133-13
*SHELFMARK MS ENG THE E 50 133-1, MS MALONE 886 133-2, MS

74

MUSAEO 131 133-3, MS LAT MISC D 77 133-4, MS ENG POET C 1
133-5, MS DON E 70 133-6, MS DON C 62 133-7, MS SHELLEY ADD E
12 133-8, MS DON D 3 133-9, MS DON E 7 133-10, MS ENG POET B 3
133-11, MS DON F 3 133-12, MS ENG MISC D 281 133-13
*PROVENANCE ENGLISH
*DATE EXECUTED 16TH/1593 133-2, 17TH/JAN 23 1646-7 133-4,
18TH/1709 133-5, 18TH/1721 133-6, 19TH/AUGUST 25 1800 133-9,
19TH/1872 133-11, 19TH 133/10 AND 12-13
*LANGUAGE ENGLISH
*AUTHOR TRAHERNE 133-1, SHAKESPEARE 133-2, DONNE 133-3, MILTON
133-4, POPE 133/5-6, BOSWELL 133-7, SHELLEY 133-8, SOUTHEY
133-9, AUSTEN/ JANE 133-10, TENNYSON 133-11, FITZGERALD/
EDWARD 133-12, GRAHAME/ KENNETH 133-13
*TYPE OF MANUSCRIPT LITERATURE/ ENGLISH 133/1-13
*CONTENTS HANDWRITING/ AUTOGRAPH OF FAMOUS ENGLISH WRITERS
133/1-13, LITERATURE/ LANDMARKS OF ENGLISH 133/1-13,

*$ABSTRACT 134
 *LIBRARY BOD
 *SLIDE SET TITLE PASSION TO PENTECOST
 *NEGATIVE REFERENCE ROLL 175E
 *RENTAL FEE SM 134 $2.60
 *COMMENTS 12 SLIDES WITH ILLUMINIATIONS FROM AN ENGLISH PSALTER
 *SHELFMARK MS GOUGH LITURG 8
 *PROVENANCE ENGLISH
 *DATE EXECUTED 14TH/C1300
 *LANGUAGE LATIN
 *ARTIST/ SCHOOL RELATED TO THE MASTER OF THE QUEEN MARY PSALTER
 *TYPE OF MANUSCRIPT PSALTER
 *CONTENTS CHRIST BEFORE HEROD AND HIGH PRIEST 134-1, PRIEST/
 HIGH WITH MITRE 134-1, CHRIST BEFORE PILATE 134-2, JEWS
 THREATEN CHRIST 134-2, FLAGELLATION 134-3, CALVARY/ ROAD TO
 134-4, CHRIST WITH MARY MAGDALENE IN GARDEN WITH OAK TREE
 134-5, ST THOMAS TOUCHING CHRIST'S WOUNDED SIDE 134-6,
 CRUCIFIXION 134-7, LONGINIUS POINTING TO HIS EYE PIERCES
 CHRIST'S SIDE 134-7, DESCENT FROM CROSS 134-8, NAILS TAKEN
 FROM CHRIST'S FEET WITH PINCERS 134-8, CHRIST IN TOMB AND MEN
 WITH PEAKED HEADDRESSES 134-9, HARROWING OF HELL 134-10, DEVIL
 ABOVE HELL MOUTH 134-10, HELL MOUTH 134-10, ASCENSION WITH
 ONLY FEET VISIBLE 134-11, ST MARY AND APOSTLES BELOW 134-11,
 PENTECOST 134-12, ST MARY AND APOSTLES SEATED 134-12

*$ABSTRACT 135
 *LIBRARY BOD
 *SLIDE SET TITLE ROMANCE OF THE ROSE
 *NEGATIVE REFERENCE ROLL 175F
 *RENTAL FEE SM 135 $3.80
 *TITLE OF MANUSCRIPT ROMANCE OF THE ROSE
 *SHELFMARK MS E MUSAEO 65
 *PROVENANCE FRENCH
 *DATE EXECUTED 14TH/C1390
 *LANGUAGE FRENCH
 *AUTHOR GUILLAUME DE LORRIS
 *TYPE OF MANUSCRIPT ROMANCE
 *CONTENTS ROMANCE OF THE ROSE 135/1-36, LITERATURE/ ROMANCE OF
 THE ROSE 135/1-36, POET RECOUNTS DREAM AND INTENTIONS OF POEM
 135-1, POET WALKS ALONG RIVER BANK 135-2, FIGURES ON GARDEN
 WALL BANISHED FROM COURTLY WORLD 135-3, LADY IDLENESS AND
 LOVER OUTSIDE GARDEN DOOR 135-4, COURTESY WITH DANCERS AND
 LOVER 135-5, LOVER AND FOUNTAIN 135-6, GOD OF LOVE AND LOVER
 AT THE FOUNTAIN 135-7, FOUNTAIN OF LOVE 135-7, GOD OF LOVE
 FIRES ARROW INTO LOVER'S EYE 135-8, GOD OF LOVE CALLS ON LOVER
 TO YIELD 135-9, GOD OF LOVE INSTRUCTS LOVER ON HIS DUTIES
 135-11, GOD OF LOVE EMBRACES NEW VASSAL THE LOVER 135-10,
 FAIR-WELCOME INVITES LOVER TO ENTER ROSE GARDEN 135-12, DANGER
 LISTENS TO LOVER AND FAIR-WELCOME 135-13, REASON DESCENDS FROM
 TOWER AND ADDRESSES LOVER 135-14, LOVER CONFIDES IN FRIEND AS
 DANGER LURKS NEARBY 135-15, JEALOUSY CHIDES FAIR-WELCOME ABOUT

LOVER 135-16, FEAR AND SHAME TALKING 135-17, DANGER FOUND BY
FEAR AND SHAME UNDER HAWTHORN TREE 135-18, JEALOUSY SUPERVISES
BUILDING OF CASTLE 135-19, CASTLE WITH WORKERS BUILDING
135-19, REASON WOOS LOVER OUTSIDE CASTLE 135-20, LOVER TALKS
TO FRIEND 135-21, SWEET TALK AND FAIR- SPEECH CONSOLE LOVER
135-22, GOD OF LOVE QUESTIONS LOVER 135-23, BARONS HARANGUED
BY GOD OF LOVE 135-24, GOD OF LOVE AND HIS BARONS 135-25,
EVIL-TONGUE APPROACHED BY FALSE-SEEMING AND ABSTINENCE 135-26,
EVIL-TONGUE'S TONGUE CUT OUT BY PILGRIM 135-27, FAIR-WELCOME
AND OLD-WOMAN IN TOWER 135-28, OLD WOMAN FORCES GIFT FROM
LOVER ON FAIR-WELCOME 135-29, FAIR-WELCOME AND OLD WOMAN
135-30, OLD WOMAN AND LOVER 135-31, DANGER DRIVES LOVER AWAY
FROM TOWER 135-32, PITY AND FRANCHISE FIGHT DANGER 135-33,
GENIUS HEARS CONFESSION OF NATURE 135-34, GENIUS AS BISHOP
URGES COMPANY TO OBEY NATURE 135-35, VENUS AIMS BOW AT FAIR
IMAGE IN CASTLE 135-36

*$ABSTRACT 136
  *LIBRARY BOD
  *SLIDE SET TITLE SAINTS
  *NEGATIVE REFERENCE ROLL 175G
  *RENTAL FEE SM 136 $3.75
  *COMMENTS 35 SLIDES TAKEN FROM ONE MS
  *TITLE OF MANUSCRIPT LIVES OF SAINTS
  *SHELFMARK MS TANNER 17
  *PROVENANCE ENGLISH
  *DATE EXECUTED 15TH
  *LANGUAGE ENGLISH/ OLD ENGLISH
  *TYPE OF MANUSCRIPT SAINTS' LIVES
  *CONTENTS ST HILARY OF AQUITAINE BISHOP OF POITIERS 136-1, ST
WOLFSTAN BISHOP OF WORCESTER 136-2, ST FABIAN POPE AND MARTYR
136-3, ST SEBASTIAN 136-4, ST AGNES 136-5, ST VINCENT OF
VALENCIA 136-6, ST JULIAN THE CONFESSOR 136-7, ST JULIAN
BISHOP OF LE MANS 136-8, ST BRIDE 136-9, ST BLAISE BISHOP OF
SEBASTE 136-10, ST AGACE/ AGATHA 136-11, ST SCHOLASTICA
136-12, ST VALENTINE 136-13, ST JULIANA 136-14, ST MATTHIAS
136-15, ST OSWALD BISHOP OF WORCESTER 136-16, ST CHAD BISHOP
OF LICHFIELD 136-17, ST GREGORY POPE 136-18, ST LONGINUS
136-19, ST PATRICK BISHOP OF ARMAGH 136-20, ST EDWARD KING OF
ENGLAND 136-21, ST CUTHBERT BISHOP OF LINDISFARNE 136-22, ST
BENET/ BENEDICT ABBOT OF MONTE CASINO 136-23, ST MARY OF EGYPT
136-24, ST ALPHEGE ARCHBISHOP OF CANTERBURY 136-25, ST GEORGE
136-26, ST MARK THE EVANGELIST 136-27, ST PETER OF VERONA
136-28, ST PHILIP THE APOSTLE 136-29, ST JACOB/ JAMES THE LESS
136-30, ST QUIRACUS/ CYRIAC BISHOP OF ANCONA 136-31, ST
BRENDAN ABBOT 136-32, ST DUNSTAN ARCHBISHOP OF CANTERBURY
136-33, ST ALDHELM/ ADHELM BISHOP OF SHERBORNE 136-34, ST
AUGUSTINE ARCHBISHOP OF CANTERBURY 136-35

*$ABSTRACT 137
  *LIBRARY BOD
  *SLIDE SET TITLE BIBLIA PAUPERAM
  *NEGATIVE REFERENCE ROLL 175I
  *RENTAL FEE SM 137 $3.00
  *COMMENTS 20 SLIDES SELECTED FROM A BLOCK BOOK COLORED BY HAND
  *TITLE OF MANUSCRIPT BIBLIA PAUPERAM
  *SHELFMARK MS AUCT M III 13
  *PROVENANCE DUTCH
  *DATE EXECUTED 15TH
  *LANGUAGE LATIN
  *TYPE OF MANUSCRIPT BIBLE
  *CONTENTS TEMPTATION OF EVE 137-1, ANNUNCIATION TO MARY 137-1,
GIDEON AND THE ANGEL 137-1, BURNING BUSH 137-2, NATIVITY
137-2, AARON'S STAFF BLOOMS 137-2, ABNER VISITS DAVID 137-3,
ADORATION OF MAGI 137-3, SOLOMON AND SHEBA 137-3, PURIFICATION
137-4, PRESENTATION IN THE TEMPLE 137-4, SAMUEL AS CHILD
BROUGHT TO ELI 137-4, CROSSING OF THE RED SEA 137-5, BAPTISM
OF CHRIST 137-5, SPIES CARRYING GRAPES 137-5, ESAU SELLS HIS

BIRTHRIGHT FOR A MESS OF POTAGE 137-6, TEMPTATION OF CHRIST
137-6, TEMPTATION OF ADAM AND EVE 137-6, WIDOW OF ZAREPATH'S
SON RESURRECTED BY ELIJAH 137-7, LAZARUS RAISED 137-7, ELISHA
RAISES SHUNAMITE'S SON 137-7, JOSEPH'S BROTHERS SELL HIM TO
ISHMAELITES 137-8, JUDAS WITH MONEY TO BETRAY CHRIST 137-8,
POTIPHAR BUYS JOSEPH 137-8, MELCHIZEDEK GIVES BREAD TO ABRAHAM
137-9, LAST SUPPER 137-9, MOSES AND THE FALL OF MANNA 137-9,
ISAAC CARRIES WOOD FOR THE SACRIFICE 137-10, CALVARY/ ROAD TO
137-10, ELIJAH AND THE WIDOW OF ZAREPATH WITH TWO STICKS
137-10, SACRIFICE OF ISAAC 137-11, CHRIST ON CROSS 137-11,
MOSES LIFTS UP THE SERPENT 137-11, CREATION OF EVE 137-12,
CHURCH BORN FROM SIDE OF CHRIST 137-12, MOSES STRIKES WATER
FROM ROCK 137-12, JOSEPH LOWERED INTO PIT 137-13, ENTOMBMENT
137-13, JONAH CAST TO THE WHALE 137-13, DAVID SLAYS GOLIATH
137-14, HARROWING OF HELL 137-14, SAMSON SLAYS LION 137-14,
SAMSON CARRIES GATES OF GAZA 137-15, RESURRECTION 137-15,
JONAH EMERGES FROM WHALE 137-16, CHRIST APPEARS TO DISCIPLES
137-16, PRODIGAL SON RETURNS 137-16, ASCENSION OF ENOCH
137-17, ASCENSION OF CHRIST 137-17, ELIJAH ASCENDS TO HEAVEN
137-17, MOSES RECEIVES THE LAW 137-18, PENTECOST 137-18, FIRE
BURNS ELIJAH'S SACRIFICE 137-18, SOLOMON'S JUDGMENT 137-19,
SECOND COMING 137-19, DAVID CONDEMNS AMELKITE 137-19, JOB'S
CHILDREN FEAST 137-20, CHRIST AND BLESSED SOULS 137-20,
JACOB'S LADDER 137-20

*$ABSTRACT 138
  *LIBRARY BOD
  *SLIDE SET TITLE CLASSICAL TEXTS LATIN
  *NEGATIVE REFERENCE ROLL 175J
  *RENTAL FEE SM 138 $3.00
  *COMMENTS 20 SLIDES SELECTED FROM 19 MSS OF CLASSICAL LATIN
  TEXTS
  *TITLE OF MANUSCRIPT CODICES LATINI ANTIQUIORES II 138-1,
  CATILINE 138-1, CHRONICON 138-2, TUSCULAN DISPUTATIONS 138-4,
  ARS AMATORIA 138-5, PROLOGUE/ PERSIUS 138-7, AENEID VIII
  138-8, ADELPHOI 138-10, GALLIC WAR 138-11, NATURAL HISTORY
  VIII 138-12, SPEECHES/ CICERO 138-14, LETTERS V-VI/ PLINY
  138-15, NATURAL HISTORY 138-17, PRO MILONE 138-19, LETTERS
  VIII/ PLINY 138-20
  *SHELFMARK MS LAT CLASS C 20 138-1, MS AUCT T 2 26 138-2, MS
  LAUD LAT 104 138-3, MS LAUD LAT 29 138-4, MS AUCT F 4 32
  138-5, MS AUCT T 1 24 138-6, MS AUCT F 1 15 138-7, MS CANON
  CLASS LAT 41 138-8, MS CANON CLASS 41 138-9, MS AUCT F 2 13
  138-10, MS HOLKHAM MISC 34 138-11, MS AUCT T 1 27 138-12, MS
  CANON CLASS LAT 30 138-13, MS D/ORVILLE 78 138-14, MS D
  HUMPHREY D I 138-15, MS AUCT F 1 13 138-16, MS AUCT O 1 2
  138/17-18, MS AUCT R SUP 3 SIGN E 138-19, MS AUCT L 4 3 138-20
  *PROVENANCE EGYPTIAN 138-1, WELSH 138-5, ENGLISH 138/7 AND 19,
  ITALIAN 138/ 8-11 AND 13-18, FRENCH 138-12
  *DATE EXECUTED 05TH 138/1-2, 09TH 138/3-5, 11TH 138/6-9, 12TH
  138/10-12, 14TH 138/13, 15TH 138/14-20
  *LANGUAGE LATIN 138/1-20, WELSH GLOSSES 138-5
  *AUTHOR SALLUST 138-1, EUSEBIUS 138-2, SIDONIUS APOLLINARIS
  138-3, CICERO 138/4 AND 14 AND 19, OVID 138-5, LIVY 138-6,
  PERSIUS 138-7, VIRGIL 138-8, JUVENAL 138-9, TERENCE 138-10,
  CAESAR 138-11, PLINY 138/12 AND 15 AND 17-18 AND 20, CATULLUS
  138-13, LUCRETIUS 138-16
  *TYPE OF MANUSCRIPT CLASSICAL LATIN TEXTS 138/1-20
  *CONTENTS HANDWRITING FROM CLASSICAL LATIN TEXTS 138/1-20,
  LATIN TEXTS 138/1-20, ILLUSTRATIONS IN TEXT OF TERENCE 138-10,
  ILLUMINATED INITIAL A IN TEXT OF LUCRETIUS 138-16

*$ABSTRACT 139
  *LIBRARY BOD
  *SLIDE SET TITLE PLANTS
  *NEGATIVE REFERENCE ROLL 175K
  *RENTAL FEE SM 139 $2.95
  *COMMENTS 19 SLIDES SELECTED FROM ENGLISH HERBAL

*TITLE OF MANUSCRIPT HERBAL
*SHELFMARK MS BODLEY 130
*PROVENANCE ENGLISH/ BURY ST EDMUNDS
*DATE EXECUTED 11TH
*LANGUAGE LATIN
*AUTHOR PSEUDO APULEIUS
*TYPE OF MANUSCRIPT HERBAL
*CONTENTS   PLANTS 139/1-19, HERBAL/ ENGLISH 139/1-19, DANDELION
139-1, WOODRUFF 139-2, OPIUM POPPY 139-3, HARTS TONGUE   139-4,
PLANTAIN   139-5,   BLACK PRYENY 139-6, RED CLOVER 139-7, TWITCH
GRASS 139-8, FLAG/   IRIS   PSEUDACORUS   139-9,   CARROT   139-10,
BRAMBLE   139-11,   GROUND   IVY 139-12, VERVAIN AND SERPENT FROM
WHICH IT GIVES PROTECTION 139-13,   HENBANE   138-14,   FOXGLOVE/
GLOVEWORT 139-15, CHAMOMILE 139-15, GROUNDPINE 139-16, RAVEN'S
FOOT 139-16, TEASEL 139-17, AGRIMONY 139-18, ALEXANDERS 139-19

*$ABSTRACT 140
*LIBRARY BOD
*SLIDE SET TITLE PARROTS
*NEGATIVE REFERENCE ROLL 175L
*RENTAL FEE SM 140 $3.00
*COMMENTS 20 SLIDES SELECTED FROM 17 MSS DEPICTING PARROTS
*TITLE   OF MANUSCRIPT AUGUSTINE DE TRINITATE 140/1-3, CALENDAR/
TREATISE ON ASTRONOMY/ WONDERS OF   THE   EAST   140-4,   BESTIARY
140/5-6   AND 8, PSALTER AND BOOK OF HOURS 140-7, BOOK OF HOURS
140/10 AND 13 AND 17-19, OVID 140-12, HISTORY OF ALEXANDER THE
GREAT   140/14-15,   AUGUSTINIAN   MISSAL   140-16,   HERBAL   AND
BESTIARY 140-20
*SHELFMARK   MS   LAUD   MISC 126 140/1-3, MS BODLEY 614 140-4, MS
BODLEY 764 140-5, MS DOUCE 88 140-6, MS LAUD LAT 82 140-7,   MS
DOUCE   151 140/8-9, MS LAUD LAT 15 140-10, MS CANON LITURG 114
140-11, MS CANON CLASS LAT 15 140-12,   MS   CANON   LITURG   8
140-13,   MS   LAUD MISC 751 140-14, MS LAUD MISC 751 140-15, MS
CANON LITURG 387 140-16, MS CANON LITURG 128 140-17, MS   DOUCE
40 140-18, MS DOUCE 135 140-19, MS ASHMOLE 1504 140-20
*PROVENANCE   FRENCH   140/1-3   AND   19, ENGLISH 140/4-10 AND 20,
ITALIAN 140/11-13 AND 18, FLEMISH 140/14-15   AND   17,   SPANISH
140-16
*DATE   EXECUTED   08TH   140/1-3,   12TH 140-4, 13TH 140/5-6, 14TH
140/7-9, 15TH 140/10-17, 16TH 140/18-20
*LANGUAGE LATIN
*TYPE OF MANUSCRIPT RELIGIOUS   TREATISE   140/1-3,   ASTRONOMICAL
TREATISE   140/4,   CALENDAR 140/4, BESTIARY 140/6 AND 8 AND 20,
PSALTER 140/7 AND 11, BOOK OF HOURS 140/10 AND 13   AND   17-19,
HISTORY 140/14-15, MISSAL 140-16, HERBAL 140-20
*CONTENTS PARROTS 140/1-20

*$ABSTRACT 141
*LIBRARY BOD
*SLIDE SET TITLE LATER MIDDLE ENGLISH MSS
*NEGATIVE REFERENCE ROLL 176A
*RENTAL FEE SM 141 $2.85
*COMMENTS   17   SLIDES   SELECTED FROM 9 MSS OF THE 14TH AND 15TH
CENTURIES
*TITLE OF MANUSCRIPT   ADVENTURE   AND   GRACE   141-3,   CANTERBURY
TALES   141-4,   ROMANCE OF KING PONTHUS OF GALICIA AND PRINCESS
OF SIDON 141-5, VERNON MS 141-6, BOKE OF THE CRAFTE OF   DYEING
141-7,   CURSOR   MUNDI   141-8,   MEDITATION   IN   VERSE   141-9,
MEDITATION EXHORTING LOVE OF GOD 141-10, GILTE LEGEND   141-11,
BIBLE/ WYCLIFFE 141-12, BIBLE/ OLD TESTAMENT 141/13-15, MASTER
OF THE GAME 141/16-17, CONFESSIO AMANTIS 141-1
*SHELFMARK   MS FAIRFAX 3 141-1, MS E MUSAEO 35 141-2, MS BODLEY
686 141-4, MS E MUSAEO 23 141-3, MS DIGBY 185   141-5,   MS   ENG
POET A   1 141-6, MS BODLEY 423 141-7, MS FAIRFAX 14 141-8, MS
RAWL A 389 141/9-10, MS DOUCE 372 141-11, MS DOUCE 369 141-12,
MS BODLEY 959 141/13-15, MS BODLEY 546 141/16-17
*PROVENANCE ENGLISH
*DATE EXECUTED 14TH 141-1, 15TH 141/2-17

78

*AUTHOR GOWER 141-1, CHAUCER 141-4, RICHARD ROLLE OF HAMPTON
   141-9
*TYPE OF MANUSCRIPT DEVOTIONAL TREATISES 141-2, BIBLE 141/12-15
*CONTENTS HANDWRITING/ EARLY ENGLISH 141/1-17, GOWER KNEELING
   141-1, HERALDRIC ARMS OF SHOTTESBROOKE OF KENT 141-3,
   HERALDRIC ARMS SWILLINGTON 141-5, HERALDRIC ARMS OF JAMES/
   LORD AUDLEY 141-16

*$ABSTRACT 142
  *LIBRARY BOD
  *SLIDE SET TITLE EARLY WORLD MAPS
  *NEGATIVE REFERENCE ROLL 177A
  *RENTAL FEE SM 142 $2.60
  *COMMENTS 12 SLIDES SELECTED FROM 11 11TH-15TH CENTURY MSS
  *SHELFMARK MS RAWL G 44 142-1, MS D/ORVILLE 77 142-2, MS RAWL G
   43 142-4, MS AUCT D 4 142-3, MS BODLEY 527 142-5, MS E MUSAEO
   223 142-6, MS TANNER 190 142-7, MS DOUCE 319 142/8-9, MS LAT
   CLASS D 14 142-10, MS AUCT D 5 14 142-11, MS DIGBY 196 142
  *PROVENANCE ENGLISH 142-3, FRENCH 142-2, ITALIAN 142/7-11
  *DATE EXECUTED 11TH 142/1-3, 12TH 142-4, 13TH 142/5-6, 14TH
   142/7-10, 15TH 142/11-12
  *TYPE OF MANUSCRIPT MAPS
  *CONTENTS MAPS/ EARLY WORLD 142/1-12, CIRCLE/ TRIPARTITE WITH
   NAMES 142-1, MAP/ NICE 142-2, CIRCLE WITH DIVIDED
   CIRCUMFERENCE INTO CURVED SEGMENTS 142-3, CIRCLE/ TRIPARTITE
   WITH FEW NAMES 142-4, CIRCLE/ DIVIDED WITH NUMEROUS NAMES
   142-5, CIRCLE/ DOUBLE AND TRIPARTITE WITH ASIA EUROPE AND
   AFRICA 142-6, MAP WITH SEA IN GREEN MOUNTAINS IN BROWN 142-7,
   CIRCLE/ TRIPARTITE 142-8, MAP/ HIGHLY COLORED 142-9,
   TRIPARTITE MAPS 142-10, CIRCLE DIVIDED 142-11, OVAL WITH THICK
   SCATTERING OF NAMES 142-12

*$ABSTRACT 143
  *LIBRARY BOD
  *SLIDE SET TITLE ALPHABET
  *NEGATIVE REFERENCE ROLL 177C
  *RENTAL FEE SM 143 $3.25
  *COMMENTS 25 SLIDES SELECTED FROM 25 12TH CENTURY MSS
  *SHELFMARK MS JESUS 93 143-1, MS RAWL C 435 143-2, MS BALLIOL 6
   143-3, MS AUCT D 2 1 143-4, MS LAUD LAT 17 143-5, MS JESUS 53
   143-6, MS JESUS 102 143-7, MS BODLEY 295 143-8, MS JESUS 93
   143-9, MS DOUCE 368 143-10, MS JESUS 52 143-11, MS BODLEY 301
   143-12, MS LAUD MISC 469 143/13 AND 23, MS JESUS 102
   143/14-15, MS JESUS 53 143-16, MS BODLEY 683 143-17, MS BODLEY
   295 143-18, MS JESUS 102 143-19, MS BALLIOL 6 143/20, MS
   BODLEY 301 143-21, MS JESUS 102 143-22, MS DIGBY 214 143-24,
   MS JESUS 93 143-25
  *PROVENANCE ENGLISH
  *DATE EXECUTED 12TH
  *AUTHOR ST AUGUSTINE 143/1 AND 3 AND 7 AND 9 AND 11-15 AND
   20-24 AND 25, ST GREGORY 143/2 AND 17 AND 24, ST JOHN
   CHRYSOSTOM 143-18
  *TYPE OF MANUSCRIPT PSALTER 143/4-5
  *CONTENTS INITIALS/ ILLUMINATED 143/1-25, INITIAL A 143-1,
   INITIAL B 143-2, INITIAL C 143-3, INITIAL D 143-4, INITIAL E
   143-5, INITIAL F 143-6, INITIAL G 143-7, INITIAL H 143-8,
   INITIAL I 143-9, INITIAL K 143-10, INITIAL L 143-11, INITIAL M
   143-12, INITIAL N 143-13, INITIAL O 143-14, INITIAL P 143-15,
   INITIAL Q 143-16, INITIAL R 143-17, INITIAL S 143-18, INITIAL
   T 143-19, INITIAL U 143-20, INITIAL V 143-21, INITIAL X
   143-22, INITIAL Y 143-23, INITIAL Z 143-24, CAPITALS/ WHOLE
   PAGE 143-25

*$ABSTRACT 144
  *LIBRARY BOD
  *SLIDE SET TITLE ARMY TRAPPINGS

*NEGATIVE REFERENCE ROLL 177D
*RENTAL FEE SM 144 $3.00
*COMMENTS 20 SLIDES SELECTED FROM PORTUGESE MS DEPICTING ARMY
 TRAPPINGS
*TITLE OF MANUSCRIPT MACHINES ET UTENSILS DE GUERRE
*SHELFMARK MS DOUCE B 2
*PROVENANCE PORTUGESE
*DATE EXECUTED 16TH/1582
*LANGUAGE FRENCH
*TYPE OF MANUSCRIPT MILITARY TEXT
*CONTENTS MILITARY TRAPPINGS 144/1-20, MILITARY EQUIPMENT
 144/1-20, FLAIL/ MODIFIED AGRICULTURAL IMPLEMENT 144-1, MAUL/
 SPIKED 144-1, CALTRAPS/ SEVEN WITH FOUR POINTS EACH 144-2,
 TRESTLE-LIKE MOBILE OBSTRUCTION WITH SPIKES 144-3, WEAPON LIKE
 PITCHFORK WITH BURNING WOOL ON SPIKE 144-4, BRIDGE/ PONTOON
 OVER RIVER 144-5, CANNON LED BY FIVE HORSES 144-6, RAM/
 BATTERING 144-7, MECHANISM TO RAISE OR LOWER CANNON 144-8,
 ANTI-PERSONNEL WEAPONS 144-9, CANNONS/ SMALL CARRIED BY WHITE
 HORSE 144-10, GUN CARRIAGE CHASSIS CARRIED BY HORSE 144-11,
 HELMETS 144-12, SWORD/ TWO EDGED 144-13, SHIELD/ CIRCULAR WITH
 SPIKE IN CENTER BOSS 144-14, DRUM WITH CROSSED DRUMSTICKS
 144-15, FIFE 144-15, BANNER HUNG FROM BUGLE 144-16, BUGLE
 144-15, BANDEROLE WITH PORTUGAL IN CARTOUCHE 144-17, HELMETS
 WITH PLUMES AND RAISED VISORS 144-18, ARMOUR/ PLATE SUIT OF
 144-19, TENT ORNAMENTED BY MALTESE CROSS 144-20

*$ABSTRACT 145
 *LIBRARY CORPUS CHRISTI COLLEGE
 *SLIDE SET TITLE TREASURES OF CORPUS CHRISTI COLLEGE
 *NEGATIVE REFERENCE ROLL 178
 *RENTAL FEE SM 145 $3.60
 *COMMENTS 32 SLIDES SELECTED FROM 3 MSS IN CORPUS CHRISTI
  COLLEGE
 *TITLE OF MANUSCRIPT HISTORIA MAJOR 145/1-12 AND 20-32, GOSPELS
  OF ST AUGUSTINE 145/13-19
 *SHELFMARK MS C C C CAMBRIDGE 16 145/1-12 AND 27-32, MS C C C
  CAMBRIDGE 26 145/20-26, MS C C C CAMBRIDGE 286 145/13-19
 *PROVENANCE ENGLISH 145/1-12 AND 20-32, ITALIAN 145/13-19
 *DATE EXECUTED 06TH 145/13-19
 *LANGUAGE LATIN 145/1-32
 *AUTHOR PARIS/ WALTER 145/1-2 AND 20-32, ST AUGUSTINE 145/13-19
 *TYPE OF MANUSCRIPT HISTORY 145/1-12 AND 20-32, GOSPELS
  145/13-19
 *CONTENTS BATTLE OF SARACENS AND CHRISTIANS AT DAMIETTA 145-1,
  SIEGE OF DAMIETTA FROM SEA 145-2, ARCHERS/ SLINGERS AND FLAIL
  145-2, ST FRANCIS SEES SERAPH OF THE STIGMATA 145-3, ST
  FRANCIS PREACHES TO THE BIRDS 145-4, WILLIAM THE MARSHALL
  UNHORSES BALDWIN OF GUISNES 145-5, DAMASCUS WITH RIVERS FARFAR
  AND ALBANA 145-6, TREATY OF COUNT OF BRITTANY AND NAZER 145-7,
  SEA-FIGHT BETWEEN PISANS AND GENOESE 145-8, HENRY III RETURNS
  TO FRANCE 145-9, QUEEN HEALS ST LOUIS WITH THE TRUE CROSS
  145-10, INNOCENT IV AT COUNCIL OF LYONS EXCOMMUNICATES EMPEROR
  145-11, ATHELSTAN GIVES BOOK TO ST CUTHBERT FROM BEDE 145-12,
  BIBLICAL SCENES IN TWELVE COMPARTMENTS 145/13-15, CHRIST'S
  MINISTRY 145/16-17, ST LUKE WITH SCENES FROM CHRIST'S MINISTRY
  145-18, CHAUCER READING FROM HIS TROILUS AND CRESSIDA 145-19,
  PALESTINE IN PARTIAL MAP 145-20, ALFRED/ KING 145-21, DUEL
  BETWEEN EDMUND IRONSIDE AND CNUT AT DEERHURST 145-22, TEMPLARS
  SHARE HORSE 145-23, TEMPLAR'S HOSPITAL FOUNDED BY MATILDA IN
  LONDON 145-23, ST AMPHIBALUS' INVENTION WITH EXCAVATION BY
  ROBERT MERCER 145-24, SALADIN DEFEATS CHRISTIANS AND CAPTURES
  TRUE CROSS 145-25, VIRGIN AND CHILD WITH TWO HEADS OF CHRIST
  145-26, ELEPHANT SENT FROM LOUIS IX TO HENRY III 145-27,
  BATTLE OF BOVINES 145-28, HUGO DE BOVES FLEES AND PHILIP OF
  FRANCE UNHORSED 145-28, SHIPWRECK OF HUGO DE BOVES 145-29,
  CHRIST/ THE VERONICA WITH ALPHA AND OMEGA 145-30, SIEGE OF
  LINCOLN 145-31, CHEMICAL WARFARE AT BATTLE OF SANDWICH 145-32

*$ABSTRACT 146
  *LIBRARY BOD
  *SLIDE   SET   TITLE RULE OF THE NUNNERY OF FRANCISCAN TERTIARIES
  AT FLORENCE
  *NEGATIVE REFERENCE ROLL 179A
  *RENTAL FEE SM 146 $2.45
  *COMMENTS 9 SLIDES SELECTED FROM FRANCISCAN RULE
  *TITLE OF MANUSCRIPT RULE OF THE NUNNERY OF THE ORDER OF
  FRANCISCAN TERTIARIES
  *SHELFMARK MS CANON LITURG 347
  *PROVENANCE ITALIAN/ FLORENCE
  *DATE EXECUTED 15TH/ AFTER 1476
  *LANGUAGE LATIN
  *TYPE OF MANUSCRIPT MONASTIC RULE/ FRANCISCAN
  *CONTENTS   HISTORIATED   INITIALS   146/1-9,   POSTULANT CLUTCHING
  ROBE KNEELING BEFORE PRIEST 146-1, POSTULANT BEING BLESSED BY
  PRIEST WHO HOLDS ROBE 146-2, POSTULANT HAVING HER HAIR CUT OFF
  146-3,   ALTAR   AND   WINDOW   IN   BACKGROUND   146-3,   POSTULANT'S
  WORLDLY HABIT REMOVED BY NUN 146-4, POSTULANT OR NOVICE BEING
  CLOTHED BY PRIEST AND NUN 146-5, NOVICE OR POSTULANT RECEIVED
  INTO ORDER 146-6, NUN KNEELING BEFORE SUPERIOR MAKING VOWS
  146-7, POPE NICHOLAS IV WITH NUNS RECEIVING RULE 146-8, POPE
  NICHOLAS IV BLESSING THREE NUNS BEFORE HIM 146-9

*$ABSTRACT 147
  *LIBRARY BOD
  *SLIDE SET TITLE BESTIAIRE D/AMOUR
  *NEGATIVE REFERENCE ROLL 180G
  *RENTAL FEE SM 147 $4.70
  *COMMENTS 54 SLIDES SELECTED FROM A COMPARISON OF LOVERS WITH
  ANIMALS
  *TITLE OF MANUSCRIPT LE BESTIAIRE D'AMOUR
  *SHELFMARK MS DOUCE 308
  *PROVENANCE FRENCH/ LORRAINE
  *DATE EXECUTED 14TH
  *LANGUAGE FRENCH
  *AUTHOR RICHARD DE FOURNIVALL
  *TYPE OF MANUSCRIPT ROMANCE BESTIARY/ MOCK
  *CONTENTS   BESTIARY/   MOCK   COMPARISON   OF   LOVERS WITH ANIMALS
  147/1-54, AUTHOR SEATED AT TABLE WRITING ON SCROLL 147-1,
  AUTHOR PRESENTING BOOK TO THREE FIGURES 147-1, MAN AND WOMAN
  TALKING 147-2, KNIGHTS IN ARMOUR BEFORE FIGURE UNDER ARCH
  147-3,   AUTHOR PRESENTS SCROLL TO ANOTHER FIGURE 147-4, BEASTS
  AND BIRDS WITH WHOM THE BOOK IS CONCERNED 147-5, KING ARMED
  AND MOUNTED LEAVES CASTLE 147-6, MUSICIANS WITH BUZINES 147-6,
  COCK ON WING WITH MAN AND WOMAN WATCHING 147-7, ASS/ WILD
  BRAYING AS MAN SHRINKS BACK 147-8, LION CONFRONTS MAN WEARING
  HOOD 147-9, CRICKET IN CAGE WITH MAN AND WOMAN POINTING
  147-10, COSTUMES/ FRENCH 14TH CENTURY 147/1-54, SWANS SINGING
  ACCOMPANIED   BY   MUSICIANS   WITH   HARPS 147-11, DOG EATING OWN
  VOMIT MAN AND WOMAN SHOCKED 147-12, WOLF BITES OWN LEG BECAUSE
  MADE NOISE BEFORE SHEEP-FOLD 147-13, WIVRE OPEN-MOUTHED AT
  SIGHT OF NAKED FIGURE 147-14, MONKEY WITH BOOTS CONFRONTED BY
  HUNTER 147-15, RAVEN FLIES AWAY FROM NEST OF FIVE BABY RAVENS
  147-16, LION EATING KILL AND MAN TURNS HEAD AWAY 147-17,
  WEASEL CONCEIVES THROUGH EAR AND GIVES BIRTH THROUGH MOUTH
  147-18,   CALADRIUS PERCHED ON SICK MAN'S BED 147-19, ASP PUTS
  EAR TO GROUND NOT TO HEAR MUSICIANS 147-20, BLACKBIRD IN CAGE
  WITH MAN AND WOMAN 147-21, MOLE COMING OUT OF HIS HILL 147-22,
  WHITE WORM NOTED FOR HIS EYESIGHT AND COUPLE 147-23, WEASEL
  GNAWING INTO MIRROR AS MAN CARRIES AWAY CUB 147-24, UNICORN
  KNEELING WITH HEAD IN VIRGIN'S LAP SPEARED 147-25, CRANES
  147-26, LION WATCHED BY TWO DOGS 147-27, ARGUS THE COWHERD
  WITH CROOK AND COW AND WOMAN 147-28, ARGUS ASLEEP AND COW
  LOOKS AT MERCURY WITH SWORD 147-29, SWALLOW FLYING TO NEST OF
  BABY SWALLOWS WITH FOOD 147-30, WEASEL REVIVES DEAD BABY
  WEASELS WITH FIRE FROM MOUTH 147-31, LION ROARS CUBS ALIVE
  147-32, PELICAN BABIES FLYING AT PARENT BIRDS 147-33, PELICAN
  BITES BREAST AND BLOOD REVIVES DEAD BIRDS 147-34, WOODPECKER/
  GREEN FLYING TO NEST WITH GREEN HERBS 147-35, SWALLOW/

L'ARONDE FLYING AFTER ITS FOOD 147-36, HEDGEHOG WITH APPLE
PICKED ON HIS SPINE 147-37, CROCODILE EATING A MAN 147-38
HYDRUS SERPENT/ DRAGON WITH SIX HEADS 147-39, HYDRUS AN
CROCODILE 147-40, MAN TALKING WITH THREE OTHERS AND SHOWIN
HEART 147-41, MAN KNEELING BEFORE LADY 147-42, SERRA UNABLE T
KEEP UP WITH BOAT 147-43, TURTLE-DOVE SEATED IN TREE AND MA
AND WOMAN WATCH 147-44, PARTRIDGE WITH EGGS STOLEN FRO
ANOTHER PARTRIDGE 147-45, PARTRIDGE BABIES RETURN TO TRU
MOTHER WHEN CALLED 147-46, OSTRICH FORGETS ABOUT EGG DEPOSITE
IN SAND 147-47, STORK'S NEST 147-48, NEST OF BIRDS SHOWN B
MAN TO WOMAN 147-49, EAGLE BREAKING BEAK AGAINST STONE 147-50
DRAGON LICKING RECUMBENT FIGURE 147-51, ELEPHANT STANDING I
THE EUPHRATES 147-52, DRAGON UNABLE TO REACH ELEPHANT 145-53
VULTURE FLYING OVER BODY OF WHITE HORSE 147-54

*$ABSTRACT 148
  *LIBRARY BOD
  *SLIDE SET TITLE ROMAN DE LA ROSE
  *NEGATIVE REFERENCE ROLL 180H
  *RENTAL FEE SM 148 $5.00
  *COMMENTS 60 SLIDES TAKEN FROM THE ROMAN DE LA ROSE
  *TITLE OF MANUSCRIPT ROMAN DE LA ROSE
  *SHELFMARK MS ASTOR A 12
  *PROVENANCE FRENCH
  *DATE EXECUTED 14TH
  *LANGUAGE FRENCH
  *AUTHOR GUILLAUME DE LORRIS AND JEAN DE MEUNG
  *TYPE OF MANUSCRIPT ROMANCE
  *CONTENTS ROMANCE OF THE ROSE 148/1-60, LITERATURE/ ROMANCE O
  THE ROSE 148/1-60, LOVER ASLEEP 148-1, HATE 148-2, VILLAIN
  148-3, FELONY 148-3, COVETOUSNESS 148-3, AVARICE 148-4, ENV
  148-4, SADNESS 148-5, OLD AGE 148-6, HYPOCRISY 148-7, POVERT
  148-8, GARDEN/ WALLED WITH BIRDS 148-9, IDLENESS OPENS TH
  DOOR 148-10, DANCE 148-11, COURTESY PLACES WREATH ON HEAD O
  MIRTH 148-12, DANCERS/ SIX HOLDING HANDS 148-13
  MUSICIANS/THREE AND DANCERS HOLDING HANDS 148-14, RICHES AN
  YOUTH 148-15, FRANCHISE AND FRIEND 148-16, COURTESY AND FRIEN
  148-16, IDLENESS AND DREAMER 148-17, YOUTH AND LOVER 148-17
  FOUNTAIN WHERE NARCISSUS DIED 148-18, GOD OF LOVE POINTS ARRO
  AT DREAMER 148-19, GOD OF LOVE EMBRACES DREAMER 148-20, GOD O
  LOVE GIVES HIS COMMANDMENTS TO THE LOVER 148-21, WELCOM
  LEADING THE DREAMER BY THE HAND 148-22, LOVER AND DANGE
  148-23, LOVER AND REASON 148-24, FRANKNESS AND PITY TALK T
  DANGER 148-25, VENUS COMES TO THE LOVER 148-26, MODESTY SPEAK
  TO DANGER 148-27, PRISON BUILT FOR WELCOME 148-28, LOVER ASK
  TO GO INTO PRISON WITH LOVER 148-29, REASON COMES TO LOVE
  148-30, REASON AND GOD OF LOVE 148-31, FORTUNE AND HER WHEE
  148-32, LOVER AND THE FRIEND 148-33, VILLAIN CHASTISES HI
  WIFE 148-34, LOVER PASSES RICHESSE AND HER COMPANION 148-35
  POVERTY/ HUNGER/ THEFT 148-36, GOD OF LOVE PUTS HAND O
  LOVER'S HEAD 148-37, MONK WRITING AT END OF PART ONE 148-38
  FAUX SEMBLANT AND ABSTINENCE AT MALEBOUCHE@S CASTLE 148-39
  FAUX SEMBLANT MURDERS MALEBOUCHE 148-40, AUTHOR SPEAKS T
  LOVER 148-41, FRANCHISE AND DANGER PREPARE TO FIGHT 148-42
  CASTLE 148-42, PITY WITH SWORD STANDS WITH FRANCHISE 148-43
  PITY AND SHAME FIGHT 148-44, DELIGHT RUNS AGAINST SHAM
  148-45, BIEN CELER JOINS THE FIGHT 148-45, FEAR FIGHTS WIT
  BIEN CELER 148-46, BOLDNESS FIGHTS FEAR 148-46, SECURITY AN
  FEAR HAVING FOUGHT SWORDS FALL TO GROUND 148-47, VENUS AN
  ADONIS SPEAK DURING HUNT 148-48, VENUS CRADLES ADONIS ON LA
  148-49, VENUS RIDES IN CHARIOT PULLED BY DOVES TO SUN 148-50
  DAME NATURE CREATES BIRDS AND ANIMALS IN HER FIGURE 148-51
  NATURE KNEELS BEFORE HER CONFESSOR 148-52, GENIUS SITS IN HI
  SHRIVING CHAIR 148-53, FIRMAMENT 148-54, MOON AND THE PLANET
  148-55, SUN 148-56, ELEMENTS/ FOUR 148-57, VENUS PREPARES T
  SHOOT ARROW AT THE ROSE 148-58, VENUS SETS CASTLE OF JEALOUS
  ON FIRE 148-59, AUTHOR STANDS BEFORE ROSE IN HER SANCTUAR
  148-60

*$ABSTRACT 149
  *LIBRARY BOD
  *SLIDE SET TITLE APOCALYPSE FROM CATHEDRAL OF THE ASSUMPTION IN
  THE KREMLIN
  *NEGATIVE REFERENCE ROLL 181A
  *RENTAL FEE SM 149 $3.40
  *COMMENTS   28   SLIDES   PHOTOGRAPHED   FROM   RECENT   SOVIET
  PUBLICATIONS
  *PROVENANCE RUSSIAN
  *DATE EXECUTED 15TH
  *TYPE OF MANUSCRIPT RUSSIAN ICON OF THE APOCALYPSE
  *CONTENTS RUSSIAN ICON OF 15TH CENTURY 149/1-28, ICON/ RUSSIAN
  149/1-28, MAN ON BLACK HORSE 149-1, LAMB ON THRONE 149-2,
  MULTITUDE WITH PALMS 149-3, ANGELS AND THE SEVEN CHURCHES
  149-4, ST MICHAEL OVERTHROWS THE DEVIL 149-5, HORSEMEN/ THREE
  149-6, HORSEMAN ON RED HORSE 149-7, HORSEMAN ON BLACK HORSE
  149-8, JOHN BEFORE THE TEMPLE AND ANGEL WITH CENSER 149-9,
  BRIDE OF THE LAMB AND ANGEL WITH JOHN 149-10, WOMAN ADORNED IN
  SUN AND FLEEING TO WILDERNESS 149-11, ANGEL IN VINEYARD
  149-11, HORSEMEN ON HORSES WITH LION'S HEADS 149-12, ANGELS/
  FOUR MEET BEFORE EUPHRATES 149-13, ANGEL ADMONISHES THE PEOPLE
  149-14, MAN ON CLOUD WITH SICKLE 149-15, PLAYERS ON PSALTERY
  149-15, RAINBOW 149-15, EVANGELIST/ SIGNS 149-15, PLAYERS ON
  THE PSALTERY 149-16, PALE HORSE AND HELL 149-17, HELL 149-16,
  PROPHETS PROPHESY 149-18, PROPHETS WILD BEAST ISSUED FROM HELL
  149-19, WHORE OF BABYLON 149-20, ANGEL CURBING WIND 149-21,
  STAR FALLING FROM CLOUD OF DARKENING SUN 149-21, ASSEMBLIES OF
  THE RIGHTEOUS BEFORE THRONE 149/22-23, JERUSALEM/ HEAVENLY
  149-24, SOULS OF THE DESTROYED 149-25, ANGELS OVERTHROWN IN
  FIERY LAKE 149-26, SATAN TAKES SOULS AFTER THEIR RESURRECTION
  149-26, DEMONS 149-27, ANTICHRIST AND HIS ARMY 149-28

*$ABSTRACT 150
  *LIBRARY BOD
  *SLIDE SET TITLE PETRARCH
  *NEGATIVE REFERENCE ROLL 181 I%1<
  *RENTAL FEE SM 150 $2.15
  *COMMENTS 3 SLIDES SELECTED FROM WORK OF PETRARCH
  *TITLE OF MANUSCRIPT TRIONFI
  *SHELFMARK MS HOLKHAM 520
  *PROVENANCE ITALIAN
  *DATE EXECUTED 15TH
  *LANGUAGE LATIN
  *AUTHOR PETRARCH
  *TYPE OF MANUSCRIPT TREATISE
  *CONTENTS LOVE TRIUMPHS 150-1, CHASTITY TRIUMPHS 150-2, DEATH
  TRIUMPHS 150-3, TRIUMPHS OF LOVE/ CHASTITY/ DEATH 150/1-3

*$ABSTRACT 151
  *LIBRARY BOD
  *SLIDE SET TITLE PORTABLE MISSAL
  *NEGATIVE REFERENCE ROLL 182A
  *RENTAL FEE SM 151 $2.50
  *TITLE OF MANUSCRIPT MISSAL
  *SHELFMARK MS C C C 282
  *PROVENANCE IRISH
  *DATE EXECUTED 12TH
  *LANGUAGE LATIN
  *TYPE OF MANUSCRIPT MISSAL
  *CONTENTS MANUSCRIPT SATCHEL/ LEATHER 151/1-4, MISSAL/ CLOSED
  151-5, INITIAL/ ILLUMINATED 151-6, INTERLACE PATTERN ON PAGES
  151/7-9, INTERLACE WITH MONSTER'S HEAD 151-10

*$ABSTRACT 152
  *LIBRARY BOD
  *SLIDE SET TITLE LEOFRIC MISSAL

*NEGATIVE REFERENCE ROLL 182B
*RENTAL FEE SM 152 $2.50
*TITLE OF MANUSCRIPT LEOFRIC MISSAL
*SHELFMARK MS BODLEY 579
*PROVENANCE FRENCH/ ARRAS OR CAMBRAI AND ENGLISH/ GLASTONBURY
*DATE EXECUTED 10TH/ WITH ADDITIONS BEFORE 979 AND 1050-72
*LANGUAGE LATIN
*TYPE OF MANUSCRIPT SACRAMENTARY/ BENEDICTINE
*CONTENTS ZODIAC/ NAMES OF IN DIAMOND PATTERN 152-1, GOD'S
RIGHT HAND WITH DATE OF EASTER 152-2, LIFE/ ALLEGORICAL FIGURE
152-3, DEATH 152-4, ORNAMENTAL DESIGN 152-5, CIRCLES/
DIAGRAMMATIC 152-6, SUUM CORDA 152-7, VERE DIGNUM 152-8,
DECORATIVE TEXT 152-9, PANELS WITH TEXT 152-10

*$ABSTRACT 153
*LIBRARY BOD
*SLIDE SET TITLE
*NEGATIVE REFERENCE ROLL 182C
*RENTAL FEE SM 153 $2.55
*TITLE OF MANUSCRIPT ROMANCE OF THE ROSE
*SHELFMARK MS DOUCE 195 153/1-4, MS SELDEN SUPRA 57 153/5-8, MS
ADD A 22 153/9-11
*PROVENANCE FRENCH
*DATE EXECUTED 15TH 153/1-4, 14TH 153/5-11
*LANGUAGE FRENCH
*AUTHOR GUILLAUME DE LORRIS AND JEAN DE MEUNG
*TYPE OF MANUSCRIPT ROMANCE
*CONTENTS ROMANCE OF THE ROSE 153/1-11, LITERATURE/ ROMANCE OF
THE ROSE 153/1-11, LOVER IN BED AND POET AT DESK 153-1,
TRISTECE 153-2, PALELARDIE 153-3, POUURETE 153-4, LOVER IN BED
153-5, LOVER DRESSING 153-5, LOVER MEDITATING 153-5, LOVER IN
GARDEN 153-5, LOVER SWEARS FEALTY TO GOD OF LOVE 153-6, HONTE
AND PEUR VISIT DANGIER SLEEPING 153-7, ABSTINENCE/ CONSTRAINT
AND FAUX SEMBLANT VISIT GOD OF LOVE 153-8, LOVER IN BED 153-9,
VIELLECE 153-10, ABSTINENCE/ CONSTRAINT AND FAUX SEMBLANT
VISIT MALEBOUCHE 153-11

*$ABSTRACT 154
*LIBRARY BOD
*SLIDE SET TITLE ASTRONOMY TRIGONOMETRY AND GEOMETRY/
MATHEMATICAL TREATISES
*NEGATIVE REFERENCE ROLL 182F
*RENTAL FEE SM 154 $3.75
*COMMENTS 35 SLIDES SELECTED FROM 5 MSS AND 3 BOOKS
*TITLE OF MANUSCRIPT TRETISE ON QUADRANT 154/12-15, THEORY OF
PLANETS 153-17, L'ART DE NAVIGUER 153/22-23, AGAYNST THE
REPROUERS OF ASTRONOMIE AND SCIENCES MATHEMATICALL 154/24-27,
ASTRONOMIA NOVA DE MOTIBUS STELLA MARIS 154/29-35
*SHELFMARK MS ASHMOLE 1522 154/1-11, MS AUCT F 3 13 154/12-15,
MS DOUCE 125 154-16, MS BODLEY 300 154-17, MS BODLEY 309
154/18-21
*PROVENANCE ENGLISH 154/1-21 AND 24-28, FRENCH 154/22-23 AND
154/29-35
*DATE EXECUTED 15TH 154/1-11 AND 17, 13TH 154/12-15, 11TH
154-16, 16TH 154/22-35
*TYPE OF MANUSCRIPT MATHEMATICAL TREATISES
*CONTENTS MATHEMATICAL TREATISES 154/1-35, ALGORISM BY JOHN DE
SACRO BOSCO 154-1, CUBES/ SQUARES/ MEANS AND ROOTS 154-1,
SPHERE BY JOHN DE SACRO BOSCO 154-2, HEAVENS WITH EARTH AT
CENTER 154-2, STAR OF DAVID 154-3, EYE SEEING OBJECT IN VESSEL
OF WATER 154-3, EYE ON EARTH SEEING SUN THROUGH VAPOR 154-3,
EARTH WITH TROPIC ZONE WITH SIGNS OF ZODIAC 154-4, ANCIENT
QUADRANT BY JOHN OF MONTPELLIER 154/5-8, QUADRANT WITH DEGREES
OF MONTH AND SIGNS OF ZODIAC 154-5, ALTITUDES OF OBELISKS
TAKEN BY QUADRANT 154/6-7, OBELISKS AND QUADRANT 154-8, SOLID
SPHERE AND SPHERICAL ASTROLABE 154-8, ASTROLABE/ DIAGRAM
154-9, CYLINDRCAL SUNDIAL MARKED WITH DEGREES 154-10, COMPASS/
MARINER'S IN LETTER ABOUT MAGNET 154-11, ZODIAC SIGNS 154-12,

QUADRANT USED TO TAKE ALTITUDES OF TOWERS 154-13, ALTITUDES OF
TOWERS 154-14, SUN'S POSITION 154-15, FIGURES/ NUMBERS AND
MEASUREMENTS 154-16, PTOLEMAIC SYSTEM OF UNIVERSE DIAGRAMMED
154-17, CHRONOLOGICAL TREATISES 154/18-21, LETTERS OF POPE
HONORIUS II TO ARCHBISHOP OF TOURS 154-18, LETTER OF BISHOP OF
LEMANS TO BISHOP OF ANGOULEME 154-18, LETTER FROM BISHOP OF
LEMANS TO BISHOP OF CHARTRES 154-18, POEM CONCERNING WALK IN
ROME 154-19, CONFESSION BY BERENGER FOR BELIEF IN REAL
PRESENCE 154-19, TABLE FOR MOVABLE FEASTS 154-19, TABLES WITH
DOMINICAL LETTERS/ LEAP-YEAR AND DAYS 154-19, BEDE'S DE
RATIONE TEMPORUM 154/20-21, PLANETARY/ DIAGRAM AND OTHER
SPHERES 154-22, WORLD/ MAP OF 154-23, QUADRANT AND SUNDIAL
154-24, SUNDIAL AND MAGNITUDES OF PLANETS 154-25, PLANETS AND
OTHER SPHERES POSITIONS 154-26, WEATHER FORECAST TEXTS
154/26-27, ZODIAC SIGNS IN MARGINS 154-27, PLANETS WITH TEXT
154-28, ASTRONOMIA NOVA 154/29-35, TITLE PAGE 154-29, VIRTUTEM
QUAE PLANETAM 154-30, DIAGRAM CHAPTER 32 154-31, CHAPTER 33
VIRTUTEM QUAE PLANETAS 154-32, EVIDENTIOR PROBATIO/ CHAPTER 24
154-33, ACCURATIS EXAMEN PROPORTIONIS ORBIUM/ CHAPTER 54
154-34, DEMONSTRATUR EX OBSERVATIONIBUS CAPITUM/ CHAPTER 55
154-35

*$ABSTRACT 155
 *LIBRARY BOD
 *SLIDE SET TITLE BURY BIBLE
 *NEGATIVE REFERENCE ROLL 183
 *RENTAL FEE SM 155 $5.15
 *TITLE OF MANUSCRIPT BURY BIBLE
 *SHELFMARK MS C C C CAMBRIDGE 2
 *PROVENANCE ENGLISH/ BURY ST EDMUNDS ABBEY
 *DATE EXECUTED 12TH/1120-48
 *LANGUAGE LATIN
 *ARTIST/ SCHOOL A PORTION OF THE BIBLE OF MAGISTER HUGO
 *TYPE OF MANUSCRIPT BIBLE
 *CONTENTS INITIAL TO JEROME'S PROLOGUE 155/1-4, CENTAUR
GALLOPING WITH SHIELD AND LANCE 155/1-4, MAN WITH WOODEN LEG
CHASING HARE 155/1-4, MERMAID WITH BLUE TAIL AND FISHES
155/1-4, INCIPIT PROLOGUE TO JEROME 155-5, INITIAL D WITH OWL
155-5, PRINCIPIO 155-6, EXODUS/ DECORATED INITIAL AT BEGINNING
OF 155-7, LEVITICUS/ DECORATED INITIAL 155-8, NUMBERS/
FRONTISPIECE 155-9, MOSES AND AARON 155-10, MOSES ADDRESSES
MEN AND AARON BEHIND 155-11, NUMBERS/ DECORATED INITIAL
155-12, EXPLICIT CAPITULA INCIPIT DEUTERONOMIUM 155-13,
DEUTERONOMY/ FRONTISPIECE 155-14, MOSES AND AARON ADDRESSING
ISRAELITES 155-15, MOSES ESTABLISHING LAW ON UNCLEAN BEASTS
155-16, DEUTERONOMY/ DECORATED INITIAL 155-17, PROLOGUE TO
JOSHUA AND JUDGES/ INITIAL 155-18, JOSHUA/ INITIAL WITH TWO
HUMAN HEADS 155-19, JUDGES/ LARGE INITIAL 155-20, RUTH/
INITIAL 155-21, KINGS/ PROLOGUE 155-22, KINGS I/ FRONTISPIECE
155-23, ELKANAH GIVES ROBES TO HANNAH AND PENNINAH 155-24, ELI
LISTENS TO PRAYING HANNAH 155-25, DECORATED INITIALS
155/26-31, KINGS I WITH LIONS AND HUMAN HEADS 155-26, KINGS II
155-27, KINGS III 155-28, KINGS IV 155-29, ISAIAH/ PROLOGUE
155-30, ISAIAH HOLDING WHITE SCROLL TO RIGHT HAND OF GOD
155-31, JEREMIAH/ PROLOGUE 155-32, JEREMIAH ON ROCKS HOLDS
WHITE SCROLL OUT TO GOD 155-34, WARRIORS WITHIN CITY WITH
HELMETS/ MAIL AND SHIELDS 155-35, JEREMIAH/ INITIAL 155-36,
BARUCH/ INITIAL 155-37, EPISTLE OF JEREMY/ INITIAL 155-38,
INCIPIT LAMENTATIONS OF JEREMIAH 155-39, EXPLICIT LAMENTATIONS
OF JEREMIAH 155-40, EZEKIEL/ VISION OF 155-41, EVANGELIST
SYMBOLS 155-42, CHRIST IN MANDORLA 155/43-44, DANIEL/ PROLOGUE
155-45, DANIEL/ INITIAL 155-46, HOSEA/ INITIAL 155-47, AMOS
PROPHETA/ ARGUMENTS TO 155-48, INCIPIT AMOS PROPHETA WITH
NIMBED AMOS 155-49, JONAH/ INITIAL 155-50, MICAH/ ARGUMENTS TO
INITIAL 155-51, NAHUM PROPHETA/ INITIAL 155-52, HABAKKUK/
ARGUMENTS TO 155-53, HABAKKUK/ INITIAL 155-54, ZEPHANIAH/
ARGUMENTS INITIAL 155-55, INCIPIT SOPHIONAS PROPHETAS/ INITIAL
155-56, HAGGAI/ ARGUMENT TO 155-57, ZECHARIAH/ INITIAL 155-58,
INCIPIT LIBER MALACHI 155-59, PROLOGUE TO JOB/ INITIAL 155-60,
JOB/ FRONTISPIECE 155-61, JOB KNEELING DIVINE HAND ABOVE AND

SONS AND DAUGHTERS 155-62, JOB SEATED ON ROCKS AND WIFE WITH
SCROLL 155-63

*$ABSTRACT 156
  *LIBRARY BOD
  *SLIDE SET TITLE GOSPELS, SELECTED DRAWINGS/ BORDERS AND
   INITIALS
  *NEGATIVE REFERENCE ROLL 184A
  *RENTAL FEE SM 156 $2.50
  *TITLE OF MANUSCRIPT GOSPELS/ BIBLE
  *SHELFMARK MS WADHAM COLLEGE 2
  *PROVENANCE ENGLISH
  *DATE EXECUTED 11TH
  *LANGUAGE LATIN
  *TYPE OF MANUSCRIPT GOSPELS
  *CONTENTS INITIAL B 156-1, ANIMAL MASK AND FOLIAGE 156-1,
   DECORATIVE FRAME 156-2, ST MATTHEW 156-3, BORDER WITH FOLIAGE
   AND STRAPWORK 156-4, INITIAL P WITH BITING BIRD'S HEAD 156-5,
   INITIAL Q 156-6, ST MICHAEL TRAMPLES CHAINED DRAGON-DEVIL
   155-6, ST LUKE'S GOSPEL/ TEXT 156-7, MARYS/ THREE AT TOMB
   155-8, ANGEL STANDS ON SLEEPING GUARDS 156-8, INITIAL H 156-9,
   INITIAL I 156-10

*$ABSTRACT 157
  *LIBRARY BOD
  *SLIDE SET TITLE HISTORICAL BOOKS OF THE BIBLE, JOSHUA TO JOB
  *NEGATIVE REFERENCE ROLL 184C
  *RENTAL FEE SM 157 $2.85
  *COMMENTS 17 SLIDES ILLUSTRATING HISTORIATED INITIALS
  *SHELFMARK MS WADHAM COLLEGE 1
  *PROVENANCE FRENCH
  *DATE EXECUTED 13TH
  *LANGUAGE LATIN
  *TYPE OF MANUSCRIPT BIBLE
  *CONTENTS GENESIS/ PROLOGUE 157-1, ST JEROME SEATED WRITING
   157-1, JOSHUA 157-2, KNIGHT WITH SHIELD 157-2, JUDGES 157-3,
   JUDGE AND SUPPLIANT 157-3, RUTH 157-4, ELIMELECH/ NAOMI AND
   THEIR TWO SONS 157-4, KINGS I 157-5, DAVID ORDERS MAN TO BE
   KILLED 157-5, KINGS II 157-6, KINGS III 157-7, DAVID OLD AND
   NOT WARM 157-7, KINGS IV 157-8, OCHOZIAS FALLS FROM WINDOW OF
   UPPER ROOM 157-8, CHRONICLES II/ PARALIPOMENON 157-9,
   ANCESTORS OF ISRAEL 157-9, CHRONICLES II 157-10, SOLOMON
   ENTHRONED 157-10, ESDRAS I 157-11, CYRUS AND JEREMIAS 157-11,
   ESDRAS II 157-12, ARTAXERXES AND CUP-BEARER 157-12, ESDRAS III
   157-13, PRIEST ASPERGES ALTAR 157-13, TOBIAS 157-14, RAPHAEL/
   ARCHANGEL AND BLIND TOBIAS WITH SON 157-14, JUDITH 157-15,
   JUDITH KILLS HOLOFERNES 157-15, ESTHER 157-16, ESTHER SPEAKING
   TO KING AND HAMAN HANGED 157-16, JOB 157-17, JOB AND WIFE AND
   COMFORTER 157-17

*$ABSTRACT 158
  *LIBRARY BOD
  *SLIDE SET TITLE DEVELOPMENT OF 15TH CENTURY HUMANISTIC SCRIPT
   AND DECORATION
  *NEGATIVE REFERENCE ROLL 184E
  *RENTAL FEE SM 158 $4.05
  *COMMENTS 41 SLIDES SELECTED FROM 26 MSS SHOWING EARLY SCRIPT
  *TITLE OF MANUSCRIPT DIALOGUES 158/1-2, GOSPELS 158/3-5, ORATOR
   158-6, ORATIONS 158/7-8, DE PRIMO BELLO PUNICO 158/9-10,
   COMEDIES 158-11, THIRD DECADE 158-12, PSALTER 158-13, COMEDIES
   158-14, SERMONS AND LETTERS OF JEROME AND AUGUSTINE 158-15,
   LIVES/ PLUTARCH 158/16-21, COMEDIES/ TERENCE 158-22, ORATIONS
   158/23-26, DE MILITIA 158-27, FIRST DECADE 158/28-29, HISTORIA
   FLORENTINA 158/30-31, CONTRA ACADEMICOS 158-32, DE OFFICIIS
   158-33, SILVAE 158-34, ORATIONS 158-35, THESAURUS 158-36,
   LETTERS 158-37, DONATUS ON TERENCE 158-38, LIVES/ PLUTARCH

```
       158/39-40, DE AMICITIA 158-41
  *SHELFMARK   MS CANON PAT LAT 105 158/1-2, MS LAUD LAT 25 158-3,
  MS CANON PAT LAT 156 158/4-5, MS LAT CLASS  D  37  158-6,  MS
  D/ORVILLE   78   158/7-8,  MS  LAUD  MISC 531 158/9-10, MS CANON
  CLASS LAT 99 158-11, MS CANON CLASS LAT 300 158-12, MS CANON
  BIBL  LAT 63 158-13, MS LAT CLASS D 6 158-14, MS CANON PAT LAT
  27 158-15, MS DOUCE 214 158/16-21, MS LAUD LAT 73 158-22, MS
  NEW COLLEGE 249 158/23-26, MS LINCOLN COLLEGE 20 158/28-29, MS
  BUCHANAN  C 1 158/30-31, MS D/ORVILLE 207 158-32, MS D/ORVILLE
  87 158-33, MS BARLOW 23 158-34, MS  LINCOLN  COLLEGE  LAT  39
  158-35,  MS  LINCOLN COLLEGE LAT 37 158-36, MS LINCOLN COLLEGE
  LAT 47 158-37, MS LINCOLN COLLEGE LAT 45 158-38, MS AUCT F 1 7
  158/39-40, MS D/ORVILLE 88 158-41
  *PROVENANCE ITALIAN/ FLORENCE
  *DATE EXECUTED 12TH 158/1-5, 15TH 158/6-41
  *LANGUAGE LATIN
  *AUTHOR ST GREGORY 158/1-2, CICERO 158/6-8 AND 23-26 AND 33 AND
  35 AND 41 BRUNI 158/9-10 AND 30-31, TERENCE  158/11  AND  22,
  LIVY  15  AND  12  AND  28-29, PLAUTUS  158-14, ST JEROME AND
  AUGUSTINE LETTERS 158-15, PLUTARCH 158/16-21 AND 39-40, ST
  AUGUSTINE  158-32, STATIUS 158-34, ST CYRIL 158-36, ST CYPRIAN
  158-37
  *TYPE OF MANUSCRIPT MISCELLANY
  *CONTENTS SCRIPT AND DECORATION IN FLORENTINE HUMANISTIC  STYLE
  158/1-41, INITIALS AND BORDERS/ DECORATIVE 158/1-41, INITIAL P
  158-2,  INITIAL  L  158-3,  INITIAL  V 158-4, INITIAL P 158-5,
  INITIAL I 158/6-7, INITIAL P 158-8, INITIAL C 158/9 AND 11 AND
  18, INITIAL V 158/10 AND 14, INITIAL M 158/12 AND 16  AND  17,
  INITIAL  B 158-13, INITIAL A 158-15, INITIAL L 158-19, INITIAL
  P 158-22, INITIAL  G  158-23,  INITIAL  E  158-24,  INITIAL  V
  158-25,  INITIAL C 158-26, INITIAL V 158-27, INITIAL F 158-28,
  INITIAL D 158-30, INITIAL E 158-32, INITIAL Q 158-33,  INITIAL
  E  158-34,  INITIAL  I  158-35,  INITIAL  B  158-36, INITIAL T
  158-37, INITIAL Q 158-39, INITIAL  O/  PORTRAIT  OF  ARISTOTLE
  158-40, ARISTOTLE PORTRAIT 158-40




 *$ABSTRACT 159
  *LIBRARY BOD
  *SLIDE  SET TITLE DEVELOPMENT OF 15TH CENTURY HUMANISTIC SCRIPT
  AND DECORATION
  *NEGATIVE REFERENCE ROLL 184F
  *RENTAL FEE SM 159 $3.15
  *COMMENTS 23 SLIDES SELECTED FROM 14 MSS AFTER 1450
  *TITLE OF MANUSCRIPT DE VAIETATE FORTUNAE 159-1, OPERA 159/2-3,
  OPERA  PHILOSOPHICA  159/4-5, PHALARIS/ LETTERS OF   159-6,
  ORATIONS  159/7-8,  CANZONIERE  AND TRIONFI 159/9-10, GEORGICS
  159-11,  ST  CYRIL  ON  JOHN  159/12-13,  TRIONFI  159/14-15,
  COMEDIES  159/16-18, CANZONIERE AND TRIFONI 159/19-20, ELEGIES
  159/21-22, STATUTES OF HOSPITAL OF ST MARIA NUOVA 159-23
  *SHELFMARK MS BUCHANAN D 4 159-1, MS CANON PAT LAT 138 159/2-3,
  MS AUCT F 1 12 159/4-5, MS RAWL  G  66  159-6,  MS  DIGBY  231
  159/7-8,  MS  CANON  ITAL 62 159/9-10, MS RAWL G 97 159-11, MS
  CANON PAT LAT 159 159/12-13, MS MONTAGUE E 1 159/14-15, MS E D
  CLARKE 28  159/16-17,  MS  CANON  CLASS  LAT  296  159-18,  MS
  MONTAGUE  D  32 159/19-20, MS CANON CLASS LAT 31 159/21-22, MS
  BODLEY 488 159-23
  *PROVENANCE ITALIAN/ FLORENTIAN
  *DATE EXECUTED 15TH
  *LANGUAGE LATIN
  *AUTHOR BRACCIOLINI/ POGGIO 159-1, LACTANTIUS  159/2-3,  CICERO
  159/4-5 AND 7-8, PETRARCH 159/9-10 AND 14-15 AND 19-20, VERGIL
  159-11,  ST  CYRIL  159/12-13, TERENCE 159/16-17, LIVY 159-18,
  PROPERTIUS 159/21-22
  *TYPE OF MANUSCRIPT MISCELLANY
  *CONTENTS SCRIPT AND DECORATION IN HUMANISTIC FLORENTINE  STYLE
  159/1-23, INITIALS AND BORDERS DECORATED 159/1-23
```

*$ABSTRACT 160
  *LIBRARY BOD
  *SLIDE SET TITLE ENGLISH ILLUMINATION OF THE LATE 14TH AND 15TH
   CENTURIES
  *NEGATIVE REFERENCE ROLL 184G
  *RENTAL FEE SM 160 $3.80
  *COMMENTS 36 SLIDES SELECTED FROM 21 MSS
  *TITLE OF MANUSCRIPT PSALTER AND HOURS 160-1, MISSAL 160-2,
   CHARTER GIVEN BY RICHARD II TO CROYLAND ABBEY 160-3, WILLIAM
   OF NOTTINGHAM'S COMMENTARY ON THE FOUR GOSPELS 160-4, LAPWORTH
   MISSAL 160-5, LI LIVRES DU GRAUNT CAAM 160/6-9, BOOK OF HOURS
   160-10, SARUM MISSAL 160/11-12, MISSAL 160/13-14, BIBLE IN
   ENGLISH 160-15, RICHARD OF HAMPOLE'S COMMENTARY ON THE PSALMS
   AND CANTICLES 160/16-17, CONFESSIO AMANTIS 160-18, BOOK OF
   HOURS 160/19-20, PORTABLE PSALTER 160/21-22, CANTERBURY TALES
   160-23, CLOSWORTH MISSAL 160-24, MISSAL 160/25-28, ABINGDON
   MISSAL 160/29-31, ABINGDON MISSAL/ WINTER PART 160-32, LIFE OF
   WILLIAM OF WYKEHAM 160-33, MIRROURE OF THE WORLD 160-34,
   STATUTES OF ENGLAND 160/35-36
  *SHELFMARK MS LAUD MISC 188 160-1, MS ASHMOLE 1831 160-3, MS
   TRINITY COLLEGE 8 160-2, MS LAUD MISC 165 160-5, MS C C C 394
   160-6, MS BODLEY 264 160/6-9, MS LAT LITURG F 2 160-10, MS
   HATTON 1 160/11-12, MS ORIEL COLLEGE 75 160/13-14, MS BODLEY
   277 160-15, MS BODLEY 953 160/16-17, MS BODLEY 294 160-18, MS
   GOUGH LITURG 6 160/19-20, MS DOUCE 18 160/21-22, MS BODLEY 686
   160-23, MS DON B 6 160-24, MS LAUD MISC 302 160/25-28, MS
   DIGBY 227 160/29-31, MS TRINITY COLLEGE 75 160-32, MS NEW
   COLLEGE 288 160-33, MS BODLEY 283 160-34, MS HATTON 10
   160/35-36
  *PROVENANCE ENGLISH
  *DATE EXECUTED 14TH AND 15TH
  *LANGUAGE LATIN 160/1-2 AND 5 AND 10-14 AND 19-22 AND 24-32,
   FRENCH 160/6-9, ENGLISH 160/3-4 AND 15 AND 18 AND 23 AND 33-36
  *AUTHOR MARCO POLO 160/6-9, RICHARD OF HAMPOLE 160/16-17, JOHN
   GOWER 160-18, CHAUCER 160-23, THOMAS CHAUNDLER 160-33
  *TYPE OF MANUSCRIPT PSALTER/ MISSAL/ BOOK OF HOURS/ BIBLE/
   CHARTER
  *CONTENTS PRESENTATION OF CHRIST IN TEMPLE 160-1, JOSEPH WITH
   DOVES IN BASKET 160-1, PRIEST AT ALTAR GIVES COMMUNION TO FOUR
   MEN 160-2, ILLUMINATION/ ENGLISH 160/1-23, KINGS GIVE CHARTER
   TO ABBOT AND MONKS 160-3, ARCHBISHOP ENTHRONED AMONG CLERICS
   160-4, CRUCIFIXION 160-5, VENICE WITH ST MARK'S/ PALACE OF
   DOGES/ WATERFRONT 160-6, PAPAL LETTERS PRESENTED TO KHAN
   160-7, MARCO POLO HEARING STORY IN PERSIA 160-8, SHEPHERD WITH
   BAGPIPES 160-8, PIETA 160-10, MASS FOR ALL SAINTS 160-11,
   CHRIST BLESSING COMPANY OF SAINTS 160-11, TRINITY AND MERCY-
   SEAT TYPE 160-12, ADORATION OF THE MAGI 160-13, CHILD PUTS
   HAND IN GOLDEN CUP 160-13, NATIVITY 160-14, VIRGIN ON
   ELABORATE COUCH WITH CANOPY 160-14, BORDER OF WYCLIFF BIBLE
   160-15, FOOL IN FEATHERED HOOD WITH BLADDER 160-16, GOD ON
   EMPTY BENCH INDICATES EMPTY PLACE BY HIM 160-17, LOVER KNEELS
   BEFORE HIS CONFESSOR 160-18, HISTORIATED INITIALS 160-19,
   REDEEMER BEARING SOULS TO HEAVEN 160-20, MAGI COMING 160-21,
   NATIVITY 160-21, DAVID KNEELING POINTS TO HIS EYES 160-22,
   FLOWER AND LEAF-MOTIFS 160-23, CRUCIFIXION WITH HILLS THOUGHT
   TO BE DORSET 160-24, ADORATION OF THE MAGI 160-25, BETHLEHEM
   AS CASTELLATED BUILDINGS 160-25, SHEPHERDS WITH SHEEP 160-25,
   ST ANDREW CRUCIFIXION 160-26, GROTESQUE FIGURES 160-27,
   ANIMALS IN PAGE BORDER 160/27-28, RESURRECTION 160-29,
   CRUCIFIXION WITH ST MARY AND ST JOHN AND TRINITY 160-30,
   ANNUNCIATION 160-31, NATIVITY WITH ASS BENDING HEAD TO LOOK
   160-32, GRISAILLE DRAWING 160-33, CLOISTER OF NEW COLLEGE
   OXFORD AND MEMBERS 160-33, FRUIT-LIKE FLOWERS IN PAGE BORDER
   160-34, INITIAL WITH A BIRD 160-35, KING EDWARD IV ENTHRONED
   SURROUNDED BY COURTIERS 160-36

*$ABSTRACT 161
  *LIBRARY BOD
  *SLIDE SET TITLE MIDDLE ENGLISH POETRY
  *NEGATIVE REFERENCE ROLL 185B

*RENTAL FEE SM 161 $2.95
*COMMENTS 19 SLIDES FROM 11 MSS DEPICTING MIDDLE ENGLISH POETRY
*TITLE OF MANUSCRIPT PRICK OF CONSCIENCE 161-1, CONFESSIO
AMANTIS 161/2-3, VERNON MS 161-4, DE PRINCIPIUM REGIMINE
161-5, TO LERNE TO DIE 161-6, TROY BOOK 161/7-15, FALL OF
PRINCES 161-16, COMPLAINT OF MARS AND VENUS 161-17, TROILUS
AND CRESSIDA 161-18, LEGEND OF GOOD WOMEN 161-19
*SHELFMARK MS DOUCE 156 161-1, MS FAIRFAX 3 161/2-3, MS ENG
POET A1 161-4, MS DOUCE 158 161-5, MS SELDEN SUPRA 53 161-6,
MS DIGBY 232 161/7-10, MS RAWL C 446 161/11-14, MS RAWL POET
223 161-15, MS BODLEY 263 161-16, MS FAIRFAX 16 161-17, MS
ARCH SELD B 24 161/18-19
*PROVENANCE ENGLISH 161/1-17, SCOTTISH 161/18-19
*DATE EXECUTED 15TH
*LANGUAGE ENGLISH
*AUTHOR ROLLE 161-1, GOWER 161/2-3, HOCCLEVE 161/5-6, LYDGATE
161/7-16, CHAUCER 161/17-19
*TYPE OF MANUSCRIPT POETRY
*CONTENTS LITERATURE/ MIDDLE ENGLISH 161/1-19, POETIC TEXTS IN
MIDDLE ENGLISH 161/1-19, DECORATIVE BORDER AND INITIAL 161-1,
DREAM OF NEBUCHADNEZZAR 161-2, POET AND HIS CONFESSOR 161-3,
PAGE OF TEXT OF POETRY 161-4, INITIAL/ DECORATIVE AND
BEGINNING OF TEXT 161-5, DEATH BED SCENE WITH DEATH AS
SKELETON WITH SPEAR 161-6, LYDGATE PRESENTING HIS BOOK TO
HENRY V 161-7, PELEUS/ KING PRAYS TO THE GODS 161-8, HECTOR
KILLS PATROCLUS 161-10, LYDGATE PRESENTS BOOK TO HENRY V
161-11, CASTLE BESIEGED BY KING PRIAM 161-12, HECTOR KILLS
PATROCLUS 161-13, AGAMEMNON AND HIS LORDS WITH TENT OF
ACHILLES 161-14, HECTOR'S SHRINE 161-14, INITIAL/ ILLUMINATED
161-15, FALL OF PRINCES/ SCENES IN MINATURE FROM TEXT 161-16,
JUPITER, MARS AND VENUS WITH PAGE OF DECORATED TEXT 161-17,
INITIAL/ HISTORIATED WITH BEGINNING OF TROILUS AND CRESSIDA
161-18, LEGEND OF GOOD WOMEN/ BEGINNING OF TEXT 161-19

*$ABSTRACT 162
*LIBRARY BOD
*SLIDE SET TITLE BRITAIN IN THE NOTITIA DIGNITATUM
*NEGATIVE REFERENCE ROLL 186B
*RENTAL FEE SM 162 $3.00
*COMMENTS 20 SLIDES FROM A HANDBOOK AND ILLUSTRATIONS OF THE
MILITARY AND CIVIL ORGANIZATION OF THE LATER ROMAN EMPIRE
*TITLE OF MANUSCRIPT NOTITIA DIGNITATUM
*SHELFMARK MS CANON MISC 378
*PROVENANCE ENGLISH
*DATE EXECUTED 15TH
*LANGUAGE LATIN
*TYPE OF MANUSCRIPT HANDBOOK OF MILITARY AND CIVIL ORGANIZATION
*CONTENTS MILITARY AND CIVIL INSIGNIA OF ROMAN EMPIRE IN
BRITAIN 162/1-20, NOTITIA DIGNITATUM/ OPENING PAGES 161-1,
INSIGNIA OF PRAEFECTUS PRAETORIO PER ITALIAS 162-2, INSIGNIA
OF THE MAGISTER PEDITUM 162-3, COMES BRITANNIAE/ TROOPS IN
BRITAIN 162/3-5, SHIELDS ON INSIGNIA OF THE MAGISTER PEDITUM
162-6, INSIGNIA OF THE MAGISTER EQUITUM AND LIST OF COMMANDERS
162-7, CAVALRY UNITS OF COMITATENSES 162/7-8, GEOGRAPHICAL
LOCATION OF THE UNITS/ DISTRIBUTIO NUMERORUM 162-9, CAVALRY
UNITS WITH COUNT OF THE BRITAINS 162-10, INSIGNIA OF THE
MAGISTER OFFICIORUM 162-11, INSIGNIA OF THE COMES SACARUM
LARGITIONUM 162-12, INSIGNIA OF COMES RERUM PRIVATARUM/ CHIEF
OF PRIVY PURSE 162-13, INSIGNIA OF PRIMICERIUS NOTARIORUM/
FIRST SECRETARY OF CHANCELLERY 162-14, INSIGNIA OF THE
VICARIUS BRITANNIARUM 162-15, INSIGNIA OF COMES LITORIS
SAXONICA PER BRITANNAIA 162-16, INSIGNIA AND STAFF OF COMES
BRITANNIAE 162-17, INSIGNIA OF THE DUX BRITANNIARUM 162-18,
INSIGNIA OF THE CONSULARIS CAMPANIAE AND HIS FORCES 162-19,
INSIGNIA OF THE PRAESES DALMATIAE AND HIS OFFICE STAFF 162-20

*$ABSTRACT 163
*LIBRARY BOD

```
*SLIDE SET TITLE ARTHURIAN LEGEND
*NEGATIVE REFERENCE ROLL 186C
*RENTAL FEE SM 163 $2.70
*TITLE OF MANUSCRIPT LANCELOT CYCLE
*SHELFMARK MS DOUCE 178
*PROVENANCE ITALIAN
*DATE EXECUTED 14TH
*LANGUAGE FRENCH
*TYPE OF MANUSCRIPT ROMANCE
*CONTENTS   ARTHURIAN   LEGEND   163/1-14,   LITERATURE/   ARTHURIAN
163/1-14,   ROMANCE/   ARTHURIAN  163/1-14,  EMPERORS  OF  ROME  FROM
TIBERIUS  TO  VESPASIANUS  163-1,  JOSEPH  PRAYING  BEFORE  ARK  SEES
VISION   OF   CHRIST   163-2,  JOSEPHO   AS   BISHOP   WITH   QUEEN
SARRACINTE  163-3,  HARROWING  OF  HELL  163-4,  CHRIST  IN  MANDORLA
WITH   BLACK  CHASM  AT  HIS  FEET  163-4,  VORTIGERN/  USURPER  POINTS
TO  MURDERERS  BUT  KNOWS  THEM  NOT  163-5,  MERLIN  ON  BLACK  HORSE
WITH  KINGS  DAN  AND  BORS  163-6,  GAWAINE  RESCUES  MOTHER  FROM  THE
SESNES   163-7,   KNIGHTS   IN   BATTLE   WITH   SESNES  NEAR  ARUNDEL
163-8,  BATTLE  AT  DANEBLAISE   WITH   KINGS   IN   CONFLICT   163-9,
ENEMIES  PLAN  TO  SUBSTITUTE  GUINIVERE  FOR  ARTHUR'S  WIFE  163-10,
LOT/  KING  AND  SONS  LEAVE  DEAD  BODIES  OF  SESNES  163-11,  RION/
KING'S  MESSENGER  ARRIVES  AT  CAMELOT  163-12,   EMPEROR   OF   ROME
RECEIVES   WORD   OF   HIS  DEFEAT  163-13,  KNIGHT  DECAPITATING  THE
OTHER  AND  DEAD  KNIGHT  AT  ALTAR  163-14


*$ABSTRACT 164
  *LIBRARY BOD
  *SLIDE SET TITLE LADIES IN ARTHURIAN LEGEND
  *NEGATIVE REFERENCE ROLL 186D
  *RENTAL FEE SM 164 $2.65
  *COMMENTS 13 SLIDES SELECTED FROM 2 MSS
  *TITLE OF MANUSCRIPT  LESTOIRE  DE  MERLIN   164/1-2,   ROMAN   DE
LANDELOT DU LAC 164/3-13
  *SHELFMARK MS DOUCE 178 164/1-2, MS DOUCE 199 164/3-13
  *PROVENANCE ITALIAN 164/1-2, FRENCH 164/3-13
  *DATE EXECUTED 14TH
  *LANGUAGE FRENCH
  *TYPE OF MANUSCRIPT ROMANCE
  *CONTENTS   ARTHURIAN   ROMANCE   164/1-13,  ROMANCE/   ARTHURIAN
164/1-13,   LITERATURE/   ARTHURIAN   164/1-13,   GARLOT/   QUEEN
CAPTURED   AND   CARRIED   OFF   ON   HORSE   164-1,  LADY  WITH  DWARF
ARRIVING  AT  ARTHUR'S  COURT  164-2,  GUINEVERE  ILL  IN   BED   GIVES
BOHORT   RING  FOR  LANCELOT  164-3,  GUINEVERE  WAVES  FROM  TOWER  TO
COUSIN  ELYZABEL  164-4,  OLD  WOMAN  GUIDING  LANCELOT  KNIGHT   AND
DAMSELS   164-5,   LADY  PEEPING  THROUGH  DOORWAY  OF  CASTLE  164-6,
QUEEN  SARSTAN/  MORGAN  DE  FEE  AND  SABILLE  APPROACH  LANCELOT
164-7,  LADY  AND  SQUIRE  GIVE  LANCELOT  NEWS  ON  ROAD  164-8,
LANCELOT  SURROUNDED  BY  DANCERS   AND   CROWNED  BY  LADY   164-9,
ELYZABEL   AND   SQUIRES  ARRIVE  AT  ABBEY  164-10,  KNIGHTS  WITH
SWORDS  DRAG  LANDOINE  BY  HER  HAIR  164-11,  LADY  IN  BED  GREETED
BY  LANCELOT  IN  PAVILLION  164-12,  ELAINE/  LANCELOT  AND  GALAHAD
ON  WAY  TO  ABBEY  164-13


*$ABSTRACT 165
  *LIBRARY BOD
  *SLIDE SET TITLE MERLIN
  *NEGATIVE REFERENCE ROLL 186E
  *RENTAL FEE SM 165 $3.45
  *COMMENTS LANCELOT CYCLE/ BRANCHES ONE/ TWO/ AND THREE
  *TITLE OF MANUSCRIPT LESTOIRE DE MERLIN
  *SHELFMARK MS DOUCE 178
  *PROVENANCE ITALIAN/ VENICE
  *DATE EXECUTED 14TH/C1300
  *LANGUAGE FRENCH
  *TYPE OF MANUSCRIPT ROMANCE
  *CONTENTS MERLIN IN ARTHURIAN LEGEND SEEN IN  14TH  CENTURY  MS
  165/1-28,   ARTHURIAN   ROMANCE  165/1-28,  ROMANCE/   ARTHURIAN
  165/1-28,  LITERATURE/  ARTHURIAN  165/1-28,  MERLIN'S   BIRTH
```

165-1, MERLIN MOUNTED AS DAN AND BERS ARRIVE AT COURT 165-2,
MERLIN TELLING DAN AND BERS OF ARTHUR'S PARENTAGE 165-3, ARMY
BROUGHT TOGETHER BY MERLIN ON BLACK HORSE 165-4, MERLIN BRINGS
ARMY TO BRITAIN 165-5, MERLIN WITH DAN AND BERS ARRIVE AT
CARMELIDE 165-6, MERLIN TELLS ARTHUR OF BATTLE WITH SESNES
165-7, MERLIN RELATES FATE OF SAGREMOR TO GAWAIN 165-8, MERLIN
RETURNS TO CARMELIDE AND TALKS WITH KNIGHTS 165-9, VIVIANE
TAUGHT MAGIC BY MERLIN 165-10, MERLIN AS SMALL BOY BRINGS
LETTER TO ARTHUR 165-11, SESNES PURSUED BY MERLIN AND KNIGHTS
OF ROUND TABLE 165-12, GAWAIN ARRANGING SHIPS AT DOVER UNDER
MERLIN'S ORDERS 165-13, DAN/ KING ASKS MERLIN TO INTERPRET
QUEEN'S DREAM 165-14, GAWAIN WELCOMED BY MERLIN AT BENWIC'S
CASTLE 165-15, MERLIN ENTERS FOREST OF ROMANIE 165-16, MERLIN
AS STAG ENTERS EMPEROR'S PALACE 165-17, MERLIN TAKES LEAVE OF
EMPEROR 165-18, MERLIN TELLS BRETEL AND ULFII OF PLANNED
TREACHERY 165-19, MERLIN LEAVING ARTHUR AND LEODEGAN TO GO TO
BLAISE 165-20, MERLIN GOES TO BLAISE HOLDING SCROLL 165-21,
MERLIN AND KINGS DAN/ BORS AND ARTHUR 165-22, ARTHUR AND DAN
AT FEAST WITH MERLIN AND MINSTREL 165-23, MERLIN BIDS FAREWELL
TO ARTHUR 165-24, MERLIN EXPLAINS DREAM TO KING PLUALIS
165-25, MERLIN BIDS ARTHUR PREPARE FOR WAR 165-26, MERLIN
ADVISES ARTHUR TO SEND MEN TO MEET MESSENGERS 165-27, SAGREMOR
ARRIVES AT MERLIN@S PRISON 165-28

*$ABSTRACT 166
 *LIBRARY BOD
 *SLIDE SET TITLE KING ARTHUR
 *NEGATIVE REFERENCE ROLL 186F
 *RENTAL FEE SM 166 $2.60
 *COMMENTS 12 SLIDES DEPICTING KING ARTHUR FROM 2 MSS
 *TITLE OF MANUSCRIPT LESTOIRE DE MERLIN 166/1-10, ROMAN DE
LANCELOT DU LAC 166/11-12
 *SHELFMARK MS DOUCE 178 166/1-10, MS DOUCE 199 166/11-12
 *PROVENANCE ITALIAN 166/1-10, FRENCH 166/11-12
 *DATE EXECUTED 14TH
 *LANGUAGE FRENCH
 *TYPE OF MANUSCRIPT ROMANCE
 *CONTENTS ARTHUR/ KING 166/1-12, ROMANCE/ ARTHURIAN 166/1-12,
LITERATURE/ ARTHURIAN 166/1-12, ARTHUR CROWNED 166-1, ARTHUR
WITH GREEN BATON AND TWO KNIGHTS 166-2, ARTHUR VICTORIUS
166-3, ARTHUR WELCOMED AT CAROHAISE 166-4, ARTHUR AND
COMPANIONS IN BOAT RETURNING TO ENGLAND 166-5, ARTHUR AT MASS
166-6, ARTHUR AMBUSHED BY KING LOT OF ORKNEY 166-7, ARTHUR
KILLS HEADLESS KING RIONS 166-8, ARTHUR WITH KNIGHTS
APPROACHES CASTLE ON AUKE 166-9, ARTHUR/ BAN AND BORS LEAVE
EACH OTHER 166-10, GAWAIN TAKING LEAVE OF ARTHUR AND GUINEVERE
166-11, ARTHUR ON WHITSUNDAY SUMMONS COMPANIONS TO TELL OF
QUEST 166-12

*$ABSTRACT 167
 *LIBRARY BOD
 *SLIDE SET TITLE LE MIREUR DU MONDE
 *NEGATIVE REFERENCE ROLL 187H
 *RENTAL FEE SM 167 $3.45
 *COMMENTS 29 SLIDES FROM A HISTORY OF THE WORLD IN TWO PARTS
 *TITLE OF MANUSCRIPT MIREUR DU MONDE
 *SHELFMARK MS DOUCE 336 167/1-24, MS DOUCE 337 167/25-29
 *PROVENANCE FRENCH
 *DATE EXECUTED 15TH
 *LANGUAGE FRENCH
 *TYPE OF MANUSCRIPT HISTORY OF THE WORLD
 *CONTENTS BORDER WITH FOUR FIGURES AND FLOWERS 167-1, CREATION
OF ADAM AND EVE 167-2, MOSES AND BURNING BUSH 167-3, HERCULES@
LABORS 167-4, HELEN ABDUCTED 167-5, TROY@S FALL 167-6,
POLYXENE MURDERED 167-7, CARTHAGE BURNED 167-8, SAMSON KILLING
PHILISTINES 167-9, ELIJAH AND AHAZ SACRIFICING 167-10, ELISHA
MOCKED AND ELIJAH BORNE TO HEAVEN IN CHARIOT 167-11, JERUSALEM
FALLS 167-12, CYRUS DEFEATING MEDES AND PERSIANS 167-13, RAPE

91

OF LUCRECE 167-14, LUCRECE@S DEATH 167-15, TARQUIN THROWN OU
OF ROME 167-16, APPIUS' GOVERNMENT 167-17, ALEXANDER AN
PHILIP OF MACEDON'S FATHERHOOD ENTHRONED 167-18, ALEXANDE
MEETING AMAZON QUEEN 167-19, ALEXANDER BURYING VICTIM 167-20
ALEXANDER'S ARMY SLAUGHTERING MYTHICAL BEASTS 167-21
ALEXANDER DRAWN ALOFT IN CAGE DRAWN BY GRIFFINS 167-22
SLAUGHTER OF MYTHICAL BEASTS BY ALEXANDER 167-23, BEASTS,
MYTHICAL 167-23, DRAGONS BATTLED BY ALEXANDER'S ARMY 167-24
ALEXANDER IN BABYLON 167-25, OLYMPIAS' DEATH 167-26, TITU
BESIEGES JERUSALEM 167-27, MONSTER 167-28, ST GREGORY/ VISIO
OF 167-29

*$ABSTRACT 168
  *LIBRARY BOD
  *SLIDE SET TITLE ANNALS OF HAINAULT
  *NEGATIVE REFERENCE ROLL 187I
  *RENTAL FEE SM 168 $2.45
  *TITLE OF MANUSCRIPT ANNALS OF HAINAULT
  *SHELFMARK MS DOUCE 205
  *PROVENANCE FRENCH
  *DATE EXECUTED 16TH/C1500
  *LANGUAGE FRENCH
  *ARTIST/ SCHOOL MASTER OF ANTOINE ROLLIN
  *AUTHOR GUYSE/ DE JACQUES TRANSLATED FROM LATIN BY JEAN LESSAB
  *TYPE OF MANUSCRIPT ANNALS
  *CONTENTS JACQUES DE GUYSE AT DESK WITH SHELF AND LECTER
  168-1, MONOGRAM AM IN GOLD FORMED FROM TWIGS AND SCROLL
  168-2, BAUDOUIN/ EMPEROR OF CONSTANTINOPLE PRESENTS DAUGHTE
  168-3, PHILIP OF NAMUR PAYS HOMAGE TO BAUDOUIN OF FLANDER
  168-4, HAINAULT RECEIVES HOMAGE OF PHILIP OF NAMUR 168-4
  BAUDOUIN/ COUNT IN COMBAT AGAINST COMTE DE NEVERS 168-5, COUR
  OF HENRY THE YOUNG 168-6, GOSSUIN DEFEATED AT D'AVESNES B
  BADOUIN 168-7, MARGUERITE/ COUNTESS AND SONS PLEAD CASE T
  KING 168-8, FRANCISCAN FRIARS/ FIRST SENT TO FLANDERS 168-9

*$ABSTRACT 169
  *LIBRARY BOD
  *SLIDE SET TITLE CREATURES
  *NEGATIVE REFERENCE ROLL 187J
  *RENTAL FEE SM 169 $3.80
  *SHELFMARK MS ASHMOLE 1525
  *PROVENANCE ENGLISH/ CANTERBURY
  *DATE EXECUTED 13TH
  *LANGUAGE LATIN
  *TYPE OF MANUSCRIPT PSALTER/ CHOIR GALLICAN
  *CONTENTS PSALTER/ ENGLISH/ 13TH 169/1-36, BIRDS/ WHITE 169-1
  HARE 169-2, DOG 169-2, APE SQUATTING 169-3, JAY/ BLUE WINGE
  169-4, FOX BLOWING TRUMPET 169-5, HARE PLAYING HARP 169-6
  BIRD/ WHITE EAGLE TYPE 169-7, CAT POUNCING ON RAT 169-8
  PARROT 169-9, HORSE/ BLUE SITTING ON HAUNCHES 169-10, HAR
  WITH HARP 169-11, FOX 169-12, CAT WITH PAWS ON SPADE AND RAT
  ALL BLUE 169-13, BIRD/ WHITE AND FOX/ YELLOW 169-14, BIRD
  LARGE WHITE 169-15, HARE SITTING 169-16, MONSTER WITH RE
  WINGS ATTACKING LION 169-17, WIVERN/ RED WITH GREEN WING
  169-18, LION/ WHITE SQUATTING 169-19, BIRDS/ WHITE 169-20, AP
  SEATED WITH KNIFE IN EACH HAND 169-21, MAGPIE 169-22, OW
  169-22, COW/ RED 169-23, FOX/ BLUE WITH SHIELD 169-24, ANIMA
  LIKE LEOPARD 169-25, BIRDS/ WHITE 169-26, FOX/ GRAY 169-27
  SQUIRREL-LIKE ANIMAL 169-28, RAM SQUATTING ON HAUNCHES 169-29
  BIRD WITH LONG BEAK/ BLUE 169-30, VULTURE 169-31, BIRD/ WHIT
  169-32, SQUIRREL/ GRAY 169-33, WIVERN/ RAM-HEADED 169-34, FIS
  169-35, FOX/ WHITE 169-36

*$ABSTRACT 170
  *LIBRARY BOD
  *SLIDE SET TITLE THIRTEENTH CENTURY ENGLISH LIFE

*NEGATIVE REFERENCE ROLL 189A
*RENTAL FEE SM 170 $3.10
*COMMENTS 22 SLIDES TAKEN FROM 9 MSS DEPICTING MEDIEVAL ENGLISH
LIFE
*SHELFMARK MS DOUCE 88 170/1-5, MS DOUCE 167 170-6, MS
UNIVERSITY COLLEGE 120 170-7, MS ASHMOLE 1511 170/8-13, MS
DIGBY 9 170-14, MS RAWL C 400 170/15-17, MS ASHMOLE 753
170-18, MS TANNER 184 170/19-21, MS AUCT D 4 17 170-22
*PROVENANCE ENGLISH
*DATE EXECUTED 13TH
*LANGUAGE LATIN
*TYPE OF MANUSCRIPT BESTIARY 170/1-13, BIBLE 170-14, MUSICAL
FRAGMENTS 170/15-17, APOCALYPSE 170/18-22
*CONTENTS   DAILY   LIFE/ MEDIEVAL 170/1-22, WHALE WITH BOATS
ALONGSIDE 170-1, MONSTROUS MEN 170-2, SCIAPOD 170-2, BEES
FLYING TO HIVE 170-3, WOMEN AND MAN WITH SICKLE 170-3, MORS/
DEATH REACHES WITH HOOK FOR MAN ON DEATHBED 170-4, JOACHIM'S
PROPHECIES ABOUT POPES 170-5, DRAGON AND ASPIDO CELONE 170-6,
HOUND/ FAITHFUL OF KING GARAMANTES 170-7, ANTELOPE HORNS IN
TREE SPEARED BY HUNTER 170-8, CATS CATCHING MICE AND CLEANING
SELVES 170-9, ANT CARRYING GRAIN AND MAKING ANTHILL   170-10,
HUNTER   WITH   BOW   AND ARROWS SHOOTING MAGPIES 170-11, SYRENE/
MERMAID HOLDING COMB AND FISH 170-12, CALADRIUS/ BIRD FACING
PATIENT   170-13,   MONKS   CHANTING   170-14, MUSICAL SETTINGS OF
ALLELUJAH/ POLYPHONY 170/15-17, ST JOHN WRITING TO CHURCHES
170-18, KNIGHT ON RED HORSE 170-19, HORSEMEN/ FOUR OF
APOCALPYSE 170-20, SATAN AND HOST ATTACK BELOVED CITY 170-21,
ANTICHRIST'S DEATH BY FIRE FROM HEAVEN 170-22, DEVILS PUSH
ANTICHRIST FROM THRONE 170-22, ANTICHRIST'S FOLLOWERS BEWAIL
DEATH OF MASTER 170-22

*$ABSTRACT 171
*LIBRARY BOD
*SLIDE SET TITLE CALENDARS
*NEGATIVE REFERENCE ROLL 189C
*RENTAL FEE SM 171 $3.25
*COMMENTS 25 SLIDES SELECTED FROM 2 MSS
*SHELFMARK MS DOUCE 8 171/1-13, MS DOUCE 12 170/14-25
*PROVENANCE FLEMISH
*DATE EXECUTED 15TH
*LANGUAGE LATIN AND ITALIAN
*TYPE OF MANUSCRIPT OFFICES/ PRAYERS FOR PRIVATE USE
*CONTENTS CALENDARS/ FLEMISH/ 15TH 171/1-25, JANUARY 171-1,
DOMESTIC SCENE MAN BY FIRE AND WOMAN PREPARES MEAL   171-1,
WINTER   WITH   SNOWY   STREET 171-1, FEBRUARY 171-2, ROCKY
LANDSCAPE WITH LABORERS AND MAN OBSERVING 171-2, MARCH 171-3,
APRIL   171-4,   COUPLE   ON   GRASSY ENCLOSURE WITH MOATED CASTLE
171-4, CASTLE AND MOAT AND MAN WITH LUTE 171-5, MAY 171-5, MEN
WITH LADDER/ TREE/ DRUM/ SCYTHE 171-6, JUNE 171-6, JULY 171-7,
GRAIN HARVESTED AND MAN WITH RAKE AND SHEAVES 171-7, AUGUST
171-8, THRESHING SCENE WITH WORKMEN 171-8, SEPTEMBER 171-9,
GRAPES PRESSED AND STORED 171-9, OCTOBER 171-10, VINTAGE
171-10, SOWING IN PREPARED FIELDS 171-11, NOVEMBER 171-11,
DECEMBER 171-12, WOMAN FEEDING SWINE AND MAN KNOCKING NUTS
FROM TREE 171-12, SLAUGHTERING PIG 171-12, PIG CLEANED AFTER
SLAUGHTERING 171-13, JANUARY 171-14, MAN AND WOMAN BEFORE
FIREPLACE 171-14, FEBRUARY 171-14, CHILDREN PLAYING ON ICE
171-14, MARCH 171-15, PRUNING AND FELLING TREES 171-15, APRIL
171-16, SHEPHERDS WITH FLOCKS AND BAGPIPER WITH DOG 171-16,
JANUARY/ SECOND PART 171-16, SNOWSTORM AND STREET SCENE
171-16, FEBRUARY 171-17, CANDLEMAS WITH PEOPLE IN CHURCH AND
PRIEST AT LECTERN 171-17, APRIL/ SECOND PART 171-17, SHEEP
SHEARING   171-17, MAY 171-18, BOAT AND PEOPLE ON HORSEBACK
171-18, JUNE 171-19, REAPING AND HAYWANE DRIVEN INTO BARN
171-19, JULY 171-20, SCYTHING GRASS AND MAKING HAY 171-20,
LOVERS IN FIELD 171-20, AUGUST 171-21, THRESHING 171-21,
MEASURING AND STORING GRAIN 171-21, SEPTEMBER 171-22, GRAPES
GATHERED 171-22, TREADING OF GRAPES AND STORAGE OF FILLED
CASKS 171-22, OCTOBER 171-23, SOWING 171-23, PLOUGHING WITH
TWO-HORSE PLOUGH 171-23, NOVEMBER 171-24, SWINE FEEDING
171-24, DECEMBER 171-25, PIG BLEEDING 171-25

*$ABSTRACT 172
 *LIBRARY BOD
 *SLIDE SET TITLE HOLKHAM HUMANISTIC MSS
 *NEGATIVE REFERENCE ROLL 189H
 *RENTAL FEE SM 172 $4.05
 *COMMENTS 41 SLIDES FROM 10 MSS
 *TITLE OF MANUSCRIPT PHILIPPICS 172/1-9, JUVENCUS 172/9-10
  SEXTUS RUFUS 172/11-12, ARS POETICA AND SERMONES 172/13-16
  CAESAR'S COMMENTARIES 172/20-24, ORATIONS OF JOHANNES LUCIDU
  CATTANCI 172/34-41
 *SHELFMARK MS HOLKHAM 388 172/1-8, MS HOLKHAM 418 172/9-10, M
  HOLKHAM 369 172/11-12, MS HOLKHAM 317 172/13-16, MS HOLKHA
  328 172/17-19, MS HOLKHAM 341 172/20-24, MS HOLKHAM 32
  172/25-26, MS HOLKHAM 331 172/27-28, MS HOLKHAM 409 172/29-33
  MS HOLKHAM 496 172/34-41
 *PROVENANCE ITALIAN
 *DATE EXECUTED 15TH
 *LANGUAGE LATIN
 *AUTHOR CICERO 172/1-12, HORACE 172/13-16, JUVENAL AND PERSIU
  172/17-19 AND 25-27, CAESAR 172/20-24, HYGIUS AND MANLIU
  172/27-33, CATTANCI/ JOHANNES LUCIDUS 172/34-41
 *TYPE OF MANUSCRIPT CLASSICAL TEXTS
 *CONTENTS HUMANISTIC SCRIPT IN FIFTEENTH CENTURY ITALIAN TEXT
  172/1-41, PALEOGRAPHY 172/1-41, DECORATIVE BORDERS AN
  INITIALS 172/1-41, INITIAL A 172-1, INITIAL N 172-2, INITIAL
  172-3, INITIAL P 172-4, INITIAL V 172-5, INITIAL M 172-6
  INITIAL E 172-7, INITIAL A 172-8, INITIAL I 172-10, INITIAL
  172-11, INITIAL P 172-12, INITIAL H 172-13, INITIAL Q 17
  172-15, INITIAL E 172-16, INITIAL S 172-17, INITIAL E 172-18
  INITIAL N AND O 172-19, INITIAL G 172-20, INITIAL OF CAESA
  172-21, ARMS OF MEDICI 172-22, RUBRIC AND INITIAL 172-23
  INITIAL C 172-24, INITIAL S 172-25, INITIAL N 172-26, INITIA
  H 172-27, INITIAL C 172-28, INITIAL L 172-29, INITIAL
  172-30, INITIAL Q 172-31, INITIAL R 172-32, DECORATED TEX
  PAGES 172/33-41

*$ABSTRACT 173
 *LIBRARY BOD
 *SLIDE SET TITLE MEDIEVAL BOOKBINDINGS
 *NEGATIVE REFERENCE ROLL 189J
 *RENTAL FEE SM 173 $2.45
 *COMMENTS 9 SLIDES SHOWING BOOKBINDING ON SEVERAL MSS
 *SHELFMARK MS BODLEY 63/86/125 173-1, MS HATTON 173-1, MS RAW
  C 163 173-2, MS BODLEY 270B 173-3, MS BODLEY 700 173-4, M
  HAMILTON 15 AND 31 173-5, MS DOUCE 367 173/6-7, MS DOUC
  BINDINGS A 2 173-8, MS LAUD MISC 529 173-9
 *PROVENANCE ENGLISH 173/1-2 AND 4 AND 9, FRENCH 173-3, GERMA
  173/5-7, ITALIAN 173-8
 *DATE EXECUTED 12TH 173/1-2, 13TH 173-3, 14TH 173-4, 15T
  173/5-9
 *CONTENTS BOOKBINDINGS/ MEDIEVAL 173/1-9, BINDINGS/ UNDECORATE
  WITH SQUARE CONSTRUCTION/ BOARDS/ TABS 173-1, BINDING O
  STAMPED CALF OVER OAK BOARDS 173-2, BINDING/ STAMPED ON RE
  SHEEPSKIN 173-3, BINDING/ PROTECTIVE WITH DONOR'S ARMS AN
  INSCRIPTION 173-4, BINDINGS/ INCISED LEATHER 173-5, BINDING
  LEATHER WITH CONTRASTING ENGRAVING 173/6-7, ARMS OF VISCONT
  AND SFORZA ON INCISED LEATHER COVER 173-8, BINDING WIT
  COMBINED INCISED AND TOOLED TECHNIQUES 173-9

*$ABSTRACT 174
 *LIBRARY BOD
 *SLIDE SET TITLE FIFTEENTH CENTURY BLIND-TOOLED BINDINGS
 *NEGATIVE REFERENCE ROLL 189K
 *RENTAL FEE SM 174 $2.80
 *COMMENTS 16 SLIDES SHOWING BINDINGS
 *SHELFMARK MS DOUCE 310 174-1, MS AUCT 5 Q 2 4 174/2-3, MS AUCT
  2 Q 3 46 174-3, MS AUCT 4 Q 6 27 174-3, MS AUCT 2 Q 3 4
  174-4, MS AUCT 5 Q 4 174-5, MS AUCT 4 Q 1 17 174-6, MS AUCT

94

SUB FEN 2 174-7, MS AUCT 2 Q INF 250 174-8, MS LYELL 45 174-9,
MS DOUCE 57 174-10, MS DOUCE 10 174-11, MS LAT THE 7 174-12,
MS GR CLASS C 96 174-13, MS BODLEY 141 174-14, MS DOUCE
BINDINGS A 1 174-15, MS KENNICOT 1 174-16
*PROVENANCE ITALIAN 174-1, GERMAN 174/2-7, AUSTRIAN 174-8,
FRENCH 174-9, DUTCH 174/10-11, ENGLISH 174/12-15, SPANISH
174-16
*DATE EXECUTED 15TH
*CONTENTS BINDINGS/ BLIND-TOOLED FROM THE 15TH CENTURY
174/1-16, BINDING OF DARK MOROCCO 174-1, BINDING IN CALF AND
STAMP WITH BINDER'S NAME 174-2, BINDER'S MARKS AND
INSCRIPTIONS 174-3, BINDINGS WITH COVER DESIGNS 174-4,
HALF-BINDING OVER OAK BOARDS WITH BEVELED BOARDS 174-5,
BINDING WITH METAL BOSSES AND CORNERS 174-6, BINDING WITH
DESIGN OF SMALL TOOLS 174-7, BINDINGS WITH FLAT BOSSES/ CLASPS
OF METAL, LABELS 174-8, STAMPED BINDING OVER BEVELLED BOARDS
174-9, PANEL-STAMPED BINDING ON RED LEATHER 174-10, BINDING
OVER OAK BOARDS 174-11, BOOKS WITH CLASPS FROM UPPER TO LOWER
BOARDS 174-12, REBACKED BINDING OF TEXT 174-13, STAPLE HOLES
IN BINDING FROM BEING CHAINED 174-14, BINDING WITH ONLY
CUT-OUT OF PANEL SURVIVING 174-15, BINDING WITH HIGHLY
GEOMETRIC ISLAMIC DECORATION 174-16

*$ABSTRACT 175
  *SLIDE SET TITLE SIXTEENTH CENTURY BLIND-TOOLED BINDINGS
  *LIBRARY BOD
  *NEGATIVE REFERENCE ROLL 189L
  *RENTAL FEE SM 175 $2.80
  *COMMENTS 16 SLIDES SHOWING BINDINGS OF SEVERAL MSS
  *SHELFMARK MS CANON GR 18 175-1, MS VET E 1 C 61 175-2, MS AUCT
  4 Q 6 27 175-3, BYW M 9 14 175-5, MS SELDEN D 21 175-6, MS
  BUCHANAN 397 175-9, MS DOUCE G 433 175-10, MS LINCOLN C 2 10
  175-11, MS RAWL C 6 175-12, MS RAWL C 779 175-13, MS LINCOLN A
  15 7 175-14, MS LINCOLN A 7 23 175-15, PRINTED BOOK MED B 1 3
  175-16
  *PROVENANCE ITALIAN 175/1-2, AUSTRIAN 175-3, GERMAN 175/4-6,
  FRENCH 175/7-9, ENGLISH 175/10-16
  *DATE EXECUTED 16TH
  *CONTENTS BLIND-TOOLED BINDINGS FROM 16TH CENTURY 175/1-16,
  BINDINGS 175/1-16, GREEK-TYPE ORNAMENTS AND SPINE TREATMENT
  WITH ITALIAN ARABESQUES 175-1, BLIND TOOLING AND LATER ADDED
  GOLD TOOLING 175-2, ABBEY'S ARMS ON BOOK COVER AND BEVELLED IN
  EDGES 175-3, PANEL STAMP OF BIBICAL SCENE ON COVER 175-4,
  RELIGIOUS PORTRAITS IN ROLL-TOOLED BORDER 175-5, ARMORIAL
  STAMP ON PIGSKIN BINDING WITH ROLLS 175-6, SS PAUL AND THOMAS
  AND BARBARA ON PANEL 175-7, ST SABASTIAN MARTYRDOM PANEL STAMP
  175-8, BINDING OF COMMENTARY ON ARISTOTLE'S ETHICS 175-8,
  CRUCIFIXION PANEL WITH ROSE AND OGIVAL ORNAMENTS 175-9,
  MEDALLION PANELS/ ENGLISH AND BELGIAN 175-10, ENGLISH ROYAL
  ARMS WITH ARABESQUES 175-10, FLAGELLATION OF CHRIST AND
  ANIMALS IN BINDING PANELS 175-11, EAGLE IN LATTICE HALF-STAMP
  PANEL OF BOOKBINDING 175-12, ST JOHN THE BAPTIST AND ST ROCH
  175-13, ST ROCH 175-13, ST BARBARA ON PANEL STAMP 175-14,
  ANIMAL STAMPS ON PANEL OF BINDING 175-14, ROYAL ARMS ON PANEL
  STAMP OF BINDING 175-15, ROLL-TOOLS ON LATE 15TH CENTURY
  BINDING 175-16

*$ABSTRACT 176
  *LIBRARY BOD
  *SLIDE SET TITLE GILT CONTINENTAL RENAISSANCE BINDINGS
  *NEGATIVE REFERENCE ROLL 189M
  *RENTAL FEE SM 176 $3.15
  *COMMENTS 23 SLIDES SHOWING BINDINGS OF VARIOUS MSS
  *SHELFMARK MS AUCT F 1 14 176-1, MS CANON CLASS LAT 167 AND 168
  176-3, MS LAUD MISC 710 176-6, MS AUCT 2 R4 176-5, MS LAUD GR
  5 176-7, MS DOUCE BB 225 176-8, MS DOUCE 170 176-9, MS AUCT N4
  11 176-10, MS DOUCE V 255 176-11, MS DOUCE S 528 176-12, MS
  DOUCE P 16 176-13, MS ARCH B F 53 176-15, MS ARCH B D 4

176-16, MS D/ORVILLE 1 176-19
*PROVENANCE ITALIAN 176/1-4 AND 6-7 AND 12-13, GERMAN 176-
FRENCH 176/9-11 AND 14-18, SPANISH 176/8 AND 22, DUTCH 176-1
BELGIAN 176-20, GERMAN 176-21, PORTUGESE 176-23
*DATE EXECUTED 16TH
*CONTENTS BINDINGS/ GILT CONTINENTAL RENAISSANCE 176/1-2
BINDING WITH EMBLEMATIC CROW OF HUNGARY 176-1, ARABESQU
KNOTWORK/ SMALL TOOLS ON PSALTER 176-2, ITALIAN BINDINGS 76-
INTERLACED LOZENGE 176-4, BINDINGS 176-5, DUCALES
CREDENTIALS OF VENETIALS 176-6, BOOKS ORNAMENTED WITH POPUL
EMBLEMS 176-7, GOLD-BACKED BOOK OF HOURS WITH POLYCHRO
BINDING 176-9, BOOK OF HOURS 176-8, PATTERNED CALF BINDI
WITH GILT TOOLING 176-10, GROLIER/ JEAN BOOK COVER MADE F
176-11, GROLIER'S MOTTO ON POLYCHROME COVER MADE FOR H
176-12, CALF BINDING INLAID WITH CITRON AND OLIVE GRE
MOROCCO 176-13, STATUTS DE L'ORDRE DE ST MICHAEL 176-1
MINIATURE REALISTIC FLOWERS ON BINDING FOR PIETRO DUO
176-15, PARISIAN FANFARE BINDING 176-16, GENEVA FRENCH BIB
176-17, BEZA'S VERSION OF THE PSALMS WITH GENEVA BINDI
176-18, APOLLORDORUS BOUND MANUSCRIPT 176-19, CABELLE
DETERMINADO/ DE OF DE LA MARCHE 176-20, ARABESQUE BORDER WI
STAMP OF RESURRECTION 176-21, MEDALLION HEADS WITH ROLL-TOOL
BORDER 176-22, DOLPHINS/ GILT AND ARMS OF BISHOP OF FA
176-23

*$ABSTRACT 177
 *LIBRARY BOD
 *SLIDE SET TITLE BAPTISM
 *NEGATIVE REFERENCE ROLL 189N1
 *RENTAL FEE SM 177 $4.45
 *COMMENTS 29 SLIDES FROM 18 MSS DEPICTING BAPTISM
 *TITLE OF MANUSCRIPT SPECULUM HUMANAE SALVATIONIS 177-14, LI
 OF CHRIST AND THE VIRGIN 177-22, ACTS OF ST MARY AND JES
 177-23
 *SHELFMARK MS CANON LITURG 190 177-1, MS LAUD MISC 740 177-
 MS AUCT D 4 8 177-3, MS LITURG 41 177-4, MS ASHMOLE 15
 177/5-6, MS RAWL A 417 177-7, MS DOUCE 29 177-8, MS DOUCE 2
 177-9, MS BODLEY 270 177-10, MS DOUCE 211 177-11, MS CAN
 BIBL LAT 58 177-12, MS DOUCE 29 177-13, MS DOUCE F 4 177-1
 MS NEW COLLEGE 322 177-15, MS C C C 410 177-16, MS CAN
 LITURG 382 177-17, MS C C C 410 177/18-19, MS LAUD MISC
 177-20, MS CANON ITAL 280 177-22, MS CANON MISC 476 177-2
 MSC C C 410 177-24, MS CANON MISC 476 177-25, MS NEW COLLE
 65 177-26, MS BODLEY 270 177-27, MS BODLEY 270 177-28, MS N
 COLLEGE 65 177-29
 *PROVENANCE ITALIAN 177/1-2 AND 8 AND 16-19 AND 22-25, ENGLI
 177/3 AND 5-6 AND 14-15 AND 26 AND 29, FRENCH 177/4 AND 7 A
 9-11 AND 20
 *DATE EXECUTED 13TH 177/5-6 AND 12, 15TH 177/1-4 AND 7 AND
 AND 20-22, 14TH 177/9 AND 16-19 AND 23 AND 26, 13TH 177/15 A
 10 AND 27-29, 16TH 177-8
 *LANGUAGE LATIN
 *TYPE OF MANUSCRIPT BENEDICTINE MANUAL 177-1, BIBLE 177/3 A
 9-12 AND 27-29, BOOK OF HOURS 177/4 AND 8, MISSAL 177-1
 BESTIARY 177/5-6, RELIGIOUS TREATISE 177-7,PSALTER 177-1
 BREVIARY/ CHOIR 177-20, APOCALYPSE 177-26
 *CONTENTS BAPTISM SCENES FROM 13TH-16TH CENTURY MSS 177/1-2
 PRIEST AT DOOR RECEIVES INFANT AND WOMAN 177-1, BAPTISM
 INFANT AND GODPARENTS HOLD CANDLE 177-2, ADULT BAPTISED SEAT
 IN SMALL FONT 177-3, ST PETER BAPTISES GROUP OF ADUL
 SPRINKLING WITH WATER 177-4, SPIRIT OF GOD MOVES OVER WAT
 177-5, WATERS BRING FORTH LIVING CREATURES 177-6, NOAH'S A
 WITH DOVE AND OLIVE BRANCH 177-7, CROSSING RED SEA A
 EGYPTIANS DROWN 177-8, PILLAR OF CLOUD GUIDES ISRAELIT
 177-9, MOSES SWEETENS THE WATER OF MARAH 177-10, WATER FR
 ROCK STRUCK BY MOSES 177-11, JOSHUA AND ISRAELITES BY RIV
 JORDAN 177-12, ELIJAH'S SACRIFICE 177-13, NAAMAN CLEANSED
 LEPROSY IN RIVER JORDAN 177-14, JONAH SWALLOWED AND DISGORG
 BY WHALE 177-15, ST JOHN BAPTISES TWO PEOPLE BY IMMERSION
 JORDAN 177-16, CHRIST BAPTISED BY ST JOHN BAPTIST 177-1

96

CHRIST AND WOMAN AT WELL AT SAMARIA 177-18, WATER FROM
CHRIST'S SIDE 177-19, RESURRECTION 177-20, CHRIST HEALS BLIND
MAN 177-21, CHRIST HEALS CRIPPLE AT POOL AT BETHESDA 177-22,
CHRIST HEALS LEPER 177-23, CHRIST HEALS A PARALYTIC 177-24,
CHRIST CASTS OUT A DEVIL FROM A POSSESSED MAN 177-25, DEMONIC
POSSESSION 177-25, WATER OF LIFE FLOWING FROM THE THRONE OF
GOD 177-26, RECEIVE CHARACTER OF CHRISTIANS THOUGH BAPTISM
177-27, CIRCUMCISION IN OLD TESTAMENT 177-28, PEOPLE SEALED
WITH MARK OF GOD 177-29

*$ABSTRACT 178
  *LIBRARY BOD
  *SLIDE SET TITLE CONFIRMATION
  *NEGATIVE REFERENCE ROLL 189N2
  *RENTAL FEE SM 178 $2.30
  *COMMENTS 6 SLIDES FROM 6 MSS DEPICTING CONFIRMATION
  *TITLE OF MANUSCRIPT FALL OF PRINCES 178-2
  *SHELFMARK MS LITURG 41 178-1, MS BODLEY 263 178-2, MS DOUCE 29
  178-3, MS LITURG 407 178-4, MS AUCT D 35 178-5, MS RAWL LITURG
  E 18 178-6
  *PROVENANCE FRENCH 178/1 AND 6, ENGLISH 178/2 AND 4-5, ITALIAN
  178-6
  *DATE EXECUTED 15TH 178/1-2 AND 6, 16TH 178-3, 13TH 178/4-5
  *LANGUAGE LATIN 178/1 AND 3-6, ENGLISH 178-2
  *AUTHOR LYDGATE/ JOHN 178-2
  *TYPE OF MANUSCRIPT BOOK OF HOURS 178/1 AND 3 AND 6, DE CASIBUS
  TRAGEDY 178-2, PSALTER 178-4, BIBLE 178-5
  *CONTENTS CONFIRMATION SCENES FROM VARIOUS MSS 178/1-6,
  CONFIRMATION BY APOSTLES OF GROUP OF PEOPLE 178-1, FALLING
  TOWER OF BABEL 178-2, MOSES RECEIVES LAW ON MOUNT SINAI 178-3,
  ANOINTING OF DAVID 178-4, ZADOC ANOINTS KING SOLOMON 178-5,
  PENTECOST 178-6, HOLY SPIRIT DESCENDS AS DOVE AND TONGUES OF
  FIRE 178-6, APOSTLES AND ST MARY 178-6

*$ABSTRACT 179
  *LIBRARY BOD
  *SLIDE SET TITLE EUCHARIST
  *NEGATIVE REFERENCE ROLL 189N3
  *RENTAL FEE SM 179 $3.00
  *COMMENTS 20 SLIDES FROM 12 MSS DEPICTING THE EUCHARIST
  *TITLE OF MANUSCRIPT PELERINAGE DE LA VIE HUMAINE 179-2,
  SPECULUM HUMANAE SALVATIONIS 179-3, MEDITATIONS ON LIFE OF
  CHRIST 179/14-16, BIBLE HISTORIALE 179/17-19
  *SHELFMARK MS LAT TH B 4 179-1, MS LAUD MISC 740 179-2, MS
  DOUCE 112 179-3, MS C C C 161 179/4 AND 11 AND 13, PRINTED
  BOOK AUCT 7Q 2 13 179-5, MS BODLEY 270 179-6, MS DOUCE 29
  179-7, MS DOUCE 311 179-8, MS BODLEY 270 179/9-11, MS AUCT D
  38 179-12, MS C C C 410 179/14-16, MS DOUCE 211 179/17-19, MS
  RAWL LITURG E 20 179-20
  *PROVENANCE ITALIAN 179/7 AND 14-19, ENGLISH 179-2, FRENCH
  179/5-6 AND 12 AND 17-20, FLEMISH 179/3-4
  *DATE EXECUTED 13TH 179/1 AND 6 AND 12, 13TH 179/17-19, 14TH
  179/5 AND 14-19, 15TH 179/2 AND 4 AND 8 AND 20, 16TH 179-7
  *LANGUAGE ENGLISH 179-2, LATIN 179/1 AND 3-20
  *AUTHOR DEGUILLEVILLE/ GUILLAUME 179-2
  *TYPE OF MANUSCRIPT DECRETALS 179-1, BOOK OF HOURS 179/3 AND
  7-8 AND 20, BIBLE 179/6 AND 22, MEDITATIONS 179/14-19
  *CONTENTS EUCHARIST SCENES 179/1-20, MASS WITH CELEBRANT
  ELEVATING HOST 179-1, PILGRIMS RECEIVE HOLY COMMUNION 179-2,
  LADY RECEIVES HOLY COMMUNION 179-3, PASCHAL MEAL EATEN BY
  ISRAELITES 179-4, CHRIST WITH SYMBOL OF OLD AND NEW COVENANT
  179-5, GOD PROVIDES QUAILS IN DESERT 179-6, MANNA IN THE
  DESERT 179-7, SPIES WITH GRAPES 179-8, ELIJAH FED BY RAVENS
  179-9, ELIJAH FED BY ANGEL 179-10, WIDOW'S OIL INCREASED
  179-11, HABAKKUK TAKES LOAVES AND PITCHER TO DANIEL 179-12,
  MELCHIZADEK GIVES BREAD AND WINE TO ABRAHAM 179-13, WATER
  TURNED INTO WINE AT CANA 179-14, CHRIST FEEDS THE FIVE
  THOUSAND 179-15, LAST SUPPER 179-16, ABEL'S SACRIFICE 179-17,

97

LEVITICAL SACRIFICE 179-18, ABRAHAM PREPARES TO SACRIFIC
ISAAC 179-19, CRUCIFIXION 179-20

*$ABSTRACT 180
 *LIBRARY BOD
 *SLIDE SET TITLE PENANCE
 *NEGATIVE REFERENCE ROLL 189N4
 *RENTAL FEE SM 180 $2.35
 *COMMENTS 7 SLIDES FROM 6 MSS SHOWING PENANCE
 *SHELFMARK MS DOUCE 131 180-1, MS DOUCE 112 180-2, MS RAW
 LITURG E 24 180-3, MS DOUCE 313 180-4, MS DOUCE 135-5, M
 DOUCE 313 180-6, MS DOUCE 256 180-7
 *PROVENANCE ENGLISH 180-1, FRENCH 180/3-6, FLEMISH 180/2 AND 7
 *DATE EXECUTED 14TH 180/1 AND 4 AND 6, 15TH 180/2-3, 16TH 180/
 AND 7
 *LANGUAGE LATIN
 *TYPE OF MANUSCRIPT PSALTER 180-1, BOOK OF HOURS 180/2-3 AND
 AND 7, MISSAL/ FRANCISCAN 180/4 AND 6
 *CONTENTS PENANCE SCENES FROM VARIOUS MSS 180/1-7, CONFESSIO
 AS WOMAN CONFESSES TO PRIEST 180-1, SERPENT/ BRAZEN 180-2
 DAVID'S REPENTENCE 180-3, REPENTENCE OF NINEVEH 180-4
 PRODIGAL SON RETURNS 180-5, ASH WEDNESDAY AND ASHE
 DISTRIBUTED TO CONGREGATION 180-5, GOOD THIEF TURNS TO CHRIS
 ON CROSS 180-7

*$ABSTRACT 181
 *LIBRARY BOD
 *SLIDE SET TITLE SACRAMENTS/ ANOINTING OF THE SICK
 *NEGATIVE REFERENCE ROLL 189N5
 *RENTAL FEE SM 181 $2.20
 *COMMENTS 4 SLIDES FROM 4 MSS DEPICTING ANOINTING OF THE SICK
 *SHELFMARK MS DOUCE 313 181-1, MS LITURG 41 181-2, MS DOUCE 25
 181-3, MS DOUCE 30 181-4
 *PROVENANCE FRENCH 181/1-2, FLEMISH 181-3, DUTCH 181-4
 *DATE EXECUTED 14TH 181-1, 15TH 181/2-4
 *LANGUAGE LATIN
 *TYPE OF MANUSCRIPT MISSAL/ FRANCISCAN 181-1, BOOK OF HOUR
 181/2-4
 *CONTENTS ANOINTING OF THE SICK 181/1-4, CHRIST'S COMPASSIO
 FOR SICK 181-1, PRIEST ANOINTS HEAD OF SICK MAN 181-1, PRIES
 AT BED OF DYING MAN 181-2, HOLY WATER 181-2, LAZARUS RAISE
 181-3, RESURRECTION 181-4, LAST JUDGMENT 181-4

*$ABSTRACT 182
 *LIBRARY BOD
 *SLIDE SET TITLE SACRAMENTS/ ORDINATION
 *NEGATIVE REFERENCE ROLL 189N6
 *RENTAL FEE SM 182 $2.40
 *COMMENTS 8 SLIDES FROM 8 MSS DEPICTING ORDINATIONS
 *SHELFMARK MS DOUCE 313 182-1, MS BODLEY 270B 182/2-3, MS DOUC
 112 182-4, MS CANON BIBL LAT 52 182-5, MS HATTON 1 182-6
 PRINTED BOOK AUCT 7 Q 2 13 182-7, MS LITURG 41 182-8
 *PROVENANCE FRENCH 182/1-4 AND 7-8, ENGLISH 182-6
 *DATE EXECUTED 13TH 182-5, 14TH 182/1 AND 7, 15TH 182/2-4 AND
 AND 8
 *LANGUAGE LATIN
 *TYPE OF MANUSCRIPT MISSAL/ FRANCISCAN 182-1, MISSAL/ ENGLIS
 182-6, BIBLE/ MORALISEE 182-2, BIBLE 182-5, BOOK OF HOURS
 AND 8
 *CONTENTS ORDINATION SCENES 182/1-8, ST MATTHIAS CONSECRATE
 BISHOP BY APOSTLES 182-1, PRIESTHOOD REQUIRES MEN TO LEAV
 WORLDLY TIES 182-2, DUPLICATE OF 182-2 182-3, AARON'S RO
 FLOWERS AS SIGN OF PRIESTHOOD 182-4, LEVITICAL SACRIFIC
 182-5, CHRIST CALLS 2 OF HIS APOSTLES 182-6, CRUCIFIXIO
 182-7, APOSTLES GO FORTH TO PREACH AND BAPTISE 182-8

*$ABSTRACT 183
  *LIBRARY BOD
  *SLIDE SET TITLE SACRAMENTS/ MARRIAGE
  *NEGATIVE REFERENCE ROLL 189N7
  *RENTAL FEE SM 183 $2.40
  *COMMENTS 8 SLIDES FROM 7 MSS DEPICTING MARRIAGE
  *TITLE OF MANUSCRIPT SPECULUM HUMANAE SALVATIONIS 183-1,
  DECRETALS OF POPE GREGORY IX 183-2, COMMENTARY ON THE SONG OF
  SONGS 183-3
  *SHELFMARK MS DOUCE 240 183-1, MS LAT TH B 4 183-2, MS LAUD
  MISC 150 183-3, MS ASHMOLE 1511 183-4, MS DOUCE 211 183-5, MS
  DOUCE 313 183/6-7, MS TANNER 184 183-8
  *PROVENANCE SPANISH/ CATALAN 183-1, ITALIAN 183-2, GERMAN
  183-3, ENGLISH 183/4 AND 8, FRENCH 183/5-7
  *DATE EXECUTED 13TH 183/1-2 AND 4 AND 8, 14TH 183/3 AND 5-7
  *LANGUAGE LATIN
  *TYPE OF MANUSCRIPT BESTIARY 183-4, BIBLE/ HISTORIALE 183-5,
  MISSAL/ FRANCISCAN 183/6-7, APOCALYPSE 183-8
  *CONTENTS MARRIAGE SCENES 183/1-8, SARA AND TOBIAS MARRIED
  183-1, WEDDING SCENE 183-2, CHRIST EMBRACES THE CHURCH AS HIS
  BRIDE 183-3, GOD CREATES EVE FROM ADAM'S SIDE 183-4, GOD MAKES
  COVENANT WITH ABRAHAM 183-6, PARABLE OF WEDDING OF KING'S SON
  183-6, PARABLE OF THE WISE AND FOOLISH VIRGINS 183-7, MARRIAGE
  OF THE LAMB 183-8

*$ABSTRACT 184
  *LIBRARY BOD
  *SLIDE SET TITLE CLASSICS THROUGH MEDIEVAL EYES
  *NEGATIVE REFERENCE ROLL 190A
  *RENTAL FEE SM 184 $2.50
  *COMMENTS 10 SLIDES FROM 6 MSS DEPICTING THE CLASSIC WRITERS
  *SHELFMARK MS BODLEY 943 184/1-3, MS CANON CLASS LAT 52
  184/4-5, MS ASHMOLE 1462 184-6, MS CANON ITAL 108 184-7, MS
  AUCT F 2 18 184/8-9, MS AUCT F 6 5 184-10
  *PROVENANCE ENGLISH 184/1-3 AND 6, ITALIAN 184/4-5 AND 7-9,
  GERMAN 184-10
  *DATE EXECUTED 12TH 184-10, 13TH 184-6, 14TH 184/4-5 AND 7,
  15TH 184/1-3 AND 8-9
  *LANGUAGE LATIN
  *TYPE OF MANUSCRIPT CLASSICAL TEXTS 184/1-10
  *CONTENTS CLASSICAL WRITERS IN MEDIEVAL MSS 184/1-10, SOCRATES
  184-1, DIOGENES 184-2, HOMER 184-3, AENEAS FIGHTS TURNUS
  184-4, OVID 184-5, HOMER AS A MEDICAL AUTHOR 184-6, VIRGIL AND
  DANTE MEET CLASSICAL POETS 184-7, CICERO 184/8-9, BOETHIUS IN
  PRISON WITH PHILOSOPHY 184-10

*$ABSTRACT 185
  *LIBRARY BOD
  *SLIDE SET TITLE EMBROIDERED BINDINGS
  *NEGATIVE REFERENCE ROLL 190B
  *RENTAL FEE SM 185 $2.30
  *COMMENTS 6 SLIDES OF 4 EMBROIDERED BINDINGS
  *SHELFMARK MS CHERRY 36 185-1, MS C MUSAEO 242 185-2, N T ENG
  1628 185-3, ARCH A D 5 185-4, DOUCE BIBLES N T ENG 1625
  185/5-7
  *PROVENANCE ENGLISH
  *DATE EXECUTED 16TH 185/1-2, 17TH 185/3-7
  *CONTENTS BINDINGS/ EMBROIDERED 185/1-7, ELIZABETH I FOR
  CATHERINE PARR 185-1, CROSS/ BRAIDED WITH INITIALS K P 185-1,
  NEW TESTAMENT COVER WORKED BY ELIZABETH I 185-2, NEW TESTAMENT
  COVER IN PINK SATIN 185-3, LANDSCAPE AND FIGURES IN WHITE
  SATIN AND GOLD 185-4, DAVID PLAYING HARP IN FLOWING WIG AND
  ROBE 185-5, DRAGON-FLY/ EMBROIDERED 185-5, ABRAHAM IN CLOTHES
  OF CHARLES II SACRIFICING SON 185-6, FIGURES IN COSTUME OF
  PERIOD OF CHARLES I 185-6, NEEDLEWORK IN TAPESTRY STITCH 185-7

*$ABSTRACT 186
 *LIBRARY BOD
 *SLIDE SET TITLE ROMANCE OF ALEXANDER
 *NEGATIVE REFERENCE ROLL 190F
 *RENTAL FEE SM 186 $2.30
 *TITLE OF MANUSCRIPT ROMANCE OF ALEXANDER
 *SHELFMARK MS BAROCCI 17
 *PROVENANCE BYZANTINE
 *DATE EXECUTED 13TH
 *LANGUAGE GREEK
 *TYPE OF MANUSCRIPT ROMANCE
 *CONTENTS ALEXANDER/ ROMANCE OF 186/1-6, ROMANCE OF ALEXAND
  186/1-6, LITERATURE/ ROMANCE OF ALEXANDER 186/1-
  NECTANEBOR'S DEATH 186-1, ALEXANDER IN FUNERAL PROCESSI
  186-1, BUCEPHALUS AND ALEXANDER IN CAGE 186-2, ALEXAND
  RIDING BUCEPHALUS 186-3, PHILIP/ KING'S NEW WIFE'S RELATIV
  KILLED BY ALEXANDER 186-4, ALEXANDER ENTERS ROME 186-5, RO
  ENTERED BY ALEXANDER 186-6

*$ABSTRACT 187
 *LIBRARY BOD
 *SLIDE SET TITLE ST JAMES OF COMPOSTELLA
 *NEGATIVE REFERENCE ROLL 190F
 *RENTAL FEE SM 187 $3.25
 *COMMENTS 25 SLIDES FROM 20 MSS DEPICTING LIFE OF ST JAMES
  COMPOSTELLA
 *TITLE OF MANUSCRIPT CHRONICLE OF FRANCE 187-11, MIROU
  HISTORIAL ABREGIE DE FRANCE 187-12, PILGRIMAGE OF ARNOLF V
  HARFFE 187-25
 *SHELFMARK MS RAWL A 417 187-1, MS DOUCE 313 187/2-5, MS LITU
  400 187-6, MS DIGBY 9 187-7, MS DOUCE 313 187-8, MS DOUCE 1
  187/9-10, MS DOUCE 217 187-11, MS BODLEY 968 187-12, MS RAWL
  939 187-13, MS DOUCE 245 187-14, MS CANON LITURG 99 187-15,
  BUCHANAN E 4 187-16, MS DOUCE 31 187-17, MS LITURG 41 187-1
  MS DOUCE 268 187-19, MS LAUD MISC 93 187-20, MS DOUCE
  187-22, MS DOUCE 311 187-23, MS RAWL LITURG 187-24, MS BODL
  972 187-25 FLEMISH 187/6 AND 9-10 AND 23, ENGLISH 187/7 A
  13, ITALIAN 187-22, GERMAN 187-25
 *DATE EXECUTED 14TH 187/2-5 AND 8 AND 13-14, 13TH 187-7, 15
  187/1 AND 6 AND 9-12 AND 15-24, 16TH 187-25
 *TYPE OF MANUSCRIPT RELIGIOUS TREATISE 187-1, MISSA
  FRANCISCAN 187/2-5 AND 8, BIBLE 187-7, BOOK OF HOURS 187/6 A
  9-10 AND 15-24, CHRONICLE 187-11, CALENDAR 187-13, BREVIA
  187-14 AND 20
 *CONTENTS ST JAMES OF COMPOSTELLA/ SCENES FROM HIS LI
  187/1-25, ST JAMES AS CHILD DRESSED AS PILGRIM 187-1, CHRI
  CALLS SS JAMES/ JOHN/ PETER/ ANDREW 187-2, SS JAMES/ JOH
  PETER WITH FISH 187-3, SS JAMES AND JOHN AS BOYS WITH CHRI
  187-4, ST JAMES AS PILGRIM PREACHING TO MEN 187-5, SS JAME
  JOHN/ PETER ASLEEP IN GETHSEMANE 187-6, ST JAMES AS PILGR
  187-7, ST JAMES AS PILGRIM EXECUTED WITH SPEAR 187-
  MARTYRDOM OF ST JAMES 187-9, MIRACLE OF TAMED BULLS 187-
  CONVERSION OF QUEEN LOUVÉ BY ST JAMES 187-10, VISION
  CHARLEMAGNE AND ST JAMES POINTS OUT WAY 187-11, VISION
  BISHOP TURPIN 187-12, ST JAMES RESCUES SOUL OF CHARLEMAG
  187-12, ST JAMES TIPS SCALES IN FAVOR OF CHARLEMAGNE 187-1
  CHARLEMAGNE 187-12, SS MARGARET/ MARY MAGDELENE/ JAMES/ ANN
  SAMPSON/ GERMAINE 187-13, ST JAMES AS PILGRIM 187/14-20 A
  24-25, MEDALLIONS OF THE SAINTS INCLUDING ST JAMES
  COMPESTELLA 187-23

*$ABSTRACT 188
 *LIBRARY BOD
 *SLIDE SET TITLE SAINTS FROM A CALENDAR
 *NEGATIVE REFERENCE ROLL 190G
 *RENTAL FEE SM 188 $3.20
 *COMMENTS 24 SLIDES FROM 1 MS DEPICTING SAINTS
 *SHELFMARK MS RAWL D 939

*PROVENANCE ENGLISH
*DATE EXECUTED 14TH/C1370
*LANGUAGE LATIN AND ENGLISH
*TYPE OF MANUSCRIPT CALENDAR/ ASTROLOGICAL AND ECCLESIASTICAL
*CONTENTS CALENDAR/ ENGLISH/ 14TH 188/1-24, CIRCUMCISION 188-1,
EPIPHANY 188-1, ST HILARY 188-1, ST MAUR 188-1, SS FABIAN AND
SEBASTIAN 188-2, ST AGNES 188-2, ST WULFSTAN 188-2, ST VINCENT
188-2, ST PAUL 188-2, ST JULIAN OF LE MANS 188-2, ST BATILDA
188-2, ST BRIDGET 188-3, PURIFICATION 188-3, ST BLAISE 188-3,
ST AGATHA 188-3, ST SCHOLASTICA 188-3, ST VALENTINE 188-3, ST
JULIANA 188-4, CATHEDRA OF ST PETER 188-4, ST MATTHIAS 188-4,
ST OSWALD 188-4, ST DAVID 188-5, ST CHAD 188-5, ST PERPETUA
188-5, ST FELICITY 188-5, ST GREGORY 188-5, ST EDWARD THE
MARTYR 188-5, ST CUTHBERT 188-6, ST BENEDICT 188-6,
ANNUNCIATION 188-6, RESURRECTION 188-6, ST GABRIEL 188-6, ST
MARY OF EGYPT 188-7, ST RICHARD OF CHICHESTER 188-7, ST
AMBROSE 188-7, ST LEO 188-7, SS TIBURTIUS AND VALERIANUS
188-7, ST ALPHEGE 188-8, ST GEORGE 188-8, LION OF ST MARK
188-8, ST VITALIS 188-8, SS PHILIP AND JAMES THE LESS 188-9,
INVENTION OF THE CROSS 188-9, ST JOHN IN CAULDRON 188-9, ST
JOHN OF BEVERLY 188-9, ST PANCRAS 188-9, ST DUNSTAN 188-10, ST
ALDHELM 188-10, ST AUGUSTINE OF CANTERBURY 188-10, ST GERMANUS
OF PARIS 188-10, ST PETRONILLA 188-10, ST BONIFACE 188-11, ST
EDMUND RICH 188-11, ST BARNABAS 188-11, ST EADBURGA 188-11, ST
BOTULPH 188-11, ST ALBAN 188-11, ST ETHELREDA 188-12, ST JOHN
THE BAPTIST 188-12, ST PETER 188-12, ST PAUL 188-12, ST
SWITHIN 188-13, ST MARTIN 188-13, ST MARTIN 188-13, ST THOMAS
188-13, ST BENEDICT 188-13, ST MILDRED 188-13, ST KENELM
188-13, ST MARGARET 188-13, ST MARGARET 188-14, ST MARY
MAGDALENE 188-14, ST JAMES THE GREAT 188-14, ST ANNE WITH THE
VIRGIN 188-14, ST SAMPSON 188-14, ST GERMANUS OF AUXERE
188-14, ST PETER 188-15, ST STEPHEN 188-15, ST OSWALD
188-15, ST SIXTUS 188-15, ST LAWRENCE 188-15, ST TIBERTIUS
188-15, ST HIPPOLYTUS 188-15, ASSUMPTION OF VIRGIN 188-15, ST
MAGNUS 188-16, ST TIMOTHY 188-16, ST BARTHOLOMEW 188-16, ST
AUGUSTINE OF HIPPO 188-16, DECOLLATION OF ST JOHN THE BAPTIST
188-16, ST FELIX 188-16, ST GILE 188-17, ST CUTHBERT 188-17,
NATIVITY OF THE VIRGIN 188-17, EXULTATION OF THE CROSS 188-17,
ST LAMBERT 188-17, ST MATTHEW 188-17, ST MAURICE 188-18, SS
COSMAS AND DAMIAN 188-18, ST MICHAEL 188-18, ST JEROME 188-18,
ST THOMAS CANTELUPE OF HEREFORD 188-19, ST LEGER 188-19, ST
FRANCIS 188-19, ST FAITH 188-19, ST OSWALD 188-19, ST DENIS
188-19, ST ETHELBURGA 188-19, ST EDWARD THE CONFESSOR 188-19,
ST MICHAEL 188-19, ST LUKE 188-19, ST FRIDESWIDA 188-19, ST
URSULA AND THE 11000 VIRGINS 188-20, ST ROMANUS 188-20, SS
SIMON AND JUDE 188-20, ST QUINTIN 188-20, ALL SAINTS 188-21,
ALL SOULS 188-21, ST LEONARD 188-21, ST MARTIN 188-21, ST
BRICE 188-21, ST EDMUND 188-21, ST HUGH OF LINCOLN 188-22, ST
EDMUND THE MARTYR 188-22, ST CLEMENT 188-22, ST CATHERINE
188-22, ST LINUS 188-22, ST ANDREW 188-22, ST NICHOLAS 188-23,
CONCEPTION OF THE VIRGIN 188-23, ST DAMASUS 188-23, ST LUCY
188-23, ST THOMAS 188-24, NATIVITY 188-24, ST STEPHEN 188-24,
ST JOHN 188-24, HOLY INNOCENTS 188-24, ST THOMAS BECKET
188-24, ST SILVESTER 188-24

*$ABSTRACT 189
 *LIBRARY BOD
 *SLIDE SET TITLE MISSAL/ SARUM SHOWING CONTINENTAL INFLUENCE ON
 DECORATION
 *NEGATIVE REFERENCE ROLL 190 I
 *RENTAL FEE SM 189 $2.80
 *COMMENTS MANY HIGHLY DECORATED AND COMPLICATED FULL PAGE
 BORDERS SHOW SOME FOREIGN INFLUENCE
 *TITLE OF MANUSCRIPT SARUM MISSAL
 *SHELFMARK MS LAUD MISC 302
 *PROVENANCE ENGLISH/ DIOCESE OF DURHAM
 *DATE EXECUTED 15TH/ MIDDLE
 *LANGUAGE LATIN
 *ARTIST/ SCHOOL ENGLISH WITH CONTINENTAL INFLUENCE ON
 DECORATION

*TYPE OF MANUSCRIPT MISSAL
*CONTENTS MISSAL/ ENGLISH/ 15TH 189/1-16, DECORATED BORDE
189/1-16, HISTORIATED INITIALS 189/1-16, GROTESQUES IN BORDE
189/1-16, MUSICAL NOTATION 189-1, BLESSING OF HOLY WATER/ TE
189-1, DAVID KNEELING TO GOD 189-2, NATIVITY 189-3, ADORATI
OF THE MAGI 189-4, RESURRECTION 189-5, ASCENSION 189-
PENTECOST 189-7, TRINITY/ MERCY-SEAT TYPE 189-8, DEDICATION
CHURCH WITH BISHOP 189-9, ST ANDREW'S CRUCIFIXION 189-1
PRESENTATION OF CHRIST IN TEMPLE 189-11, ST JOHN THE BAPTI
189-12, ASSUMPTION OF VIRGIN 189-13, NATIVITY OF THE VIRG
189-14, CHRIST/ SEATED BLESSING 189-15, ST THOMAS 189-16

*$ABSTRACT 190
 *LIBRARY BOD
 *SLIDE SET TITLE BESTIARY
 *NEGATIVE REFERENCE ROLL 190K
 *RENTAL FEE SM 190 $4.00
 *SHELFMARK MS LAUD MISC 247
 *PROVENANCE ENGLISH
 *DATE EXECUTED 12TH/C1120-30
 *LANGUAGE LATIN
 *TYPE OF MANUSCRIPT BESTIARY
 *CONTENTS BESTIARY 190/1-40, LED/ LION 190-1, ANTELOPES SAWI
 TREE WITH HORNS 190-2, TEXT OF BESTIARY 190-3, LAPIDA
 IGNIFERI/ FIRESTONES MEETING 190-4, FIRESTONES MEETING 190-
 SERRA EATING FISH 190-5, CALADRIUS HOVERS OVER PATIENT IN B
 190-6, PELICAN WITH YOUNG ATTACKING PARENTS 190-7, NICTICORA
 NIGHT HERON WITH OWL'S HEAD AND HUMAN EYES 190-8, AQUIL
 EAGLE WITH WINGS OUTSTRETCHED 190-9, PHOENIX/ FENIX PREENI
 BREAST 190-10, HOOPOE/ HUPUPA WITH YOUNG 190-11, SIREN A
 CENTAUR/ SYRENE ET ONOCENTAURI 190-12, HEDGEHOG/ HERINACI
 EATING GRAPES ON SPIKES 190-13, IBIS/ YBEX EATING FISH 190-1
 FOX/ VULPIS FEIGNING DEATH TO ATTRACT PREY 190-15, UNICOR
 RHINOCEROS LEAPING INTO VIRGIN'S LAP AND SPEARED 190-1
 BEAVER/ CASTOR WITH HUNTSMAN BLOWING HORN 190-17, HYAEN
 HIENA VOMITTING 190-18, HYDRUS SWALLOWED AND BREAKS O
 190-19, HYDRUS 190-20, GOAT/ WILD CAPREA STEPPING TO HIGH
 PASTURE 190-21, ASS/ WILD ONAGER 190-21, MONKEYS/ SIM
 190-22, COOT/ FULICA GAZES UPWARDS 190-23, PANTHER/ PANTE
 BELCHING FOLLOWED BY ANIMALS 190-24, WHALE/ ASPEDOCHELONE WI
 SHIP WITH DRAGON FIGUREHEAD 190-25, PARTRIDGE WITH WI
 UPRAISED 190-26, WEASEL/ MUSTELA LEAPING FORWARD 190-27, API
 ASP WITH TAIL APPROACHING EAR 190-28, OSTRICH/ ASSIDA WI
 CAMEL FEET HEAD TO GROUND 190-29, STAG/ CERVUS WITH TONG
 OUTSTRETCHED EATS SNAKE 190-30, SALAMANDER/ SALAMANDRA 190-3
 DOVES/ COLOMBE FIVE 190-32, PERINDEUS TREE WITH DRAGON EATI
 LEAF 190-33, TEXT AND PERINDEUS 190-34, ELEPHANTS 190-3
 DRAGON 190-33, ADAM AND EVE 190-36, DRAGON ATTACKS ELEPHAN
 190-37, AMOS/ PROPHET WITH GOATS 190-38, ADAMANT/ EARTH WI
 JEWELS EMBEDDED 190-39, CONCHUS/ SHELL IN TWO HALVES UND
 WATER 190-40

*$ABSTRACT 191
 *LIBRARY BOD
 *SLIDE SET TITLE EMBROIDERED BINDINGS
 *NEGATIVE REFERENCE ROLL 194A
 *RENTAL FEE SM 191 $2.95
 *SHELFMARK MS BODLEY 883 191-1, MS ASTOR D 1 191-2, MS CHERE
 36 191/3-4, MS BODLEY 660 191-5, MS E MUSAEO 242 191-6, M
 DOUCE ENG 1583 191-7, BIBLE ENG 1617 191-8, ARCH GE 36 191-9
 NEW TESTAMENT ENG 1628 191-10, PS VERSE 1638 191-10, GIBSON
 AND 12 191-12, MS BIB ENG 1633 191-13, BIBLE ENG 1634 191-13
 MS TANNER 67 191/14-15, ARCH A 191-16, MS DOUCE BIB NT EN
 1625 191-17, GIBSON 2 AND 6 191-19
 *PROVENANCE ENGLISH
 *DATE EXECUTED 16TH 191/1-7, 17TH 191/8-18, 18TH AND 19
 191/19
 *TYPE OF MANUSCRIPT BIBLE 191/6-8 AND 10-18, BOOK OF COMMO

102

PRAYER 191-15
*CONTENTS BINDINGS/ EMBROIDERED 191/1-19, BINDING OF RED VELVET
ON FRENCH POEM 191-1, BINDING WITH ARMS OF FRANCOIS KING OF
FRANCE 191-2, EMBROIDERY ON BOOK DONE BY ELIZABETH I 191/3-4,
SILVERWORK BINDING ON RED SATIN 191-5, NEW TESTAMENT WITH
NOTES AND INITIAL OF ELIZABETH I 191-6, BIBLE GIVEN BY PRINTER
TO ELIZABETH I 191-7, BOOK OF COMMON PRAYER 191-8, BIBLE
191-8, BACON'S ESSAYS WITH PORTRAIT OF VILLIERS DUKE OF
BUCKINGHAM 191-9, CAMBRIDGE NEW TESTAMENT AND PSALM BOOK
191-10, PETIT-POINT TAPESTRY STITCH EMBROIDERY ON CANVAS
191-11, DOS A DOS NEW TESTAMENT 191-12, BIBLES WITH EMBROIDERY
OF COLORED SILKS 191-13, PETITION ON BEHALF OF MILLINERS AND
EMBROIDERERS 191-14, EMBROIDERED PLENTY AND PEACE 191/15-16,
DAVID/ ISAAC AND ABRAHAM ON SATIN BINDING 191-17, NEEDLEWORK
IN TAPESTRY STITCH 191-18, BOOKS WITH VELVET BINDINGS AND
INITIALS M D 191-19

*$ABSTRACT 192
*LIBRARY BOD
*SLIDE SET TITLE PORTUGESE PORTOLANOS
*NEGATIVE REFERENCE ROLL 194B
*RENTAL FEE SM 192 $2.75
*COMMENTS MAPS SHOWING SIX SHIPS OF VARIOUS TYPES IN THE
ATLANTIC
*TITLE OF MANUSCRIPT PORTUGALIAE MONUMENTA CARTOGRAPHICA
192/1-7, DOMINGOS TOIXOIRA 192/8-15
*SHELFMARK MS KL 111 192/1-7, MS KL 110 192/8-15
*PROVENANCE PORTUGESE
*DATE EXECUTED 16TH/C1550 192/1-7, 16TH/C1570 192/8-15
*LANGUAGE LATIN
*TYPE OF MANUSCRIPT MAPS
*CONTENTS MAPS OF ATLANTIC AND THE AMERICAS 192/1-15, ATLANTIC
AND AMERICA 192-1, ATLANTIC/ BRITAIN/ EUROPE/ AND AFRICA
192-2, VIRGIN AND CHILD AND NORTH AND CENTRAL AMERICA 192-3,
SOUTH AMERICA AND WEST INDIES 192-4, EUROPE AND NORTH AFRICA
192-5, WEST AFRICA 192-6, AFRICA/ WEST WITH CASTLE/ HUTS/
ANIMALS 192-7, ATLANTIC AND AMERICA 192-8, AMERICA/ NORTH AND
WEST INDIES 192-10, ATLANTIC/ BRITAIN/ EUROPE/ AFRICA 192-9,
AMERICA/ SOUTH AND CENTRAL 192-11, WEST INDIES AND CENTRAL
AMERICA 192-12, EUROPE/ WESTERN AND NORTH AFRICAN COAST
192-13, AFRICA/ WEST COAST 192-14, AFRICA/ WEST WITH CASTLES/
PALMS AND WORDS CONGO/ AMINA 192-15

*$ABSTRACT 193
*LIBRARY BOD
*SLIDE SET TITLE MAGI
*NEGATIVE REFERENCE ROLL 194D
*RENTAL FEE SM 193 $3.55
*COMMENTS 31 SLIDES SELECTED FROM 26 MSS DEPICTING THE MAGI
*TITLE OF MANUSCRIPT INFANCY OF CHRIST 193/3-6, SPECULUM
HUMANAE SALVATIONIS 193/7-9
*SHELFMARK MS CANON LITURG 393 193/1-2, MS SELDEN SUPRA 38
193/3-6, MS DOUCE F 4 193/7-8, MS DOUCE 204 193-9, MS CANON
LITURG 382 193-10, MS CANON LITURG 258 193-11, MS DOUCE 10
193-12, MS CANON LITURG 91 193-13, MS CANON LITURG 123 193-14,
MS BUCHANAN E 5 193-15, MS DOUCE 51 193-16, MS BUCHANAN E 18
193-17, MS DOUCE 256 193-18, MS DOUCE 48 193-19, MS BUCHANAN E
2 193-20, MS RAWL LITURG E 24 193-21, MS CANON LITURG 76
193-22, MS RAWL LITURG E 20 193-23, MS RAWL LITURG E 14
193-24, MS RAWL LITURG F 26 193-25, MS CANON LITURG 99 193-26,
MS LITURG 58 193-27, MS GOUGH LITURG 11 193-28, MS DOUCE 268
193-29, MS CANON LITURG 283 193-30, MS DOUCE 135 193-31
*PROVENANCE ENGLISH 193/1-8, SPANISH 193-9, ITALIAN 193/10-12,
FLEMISH 193/13-18, FRENCH 193/19-31
*DATE EXECUTED 13TH 193/1-2 AND 19, 14TH 193/3-6 AND 10, 15TH
193/7-9 AND 11-18 AND 21-29, 16TH 193/30-31
*LANGUAGE LATIN
*TYPE OF MANUSCRIPT PSALTER 193/1-2 AND 19, MISSAL 193-10,

BREVIARY 193-12, BOOK OF HOURS 193/11 AND 13-18 AND 20-31
*CONTENTS MAGI 193/1-31, MAGI ASK HEROD THE WAY 193-1
ADORATION OF THE MAGI 193/2 AND 9-31, NATIVITY 193-3, MAGI'
JOURNEY 193-4, MAGI VISIT HEROD 193-5, MAGI'S DREAM 193-6
THREE MEN BRING WATER TO DAVID 193-7, MAGIFOLLOW THE STA
193-8, BAPTISM OF CHRIST 193-10, ST JOSEPH WARMS HANDS BY
BRAZIER 193/13, AGES/ THREE OF MAN 193/14 AND 17, AGES/ THRE
OF MAN 193/20 AND 24 AND 27-28, KING/ BLACK 193/18 AND 26 AN
30-31, STAR AND CAMEL IN BORDER 193-19, MANGER OX AND AS
193-21, VIRGIN SITTING ON MAT OUTDOORS 193-22, SHEPHER
WATCHING 193-23, CHRIST CHILD ACCEPTS GIFT 193-29, ST JOSEP
STOWS GIFTS IN CHEST 193-30

*$ABSTRACT 194
  *LIBRARY BOD
  *SLIDE SET TITLE ST ANNE
  *NEGATIVE REFERENCE ROLL 194F
  *RENTAL FEE SM 194 $2.20
  *SHELFMARK MS DOUCE D 13 194-1, MS ORIEL COLLEGE 75 194-2, M
  TRINITY COLL 8 194-3, MS C C C 161 194/4 AND 10, MS DOUCE F
  194-5, MS LITURG 401 194-6, MS BODLEY 596/B 194-7, MS LITUR
  98 194/8 AND 13, MS RAWL LITURG G 3 194-9, MS AUCT D 4
  194-11, MS LITURG 401 194-12, MS LAUD LAT 15 194-14
  *PROVENANCE ENGLISH
  *DATE EXECUTED 14TH 194/1 AND 3 AND 11, 15TH 194/2 AND 4-10 A
  12-14
  *LANGUAGE LATIN
  *TYPE OF MANUSCRIPT MISSAL 194/2-3, SPECULUM HUMAN
  SALVATIONIS 194/4-5 AND 10, BOOK OF HOURS 194/6 AND 8-9 A
  11-14, LIFE OF THE VIRGIN 194-7
  *CONTENTS ST ANNE 194/1-14, ST ANNE IN HEADRESS AND ROBE 194-1
  ST JOACHIM ROBED BEFORE GOLDEN GATE 194-1, BIRTH OF THE VIRG
  194-2, ST ANNE RECEIVES BABY FROM MIDWIFE 194-2, VIRGIN
  BIRTH AND ST ANNE HOLDS BABY 194-3, BIRTH OF VIRGIN 194-4, S
  ANNE HANDING VIRGIN TO ST JOACHIM 194-4, ST ANNE OFFERS BREA
  TO NIMBED VIRGIN 194-5, PRESENTATION OF VIRGIN 194-6
  PRESENTATION OF VIRGIN WITH ANNE AND JOACHIM WATCHING 194-
  ST ANNE AND JOACHIM WATCH VIRGIN AT TEMPLE 194-8, PRESENTATIO
  OF VIRGIN WITH NIMBED ST ANNE 194-9, PRESENTATION OF VIRG
  194-10, ST ANNE IN THREE-TIERED MINIATURE OF SAINTS 194-11, S
  ANNE TEACHES VIRGIN TO READ 194-12, ST ANNE BEHIND VIRG
  FEEDING CHILD 194-13, ST ANNE BESIDE VIRGIN AND CHILD 194-14

*$ABSTRACT 195
  *LIBRARY BOD
  *SLIDE SET TITLE INITIALS BY FELLOW-ARTISTS OF DE BRAILLES
  *NEGATIVE REFERENCE ROLL 195C
  *RENTAL FEE SM 195 $3.00
  *TITLE OF MANUSCRIPT DE BRAILES PSALTER
  *SHELFMARK MS NEW COLLEGE 322
  *PROVENANCE ENGLISH
  *DATE EXECUTED 13TH
  *LANGUAGE LATIN
  *ARTIST/ SCHOOL DE BRAILES AND FELLOW-ARTISTS
  *TYPE OF MANUSCRIPT PSALTER
  *CONTENTS PSALTER INITIALS 195/1-20, INITIALS/ DECORAT
  195/1-20, INITIAL Q/ QUARE FREMUERUNT 195-1, MEN WITH HAN
  RAISED IN EXHORTATION 195-1, INITIAL D/ DOMINE QU
  MULTIPLICATI 195-2, MAN SEATED POINTING UPWARDS 195-2, INITI
  D/ DOMINE DEUS MEUS 195-3, MAN SEATED TEACHING FROM BO
  195-3, INITIAL D/ DIXIT INSIPIENS 195-4, MAN SEATED HOLDI
  SCROLL 195-4, INITIAL D/ DOMINUS QUIS HABITABIT 195-5, M
  SEATED HOLDING BOOK 195-5, INITIAL D/ DILIGEM TE DOMINE 195-
  MAN SEATED HOLDING BOOK 195-6, INITIAL C/ CAELI ENARRA
  195-7, BISHOP SEATED HOLDING STAFF 195-7, INITIAL D/ DEUS DE
  MEUS 195-8, MAN SEATED HOLDING BOOK 195-8, INITIAL D/ DOMI
  EST TERRA 195-9, MAN SEATED READING 195-9, INITIAL A/ AD
  DOMINE 195-10, MAN SEATED HOLDING BOOK 195-10, INITIAL

104

AFFERTE DOMINO 195-11, MAN SEATED TEACHING OR JUDGING 195-11,
INITIAL N/ NOLI AEMULARI 195-12, MAN SEATED POINTING UPWARDS
195-12, INITIAL D/ DEUS DEORUM 195-13, MAN SEATED WEARING
SKULL-CAP 195-13, INITIAL S/ SI VERE UTIQUE 195-14, MAN WITH
HANDS RAISED AS IF EXPOUNDING 195-14, INITIAL D/ DEUS DEUS
MEUS 195-15, MAN SEATED TEACHING 195-15, INITIAL D/ DEUS
VENERUNT 195-16, CHRIST STANDING BESIDE CHURCH 195-16, INITIAL
B/ BENEDIIO ANIMA 195-17, MAN HOLDING BOOK AND OWL IN MARGIN
195-17, INITIAL F/ FECI JUDICHM 195-18, MAN HOLDING SCROLL
195-18, INITIAL A/ AD DOMINUM 195-19, MAN SEATED 195-19,
INITIAL L/ LEVAVI OCULOS 195-19, MAN WITH HANDS RAISED 195-19,
INITIAL A/ AD TE LEVAVI 195-20, HOODED MAN WITH HANDS RAISED
195-20, INITIAL N/ NISI QUIA DOMINUS 195-20, MAN SEATED
READING SCROLL 195-20

*$ABSTRACT 196
 *LIBRARY BOD
 *SLIDE SET TITLE BOCCACCIO
 *NEGATIVE REFERENCE ROLL 196B
 *RENTAL FEE SM 196 $2.50
 *COMMENTS MADE FOR JOHN/ DUKE OF BERRY, ILLUSTRATIONS FROM
 LAURENT DE PREMIERFAIT'S FRENCH TRANSLATION OF DES CAS DES
 NOBLES HOMMES ET FEMMES
 *TITLE OF MANUSCRIPT DES CAS DES NOBLES HOMMES ET FEMMES
 *SHELFMARK MS BODLEY 265
 *PROVENANCE FRENCH
 *DATE EXECUTED 15TH/C1420
 *LANGUAGE FRENCH
 *AUTHOR BOCCACCIO/ TRANSLATED BY LAURENS DE PREMIERFAIT
 *ARTIST/ SCHOOL ATELIER OF THE TERENCE DES DUCS
 *TYPE OF MANUSCRIPT LITERATURE
 *CONTENTS LITERATURE/ BOCCACCIO 196/1-10, COURT OF THE POPE
 196-1, COURT OF KING OF FRANCE 196-1, PRESENTATION OF BOOK TO
 JEAN DUKE OF BERRY 196-1, WORKMEN WITH TOOLS 196-1, AUTHOR AT
 LECTERN 196-2, ADAM AND EVE 196-2, SAULOS DEATH AND AN
 EXECUTION 196-3, CROSSROADS MARKED WITH STONE CROSS 196-4,
 POURETE BENDS OVER FIGURE OF FORTUNE 196-4, POURETE TIES
 FORTUNE TO PILLAR 196-4, MANLIUS AND ASSISTANT THROW GAUL INTO
 TIBER 196-5, ROMANS STANDING BELOW TOWER 196-5, SELEUCUS AND
 ANTIOCHUS/ UNFORTUNATE BROTHERS 196-6, MEN HUNG ON GIBBET AND
 TWO BEHEADED 196-7, MARK ANTHONY'S SON ANTHONY KILLED BEFORE
 STATUE OF CAESAR 196-8, PETRARCH DEBATES WITH BOCCACCIO ON HIS
 DEATHBED 196-9, BRUNECHILDE TIED TO THREE HORSES AND TORN
 ASUNDER 196-10

*$ABSTRACT 197
 *LIBRARY BOD
 *SLIDE SET TITLE THIRD HOLKHAM MISCELLANY
 *NEGATIVE REFERENCE ROLL 196F
 *RENTAL FEE SM 197 $4.55
 *TITLE OF MANUSCRIPT DE CONSOLATIONE PHILOSOPHIAE 197/1-3,
 MISSALE ROMANUM 197/4-9, DE AMICITIA 197/10-11, SATIRES OF
 FRANCESCO FILELFO 197/12-14, RHETORICAL WORKS 197-15, APPIANUS
 197/16-22, SALLUST 197/23-26, JOSEPHUS 197/27-28, ETHICS AND
 POLITICS OF ARISTOTLE 197/33-35, LETTERS OF ST JEROME
 197/36-38, BRUNI/ LEONARDO WORKS OF 197-39, CASTIGLIONCHO/
 LAPO DA WORKS OF 197-40, LETTERS OF PHALARIS 197-42,
 PHILOSOPHICAL WORKS 197/43-45, BOOK OF HOURS 197/46-151
 *SHELFMARK MS HOLKHAM 402 197/1-3, MS HOLKHAM 35 197/4-9, MS
 HOLKHAM 386 197/10-11, MS HOLKHAM 431 197/12-14, MS HOLKHAM
 375 197-15, MS HOLKHAM 364 197/16-22, MS HOLKHAM 366
 197/23-26, MS HOLKHAM 454 197/27-28, MS HOLKHAM 346 197/29-32,
 MS HOLKHAM 444 197/33-35, MS HOLKHAM 126 197/36-38, MS HOLKHAM
 478 197-39, MS HOLKHAM 488 197/40, MS HOLKHAM 365 197-41, MS
 HOLKHAM 452 197-42, MS HOLKHAM 383 197/43-45, MS HOLKHAM 42
 197/46-51
 *PROVENANCE ITALIAN
 *DATE EXECUTED 15TH

*AUTHOR BOETHIUS 197/1-3, CICERO 197/10-11 AND 43-45, FILELF(
FRANCESCO 197/12-14, DICTYS CRETENSIS 197/16-22, SALLUS
197/23-26, JOSEPHUS 197/27-28, LIVY 197/29-32, ARISTOTI
197/33-35, ST JEROME 197/36-38, BRUNI/ LEONARDO 197-39
CASTIGLIONCHO 197-40, QUINTUS CURTIUS 197-41, PHALARIS 197-42
*TYPE OF MANUSCRIPT MISCELLANY
*CONTENTS MANUSCRIPT/ MISCELLANY ITALIAN 197/1-51, INITIAL
197-1, INITIAL I 197-2, INITIAL D 197-3, PAGE/ WHOLE 197-4
PAGE/ TOP HALF 197-5, INITIAL P 197-6, CRUCIFIXION 197-
INITIAL T 197-8, INITIAL E 197-9, INITIAL O 197-10, INITIAL
197-11, INITIAL I 197-12, INITIAL O 197-13, INITIAL N 197-1
INITIAL C 197-15, INITIAL D 197/16 AND 21, INITIAL C 197-1
INITIAL I 197-18, INITIAL S 197-19, INITIAL I 197-20, INITI
A 197-22, PAGE/ FIRST 197-23, INITIAL F 197-24, BORDER WI
PEACOCK 197-25, INITIAL B 197-26, INITIAL N 197-27, INITIAL
197-28, PAGE/ WHOLE 197-29, INITIAL F AND GOLD HEAD 197-30
BORDER AND ARMS 197-31, INITIAL H 197-32, INITIAL I 197-3
INITIAL O 197-34, INITIAL D 197-35, PAGE/ WHOLE 197-36
INITIAL O 197-37, INITIAL P 197-38, INITIAL V 197-39, INITI
V 197-40, INITIAL I 197-41, INITIAL O 197/43-44, INITIAL
197-45, INITIAL D 197/46-48 AND 50-51, INITIAL S 197-49

*$ABSTRACT 198
    *LIBRARY BOD
    *SLIDE SET TITLE BERKSHIRE DOMESDAY BOOK
    *NEGATIVE REFERENCE ROLL 196J
    *RENTAL FEE SM 198 $2.80
    *COMMENTS 10 SLIDES FROM FOLIO 56 OF THE ORIGINAL MS
    *TITLE OF MANUSCRIPT BERKSHIRE DOMESDAY BOOK
    *SHELFMARK DOMESDAY BOOK OF GREAT SURVEY OF ENGLAND OF WILLI
    CONQUEROR
    *PROVENANCE ENGLISH
    *DATE EXECUTED 11TH
    *TYPE OF MANUSCRIPT SURVEY OF ENGLISH POPULATION
    *CONTENTS DOMESDAY BOOK 198/1-16, TENANTS/ LIST OF 198-1, KI
    198/2-4, BISHOPS OF WINCHESTER/ SALIABURY/ DURHAM 198-
    BISHOPS OSBERN/ COUTANCES 198-6, ABBEY OF ABINGDON 198-
    ABINGDON CHURCH 198-7, ABINGDON CHURCH/ GLASTONBUR
    WESTMINSTER 198-8, WINCHESTER/ CHESTER/ BATTLE ABBEY 198-
    AMESBURY CHURCH/ COUNT OF EVREUX/ WALTER GIFARD 198-9, HEN
    DE FERIERES/ WILLIAM SON OF ANSCULF 198-10, WILLIAM DE O
    WILLIAM PEVREL/ WALTER SON OF PONZ 198-11, WALTER SON
    OTHER/ GILBERT DE BRETEVILLE 198-12, GILBERT DE GAND/ GEOFFR
    DE MANNEVILLE/ ROBERT DE OILGI 198-13, ROGER DE IVERI/ ROG
    DE LACI 198-14, HUMPHREY THE CHAMBERLAIN 198-15, STEPHEN S
    OF EIRARD 198-16

*$ABSTRACT 199
    *LIBRARY BOD
    *SLIDE SET TITLE LYDGATE
    *NEGATIVE REFERENCE ROLL 196K
    *RENTAL FEE SM 199 $2.40
    *COMMENTS ILLUSTRATIONS FROM 6 MSS
    *SHELFMARK MS DIGBY 232 199-1, MS DIGBY 230 199/2-4, MS DIG
    230 199-5, MS RAWL C446 199-6, MS ASHMOLE 46 199-7, MS ASHMO
    46 199-8
    *PROVENANCE ENGLISH
    *DATE EXECUTED 15TH
    *LANGUAGE ENGLISH
    *AUTHOR LYDGATE/ JOHN
    *TYPE OF MANUSCRIPT ROMANCE
    *CONTENTS LYDGATE/ ILLUSTRATIONS FROM MSS OF HIS WORKS 199/1-
    LITERATURE/ LYOGATE 199/1-8, TROY BOOK 196-1, PRIAM BESIEGI
    CITY 199-1, SIEGE OF THEBES 199/2-4, INITIAL W/ WHANNE 199-
    SIEGE OF JERUSALEM 199-5, SIEGE OF TROY 199-6, PELLEUS/ KI
    CROWNED IN BLUE 199-6, LIFE AND MARTYRDOM OF ST EDMUND 199-
    ST EDMUND ENTHRONED 199-7, LIFE AND MARTYRDOM OF ST EDMUN
    TEXT 199-8

106

```
*$ABSTRACT 200
 *LIBRARY BOD
 *SLIDE SET TITLE HERMITS
 *NEGATIVE REFERENCE ROLL 198D
 *RENTAL FEE SM 200 $2.50
 *COMMENTS 10 SLIDES OF HERMITS FROM 7 MSS
 *SHELFMARK   MS  UNIVERSITY  COLLEGE   165   200/1-2, MS DOUCE 199
 200-3, MS DIGBY 223 200-4, MS DOUCE 215 200-5, MS RAWLINSON  Q
 B 6 200/6-8, MS ASHMOLE 828 200-9, MS AUCT D 4 4 200-10
 *PROVENANCE  ENGLISH  200/1-2  AND  10, FRENCH 200/3-8, FLEMISH
 200-9
 *DATE EXECUTED 12TH 200/1-2, 14TH 200/3-10
 *TYPE OF MANUSCRIPT ROMANCE 200/3-9, PSALTER AND HOURS 200-10
 *CONTENTS HERMITS 200/1-10,  RAVENS  MAKE  AMENDS  TO  CUTHBERT
 200-1,  CUTHBERT TELLS OF DEATH TO HEREBERHT THE HERMIT 200-2,
 HERMITAGE 200-3, HERMIT  EXHORTS  LANCELOT  200-4,  HERMIT  IN
 WICKER  HUT HEARS LANCELOT'S CONFESSION 200-5, HERMIT 200/6-8,
 HERMIT MEETS LANCELOT 200-9, HERMIT TO WHOM ABBESS'S CHILD  TO
 BE ENTRUSTED 200-10


*$ABSTRACT 201
 *LIBRARY BOD
 *SLIDE SET TITLE LANCELOT WITH HERMITS
 *NEGATIVE REFERENCE ROLL 198J
 *RENTAL FEE SM 201 $2.50
 *COMMENTS 10 SLIDES FROM 4 MSS DEPICTING LANCELOT WITH HERMITS
 *TITLE OF MANUSCRIPT ROMANCE OF LANCELOT DU LAC
 *SHELFMARK   MS  ASHMOLE  828  201/1-5, MS DIGBY 223 201/6-7, MS
 DOUCE 215 201-8, MS RAWLINSON Q B 6 201/9-10
 *PROVENANCE FLEMISH 201/1-5, FRENCH 201/6-10
 *LANGUAGE FRENCH
 *TYPE OF MANUSCRIPT ROMANCE
 *CONTENTS ROMANCE OF  LANCELOT   DU  LAC   201/1-10,  LITERATURE/
 LANCELOT   DU  LAC   201/1-10,  LANCELOT  WITH HERMITS 201/1-10,
 HERMITS 201/1-10, LANCELOT AND THE LADY OF THE LAKE AT  DINNER
 201-1,  LANCELOT MEETS HERMIT 201-2, LANCELOT AWAKES IN LITTER
 201-3, LANCELOT SEATED ON FLOOR BESIDE LADY OF MALEHAUT 201-4,
 LANCELOT AND QUEEN EMBRACE 201-5, LANCELOT WITH DAMSEL  COMING
 FOR  HIM  201-6,  LANCELOT  EXHORTED BY HERMIT 201-7, LANCELOT
 CONFESSES  TO  HERMIT  201-8,  LANCELOT  MEETS  HERMIT  201-9,
 LANCELOT TRAVELS WITH DAMSEL AND SQUIRE 201-10


*$ABSTRACT 202
 *LIBRARY BOD
 *SLIDE SET TITLE HERALDIC BRASS RUBBINGS
 *NEGATIVE REFERENCE ROLL 200B
 *RENTAL FEE SM 202 $2.60
 *COMMENTS  12 SLIDES OF BRASS RUBBINGS GIVEN TO THE BODLEIAN BY
 MAJOR H F OWEN-EVANS IN 1966
 *PROVENANCE ENGLISH
 *CONTENTS BRASS RUBBINGS 202/1-12, HERALDIC BRASS  RUBBINGS  OF
 16TH  CENTURY TOMBS 202/1-12, SIR ROGER LE STRANGE/ HUNSTANTON
 NORFOLK 1506 202-1, ANTHONYE FETYPLACE/  SWINBROOK  OXON  1510
 202-2,  ANTHONY HANSART WITH WIFE CAMBS 1517 202-3, JOHN TERRI
 AND WIFE LETTYS/ NORWICH 1524  202-4,  JOHN  SACHEVERELL  WITH
 WIFE  MORLEY/  DERBS  1525  202-5,  ANDREW  AND  ELLEN EVYNGAR
 BARKING 1530 202-6, SIR EDMUND TAME AND WIVES GLOS 1534 202-7,
 SIR WILLIAM GASCOIGNE AND WIFE ELIZABETH 202-8,  WIFE/  SECOND
 OF SIR WILLIAM GASCOIGNE 1540 202-9, SIR ROBERT DYMOKE/ KING'S
 CHAMPION  1545  202-10,  SIR  RALPH  VERNEY AND WIFE ELIZABETH
 HERTS 1546 202-11, JOHN SHELLEY AND  WIFE  MARY/  SUSSEX  1550
 202-12


*$ABSTRACT 203
 *LIBRARY BOD
 *SLIDE SET TITLE ATLAS OF VICOMTE DE SANTAREM
```

107

*NEGATIVE REFERENCE ROLL 200C
*RENTAL FEE SM 203 $2.85
*COMMENTS ATLAS COMPILED AND EXECUTED UNDER THE DIRECTION OF
VICOMTE DE SANTAREM PARIS 1849
*TITLE OF MANUSCRIPT ATLAS COMPOSE DE MAPMONDES/ DE PORTULANS/
DE CARTES/ HYDROGRAPHIQUES/ HISTORIQUES
*PROVENANCE FRENCH
*DATE EXECUTED 19TH/ FROM 15TH AND 16TH CENTURY MAPS
*LANGUAGE FRENCH
*TYPE OF MANUSCRIPT ATLAS
*CONTENTS ATLAS 203/1-17, MAPS 203/1-17, MAP OF THE WORLD FROM
MERINO SANUTO 203-1, MAP OF THE WORLD BY JOHANES LEARDUS OF
VENICE 203-2, MAP OF THE WORLD 203-3, GLOBE BY MARTIN BEHAIM
IN DIAMETRO 203-4, WORLD MAP FROM THE 15TH CENTURY 203-5,
AFRICA ON FRENCH MAP OF WORLD FROM 1508 203-6, AFRICA ON LATIN
MAP OF WORLD/ ROME 1553 203-7, WEST AFRICA/ BIAFRA ON
PORTUGESE MAP 1513 203-8, BIAFRA ON MAP OF JOAN MARTINES
203/9-10, BIAFRA 203/11-15 AND 17, WEST COAST OF AFRICA
203/11-17, LEASSEURX/ GUILLAUME DE DIEPPE MAP OF 1601 203-11,
JEAN DUPONT DE DIEPPE 1625 MAP OF 203-12, JEAN GUERARD DE
DIEPPE 1631 MAP OF 203-13, JACQUES DE VAUX 1553 MAP OF 203-14,
MAP/ ENTIRE 203-15, JUEN DE LA COZA PILOT FOR CHRITOPHE COLOMO
1493 203-16, MAP OF WORLD FROM WEIMAR 203-17

*$ABSTRACT 204
  *LIBRARY BOD
  *SLIDE SET TITLE ST MARGARET FROM A BOOK OF HOURS
  *NEGATIVE REFERENCE ROLL 202B
  *RENTAL FEE SM 204 $2.55
  *COMMENTS WRITTEN FOR A MEMBER OF THE FAMILY OF LA FRESNAY
  D'AIGNAN, NORMANDY, WHO KNEELS BEFORE ST JOHN BAPTIST
  *SHELFMARK MS RAWL LITURG E 12
  *PROVENANCE FRENCH/ NORMANDY
  *DATE EXECUTED 15TH/ FIRST HALF
  *LANGUAGE LATIN AND FRENCH
  *TYPE OF MANUSCRIPT BOOK OF HOURS/ USE OF BAYEUX
  *CONTENTS BOOK OF HOURS/ FRENCH/ 15TH 204/1-11, ST MARGARET
  204/1-11, NURSE CONVERTS ST MARGARET 204-1, MESSENGER FROM
  OLIBRIUS BEFORE ST MARGARET 204-2, ST MARGARET BEFORE OLIBRIUS
  204-3, TORTURE OF ST MARGARET 204-4, IMPRISONMENT OF ST
  MARGARET 204-5, DRAGON ENCOUNTERED BY ST MARGARET 204-6, ST
  MARGARET EMERGES FROM DRAGON 204-7, DEVIL SLAIN BY ST MARGARET
  204-8, ST MARGARET WARNED OF APPROACHING DEATH 204-9,
  EXECUTION OF ST MARGARET 204-10, BURIAL OF ST MARGARET 204-11

*$ABSTRACT 205
  *LIBRARY BOD
  *SLIDE SET TITLE BOOKS OF HOURS/ A COLLECTION OF FRAGMENTS
  *NEGATIVE REFERENCE ROLL 203A
  *RENTAL FEE SM 205 $3.10
  *SHELFMARK MS DOUCE D 19
  *PROVENANCE DUTCH
  *DATE EXECUTED 15TH/C1420-30
  *LANGUAGE LATIN
  *TYPE OF MANUSCRIPT BOOK OF HOURS
  *CONTENTS BOOK OF HOURS/ DUTCH/ 15TH 205/1-22, INITIALS/
  ILLUMINATED 205/1-22, INITIAL D/ DEUS 205/1-6 AND 8-13 AND
  15-16 AND 18-20 AND 22, INITIAL C/ CONUERTE 205/7 AND 14 AND
  21, VISITATION 205-1, ST CATHERINE IN BORDER 205-1, NATIVITY
  205-2, ST GENEVIEVE IN BORDER 205-2, ANGEL AND TWO SHEPHERDS
  205-3, ST PETER IN BORDER 205-3, ADORATION OF THE MAGI 205-4,
  ST APOLLONIA 205-4, FLIGHT INTO EGYPT 205-5, ST GEORGE WITH
  DRAGON 205-5, PRESENTATION IN THE TEMPLE 205-6, ST PAUL IN
  BORDER 205-6, CORONATION OF VIRGIN 205-7, ST ANTHONY THE ABBOT
  205-7, BETRAYAL OF CHRIST 205-8, ANGEL WITH CROSS IN BORDER
  205-8, CHRIST CROWNED WITH THORNS 205-9, ANGEL WITH PILLAR AND
  SCOURGES 205-9, CHRIST CROWNED WITH THORNS 205-9, CRUCIFIXION
  205-12, ANGEL WITH SPONGE AND PAIL IN BORDER 205-12, SCOURGING

OF CHRIST 205-11, ANGEL WITH CROWN OF THORNS IN BORDER 205-11,
DEPOSITION 205-13, ANGEL WITH THIRTY PIECES OF SILVER ON TRAY
205-13, ENTOMBMENT 205-14, ANGEL WITH TORCH AND LANTERN
205-14, TRINITY 205-15, ST JOHN EVANGELIST IN BORDER 205-15,
ABRAHAM AND THE ANGELS 205-16, ST CHRISTOPHER IN BORDER
205-16, EZEKIEL'S VISION OF THREE DOVES 205-17, ST APOLLONIA
IN BORDER 205-17, ADAM'S BODY HELD BY TWO ANGELS 205-18,
TRINITY 205-18, ST ANDREW 205-18, DAVID WITH HARP AS PSALMIST
205-19, ST PETER HOLDS FISH 205-19, VISION OF ISAIAH 205-20,
JEREMIAH 205-21, ST THOMAS HOLDING A SPEAR 205-21, CHRIST
ENTHRONED BLESSING HOLDING ORB 205-22, ST JOHN EVANGELIST WITH
CHALICE 205-22

*$ABSTRACT 206
  *LIBRARY BOD
  *SLIDE SET TITLE SENECA/ PHILOSOPHICAL WORKS AND TRAGEDIES
  *NEGATIVE REFERENCE ROLL 203B
  *RENTAL FEE SM 206 $2.70
  *COMMENTS GIVEN BY MELISSUS TO JUSTUS LIPSIUS, WHO EDITED
  SENECA IN ANTWERP IN 1605 USING THIS MS
  *SHELFMARK MS HOLKHAM 390
  *PROVENANCE ITALIAN
  *DATE EXECUTED 14TH/ SECOND QUARTER
  *LANGUAGE LATIN
  *AUTHOR SENECA
  *TYPE OF MANUSCRIPT PHILOSOPHICAL WORKS AND TRAGEDIES
  *CONTENTS SENECA/ ILLUSTRATIONS OF HIS WORKS 206/1-14,
  CLASSICAL WRITINGS/ SENECA 206/1-14, TITLE PAGE 206-1, ST
  JEROME DISPLAYING REFERENCE TO SENECA 206-1, SENECA WRITING TO
  LUCILIUS 206-2, DRAGON/ ORNAMENTAL 206-3, REMEDISS FORTUITORUM
  AD GALLIONEM 206-4, SEVEN LIBERAL ARTS 206-5, DE MORIBUS
  206-6, DE BENEFICIIS 206-7, DE PREVEDENTIA DEI 206-8,
  TRANQUILLITY OF SOUL 206-9, DE BREVITATE VITE 206-10, AD
  MARCIAM 206-11, AD HEBIAM MATREM DE CONSOLATIONE 206-12, DE
  MORTE DIVI CLAUDII 206-13, HERCULES FURENS 206-14

*$ABSTRACT 207
  *LIBRARY BOD
  *SLIDE SET TITLE MILITARY TREATISE
  *NEGATIVE REFERENCE ROLL 203D
  *RENTAL FEE SM 207 $2.60
  *SHELFMARK MS DOUCE 186
  *PROVENANCE GERMAN
  *DATE EXECUTED 16TH
  *LANGUAGE GERMAN
  *TYPE OF MANUSCRIPT MILITARY TREATISE
  *CONTENTS MILITARY TREATISE/ GERMAN 207/1-12, ARMS OF CITY OF
  NUREMBURG 207-1, TURK STANDING ON PORCH 207-2, BADGES/
  MILITARY 207/3-7, HAMMERS CROSSED IN WREATH WITH PENDANT
  SHIELD 207-3, BANNERS CROSSED 207-4, FALCON IN WREATHS WITH
  PENDANT SHIELDS 207-4, HORSE AND MONOGRAM IHS IN WREATHS
  207-5, MEDAL OF VIRGIN 207-5, SOLDIER ARMOURED 207-6, STAVES
  CROSSED 207-6, STAFF UPRIGHT 207-6, SWORDS CROSSED 207-6,
  HERMIT BLESSES PILGRIM 207-8, KEYS AND AXES CROSSED 207-7,
  HERALD WITH TABARD WITH ROYAL EAGLE 207-9, MILITARY
  STORE-KEEPER WITH ELABORATE UNIFORM 207-10, INFANTRY OFFICER
  IN ELABORATE COSTUME 207-11, ST GEORGE'S CROSS SURROUNDED BY
  GREEN LAUREL WREATH 207-12

*$ABSTRACT 208
  *LIBRARY BOD
  *SLIDE SET TITLE MASONS CARPENTERS AND ARTICLES ON FREEMASONRY
  *NEGATIVE REFERENCE ROLL 203F
  *RENTAL FEE SM 208 $3.00
  *COMMENTS 20 SLIDES DEPICTING MASONS AND CARPENTERS FROM 15 MSS
  AND 2 PRINTED BOOKS

*TITLE OF MANUSCRIPT HESPERIS 208-10, NATURAL HISTORY OF
STAFFORDSHIRE 208-16, GRAND MYSTERY OF FREE-MASONS DISCOVERED
208/17-18
*SHELFMARK MS RAWL G 126 208-1, MS E D CLARKE 31 208-2, MS
CANON BIBL LAT 57 208-3, MS AUCT D 5 17 208-4, MS CANON BIBL
LAT 92 208-5, MS TRINITY COLLEGE 53 208-6, MS CANON BIBL LAT
36 208-7, MS DOUCE 6 208-8, MS LAT LITURG B 1 208-9, MS CANON
CLASS LAT 81 208-10, MS BODLEY 850 208-11, MS BODLEY 596/B
208-12, MS ADD A 211 208/13-15, MS RAWL C 36 208/17-18
*PROVENANCE ENGLISH 208/1 AND 11-20, FRENCH 208/2 AND 4-6,
ITALIAN 208/3 AND 7 AND 9-10, FLEMISH 208-8
*DATE EXECUTED 13TH 208/4-7, 14TH 208/1-3 AND 8, 15TH 208/9-12,
17TH 208/13-16, 18TH 208/17-20
*AUTHOR BASINIO DE BARANI 208-10, PLOT/ DR R 208-16
*TYPE OF MANUSCRIPT BIBLE 208/1-7, PSALTER 208/8-9, BOOK OF
HOURS 208-11, LIFE OF THE VIRGIN 208-12
*CONTENTS MASONS 208/1-20, CARPENTERS 208/1-20, FREEMASONRY/
COMMENTS ON 208/13-20, MASONS BUILDING TEMPLE 208-1, MASONS
BUILDING TEMPLE 208-2, MASON WITH HAMMER AND CHISEL 208-3,
MASON WITH HAMMER 208-4, MASONS OF CYRUS BUILD TEMPLE 208-5,
MASONS WITH HAMMER AND TROWEL 208-6, MASON REBUILDING TEMPLE
208-7, MASON 208-8, MASON ADDS BRICKS TO BUILDING 208-9,
MASONS PREPARING BLOCKS OF STONE 208-10, CARPENTER AT THE
CRUCIFIXION 208-11, ST JOSEPH AND HIS CARPENTER TOOLS 208-12,
ELIAS ASHMOLE DESCRIBES ADMISSION TO THE FREEMASONS 208-13,
ASHMOLE DESCRIBES SUMMONS TO APPEAR AT FREEMASONS HALL
208/14-15, FREEMASON'S CUSTOMS DESCRIBED 208-16, TITLE PAGE OF
GRAND MYSTERY OF FREEMASONS 208-17, EXTRACT FROM WORK ON
FREEMASONS ABOVE 208-18, FREEMASON CATECHISM/ EXTRACT 208-19,
FREEMASON CATECHISM/ EXTRACT 208-20

*$ABSTRACT 209
  *LIBRARY BOD
  *SLIDE SET TITLE LEISURE ACTIVITIES
  *NEGATIVE REFERENCE ROLL 203G
  *RENTAL FEE SM 209 $2.70
  *TITLE OF MANUSCRIPT ROMANCE OF ALEXANDER
  *SHELFMARK MS BODLEY 264
  *PROVENANCE FLEMISH
  *DATE EXECUTED 14TH/C 1338-1344
  *LANGUAGE FRENCH
  *ARTIST/ SCHOOL JEHAN DE GRISE
  *TYPE OF MANUSCRIPT ROMANCE
  *CONTENTS ROMANCE OF ALEXANDER 209/1-14, LITERATURE/ ROMANCE OF
  ALEXANDER 209/1-14, LEISURE ACTIVITIES 209/1-14, TRAPPING
  BIRDS WITH CAGE AND DECOY 209-1, GAME OF DRAUGHTS PLAYED BY
  LADY AND PAGE 209-2, SWORD FIGHTING AS GAME 209-3, GAME
  SIMILAR TO BLIND MAN'S BLUFF 209-4, HORSE AND APE PERFORMING
  209-5, PUPPET SHOW 209-6, WOMEN HAWKING FOR DUCKS 209-7,
  TRIUMPHAL PROCESSION OF VICTOR OF COCK FIGHT 209-8, TILTING AT
  QUINTAIN FROM ROWING BOAT 209-9, FIGHTING GAMES 209-10, GOAT
  PERFORMING/ DANCING TO DRUM 209-11, TUG OF WAR GAME 209-12,
  GAME OF CHESS WITH PEACOCKS AND DOGS BY PLAYERS 209-13, SOW
  PERFORMING WITH LITTER OF PIGLETS 209-14

*$ABSTRACT 210
  *LIBRARY BOD
  *SLIDE SET TITLE WORK
  *NEGATIVE REFERENCE ROLL 203H
  *RENTAL FEE SM 210 $3.00
  *TITLE OF MANUSCRIPT ROMANCE OF ALEXANDER
  *SHELFMARK MS BODLEY 264
  *PROVENANCE FLEMISH
  *DATE EXECUTED 14TH/C 1338-1344
  *LANGUAGE FRENCH
  *ARTIST/ SCHOOL JEHAN DE GRISE
  *TYPE OF MANUSCRIPT ROMANCE
  *CONTENTS WORK 210/1-20, ROMANCE OF ALEXANDER 210/1-20,

LITERATURE/ ROMANCE OF ALEXANDER 210/1-20, PEASANT WORKING
WITH SCYTHE 210-1, SWORDSMITH BURNISHING LARGE SWORD 210-2,
DYERS AT WORK 210-3, COOKS AT SALTIRE INN 210-4, SMITHS
WORKING AT FORGE 210-5, BLACKSMITHS SHOEING HORSE 210-6,
BLACKSMITHS WORKING ANVIL 210-7, SWORDSMITHS MAKING HUGE SWORD
210-8, SWORDSMITHS SHARPENING SWORD 210-9, LONGBOWS BEING MADE
210-10, INNKEEPER SERVES CUSTOMER AT SALTIRE INN 210-11,
METALWORKERS MAKING HELMET 210/12-13, HELMET/ TOURNAMENT MADE
AND DECORATED 210/14-15, COOKS BASTING ROASTING BIRDS ON SPIT
210-16, MILITARY ENGINEERS WITH CATAPULT 210-17, MILITARY
ENGINEERS WITH BALLISTA 210-18, PROVISIONERS IN CAMP/ BAKER'S
SHOP 210-19, PROVISIONERS IN CAMP COOKING AT SALTIRE INN
210-20

*$ABSTRACT 211
  *LIBRARY BOD
  *SLIDE SET TITLE MEDIEVAL PEOPLE
  *NEGATIVE REFERENCE ROLL 203I
  *RENTAL FEE SM 211 $2.60
  *TITLE OF MANUSCRIPT ROMANCE OF ALEXANDER
  *SHELFMARK MS BODLEY 264
  *PROVENANCE FLEMISH
  *DATE EXECUTED 14TH/C1338-1344
  *LANGUAGE FRENCH
  *ARTIST/ SCHOOL JEHAN DE GRISE
  *TYPE OF MANUSCRIPT ROMANCE
  *CONTENTS ROMANCE OF ALEXANDER 211/1-12, LITERATURE/ ROMANCE OF
  ALEXANDER 211/1- 12, MEDIEVAL PEOPLE 211/1-12, YOUNG PEOPLE IN
  FINE COSTUMES 211-1, KNIGHT ON HORSEBACK WITH ATTENDANTS
  211-2, KNIGHT ON HORSEBACK WITH BEARDED COUNCILLORS 211-3,
  WOMAN WITH TWO SMALL BOYS 211-4, DOCTOR/ ASSISTANT AND PATIENT
  211-5, FRIAR PREACHING FROM PULPIT 211-6, WEDDING PROCESSION
  211-7, WEDDING AT DOOR OF CHURCH 211-8, KING IN SHIP WITH
  PEOPLE INCLUDING OARSMEN 211-9, KING IN SHIP WITH CARVED PROW
  211-10, MOURNERS IN STRIPED COSTUMES 211/11-12

*$ABSTRACT 212
  *LIBRARY BOD
  *SLIDE SET TITLE ALPHABET OF ST ANNE
  *NEGATIVE REFERENCE ROLL 204N
  *RENTAL FEE SM 212 $2.70
  *SHELFMARK MS CANON MISC 476 212/1-3 AND 5 AND 8-13, MS CANON
  LITURG 286 212/4 AND 7, MS CANON LITURG 206 212-6, MS LAUD
  MISC 93 212-14
  *PROVENANCE ITALIAN 212/1-3 AND 5-6 AND 8-13, GERMAN 212/4 AND
  7, FRENCH 212-14
  *DATE EXECUTED 14TH 212/1-3 AND 5 AND 8-13, 15TH 212/4 AND 6-7,
  16TH 212-14
  *LANGUAGE LATIN
  *TYPE OF MANUSCRIPT ACTS OF ST MARY AND JESUS 212/1-3 AND 5 AND
  13-18, BREVIARY/ PORTABLE 212/4 AND 6-7, BREVIARY/ CHOIR
  FESTIVE 212-14
  *CONTENTS ST ANNE/ ALPHABET OF 212/1-14, ALPHABET OF ST ANNE
  212/1-14, INITIALS/ HISTORIATED OF ST ANNE 212/1-14, JOACHIM'S
  OFFERING REJECTED 212-1, RAPHAEL/ ARCHANGEL TELLS JOACHIM THAT
  ANNE TO HAVE CHILD 212-2, RAPHAEL/ ARCHANGEL TELLS ANNE SHE
  WILL HAVE CHILD 212-3, JOACHIM AND ANNE MEET AT GOLDEN GATE
  212-4, IMMACULATE CONCEPTION OF VIRGIN MARY 212-5, BIRTH OF
  VIRGIN MARY 212-6, BIRTH OF VIRGIN MARY 212-7, JOACHIM
  REJOICES AT BIRTH OF VIRGIN MARY 212-8, ANNE REJOICES AT BIRTH
  OF VIRGIN MARY 212-9, SIGNS IN HEAVEN AT BIRTH OF VIRGIN MARY
  212-10, PRESENTATION OF VIRGIN MARY IN TEMPLE 212-11,
  CONSECRATION OF VIRGIN MARY 212-11, VIRGIN MARY BROUGHT BACK
  TO TEMPLE AT SEVEN 212-12, BETROTHAL OF VIRGIN MARY 212-13, ST
  ANNE TEACHES VIRGIN MARY TO READ 212-14

111

*$ABSTRACT 213
  *LIBRARY BOD
  *SLIDE SET TITLE LAST SUPPER
  *NEGATIVE REFERENCE ROLL 204O
  *RENTAL FEE SM 213 $2.50
  *TITLE OF MANUSCRIPT SPECULUM HUMANAE SALVATIONIS 213-8,
  MEDITATIONS ON THE LIFE OF CHRIST 213-10
  *SHELFMARK MS CANON BIBL LAT 61 213-1, MS AUCT D 4 8 213-3, MS
  DOUCE 38 213-3, MS DOUCE 38 213-4, MS LITURG 196 213-5, MS
  DOUCE 313 213-6, MS LAUD MISC 3 213-7, MS CANON LITURG 352
  213-9, MS C C C 410 213-10
  *PROVENANCE DALMATIAN 213-1, LEVANTINE 213-2, ENGLISH 213/3 AND
  7, FLEMISH 213/4-5, FRENCH 213-6, BOHEMIAN 213-8, ITALIAN
  213/9-10
  *DATE EXECUTED 11TH 213-1, 13TH 213/2-5, 14TH 213/6-10
  *LANGUAGE LATIN
  *TYPE OF MANUSCRIPT LECTIONARY/ MASS 213-1, BIBLE 213-3,
  PSALTER 213/4-5, MISSAL 213/6 AND 9, BREVIARY 213-7, SPECULUM
  HUMANAE SALVATIONIS 213-8, MEDITATIONS 213-10
  *CONTENTS LAST SUPPER 213/1-10, DRAWING/ HALF PAGE 213-1, JUDAS
  STANDS IN FRONT OF TABLE TALKING TO CHRIST 213-2, INITIAL TO
  REVELATION 213-3, INITIAL TO PSALM DOMINUS ILLUMINATIO 213-4,
  INITIAL TO PSALM DIXIT INSIPIENS 213-5, CHRIST GIVES BREAD TO
  JUDAS 213-6, ST JOHN ASLEEP ON CHRIST@' LAP 213-7, DRAWING IN
  RED AND BROWN INK 213-8, ST JOHN LEANS AGAINST CHRIST'S BREAST
  213-9, CHRIST BREAKS BREAD 213-10

*$ABSTRACT 214
  *LIBRARY BOD
  *SLIDE SET TITLE ROTA NOVA OF GUIDO FABA
  *NEGATIVE REFERENCE ROLL 204P
  *RENTAL FEE SM 214 $2.15
  *TITLE OF MANUSCRIPT ROTA NOVA
  *SHELFMARK MS NEW COLLEGE 255
  *PROVENANCE ITALIAN
  *DATE EXECUTED 13TH
  *LANGUAGE LATIN
  *TYPE OF MANUSCRIPT ROTA NOVA
  *CONTENTS WHEEL OF FORTUNE 214-1, FORTUNE'S WHEEL 214-1, ANGEL
  AND MONK 214-1, FOUNTAIN OF RHETORIC WITH ANGEL POINTING TO IT
  214-2, HEAVENS WITH SUN/ MOON AND EIGHT STARS 214-3

*$ABSTRACT 215
  *LIBRARY BOD
  *SLIDE SET TITLE KINGS OF ENGLAND FROM EDWARD THE CONFESSOR TO
  EDWARD I
  *NEGATIVE REFERENCE ROLL 205B
  *RENTAL FEE SM 215 $2.60
  *SHELFMARK MS BODLEY ROLLS 3
  *PROVENANCE ENGLISH
  *DATE EXECUTED 13TH/ LATE
  *LANGUAGE ENGLISH
  *TYPE OF MANUSCRIPT HISTORY
  *CONTENTS KINGS OF ENGLAND EDWARD THE CONFESSOR TO EDWARD I
  215/1-12, MEDALLIONS OF KINGS OF ENGLAND 215/1-12, EDWARD THE
  CONFESSOR 215-1, HAROLD 1066 215-2, WILLIAM THE CONQUEROR
  1066-1087 215-3, WILLIAM II 1087-1100 215-4, HENRY I 1100-1135
  215-5, STEPHEN 1135-1154 215-6, HENRY II 1154-1189 215-7,
  HENRY/ YOUNG CROWNED 1183 NEVER REIGNED 215-8, RICHARD I
  1189-1199 215-9, JOHN 1199-1216 215-10, HENRY III 1216-1272
  215-11, EDWARD I 1272-1307 215-12

*$ABSTRACT 216
  *LIBRARY BOD
  *SLIDE SET TITLE MAPS
  *NEGATIVE REFERENCE ROLL 205B

*RENTAL FEE SM 216 $2.65
*TITLE OF MANUSCRIPT OPUS DE NATURA RERUM 216/1-2,
POLYCHRONICON OF RANULF HIGDEN 216-3, DIALOGI CUM MOYSE JUDAEO
216/4-5, HISTRIA TROIANA 216-10, METAMORPHOSES 216/11-12
*SHELFMARK MS AUCT F 2 20 216/1-2, MS TANNER 170 216-3, MS LAUD
MISC 356 216/4-5, MS ASHMOLE 1352 216/6-9, MS RAWL B 214
216-10, MS DOUCE 117 216/11-12, MS GOUGH MAPS 230 216-13
*PROVENANCE FRENCH 216/1-2 AND 4-9 AND 11-12, ENGLISH 216/3 AND
10 AND 13
*DATE EXECUTED 13TH 216/1-2, 14TH 216-3, 15TH 216/4-10, 16TH
216/11-12, 18TH 216-13
*LANGUAGE LATIN
*AUTHOR ST ISIDORE OF SEVILLE 216/1-2, RANULF HIGDEN 216-3,
ALPHONSI/ PETRUS 216/4-5, OVID 216/11-12
*TYPE OF MANUSCRIPT MAPS
*CONTENTS MAPS OF THE EARTH 216/1-13, ZONES OF THE EARTH 216-1,
CONTINENTS THREE 216-2, MAP OF THE WORLD 216-3, MAP CIRCULAR
216-4, MAP/ CIRCULAR 216-5, BAY OF BISCAY/ ATLAS AND CALENDAR
216-6, FRANCE/ NORTH COAST ON MAP 216-7, ENGLAND/ MAP 216-8,
IRELAND/ MAP 216-9, CLIMATE ZONES OF EAST 216-10, ZONES OF THE
EARTH/ FIVE 216-11, WINDS/ FOUR REGIONS 216-12, ANTIDILUDIAN
SPHERE 216-13

*$ABSTRACT 217
*LIBRARY BOD
*SLIDE SET TITLE OVID HEROIDES
*NEGATIVE REFERENCE ROLL 205G
*RENTAL FEE SM 217 $3.10
*COMMENTS NORMAN FRENCH TRANSLATION BY OCTAVIAN DE ST GELAIS/
BISHOP OF ANGOULEME
*TITLE OF MANUSCRIPT HEROIDES
*SHELFMARK MS BALLIOL 383
*PROVENANCE FRENCH
*DATE EXECUTED 15TH
*LANGUAGE NORMAN FRENCH
*AUTHOR OVID/ TRANSLATED BY OCTAVIAN DE ST GELAIS BISHOP OF
ANGOULEME
*TYPE OF MANUSCRIPT LETTERS
*CONTENTS LOVE-LETTERS OF FAMOUS WOMEN 217/1-22, LITERATURE/
OVID 217/1-22, ALEXANDER THE GREAT STANDS BEFORE THRONE 217-1,
PENELOPE SENDING LETTER TO ULYSSES BY BOATMAN 217-2, PHYLLIS
LOOKING TOWARDS THE SEA TO ESPY DEMOPHON RETURNING 217-3,
BRISEIS TO ACHILLES COMPLAINS 217-4, PHAEDRA WRITING TO
HIPPOLYTUS OF HER PLEASURE IN HUNTING 217-5, OENONE TO PARIS
AS SHE SEES HIM WITH HELEN 217-6, HYSIPHILE TO JASON LEARNS OF
FAITHLESSNESS 217-7, DIDO WRITES TO AENEAS 217-8, HERMIONE
TELLS OZASTES HOW PYRRHUS HOLDS HER AGAINST WILL 217-9,
DEIANEIRA SENDING LETTER TO HERCULES 217-10, ARIADNE WATCHES
THESEUS' SHIP SAIL AWAY 217-11, CANACE TO MACAREUS AS RECEIVES
SWORD TO KILL SELF 217-12, MEDEA TO JASON UPBRAIDING HIM FOR
NEW BRIDE 217-13, LAODAMRA BEWAILS ABSENCE OF HUSBAND
PROTESILAUS AT TROY 217-14, HYPERMNESTRA TELLS BROTHER LYCEUS
SHE IS IMPRISONED 217-15, PARIS TO HELEN BEGGING HER TO BECOME
HIS 217-16, HELEN WITH ATTENDANTS CLYMENE AND AETHRA WRITING
TO PARIS 217-17, LEANDER TO HERO EXPLAINS SEA TO ROUGH FOR
SWIMMING 217-18, HERO REPLIES TO LEANDER WITH DEAD DOLPHIN ON
SHORE 217-19, ACONTIUS LETTER TO CYDIPPE 217-20, CYDIPPE IN
REPLY SPEAKS OF HER LANGOUR 217-21, SAPPHO TO PHAON BEWAILING
HIS FAITHLESSNESS 217-22

*$ABSTRACT 218
*LIBRARY BOD
*SLIDE SET TITLE HERMITS
*NEGATIVE REFERENCE ROLL 205I
*RENTAL FEE SM 218 $2.40
*TITLE OF MANUSCRIPT TRETYSE OF PARCE MICHI DOMINE 218-3
*SHELFMARK MS LAUD MISC 528 218-1, MS RAWL C 149 218-2, MS
DOUCE 322 218-3, MS LAUD LAT 15 218-4, MS BODLEY 850 218-5, MS

113

RAWL LITURG G 3 218-6, MS LITURG 98 218/7-8
*PROVENANCE ENGLISH 218/1-6, FLEMISH 218/7-8
*DATE EXECUTED 15TH 218/1 AND 3-8, 12TH 218-2
*LANGUAGE LATIN 218/2 AND 4-8, ENGLISH 218/1 AND 3
*AUTHOR ROLLE/ RICHARD 218/1 AND 3
*TYPE OF MANUSCRIPT POETRY 218/1 AND 3, MISCELLANY 218-2, BOOK
OF HOURS 218/4-8
*CONTENTS HERMITS 218/1-8, RICHARD ROLLE WITH ANOTHER HERMIT
218-1, ST MARY MAGDALENE AS PENITENT 218-2, POET LYING IN
FIELD/ RICHARD ROLLE 218-3, ST JEROME WRITING 218-4, ST JEROME
WITH LION 218/5-7, ST MARY MAGDALENE IN DESERT LANDSCAPE 218-8

*$ABSTRACT 219
*LIBRARY BOD
*SLIDE SET TITLE FALL OF MAN
*NEGATIVE REFERENCE ROLL 205J
*RENTAL FEE SM 219 $2.35
*TITLE OF MANUSCRIPT CALENDAR
*SHELFMARK MS RAWL D 939
*PROVENANCE ENGLISH
*DATE EXECUTED 14TH/C1370
*LANGUAGE LATIN AND ENGLISH
*TYPE OF MANUSCRIPT CALENDAR
*CONTENTS FALL OF MAN 219/1-7, CALENDAR/ ENGLISH 219/1-7,
TEMPTATION OF ADAM AND EVE AND EXPULSION 219-1, ADAM WITH
SPADE EVE WITH DISTAFF IN FIGLEAVES 219-2, ADAM AND EVE AS
PEASANTS DIG AND SPADE 219-3, SACRIFICES OF CAIN AND ABEL
219-4, CAIN KILLS ABEL WITH JAWBONE 219-4, DEATH OF ADAM
219-5, ADAM IN LIMBO 219-5, CHRIST HARROWING HELL AND RESCUING
ADAM 219-6, CHRIST AS LIFE AND DEVIL AS DEATH 219-7

*$ABSTRACT 220
*LIBRARY BOD
*SLIDE SET TITLE SPANISH MANUSCRIPTS 12TH TO 18TH CENTURIES
*NEGATIVE REFERENCE ROLL 2050
*RENTAL FEE SM 220 $3.95
*COMMENTS ILLUSTRATIONS FROM SPANISH MSS DESCRIBED BY PACHT AND
ALEXANDER IN VOL 1 OF ILLUMINATED MANUSCRIPTS IN THE BODLEIAN
LIBRARY
*TITLE OF MANUSCRIPT ALFRAGANUS DE MOTIBUS PLANETARUM 220/3-4,
TABULAE ASTRONMIC 220/6-12, CHARTER OF PRIVILEDGES GRANTED TO
SEVILLE 220-15, PARAPHRASE OF NICOMACHEAN ETHICS OF ARISTOTLE
220/16-17, LIBRO DE LAS ARMILLAS 220-25, RULES AND
CONSTITUTIONS OF ST PETER/ MARTYR/ MADRID 220/27-29,
PRIVILEDGES AND STATUTES OF COLLEGE OF SURGEONS BARCELONA
220/30-32
*PROVENANCE SPANISH
*DATE EXECUTED 12TH 220-1, 13TH 220/3-4, 14TH 220/2 AND 6-12,
15TH 220/13-25, 16TH 220/26-33
*LANGUAGE LATIN AND SPANISH
*AUTHOR JACOBUS BONA DIES 220/6-12, ALPHONSO THE WISE 220-25
*TYPE OF MANUSCRIPT GOSPEL LECTIONARY 220-1, CHARTERS 220/2 AND
15, ASTRONOMICAL TEXTS 220/3-12, PSALTER 220/13-14, PSALTER/
CARTHSIAN 220/18-19, BOOK OF HOURS/ AUGUSTINIAN 220/20,
MISSAL/ AUGUSTINIAN 220-20, ASTRONOMICAL TRACTS 220-26,
ANTIPHONAL/ FRANCISCAN 220-33
*CONTENTS SPANISH MANUSCRIPTS/ MISCELLANY 220/1-39, DECORATED
TEXT 220-1, CHARTERS 220-2, INITIAL Q 220-3, ECLIPSES
ILLUSTRATED 220-4, ST JAMES THE GREAT WITH VIRGIN AND CHILD
220-5, ZODIAC WITH ARIES 220-6, ZODIAC 220/6-12, TAURUS AND
GEMINI 220-7, CANCER AND LEO 220-8, VIRGO AND LIBRA 220-9,
SCORPIO AND SAGITTARIUS 220-10, CAPRICORN AND AQUARIUS 220-11,
PISCES 220-12, BORDER AND INITIALS DECORATED 220/13-17, BEATUS
PAGE/ DECORATED WITH PEACOCKS IN BORDER 220-18, GRISAILLE
MINIATURE OF DAVID 220-19, COCK/ HEN/ APE IN DECORATED BORDER
220-20, NOVICE ADMITTED INTO NUNNERY/ CEREMONY OF 220-21,
MUSIC FOR ATOLLITE PORTAS 220-22, ARMS SUPPORTED BY ANGELS
220-23, ARMS SUPPORTED BY DRAGONS 220-24, DIAGRAM FOR

MEASURING HEIGHTS 220-25, DIAGRAMS OF ASTRONOMY 220-26, ST
JOHN WITH EAGLE 220-27, ST LUKE AND ST MATTHEW WITH EMBLEMS
220-28, CROSS/ EMPTY AND SYMBOLS OF PASSION 220-29, SS COSMAS
AND DAMIAN 220-30, CRUCIFIXION 220-31, DOVE/ EVANGELISTS/
COSMAS AND DAMIAN IN BORDER 220-31, VIRGIN ON CRESCENT MOON
WITH HER SYMBOLS 220-32, INITIAL WITH CHALICE AND HOST 220-33

*$ABSTRACT 221
  *LIBRARY BOD
  *SLIDE SET TITLE SAINTS
  *NEGATIVE REFERENCE ROLL 205L
  *RENTAL FEE SM 221 $2.75
  *SHELFMARK MS CANON LITURG 343
  *PROVENANCE ITALIAN/ VENICE OR PADUA
  *DATE EXECUTED 16TH/C1500
  *LANGUAGE LATIN
  *ARTIST/ SCHOOL SCHOOL OF BENEDETTO BORDONE OF PADUA
  *TYPE OF MANUSCRIPT BREVIARY/ CISTERCIAN
  *CONTENTS SAINTS 221/1-15, ST STEPHEN 221-1, ST AGNES WITH LAMB
  221-2, ST AGATHA WITH PAIR OF PINCERS 221-3, ST APOLLONIA AND
  ST SCHOLASTICA 221-4, ST HELENA HOLDING THE CROSS 221-5, ST
  MARGARET OF ANTIOCH EMERGING FROM DRAGON 221-6, ST
  MARYMAGDALENE WASHING CHRIST'S FEET 221-7, ST LAWRENCE HOLDING
  GRIDIRON AND BOOK 221-8, DORMITION OF VIRGIN MARY 221-9, ST
  BERNARD WITH VIRGIN AND CHILD 221-10, CHRIST AND THREE
  DISCIPLES AT MEAL 221-11, ST MICHAEL SLAYS DRAGON 221-12, ST
  FRANCIS WITH CROSS AND BOOK SHOWS STIGMATA 221-13, ST URSULA
  HOLDING CROSS-BANNER AND BOOK 221-14, ST CATHERINE OF
  ALEXANDRIA HOLDING HER WHEEL 221-15

*$ABSTRACT 222
  *LIBRARY BOD
  *SLIDE SET TITLE JOHANNES DE BADO AUREO TRACTATUS DE ARMIS
  *NEGATIVE REFERENCE ROLL 205Q
  *RENTAL FEE SM 222 $2.70
  *TITLE OF MANUSCRIPT DE ARTE HERALDICA
  *SHELFMARK MS LAUD MISC 733
  *PROVENANCE ENGLISH
  *DATE EXECUTED 15TH/C1440-50
  *LANGUAGE ENGLISH
  *AUTHOR JOHANNES DE BADO AUREO
  *TYPE OF MANUSCRIPT HERALDRY
  *CONTENTS HERALDRY 222/1-14, KING OF ARMS AND TWO OTHER MEN
  222-1, LYON AND LYONARD 222-2, PARD/ HERT AND BOAR 222-3,
  DOGGE/ DRAGON/ HORS/ BERE AND EGLE 222-4, FFAUCON/ OULE/
  DOWVE/ CROWE/ SWAN 222-5, COK/ GRYPHON/ MERLION/ LUCE 222-6,
  CRABBE AND SHIELD CHARGED WITH CROSSES 222-7, SHIELDS CHARGED
  WITH CROSSES 222-8, SHIELDS SHOWING VARIOUS CHARGES 222/9-13,
  TREATISE END WITH DECORATED EXPLICIT 222-14, COURT OF EMPEROR
  DIOCLETIAN/ MINATURE 222-14

*$ABSTRACT 223
  *LIBRARY BOD
  *SLIDE SET TITLE CHRONICLE OF ENGLAND
  *NEGATIVE REFERENCE ROLL 205R
  *RENTAL FEE SM 223 $2.60
  *TITLE OF MANUSCRIPT CHRONICLE OF ENGLAND
  *SHELFMARK MS LAUD MISC 733
  *PROVENANCE ENGLISH
  *DATE EXECUTED 15TH/C1440-50
  *LANGUAGE ENGLISH
  *TYPE OF MANUSCRIPT CHRONICLE
  *CONTENTS CHRONICLE OF ENGLAND 223/1-12, HISTORICAL FIGURES OF
  ENGLAND 223/1-12, DIOCLETIAN WITH COURTIERS AND DAUGHTERS
  223-1, WILD MEN APPEAR FROM FOREST 223-1, BRUTE AND HIS PEOPLE
  ARRIVE ON ISLE OF ALBYON 223-2, GIANT GOGMAGOG'S BODY CARRIED

TO WATER 223-2, CONSTANTINE WITH SHIELD BEARING LETTERS SPQR
223-3, ST URSULA AND KING GOWAN 223-4, ST ALBAN REPRESENTED BY
ANGEL WITH HERALDIC SHIELD 223-5, HENGEST CARRYING SHIELD AND
SPEAR 223-6, KING ARTHUR WITH HERALDIC SHIELD 223-7, ST
OSWOLDE REPRESENTED BY ANGEL WITH SHIELD 223-8, ST EDMOND
REPRESENTED BY ANGEL WITH SHIELD 223-9, ST EDWARD MARTYR
REPRESENTED BY ANGEL WITH SHIELD 223-10, ST EDWARD THE
CONFESSOR REPRESENTED BY ANGEL WITH SHIELD 223-11, BATTLE OF
HASTINGS AND OR TUNBRIDGE 223-12, ARMS OF WILLIAM AND HAROLD
APPEAR ON TWO STANDARDS 223-12, HAROLD/KING 223-12

*$ABSTRACT 224
  *LIBRARY BOD
  *SLIDE SET TITLE FIFTEENTH CENTURY PEOPLE
  *NEGATIVE REFERENCE ROLL 205S
  *RENTAL FEE SM 224 $3.50
  *TITLE OF MANUSCRIPT BOOK OF HOURS
  *SHELFMARK MS CANON LITURG 283
  *PROVENANCE FRENCH/ NORMANDY
  *DATE EXECUTED 15TH
  *LANGUAGE LATIN
  *ARTIST/ SCHOOL ATELIER OF THE ROYAL GOLD CUP IN BRITISH MUSEUM
  *TYPE OF MANUSCRIPT BOOK OF HOURS/ USE OF EVREUX
  *CONTENTS BOOK OF HOURS/ FRENCH/ 15TH 224/1-30, PEOPLE/
  FIFTEENTH CENTURY 224/1-30, OCCUPATIONS OF THE MONTHS
  224/1-12, ZODIAC/ SIGNS OF 224/1-12, MAN FEASTING 224-1,
  AQUARIUS 224-1, MAN STANDING BY FIRE 224-2, PISCES 224-2,
  PRUNING 224-3, ARIES 224-3, PICKING FLOWERS 224-4, TAURUS
  224-4, HAWKING 224-5, GEMINI IN BASKET 224-5, SHEEP CARRIED TO
  BE SHORN 224-6, CANCER/ AS LOBSTER 224-6, SHARPENING SCYTHE
  224-7, LEO 224-7, HARVESTING CORN 224-8, VIRGO 224-8, SOWING
  SEED 224-9, LIBRA 224-9, PRESSING GRAPES 224-10, SCORPIO
  224-10, KILLING PIG 224-11, SAGITTARIUS 224-11, BAKING 224-12,
  CAPRICORN 224-12, BOY ON HOBBY HORSE TEASES LARGE BIRD 224-13,
  COURTING COUPLE 224-14, SPEARMAN/ NAKED ATTACKS BIRD 224-15,
  SHEPHERDS IN ANNUNCIATION SCENE 224-16, NAKED WOMAN WITH LONG
  AUBURN HAIR 224-17, ARCHER SHOOTING DRAGON 224-18, BIRD
  ATTACKS BOY 224-19, BAGPIPES PLAYED BY MAN TO BIRD 224-20, APE
  WITH CANNON AND BOY WITH BIRD 224-21, CELEBRATION OF MASS
  224-22, ARCHER SHOOTING LONG-EARED OWL 224-23, PEASANT COUPLE
  TRAVELING PERHAPS PILGRIMS 224-24, MAN WITH PRUNING KNIFE AND
  WOMAN SET TRAPS 224-25, BOY DRESSED IN WHITE TUNIC AND PINK
  COAT 224-26, BAGPIPES PLAYED BY WOMAN TO MAN SETTING BIRD NETS
  224-27, MAN HOLDS PRUNING KNIFE IN MOUTH WHILE BREAKING
  BRANCHES 224-28, STRAWBERRIES PICKED BY BOY IN PINK COAT
  224-29, MAN IN BLUE SOCKS CROSSES POND ON STILTS 224-30

*$ABSTRACT 225
  *LIBRARY BOD
  *SLIDE SET TITLE OCCUPATIONS OF THE MONTHS
  *NEGATIVE REFERENCE ROLL 206A
  *RENTAL FEE SM 225 $2.60
  *SHELFMARK MS AUCT D 4 2
  *PROVENANCE FLEMISH/ GHENT OR BRUGGES
  *DATE EXECUTED 13TH/ THIRD QUARTER
  *LANGUAGE LATIN
  *TYPE OF MANUSCRIPT PSALTER/ PORTABLE
  *CONTENTS OCCUPATIONS OF THE MONTHS 225/1-12, CALENDAR
  225/1-12, JANUARY 225-1, MAN IN WINGED HEADRESS DRINKS FROM
  BARREL NEAR FIREPLACE 225-1, FEBRUARY 225-2, CANDLEMAS 225-2,
  WOMAN IN FUR-LINED CLOAK CARRYING STRIPED CANDLE 225-2, MARCH
  225-3, PEASANT TREE-CUTTING 225-3, APRIL 225-4, YOUTH IN PINK
  ROBE CARRYING BRANCHES 225-4, MAY 225-5, NOBLEMAN RIDING
  DAPPLE-GRAY HORSE HAWKING 225-5, JUNE 225-6, PEASANT CARRYING
  BUNDLE OF RUSHES 225-6, JULY 225-7, PEASANT SCYTHING GRASS
  225-7, AUGUST 225-8, PEASANT REAPING CORN WITH SICKLE 225-8,
  SEPTEMBER 225-9, PEASANT GATHERING GRAPES WITH A SICKLE 225-9,
  OCTOBER 225-10, SOWING GRAIN FROM CLOTH SLING 225-10, NOVEMBER

225-11, ACORNS KNOCKED DOWN TO FEED PIGS 225-11, DECEMBER
225-12, PIG SLAUGHTERED BY PEASANT WITH AXE 225-12'

*$ABSTRACT 226
 *LIBRARY BOD
 *SLIDE SET TITLE OCCUPATIONS OF THE MONTHS
 *NEGATIVE REFERENCE ROLL 206C
 *RENTAL FEE SM 226 $2.60
 *SHELFMARK MS LAUD LAT 84
 *PROVENANCE FLEMISH
 *DATE EXECUTED 14TH/ FIRST QUARTER
 *LANGUAGE LATIN
 *TYPE OF MANUSCRIPT PSALTER/ GALLICAN
 *CONTENTS   OCCUPATIONS   OF   THE   MONTHS   226/1-12,   CALENDAR
 226/1-12, JANUARY 226-1, JANUS AT TABLE FEASTING 226-1,
 FEBRUARY 226-2, MAN SEATED BY FIRE COOKING 226-2, MARCH 226-3,
 PEASANT   PRUNING WITH SICKLE 226-3, APRIL 226-4, YOUNG MAN IN
 FUR-TRIMMED ROBE HOLDING FLOWERS 226-4, MAY 226-5, NOBLEMAN ON
 DAPPLE-GRAY HORSE HAWKING 226-5, JUNE 226-6, PEASANT IN STRAW
 HAT SCYTHING GRASS 226-6, JULY 226-7, PEASANT CARRYING BUNDLE
 OF RUSHES OR FAGGOTS 226-7, AUGUST 226-8, CORN REAPED BY
 PEASANT   WITH SICKLE 226-8, SEPTEMBER 226-9, GRAPES HARVESTED
 BY TWO PEASANTS 226-9, OCTOBER 226-10, PEASANT SOWING GRAIN
 FROM CLOTH SLING 226-10, NOVEMBER 226-11, PEASANT KNOCKING
 DOWN ACORNS TO FEED PIGS 226-11, DECEMBER 226-12, PEASANT
 KILLING PIG WITH AXE 226-12

*$ABSTRACT 227
 *LIBRARY BOD
 *SLIDE SET TITLE BOOK OF HOURS
 *NEGATIVE REFERENCE ROLL 206F
 *RENTAL FEE SM 227 $2.75
 *COMMENTS MADE FOR ELEANORA IPPOLITA GONZAGA, WIFE OF FRANCESCO
 MARIA 1, DUKE OF URBINO
 *SHELFMARK MS DOUCE 29
 *PROVENANCE ITALIAN/ URBINO OR MANTUA
 *DATE EXECUTED 16TH/C1530-38
 *LANGUAGE LATIN
 *ARTIST/ SCHOOL VINCENZO RAIMOND
 *TYPE OF MANUSCRIPT BOOK OF HOURS/ USE OF ROME
 *CONTENTS BOOK OF HOURS/ ITALIAN/ 16TH 227/1-15, BIBLICAL
 TYPOLOGY 227/1-15, BINDING OF RED VELVET WITH DECORATED ENAMEL
 CLASPS 227-1, ARMS OF DELLA ROVERE IMPALING GONZAGA 227-2,
 DEDICATION TO LEONORE GONZAGA URBINI DUCI 227-2, GOD GIVES LAW
 TO MOSES 227-3, ANNUNCIATION TO VIRGIN 227-3, SS ANNE AND
 JOACHIM MEET AT GOLDEN GATE 227-4, VISITATION 227-4, NATIVITY
 OF ST JOHN BAPTIST 227-5, NATIVITY OF CHRIST 227-5, JACOB'S
 DREAM 227-6, ANNUNCIATION TO SHEPHERDS 227-6, KING SOLOMON AND
 THE QUEEN OF SHEBA 227-7, ADORATION OF THE MAGI 227-7,
 PRESENTATION OF SAMUEL 227-8, PRESENTATION OF CHRIST 227-8,
 EXODUS/ ISREALITES CROSSING RED SEA 227-9, FLIGHT INTO EGYPT
 227-9, SOLOMON'S DREAM 227-10, CHRIST CHILD WITH DOCTORS IN
 TEMPLE 227-10, ISRAELITES GATHER MANNA 227-11, LAST SUPPER
 227-11, DESTRUCTION OF SODOM AND GOMORRAH 227-12, DAVID
 PLAYING 227-12, FALL OF MAN 227-13, EXPULSION OF ADAM AND EVE
 FROM PARADISE 227-13, ENTOMBMENT 227-13, CHRIST BEARING THE
 CROSS ON ROAD TO CALVARY 227-14, SACRIFICE OF ABRAHAM 227-14,
 SACRIFICE OF ELIJAH 227-15, PENTECOST WITH VIRGIN AND APOSTLES
 227-15

*$ABSTRACT 228
 *LIBRARY BOD
 *SLIDE SET TITLE MUSICAL INSTRUMENTS
 *NEGATIVE REFERENCE ROLL 207A
 *RENTAL FEE SM 228 $2.30
 *COMMENTS 6 SLIDES FROM 3 COLLEGE MSS IN OXFORD

117

*SHELFMARK MS EXETER COLLEGE 47 228/1-2, MS ST HILDA'S COLLEGE
 1 228/3-6, MS NEW COLLEGE 7 228-6
*PROVENANCE FRENCH 228/1-2, DUTCH 228/3-5, ENGLISH 228-6
*DATE EXECUTED 13TH/ 1220-30 228-6, 14TH 228/1-2, 15TH 228/3-5
*LANGUAGE LATIN
*TYPE OF MANUSCRIPT PSALTER 228/1-2, BOOK OF HOURS 228/3-5,
 PSALTER 228-6
*CONTENTS MUSICAL INSTRUMENTS 228/1-6, MUSICIAN/ GROTESQUE WITH
 CURVED WIND INSTRUMENT AND TABOR 228-1, GROTESQUE MUSICIAN/
 DEVIL WITH FIDDLE 228-2, SINGERS AND LUTISTS 228-3, CHRIST
 CHILD AND MUSICAL ANGELS MAKE MUSIC 228-4, ANGELS PLAY TO
 CHILD WITH DOVE 228-5, INITIAL E/ EXULTATE DEO 228-6, TRUMPET/
 VIOLA/ HANDBELLS PLAYED BEFORE GOD 228-6

*$ABSTRACT 229
 *LIBRARY BOD
 *SLIDE SET TITLE CREATION
 *NEGATIVE REFERENCE ROLL 207C
 *RENTAL FEE SM 229 $2.85
 *COMMENTS 17 SLIDES FROM BIBLE DEPICTING CREATION GENESIS
 *TITLE OF MANUSCRIPT BIBLE MORALISEE
 *SHELFMARK MS BODLEY 270B
 *PROVENANCE FRENCH
 *DATE EXECUTED 13TH/C1250
 *LANGUAGE LATIN
 *ARTIST/ SCHOOL FRENCH ROYAL WORKSHOPS
 *TYPE OF MANUSCRIPT BIBLE MORALISEE
 *CONTENTS CREATION 229/1-17, CREATOR 229-1, CREATION OF HEAVEN
 AND EARTH AND LIGHT 229-2, GOD DIVIDES LIGHT FROM DARKNESS
 229-3, GOD MAKES THE FIRMAMENT IN THE WATERS 229-4, GOD
 DIVIDES THE WATERS BY THE FIRMAMENT 229-5, WATERS GATHERED
 229-6, DRY LAND 229-7, FISHES/ BIRDS/ BEASTS/ REPTILES 229-8,
 HERB YIELDING SEED 229-9, TREE BEARING FRUIT 229-10, GOD MADE
 SUN/ MOON/ STARS 229-11, CREATION OF REPTILES AND BIRDS
 229-12, ANIMALS/ ALL CREATED BY GOD 229-13, GOD CREATES MAN IN
 HIS LIKENESS 229-14, GOD GAVE MAN FRUITS OF EARTH TO EAT
 229-15, SEVENTH DAY GOD RESTING FROM LABORS 229-16, RIVERS/
 FOUR OF EDEN 229-17

*$ABSTRACT 230
 *LIBRARY BOD
 *SLIDE SET TITLE TREASURES OF MERTON COLLEGE OXFORD
 *NEGATIVE REFERENCE ROLL 207H
 *RENTAL FEE SM 230 $3.05
 *COMMENTS 21 SLIDES FROM 16 MSS IN MERTON COLLEGE OXFORD
 *TITLE OF MANUSCRIPT PETER PRIOR OF FLORENCE ON THE PSALMS
 230-8, JEROME ON THE PROPHETS 230-9, SUMMA I 230-11, PETER
 LOMBARD ON EPISTLES 230-12
 *SHELFMARK MS MERTON COLLEGE A 2 7 230-1, MS MERTON COLLEGE A 3
 3 230-2, MS MERTON COLLEGE A3 1 230/3-4, MS MERTON COLLEGE B 3
 1 230-5, MS MERTON COLLEGE B 3 4 230-6, MS MERTON COLLEGE B 2
 3 230-7, MS MERTON COLLEGE C 2 2 230-8, MS MERTON COLLEGE N 2
 11 230-9, MS MERTON COLLEGE H 3 10 230-10, MS MERTON COLLEGE I
 1 2 230-11, MS MERTON COLLEGE I 3 4 230-12, MS MERTON COLLEGE
 K 1 7 230/13-16, MS MERTON COLLEGE L 3 8 230-17, MS MERTON
 COLLEGE O 1 10 230/18-19, MS MERTON COLLEGE O 3 6 230-20
 *PROVENANCE ENGLISH 230/1-2 AND 6-11 AND 13-20, FRENCH 230/5
 AND 12, ITALIAN 230-3, GERMAN 230-21
 *DATE EXECUTED 13TH 230/1-2 AND 7 AND 11 AND 20, 14TH 230/3-4
 AND 10-12, 15TH 230/6 AND 8 AND 13-16 AND 18, 16TH 230-21
 *LANGUAGE LATIN
 *AUTHOR ORIGEN 230-2, SENECA 230/3-4, AUGUSTINE 230-5, JEROME
 230/6 AND 9, PETER PRIOR OF FLORENCE 230-8, GROSSETESTE
 230-10, AQUINAS 230/11-12, WILLIAM OF NOTTINGHAM 230-17,
 JOHANNITUS ISAGOGE 230/18-19
 *TYPE OF MANUSCRIPT MISCELLANY
 *CONTENTS ILLUMINATED MSS FROM MERTON COLLEGE OXFORD 230/1-21,
 GOSPEL OF ST MATTHEW/ BEGINNING 230-1, INITIAL P 230-2, TEXT

118

OF SENECA 230-3, CROWNED FIGURE 230-4, ST AUGUSTINE AND
NATIVITY 230-5, ARMS OF FITZJAMES OF DORSET AND SOMERSET
230-6, HARES AND MASKS IN DECORATION 230-7, FRONTISPIECE
230-8, TEXT OF JEROME 230-9, BISHOP'S HEAD ON PAGE 230-10,
AQUINAS WITH CROSS PREACHES TO PEOPLE 230-11, CRUCIFIXION AND
HOUNDS HUNTING 230-12, MAGNA CARTA AND EAGLE 230-13, STATUTES
OF EDWARD III 230-14, LEOPARD 230-14, STATUTES OF HENRY V
230-15, STAG 230-15, STATUTES OF HENRY VI 230-16, PORTRAIT OF
HENRY VI 230-16, INITIAL WITH BORDER 230-17, INITIAL DECORATED
230-18, INITIAL 230-19, ROMANS/ EPISTLE TO 230-20, BINDING
MADE FOR PRINCE-BISHOP OF WURZBURG 230-21

*$ABSTRACT 231
 *LIBRARY BOD
 *SLIDE SET TITLE VULGATE INITIALS
 *NEGATIVE REFERENCE ROLL 207I
 *RENTAL FEE SM 231 $4.30
 *SHELFMARK MS MERTON COLLEGE H 2 2
 *PROVENANCE ENGLISH
 *DATE EXECUTED 13TH
 *LANGUAGE LATIN
 *TYPE OF MANUSCRIPT BIBLE
 *CONTENTS INITIALS/ VULGATE 231/1-46, PROLOGUE TO VULGATE
231-1, ST JEROME SEATED AT DESK WITH SCROLL AND BOOKS 231-1,
GENESIS 231-2, CREATION/ FALL OF ADAM AND EVE 231-2,
ANNUNCIATION/ CRUCIFIXION/ HARROWING OF HELL 231-2, EXODUS
231-3, MOSES AND BURNING BUSH 231-3, LEVITICUS 231-4, PRIEST
SACRIFICES OX AND ATTENDANT CATCHES IN CHALICE 231-4, NUMBERS
231-5, BALAAM'S ASS TURNS TO SPEAK TO PROPHET 231-5,
DEUTERONOMY 231-6, MOSES WITH TABLETS OF LAW SPEAKS TO
ISRAELITES 231-6, JOSUE 231-7, JOSHUA KNEELS BEFORE GOD 231-7,
JUDGES 231-8, SAMSON KILLS LION 231-8, RUTH 231-9, NAOMI
ABOVE/ BELOW RUTH AND BOAZ REAPING 231-9, KINGS I 231-10,
HANNAH KNEELS BEFORE ELI WHO BLESSES HER 231-10, KINGS II
231-11, SAUL KILLED BY THE AMALEKITE 231-11, KINGS III ABISHAG
BROUGHT TO DAVID TO WARM HIM 231-12, KINGS IV 231-13, ELIJAH
ASCENDS TO HEAVEN IN CHARIOT 231-13, PARALIPOMENON I 231-14,
DAVID KNEELING APPOINTED KING 231-14, PARALIPOMENON II 231-15,
TEMPLE REBUILT AND MEASURING WITH PLUMBLINE 231-15, ESDRAS I
231-16, SOLOMON ENTHRONED RECEIVES QUEEN OF SHEBA 231-16,
ESDRAS II 231-17, ARTAXERXES SPEAKS TO NEHEMIAH 231-17, TOBIAS
231-18, TOBIAS AND ANGEL RAPHAEL 231-18, JUDITH 231-19, JUDITH
CUTS HEAD OFF SLEEPING HOLOFERNES 231-19, ESTHER 231-20,
AHASUERUS RECEIVES ESTHER 231-20, JOB 231-21, JOB COVERED WITH
SORES ON DUNGHEAP WITH SCOLDING WIFE 231-21, PSALM I 231-22,
DAVID PLAYING HARP 231-23, DOEG THE EDOMITE KILLS PRIEST AS
SAUL ORDERED 231-23, PSALM 52 231-23, FOOL HOLDING BAUBLE ON
STICK 231-23, PSALM 68 231-24, DAVID PRAYS TO GOD TO SAVE HIM
FROM WATERS 231-24, PSALM 80 231-25, DAVID PLAYING ON BELLS
231-25, PSALM 97 231-26, CHORISTERS SINGING ONE COVERING EAR
WITH HAND 231-26, PSALM 109 231-27, TRINITY WITH DOVE BETWEEN
FATHER AND SON 231-27, PROVERBS 231-28, SOLOMON INSTRUCTS
YOUNG MAN 231-28, ECCLESIASTES 231-29, PREACHER DREAMS OF
VANITY AS WOMAN WITH MIRROR 231-29, CANTICLE 231-30, VIRGIN
KISSING CHRIST CHILD ON HER LAP 231-30, WISDOM 231-31, SOLOMON
ENTHRONED TEACHING 231-31, ECCLESIASTICUS 231-32, CROWNED MAN
SEATED WITH HANDS RAISED IN AIR 231-32, ISAIAS 231-33, ISAIAH
SAWED ASUNDER 231-33, JEREMIAS 231-34, JEREMIAH CONTEMPLATES
JERUSALEM 231-34, EZEKIEL 231-35, MAN ABOUT TO EXECUTE
KNEELING FIGURE 231-35, DANIEL 231-36, DANIEL IN LION'S DEN
231-36, AMOS 231-37, AMOS HOLDING SCROLL MINDING FLOCK 231-37,
NAHUM 231-38, NAHUM PROPHESIES FALL OF NINEVEH 231-38, HABACUC
231-39, GOD DICTATES TO HABACUC AS HE WRITES 231-39, MALACHIAS
231-40, MALACHI SEATED HOLDING SCROLL 231-40, MACCABEES II
231-41, LETTER FROM JEWS IN JERUSALEM TO JEWS IN EGYPT 231-41,
MATTHEW 231-42, JESSE TREE WITH ONLY CHRIST IN ITS BRANCHES
231-42, LUKE 231-43, ST LUKE SEATED WRITING ON SCROLL WITH OX
BELOW 231-43, JOHN 231-44, ST JOHN HOLDING BOOK 231-44, ROMANS
231-45, ST PAUL SEATED WITH SWORD AND CHURCH 231-45,
APOCALYPSE 231-46, CHRIST ENTHRONED WITH SEVEN TALL
CANDLESTICKS 231-46

*$ABSTRACT 232
  *LIBRARY BOD
  *SLIDE SET TITLE ARISTOTLE DE HISTORIIS ANIMALIUM
  *NEGATIVE REFERENCE ROLL 207J
  *RENTAL FEE SM 232 $2.65
  *TITLE OF MANUSCRIPT DE HISTORIIS ANIMALIUM
  *SHELFMARK MS MERTON COLLEGE O 1 3
  *PROVENANCE ENGLISH
  *DATE EXECUTED 13TH OR 14TH
  *LANGUAGE LATIN
  *AUTHOR ARISTOTLE
  *TYPE OF MANUSCRIPT BESTIARY
  *CONTENTS BESTIARY 232/1-13, INITIALS 232/1-13, LION/ SQUIRREL,
  HARE/ HOUND AND HOUNDS CHASING STAG 232-1, SQUIRREL EATING NU'
  232-2, HOUND CHASES HARE 232-2, BIRDS IN TREE/ FISH IN WATER,
  HOUND AND HARE 232-3, FISH/ HARE/ HOUND 232-4, CATTLE MATING,
  HARE AND DOGS 232-5, ANIMALS AND BIRD/ HORSE/ HYENA/ LIO'
  232-6, HORSE/ FOX/ HARE/ DONKEY 232-7, SHEEP/ HARES/ BIRDS,
  PELICAN/ BEES AND BEEHIVE 232-8, LOVERS AND WOMAN ROCKING
  CRADLE 232-9, LOVERS AND WOMAN NURSING BABY BY FIREPLAC]
  232-9, LOVERS IN BED 232-10, DOG AND BIRDS 232-11, GOD HOLDIN(
  GLOBE TREES AND WATER CLEARLY MARKED 232-12, SEPARATE PARTS OI
  VARIOUS ANIMALS 232-13, HEADLESS ANIMALS 232-13

*$ABSTRACT 233
  *LIBRARY BOD
  *SLIDE SET TITLE ENCYCLOPEDIA OF VINCENT OF BEAUVAIS
  *NEGATIVE REFERENCE ROLL 207K
  *RENTAL FEE SM 233 $2.75
  *TITLE OF MANUSCRIPT ENCYCLOPEDIA OF VINCENT OF BEAUVAIS
  *SHELFMARK MS MERTON COLLEGE M 2 7-10
  *PROVENANCE FRENCH
  *DATE EXECUTED 14TH
  *LANGUAGE FRENCH
  *AUTHOR VINCENT OF BEAUVAIS
  *TYPE OF MANUSCRIPT ENCYCLOPEDIA
  *CONTENTS INITIALS/ DECORATED 233/1-15, ENCYCLOPEDIA 233/1-15
  AUTHOR SEATED AT LECTERN WRITING BOOK 233-1, CHRIST ENTHRONE]
  BLESSING 233-2, MOSES HORNED INSTRUCTS ISRAELITES FROM TABLE'
  OF LAWS 233-3, CYRUS GIVES ORDERS TO TROOPS/ NEARBY SIT:
  SCRIBE 233-4, PHILIP OF MACEDON ENTHRONED WITH SWORD 233-5
  INITIAL I INFILLED WITH FOLIAGE 233-6, NATIVITY OF CHRIST WIT!
  ENTHRONED QUEEN IN BACKGROUND 233-7, DORMITION OF VIRGI]
  233-8, CLAUDIUS HOLDING SWORD ADDRESSED GROUP OF PEOPLE 233-9,
  SIEGE OF JERUSALEM WITH HORSEMEN ATTACKING TOWER 233-10
  DIOCLETIAN CONDEMNS TWO MARTYRS TO BE BEHEADED 233-11
  MAXIMIAN SENTENCES SEVERAL MEN TO BE BEHEADED 233-12, AVEMU
  PERSECUTES CHRISTIANS IN INDIA 233-13, MONK CONFOUNDS KIN'
  233-13, THEODOSIUS IN A D 381 ESTABLISHES KINGDOMS 233-14
  CHARLEMAGNE GIVES ORDERS TO TWO MEN/ ONE CROWNED 233-15

*$ABSTRACT 234
  *LIBRARY BOD
  *SLIDE SET TITLE ENGLISH ROMANESQUE INITIALS
  *NEGATIVE REFERENCE ROLL 208A
  *RENTAL FEE SM 234 $2.60
  *SHELFMARK MS AUCT E INF 2 234/1-9, MS AUCT D 2 15 234/10-12
  *PROVENANCE ENGLISH
  *DATE EXECUTED 12TH
  *LANGUAGE LATIN
  *TYPE OF MANUSCRIPT BIBLE 234/1-9, GOSPELS 234/10-12
  *CONTENTS INITIALS/ ENGLISH ROMANESQUE 234/1-12, BEATU:
  INITIALS 234/1-2, INITIAL Q PSALM 51 234-3, INITIAL D PSAL
  101 234-4, INITIAL D PSALM 109 234-5, INITIAL P PROVERB:
  234-6, INITIAL A PARALIPOMENON I 234-7, INITIALS C AND
  TOBIAS 234-8, INITIAL L ST MATTHEW 234-9, INITIAL L ST MATTHE
  234-10, INITIAL I ST MARK 234-11, INITIAL I ST JOHN 234-12

*$ABSTRACT 235
  *LIBRARY BOD
  *SLIDE SET TITLE OVID METAMORPHOSES
  *NEGATIVE REFERENCE ROLL 208B
  *RENTAL FEE SM 235 $2.70
  *COMMENTS SEE   W.   O.   HASSALL,   THE   HOLKHAM   LIBRARY
   ILLUMINATIONS   AND   ILLUSTRATIONS IN THE MANUSCRIPT LIBRARY OF
   THE EARL OF LEICESTER, 1970.
  *TITLE OF MANUSCRIPT METAMORPHOSES
  *SHELFMARK MS HOLKHAM 324
  *PROVENANCE FLEMISH
  *DATE EXECUTED 15TH/C1497
  *LANGUAGE LATIN
  *AUTHOR OVID
  *TYPE OF MANUSCRIPT LITERATURE
  *CONTENTS METAMORPHOSES OF   OVID 235/1-14, LITERATURE/ OVID
   235/1-14, PHATETHON CRASHES FATHER'S CAR 235-1, PYRAMUS AND
   THISBE/ MULBERRY CHANGES   COLOR 235-2, ARACHNE AND PALLAS
   235-3,   ARACHNE TALKING   SEATED 235-4,   ARACHNE'S CHALLENGE
   235-5, ARACHNE TURNED INTO SPIDER AFTER WEAVING CONTEST 235-6,
   ORPHEUS AND EURIDICE AND PLUTO ENTHRONED 235-7, EURIDICE TAKEN
   TO HADES BY DRAGONS 235-8, ORPHEUS PLEADS WITH PLUTO FOR
   EURIDICE@S RELEASE 235-9, ORPHEUS STONED BY MAENADS 235-10,
   MIDAS TURNS ALL HE TOUCHES TO GOLD 235-10, MIDAS AND HIS
   GOLDEN TOUCH 235-12, ORPHEUS STONED BY MAENADS 235-11, OVID
   SPEAKS ON LOVE TO SEATED COUPLES 235-13, FATE OF LOVERS
   LEANDER/ PYRAMUS/ THISBE/ AND SAPPHO 235-14

*$ABSTRACT 236
  *LIBRARY BOD
  *SLIDE SET TITLE ILLUSTRATIONS OF THE SEVEN DEADLY SINS
  *NEGATIVE REFERENCE ROLL 208E
  *RENTAL FEE SM 236 $3.20
  *TITLE OF   MANUSCRIPT LA   VIGNE   DE   NOSTRE SEIGNEUR 236/1-6,
   PELERINAGE DE   VIE   HUMAINE   236/7-11,   REFORMATIO LANGUENTIS
   ANIMAE 236/12-15, DE QUINQUE SEPTENIS 236/16-18, MIRROR OF THE
   WORLD 236/19-24
  *SHELFMARK   MS DOUCE 134 236/1-6, MS DOUCE 300 236/7-8, MS LAUD
   MISC 740   236/9-11,   MS   DOUCE   373   236/12-15,   MS   LAT C 2
   236/16-18, MS BODLEY 283 236/19-24
  *PROVENANCE FRENCH 236/1-8, ENGLISH 236/9-11 AND 16-18, FLEMISH
   236/12-15, ENGLISH AND DUTCH 236/19-24
  *DATE   EXECUTED   13TH   236/16-18, 15TH 236/1-11 AND 19-24, 16TH
   236/12-15
  *LANGUAGE FRENCH 236/1-8, ENGLISH   236/9-11 AND 19-24, LATIN
   236/12-18
  *AUTHOR DEGUILLEVILLE/ GUILLAUME DE 236/7-11
  *TYPE OF MANUSCRIPT PELERINAGE LITERATURE
  *CONTENTS   SEVEN DEADLY SINS 236/1-24, PUNISHMENT OF ENVIOUS IN
   HELL 236-1, WRATHFUL 236-2, SLOTHFUL 236-3, AVARICIOUS 236-4,
   GLUTTONS   236-5,   LECHERS 236-6, SLOTH APPROACHES 236-7, WRATH
   236-8, SLOTH 236-9, ENVY 236-10, COVETOUSNESS 236-11, ARBOR
   BIS MORTUA 236/12-13, ECCE HOMO WITH NAMES OF SINS ON CORPSE
   236-14, SPECULUM PATIENTIAE WITH SEVEN DEADLY SINS AT TABLE
   236-15, SEVEN DEADLY SINS 236-15, WHEEL 236-16, ACCIDIA IN
   MEDALLION 236-17, IRA IN MEDALLION 236-18, LECHERY 236-19,
   PRIDE 236-20, WRATH 236-21, SLOTH 236-22, AVARICE 236-23,
   GLUTTONY 236-24

*$ABSTRACT 237
  *LIBRARY BOD
  *SLIDE SET TITLE ILLUSTRATIONS FROM PORTABLE PSALTER I
  *NEGATIVE REFERENCE ROLL 208H
  *RENTAL FEE SM 237 $3.80
  *SHELFMARK MS DOUCE 5
  *PROVENANCE FLEMISH/ GHENT
  *DATE EXECUTED 14TH/C1320-30
  *LANGUAGE LATIN

121

*TYPE OF MANUSCRIPT PSALTER/ PORTABLE
*CONTENTS PSALTER/ ILLUSTRATIONS FROM   237/1-36,   CALENDAR
237/1-8, JANUARY 237-1, FEBRUARY 237-2, APES/ HARE WITH
BAGPIPES/ MAN BY FIRE/ 237-2, WOMAN WITH JAR ON HEAD/ APE WITH
JUG/ BOY ROASTING BIRD 237-1, SKATING AND TOBOGGANING AND
PRIEST BLESSING TREE 237-3, APRIL 237-4, LADY BIDS FAREWELL TO
HORSEMAN AND ATTENDANT/ SQUIRE KNEELS 237-4, MAY 237-5, HUNTER
SHOOTS DEER/ SWORDSMAN/ GRAPE HARVEST 237-5, OCTOBER 237-6,
PIGS FED WITH ACORNS/ APE PRODS HARE WITH POLE 237-6, NOVEMBER
237-7, APE CARRYING PAILS ON YOKE/ SPARROW/ PIG KILLED 237-7,
DECEMBER 237-8, HARES/ KITCHEN WITH OVEN AND COOKS 237-8,
ANNUNCIATION TO VIRGIN 237-9, VISITATION 237-10, PRESENTATION
IN TEMPLE 237-11, ANNUNCIATION TO SHEPHERDS 237-12, NATIVITY
WITH OX AND ASS IN BACKGROUND 237-13, MASSACRE OF INNOCENTS
WITH ENTHRONED HEROD GIVING ORDERS 237-14, PALM SUNDAY WITH
CHRIST RIDING INTO JERUSALEM ON ASS 237-15, TRINITY 237-16,
BEATUS INITIAL WITH DAVID PLAYING HARP AND KILLING GOLIATH
237-16, DAVID SLAYS GOLIATH 237-16, BAGPIPER AND TUMBLER
237-16, GROTESQUES/ ONE PLAYING FIDDLE AND ONE A TRIANGLE
237-17, BIRD'S HEAD/ ANGEL'S BUST/ HOODED MAN/ MAN WITH HAT
237-18, APE FALLS FROM HORSE/ APE DRESSED AS BISHOP 237-19,
GROTESQUE HEADS/ BLUE TIT 237-19, SOLDIER WITH SHIELD AND
HELMET 237-19, WOMAN IN RED DRESS/ MAN WITH POINTED HAT
237-20, APE CROUCHES BEFORE HALF FIGURE OF BISHOP 237-20,
WOMAN'S HEAD IN INITIAL V 237-21, MAN DRAWS SWORD TO KILL
LION/ HARE AND FINCH 237-21, BEARDED HEAD WITH POINTED HAT AND
ANIMAL HEADS 237-21, MAN DIPS POLE INTO PAIL 237-22, INITIAL B
WITH MAN PREPARING TO KILL PIG 237-23, UNICORN'S HEAD/ BIRD'S
HEAD/ GREEN ANIMAL'S HEAD 237-23, MAN WITH AXE/ BIRD'S HEAD/
UNICORN'S HEAD 237-24, APE WITH AXE FIGHTING WITH SWORDSMAN
237-25, MAN WITH AXE 237-24, SPARROW/ HARE/ HOODED HUMAN HEAD/
BIRD'S HEAD 237-25, UNICORN'S HEAD/ HARE'S HEAD 237-26
TRUMPET PLAYED BY ANIMAL HEAD 237-26, APE WITH BOWL AND SPOON/
HARE/ UNICORN'S HEAD 237-27, PIPER AND DANCING GIRL/ MAN AND
UNICORN'S HEAD 237-28, MESSENGER COMES TO ARMED KNIGHT 237-29,
EEL/ BIRDS/ ANIMAL AND HUMAN HEADS 237-30, HEADS OF UNICORN,
BIRDS/ ANIMALS 237-30, HUMAN HEADS WITH HATS AND ANIMAL HEADS
237-31, BEARDED HEAD AND WOMAN WITH HAWK ON HER WRIST 237-32,
JESTER/ ANIMAL AND BIRD HEADS 237-33, APE WITH SHIELD AND
LANCE TILTING AT QUINTAIN 237-34, TILTING 237-34, HARE DRESSED
IN CHAUSABLE 237-34, SERPENT-LIKE CREATURES AND BIRD'S HEADS
237-34, TONSURED MONK'S HEAD AND UNICORN HEADS AND ANIMAL
HEADS 237-35, APE STANDING ON HANDS 237-36, NAKED MAN BITTEN
BY SERPENT 237-36, HARE AND GREAT TIT 237-36, HEADS OF HUMANS,
UNICORN/ AND ANIMALS 237-36

*$ABSTRACT 238
*LIBRARY BOD
*SLIDE SET TITLE EXAMPLES OF POST-MEDIEVAL BOOK PRODUCTION
*NEGATIVE REFERENCE ROLL 208I
*RENTAL FEE SM 238 $3.10
*COMMENTS 22 SLIDES DEPICTING VARIOUS PRINTING PROCESSES
*TITLE OF MANUSCRIPT ACTES AND MONUMENTS 238-1, MECHANICK
EXERCISES 238-2, SELECT MAGAZINE 238-3, QUADS FOR AUTHORS
238-4, IRISH MELODIES 238-5, DE HUMANI CORPORIS FABRICA 238-6,
SCULPTURA 238-7, HISTORY OF BRITISH BIRDS 238-8, VOYAGE AROUND
GREAT BRITAIN 238-9, TREATISE ON LITHOGRAPHY 238/10-13, ESSAY
ON PRINTING IN CHIARO-OSCURO 238-13, SUMMER 238-14, MICROCOSM
OF LONDON 238-15, DR SYNTAX IN SEARCH OF THE PICTURESQUE
238-16, HORTUS GRAMINEUS WODERNENSIS 238-17, DORSETSHIRE
PHOTOGRAPHICALLY ILLUSTRATED 238-18, BOTANICAL MAGAZINE
238-19, BIRDS OF GREAT BRITAIN 238-21, SEAT OF WAR/ SKETCHES
MADE IN THE CRIMEA 238-21, ALHAMBRA VOL I 238-22
*PROVENANCE ENGLISH
*DATE EXECUTED 16TH 238/1 AND 6, 17TH 238/2 AND 7, 18TH 238/8
AND 13, 19TH 238/3-5 AND 9-12 AND 14-20 AND 22, 20TH 238-21
*LANGUAGE ENGLISH 238/1-5 AND 8-16 AND 18-22, LATIN 238/6-7 AND
17
*AUTHOR FOX/ J 238-1, MOXON/ J 238-2, TUER/ W 238-4, MOORE/ T
238-5, VESALIUS 238-6, EVELYN/ J 238-7, BEWICK/ T 238-8,

DANIELL/ W 238-9, SENEFELDER/ A 238/10-12, JACKSON/ J B
238-13, MUDIE/ R 238-14, ACKERMANN/ R 238-15, ROWLANDSON/ T
AND COMBE/ W 238-16, SINCLAIR/ G 238-17, POUNCY/ J 238-18,
GOULD/ J 238-20, SIMPSON/ W 238-21, JONES/ O 238-22
*TYPE OF MANUSCRIPT MISCELLANY/ PRINTING PROCESSES
*CONTENTS PRINTING PROCESSES OF POST-MEDIEVAL BOOK PRODUCTION
238/1-22, BOOK PRODUCTION 238/1-22, SKELETON ILLUSTRATION
238-6, OSPREY IN WOOD ENGRAVING 238-8, SHIPS ON THE CLYDE
238-9, ITALIAN SCENE 238-14, GREAT HALL OF BANK OF ENGLAND
238-15, DACTYLIS GLOMERATA 238-17, GATEHOUSE OF WOLVETON OR
WOLTON HOUSE 237-18, CEREUS NAPOLEONIS 238-19, OWL/ ENGLISH
238-20, CHARGE OF THE LIGHT BRIGADE 238-21, ALHAMBRA/ PAINTING
ON CEILING OF HALL OF JUSTICE 238-22

*$ABSTRACT 239
  *LIBRARY BOD
  *SLIDE SET TITLE ALCHEMY
  *NEGATIVE REFERENCE ROLL 209
  *RENTAL FEE SM 239 $2.70
  *TITLE OF MANUSCRIPT THETRUM CHEMICUM BRITANNICUM 239/2-6,
  ALCHEMICAL POEM 239/7-14
  *SHELFMARK MS ASHMOLE 1445 239-1, MS ASHMOLE 971 239/2-6, MS
  ADD A 287 239/7-14
  *PROVENANCE ENGLISH 239/1-6, GERMAN 239/7-14
  *DATE EXECUTED 16TH-17TH 239-1, 17TH 239/2-14
  *TYPE OF MANUSCRIPT ALCHEMICAL TREATISES
  *CONTENTS ALCHEMICAL ELIXIR FOR AN ELIXIR 239-1, AUTHOR
  PRESENTS BOOK TO PATRON 239-2, ALCHEMICAL TEXTS 239/1-14,
  PHILOSOPHERS GEBER/ ARISTOTLE/ RHOZES/ AND HERMES 239-1,
  ALCHEMISTS/ FOUR AT WORK 239-4, ASTROLOGICAL TABLE WITH SEATED
  FIGURES 239-6, CALVARY SCENE SET IN DETAILED LANDSCAPE 239-7,
  ALCHEMIST SURROUNDED BY BOOKS AND APPARATUS 239-8, ALCHEMIST
  AND ASSISTANTS AT WORK ONE WITH BALANCE 239-9, AGES/ FIVE OF
  MAN 239-10, ELEMENTS AIR/ WATER/ EARTH/ FIRE 239-11, FIRE
  SYMBOLIZED LIKE THE EVANGELISTS 239-11, DRAGON/ GREEN SLAIN BY
  ARMOURED SOLDIERS 239-12, PLANETS SATURN/ LUNA/ MERCURY/ MARS
  IN SYMBOLIC FIGURES 239-13, ALCHEMICAL APPARATUS WITH MAN IN
  BLACK 239-14, BOY'S HEAD APPEARS ABOVE GROUND 239-14

*$ABSTRACT 240
  *LIBRARY BOD
  *SLIDE SET TITLE IMPORTANT EARLY TEXTS
  *NEGATIVE REFERENCE ROLL 211H
  *RENTAL FEE SM 240 $2.75
  *COMMENTS 15 SLIDES FROM 11 MSS OF THE 6TH-14TH CENTURIES
  *TITLE OF MANUSCRIPT LAUDIAN ACTS 240-1, RULE OF ST BENEDICT
  240-2, ST DUNSTAN'S CLASSBOOK 240/3-4, ALFRED'S OLD ENGLISH
  TRANSLATION OF GREGORY'S CURS PASTORALIS 240-5, ALFRED'S OLD
  ENGLISH TRANSLATION OF BEDE'S HISTORIA ECCLESIASTICA 240/6-7,
  CAEDMON GENESIS 240-8, ANGLO-SAXON CHRONICLE 240/9-10, CHANSON
  DE ROLAND 240-11, ORMULUM 240-12, OWL AND THE NIGHTINGALE
  240-13, SOUTH-ENGLISH LEGENDARY 240-14, WYCLIF BIBLE 240-15
  *SHELFMARK MS LAUD GR 35 240-1, MS HATTON 48 240-2, MS AUCT F 4
  32 240/3-4, MS HATTON 20 240-5, MS TANNER 10 240/6-7, MS
  JUNIUS 11 240-8, MS LAUD MISC 636 240/9-10, MS DIGBY 23
  240-11, MS JUNIUS 1 240-12, MS JESUS COLLEGE 29 240-13, MS
  LAUD MISC 108 240-14, MS BODLEY 959 240-15
  *PROVENANCE ENGLISH
  *DATE EXECUTED 06TH/C668 240-1, 08TH/C700 240-2, 09TH/C820
  240/3-4, 09TH/C890-7 240-5, 10TH 240/6-7, 11TH/C1000 240-8,
  12TH 240/9-11, 13TH/C1200 240/11-12, 13TH 240-13, 14TH
  240/14-15
  *LANGUAGE LATIN 240/1-4, ENGLISH 240/5-10 AND 12-15,
  ANGLO-NORMAN 240-11
  *TYPE OF MANUSCRIPT MISCELLANY/ EARLY ENGLISH MSS
  *CONTENTS ENGLISH TEXTS/ EARLY 240/1-15, LATIN AND GREEK TEXTS
  IN PARALLEL COLUMNS 240-1, PASSAGE DESCRIBING OBSERVANCES IN
  WINTER 240-2, RUNIC ALPHABET 240-3, OVID SECTION OPENING

123

240-4, CHAPTER 1 OPENING 240-5, LETTER FROM GREGORY T
AUGUSTINE ANSWERING QUESTIONS 240/6-7, GOD ENTHRONED ABOV
CHAOS AND BEGINNING OF TEXT 240-8, ANGLO-SAXON CHRONICLE WIT
EARLIEST MENTION OF OXFORD 240-9, ANNALS 240-10, CHARLEMAGNE'
TRIUMPHANT REVENGE AND MIRACLE OF SUN 240-11, ORMULUM PREFACE
INTRODUCTION AND BEGINNING 240-12, OWL AND NIGHTINGAL
REFERENCE TO PRESUMED AUTHOR 240-13, LIVES OF THE SAINTS/ S
CHRISTOPHER 240-14, WYCLIF BIBLE/ BEGINNING OF PSALMS 240-15

*$ABSTRACT 241
  *LIBRARY BOD
  *SLIDE SET TITLE DRAMA THE CORNISH PASSION PLAYS
  *NEGATIVE REFERENCE ROLL 211I
  *RENTAL FEE SM 241 $2.75
  *TITLE OF MANUSCRIPT CORNISH PASSION PLAYS
  *SHELFMARK MS E MUSAEO 160 241/1-4, MS DIGBY 133 241/5-8, M
  BODLEY 791 241/9-12, MS BODLEY 219 241/13-15
  *PROVENANCE ENGLISH
  *DATE EXECUTED 15TH 241/9-15, 16TH 241/1-8
  *LANGUAGE LATIN AND ENGLISH
  *TYPE OF MANUSCRIPT PASSION PLAYS/ CORNISH
  *CONTENTS PASSION PLAYS/ CORNISH 241/1-15, DRAMA/ CORNIS
  PASSION PLAYS 241/1-15, LITERATURE/ PASSION PLAYS 241/1-15
  BURIAL AND RESURRECTION 241/1-4, PLAY OF ST MARY MAGDALEN
  241/5-7, NAMES OF CAST/ STAGE DIRECTION/ NAME OF SCRIBE 241-8
  ORIGO MUNDI 241-9, DIAGRAM OF STAGE 241/11-12, JORDAN'
  CREATION OF WORLD 241-13, GABRIEL/ GOD/ LUCIFER 241-13, STAG
  DIRECTIONS 241-14, FALL OF LUCIFER 241/14-15, LUCIFER/FAL
  241/14-15

*$ABSTRACT 242
  *LIBRARY BOD
  *SLIDE SET TITLE MEDIEVAL MUSIC
  *NEGATIVE REFERENCE ROLL 156A
  *RENTAL FEE SM 242 $5.10
  *COMMENTS 62 SLIDES WITH CAROLS AND SONGS IN ENGLISH AND LATI
  POSSIBLY FROM ST GEORGE'S CHAPEL WINDSOR 1425-40
  *SHELFMARK MS ARCH SELD B 26
  *PROVENANCE ENGLISH/ PERHAPS FROM ST GEORGE'S CHAPEL WINDSOR
  *DATE EXECUTED 15TH/C1425-1440
  *LANGUAGE LATIN AND ENGLISH
  *TYPE OF MANUSCRIPT MUSICAL TEXTS
  *CONTENTS MUSICAL TEXTS 242/1-62, CAROLS AND SONGS 242/1-62
  MATER ORA FILIUM NO BIS DONET GAUDIUM 242-1, SANCTA MARI
  VIRGO INTERCEDE 242/2-4, I PRAY YOU ALLE 242-5, AVE REGIN
  COLORUM 242/6-7, BEATA MATER TE INNPUTA 242-8, NOEL SYNG W
  BOTH AL AND SOM 242-9, A MAN A SAY A SAY A SAY 242-10, GOƏDA
  MY LORD SYRE CHRISTEMASSE 242-11, MILES CHRISTI GLORIOS
  242/13-14, OF A ROSE SYNGE WE 242-14, ALLELUYA NOW WEL MAY W
  242-15, SYNGE WE TO THIS MERY CUMPANE 242-16, OMNES UN
  GAUDEMAS 242-17, REGINA COELI LETARE 242-18, DEO GRACIA
  PERSOLVAMUS 242-19, AVE REGINA CELORUM 242-20, FUNDE VIRGO TE
  BEATA 242-21, ALMA REDEMPTORIS MATER 242-22, AVE DOMINA CEI
  REGINA 242-23, NOWEL NOWEL OWT OF YOR SLPEPE ARYSE AND WAK
  242-24, MAKE YOU JOY NOW IN THIS FEST 242-25, WHAT TYDYNGE
  BRYNGEST THOU MESSANGER 242-26, ALLEYUA PRE VIRGINE MARI
  242-27, AVE MARIA COLORUM 242/28-29, DEO GRACIAS ANGLI
  242-30, AS I LAY UP ON A NIGHT 242/31-32, THE MERTHE OF ALL
  THIS LONDE 242-33, GLAD AND BLITHE MOTE YOU BE 242/34-35
  NESCIENS MARIA VIRGO 242-36, SANCTA MARIA VIRGO INTERCED
  242-37, ALLEYUA A NYWE WERKE IS COME 242/38-39, GAUDE TERR
  TENEBROSA 242-40, HAL MARY FUL OF GRACE 242-41, A HEVENL
  SONGE Y DERE WEL SAY 242-42, HAYL GODYS SONE IN TRINIT
  242-43, DAVID EX PROGENIE 242-44, VERBUM CARO FACTUM ES
  242-45, NOVUS SOL DE VIRGINE 242-46, AVE MARIA GRACIA 242-47
  NESCIENS MATER VIRGO 242-48, ECCE QUOD NATURA 242-49, NOWE
  NOWEL TO US YE BORN 242-50, LAUS HONOR VIRTUS GLORIA 242-51
  BLESSID BE THAT LORD IN MAGESTE 242-52, VENI REDEMPTOR GENCIU

242-53, ABYDE Y HOPE HIT BE THE BESTE 242-54, ETERNE REX
ALTISSIME 242-55, SPECIOSA FACTA EST 242/56-57, TOTA PULCHRA
EST 242/58-59, TAPPSTER DRYNGKER FYLL A NOTHER ALE 242-60, WEL
COM BE YE WHEN YE GOD 242-61, MUSICAL SCRIBBLES IN A LATER
HAND 242-62

*$ABSTRACT 243
  *LIBRARY BOD
  *SLIDE SET TITLE MEDICAL AND PLANT ILLUSTRATIONS
  *NEGATIVE REFERENCE ROLL 186H
  *RENTAL FEE SM 243 $5.30
  *SHELFMARK MS ASHMOLE 1462
  *PROVENANCE ENGLISH
  *DATE EXECUTED 12TH
  *LANGUAGE LATIN
  *TYPE OF MANUSCRIPT SCIENTIFIC
  *CONTENTS MEDICAL ILLUSTRATIONS 243/1-66, PLANT ILLUSTRATIONS
243/1-66, HERBAL 243/1-66, MEDICAL PICTURES WITH FIGURES
243-1, MEDICAL PICTURE WITH RECUMBENT AND STANDING FIGURES
243-2, SURGEONS OPERATING ON EYE AND NOSE 243-2, ANTONIUS MUSA
ON BETONY 243-3, BETOYNE BETONICA 243-3, BALD MAN DEFENDING
SELF FROM DOG WITH SWORD 243-4, APULEIUS HERBAL 243-4, DRAGON
AND SCORPION FOUGHT BY MAN WITH AXE 243-5, QUINQUE FOLIUM/ PES
COLUMBE 243-5, VERVAIN 243-6, SERPENT STABBED BY MAN HOLDING
HERBE VERMINACIA 243-6, HENBANE/ MAN AND MAD DOG WITH
SIMPHONIACA 243-6, SNAKEWEED/VIPERINE 243-7, MUGWEED OR
MUGWORT 243-7, ARTHEMESIA MATRICARIA 243/7-8, DIANA HANDING
ARTEMESIA TO CHIRON 243-8, DRAGDAUNCE/ DRACONTA AND
SERPENDINE/ DRAGONS AND ORCHIS 243-9, GENTIANA/ CYCLAMINOS
243-9, KNOTGRASS/ PROSPERINA 243-10, SMEARWORT 243-10,
NASTURTIUM 243-10, SOURE DEWE AND GLOVEWORT/ APOLLINARIS
243-11, CHAMOMILE AND CAMEDRIS 243-11, SERPENT STABBED BY MAN
243-11, TEASEL/ RAVENSFOOT/ DANEWORT 243-12, SYNACHE/ WILDE
LETUSE AND SMALL BIRD ON LEAF 243-12, AGRIMONY 243-13,
CENTAUR/ CHIRON/ CURMEL 243-13, LESSER CURMEL/ BEET/
STRAWBERRY 243-14, MARSH MALLOW/ HORSETAIL/ WILDE MAWE 243-15
TUNGE 243-15, HOREHOUND/ FOXES FOOT 243-16, HOUSE LEEK
243-17, HOMER WITH MERCURY HOLDING PLANT IMMOLUM 243-17,
ELETRPION/ CRIAS/ MAIDENHAIR 243-17, SPERWORTH/ WILD POPPY/
OPIUM POPPY/ DROPWORT 243-18, NARCISSUS/ HUNDESTUNGE/
HARTSTONGUE/ POLEION 243-18, BUTCHER'S BROOM/ CONFREY
HARESFOOT 243-19, DITTANY/ SOLAGO MAIOR/ AFRICAN MARIGOLD
243-20, PEONIA/ VERVAIN/ COLUMBINA 243-20, BLACK BRYONY/ WATER
LILY/ WOAD/ RUSTICORUM 243-21, WILD GARLIC 243-21, MULLEIN/
CELENDINE/ GROUNDSEL 243-22, ASPLENUM/ TWITCH GRASS/ FLAG/ ROS
MARYN 243-23, CARROT/ CHEADLE/ EVERFERN/ ASPARAGAS OFFICINALIS
243-24, SAVIN/ HOUND'S HEAD/ BRAMBLE 243-25, YARROW/ WATER
MENTE/ MAN DRAWING SWORD AGAINST MAD DOG 243-26, DANEWORT/
PENNYROYAL 243-27, CATMINT/ CAMMOCK/ HORSHELLE 243-28,
SUNDCORN/ IVY 243-28, ORGANY/ WORMWOOD/ SAGE/ CORIANDER
243-29, PURSLANE/ CHERVIL/ WATER MINT 243-30, ALEXANDERS/
WHITE LILY/ SPURGE 243-20, DRAGON FOUGHT BY MAN 243-30,
SONCHUS/ WODE THISTEL/ LUPINUS 243-31, LUTEUS/ LACTERIDES/
WILDE LETUSE/ CUCUMBER 243-31, WILD HEMP/ WILD RUE 243-32,
CINQUEFOIL/ WILD BASIL 243-32, APION/ CROWFOOT/ IVY/ CORN
MINT/ HOUSE LEK/ DILL 243-33, PERSIL/ BRASICA SALVATICA
243-34, MANDRAKE WITH NAKED FIGURE/ LEAVES GROWING FROM HEAD
243-35, STAG 243-36, QUADRUPED 243-37, STAG 243-38, HARE
EATING HERB 243-39, FOX AND SHE-GOAT 243-40, WOLF AND DOG
243-41, DONKEY/ MULE/ HORSE 243-42, RAM AND HE-GOAT 243-43,
NAKED YOUTH USING CHAMBER-POT IN PRESENCE OF LADY 243-44, CAT/
KRILLOS/ WEASELS/ MICE/ PARTRIDGE/ CORVUS/ RAVEN/ COCK 243-45,
HEN 243-46, DOVE/ GOOSE/ SWALLOW 243-47, DIOSCORIDES/ HERBE
FEMINA/ BUGLOSUS/ ACHANTUM 243-48, SALVIA/ CYMINOA/
CAMMELLEON/ HERPULLOS 243-49, CAMEROPS/ POLYGAROS/ SARSUCON/
CESTROS 243-50, ARISTOCHIA/ STCAS/ ADIANTES/ MANDRAGORA
FEMINEA 243-51, THASPIS/ SYSIMBRION/ CELIDONA/ CAMOMODROS
243-52, SIDERITIS/ FLOMMOS/ LYNOZOSTIS/ ANTHERENON/ BRITANNICA
243-53, PUSILLIOS/ MELENA/ TRIBULOSA/ CONZIA 243-54, STRIGNOS/
BUTALION/ IFFERITIS/ HYPPIRES 243-55, AYZOS/ TITIMALLOS/

125

ELYOTROPIOS/ SCOLYBOS/ ACHILLEA 243-56, STAPHISA/ CAMELLEIA
CEIOS 243-57, ALCIBIADIOS/ SPLENIOS/ COLOPENDARIOS 243-57
TRITIMALLOS/ CLITIRIZA/ BULBUS RUFUS/ DRACONTEA FEMINA 243-58
MEOCHON/ COLOCINTHOS/ COLLOQUINTULA 243-59, YPERION/ LAPATIUM
ELYTROPIUM/ ARNOGLOSOS 243-60, CAMELEUCE/ SEYLLA/ SQUILLA
ERINGION 243-61, VERVENA/ STRUCION/ DELPHION 243-62
CENTIMORBIA/ ANCA/ CINOBATHOS/ CAPPARRA/ AUROSA/ 243-63
ANAGALLIUS/ PANATIA/ VIOLA PURPUREA 243-64, ZAMLENTIO
FEMINEA/ SAMALENTION MASCULINE/ SYON 243-64, LUCANIS
ABROTANUM ERACLEON 243-65, APATYNA/ PYLANTROPOS/ ORIGANU
243-66

*$ABSTRACT 244
 *LIBRARY BOD
 *SLIDE SET TITLE ASTRONOMICAL TREATISE
 *NEGATIVE REFERENCE ROLL 130A
 *RENTAL FEE SM 244 $3.90
 *SHELFMARK MS DIGBY 83
 *PROVENANCE ENGLISH
 *DATE EXECUTED 12TH/ MIDDLE
 *LANGUAGE LATIN
 *TYPE OF MANUSCRIPT ASTRONOMICAL TREATISE
 *CONTENTS ASTRONOMICAL TREATISE 244/1-38, SERPENT-LIKE DRAGO
 POINTED TO IN CIRCLE 244-1, BOOTES/ WOMAN HOLDING LEAF AN
 STARRED SPHERE 244-2, ENGONASIN/ HOLDING DRAGON AND CLU
 244-3, LYRA/ EIGHT STRINGS 244-4, CYGNUS 244-5, CEPHEUS SEATE
 CROWNED WITH BRANCH IN HAND 244-6, CASSIOPEIA CROWNED WIT
 HANDS UPRAISED 244-7, ANDROMEDA HANDS BOUND 244-8, PERSEU
 WINGED HOLDING MEDUSA'S HEAD ON PIKE 244-9, PLEIADES AN
 HEIADES AND TWO CIRCLES WITH SEVEN CIRCLES 244-10, HERCULE
 SERPENT ENTWINED AROUND NAKED BODY 244-11, HENIOCHUS WIT
 STAG-LIKE HEAD 244-12, URSA MAJOR AND MINOR 244-12, AQUIL
 244-13, PISCES 244-14, PEGASUS 244-15, DELTOTON/ TRIANGLE I
 GOLD AND STYLISED VINES 244-16, ARIES WITH SHAGGY COAT/ CURLE
 HORNS/ RED COLORING 244-17, TAURUS/ SPIRITED DRAWING COLORE
 OCHRE 244-18, GEMINI/ PAIR OF YOUNG GIRLS IN GREEN DRESSE
 244-19, CANCER WITH LION'S MASK AND CLAWS 244-20, VIRGO A
 DRAPED WOMAN WITH BRANCH 244-22, LIBRA HELD IN HAND OF SCORPI
 WITH LION'S MASK 244-23, LEO 244-21, SAGITTARIUS AS CENTAU
 WITH BOW AND ARROW 244-24, CAPRICORN WITH FISHTAIL AN
 FOREPART OF GOAT 244-25, AQUARIUS/ NAKED WOMAN IN LOIN-CLOT
 POURING WATER FROM VASE 244-26, PISCES AS PAIR OF FISH END T
 END 244-27, ORION HOLDING SWORD AND BRANCH 244-28, LEPU
 244-29, CANIS 244-30, CANIS MINOR RUNS UP MARGIN 244-31, ARG
 IN VESSEL WITHOUT BOW 244-32, AQUARIUS/ WOMAN POURING WATE
 FROM VASE 244-33, CENTAUR WITH LION-SKIN OVER SHOULDER AN
 CONEY BY LEGS 244-34, CETUS/ FISH-LIKE CREATURE WITH TUSK
 244-35, PISCES CALLED NIGHT-FISH IN TEXT 244-36, ARA
 ALTAR-LIKE STRUCTURE DRAPED IN CLOTH 244-37, HYDRA
 SEVEN-HEADED DRAGON WITH CRATER AND CORVUS 244-38, DRAGO
 244-38

*$ABSTRACT 245
 *LIBRARY BOD
 *SLIDE SET TITLE TREATISES ON THE ASTROLABE
 *NEGATIVE REFERENCE ROLL 182I
 *RENTAL FEE SM 245 $2.80
 *TITLE OF MANUSCRIPT ON THE ASTROLABE 245/1-8, TREATISE ON TH
 ASTROLABE 245/9-16
 *SHELFMARK MS ASHMOLE 1522 245/1-8, MS RAWL D 913 245/9-16
 *PROVENANCE ENGLISH
 *DATE EXECUTED 14TH 245/1-8, 15TH 245/9-16
 *LANGUAGE ENGLISH
 *AUTHOR MESSEHALACH 245/1-8, CHAUCER 245/9-16
 *TYPE OF MANUSCRIPT SCIENTIFIC
 *CONTENTS ASTROLABE/ TREATISES ON 245/1-16, ASTROLABE 245-1
 INDICES OR POINTERS CALLED ALLIDADA 245-2, INDICES/ MARKE
 HOURS 1-6 AND INFINITE SHADE 245-3, ROD OR WEDGE TO HOL

TABLES 245-4, INSCRIPTION OF CIRCUMCIRCLES OF THE WHOLE
DECLINATION 245-5, ZODIAC INSCRIPTION AND DIVISION BY ARCS
245-6, INSCRIPTION OF FIXED STARS FROM THEIR LATITUDES 245-7,
SPIDER'S WEB/ VALZAGORA/ ALHANTABUZ 245-8, CHAUCER'S TREATISE
ON THE ASTROLABE/ PROLOGUE 245-9, TEXT OF CHAUCER'S TREATISE
245-10, ASTROLABE/BACK 245-12, ALIDADA/ RULE/ AXLE/ HORSE
POINTERS 245-13, ASTROLABE/ BELLY 245-14, CIRCLES CALLED
ALMICANTERAS AND AZIMUTHS FROM ZENITH 245-15, TEXT/ FINAL PAGE
245-16

*$ABSTRACT 246
 *LIBRARY BOD
 *SLIDE SET TITLE MATHEMATICAL MANUSCRIPTS
 *NEGATIVE REFERENCE ROLL 182D-E
 *RENTAL FEE SM 246 $4.10
 *TITLE OF MANUSCRIPT PSEUDO-BOETHIUS ON GEOMETRY 246/7-13,
 LIBER EXPERIMENTARIUS 246-14, BIBLE MORALISEE 246-15,
 RETARDATION OF OLD AGE 246/16-17, GEOMETRICAL TREATISE
 246/18-37, CASTLE OF KNOWLEDGE 246-37, NOTES ON MATHEMATICAL
 PROBLEMS 246-42
 *SHELFMARK MS D/ORVILLE 301 246/1-6, MS DOUCE 125 246/7-13, MS
 ASHMOLE 304 246-14, MS BODLEY 270B 246-15, MS BODLEY 211
 246/16-17, MS CANON ITAL 197 246/18-37, MS SAVILE B AND H AND
 K 246/39-41, MS RAWL D 471 246-42
 *PROVENANCE FRENCH 246/1-6 AND 14-15, ENGLISH 246/7-13 AND
 16-17 AND 38-42, ITALIAN 246/18-37
 *DATE EXECUTED 09TH/888 246/1-6, 10TH 246/7-13, 13TH 246/14-15,
 15TH 246/18-37, 16TH/1556 246-38
 *LANGUAGE LATIN AND ENGLISH
 *AUTHOR EUCLIDE 246/1-6, PYTHAGORAS 246-14, ROGER BACON
 246/16-17, MELETO OF BRESCIA OR BELO MOILTTA 246/18-37, ROBERT
 RECORDE 246-38, ISSAC NEWTON 246-42
 *TYPE OF MANUSCRIPT MATHEMATICAL TREATISES
 *CONTENTS MATHEMATICAL TREATISES 246/1-42, ELEMENTA II 246-1,
 ELEMENTA III 246-2, ELEMENTA XI 246/3-4, ELEMENTA XII 246/5-6,
 DIAGRAMS OF INTEREST FOR SURVEYING 246/7-8, GEOMETRICAL
 FIGURES/ COLORED 246/9-13, PYTHAGORAS 246-14, WATER CLOCK ONLY
 KNOWN PICTURE 246-15, BACON PRESENTING WORK TO PATRON 246-16,
 BACON/ ROGER AND PUPIL 246-17, MEASURING TOWER WITH QUADRANT
 246-18, BOOK MEASUREMENT MADE WITH TWO RODS 246-19,
 MEASUREMENT OF TOWER BY QUADRANT/ MIRROR/ SHADOW 246-20,
 HEIGHT OF INACCESSIBLE TOWER MEASURED BY MIRROR 246-21,
 QUADRANT MEASUREMENTS OF TOWER 246-22, MEASUREMENTS INVOLVING
 CASTLE/ TOWER/ LADDER 246-23, DIVISION BETWEEN BROTHERS OF
 GARDEN WITH TOWERS 246-24, PROBLEM OF MEASURING FALLEN TREE
 OVER RIVER 246-25, MEASURING LENGTH OF FIELD AND DEPTH OF WELL
 246-26, ASCERTAINING CAPACITY OF PAVILLION 246-27, AX STROKES
 TO FELL TREE AND ERECT COLUMN 246-28, PROBLEM OF OPENINGS IN
 ROOM AND MEASUREMENTS OF CARPETS 246-29, EXCAVATION
 MEASUREMENT AND VOLUME PROBLEM IN WELLS 246-30, MEASUREMENT OF
 STORAGE VOLUME 246-31, VOLUME MEASURE AND PROBLEM OF SACKS OF
 VARYING CAPACITY 246-32, CAPACITIES OF VARIOUS CASKS AND
 BARRELS 246-33, AREAS OF SEVERAL TOWNS EACH SURROUNDED BY WALL
 246-34, PROBLEMS OF VOLUME WITH STONES AND MILLSTONES 246-35,
 PROBLEM WITH TWO COFFINS OR SARCOPHAGI 246-36, SPHERES AND
 CUBES 246-37, TITLE PAGE OF CASTLE OF KNOWLEDGE 246-38,
 BINDINGS OF BOOKS BELONGING TO JOHN WALLUS 246/39-42, BACKS OF
 BOOKS 246/39-42, NEWTON'S NOTES ON MATHEMATICAL PROBLEMS
 246-42

*$ABSTRACT 247
 *LIBRARY BOD
 *SLIDE SET TITLE BYZANTINE ILLUMINATION I
 *NEGATIVE REFERENCE ROLL 102A
 *RENTAL FEE SM 247 $4.70
 *TITLE OF MANUSCRIPT MENOLOGION
 *SHELFMARK MS GR THEF 1
 *PROVENANCE GREEK/ THESSALY

*DATE EXECUTED 14TH
*LANGUAGE GREEK
*TYPE OF MANUSCRIPT CATALOGUE OF SAINTS
*CONTENTS ANNUNCIATION/ NATIVITY/ ANGELS AND SHEPHERDS 247-1
MAGI/ JOSEPH/ CHRIST WASHED 247-1, PRESENTATION IN TEMPLE AN
BAPTISM OF CHRIST 247-2, TRANSFIGUATION AND DEPOSITION AN
LAMENTATION 247-3, HARROWING OF HELL AND ASCENSION 247-4
PENTECOST AND DEATH OF VIRGIN 247-5, SS MAMMAS/ NESTEUTOS
ANTHIMUS/ BABYLAS/ ZACHARIAS 247-6, SS MICHAEL/ SOZON/ BIRT
OF VIRGIN/ JOACHIM AND ANNA 247-6, SS METRODORA/ MENODORA
NYMPHORA/ THEODORA/ AUTONOMOS 247-7, ELEVATION OF CROSS 247-8
SS NICHOLAS/ EUPHEMIA/ SOPHIA/ EUMENIUS 247-8, TROPHIMUS
EUSTACE/ QUDRATUS 247-8, SS PHOCAS/ THECLA/ EUPHROSINE/ JOH
DIVINE 247-9, SS CALLISTRATAS/ CHARITON/ CYRIACUS/ ZACHARIA
IN TEMPLE 247-9, SS GREGORY/ ANANIAS/ CYPRIAN/ DIONYSIUS
HIEROTHEUS/ CHARITAN 247-10, SS THOMAS THE APOSTLE/ SERGIU
AND BACCHUS 247-10, SS PELAGIA/ JAMES/ EULAMPIUS/ PHILIP
TARACHUS/ PROBUS 247-11, SS PAPYLAS/ CARPAS/ NAZARIUS/ LUCIANU
247-11, SS LONGINUS/ HOSEA/ LUKE THE EVANGELIST/ JOEL 247-12
SS ARTEMIUS/ HILARY/ ABERICUS/ JAMES BROTHER OF CHRIST 247-12
SS ARETHAS/ NOLARII/ DEMETRIUS/ NESTOR/ TERENTIUS 247-13, S
ANATASIA/ ZENOBIUS/ ZENOBIA/ EPIMACHUS 247-13, SS COSMAS
DAMIAN/ AEINDYNUS/ ACEPSIMAS 247-14, SS EPISTERA/ PAUL/ JEROM
SYNAXIS 247-14, SS MATRONA/ ERASTUS/ VINCENT/ JOHN C
ALEXANDRIA 247-15, SS JOHN CHRYSOSTOM/ SOLIDUS 247-15,
PHILIP THE APOSTLE/ MATTHEW APOSTLE AND EVANGELIST 247-15, S
GREGORY/ PLATO/ ABODIAH/ PROCULUS 247-16, PRESENTATION C
VIRGIN 247-16, SS PHILEMON/ AMPHILOCHUS/ AERAGANTINUS
KATHERINE 247-16, SS PETER AND CLEMENT/ ALYPIUS/ 247-17, S
JAMES PERSES/ STEPHEN THE YOUNGER 247-17, PARAMONUS/ ANDRE
THE APOSTLE/ NAHUM 247-17, SS HABAKKUK/ ZEPHANIAH/ BARBARA
SABAS 247-18, SS NICHOLAS/ AMBROSE PATAPIUS/ ANNE 247-18,
EUGRAPHUS/ HERMOGENES/ DANIEL STYLITES 247-19, SS SPYRIDON
EUSTRATIUS/ THRYSUS 247-19, SS ELEUTHERIUS/ ANACEUS/ DANIE
247-19, SHADRACH/ MECHACH/ ADEDNEGO 247-19, SS ANASTASIA/ TH
MARTYRS OF CRETE/ EUGENIA/ NATIVITY 247-20, SS JOSEPH
STEPHEN/ ENDES/ DOMNA 247-21, MARTYRS 20000/ HOLY INNOCENT
247-21, SS SYLVESTER/ MALACHI/ GORDIUS AND MYSTAE/ THROPOM
247-22, SS PROCTROMUS/ DOMINICA/ POLYEUCTUS/ BAPTISM OF CHRI
247-22, SS GREGORY OF NYSSA/ THEODOSIUS/ TATIANA 247-23, S
STRALORICUS AND HENNYLUS 247-23, SS JOANNES CALYBITES/ ABBOT
OF SINAI/ ST PETER'S CHAIR 247-23, ST ANTHONY 247-23, S
ATHANASIUS/ MACARIUS/ EURPHYMIUS/ MAXIMUS/ CLEMENT/ ANASTASI
247-24, SS PERSES/ AGATHANGELUS/ XENO/ GREGORY 247-24, S
XENOPHON/ CHRYSOSTOM/ EPHRAIM/ RELICS OF IGNATIUS 247-25, S
CYRUS/ JOAN/ THREE ARCHBISHOPS/ TRYPHON 247-25, SS TIMOTHY
RELICS OF EUGENIA/ POLYCARP/ HEAD OF PRODOMUS 247-27, S
PARASIUS/ PROPHYRIUS/ PROCOPIUS/ BASILIUS/ CASSIANUS 247-28
SS EUDOXIA/ THEODOTUS/ EUTROPIUS/ GERASIMOS 247-29, SS CONOM
42 MARTYRS/ EPHRAIM OF CHESON/ THEOPHYLACTUS 247-30, S
QUADRATUS/ SOPHRONIUS/ 40 MARTYRS/ THEOPHANES 247-30, S
EICOPHORUS/ BENDICTUS/ AGAPIUS/ SABINUS/ ALEXIUS/ MAN OF GC
247-31, SS CYRILLUS/ CHRYSANTHUS 247-31, SLAUGHTER OF FATHEI
IN LAUROI OF ST SABAS 247-31, ST SABAS 247-31, SS JACOBU
BASILIUS/ NICON AND 11 MARTYRS/ ANNUNCIATION 247-32,
GABRIEL/ METRONA/ MARCUS OF ARETHUSA 247-32, SS BARACHESIU
CLIMACUS/ HYPATIUS 247-33, SS MARIA AEGYPTICA/ TITUS/ SOZIM
247-33, ST NICETUS OF MALICION 247-33, SS JOSEPH HYMNOGRAPHUS
AGATHOPUS/ EUTYCHIUS/ GEORGIUS OF LESBOS 247-34, S
HERODIANUS/ ZUPSYTHIUS/ TERENTIUS/ ANTIPAS 247-34, S
BASILIUS/ ARTEMON/ MARTINUS/ ARISTARCHUS/ IRENE/ CHIONI
247-35, SS SIMEON PORSA/ SABBAS/ PALAISTAURITES 247-35, S
THEODORUS/ TRICHINAS/ JANNUARIUS/ THEODORUS 247-36, S
GEORGIUS/ SABAS/ STRATELATES 247-36, SS MARCUS/ BASILEIUS
SIMEON 247-36, SS JACOBUS/ MAMNON/ JAMES/ JERMIAH/ ATHANASIUS
TIMOTHEUS 247-37, SS PELAGIA/ IRENE/ JOB/ SIGN OF CROS
247-38, SS JOHN THE DIVINE/ ARSENIUS/ ISAIAH/ SIMON ZELOTES
MOCTIUS 247-38, SS EPIPHANIUS/ GLYCERIA/ ISIDORUS 247-39,
PATHAMIUS/ THEODORUS/ ANDRONIKUS/ THEODOTUS 247-39, S
PATRICIUS OF PRUSA 247-39, SS THALELAEUS/ CONSTANTINE AN
HELENA/ BASILISCUS 247-40, SS MICHAEL OF SYNNAD
TLAMMASTORITES 247-40, SS CARPUS/ HAND OF BAPTIST/ THERAPO

128

247-40, SS HELLADIUS/ THEODOSIA/ ISAAC DAMLATA/ HERMIAS
247-41, SS JUSTINUS/ NICEPHORUS/ LUCILLIANUS OF METROPHANES
247-41, SS DOROTHEUS/ BESSARION/ THEODOTUS/ THEODORUS
STRATELATES 247-42, SS CYRILLUS/ TIMOTHEUS/ BARTHOLOMAEUS/
ONAPHRIUS 247-42, SS AQUILINO/ METHODIUS/ AMOS/ TYCHORIN/
SABEL AND OTHERS 247-43, SS LEONTIUS/ JUDAS/ METHODIUS OF
PATORA 247-43, SS JULIANUS/ EUSEBIUS/ AGRIPPINA 247-44, SS
PRODROMUS AND PHEARONIA 247-44, SS DAVID OF THESSALONIKA/
SAMPSON/ JOHN IN CYPRUS 247-44, SS PETER AND PAUL/ 12
APOSTLES/ COSMAS AND DAMIAN 247-45, SS HYACINTHUS/ ANDREAS OF
CRETE/ LAMPACLUS 247-45, SS SISOES/ THOMAS/ PROCOPIUS/
PANCRATIUS 247-46, MARTYRS OF NICIPOLIS/ EUPHOMIA 247-46, SS
PROCULUS/ HILARIA/ STEPHANUS SABBATITES 247-46, SS SQUILA/
CYRICAS/ ATHENOGENES/ MARIA/ AEMILIANUS 247-47, SS DIUS AND
MACRIN/ ELIAS/ SIMEON 247-47, SS MARY MAGDALENE/ TROPHIMUS/
CHRISTIAN/ ANNA/ HERMOLAUS 247-48, SS PANTELOEMEN/ TIMON/
CALLIPICUS 247-48, SS SILVANUS/ EUDOKIMUS/ MACCHABAEI ELEZER/
EUSIGNIUS 247-49, SS STEPHANUS/ FAUSTUS/ DALMATI/ CHILDREN OF
EPHESUS 247-49, SS DOMATIUS/ AEMILIANUS/ MATHIAS/ LAURENTIUS/
EUPLOUS 247-50, SS PHOTIUS/ MAXIMUS/ TRANSFIGURATION 247-50,
SS MICHAUS/ VIRGIN/ DIOMEDES/ MYRON/ PHLORUS/ LAURUS 247-51,
SS ANDREAS THE SOLDIER/ SAMUEL/ THADAEUS 247-51 SS
AGATHONICUS/ LUPUS/ EUGYCHOS/ BARTHOLOMAEUS/ ADRIANUS 247-52,
SS POEMEN/ MOSES AETHIOP/ DEATH OF PRODROMUS 247-52, SS
ALEXANDER OR PAULUS/ GIRDLE OF VIRGIN 247-53, ST DEMETRIUS/
LIFE OF 247-54

*$ABSTRACT 248
  *LIBRARY BOD
  *SLIDE SET TITLE ST BARBARA
  *NEGATIVE REFERENCE ROLL 138A
  *RENTAL FEE SM 248 $2.55
  *SHELFMARK MS DOUCE 152 248-1, MS RAWL LITURG F 31 248-2, MS
   CANON LITURG 99 248-3, MS DOUCE 276 248-4, MS RAWL LITURG E 14
   248-5, MS RAWL LITURG E 36 248-6, MS DOUCE 8 248-7, MS DOUCE
   219 248-8, MS DOUCE 223 248-9, MS AUCT D INF 2 13 248-10, MS
   DOUCE 381 248-11
  *PROVENANCE FRENCH 248/1-6, FLEMISH 248/7-9, ENGLISH AND DUTCH
   248-10, DUTCH 248-11
  *DATE EXECUTED 14TH 248-1, 15TH 248/3-5 AND 7-11, 16TH 248-6
  *LANGUAGE LATIN
  *CONTENTS ST BARBARA IN DIFFERENT MSS 248/1-11

*$ABSTRACT 249
  *LIBRARY BOD
  *SLIDE SET TITLE PSALTER OF RICHARD ROLLE
  *NEGATIVE REFERENCE ROLL 146B
  *RENTAL FEE SM 249 $2.50
  *TITLE OF MANUSCRIPT PSALTER OF RICHARD ROLLE
  *SHELFMARK MS BODLEY 953
  *PROVENANCE ENGLISH/ SOUTHERN
  *DATE EXECUTED 14TH
  *LANGUAGE LATIN
  *TYPE OF MANUSCRIPT COMMENTARY ON PSALTER
  *CONTENTS PSALTER 249/1-11, INITIALS/ DECORATED 249/2-11, TITLE
   249-1, INTRODUCTION 249-2, PSALM 1/ BEATUS VIR 249-3, DAVID
   CROWNED PLAYING HARP 249-3, PSALM 26/ DOMINUS ILLUMINATIO MEA
   249-4, DAVID CROWNED POINTING TO EYES 249-4, PSALM 38/ DIXIT
   CUSTODIAM 249-5, FOOL ON BENCH WITH BLADDER ON STICK 249-6,
   PSALM 52/ DIXIT INSIPIENS 249-6, DAVID POINTING TO MOUTH
   249-5, PSALM 68/ SALVUM ME FAC 249-7, DAVID ALMOST COMPLETELY
   SUBMERGED IN WATER 249-7, PSALM 80/ EXULTATE 249-8, BELLS
   PULLED BY MAN IN WHITE SURPLICE 249-8, PSALM 97 CANTATE DOMINO
   249-9, CHOIRISTERS IN WHITE SURPLICES SING FROM BOOK ON STAND
   249-9, PSALM 109/ DIXIT DOMINUS 249-10, GOD THE FATHER
   INDICATES PLACE ON HIS RIGHT HAND 249-10, CANTICLE/ CONFITEBOR
   TIBI 249-11, ARMS WITH MITRE AND CREST 249-11

129

*$ABSTRACT 250
  *LIBRARY BOD
  *SLIDE SET TITLE GENEALOGICAL HISTORY FROM BRUTE TO EDWARD I
  *NEGATIVE REFERENCE ROLL 169E
  *RENTAL FEE SM 250 $2.85
  *SHELFMARK MS BODLEY ROLLS 3
  *PROVENANCE ENGLISH/ BELONGED TO ST MARY'S YORK
  *DATE EXECUTED 13TH
  *LANGUAGE LATIN
  *TYPE OF MANUSCRIPT GENEALOGY
  *CONTENTS GENEALOGY OF HISTORY FROM BRUTE TO EDWARD I 250/1-17
   HISTORY/ ENGLISH 250/1-17, TROJAN WAR/ TWENTY MEDALLION
   250/1-7, KINGS AND SUB-KINGS/ SOME WITH ARMS 220 PORTRAIT
   250/8-16, PELIAS AND JASON 250-1, JASON ASKS FRIENDS T
   ACCOMPANY HIM 250-1, JASON GOES ON BOARD WITH ARGO 250-2
   JASON'S SHIP REACHES PHRYGIA 250-3, LAOMEDON CONFRONTS THE
   AND GOLDEN FLEECE CARRIED ON BOARD 250-4, BATTLE OF HESION
   WITH CAVALRY 250-5, PARIS ELOPES WITH HELEN AND SIEGE OF TRO
   250-5, AENEAS SAILS TO LATINUS/ BRUTUS IN EXILE SEES PANDRIM
   250-6, PANDRASIUS GIVES BRUTUS DAUGHTER AND SAILS TO ISLAN
   250-7, KINGS BRUTUS/ LOCRINUS/ GWENDOLA/ MADAN/ MENPRITU
   250-8, KINGS EBRANCU/ BRUTUS/ LEIL/ RUDHUDIBRAS 250-8, KINC
   GLADUD/ LEIR/ CORDILLA/ CUNEDAGINS 250-8, KINGS GURGUNPIUS
   RIRVALD/ LAGO/ KYNEMARCUS/ GORBODIANUS 250-8, KINGS DUNWALI
   GELLMUS/ GURGINTE/ GWELIN/ MARCIA/ SISILLEUS 250-8, KINC
   KYMARUS/ DAMIUS/ MORNIDUS/ GORBADIMUS/ ARGALT 250-9, KINC
   ELIDURUS/ REGUM/ MARGANUS/ CUMANYS TEWLLO 250-9, KINGS RUNC
   GEROANS/ CATELLUS/ CAILLUS/ PORREX 250-9, KINGS CHERIM
   SULGENTIUS/ CLERIDIUS/ ANDRAGIUS 250-9, KINGS BRIAMISANDRA
   CLEDACUS/ CLOTENUS/ GURINCIUS 250-9, KINGS MERIANUS/ BLEDANC
   CAPOENUS/ SISILLIUS 250-10, KINGS BLAGABERD/ ARCHIMAIL/ ELDC
   250-10, KINGS REDION/ REDOLCHIUS/ SAMUL/ PYR 250-10, KINC
   ELIGNELLUS/ ELY/ LUD/ CASSIBLANUS 250-10, KINGS GENUANTIUS
   KYNELMUS/ GUYDENUS/ ARMIGARUS 250-10, KINGS MARIUS/ COILLUS
   LUCIUS/ SEVERUS 250-10, KINGS BASIANUS/ CARAUSIUS/ ALYCTUS
   AESCLEPIODOCUS 250-11, KINGS COLE/ CONSTANTINUS/ CONSTANTINE
   OCTAVIUS/ TRAHERNE 250-11, KINGS OCTAVIUS/ MAXIMILIANUS
   GRACIANUS/ CONSTANTINUS 250-11, KINGS CONSTANS/ VORTIGERNES
   AURELIUS/ AMBROSIUS 250-11, KINGS UTER PENDRAGON/ ARTHURUS
   CONSTANTIUS/ AURELIUS 250-11, KINGS VORTIPORUS/ MALGC
   CATERICUS/ CADUANUS 250-11, KINGS CADWALLO/ CADULODRUS
   HENGISTUS 250-12, KINGS ESCA/ HILDA/ ELLA/ ECTA TO EDWINU
   250-12, KINGS AETHELBERTUS TO OSWYN 250-13, KINGS ERKENBERTM
   TO ALFREDUS/ LOTARIUS TO EADBRICTUS 250-13, KINGS AIDRECHTM
   TO MOLEDELWALDUS 250-14, KINGS EDBRICTUS TO ALWOLDUS/ EGBERTU
   TO EDELBREDUS 250-14, KINGS ATHELWULFAS/ ETEHBALDUS/ EDDREDUS
   ALFREDUS 250-15, KINGS EDWARDUS/ ETHELSTANUS/ EDMUNDUS
   EDREDUS/ EDWYNUS 250-15, KINGS EDGARUS/ EDWARDUS/ ETHELREDUS
   EDMUNDUS 250-15, KINGS CNUTUS/ HARALDUS/ HARDECNUTUS/ EDWARDU
   250-15, KINGS HARALDUS/ WILLIELMUS 250-15, KINGS WILLIOLMUS
   HENRICUS/ STEPHANUS/ HENRICUS 250-15, KINGS RICARDUS
   JOHANNES/ HENRICUS/ EDWARDUS 250-16, POWELL ROLL OF ARM
   250-17

*$ABSTRACT 251
  *LIBRARY BOD
  *SLIDE SET TITLE MEDICAL WRITINGS
  *NEGATIVE REFERENCE ROLL 153A
  *RENTAL FEE SM 251 $3.00
  *COMMENTS MEDICAL WRITINGS/ PRESCRIPTIONS AND DRAWINGS
  *SHELFMARK MS ASHMOLE 399
  *PROVENANCE ENGLISH
  *DATE EXECUTED 13TH/C1292
  *LANGUAGE LATIN
  *TYPE OF MANUSCRIPT MEDICAL WRITING
  *CONTENTS MEDICAL WRITINGS/ PRESCRIPTIONS/ DRAWINGS 251/1-20
   ANATOMY OF FEMALE GENITALIA 251-1, CHILD IN WOMB/ DIAGRAMS C
   POSSIBLE PRESENTATIONS 251-2, CHILD IN WOMB/ POSSIBL
   PRESENTATION INCLUDING HAND 251-3, DIAGRAMS OF CHILD IN WOMB
   TWINS AND TRANSVERSE LIE 251-4, CHIROMATIC DRAWINGS OF HANI

130

251-5, VEINS IN DIAGRAM OF BODY 251-6, DIAGRAM OF BODY
251/6-12, ARTERIES 251-7, BONES/ INCLUDING DENTAL CHART 251-8,
NERVES 251-9, MUSCLES 251-10, EXCRETORY AND DIGESTIVE SYSTEM
251-11, HEART/ LUNG/ LIVER/ AND OTHER INTESTINES 251-12,
ANATOMY OF MALE GENITALIA 251-13, ATTEMPTS TO REVIVE SWOONING
WOMAN PATIENT 251-14, PATIENT IN BED SURROUNDED BY PHYSICIAN
AND ATTENDANTS 251-15, PATIENT RECOVERING 251-15, WOMAN
PATIENT IN BED WITH PHYSICIAN AND ATTENDANTS AROUND 251-16,
DISSECTION OF FEMALE CORPSE/ DISSECTOR DISTURBED 251-17,
PHYSICIAN CONSULTED BY WOMEN PATIENTS AND RIDING AWAY 251-18,
DIAGRAM OF HANDS 251-19, ZODIACAL CIRCLE AND SMALLER CIRCLES
IN CORNERS OF PAGE 251-20

*$ABSTRACT 252
  *LIBRARY BOD
  *SLIDE SET TITLE PSALTER
  *NEGATIVE REFERENCE ROLL 161F
  *RENTAL FEE SM 252 $3.30
  *COMMENTS 26 SLIDES FROM PSALTER ALSO CONTAINING 20 NEW
  TESTAMENT SCENES
  *SHELFMARK MS GOUGH LITURG 2
  *PROVENANCE ENGLISH/ NORTH
  *DATE EXECUTED 13TH/C1200
  *LANGUAGE LATIN
  *TYPE OF MANUSCRIPT PSALTER
  *CONTENTS PSALTER 252/1-16, NEW TESTAMENT SCENES 252/1-21,
  ANNUNCIATION 252-1, VISITATION 252-2, NATIVITY 252-3, ANGEL
  APPEARS TO SHEPHERDS 252-4, ADORATION OF MAGI 252-5,
  PRESENTATION OF CHRIST IN TEMPLE 252-6, FLIGHT INTO EGYPT
  252-7, MAGI VISIT HEROD 252-8, MASSACRE OF INNOCENTS 252-9,
  MARRIAGE FEAST AT CANA 252-10, BAPTISM OF CHRIST 252-11,
  CHRIST TEMPTED TO TURN STONES INTO BREAD 252-12, CHRIST
  TEMPTED TO THROW HIMSELF FROM TEMPLE PINNACLES 252-13, SATAN
  ROUTED 252-14, LAST SUPPER 252-15, BETRAYAL 252-16,
  FLAGELLATION OF CHRIST 252-17, CRUCIFIXION 252-18, TOMB/ EMPTY
  252-19, ASCENSION 252-20, HOLY GHOST COMES 252-21, DAVID WITH
  MUSICIANS 252-22, DAVID EMBRACED BY DEMON 252-23, WARRIOR
  MOUNTED WITH SHIELD AND PENNANT 252-24, MEN IN BOAT 252-25,
  KING SEATED HOLDING SWORD 252-26

*$ABSTRACT 253
  *LIBRARY BOD
  *SLIDE SET TITLE ROMANESQUE ILLUMINATION II
  *NEGATIVE REFERENCE ROLL 131B
  *RENTAL FEE SM 253 $5.40
  *TITLE OF MANUSCRIPT CONSOLATION OF PHILOSOPHY 253/1-2,
  COMMENTARY ON THE PSALMS 253/3-8, LIFE OF ST CUTHBERT 253/9-66
  *SHELFMARK MS AUCT F 6 5 253/1-2, MS BODLEY 269 253/3-8, MS
  UNIVERSITY COLLEGE 165 253/9-66, MS C C C 2 253/67-68
  *PROVENANCE ENGLISH
  *DATE EXECUTED 12TH/C1140-1150
  *LANGUAGE LATIN
  *AUTHOR BOETHIUS 253/1-2, ST AUGUSTINE 253/3-8, BEDE 253/9-66
  *TYPE OF MANUSCRIPT PHILOSOPHICAL TEXT 253/1-2, COMMENTARY ON
  PSALMS 253/3-8, SAINT'S LIFE 253/9-66, PSALTER 253/67-68
  *CONTENTS ROMANESQUE MANUSCRIPTS 253/1-68, INITIAL C/ BOETHIUS
  SEATED WRITING BOOK 253-1, BOETHIUS LISTENING TO PHILOSOPHY/
  ARCHITECTURAL BORDER 253-2, VIRGIN ENTHRONED/ CHRIST CHILD ON
  KNEE 253-3, INITIAL E/ FLORIATED 253-4, DOG/ BARKING 253-5,
  ANIMAL GROTESQUE WITH TWISTED TAIL 253-6, INITIAL P/ FLORIATED
  253-7, BIRD HOLDING LEAF IN BEAK 253-8, BEDE WRITING AND
  GIVING BOOK TO BISHOP OF LINDISFARNE 253-9, INITIAL OF
  PROLOGUE/ BEDE WRITING 253-10, FIGHT 253-11, INITIAL/
  ORNAMENTAL 253-12, ST CUTHBERT'S KNEE CURED BY ANGEL 253-13,
  PRAYER CHANGES WIND 253-14, ST AIDAN CARRIED TO HEAVEN 253-15,
  ST CUTHBERT DIVINELY FED ON JOURNEY 253-16, ST CUTHBERT HAILED
  BY BOISIL AT MONASTERY GATE 253-17, ANGEL SERVES HEAVENLY
  BREAD 253-18, BOISIL PROPHESIES ON HIS DEATHBED 253-19, ST

*$ABSTRACT 254
 *LIBRARY BOD
 *SLIDE SET TITLE SPORTS AND PASTIMES OF MEDIEVAL FLANDERS
 *NEGATIVE REFERENCE ROLL 93
 *RENTAL FEE SM 254 $3.40
 *TITLE OF MANUSCRIPT ROMANCE OF ALEXANDER
 *SHELFMARK MS BODLEY 264
 *PROVENANCE FLEMISH
 *DATE EXECUTED 14TH/C1338-44
 *LANGUAGE FRENCH
 *ARTIST/ SCHOOL JEHAN DE GRISE
 *TYPE OF MANUSCRIPT ROMANCE
 *CONTENTS GAMES AND PASTIMES OF MEDIEVAL FLANDERS 254/1-2
 ROMANCE OF ALEXANDER 254/1-28, LITERATURE/ ROMANCE
 ALEXANDER 254/1-28, SPORTS 254/1-28, ROMANCE OF ALEXANDE
 ILLUSTRATIONS FROM 254/1-28, CITTERN PLAYED BY BOY FOR DANCE
 254-1, MASKS OF DEER/ RABBIT/ WOLF WORN BY BOYS 254-1, MO
 WITH BAT LOOKS AT NUN WITH BALL 254-2, WOMAN WITH VESSEL
 THREATENED WITH CLUB BY BOY 254-3, BUTTERFLY ON POT AND S
 CHILDREN IN CIRCLE 254-3, BAGPIPES AND BOYS WITH SHIELDS
 DONKEY TILT 254-4, COCK FIGHT WATCHED BY CHILDREN 254-5, GA
 BETWEEN PAIRS OF CHILDREN 254-6, GLOVE PUPPET SHOW
 BATTLEMENTED STAGE 254-7, HOODED MAN KNEELS TO DRAW BOW
 SHOOT HARES 254-8, GAME OF BOWLS 254-9, TOPS WHIPPED BY BO
 FACING EACH OTHER 254-10, DICE BOARD BETWEEN TWO BOYS 254-1
 STILTS PLAYED WITH BY TWO BOYS 254-12, MUMMING/ BOY WITH TAB
 AND PIPE/ ONE AS STAG 254-14, SWORD AND WHEEL BALANCI
 254-15, SWING PLAYED ON BY TWO BOYS 254-16, HUNTER HUNTED/ B
 ON BACK OF HUMAN-SIZED HARE 254-17, REVOLVING QUINTAIN US
 FOR TILTING PRACTICE 254-18, FIXED QUINTAIN USED FOR TILTI

PRACTICE 254-19, SADDLED AND BRIDLED HORSE KICKS YOUTH WITH
DRUM 254-20, MERELLES/ BOARD GAME PLAYED BY YOUTH AND MAIDEN
254-21, CHESS/ OR SIMILAR BOARD GAME PLAYED 254-22, MUMMERS IN
LONG-TAILED HOODS DANCING 254-23, BLIND MAN'S BLUFF PLAYED BY
FOUR GIRLS 254-24, DRUM PLAYED BY HORSE AND HELD BY BOY
254-25, MUSICIANS/ BAND WITH CITTERN/ HARP/ FIDDLE/ PSLATERY
254-26, MUSICIANS WITH BAGPIPES/ HURDY-GURDY/ FIDDLE/ CORNET/
ORGAN 254-27, MUMMERS WITH HEADS OF ASS/ MONKEY/ GOAT/ OX/
VULTURE 254-28

*$ABSTRACT 255
 *LIBRARY BOD
 *SLIDE SET TITLE FLEMISH ILLUMINATION IV/ HAWKING AND HUNTING
 *NEGATIVE REFERENCE ROLL 121A
 *RENTAL FEE SM 255 $3.00
 *COMMENTS 20 SLIDES WITH GOOD ILLUSTRATIONS OF COURTLY LIFE AND
 CUSTOMS
 *TITLE OF MANUSCRIPT BOOK OF HOURS
 *SHELFMARK MS DOUCE 219-220
 *PROVENANCE FLEMISH
 *DATE EXECUTED 15TH 1480-90
 *LANGUAGE LATIN
 *ARTIST/ SCHOOL MASTER OF MARY OF BURGUNDY
 *TYPE OF MANUSCRIPT BOOK OF HOURS/ DOMINICAN USE
 *CONTENTS BOOK OF HOURS/ FLEMISH/ 15TH 255/1-20, FLEMISH
 ILLUMINATION 255/1-20, HAWKING AND HUNTING 255/1-20, COURTLY
 LIFE AND CUSTOMS 255/1-20, BOOK OF HOURS 255/1-20, FALCONER
 KNEELS BEFORE LADY IN BROCADE DRESS 255-1, FALCONER PULLING ON
 GLOVES AND TWO FALCONS 255-2, HUNTSMAN BLOWING HORN/ AND DOG
 255-3, HUNTSMAN WHISTLES TO RUNNING GREYHOUND 255-4, FALCONER
 WITH BIRDS ON WRIST AND GREYHOUND 255-5, FALCONER LURES FALCON
 BACK 255-6, HUNTSMAN RUNNING TOWARDS DOGS WITH RETRIEVED BIRD
 255-7, HUNTSMAN WITH DEAD GAME BIRD 255-8, LADY RECEIVES DEAD
 GAME BIRD FROM KNEELING HUNTSMAN 255-9, LADIES EXAMINE DEAD
 GAME BIRD 255-10, LADIES ADMIRE HEADRESS/ SEWING BASKET ON
 GROUND 255-11, OSTRICH FEATHER CREST HELD BY LADY 255-12,
 MONKEY ARMED BY LADY WITH SPEAR AND HELMET 255-13, UNICORN
 TRAPPINGS ADJUSTED BY LADY BRIDLE HELD BY MONKEY 255-14,
 MONKEYS ON UNICORN AND STAG 255-16, TOURNAMENT BETWEEN MONKEYS
 AND WILD MEN IN UNIQUE MINATURE 255-17, MONKEY ON BOAR BLOWS
 TRUMPET AT TWO HARES 255-18, GRIFFIN MOUNTED BY WILD MAN
 CARRYING SPEAR 255-19, LION WITH HELMET/ MONKEY ON PILLION ON
 UNICORN 255-20

*$ABSTRACT 256
 *LIBRARY BOD
 *SLIDE SET TITLE BOTANICAL ILLUSTRATION
 *NEGATIVE REFERENCE ROLL 123
 *RENTAL FEE SM 256 $2.90
 *COMMENTS 18 SLIDES FROM 4 MSS AND PRINTED BOOKS
 *TITLE OF MANUSCRIPT FLORA GRAECA 256/6-7, FLORA GRAECA
 256/8-10, FLORA GRAECA 256/11-15, CURTIS@ BOTANICAL MAGAZINE
 256/16-18
 *SHELFMARK MS DOUCE 223 256/1-5, MS SHERARD 241 256/6-7, MS
 SHERARD 242 256/8-10, MS SHERARD 245 256-11, PRINTED EDITION
 VOL I/ III/ IX/ X 256/12-15, CURTIS'S BOTANICAL MAGAZINE VOL
 I/ 171 256/16-18
 *PROVENANCE FLEMISH 256/1-5, ENGLISH 256/6-18
 *DATE EXECUTED 15TH/C1480 256/1-5, 18TH 256/16-18, 19TH
 256/6-15
 *LANGUAGE LATIN AND ENGLISH
 *ARTIST/ SCHOOL MASTER OF MARY OF BURGUNDY 256/1-5
 *TYPE OF MANUSCRIPT BOOK OF HOURS 256/1-5, BOTANICAL TEXTS
 256/6-18
 *CONTENTS BOTANICAL ILLUSTRATION 256/1-18, FLOWERS 256/1-18,
 PANSIES/ VIOLETS/ STRAWBERRIES IN BORDER 256-1, PEA PLANT/
 PRIMROSES 256-2, ASSUMPTION 256-3, ACANTHUS/ HEARTSEASE/
 STRAWBERRIES 256-3, ACANTHUS/ HEARTSEASE/ PIMPERNEL/ CAMPION

256-4, ST CATHERINE OF ALEXANDRIA 256-5, BUTTERFLIES A
ACANTHUS FLOWERS/ PINKS/ SPEEDWELLS 256-5, ATHENS
FRONTISPIECE 256-6, HYPERICUM REPENS 256-7, SCABIOSA 256-
MORINA AND PERSICA 256-9, CINERARIA/ MARITIMA 256-10, IR
FLORENTINA 256-11, MONS PARNASSAS ON TITLE PAGE 256-12, NERI
OLEANDER 256-13, CINERARIA MARITMA 256-14, DELPHI ON TIT
PAGE 256-15, GERANIUM PELTATUM/ IVY-LEAFED GERANIUM 256-1
FRANKLIN'S TARTAR/ VARIETY OF CARNATION 256-17, COTONEASTE
WATERI 256-18

*$ABSTRACT 257
  *LIBRARY BOD
  *SLIDE SET TITLE ENGLISH ILLUMINATION/ THE ORMESBY PSALTER
  *NEGATIVE REFERENCE ROLL 139D
  *RENTAL FEE SM 257 $2.60
  *TITLE OF MANUSCRIPT ORMESBY PSALTER
  *SHELFMARK MS DOUCE 366
  *PROVENANCE ENGLISH
  *DATE EXECUTED 14TH/C1300
  *LANGUAGE LATIN
  *TYPE OF MANUSCRIPT PSALTER
  *CONTENTS PSALTER 257/1-12, BORDER DETAILS FROM PSALT
  257/1-12, INITIAL TO PSALM 38/ DIXI CUSTODIAM 257-1, CHRI
  BEFORE PILATE 257-1, INITIAL TO PSALM 68/ SALVUM ME FAC 257-
  JONAH AND THE WHALE 257-2, INITIAL TO PSALM 98/ EXULTA
  257-3, DAVID WITH BELLS AND MUSICIANS 257-3, BORDER DETAI
  257/4-12, UNICORN HUNTED 257-4, GOODWIFE'S STOLEN COCK 257-
  RIDDLE 257-6, RIDDLE OF WOLF/ LAMB/ AND GREEN FOOD 257-
  SNAIL FRIGHTENS MAN 257-8, DRAGON AND KNIGHT/ DUEL OF HAR
  257-10, MAN WITH VINE 257-11, GIFT OF RING 257-12

*$ABSTRACT 258
  *LIBRARY BOD
  *SLIDE SET TITLE FRENCH ILLUMINATION/ ROMANCE OF RENART A
  ISENGRIN
  *NEGATIVE REFERENCE ROLL 140B
  *RENTAL FEE SM 258 $2.35
  *TITLE OF MANUSCRIPT ROMANCE OF RENART AND ISENGRIN
  *SHELFMARK MS DOUCE 360
  *PROVENANCE FRENCH
  *DATE EXECUTED 14TH/ 1339
  *LANGUAGE FRENCH
  *TYPE OF MANUSCRIPT ROMANCE
  *CONTENTS ROMANCE/ SCENES FROM RENART AND ISENGRIN 258/1-
  LITERATURE/ ROMANCE OF RENART 258/1-7, JUDGMENT OF RENA
  258-1, RENART CHASED BY WOMAN AND HUSBAND 258-2, ISENGR
  DESCENDS WELL AND PULLS RENART ON TOP 258-3, ASS/ SHEEP/ F
  DRESSED AS PILGRIMS 258-4, BEAR DEMANDS PEASANT'S BE
  BULLOCK/ PEASANT CONSULTS RENART 258-5, RENART TIES
  SLEEPING ISENGRIN/ SHOWN TWICE 258-6, MONK ARMED WITH CL
  CHASES RENART 258-7

*$ABSTRACT 259
  *LIBRARY BOD
  *SLIDE SET TITLE MOLDAVIAN/ BYZANTINE ILLUMINATION
  *NEGATIVE REFERENCE ROLL 140C
  *RENTAL FEE SM 259 $2.40
  *COMMENTS 8 SLIDES FROM SLAVONIC AND GREEK GOSPELS WRITTEN
  1429 AT THE MONASTERY OF NEAMTZYN
  *SHELFMARK MS CANON GR 122
  *PROVENANCE MOLDAVIAN/ BYZANTINE
  *DATE EXECUTED 15TH/ 1429
  *LANGUAGE SLAVONIC AND GREEK
  *TYPE OF MANUSCRIPT GOSPELS
  *CONTENTS ILLUMINATION/ MOLDAVIAN 259/1-8, GOSPEL ILLUMINATI
  259/1-8, ST MATTHEW 259-1, ST MATTHEW'S GOSPEL 259-2, ST MA

259-3, ST MARK'S GOSPEL 259-5, ST LUKE 259-5, ST LUKE'S GOSPEL
259-6, ST JOHN 259-7, ST JOHN'S GOSPEL 259-8

*$ABSTRACT 260
 *LIBRARY BOD
 *SLIDE SET TITLE VIRGIL GEORGICS
 *NEGATIVE REFERENCE ROLL 145A
 *RENTAL FEE SM 260 $2.20
 *TITLE OF MANUSCRIPT GEORGICS
 *SHELFMARK MS RAWL G 98
 *PROVENANCE ITALIAN/ MILAN
 *DATE EXECUTED 15TH
 *LANGUAGE LATIN
 *ARTIST/ SCHOOL MASTER OF THE VITAE IMPERATORUM
 *AUTHOR VIRGIL
 *TYPE OF MANUSCRIPT CLASSICAL LITERATURE
 *CONTENTS CLASSICAL LITERATURE/ EXAMPLE OF VIRGIL'S GEORGICS
 260/1-4, LITERATURE/ VIRGIL 260/1-4, PLOUGHING AND SOWING
 260-1, VIRGIL WRITING IN INITIAL 260-1, TENDING VINES AND
 VIRGIL IN INITIAL 260-2, VIRGIL IN INITIAL 260/1-4, SHEPHERD
 AND SHEEP AND COWHERD AND COWS 260-3, BEEKEEPERS/ BEEHIVES/
 EXTRACTION OF HONEY 260-4

*$ABSTRACT 261
 *LIBRARY BOD
 *SLIDE SET TITLE DUTCH BOOK OF HOURS
 *NEGATIVE REFERENCE ROLL 151B
 *RENTAL FEE SM 261 $2.30
 *SHELFMARK MS ST HILDA'S COLLEGE I
 *PROVENANCE DUTCH
 *DATE EXECUTED 15TH/ LATE
 *LANGUAGE LATIN
 *TYPE OF MANUSCRIPT BOOK OF HOURS
 *CONTENTS BOOK OF HOURS 261/1-6, VIRGIN AND CHILD ON CRESCENT
 MOON 261-1, CORONATION OF VIRGIN 261-2, ROAD TO CALVARY 261-3,
 MAN OF SORROWS 261-4, DAVID PRAYING 261-5, SOULS IN TORMENT
 261-6

*$ABSTRACT 262
 *LIBRARY BOD
 *SLIDE SET TITLE ILLUSTRATING PROVERBS TO THE APOCALYPSE
 *NEGATIVE REFERENCE ROLL 152B
 *RENTAL FEE SM 262 $3.35
 *TITLE OF MANUSCRIPT BIBLE HISTORIALE
 *SHELFMARK MS DOUCE 212
 *PROVENANCE FRENCH/ PARIS
 *DATE EXECUTED 14TH/ EARLY
 *LANGUAGE FRENCH
 *AUTHOR DESMOULINS/ GUYART
 *TYPE OF MANUSCRIPT BIBLE HISTORIALE
 *CONTENTS APOCALYPSE/ ILLUSTRATING PROVERBS TO 262/1-27,
 SOLOMON WRITING OPENING WORDS TO BOOK 262-1, VIRGIN AND CHILD
 262-2, SOLOMON EXHORTING JUDGES OF EARTH TO LOVE JUSTICE
 262-3, ISAIAH SEATED HOLDING BOOK AND ANGEL HOLDING SCROLL
 262-4, JEREMIAH RECEIVING GOD'S WORD 262-5, JEREMIAH MOURNING
 OVER JERUSALEM 262-6, KING JOACHIM OF JUDAH LED AS PRISONER TO
 BABYLON 262-7, HOSEA RECEIVES GOD'S WORD FROM ANGEL 262-8,
 MICAH RECEIVES GOD'S WORD FROM ANGEL 262-9, HABAKKUK RECEIVES
 GOD'S WORD FROM ANGEL 262-10, ZACHARIAH RECEIVES GOD'S WORD
 FROM MAN ON HORSEBACK 262-11, GENERATIONS OF CHRIST 262-12, ST
 MARK SEATED WRITING WITH LION 262-13, ST LUKE SEATED WRITING
 WITH OX 262-14, ST JOHN SEATED WRITING WITH EAGLE 262-15, ST
 PAUL 262-16, ST PAUL SPEAKING TO TIMOTHY 262-17, ST PAUL
 BEFORE GATES OF EPHEUS 262-18, ST PAUL SEATED WRITING
 262/19-20 AND 22-23, TIMOTHY 262-19, TIMOTHY LISTENING 262-20,
 ST PAUL HANDS BOOK TO TIMOTHY OR MESSENGER 262-21, TITUS WITH

135

BOOK 262-22, EPISTLE TO PHILEMON 262-23, CONVERSION OF ST PA▮
262-24, ST JOHN WRITING EPISTLE TO LADY ELECT 262-25, ST JO▮
KNEELING IN PRAYER AND GAIUS WITH BOOK 262-26, ST JOHN SE▮
VISION OF SON OF MAN 262-27

*$ABSTRACT 263
  *LIBRARY BOD
  *SLIDE SET TITLE HERBAL AND BESTIARY/ A CHILD'S PRIMER
  *NEGATIVE REFERENCE ROLL 156B
  *RENTAL FEE SM 263 $6.65
  *TITLE OF MANUSCRIPT PATTERN BOOK
  *SHELFMARK MS ASHMOLE 1504
  *PROVENANCE ENGLISH
  *DATE EXECUTED 16TH/C 1520-30
  *LANGUAGE ENGLISH
  *TYPE OF MANUSCRIPT HERBAL AND BESTIARY, PATTERN BOOK
  *CONTENTS HERBAL 263/1-54, BESTIARY 263/55-93, APPLE TREE A▮
  BEL 263-1, ASPHODEL/ NARCISSUS/ WOOD AVENS/ CATERPILLAR 263-▮
  GROUND IVY AND ADDER'S TONGUE 263-3, BEANS AND BORAGE 263-▮
  BETONY AND BUGLOSS 263-5, BARBERRY AND BROOM 263-6, BAUIRE A▮
  BASIL 263-7, COWSLIP AND COCKLE 263-8, COLUMBINE AND OXL▮
  263-9, CAMOMILE AND CALAMINT 263-10, CUMFREY AND DAISY 263-1▮
  DEADLY NIGHTSHADE AND DETEYRE 263-12, DANDELION AND EGLANTI▮
  263-13, MARIGOLD AND CROMWELL 263-14, DAFFODIL AND CARNATI▮
  263-15, HEMP AND HOPS 263-16, HENBANE AND HART'S TONG▮
  263-17, HYSSOP AND JUNIPER 263-18, JENESTRE AND KNAPWE▮
  263-19, LILY AND LAVENDER 263-20, OXTONGUE AND LINSEED 263-2▮
  MADDER AND BELLADONA 263-22, MALLOW AND MINT 263-23, NETT▮
  AND CATMINT 263-24, ORPINE LIVELONG AND KING FERN 263-2▮
  HELLEBORE AND IRIS 263-26, FOXGLOVE AND FENNEL 263-27, EYESE▮
  AND ROSEMARY 263-28, RUSHES AND WILD GARLIC 263-29, RUE A▮
  SAFFRON 263-30, SPERAGE AND SAGE 263-31, CLOVER AND ST JOHN'▮
  WORT 263-32, THISTLE AND TEAZLE 263-33, VIOLET AND WOODRU▮
  263-34, PLAITAIN AND TANSY 263-35, ALDER AND ASPEN 263-36, A▮
  AND ALMOND 263-37, BLACKBERRY AND BIRCH 263-38, BOX A▮
  POMEGRANATE 263-39, IVY AND LIME 263-40, LAUREL AND MULBER▮
  263-41, MISTLETOE AND OLIVE 263-42, OAK AND PINE 263-43, PEA▮
  AND PRUNE 263-44, PEA AND ROSE 263-45, SORBUS AND VINE 263-4▮
  WALNUT AND CHERRY 263-47, PIMPERNEL/ AND STYLIZED DESI▮
  263-48, BOTANICAL SHAPES IN STYLIZED DESIGN 263/49-54, ASPI▮
  AND APE 263-55, ALDYE AND EAGLE 263-56, BEAR AND BLOODHOU▮
  263-57, CONEY AND BEAVER 263-58, GOAT AND CAMEL 263-59, CA▮
  263-60, DRAGON AND DROMEDARY 263-61, DOGS 263-62, ELEPHA▮
  263-63, DOGS 263-64, GRIFFON AND GREYHOUND 263-65, HORSE A▮
  HARE 263-66, HORSE AND HART 263-67, HARE AND HIND 263-6▮
  HARTS 263-69, UNICORNS 263-70, IBEX AND HART 263-7▮
  COCKATRICE AND CROCODILE 263-72, LIONS 263-73, LYNX AND LIZA▮
  263-74, PEACOCK AND OSTRICH 263-75, REINDEER AND PANTH▮
  263-76, TIGER AND RAM 263-77, RATS 263-78, SCROLL ALPHAB▮
  263/79-85, ALPHABET BASED ON HUMAN FORMS 263-86, COAT OF ARM▮
  OF WALDEGRAVE 263-87, COAT OF ARMS OF EMPEROR CHARLES ▮
  263-88, DESIGN BASED ON BOTANICAL SHAPES 263/89-90, COAT ▮
  ARMS SURROUNDED BY GARTER 263-91, COAT OF ARMS OF JOHN DE VE▮
  263-92, INDEX 263-93

*$ABSTRACT 264
  *LIBRARY BOD
  *SLIDE SET TITLE MIROUER HISTORIAL ABREGIE DE FRANCE
  *NEGATIVE REFERENCE ROLL 159D
  *RENTAL FEE SM 264 $2.85
  *COMMENTS COMPILED FOR CHARLES D'ANJOU, COUNT OF MAINE, A▮
  EXECUTED FOR HIS SECOND WIFE, ISABEL OF LUXEMBOURG
  *TITLE OF MANUSCRIPT MIROUER HISTORIAL ABREGIE DE FRANCE
  *SHELFMARK MS BODLEY 968
  *PROVENANCE FRENCH AND LATIN
  *DATE EXECUTED 15TH/ BEFORE 1472
  *LANGUAGE FRENCH
  *TYPE OF MANUSCRIPT HISTORY

*CONTENTS HISTORY OF FRANCE/ SCENES OF 264/1-17, PROLOGUE WITH
GOD CROWNING KNEELING KING OF FRANCE 264-1, ROYAL ARMS OF
FRANCE ENCIRCLED BY TWO LILY SPRAYS 264-2, INITIAL/ FLORIATED
WITH FULL FLORAL BORDER 264-3, MAHOMET RECLINING IN GARDEN
264-4, SARACENS PLAYING WHILE ARMED MEN ENTER MOSQUE 264-5,
EMPEROR CONSTANTINE IV ENTHRONED WITH CLERICS 264-6, POPE
STEPHEN II CROWNS PEPIN AND HIS SONS 264-7, CHARLEMAGNE AND
HIS BROTHER KARLOMANNUS 264-8, MONKS OF ST MARTIN OF TOURS
KILLED 264-9, CHARLEMAGNE ENTHRONED HOLY ROMAN EMPEROR WITH
THREE SONS 264-10, VISION OF BISHOP TURPIN 264-11, ST JAMES
RESCUES SOUL OF CHARLEMAGNE FROM DEVILS 264-12, LOUIS THE
PIOUS ENTHRONED WITH FOUR SONS 264-13, DEVILS RUSH TO AIX TO
CLAIM SOUL OF CHARLEMAGNE 264-11, FORTENAY/ BATTLE OF 264-14,
HUGH CAPET AND SON ROBERT 264-15, HASTINGS/ BATTLE OF 264-16,
UNION OF CAPET LINE WITH DESCENDANTS OF CHARLEMAGNE 264-17

*$ABSTRACT 265
  *LIBRARY BOD
  *SLIDE SET TITLE LAPWORTH MISSAL
  *TITLE OF MANUSCRIPT LAPWORTH MISSAL
  *NEGATIVE REFERENCE ROLL 161
  *RENTAL FEE SM 265 $2.20
  *SHELFMARK MS C C C 394
  *PROVENANCE ENGLISH
  *DATE EXECUTED 14TH/ 1398
  *LANGUAGE LATIN
  *TYPE OF MANUSCRIPT MISSAL
  *CONTENTS MISSAL/ LAPWORTH 265/1-4, TEXT AND BORDERS AT
  BEGINNING OF TEMPORAL 265-1, CRUCIFIXION 265-2, INITIALS AND
  TEXT 265/3-4, MASS OF THE TRINITY 265-3, SANCTORALS/ BEGINNING
  265-4

*$ABSTRACT 266
  *LIBRARY BOD
  *SLIDE SET TITLE GAMES/ CHILDREN/ TOYS
  *NEGATIVE REFERENCE ROLL 162B
  *RENTAL FEE SM 266 $5.55
  *COMMENTS 71 SLIDES SELECTED FROM 16 MSS
  *TITLE OF MANUSCRIPT FONTES MEMORABILIUM 266/14 AND 69-70, LA
  COCHE OU LE DEBAT DE L'AMOUR 266-71, BEDE LIFE OF ST CUTHBERT
  266-1, ROMAN DE LANCELOT DU LAK 266-3, MEMORABILIA 266-11
  *SHELFMARK MS UNIVERSITY COLLEGE 165 266-1, MS DOUCE 118 266-2,
  MS ASHMOLE 828 266-3, MS DOUCE 5 266/4-6, MS DOUCE 6 266/7-10,
  MS DOUCE 202 266-11, MS DOUCE 62 266/12-13, MS BALLIOL 238E
  266/14 AND 69-70, MS DOUCE 8 266-15, MS DOUCE 135 266/16-29,
  MS DOUCE 276 266/30-65, MS BODLEY 602 266-66, MS AUCT D 4 17
  266-67, MS DOUCE 48 266-68, MS DOUCE 91 266-71
  *PROVENANCE ENGLISH 266/1 AND 66-67, FRENCH 266/2 AND 11-13 AND
  16-65 AND 68 AND 71, FLEMISH 266/3-10 AND 15, GERMAN 266/14
  AND 69-70
  *DATE EXECUTED 12TH 266/1 AND 66, 13TH 266/67-68, 14TH
  266/2-10, 15TH 266/11-15 AND 30-65 AND 69-71, 16TH 266/16-29
  *LANGUAGE LATIN
  *AUTHOR BEDE 266-1, VALERIUS MAXIMUS 266-11, DOMINICUS BANDINUS
  OF AREZZO 266/14 AND 69-70
  *TYPE OF MANUSCRIPT SAINT'S LIFE 266-1, PSALTER 266/2 AND 4-10,
  ROMANCE 266-3, VOTIVE OFFICES 266-15, BOOK OF HOURS 266/16-65
  AND 68, BESTIARY 266-66, APOCALYPSE 266-67
  *CONTENTS GAMES/ CHILDREN/ TOYS 266/1-71, ST CUTHBERT PLAYS
  SHINTY 266-1, HOBBY-HORSE 266-2, JUGGLING WITH TWO GOLDEN
  PLATES 266-3, SKATES AND TOBOGGAN AND BOYS 266-4, JOUSTING
  266-5, HOOP AND STICK AND FIGURE 266-6, SPINNING A TOP 266-7,
  BALL BOWLED TO BLIND BATSMAN 266-8, MONKEY ON STICK AND
  NINEPINS 266-9, MONKEY ON STILTS 266-10, WRESTLING OUTSIDE
  GYMNASIUM 266-11, BALL GAME 266-12, BALL GAME 266-13,
  CROQUET-LIKE GAME 266-14, CHILD SPINNING TOP 266-15, HOCKEY
  PLAYED BY FIVE CHILDREN 266-16, BLIND MAN'S BLUFF 266-17,
  PICK-A-BACK AND BLIND MAN'S BLUFF 266-18, BALL GAME 266-19,

137

SNOWBALLING 266-20, CHILD TRYING TO CATCH INSECT 266-21, B
266-22, BOYS PLAYING WITH BALL AND DEATH SEIZES ONE 266-2
CHILD IN CRADLE 266-24, BOY FOWLING WITH LONG-BOW 266-25, B
FOWLING WITH CROSS-BOW 266-26, BOY FOWLING 266-27, BIRDNESTI
266-28, BOY PICKING APPLES FROM TREE 266-29, SWIMMING A
SHOOTING AT POPINJAY 266-30, NAKED CHILDREN PLAYING 266-3
SCHOOLMASTER WITH BIRCH 266-32, PLAYING BOWLS 266-33, FIRI
GUNS AT TARGET AND ARCHERY PRACTICE 266-34, CHILDREN HOPPI
AND HOLDING OTHER'S FOOT 266-35, PIPE AND TABOR PLAYER A
TUMBLERS 266-36, PICKING APPLES 266-37, BEARS PLAYING GA
266-38, PIPE AND TABOR AND COUNTRY DANCE 266-39, GYMNASTIC
NAKED 266-40, FENCING WITH SWORD AND BUCKLER 266-41, PLAYI
BOWLS IN HURLING ALLEY 266-42, FIGURES ON GROUND PULLING STI
BETWEEN THEM 266-43, MORRIS DANCING 266-44, MAN IN CLOGS A
CHILDREN WITH WHIRLIGIGS 266-45, DOGS AND CHILDREN FIGHTI
AND BOY ON STILTS 266-46, ROWING AND SAILING CHILDREN 266-4
BLIND MAN'S BLUFF 266-48, FISHING WITH NET 266-49, CHILDR
PLAYING GAME OF STATUES OR QUEENIE 266/50-51, HOPPING 266-5
SHOOTING A WATERFOWL 266-54, ARCHERY PRACTICE 266-55, GAME
HOT COCKLERS 266-56, SHOOTING WITH BOW AND CROSS-BOW 266-5
FIGHTING WITH PLANTS 266-58, PROCESSION CARRYING RATTL
266-59, WOMAN COOKING 266-60, CHILD IN CRADLE 266-60, WOM
NURSING BABY 266-61, SCHOOLMASTER WITH BIRCH AND CHILDREN WI
WHIRLIGIGS 266-62, CHILDREN DOING GYMNASTICS 266-63, BALL GA
PLAYED BY CHILDREN 266-24, HOBBY-HORSES AND BOY 266-65, HOOD
CHILD CARRYING TWO BIRDS 266-66, FOOL WITH BLADDER ON STI
266-67, BOY WITH BIRD'S NEST 266-68, SCHOOLMASTER WHIPPI
SMALL BOY 266-68, BOYS CLIMBING TREE 266-70, BOYS WRESTLI
266-71

*CONTENTS PRIVATE PRAYERS AND DEVOTIONS 267/1-37, TITLEPAGE A
ARMS OF SCEPEAUX FAMILY 267-1, ANNUNCIATION 267-2, ST JOSE
OFFERS FRUIT TO CHRIST CHILD 267-3, ITALIAN BEAUTY/ TWO TYP
267-4, CRUCIFIXION 267-5, LOMBARDY/ A BEAUTY OF 267-
CORONATION OF VIRGIN 267-7, VIRGIN SUPPORTS CHRIST AFT
CRUCIFIXION 267-8, ST CHRISTOPHER CARRIES CHRIST CHILD 267-
ST SEBASTIAN/ MARTYRDOM 267-10, FLORENCE/ A BEAUTY OF 267-1
ST NICHOLAS REVIVES THE THREE CHILDREN IN PICKLING TUB 267-1,
VENICE/ A BEAUTY OF 267-13, ST CLAUDE BLESSES THE CHILD WI
WAS HANGED 267-14, ST ROCH SHOWS PLAGUE SPOT TO ANGEL 267-1
ST HUBERT KNEELS BEFORE CRUCIFIX BETWEEN STAG'S ANTLE
267-16, FERRARESE/ A BEAUTY OF PERHAPS 267-17, ST MARGARET
ANTIOCH BESIDE DRAGON 267-18, ST APPOLLONIA TORTURED 267-1
ST MARY MAGDALENE 267-20, GENOA/ A BEAUTY OF 267-21, SCEPEA
FAMILY KNEELS BEFORE SYMBOLS OF PASSION 267-22, GOD IN MAJES
267-23, ROME/ A BEAUTY OF 267-24, CRUCIFIXION 267-25, SPAIN/
BEAUTY OF 267-26, CHRIST AFTER SCOURGING SHOWN BY PILA
267-27, MEMBER OF SCEPEAUX FAMILY KNEELS BEFORE CHRIST 267-2
CHRIST IN GARDEN WITH DISCIPLES 267-29, TRINITY 267-30, CHRI
STANDS IN GARDEN 267-31, NAPLES/ A BEAUTY OF 267-32,
GREGORY SAYING MASS 267-33, ST LOUIS OR CONSTANTINE KNEE
BEFORE VIRGIN AND CHILD 267-34, FIGURE IN CROWN AND WHI
LEANING ON CROSS 267-35, CHRIST RISEN SEATED ON COFF
DISPLAYING WOUNDS 267-36, ARCHANGEL GABRIEL 267-37, GABRI
267-37

*$ABSTRACT 268
  *LIBRARY BOD
  *SLIDE SET TITLE ROMANESQUE LIFE OF CHRIST
  *NEGATIVE REFERENCE ROLL 165A
  *RENTAL FEE SM 268 $2.25
  *TITLE OF MANUSCRIPT LIFE OF CHRIST
  *SHELFMARK MS DOUCE 293
  *PROVENANCE ENGLISH
  *DATE EXECUTED 12TH
  *LANGUAGE LATIN
  *TYPE OF MANUSCRIPT LIFE OF CHRIST
  *CONTENTS LIFE OF CHRIST 268/1-5, ANNUNCIATION 268-1, NATIVITY
  WITH ANGEL SWINGING CENSER OVER BED 268-2, MIDWIFE 268-2,
  SHEPHERDS AND GOAT AND SHEEP   268-3, ADORATION OF THE MAGI
  268-4, FLIGHT INTO EGYPT 268-5

*$ABSTRACT 269
  *LIBRARY BOD
  *SLIDE SET TITLE GREGORY OF NAZIANUS
  *NEGATIVE REFERENCE ROLL 166A
  *RENTAL FEE SM 269 $2.80
  *COMMENTS SIXTEEN SERMONS OF GREGORY OF NAZIANUS PRECEDED BY
  ONE OF CHRYSOSTOM
  *SHELFMARK MS ROE 6
  *PROVENANCE BYZANTINE
  *DATE EXECUTED 13TH
  *LANGUAGE GREEK
  *AUTHOR GREGORY OF NAZIANUS
  *TYPE OF MANUSCRIPT SERMONS
  *CONTENTS SERMONS OF GREGORY NAZIANUS 269/1-16, CHRYSOSTOM
  SEATED WRITING 269-1, ANASTASIS 269-2, CHRIST IN HEAVEN WITH
  TWO ANGELS 269-3, PREACHER STANDING ON THE EARTH 269-3,
  PAPHLAGONIAN MARTYR MAMMAS 269-4, PENTECOST WITH THE DISCIPLES
  269-5, NATIVITY WITH ANGELS/ MAGI/ SHEPHERDS/ WOMEN WASHING
  CHILD 269-6, ST BASIL ON HIS BIER WITH MOURNERS 269-7, BAPTISM
  OF CHRIST 269-8, MARTYRS/ NINE IN HEAVEN 269-9, ST GREGORY OF
  NYSSA LISTENING TO ST GREGORY NAZIANZUS 269-10, ST GREGORY
  PREACHING TO 150 BISHOPS 269-11, ST ATHANASIUS 269-12, ST
  GREGORY PREACHING TO GROUP OF MEN 269-13, ELEAZAR AND WIFE AND
  SEVEN SONS 269-14, ST GREGORY 269-15, ST GREGORY EXHORTING THE
  PEOPLE 269-16

*$ABSTRACT 270
  *LIBRARY BOD
  *SLIDE SET TITLE HOURS
  *NEGATIVE REFERENCE ROLL 166D
  *RENTAL FEE SM 270 $2.85
  *SHELFMARK MS CANON LITURG 116 270/1-7, MS CANON LITURG 118
  270/8-17
  *PROVENANCE FLEMISH
  *DATE EXECUTED 15TH/C1400
  *LANGUAGE LATIN
  *ARTIST/ SCHOOL HERMAN SCHEERRE, MASTER OF BEAUFORT SAINTS
  *TYPE OF MANUSCRIPT BOOK OF HOURS/ USE OF ROME
  *CONTENTS BOOKS OF HOURS/ FLEMISH/ 15TH 270/1-17, PENTECOST
  270-1, VIRGIN AND CHILD 270-2, CRUCIFIXION 270-3, ANNUNCIATION
  270-4, PAGE/ WHOLE AND BORDER 270-5, LAST JUDGMENT 270-6,
  ANNUNCIATION 270-7, ST JOHN THE BAPTIST 270-8, ST MARY
  MAGDALENE 270-9, ST CHRISTOPHER 270-10, ST CATHERINE 270-11,
  ST AGNES 270-12, CRUCIFIXION 270-13, PAGE/ WHOLE WITH TEXT
  270-14, VIRGIN AND CHILD 270-15, LAST JUDGMENT 270-16, VIGIL
  OF THE DEAD 270-17

*$ABSTRACT 271
  *LIBRARY BOD
  *SLIDE SET TITLE HOURS/ DUTCH

139

*NEGATIVE REFERENCE ROLL 166E
*RENTAL FEE SM 271 $2.60
*SHELFMARK MS CANON LITURG 276
*PROVENANCE DUTCH
*DATE EXECUTED 15TH/ EARLY
*LANGUAGE LATIN
*ARTIST/ SCHOOL HERMAN SCHEERRE
*TYPE OF MANUSCRIPT BOOK OF HOURS/ USE OF ROME
*CONTENTS BOOK OF HOURS/ DUTCH/ 15TH 271/1-12, ANNUNCIATION
271-1, AGONY IN THE GARDEN 271-2, VISITATION 271-3, CHRIST
BEFORE PONTIUS PILATE 271/4-5, FLAGELLATION 271-6, ROAD TO
CALVARY 271-7, CRUCIFIXION 271-8, LAST JUDGMENT 271-9, VIGIL
OF THE DEAD 271-10, BORDER WITH TEXT 271-11, DEPOSITION AND
FACING BORDER 271-12

*$ABSTRACT 272
  *LIBRARY BOD
  *SLIDE SET TITLE MACROBIUS
  *NEGATIVE REFERENCE ROLL 218E
  *RENTAL FEE SM 272 $2.15
  *TITLE OF MANUSCRIPT DE SOMNIO SCIPIONIS
  *SHELFMARK MS CANON CLASS LAT 257
  *PROVENANCE ITALIAN/ BOLOGNA
  *DATE EXECUTED 14TH/ 1383
  *LANGUAGE LATIN
  *TYPE OF MANUSCRIPT COMMENTARY ON CICERO'S SOMNIUM SCIPIONIS
  *CONTENTS MACROBIUS/ COMMENTARY ON SOMNIUM SCIPIONIS 272/1-3,
  DREAMS/ TREATISE ON 272/1-3, SOMNIUM SCIPIONIS/ MACROBIUS
  COMMENTARY 272/1-3, MACROBIUS PORTRAIT 272-1, SCIPIO AND KING
  MASINISSA 272-1, HEAVENLY SPHERES 272-1, SCIPIO ASLEEP IN BED
  272-2, HEAVENLY SPHERE/ ROME AND CARTHAGE IN CENTER 272-2,
  ROME AND CARTHAGE IN HEAVENLY SPHERE 272-2, MACROBIUS WRITING
  AT DESK 272-3

*$ABSTRACT 273
  *LIBRARY BOD
  *SLIDE SET TITLE HOURS/ ENGLISH
  *NEGATIVE REFERENCE ROLL 166F
  *RENTAL FEE SM 273 $2.85
  *SHELFMARK MS GOUGH LITURG 6 273/1-8, MS RAWL LITURG D 1
  273/9-17
  *PROVENANCE ENGLISH
  *DATE EXECUTED 15TH/ EARLY
  *LANGUAGE LATIN
  *ARTIST/ SCHOOL HERMAN SCHEERRE
  *TYPE OF MANUSCRIPT BOOK OF HOURS/ SARUM USE
  *CONTENTS BOOK OF HOURS 273/1-17, PETER STRIKING OFF EAR OF
  MALCHUS 273-1, CHRIST BEFORE PONTIUS PILATE 273-3, ROAD TO
  CALVARY 273-4, DEPOSITION 273-5, ENTOMBMENT 273-6, GOD
  CARRYING SOULS TO HEAVEN 273-7, INITIAL/ DECORATED AND BORDER
  273-8, AGONY IN GARDEN 273-9, CHRIST HEALING MALCHUS' EAR
  273-10, DEPOSITION 273-11, ENTOMBMENT 273-12, OFFICE OF THE
  DEAD 273-13, GOD BEARING SOULS TO HEAVEN 273-14, CRUCIFIXION
  IN INITIAL 273-15, INITIAL WITH VIRGIN AND CHILD AND ST JOHN
  EVANGELIST 273-16, INITIAL/ HISTORIATED 273/15-17

*$ABSTRACT 274
  *LIBRARY BOD
  *SLIDE SET TITLE BONA SFORZA HOURS
  *NEGATIVE REFERENCE ROLL 166G
  *RENTAL FEE SM 274 $2.75
  *COMMENTS MADE FOR BONA SFORZA/ WIFE OF KING OF POLAND
  *TITLE OF MANUSCRIPT BONA SFORZA HOURS
  *SHELFMARK MS DOUCE 40
  *PROVENANCE GERMAN
  *DATE EXECUTED 16TH/1527-8

140

*LANGUAGE LATIN
*ARTIST/ SCHOOL STANISLAS OF MOGILA
*TYPE OF MANUSCRIPT BOOK OF HOURS/ USE OF ROME
*CONTENTS BOOK OF HOURS 274/1-15, AGONY IN GARDEN 274-1,
INITIALS SBP 274-1, ANNUNCIATION 274-2, ARMS OF
SFORZA-VISCONTI 274-2, VISITATION 274-3, NATIVITY 274-4, ANGEL
APPEARS TO SHEPHERDS 274-5, ADORATION OF MAGI 274-6,
PRESENTATION IN TEMPLE 274-7, FLIGHT INTO EGYPT 274-8,
MASSACRE OF INNOCENTS 274-9, VIRGIN AND CHILD 274-10, GOD
APPEARS TO DAVID AS HE KNEELS IN PRAYER 274-11, LAST JUDGMENT
274-12, CRUCIFIXION 274-13, STABAT MATER 274-14, PENTECOST
274-15

*$ABSTRACT 275
*LIBRARY BOD
*SLIDE SET TITLE FLORENTINE SCRIBES OF FIRST HALF OF FIFTEENTH
CENTURY
*NEGATIVE REFERENCE ROLL 1661
*RENTAL FEE SM 275 $3.00
*TITLE OF MANUSCRIPT LETTERS 275-1, DE ORATORE 275-2, PRO C
RABIRIO POSTUMO 275-3, CATIL I DE LEGE AGRARIA 275/4-5, DE
ORATORE 275-6, DE SACERDOTE CHRISTI 275/8-9, VERRINES 275-10,
NATURAL HISTORY 275-13, DE SENECTUTTE 275/14 AND 16, LETTERS
275/17-18
*SHELFMARK MS LAUD LAT 70 275-1, MS LAT CLASS D 37 275-2, MS
D/ORVILLE 78 275-3, MS NEW COLLEGE 249 275/4-5, MS BALLIOL
248E 275-6, MS BALLIOL 154 275-7, MS BALLIOL 78B 275/8-9, MS
BALLIOL 248B 275-10, MS CANON CLASS LAT 274 275-11, MS DIGBY
231 275-12, MS BALLIOL 249 275-13, MS AUCT F 1 12 275-14, MS
NEW COLLEGE 277 275-15, MS BALLIOL 248D 275-16, MS BALLIOL
248C 275-17, MS LINCOLN COLLEGE LAT 42 275-18, MS LINCOLN
COLLEGE LAT 47 275-19, MS LINCOLN COLLEGE LAT 59 275-20
*PROVENANCE ITALIAN/ FLORENCE
*DATE EXECUTED 15TH
*LANGUAGE LATIN
*AUTHOR SENECA 275-1, CICERO 275/2-6 AND 10 AND 12 AND 14 AND
16-18, CHRYSOSTOM/ JOHN 275-7, JOHANNES CLIMACUS 275/8-9,
VEGETIUS 275-11, PLINY 275-13, LIVY 275-15, CYPRIAN 275-19,
AULUS GELLIUS 275-20
*ARTIST/ SCHOOL GIOVANNI ARETINO 275-3, ANTONIO DI MARIO
275/4-9, GHERARDO DE CIRIAGIO 275-10
*TYPE OF MANUSCRIPT MISCELLANY
*CONTENTS SCRIBES/ FLORENTINE 275/1-20, HANDWRITING/ FLORENTINE
275/1-20, PALEOGRAPHY 275/1-20, SCRIPT 275/1-20, INITIAL/
HUMANISTIC 275-2, INITIAL 275/2-5 AND 10-20, CAPITALS/ GOLD
275-7

*$ABSTRACT 276
*LIBRARY BOD
*SLIDE SET TITLE ST AUGUSTINE/ COMMENTARIES ON THE PSALMS
*NEGATIVE REFERENCE ROLL 167B
*RENTAL FEE SM 276 $2.35
*TITLE OF MANUSCRIPT COMMENTARIES ON THE PSALMS
*SHELFMARK MS BODLEY 269
*PROVENANCE ENGLISH/ EYNSHAM
*DATE EXECUTED 12TH
*LANGUAGE LATIN
*AUTHOR ST AUGUSTINE
*TYPE OF MANUSCRIPT COMMENTARY
*CONTENTS ST AUGUSTINE/ COMMENTARIES ON PSALMS 276/1-7, VIRGIN
AND CHILD IN EIGHT-SHAPED FIGURE 276-1, VIRGIN AND CHILD
276/2-3, CAPITAL E WITH HEADS OF ANIMALS/ MEN AND LEAVES
276-4, INITIAL E 276-5, INITIAL P 276-6, DRAGON IN BORDER
276-6, INITIAL B IN RED INK AND PURPLE FLOURISHES 276-7

*\$ABSTRACT 277
  *LIBRARY BOD
  *SLIDE SET TITLE ST JEROME/ COMMENTARY ON ISAIAH
  *NEGATIVE REFERENCE ROLL 167E
  *RENTAL FEE SM 277 $2.60
  *TITLE OF MANUSCRIPT COMMENTARY ON ISAIAH
  *SHELFMARK MS BODLEY 717
  *PROVENANCE ENGLISH/ EXETER
  *DATE EXECUTED 12TH/ EARLY
  *LANGUAGE LATIN
  *AUTHOR ST JEROME
  *TYPE OF MANUSCRIPT COMMENTARY
  *CONTENTS ST JEROME'S COMMENTARY ON ISAIAH 277/1-12, ISAIAH
  HOLDING SCROLL IN HANDS UNDER ARCH 277-1, ISAIAH/ FACE AND
  BUST 277-2, ST JEROME WRITING AND ST EUSTOCHIUM 277/3-4,
  INITIAL E WITH ACANTHUS AND ANIMAL INTERLACE 277-5, INITIAL OF
  MARY 277-6, INITIAL OF JEROME 277-7, INITIAL U WITH CHRIST AND
  DISCIPLES AND ISAIAH 277-8, INITIAL U AND INITIAL P WITH EAGLE
  IN LOOP 277-9, INITIAL P WITH ACANTHUS LEAVES AND ANIMAL'S
  HEADS 277-10, HUGO PICTOR/ ILLUMINATOR OF MANUSCRIPT'S
  SELF-PORTRAIT 277-12

*\$ABSTRACT 278
  *LIBRARY BOD
  *SLIDE SET TITLE ROMANESQUE LIFE OF CHRIST AND PSALTER
  *NEGATIVE REFERENCE ROLL 167F
  *RENTAL FEE SM 278 $2.60
  *SHELFMARK MS DOUCE 293
  *PROVENANCE ENGLISH/ DURHAM
  *DATE EXECUTED 12TH
  *LANGUAGE LATIN
  *TYPE OF MANUSCRIPT LIFE OF CHRIST AND PSALTER
  *CONTENTS ROMANESQUE LIFE OF CHRIST AND PSALTER 278/1-12,
  PRESENTATION IN TEMPLE 278-1, SIMEON/ DOVES/ VIRGIN AND CHILD/
  SERVANT 278-1, LAST SUPPER/ CHRIST WASHING FEET OF PETER AND
  DISCIPLES 278-2, BETRAYAL OF CHRIST WITH JUDAS EMBRACING HIM
  278-3, CROWN OF THORNS PLACED ON CHRIST'S HEAD 278-4,
  FLAGELLATION WITH CHRIST TIED AND BLINDFOLDED 278-5,
  CRUCIFIXION WITH VIRGIN MARY AND ST JOHN 278-6, CHRIST ON
  CROSS 278-7, VIRGIN WITH CHILD 278-8, VIRGIN ENTHRONED WITH
  CHILD 278-9, CHRIST ENTHRONED WITH SYMBOLS OF FOUR EVANGELISTS
  IN CORNER 278-10, CHRIST 278-11, INITIAL/ GOLD FILLED WITH RED
  AND PURPLE INTERLACE 278-12

*\$ABSTRACT 279
  *LIBRARY BOD
  *SLIDE SET TITLE DANCES FROM THE ROMANCE OF ALEXANDER
  *NEGATIVE REFERENCE ROLL 168B
  *RENTAL FEE SM 279 $2.50
  *TITLE OF MANUSCRIPT ROMANCE OF ALEXANDER
  *SHELFMARK MS BODLEY 264
  *PROVENANCE FLEMISH
  *DATE EXECUTED 14TH
  *LANGUAGE FRENCH
  *ARTIST/ SCHOOL JEHAN DE GRISE
  *TYPE OF MANUSCRIPT ROMANCE
  *CONTENTS ROMANCE OF ALEXANDER 279/1-10, LITERATURE/ ROMANCE OF
  ALEXANDER 279/1-10, DANCES 279/1-10, FIGURES WEARING HOODS
  279-1, LEAPING FIGURES WITH THREE TRUMPETERS 279-2, BEASTS
  WITH CHAIN AND BEAST PLAYING INSTRUMENT 279-3, DANCING FIGURES
  IN HOODS 279-4, LADIES ACCOMPANIED BY VIOL PLAYER 279-5,
  COUPLES DANCING WITH ANIMALS/ DRUMMER/ MAN 279-6, HAND BELL
  RINGER/ COUPLE/ LADY/ DRUMMER/ ANIMAL 279-7, DRUMMER/ MAN
  DANCING WITH BEAR/ CHAINED BEAST 279-8, VIOL PLAYER/ DANCERS/
  PORTATIVE ORGAN/ LADIES IN CIRCLE 279-9, DRUMMER AND SEVEN
  DANCING MEN/ CYMBALIST 279-10, LADIES DANCING/ MAN WITH BELLS
  279-10

*$ABSTRACT 280
  *LIBRARY BOD
  *SLIDE SET TITLE FIFTEENTH CENTURY BOOKS OF HOURS
  *NEGATIVE REFERENCE ROLL 168G
  *RENTAL FEE SM 280 $4.30
  *SHELFMARK MS DOUCE 93 280/1-37, MS LITURG 100 280/38-44, MS
  BARLOW 47 280-45, MS CANON LITURG 252 280-46
  *PROVENANCE DUTCH/ UTRECHT 280/1-37, FRENCH 280/38-45, FLEMISH/
  BRUGGES 280-46
  *DATE EXECUTED 15TH
  *LANGUAGE LATIN
  *TYPE OF MANUSCRIPT BOOK OF HOURS
  *CONTENTS BOOKS OF HOURS 280/1-46, SS JOHN AND LUKE WRITING
  280-1, ANNUNCIATION AND VIRGIN IN PRAYER 280-2, VISITATION
  280-3, NATIVITY AND ADORATION 280-4, ADORATION OF MAGI 280-5,
  PRESENTATION IN THE TEMPLE 280-6, FLIGHT INTO EGYPT 280-6,
  MASSACRE OF INNOCENTS 280-7, CHRIST AMONG THE DOCTORS 280-8,
  DEATH OF VIRGIN AND ASSUMPTION 280-9, TRINITY 280-10, LAST
  JUDGMENT 280-11, DAVID WITH HARP 280-11, FUNERAL SERVICE WITH
  THREE QUICK AND THREE DEAD KINGS 280-12, BETRAYAL OF CHRIST
  280-13, CHRIST BEFORE PILATE AND ROAD TO CALVARY 280-14,
  CHRIST BEING NAILED TO CROSS 280-15, DESCENT FROM CROSS/
  ENTOMBMENT/ ASCENSION 280-16, VIRGIN AND CHILD ENTHRONED AND
  CORONATION OF VIRGIN 280-17, VIRGIN AND CHILD STANDING ON
  CRESCENT MOON 280-18, ST VERONICA'S HANDKERCHIEF 280-19, MASS
  OF ST GREGORY 280-19, PENTECOST 280-20, ST BERNARD 280-21, ST
  MICHAEL SLAYING DRAGON WITH ST JOHN BAPTIST 280-22, ST JOHN
  EVANGELIST/ ST ANDREW/ ST CHRISTOPHER 280-23, ST JAMES AS
  PILGRIM 280-23, ST NICHOLAS/ ST GEORGE SLAYING DRAGON/ ST
  SEBASTIAN 280-24, SS ANTHONY/ BARBARA/ CATHERINE/ MARY
  MAGDALENE 280-25, SS ANNE/ MARGARET/ BRIGITTE/ DOROTHY 280-26,
  SS NICASIUS/ JUOCUS/ ALL ANGELS AND ST MARTIN 280-27, ST
  LEONARD/ ST GERTRUDE/ APPOLONIA/ AND 10000 VIRGINS 280-28, SS
  BLAISE/ AGATHA/ QUINTIN 280-29, ST LAURENCE 280-30,
  CRUCIFIXION WITH MARY THE VIRGIN/ ST JOHN EVANGELIST/ CHURCH
  280-31, ST ANASTAIUS 280-32, BEAR AND BIRD IN BORDER 280-33,
  WRESTLERS AND FIGURE WITH SWORD 280-35, VIRGIN ON CRESCENT
  MOON WITH CHRIST CHILD 280-35, CHRIST HOLDING ORB 280-36, MAN
  OF SORROWS/ WHITE DOG IN BORDER 280-27, ANNUNCIATION 280-38,
  CRUCIFIXION 280-39, PENTECOST 280-40, PENITENTIAL PSALMS
  280-41, FUNERAL SERVICE 280-42, DECORATIVE BORDER 280-45,
  VIRGIN HOLDING CHILD 280-46

*$ABSTRACT 281
  *LIBRARY BOD
  *SLIDE SET TITLE SACRAMENTARY
  *NEGATIVE REFERENCE ROLL 169D
  *RENTAL FEE SM 281 $2.45
  *TITLE OF MANUSCRIPT GREGORIAN SACRAMENTARY
  *SHELFMARK MS CANON LITURG 319
  *PROVENANCE GERMAN/ REICHENAU
  *DATE EXECUTED 10TH
  *LANGUAGE LATIN
  *TYPE OF MANUSCRIPT SACRAMENTARY
  *CONTENTS SACRAMENTARY GERMAN 281/1-9, INITIAL IN GOLD AND
  INTRODUCTION 281-1, CRUCIFIXION 281-2, NATIVITY ABOVE AND
  SHEPHERDS BELOW 281-3, ANGEL ADDRESSING THREE MARYS AT EMPTY
  TOMB 281-4, ASCENSION 281-5, PENTECOST 281-6, INITIAL/ SMALL
  COLORED AND WHOLE PAGE SHOWN 281/7-9

*$ABSTRACT 282
  *LIBRARY BOD
  *SLIDE SET TITLE LIFE OF CHRIST FROM A BOOK OF HOURS
  *NEGATIVE REFERENCE ROLL 169G
  *RENTAL FEE SM 282 $2.65
  *COMMENTS BOOK OF HOURS BELIEVED TO HAVE BELONGED TO HENRY VII
  AND HENRY VIII
  *SHELFMARK MS AUCT INF D 2 11

143

*PROVENANCE FRENCH/ NORMANDY
*DATE EXECUTED 15TH/C1440-50
*LANGUAGE LATIN AND FRENCH
*ARTIST/ SCHOOL MASTER OF SIR JOHN FASTOLF
*TYPE OF MANUSCRIPT BOOK OF HOURS/ USE OF SARUM
*CONTENTS BOOK OF HOURS/ FRENCH/ 15TH 282/1-13, LIFE OF CHRIST
282/1-13, VISITATION 282-1, NATIVITY 282-2, ANGELS AND
SHEPHERDS 282-3, ADORATION OF THE MAGI 282-4, PRESENTATION IN
THE TEMPLE 282-5, FLIGHT INTO EGYPT 282-6, BETRAYAL OF CHRIST
282-7, CHRIST BEFORE PILATE 282-8, FLAGELLATION 282-9, ROAD TO
CALVARY 282-10, CRUCIFIXION 282-11, DESCENT FROM CROSS 282-12,
ENTOMBMENT 282-13

*$ABSTRACT 283
  *LIBRARY BOD
  *SLIDE SET TITLE VULGATE BIBLE
  *NEGATIVE REFERENCE ROLL 171A
  *RENTAL FEE SM 283 $3.25
  *SHELFMARK MS AUCT D 3 5
  *PROVENANCE ENGLISH
  *DATE EXECUTED 13TH/ MIDDLE
  *LANGUAGE LATIN
  *TYPE OF MANUSCRIPT BIBLE/ VULGATE
  *CONTENTS BIBLE/ VULGATE 283/1-78, SYNAGOGUE WITH STONE TABLET
AND BROKEN LANCE 283-1, ST JEROME WRITING 283-2, INITIAL I/
GOD SEATED AND SIX DAYS OF CREATION 283-3, CREATION 283-3,
MOSES HORNED LEADING ISRAELITES 283-4, SACRIFICE OF KID AND
CALF 283-5, MOSES COUTS ISRAELITES 283-6, MOSES GIVES LAW TO
ISRAELITES 283-7, JOSHUA EXHORTS ISRAELITES 283-8, JUDGE AND
PEOPLE 283-9, HANNAH AND ELKANAH OFFER SAMUEL TO ELI 283-10,
DAVID LAMENTS SAUL AND JONATHAN 283-11, ZADOC ANOINTS SOLOMON
283-12, AHAZIAH VISITED BY ELIJAH 283-13, ADAM AND HIS
DESCENDANTS 283-14, SOLOMON 283-15, EZRA WRITING 283-16,
NEHEMIAH BEFORE ARTAXERXES 283-17, TOBIT ASLEEP/ TOBIT AND
TOBIAS IN FOREGROUND 283-18, JUDITH ABOUT TO CHOP OFF
HOLOFERNE'S HEAD 283-19, HAMAN ON CROSS 283-20, JOB 283-21,
DAVID AND LION/ DAVID AND HARP 283-22, BEATUS VIR 283-22,
INITIAL I/ ILLUMINATION MEA/ DAVID AND GOD 283-23, INITIAL D/
DIXIT CUSTODIAM/ DAVID POINTS TO MOUTH 283-24, INITIAL Q/ QUID
GLORIARIS 283-25, DAVID AND GOLIATH/ FOOL 283-25, INITIAL S/
SALVUM ME FAC/ DAVID IN WATER 283-26, INITIAL L/ LAUDATE DEO
AND EXULTATE DEO 283-27, JACOB WRESTLES WITH ANGEL 283-27,
DAVID SEATED AT DESK/ FRIAR KNEELING 283-28, INITIAL C/
CANTATE 283-28, INITIAL D/ DOMINE EXAUDI 283-28, INITIAL D/
DIXIT DOMINUS 283-29, SOLOMON 283/30-31, SONG OF SONGS 283-32,
MAN BEFORE JUDGE 283-33, PREACHER 283-34, ISAIAH'S DEATH
283-35, JEREMIAH 283-36, LAMENTATIONS 283-37, EZEKIEL BEFORE
BABYLON 283-38, NEBUCHADNEZZAR'S DREAM 283-39, HOSEA 283-40,
JOEL 283-41, AMOS 283-42, OBADIAH 283/43-44, JONAH 283-44,
MICAH 283-45, NAHUM AND HAND OF GOD 283-46, HABAKKUK OFFERS
FOOD TO DANIEL IN LION'S DEN 283-47, ZEPHANIAH 283-48, HAGGAI
283-49, ZECHARIAH 283-50, MALACHI 283-51, MATHATHIAS WITH SONS
AND ISRAELITES 283-52, MACCABEUS GIVES BOOK FOR EGYPT 283-53,
CHURCH AS CROWNED WOMAN 283-54, JESSE/ TREE 283-55, ST MARK'S
LION 283-56, ST LUKE'S OX 283-57, ST JOHN'S EAGLE 283-58,
ASCENSION 283-59, CONVERSION OF ST PAUL 283-60, ST PAUL BLIND
LED TO WALLS OF DAMASCUS 283-61, ST PAUL PRAYS 283-62, ST PAUL
RECOVERS HIS SIGHT 283-63, ST PAUL 283-64, ST PAUL AT LYSTRA
283-65, ST PAUL BAPTISED 283-66, ST PAUL PREACHING 283-67, ST
PAUL DRIVEN OUT OF ASIAN CITY 283-68, ST PAUL GIVES BOOK TO
MESSENGER 283-69, ST PAUL 283-70, ST PAUL ADDRESSES TITUS
283-71, ST PAUL'S MARTYRDOM/ HAND OF GOD 283-72, ST JAMES
283-73, ST PETER 283-74, ST PETER AND HAND OF GOD 283-75, ST
JOHN IN CHURCH 283-76, ST JUDE 283-77, ST JOHN 283-78

*$ABSTRACT 284
  *LIBRARY BOD
  *SLIDE SET TITLE PAGES FROM A PSALTER

*NEGATIVE REFERENCE ROLL 171B
*RENTAL FEE SM 284 $3.00
*SHELFMARK MS DOUCE 293
*PROVENANCE ENGLISH/ NORTH POSSIBLY DURHAM
*DATE EXECUTED 12TH/C1170-83
*LANGUAGE LATIN
*TYPE OF MANUSCRIPT PSALTER
*CONTENTS PSALTER 284/1-20, TOMB AND APOSTLES WITH SOLDIERS   ON
GROUND 284-1, HARROWING OF HELL AND CHRIST BEFORE HELL'S MOUTH
284-2, RESURRECTION WITH ANGEL APPEARING TO THREE MARYS 284-3,
PSALM I/ BEATUS VIR 284-4, INITIAL/ DECORATIVE 284/5 AND 8-9
AND 17-18 AND 20, INITIAL/ INHABITED 7 AND 10-11 AND 19, DEUS
DEUS MEUS 284-5, DOMINUS ILLUMINATIO MEA WITH DAVID UNDER ARCH
HANDS CROSSED 284-6, DIXI CUSTODIAM 284-7, QUID GLORIARIS
284-8, DIXIT INSIPIENS 284-9, SALVUM ME FAC 284-10, EXULTATE
284/11-12, CANTATE DOMINO/ MEN WITH ANGEL'S HEAD AND WINGS
284-13, DIXIT DOMINUS/ FATHER AND SON SEATED 284-14, DILEXI
QUONIAM 284-15, LETATUS SUM/ WINGED SERPENT FORMS INITIAL
284-16, NISI DOMINUS 284-17, MEMENTO DOMINE 284-18, CONFITEBOR
TIBI DOMINE 284-19, BENEDICTUS 284-20

*$ABSTRACT 285
  *LIBRARY BOD
  *SLIDE SET TITLE AUGUSTINIAN PSALTER/ PSALM INITIALS
  *NEGATIVE REFERENCE ROLL 171C
  *RENTAL FEE SM 285 $2.50
  *SHELFMARK MS LITURG 198
  *PROVENANCE ENGLISH/ NORTHEAST
  *DATE EXECUTED 14TH
  *LANGUAGE LATIN
  *TYPE OF MANUSCRIPT PSALTER/ AUGUSTINIAN
  *CONTENTS PSALTER 285/1-10, INITIALS/ PSALM 285/1-10, BEATUS
VIR/ EVANGELISTS/ VIRGIN AND CHILD/ JESSE AND DAVID 285-1,
DOMINUS ILLUMINATIO MEA/ DAVID KNEELING POINTS TO EYES 285-2,
DIXI CUSTODIAM/ DAVID POINTS TO MOUTH 285-3, QUID GLORIARIS
285-4, GOLIATH AS KNIGHT SLAIN BY DAVID 285-4,   DIXIT
INSIPIENS/ DAVID THRUSTS SWORD INTO HIS HEART 285-5, SALVUM ME
FAC/ JONAH IN MOUTH OF WHALE 285-6, EXULTATE/ DAVID WITH
CLAW-HAMMER STRIKES BELLS 285-7, CANTATE DOMINO/ ROBED FIGURES
IN FRONT OF LECTERN 285-8, DOMINE EXAUDI/ WOMAN IN PRAYER
BEFORE ALTAR AND PORTRAIT 285-9, DIXIT DOMINUS/ SEATED FIGURES
OF GOD 285-10

*$ABSTRACT 286
  *LIBRARY BOD
  *SLIDE SET TITLE PSALM INITIALS FROM A BENEDICTINE CHOIR
PSALTER
  *NEGATIVE REFERENCE ROLL 171D
  *RENTAL FEE SM 286 $2.45
  *SHELFMARK MS AUCT D 2 2
  *PROVENANCE ENGLISH/ CANTERBURY/ CHRIST CHURCH CATHEDRAL PRIORY
  *DATE EXECUTED 14TH/ AFTER 1320
  *LANGUAGE LATIN
  *TYPE OF MANUSCRIPT PSALTER/ BENEDICTINE CHOIR/ GALLICAN USE
  *CONTENTS PSALTER 286/1-9, INITIALS/ PSALM 286/1-9, BEATUS VIR/
DAVID PLAYING HARP/ DAVID BEFORE GOLIATH 286-1, DOMINUS
ILLUMINATIO/ DAVID POINTS TO EYES 286-2, DIXI CUSTODIAM/ DAVID
CROWNED KNEELING WITH SCEPTER 286-3, QUID GLORIARIS / DAVID
AND FOOL 286-4, DIXIT INSIPIENS/ SUICIDE/ SAUL PLUNGES SWORD
INTO BREAST 286-5, SALVUM ME FAC/ JONAH AND WHALE/ NINEVEH
286-6, EXULTATE/ DAVID AND ANGELS MAKING MUSIC/   ORGAN/
BELLOWS/ BELLS 286-7, CANTATE/ MONKS IN COPES SINGING FROM
BOOK ON LECTERN 286-7, DIXIT DOMINUS/ TRINITY/ GOD WITH CHRIST
AND HOLY GHOST 286-9

145

*$ABSTRACT 287
  *LIBRARY BOD
  *SLIDE SET TITLE LIFE OF CHRIST AND PSALM INITIALS
  *NEGATIVE REFERENCE ROLL 171E
  *RENTAL FEE SM 287 $2.95
  *SHELFMARK MS GOUGH LITURG 8
  *PROVENANCE ENGLISH
  *DATE EXECUTED 14TH/C1300
  *LANGUAGE LATIN
  *ARTIST/ SCHOOL RELATED TO MASTER OF THE QUEEN MARY PSALTER
  *TYPE OF MANUSCRIPT LIFE OF CHRIST
  *CONTENTS LIFE OF CHRIST 287/1-19, PSALM INITIALS 287/1-19,
  NATIVITY/ MARY ASLEEP IN FOREGROUND/ OX/ ASS 287-1, GLORIA IN
  EXCELSIS/ SHEPHERDS AND SHEEP 287-2, MASSACRE OF INNOCENTS
  287-3, BAPTISM OF CHRIST/ ANGEL HOLDING HIS ROBES 287-4,
  JOSEPH AT FOOT OF BED WITH VIRGIN/ BARE-FOOTED MAN 282-5,
  ANGEL WARNS JOSEPH 287-6, TEMPTATION/ DEVIL OFFERS STONES TO
  JESUS 287-7, CHRIST'S TRIUMPHAL ENTRY INTO JERUSALEM 287-8,
  MAGI/ ELDEST KNEELS CROWN ON FLOOR 287-9, MAGI IN BED WARNED
  BY ANGEL 287-10, PRESENTATION OF CHRIST 287-11, FLIGHT INTO
  EGYPT/ IDOLS FALL DOWN 287-12, CHRIST IN GARDEN OF GETHSEMANE
  287-13, BETRAYAL/ ST PETER CUTTING OFF MALCHUS@ EAR 287-14,
  DOMINUS ILLUMINATIO MEA/ MEN ANNOINT DAVID 287-15, DIXIT
  INSIPIENS/ DAVID AND FOOL WITH GOD'S HEAD ABOVE 287-16, SALVUM
  ME FAC 287-17, DAVID IN WATER CALLS FOR GOD TO HELP 287-17,
  EXULTATE/ DAVID PLAYING ON SET OF BELLS 287-18, DIXIT DOMINUS/
  TRINITY 287-19

*$ABSTRACT 288
  *LIBRARY BOD
  *SLIDE SET TITLE BATHS IN NATIVITY SCENES
  *NEGATIVE REFERENCE ROLL 171H
  *RENTAL FEE SM 288 $2.35
  *SHELFMARK MS LAUD MISC 93 288-1, MS DOUCE 313 288-2, MS RAWL B
  484 288-3, MS RAWL LITURG E 12 288-4, MS CANON ITAL 280
  288/5-7
  *PROVENANCE FRENCH 288/1-2 AND 4, ENGLISH 288-3, ITALIAN
  288/5-8
  *DATE EXECUTED 10TH 288-3, 14TH 288-2, 15TH 288/1 AND 4-7
  *LANGUAGE LATIN
  *TYPE OF MANUSCRIPT MISCELLANY
  *CONTENTS BATHS IN NATIVITY SCENES 288/1-7, NATIVITY SCENES
  288/1-7, VIRGIN BEING WASHED IN OVAL BATH TUB 288-1, VIRGIN
  BEING WASHED IN TROUGH-SHAPED BATH TUB 288-2, BATHING OF
  CHRIST CHILD IN ROUND TUB 288-3, WASHING OF INFANT CHRIST/
  WATER TUB AND JUG 288-4, CHRIST BEING WASHED IN BATHTUB 288-5,
  CHRIST BEING WASHED OVER BATHTUB 288-7

*$ABSTRACT 289
  *LIBRARY BOD
  *SLIDE SET TITLE WASHING OF HANDS
  *NEGATIVE REFERENCE ROLL 172F
  *RENTAL FEE SM 289 $2.70
  *TITLE OF MANUSCRIPT ROMAN DE LA ROSE 289/1 AND 3, ROMANS DE
  CASSAMUS OF LES VOEUX DU PAON 288-2, MEDITATIONS ON LIFE OF
  CHRIST 289-4, SPECULUM HUMANAE SALVATIONIS 289-5
  *SHELFMARK MS SELDEN SUPR 57 289-1, MS DOUCE 308 289-2, MS
  DOUCE 371 289-3, MS C C C 410 289-4, MS C C C 161 289-5, MS
  DOUCE 93 289-6, MS LITURG 400 289-7, MS DOUCE 39 289-8, MS
  DOUCE 51 289-9, MS BUCHANAN E 4 289-10, MS LITURG 41 289-11,
  MS DOUCE 14 289-12, MS CANON ITAL 280 289/13-14
  *PROVENANCE FRENCH 289/1-3 AND 8 AND 10-11, ENGLISH 289-5,
  FLEMISH 289/7 AND 9, ITALIAN 289/4 AND 12-14
  *DATE EXECUTED 14TH 289/1-2 AND 4 AND 8, 15TH 289/3 AND 5-7 AND
  9-14
  *LANGUAGE FRENCH 289/1-3, LATIN 289/4-14
  *TYPE OF MANUSCRIPT ROMANCE 289/1-3, BOOK OF HOURS 289/6-12,
  LIFE OF THE VIRGIN 289/13-14

*CONTENTS WASHING OF HANDS 289/1-14, WASH BASIN ON STAND IN
AUTHOR'S BEDROOM 289-1, BOYS HOLD BOWL AND POUR WATER FOR
ALEXANDER 289-2, MAN WASHES HANDS IN BASIN ATTACHED TO CURIOUS
WASHSTAND 289-3, MEDITATIONS ON LIFE OF CHRIST 289-4, SPECULUM
HUMANAE SALVATIONIS 289-5, BOOK OF HOURS 289/5-12, LIFE OF
VIRGIN 289/12-14

*$ABSTRACT 290
 *LIBRARY BOD
 *SLIDE SET TITLE HERBAL
 *NEGATIVE REFERENCE ROLL 173D
 *RENTAL FEE SM 290 $2.80
 *TITLE OF MANUSCRIPT HERBAL
 *SHELFMARK MS ASHMOLE 1462
 *PROVENANCE ENGLISH
 *DATE EXECUTED 12TH
 *LANGUAGE LATIN AND ENGLISH
 *TYPE OF MANUSCRIPT HERBAL
 *CONTENTS HERBAL 290/1-16, VERVAIN/ SERPENT STABBED BY MAN
 290-1, ARTHEMESIA/ DIANA HANDING TWO TO CHIRON THE CENTAUR
 290-2, DRACONTEA/ SERPENTINE/ SATYRION CHRISTI 290-3, GENTIAN/
 CYCLAMINOS/ ERTHNOTE 290-3, CENTUM CAPITA/ AFFODILE/ CENTAUR/
 CENTAURIA MAIOR 290-4, BEET/ MAD DOG FOUGHT WITH SWORD/
 STRAWBERRY 290-5, ALTEA BISMALUS/ MARSH MALLOW/ HORSETAIL
 290-6, MALYA SYLVESIS/ OX TUNGE 290-6, GALLITRICUM/ HOUSE
 LEEK/ HOMER WITH IMMOLUM 290-7, DITTANY/ HELIOTROPIUM
 EUORPAEUM 290-8, AFRICAN MARIGOLD/ PEONIA/ VERVAIN 290-8, RED
 CLOVER/ WOAD/ RUSTICORUM 290-9, SAGE/ CRIANDER 290-10, WODE
 THISTEL/ SONCHUS/ LUPINUS LUTEUS 290-11, WILDE LETUSE/
 CUCUMBER 290-11, MANDRAKE/ NUDE WITH LEAVES FROM HEAD 290-12,
 SARSUCIN/ CESTROS 290-13, ADIANTOS/ MANDRAKE FEMALE 290-14,
 LYNOZOSTIS/ ANTHERENON 290-15, BULBUS RUFUS/ DRACONTEA 290-16

*$ABSTRACT 291
 *LIBRARY BOD
 *SLIDE SET TITLE VESTMENTS 13TH-15TH CENTURIES
 *NEGATIVE REFERENCE ROLL 173G
 *RENTAL FEE SM 291 $3.15
 *SHELFMARK MS BODLEY 39 291/1-2, MS BODLEY 912 291/3-5, MS
 TRINITY COLL 291-6, MS DOUCE 291-7, MS BODLEY 966 291-8, MS
 BODLEY 968 291-9, MS LAUD MISC 302 291-10, MS DOUCE 278
 291-11, MS DOUCE 118 291-12, MS DOUCE 245 291-13, MS ORIEL
 COLLEGE 75 291-14, MS GOUGH LITURG 15 291-15, MS DOUCE 217
 291-16, MS DOUCE 104 291-17, MS BUCHANAN E 13 291-18, MS RAWL
 A 417 291-19, MS GOUGH LITURG 12 291-20, MS DOUCE 77 291-21,
 MS ADD A 185 291-22, MS DOUCE 266 291-23
 *PROVENANCE ENGLISH 291/1-6 AND 14 AND 17, FRENCH 291/7-13 AND
 16 AND 19-22, FLEMISH 291/15 AND 23
 *DATE EXECUTED 13TH 291/1-2, 14TH 291/3-6 AND 12-13, 15TH
 291/7-11 AND 14-23
 *LANGUAGE LATIN
 *TYPE OF MANUSCRIPT MISCELLANY
 *CONTENTS VESTMENTS 291/1-23, ABBOT ALAN DE NESSE WITH CROZIER
 AND MITRE 291-1, STEPHEN/ FIRST ABBOT OF ST MARY'S ABBEY YORK
 291-2, BISHOP CROWNING EDWARD 291-3, BISHOP CROWNING WILLIAM
 291-4, HENRY CROWNED BY BISHOP 291-5, BISHOP ASPERGES CHURCH
 AT DEDICATION 291-6, CARDINAL/ ARCHBISHOPS/ BISHOPS BEFORE
 EMPEROR CONSTANTINE IV 291-8, BISHOPS AT CORONATION OF CHARLES
 LE BEL 291-7, POPE STEPHEN II CROWNS PEPIN AND HIS SONS 291-9,
 BISHOP WITH MITRE AND CROZIER IN FRONT OF CHURCH 291-10,
 ELECTION OF EMPEROR WITH BISHOPS/ EMPEROR CROWNED 291-11,
 PRIEST WITH GOLD NIMBUS WEARING ALB SWINGS CENSER 291-12,
 PRIEST ELEVATES HOST WEARING RED CHAUSABLE AND ALB 291-13,
 PRIEST WEARING COPE CARRYING MONSTRANCE IN PROCESSION 291-14,
 PRIEST IN BURIAL SCENE WITH GOLD COPE OVER CASSOCK 291-15,
 PRIEST WEARING ALB CELEBRATES MARRIAGE OUTSIDE CHURCH DOOR
 291-16, PRIEST HOLDS PARDON WITH SEAL 291-17, PRIEST ABOUT TO
 ASPERGE GRAVE/ DEACON IN BLUE DALMATIC 291-18, PRIEST WEARING

147

CHAUSABLE SAYS MASS BEFORE POPE 291-19, PRIEST AND CHOIR IN
WHITE SURPLICES OVER RED CASSOCKS 291-20, DEACON AND
SUB-DEACON AT MASS FOR THE DEAD 291-21, DEACON HOLDS BOOK FOR
BISHOP AT FUNERAL SERVICE 291-22, DEACON AND SUB-DEACON KNEEL
BEHIND PRIEST AT MASS 291-23

*$ABSTRACT 292
  *LIBRARY BOD
  *SLIDE SET TITLE BIBLIA PAUPERAM
  *NEGATIVE REFERENCE ROLL 173I
  *RENTAL FEE SM 292 $4.00
  *TITLE OF MANUSCRIPT BIBLIA PAUPERAM
  *SHELFMARK MS AUCT M III 13
  *PROVENANCE DUTCH
  *DATE EXECUTED 15TH
  *LANGUAGE LATIN
  *TYPE OF MANUSCRIPT BIBLIA PAUPERAM
  *CONTENTS   BIBLIA   PAUPERAM   291/1-40,   TYPOLOGICAL   SCENES
292/1-40, TEMPTATION TO EVE/ ANNUNCIATION TO MARY/ GIDEON AND
ANGEL   292-1,   BURNING   BUSH/   NATIVITY/   AARON'S   STAFF BLOOM
292-2, ABNER VISITS DAVID/ ADORATION BY THREE KINGS 292-3,
SOLOMON AND SHEBA 292-3, PURIFICATION/ PRESENTATION IN THE
TEMPLE 292-4, CHILD SAMUEL BROUGHT TO ELI 292-4, JACOB LEAVES
ISAAC AT REBECCAH'S WORD/ FLIGHT INTO EGYPT 292-5, DAVID FLEES
SAUL HELPED BY MICHAL 292-5, MOSES AND THE GOLDEN CALF/ FALL
OF IDOLS 292-6, TABERNACLE AND IDOL OF DAGON FALLS 292-6, SAUL
SLAYS PRIESTS OF LORD/ MASSACRE OF INNOCENTS 292-7, ATHALIAH
SLAUGHTERS ROYAL CHILDREN 292-7, DAVID PRAYS BEFORE RETURNING
AFTER DEATH OF SAUL 292-8, RETURN FROM EGYPT/ JACOB WITH
FLOCKS 292-8, CROSSING RED SEA/ BAPTISM/ SPIES CARRYING GRAPES
292-9, ESAU SELLS BIRTHRIGHT FOR MESS OF POTAGE 292-10,
TEMPTATION OF CHRIST 292-10, TEMPTATION OF EVE 292-10, WIDOW
OF ZAREPATH'S SON RESURRECTED BY ELIJAH 292-11, RAISING OF
LAZARUS/ ELISHA RAISES SHUNAMITE'S SON 292-11, ABRAHAM
ENTERTAINS THREE ANGELS 292-12, TRANSFIGURATION 292-12,
SHADRACH MESHACH AND ABENDEGO 292-12, DAVID CONFESSES TO
NATHAN/ MARY AT FEET OF CHRIST 292-13, MIRIAM SISTER OF MOSES
MADE LEPROUS 292-13, DAVID SHOWS GOLIATH'S HEAD/ TRIUMPHAL
ENTRY INTO JERUSALEM 292-14, ELISHA RECEIVES NAAMAN 292-14,
PERSIAN KING ALLOWS REBUILDING OF TEMPLE 292-15, CHRIST DRIVES
MONEY-LENDERS OUT OF TEMPLE 292-15, JUDAS MACCABEUS PURIFIES
TEMPLE 292-15, JOSEPH SOLD MESSENGER SENT TO JACOB 292-16,
TRIAL OF CHRIST/ ABSALOM AS JUDGE 292-16, JOSEPH'S BROTHERS
SELL HIM/ JUDAS/ POTIPHAR BUYS JOSEPH 292-17, MELCHIZEDEK
GIVES ABRAHAM BREAD/ LAST SUPPER 292-18, MOSES FALL OF MANNA
292-18, MICIAH PROPHESIES FALL OF AHAB AND JEHOSHAPHAT 292-19,
JESUS TO GETHSEMANE/ KING THREATENS ELISHA'S HEAD 292-19,
FOOLISH VIRGINS/ SOLDIERS FALL BACKWARDS AT GETHSEMANE 292-20,
LUCIFER FALLS 292-20, JOAB SLAYS ABNER/ JUDAS/ TRYPHON
DECEIVES JONATHAN 292-21, JEZEBEL THREATENS ELIJAH 292-22,
CHRIST BEFORE PILATE 292-22, BABYLONIANS DEMAND DANIEL 292-22,
HAM MOCKS NOAH/ BUFFETING OF CHRIST/ CHILDREN MOCK ELISHA
292-23, ISAAC CARRIES WOOD FOR SACRIFICE/ ROAD TO CALVARY
292-24, MOSES LIFTS UP SERPENT 292-25, ELISHA AND WIDOW OF
ZAREPATH WITH TWO STICKS 292-24, SACRIFICE OF ISAAC/ CHRIST ON
CROSS 292-25, CREATION OF EVE/ CHRIST ON CROSS/ MOSES STRIKES
ROCK 292-26, JOSEPH LOWERED INTO PIT 292-27, ENTOMBMENT/ JONAH
CAST TO WHALE 292-27, DAVID SLAYS GOLIATH/ HARROWING OF HELL/
SAMSON SLAYS LION 292-28, SAMSON WITH GATES/ RESURRECTION/
JONAH EMERGES FROM WHALE 292-29, REUBEN SEEKS BROTHER/ WOMEN
AT TOMB/ BRIDE SEEKS BELOVED 292-30, DANIEL IN LION'S DEN
292-31, MARY MAGDALENE KNEELS TO CHRIST IN GARDEN 292-31,
BRIDE FINDS HER BELOVED 292-31, JOSEPH DECLARES SELF/ ST
THOMAS TOUCHES CHRIST'S SIDE 292-32, RETURN OF PRODIGAL SON
292-32, GIDEON AND ANGEL/ JACOB AND ANGEL 292-33, CHRIST
APPEARS TO DISCIPLES 292-32, ASCENSION OF ENOCH/ ASCENSION OF
CHRIST AND ELIJAH 292-34, MOSES RECEIVES LAW/ PENTECOST/ FIRE
BURNS ELIJAH'S SACRIFICE 292-35, BATHSHEBA AND SOLOMON
ENTHRONED/ CORONATION OF VIRGIN 292-36, ESTHER AND AHASUERUS
292-36, JUDGMENT OF SOLOMON/ SECOND COMING/ DAVID CONDEMNS

AMALEKITE 296-37, KORATH/ DATHAN/ ABIRAM/ DEVIL LEADS DAMNED
BY CHAIN 292-38, DESTRUCTION OF SODOM AND GOMORRAH 292-38,
FEAST OF JOB'S CHILDREN 292-39, CHRIST GATHERS BLESSED SOULS
292-39, JACOB'S LADDER 292-39, DAUGHTER OF SION FINDS
BRIDEGROOM/ CHRIST CROWNS CHURCH 292-40, ANGEL PROMISES
MANOAH'S WIFE A SON 292-40

*$ABSTRACT 293
  *LIBRARY BOD
  *SLIDE SET TITLE CLASS DISTINCTIONS
  *NEGATIVE REFERENCE ROLL 174C
  *RENTAL FEE SM 293 $2.60
  *COMMENTS CONTRAST BETWEEN COURTLINESS AND UNCOURTLINESS FROM
  THE ROMANCE OF THE ROSE
  *TITLE OF MANUSCRIPT ROMANCE OF THE ROSE
  *SHELFMARK MS DOUCE 332
  *PROVENANCE FRENCH
  *DATE EXECUTED 14TH
  *LANGUAGE FRENCH
  *AUTHOR GUILLAUME DE LORRIS AND JEAN DE MEUNG
  *ARTIST/ SCHOOL PARIS
  *TYPE OF MANUSCRIPT ROMANCE
  *CONTENTS CLASS DISTINCTIONS 293-1-12, ROMANCE OF THE ROSE
  293/1-12, LITERATURE/ ROMANCE OF THE ROSE 293/1-12, VILLAINEY
  293-1, COVETOUSNESS 293-2, AVARICE 293-3, OLD AGE 293-4,
  POVERTY 293-5, IDLENESS IN THE DOOR 293-6, CAROLE IN GARDEN
  293-7, REASON CHASTISES LOVER 293-8, OLD WOMAN ADDRESSES
  BEL-ACUEIL ON BENCH 293-9, FRANKNESS FIGHTS DANGIER 293-10,
  FEAR AND SHAME REPROACH DANGIER 293-11, VENUS IN HER CARRIAGE
  292-12

*$ABSTRACT 294
  *LIBRARY BOD
  *SLIDE SET TITLE FURNITURE AND WOODWORK
  *NEGATIVE REFERENCE ROLL 174D
  *RENTAL FEE SM 294 $2.45
  *COMMENTS 9 SLIDES TAKEN FROM THE ROMANCE OF THE ROSE
  *TITLE OF MANUSCRIPT ROMANCE OF THE ROSE
  *SHELFMARK MS DOUCE 332
  *PROVENANCE FRENCH
  *DATE EXECUTED 14TH
  *LANGUAGE FRENCH
  *AUTHOR GUILLAUME DE LORIS AND JEAN DE MEUNG
  *ARTIST/ SCHOOL PARIS
  *TYPE OF MANUSCRIPT ROMANCE
  *CONTENTS WOODWORK AND FURNITURE 294/1-9, ROMANCE OF THE ROSE
  294/1-9, LITERATURE/ ROMANCE OF THE ROSE 294/1-9, CURTAINED
  BED/ ROUND CHAIR/ PLAITED RUSH MAT 294-1, ALTAR WITH FRINGED
  CLOTH/ SEAT AND DESK/ CURTAIN 294/2-3, WHEEL 294-4, BIRD CAGE
  294-5, EEL POT 294-6, BED WITH BOLSTER AND PILLOWS 294-7,
  CHAIR AND ALTAR WITH CLOTH 294-8, GALLOWS 294-9

*$ABSTRACT 295
  *LIBRARY BOD
  *SLIDE SET TITLE DOMESTIC LIFE
  *NEGATIVE REFERENCE ROLL 174G
  *RENTAL FEE SM 295 $2.55
  *COMMENTS TAKEN FROM THE ROMANCE OF THE ROSE
  *TITLE OF MANUSCRIPT ROMANCE OF THE ROSE
  *SHELFMARK MS DOUCE 332
  *PROVENANCE FRENCH
  *DATE EXECUTED 14TH
  *LANGUAGE LATIN
  *AUTHOR GUILLAUME DE LORRIS AND JEAN DE MEUNG
  *ARTIST/ SCHOOL PARIS
  *TYPE OF MANUSCRIPT ROMANCE

*CONTENTS DOMESTIC LIFE 295/1-11, ROMANCE OF THE ROSE 295/1-11,
LITERATURE/ ROMANCE OF THE ROSE 295/1-11, LOVER IN THE BEDROOM
SCENE 295-1, HATRED ON STONE BENCH 295-2, COVETOUSNESS WITH
CLOTHES-LINE AND CHESTS OF TREASURE 295-3, AVARICE AND
CLOTHES-LINE 295-4, OLD AGE AND FIREPLACE 295-5, HYPOCRISY AND
DRAPED ALTAR 295-6, JOHN DE MEUNG/ PORTRAIT 295-7, RICHESE AND
CROWNED LADY AND DOG 295-8, BIRD IN CAGE PLOTS FOR FREEDOM
295-9, FISH IN WICKER TRAP PLOTS FOR FREEDOM 295-10, BEDROOM
SCENE WITH WIFE TRYING TO FIND HUSBAND'S SECRETS 295-11

*$ABSTRACT 296
  *LIBRARY BOD
  *SLIDE SET TITLE ENGLISH RURAL LIFE
  *NEGATIVE REFERENCE ROLL 175H
  *RENTAL FEE SM 296 $4.55
  *COMMENTS A COMPANION TO BODLEIAN PICTURE BOOK 14
  *SHELFMARK MS AUCT D 3 2 296-1, MS NEW COLLEGE 130 296-2, MS
  BODLEY 546 296-3, MS ASHMOLE 1504 296/4 AND 13 AND 45 AND 50,
  MS BODLEY 764 296/5 AND 9 AND 10 AND 18, MS NEW COLLEGE 65
  296-6, MS BODLEY 602 296/7 AND 23 AND 44 AND 46, MS ASHMOLE
  1511 296/9 AND 16, MS GOUGH LITURG 7 296-11, MS DOUCE 88
  296/12 AND 19 AND 34, MS AUCT D 2 6 296/14 AND 20 AND 26 AND
  37 AND 33 AND 36 AND 28, MS GOUGH LITURG 2 296-17, MS ASHMOLE
  762 296-21, MS DOUCE 366 296-22, MS JUNIUS 11 296-24, MS TOP
  LINCS D 1 296-25, MS DOUCE 104 296/27 AND 49, MS BODLEY 130
  296-30, MS ASHMOLE 1431 296-32, MS C C C 157 296-35, MS
  UNIVERSITY COLLEGE 100 296-38, MS GOUGH LITURG 7 296-39, MS C
  C C 285 296/40-41 AND 45, MS SELDEN SUPRA 38 296-42, MS LITURG
  104 296-47
  *PROVENANCE ENGLISH
  *TYPE OF MANUSCRIPT MISCELLANY
  *CONTENTS RURAL LIFE/ ENGLISH 296/1-51, MAN AND WOMAN DANCING
  296-1, CAT WITH RAT 296-2, HUNTING PARTY 296-3, WINDMILL
  296-4, MULE AND WATER MILL 296-5, BIRDS 296-6, PARTRIDGE AND
  CHICKS 296-7, DOVECOTE 296-8, BEES FLYING INTO HIVE 296-9,
  WOMAN MILKING COW 296-10, MARKETING 296-11, SHOEING A HORSE
  296-12, ASS WITH PACK LOAD 296-13, PIG KILLED BY MAN 296-14,
  BOAR 296-15, COW AND CALF 296-16, SHEPHERDS AND FLOCK 296-17,
  FLOCK OF SHEEP 296/18-19, MAN SHEARING SHEEP 296-20, RAM
  296-21, MAN WITH LAMB AND WOLF 296-22, GOATS AND DEER 296-23,
  PLOUGHING WITH OXEN 296-24, PLOUGH DIAGRAM 296-25, MAN WITH
  SPADE AND HORN 296-26, MAN DIGGING 296-27, SOWER 296-28,
  LOPPING TREES 296-29, THISTLE 296-30, THISTLES BEING CUT
  296-31, COUCH GRASS 296-32, HAWKING 296-33, DOG CHASING HARE
  296-34, MAN WITH TOOLS 296-35, TOOLS 296-36, MAN WITH SCYTHE
  296-37, HARVESTING WITH SICKLE 296-38, HARVESTING 296-39,
  HAYMAKING 296-40, THRESHING 296-41, HARVESTING 296-42, FOX
  EATING BIRD 296-43, STAG AND DOE 296-43, FOX 296-45, GEESE
  296-46, DOGS 296-47, FIRESIDE 296-48, MAN DRINKING 296-49,
  WOMAN SPINNING 296-50, MAN AND WOMAN 296-51

*$ABSTRACT 297
  *LIBRARY BOD
  *SLIDE SET TITLE BIBLE
  *NEGATIVE REFERENCE ROLL 176D
  *RENTAL FEE SM 297 $7.60
  *COMMENTS 112 SLIDES FROM 13TH CENTURY BIBLE
  *TITLE OF MANUSCRIPT BIBLE
  *SHELFMARK MS CANON BIBL LAT 56
  *PROVENANCE ITALIAN/ CREMONA
  *DATE EXECUTED 13TH/1265
  *LANGUAGE LATIN
  *AUTHOR WRITTEN BY LANFRANCUS DE PANCIS DE CREMONA
  *TYPE OF MANUSCRIPT BIBLE
  *CONTENTS BIBLE/13TH PICTURES 297/1-112, ICONOGRAPHY/ BIBLICAL
  297/1-112, INITIALS/ HISTORIATED 297/1-112, ST JEROME WRITES
  TO AMBROSIUS 297-1, ST JEROME WRITES PREFACE ON PENTATEUCH
  297-2, CREATION 297-3, GENESIS 297-3, JACOB AND SONS OF ISRAEL

ZOOMORPHIC 297-109, INITIAL T/FLORIATED 297-110, INITIAL
V/FLORIATED 297-111, INITIAL Z 297-112

*$ABSTRACT 298
  *LIBRARY BOD
  *SLIDE SET TITLE FRENCH BOOK OF HOURS
  *NEGATIVE REFERENCE ROLL 177H
  *RENTAL FEE SM 298 $2.95
  *SHELFMARK MS CANON LITURG 43
  *PROVENANCE FRENCH/ USE OF BOURGES
  *DATE EXECUTED 15TH/C1470-80
  *LANGUAGE LATIN AND FRENCH
  *ARTIST/ SCHOOL MAITRE FRANCOIS
  *TYPE OF MANUSCRIPT BOOK OF HOURS/ USE OF BOURGES
  *CONTENTS BOOK OF HOURS/ FRENCH/ 15TH 298/1-19, SCRIPTURAL
  SCENES 298/1-19, ANGELS WITH MUSICAL INSTRUMENTS IN BORDERS
  298/1-19, ARCHITECTURAL BORDERS 298/1-19, VIRGIN AND CHILD/
  ANGELS/ MUSICAL INSTRUMENTS 298-1, ST MATTHEW/ CHRIST 298-1,
  ST MARK WITH LION/ BISHOPS 298-2, VISITATION/ ANNUNCIATION/
  GOD/ LANDSCAPE 298-3, PRESENTATION/ TWO MARYS 298-5,
  CORONATION OF VIRGIN 298-4, CRUCIFIXION 298-8, DAVID WITH GOD/
  AND HOLDING HEAD OF ISHBAAL 298-9, DEATH WITH SKULLS OF
  VICTIMS 298-10, BETRAYAL OF CHRIST/ MALCHUS INCIDENT 298-11,
  NATIVITY 298-12, ANNUNCIATION 298-13, ADORATION OF THE MAGI
  298-14, FLIGHT INTO EGYPT 298-15, PIETA 298-16, VISITATION
  298-17, VIRGIN HAVING PORTRAIT PAINTED/ WINGED OX/ CHRIST
  298-18, DIANA'S CHIEF PRIEST AND CRIMINALS 298-19, SERPENT AND
  ST JOHN WRITING ON PATMOS WITH EAGLE 298-19

*$ABSTRACT 299
  *LIBRARY BOD
  *SLIDE SET TITLE MINISTRY OF CHRIST
  *NEGATIVE REFERENCE ROLL 177I
  *RENTAL FEE SM 299 $2.55
  *TITLE OF MANUSCRIPT VITA GLORIOSISSIME VIRGINIS MARIAE
  *SHELFMARK MS CANON MISC 476
  *PROVENANCE ITALIAN/ VENICE
  *DATE EXECUTED 14TH
  *LANGUAGE LATIN
  *TYPE OF MANUSCRIPT ACTS OF ST MARY AND JESUS
  *CONTENTS ST MARY AND JESUS 299/1-11, JOHN BAPTIZES JESUS IN
  WATER 299-1, HOLY GHOST DESCENDS ON JESUS 299-1, DEVIL TEMPTS
  JESUS IN WILDERNESS 299-2, JESUS GATHERS DISCIPLES 299-3,
  MARRIAGE FEAST AT CANA 299-4, CHRIST HEALS SICK MAN AT
  CAPERNAUM 299-5, CHRIST FREE MEN OF DEVILS 299-6, HEALING OF
  WIDOW'S SON 299-7, JAIRUS'S DAUGHTER RAISED FROM DEAD 299-8,
  EMORYSA FREED FROM BLOODY FLUX 299-9, LAZARUS RAISED FROM DEAD
  299-10, MARY MAGDALENE WASHES FEET OF CHRIST 299-11

*$ABSTRACT 300
  *LIBRARY BOD
  *SLIDE SET TITLE PASSION
  *NEGATIVE REFERENCE ROLL 177J
  *RENTAL FEE SM 300 $4.15
  *TITLE OF MANUSCRIPT ACTS OF ST MARY AND JESUS
  *SHELFMARK MS CANON MISC 476
  *PROVENANCE ITALIAN/ VENICE
  *DATE EXECUTED 14TH
  *LANGUAGE LATIN
  *TYPE OF MANUSCRIPT ACTS OF ST MARY AND JESUS
  *CONTENTS ST MARY AND JESUS ACTS OF 300/1-43, PASSION OF CHRIST
  300/1-53, LAST SUPPER/ CHRIST HANDS SOP TO JUDAS 300-1, JOHN
  SLEEPS ON CHRIST'S ARM 300-1, CHRIST WASHING FEET OF DISCIPLES
  300-2, DISCIPLES KNEEL TO RECEIVE BREAD FROM CHRIST 300-3,
  JUDAS GOES TO PRIESTS 300-4, CHRIST FORTELLS PETER'S BETRAYAL
  300-5, CHRIST AT PRAYER WITH SWEAT AND BLOOD OF CHALICE 300-6,

152

JUDAS KISSES CHRIST 300-7, PETER CUTS OFF EAR OF MALCHUS
300-8, SOLDIERS LEAD BOUND CHRIST BY ROPE 300-9, CHRIST MOCKED
AND BEARD TORN OUT 300-10, DENIAL BY PETER 300-11, CHRIST
BEFORE CAPAIAPHAS 300-12, CHRIST BEFORE PILATE 300-13, CHRIST
BEFORE HEROD 300-14, JUDAS HANGING 300-15, FLAGELLATION
300-16, CHRIST STRUCK WITH REED 300-17, CHRIST BEFORE PILATE
300-18, PILATE'S WIFE INTERCEDES FOR CHRIST 300-19, JEWS
GIVING MONEY FOR CONDEMNATION OF CHRIST 300-20, CHRIST
CARRYING CROSS 300-21, SIMON OF CYRENE COMPELLED TO CARRY
CROSS 300-22, MARY TOLD SON TAKEN AWAY 300-22, MARY SEES SON
LED TO CRUCIFIXION 300-23, CHRIST CONSOLED BY MOTHER 300-24,
CHRIST STRIPPED OF HIS GARMENTS 300-25, CHRIST NAILED TO CROSS
300-26, CHRIST PRAYS FOR HIS CRUCIFIERS 300-27, VIRGIN'S GRIEF
AT CRUCIFIXION 300-27, SORROW OF VIRGIN/ CROSS RAISED/ SORROW
AND MOCKERY 300-28, SOLDIERS DIVIDE GARMENTS 300-29, MARY AND
ST JOHN AT FOOT OF CROSS 300-29, CHRIST ON CROSS COMMENDS
MOTHER TO ST JOHN 300-31, CHRIST ON CROSS CONSOLED BY MOTHER
300-31, JEWS BLASPHEME CHRIST ON CROSS 300-32, DEATH OF GOOD
AND BAD THIEVES 300-33, VINEGAR BROUGHT TO CHRIST AND MARYS
MOURN 300-34, SISTERS OF VIRGIN LAMENT 300-35, PORTENTS OF
PASSION/ EARTHQUAKE AND FLOOD 300-36, CHRIST'S SIDE PIERCED BY
SWORD 300-37, CENTURION DECLARES CHRIST SON OF GOD 300-37,
NICODEMUS AND JOSEPH TAKE CHRIST'S BODY AWAY 300-38, MARY
MOURNS DEATH OF SON 300-39, TOMB AS LOCKED CHEST 300-40, ST
JOHN TAKES MARY TO HOSPICE 300-41, GUARDS SLEEP OUTSIDE TOMB
300-42, CHRIST DESCENDS INTO HELL 300-43

*$ABSTRACT 301
  *LIBRARY BOD
  *SLIDE SET TITLE RESURRECTION APPEARANCES
  *NEGATIVE REFERENCE ROLL 177K
  *RENTAL FEE SM 301 $2.85
  *COMMENTS 17 SLIDES FROM ACTS OF ST MARY AND JESUS
  *TITLE OF MANUSCRIPT ACTS OF ST MARY AND JESUS
  *SHELFMARK MS CANON MISC 476
  *PROVENANCE ITALIAN/ VENICE
  *DATE EXECUTED 14TH
  *LANGUAGE LATIN
  *TYPE OF MANUSCRIPT ACTS OF ST MARY AND JESUS
  *CONTENTS RESURRECTION APPEARANCES OF CHRIST 301/1-17, CHRIST/
RESURRECTION APPEARANCES 301/1-17, CHRIST RISES FROM DEAD
301-1, SOLDIERS SLEEPING BY TOMB 301-1, WOMEN TOLD BY ANGEL OF
CHRIST'S RESURRECTION 301-1, CHRIST APPEARS TO HIS MOTHER
301-2, CHRIST APPEARS TO JOSEPH OF ARIMETHEA IN PRISON 301-3,
PETER AND JOHN ARRIVE AT EMPTY TOMB 301-4, CHRIST APPEARS TO
MARY MAGDALENE 301-5, CHRIST APPEARS TO MARY MAGDALENE AND
OTHER WOMEN 301-6, CHRIST APPEARS TO PETER 301-7, CHRIST
APPEARS TO TWO DISCIPLES OUTSIDE EMMAUS 301-8, CHRIST APPEARS
TO APOSTLE JAMES 301-9, CHRIST APPEARS TO DISCIPLES WITH
THOMAS ABSENT 301-10, CHRIST APPEARS TO DISCIPLES WITH THOMAS
PRESENT 301-11, CHRIST APPEARS TO DISCIPLES FISHING WITH NET
301-12, CHRIST ON ROCK APPEARS TO DISCIPLES ON MOUNT TABOR
301-13, CHRIST APPEARS TO DISCIPLES AT MEAL AND BLESSES FISH
301-14, VIRGIN MARY LEADS DISCIPLES TO MOUNT OF OLIVES 301-15,
CHRIST COMFORTS MARY AND ASSURES HER OF ASSUMPTION 301-16,
ASCENSION OF CHRIST WATCHED BY DISCIPLES AND MARY 301-17

*$ABSTRACT 302
  *LIBRARY BOD
  *SLIDE SET TITLE NATIVITY
  *NEGATIVE REFERENCE ROLL 177L
  *RENTAL FEE SM 302 $2.65
  *TITLE OF MANUSCRIPT MEDITATIONS ON LIFE OF CHRIST
  *SHELFMARK MS C C C 410
  *PROVENANCE ITALIAN
  *DATE EXECUTED 14TH
  *LANGUAGE LATIN
  *TYPE OF MANUSCRIPT MEDITATIONS ON LIFE OF CHRIST

*CONTENTS NATIVITY 302/1-13, ANNUNCIATION TO VIRGIN 301-1,
VIRGIN AND GABRIEL KNEEL 302-2, VISITATION WITH ZACHRIAS/
JOSEPH/ ELIZABETH/ VIRGIN 302-3, MIDWIFE ATTENDS ELIZABETH
320-4, VIRGIN WASHES JOHN BAPTIST AT TUB 302-4, ANGEL
ADDRESSES JOSEPH IN HIS SLEEP 302-5, JOSEPH ADDRESSES VIRGIN
302-6, OFFICIAL AT BETHLEHEM QUESTIONS MARY AND JOSEPH 302-7,
VIRGIN RECLINING WITH CHILD IN CRIB 302-8, ANNUNCIATION TO
SHEPHERDS 302-9, VIRGIN AND CHILD AND OX/ ASS/ JOSEPH 302-10,
VIRGIN AND CHILD AND OX/ ASS 302-11, CIRCUMCISION OF CHRIST
AND JOSEPH WATCHES 302-11, KING/ FIRST OFFERS GIFT TO JESUS
302-12, KINGS/ THREE RIDE AWAY 302-13

*$ABSTRACT 303
  *LIBRARY BOD
  *SLIDE SET TITLE MINISTRY
  *NEGATIVE REFERENCE ROLL 177M
  *RENTAL FEE SM 303 $3.00
  *TITLE OF MANUSCRIPT MEDITATIONS ON LIFE OF CHRIST
  *SHELFMARK MS C C C 410
  *PROVENANCE ITALIAN
  *DATE EXECUTED 14TH
  *LANGUAGE LATIN
  *TYPE OF MANUSCRIPT MEDITATIONS ON LIFE OF CHRIST
  *CONTENTS MINISTRY OF CHRIST 303/1-20, BAPTISM OF CHRIST WITH
ANGELS HOLDING CLOTHES 303-1, AXE LAID AT ROOT OF TREE 303-1,
CHRIST PRAYS IN WILDERNESS AND GOD'S HAND APPEARS 303-2,
ANGELS MINISTER TO CHRIST/ JOHN BAPTIST 303-3, ANDREW/ APOSTLE
OF JOHN/ ST PETER WITH JESUS 303-3, MARRIAGE AT CANA AND
MIRACLE OF WATER TO WINE 303-4, SERMON ON MOUNT 303-5, CHRIST
FEEDING POOR AND CRIPPLED 303-6, CHRIST HEALING SIMON'S
MOTHER-IN-LAW AND SHE PREPARES MEAL 303-7, CHRIST HEALS WOMAN
WITH ISSUE OF BLOOD 303-8, CHRIST DISCUSSING DEATH OF BAPTIST
WITH VIRGIN 303-9, CHRIST AND WOMAN OF SAMARIA AT WELL 303-10,
CHRIST PURSUED AND TO BE STONED BY MOB 303-11, CHRIST FLEEING
CROWD WHO WISH TO MAKE HIM KING 303-12, CHRIST PRAYING ON
MOUNTAIN AND DISCIPLES IN BOAT 303-13, DISCIPLES ASLEEP IN
BOAT AND PETER WALKS ON WATER 303-14, CHRIST DRIVING MONEY
CHANGER AND DOVE SELLER FROM TEMPLE 303-15, CHRIST HEALING
PARALYTIC AT SILOAM 303-16, CHRIST HEALING BLIND MAN BY
PUTTING CLAY ON EYES 303-17, LAZARUS RAISED BY CHRIST/
DISCIPLE/ MARY AND MARTHA 303-18, JESUS AND DISCIPLES AT
SUPPER AT SIMON'S HOUSE 303-19, MARY MAGDALENE ANOINTS JESUS'
FEET 303-19, ENTRY INTO JERUSALEM 303-20

*$ABSTRACT 304
  *LIBRARY BOD
  *SLIDE SET TITLE PASSION
  *NEGATIVE REFERENCE ROLL 177N
  *RENTAL FEE SM 304 $2.85
  *TITLE OF MANUSCRIPT MEDITATIONS ON LIFE OF CHRIST
  *SHELFMARK MS C C C 410
  *PROVENANCE ITALIAN
  *DATE EXECUTED 14TH
  *LANGUAGE LATIN
  *TYPE OF MANUSCRIPT MEDIATIONS ON LIFE OF CHRIST
  *CONTENTS PASSION OF CHRIST 304/1-17, ENTRY INTO JERUSALEM
304-1, LAST SUPPER WITH JUDAS WITHOUT HALO 304-2, CHRIST
WASHES PROTESTING DISCIPLES' FEET 304-3, JUDAS RECEIVING BRIBE
FROM TWO MEN 304-4, CHRIST GIVING SERMON ON WAY TO GETHSEMANE
AND DISCIPLES 304-5, WOMAN ATTEMPTS TO CALL CHRIST BACK 304-5,
CHRIST PRAYS APART WHILE DISCIPLES SLEEP 304-6, CHRIST'S AGONY
IN THE GARDEN/ ANGEL APPEARS 304-7, SOLDIERS COME TO ARREST
CHRIST 304-8, JUDAS BETRAYS CHRIST WITH KISS 304-8, PETER CUTS
OFF EAR OF MAN 304-8, CHRIST CHAINED TO PILLAR 304-9, CHRIST
DISMISSED BY PILATE 304-10, CHRIST SCOURGED BY SOLDIERS
304-10, PILATE INSTRUCTS SOLDIERS TO REMOVE CHRIST'S GARMENT
304-11, CHRIST MET BY WOMAN ON WAY TO CALVARY 304-12, SIMON OF
CYRENE TAKES CROSS 304-12, CHRIST STRIPPED OF GARMENT AT FOOT

OF CROSS 304-13, CRUCIFIXION AND SPONGE OFFERED TO CHRIST
304-14, SOLDIERS PIERCE CHRIST'S SIDE AND MARY AND JOHN
ENTREAT 304-15, JOSEPH AND NICODEMUS LOWER BODY FROM CROSS
304-16, CHRIST'S UNSWATHED BODY LOWERED INTO TOMB 304-17

*$ABSTRACT 305
  *LIBRARY BOD
  *SLIDE SET TITLE RESURRECTION AND APPEARANCES
  *NEGATIVE REFERENCE ROLL 177P
  *RENTAL FEE SM 305 $2.65
  *TITLE OF MANUSCRIPT MEDITATIONS ON LIFE OF CHRIST
  *SHELFMARK MS C C C 410
  *PROVENANCE ITALIAN
  *LANGUAGE LATIN
  *TYPE OF MANUSCRIPT MEDITATIONS ON LIFE OF CHRIST
  *CONTENTS RESURRECTION AND APPEARANCES OF CHRIST 305/1-13,
  CHRIST'S BODY LOWERED INTO TOMB 305-1, CHRIST DESCENDING TO
  HOLY FATHERS IN HELL 305-2, HARROWING OF HELL 305-2, CHRIST
  PLACING HOLY FATHERS IN PARADISE 305-2, RESURRECTION WITH
  CHRIST HOLDING ORB RISING FROM TOMB 305-4, JESUS APPEARS FIRST
  TO HIS MOTHER 305-5, MARYS/ THREE SPEAK TO ANGEL SEATED ON
  TOMB 305-5, PETER AND JOHN LOOKING INTO EMPTY TOMB 305-6,
  JESUS WITH PICKAXE APPEARS TO MARY MAGDALENE 305-7, CHRIST
  DELIVERS JOSEPH OF ARIMETHEA FROM PRISON 305-8, CHRIST HANDS
  JAMES THE LESS CAKE OF BREAD 305-9, CHRIST APPEARS TO
  DISCIPLES ON ROAD TO EMMAUS 305-10, THOMAS TOUCHES CHRIST'S
  WOUNDS ON SIDE AND HANDS 305-11, CHRIST APPEARS TO DISCIPLES
  AT SEA OF GALILEE 305-12, ASCENSION WATCHED BY DISCIPLES AND
  MARY 305-13

*$ABSTRACT 306
  *LIBRARY BOD
  *SLIDE SET TITLE FACE OF GOD I
  *NEGATIVE REFERENCE ROLL 179B
  *RENTAL FEE SM 306 $2.90
  *SHELFMARK MS BODLEY 602 306-1, MS RAWLINSON G 21 306-2, MS
  LITURG 104 306-3, MS RAWLINSON G 185 306/4-7, MS GOUGH LITURG
  18 306/8-9, MS C C C 18 306-10, MS LITURG 198 306-11, MS
  RAWLINSON LITURG F 28 306-12, MS CANON LITURG 63 306-13, MS
  DOUCE D 13 306-14, MS CANON BIBL LAT 49 306-15, MS CANON
  LITURG 151 306-16, MS CANON MISC 476 306-17, MS ADD C 265
  306-18
  *PROVENANCE ENGLISH 306/1-11, FRENCH 306/12-13, ITALIAN
  306/14-18
  *DATE EXECUTED 13TH 306-1, 14TH 306/2-13 AND 15-18, 15TH 306-14
  *LANGUAGE LATIN
  *TYPE OF MANUSCRIPT BESTIARY 306-1, PSALTER 306/2-11 AND 14 AND
  16, BOOK OF HOURS 306/12-13, BIBLE 306-15, ACTS OF ST MARY AND
  JESUS 306-17, SUMMA THEOLOGIA 306-18
  *CONTENTS FACES OF GOD 306/1-18, GOD/ FACES 306/1-18, CHRIST
  WITH CRUCIFORM HALO 306-1, INITIAL A WITH GOD'S HEAD WITHOUT
  HALO 306-2, CHRIST RISEN ON MARBLE THRONE DISPLAYS WOUNDS
  306-3, INITIAL D WITH CHRIST'S FACE WITH CROOKED BEARD 306-4,
  INITIAL D WITH CHRIST ON WOODEN THRONE 306-5, CHRIST
  SURROUNDED BY RAINBOW BLESSES MONASTIC MUSICIANS 306-6,
  MUSICIANS 306-6, INITIAL D WITH GOD ENTHRONED 306-7,
  CRUCIFIXION 306-8, CHRIST ENTHRONED WITH ORB BLESSING 306-9,
  TRINITY 306-10, CHRIST BLESSES PRAYING WOMAN 306-11, GOD
  ENTHRONED WEARING RED-LINED BLUE CLOAK 306-12, GOD BETWEEN TWO
  ALTARS/ OLD AND NEW LAW 306-13, GOD LOOKS FROM SKY AT UNSEEN
  ST BRUNO 306-14, ST BRUNO 306-14, INITIAL V WITH CHRIST'S HEAD
  IN CRUCIFORM HALO 306-15, GOD APPEARS FROM SKY TO DAVID
  306-16, CHRIST IN TOGA-LIKE ROBE WITH SCROLL 306-17, INITIAL Q
  WITH CHRIST IN STIFF BYZANTINE STYLE 306-18

*$ABSTRACT 307
  *LIBRARY BOD
  *SLIDE SET TITLE FACE OF GOD II
  *NEGATIVE REFERENCE ROLL 179C
  *RENTAL FEE SM 307 $4.25
  *SHELFMARK MS RAWLINSON LITURG D 1 307/1-2, MS LAUD LAT 1
  307-3, MS CANON LITURG 276 307-4, MS CANON LITURG 118 307-5
  MS CANON LITURG 92 307/6-7, MS CANON LITURG 91 307-8, MS DOUC
  30 307-9, MS DOUCE 20 307-10, MS DOUCE 51 307-11, MS DOUCE 31
  307/12-17, MS DOUCE 266 307-18, MS DOUCE 112 307-19, MS CANO
  LITURG 75 307-20, MS LITURG 100 307/21-22, MS RAWLINSON LITUR
  E 12 307/23-25, MS BUCHANAN E 14 307-26, MS LITURG 29 307-27
  MS CANON LITURG 43 307-28, MS LITURG 59 307-29, MS DOUCE 13
  307/30-31, MS CANON LITURG 99 307/32-34, MS BUCHANAN E   1
  307-35, MS CANON LITURG 349 307-36, MS CANON ITAL 164 307-37
  MS CANON LITURG 369 307/38-39, MS CANON LITURG 283 307-40, M
  CANON LITURG 383 307-41, MS DOUCE 14 307-42, MS DOUCE 4
  307/43-44, MS DOUCE 19 307-45
  *PROVENANCE ENGLISH   307/1-3,   FLEMISH   307/4-19,   FRENC
  307/20-35, ITALIAN 307/36-42 AND 45, POLISH 307-43
  *DATE EXECUTED 15TH 307/1-41, 16TH 307/42-45
  *LANGUAGE LATIN
  *TYPE OF MANUSCRIPT BOOK OF HOURS 307/1-35 AND 42-35, MISSA
  307/36 AND 38-39, BREVIARY 307-41, LETTERA CONSOLATORIA 307-3
  *CONTENTS FACE OF GOD 307/1-45, GOD/ FACES 307/1-45, INITIAL
  WITH GOD GATHERING SOULS OF THE JUST 307-1, INITIAL A WIT
  CHRIST CROWNED WITH THORNS 307-2, CHRIST AS MAN OF SORROW
  WITH INSTRUMENTS OF PASSION 307-3, FLAGELLATION OF CHRIS
  307-4, LAST JUDGMENT IN INSERTED MINIATURE 307-5, CORONATIO
  OF VIRGIN 307-6, TRINITY/ GNADENSTUHL TYPE 307-7, CHRIST A
  MAN OF SORROW 307-8, HOLY FACE 307/9-11 AND 17-19, TRINIT
  307/12 AND 23 AND 27 AND 32 AND 44-45, LAST SUPPER WITH CHRIS
  GIVING BREAD TO JUDAS 307-13, INFANT CHRIST ON MOTHER'S LA
  307-14, CHRIST'S DEATH 307-15, GOD LEANS FROM SKY TO HEA
  DAVID'S PRAYER 307-16, CORONATION OF VIRGIN 307-20, CRUCIFIE
  CHRIST 307-21, GOD THE FATHER 307-22, CORONATION OF VIRGI
  307-24, PIETA WITH INSTRUMENTS OF PASSION HELD BY ANGEL
  307-25, CRUCIFIXION 307-26, GOD AS POPE ENTHRONED BLESSIN
  VIRGIN 307-28, CRUCIPIXION 307-29, CHRIST ENTHRONED 307-30
  CHRIST ENTHRONED 307-31, GOD THE FATHER AS ELDERLY KIN
  307-33, GOD THE SON AS YOUNG BEARDED MAN WITH ORB 307-34
  CHRIST LED BEFORE PILATE 307-35, CHRIST'S HEAD WITH CRUCIFOR
  HALO 307-26, CHRIST RISING FROM TOMB 307-37, CRUCIFIXIO
  307-38, CHRIST RISEN WITH BANNER 307-39, GOD THE FATHE
  ENTHRONED 307-40, INITIAL E WITH CHRIST IN MAJESTY 307-41
  CHRIST AS MAN OF SORROWS WITH SYMBOLS OF PASSION 307-42
  CHRIST'S AGONY IN THE GARDEN 307-43

*$ABSTRACT 308
  *LIBRARY BOD
  *SLIDE SET TITLE ALLEGORY FROM THE ROMANCE OF THE ROSE
  *NEGATIVE REFERENCE ROLL 179D
  *RENTAL FEE SM 308 $2.70
  *TITLE OF MANUSCRIPT ROMANCE OF THE ROSE
  *SHELFMARK MS SELDEN SUPRA 57
  *PROVENANCE FRENCH
  *DATE EXECUTED 14TH/C1350
  *LANGUAGE FRENCH
  *AUTHOR GUILLAUME DE LORRIS AND JEAN DE MEUNG
  *TYPE OF MANUSCRIPT ROMANCE
  *CONTENTS ALLEGORY 308/1-14, ROMANCE OF THE ROSE 308/1-14
  LITERATURE/ ROMANCE OF THE ROSE 308/1-14, HATRED AS THIN/ UGL
  WOMAN 308-1, VILLAINY AS UGLY WOMAN KICKING ADMIRER 308-2
  COVETOUSNESS AS WOMAN WITH OUTSTRETCHED HANDS 308-3, AVARIC
  AS WOMAN LOOKING AT WORNOUT GARMENTS ON LINE 308-4, ENVY A
  WOMAN WITH RED HOOD 308-5, SADNESS AS GIRL TEARING HAIR 308-6
  OLD AGE AS CRIPPLE ON CRUTCHES 308-7, HYPOCRISY 308-8, POVERT
  308-9, IDLENESS AS GIRL AT GATE 308-10, LOVE AS CROWNED GO
  WITH COURTIERS 308-11, REASON AS CROWNED WOMAN PLEADING WIT
  LOVER 308-12, RICHNESS AS WOMAN WITH FINE GARMENTS 308-13

ABSTINENCE AS WOMAN IN NUN'S GARMENTS 308-14, FALSE-SEEMING
DRESSED AS FRIAR 308-14

*$ABSTRACT 309
  *LIBRARY BOD
  *SLIDE SET TITLE MEN'S DRESS
  *NEGATIVE REFERENCE ROLL 179E
  *RENTAL FEE SM 309 $2.35
  *TITLE OF MANUSCRIPT ROMANCE OF THE ROSE
  *SHELFMARK MS SELDEN SUPRA 57
  *PROVENANCE FRENCH
  *DATE EXECUTED 14TH/C1350
  *LANGUAGE LATIN
  *AUTHOR GUILLAUME DE LORRIS AND JEAN DE MEUNG
  *TYPE OF MANUSCRIPT ROMANCE
  *CONTENTS MEN'S DRESS 309/1-7, COSTUME 309/1-7, ROMANCE OF THE
  ROSE 309/1-7, LITERATURE/ ROMANCE OF THE ROSE 309/1-7, YOUNG
  MAN DRESSING 309-1, LOVER WEARING TIPPET WITH FRINGE SPEAKS TO
  IDLENESS 309-2, FRIEND IN STRIPED AND BUTTONED TUNIC TALKS TO
  LOVER 309-3, MESSENGER IN PINK TUNIC WAITS ON GOD OF LOVE
  309-4, JEAN DE MEUNG ADDRESSES THREE MEN 309-5, POSTILLION OF
  VENUS CARRIAGE 309-6, LOVER RICHLY DRESSED IN TUNIC/ TIPPET/
  SHOVEL HAT 309-7

*$ABSTRACT 310
  *LIBRARY BOD
  *SLIDE SET TITLE CALENDAR STARS AND MARVELS OF THE EAST
  *NEGATIVE REFERENCE ROLL 179F
  *RENTAL FEE SM 310 $4.00
  *SHELFMARK MS BODLEY 614
  *PROVENANCE ENGLISH
  *DATE EXECUTED 12TH/ FIRST HALF
  *LANGUAGE LATIN
  *TYPE OF MANUSCRIPT CALENDAR/ MARVELS
  *CONTENTS CALENDAR 310/1-40, STARS OF THE EAST 310/1-40,
  MARVELS OF THE EAST 310/1-40, SCHOLARS WITH ONE MEASURING SUN
  310-1, JANUARY WITH JANUS FEASTING BY CAULDRON 310-2, FEBRUARY
  WITH MAN WARMING FEET BY BELLOWS 310-3, MARCH WITH FIGURES
  PRUNING WITH BILLHOOKS 310-4, CAPITALS S AND L/ TEXT ABOUT SUN
  AND MOON 310-5, SUN GOD IN CHARIOT DRAWN BY HORSES 310-6, MOON
  GODDESS IN CHARIOT DRAWN BY BULLS 310-6, TAURUS/ GEMINI/
  CANCER 310-7, LEO/ VIRGO/ SCORPIO 310-8, SAGITTARIUS/
  CAPRICORNUS 310-9, AQUAIUS/ PISCES 310-10, MARS/ SATURN/
  JUPITER/ SOL/ VENUS/ LUNA/ MERCURY 310-11, ARCTOPHYLAX/
  SERPENT/ CROWN 310-12, ENGONASIN/ DRAGON/ LYRE/ SWAN 310-13,
  CEPHEUS/ CASSOPEIA ON THRONES 310-14, ANDROMEDA/ PERSEUS/
  MEDUSA'S HEAD/ PLEIADES/ ELECTRA 310-15, HYADES/ OPHRYUCUS
  310-16, CHARIOTEER/ ARROW/ EAGLE 310-17, DOLPHIN/ PEGASUS
  310-18, HARE/ DOG/ ANTICANIS/ ARGO 310-20, DELTOTON/ ORION
  310-19, ERIDANUS/ CANOPUS/ CENTAUR 310-21, WHALE/ PISCES
  NOTHIUS/ COMET 310-22, HEADS OF THE WINDS/ RAINBOW ABOVE
  CLOUDS 310-23, ASTRONOMER WITH ASTROLABE/ SHEEP LIKE OXEN
  310-24, ASTROLABE 310-24, HENS/ BEAST WITH TWO HEADS AND EIGHT
  LEGS 310-25, SERPENT/ DONKEYS/ SERPENTS 310-26, DOG-HEADED
  MAN/ BEARDED DWARF/ RED ANTS SHAPED LIKED DOGS 310-27, ANTS
  EAT MALE CAMEL/ GOLD SEEKER ESCAPES ON CAMEL 310-28, GIANT
  NAKED WITH LIONS HEAD/ LERTEX WITH DONKEY'S EARS 310-29, MAN
  WITH FACE ON CHEST 310-29, SERPENTS/ MAN WITH BODY OF WILD ASS
  310-30, LAND OF SUN AND LAND OF MOON 310-31, LAND WITH TREES
  LIKE LAUREL AND OLIVE 310-31, GIANT ACCOSTS/ CATCHES/ EATS AND
  MOURNS STRANGER 310-31, WHITE MAN GATHERS EARS/ MAN WITH HORN
  310-32, PRIEST IN TEMPLE OF BEL 310-32, MEN SPEAK BY MOUNTAIN
  OF RED SEA RULERS 310-33, HUNTRESS/ BEARDED WITH HOUNDS
  310-33, MAN EATING FLESH OF HORRIBLE BEAST HE HAS SLAIN
  310-33, LAND OF HOSPITABLE KINGS 310-34, TREES BEARING GEMS
  310-34, ETHIOPIANS/ BED OF IVORY/ PHOENIX 310-35, NEGROES ON
  VOLCANO/ MAMBRES RAISED FROM HELL 310-36, MAMBRES IN HELL
  310-36, JOHN THE MAGICIAN 310-36, UNICORN LANCED IN VIRGIN'S

LAP 310-37, SERPENTS GUARD GOLDEN MOUNTAINS OF INDIA 310-3
CHAMELEON WITH CAMEL'S HEAD AND HORSE'S NECK 310-37, BROTHE
FIGHT WHILE SISTER WEEPS BY HEALING SPRING 310-38, SCIOPOD (
ETHIOPIA SHADED FROM SUN BY FOOT 310-38, LIBYAN ANTAPODES A
UPPOPOD OF SCYTHIA 310-38, HERMAPHRODITE WITH FEMALE LE
BREAST 310-39, MONSTROUS MAN SHELTERS FROM SUN WITH HUGE LOW
LIP 310-39, SATYR AND PARROT 310-39, WOMEN FIXED BY SPELL
SOIL 310-40, RESCUER PULLS OFF SISTER'S ARM TRYING TO HE
310-40

*$ABSTRACT 311
 *LIBRARY BOD
 *SLIDE SET TITLE CHILDHOOD OF CHRIST
 *NEGATIVE REFERENCE ROLL 179G
 *RENTAL FEE SM 311 $4.50 TITLE OF MANUSCRIPT GESTA INFANTI
 SALVATORIS
 *SHELFMARK MS DOUCE 237
 *PROVENANCE FRENCH
 *DATE EXECUTED 15TH/C1470-80
 *LANGUAGE FRENCH
 *TYPE OF MANUSCRIPT LIFE OF CHRIST
 *CONTENTS CHRIST/ CHILDHOOD 311/1-50, INFANCY OF CHRI
 311/1-50, JOACHIM WATCHING FLOCKS FROM DOOR 311-1, PRIE
 REJECTS SACRIFICE OF JOACHIM AND ANNA AT TEMPLE 311-2, ANG
 FORETELLS BIRTH OF MARY TO ANNA 311-3, ANGEL ASKS JOACHIM
 RETURN TO ANNA 311-4, JOACHIM PROSTRATES SELF BEFORE SACRIFI(
 311-5, VIRGIN'S BIRTH 311-6, MARY AS CHILD PRAYS IN TEMP
 311-7, VIRGIN MARY WEAVING 311-8, MARY BEFORE ALTAR READI
 BOOK TO MOTHER AND GIRLS 311-9, ANGEL BRINGS FOOD TO MARY W
 HAS BOOK 311-10, PRIEST SENDS MESSENGERS FOR SUITORS FOR MA
 311-11, JOSEPH HANDS ROD TO PRIEST AND UNMARRIED JEWS BEHI
 311-12, JOSEPH RECEIVES ROD BACK WITH DOVE AND WHITE FLOWE
 311-13, JOSEPH WITH ROD LEAVES TEMPLE 311-14, BETHROTHAL (
 MARY AND JOSEPH 311-15, GABRIEL APPEARS TO MARY AS SHE WEAV
 311-16, MARY TURNS TO LOOK AT GABRIEL WHILE PRAYING 311-1
 JOSEPH GIVEN WATER DURING TRIAL BY PRIESTS 311-18, MARY A
 INFANT JESUS AS JOSEPH AND ANGELS WATCH 311-19, MARY A
 JOSEPH BESIDE INFANT JESUS/ OX AND ASS 311-20, PRESENTATION (
 CHRIST IN TEMPLE 311-21, MASSACRE OF HOLY INNOCENTS 311-2
 FLIGHT INTO EGYPT WITH HOLY FAMILY RESTING 311-23, HOLY FAMI
 ENTER TEMPLE AND IDOLS FALL 311-24, JESUS AT FIVE PLAYS
 JORDAN 311-25, JESUS COMMANDS SPARROWS HE HAS MADE TO FLY AW
 311-26, JESUS EXPLAINS TO JOSEPH WHY HE CURSED BOY 311-2
 JESUS REVIVES BOY HE CURSED 311-28, ZACHARIAS TELLS MARY A
 JOSEPH HE WILL TEACH JESUS 311-29, ZACHARIAS INSTRUCTS JES
 FROM LARGE BOOK 311-30, JESUS REVIVES ZENO WHO FELL TO H
 DEATH 311-31, JESUS CARRIES WATER IN CLOAK AFTER BREAKI
 PITCHER 311-32, LIONS ADORE JESUS AT JORDAN 311-33, JES
 TELLS LIONS TO GO IN PEACE 311-34, JESUS HELPS JOSEPH
 CARPENTER'S SHOP 311-35, JESUS STRIKES DEAD TEACHER W
 BIRCHED HIM 311-36, JESUS AT SCHOOL/ TEACHERS AMAZED BY H
 KNOWLEDGE 311-37, JESUS GIVES GRACE TO DEAD MAN 311-38, JES
 CURES JACQUES OF SNAKE BITE 311-39, JESUS BLESSES FOOD F(
 RELATIONS 311-40, JESUS RESCUES BOY FROM TOWER 311-41, FATH
 OF RESCUED BOY COMPLAINS ABOUT JESUS 311/42-43, JESUS TUR
 SOWER'S WHEAT INTO STONE 311-44, JESUS TELLS PALM TREE
 SHADE MARY AND JOSEPH 311-45, JESUS SLIDES DOWN SUNBE
 311-46, JESUS KILLS BOY WHO STRUCK HIM AND FATHER COMPLAI
 311-47, JESUS STRIKES HIS ACCUSERS BLIND 311-47, JESUS ACCUS
 OF KILLING BOY/ RESTORES TO LIFE 311-48, JESUS HEALS SEVER
 FOOT 311-49, JESUS FETCHES WATER AND THROWN PITCHER UNBROK
 311-50

*$ABSTRACT 312
 *LIBRARY BOD
 *SLIDE SET TITLE DOMESTIC LIFE
 *NEGATIVE REFERENCE ROLL 179H
 *RENTAL FEE SM 312 $2.50

*TITLE OF MANUSCRIPT ROMANCE OF THE ROSE
*SHELFMARK MS DOUCE 364
*PROVENANCE FRENCH
*DATE EXECUTED 15TH/C1460
*LANGUAGE FRENCH
*AUTHOR GUILLAUME DE LORRIS AND JEAN DE MEUNG
*TYPE OF MANUSCRIPT ROMANCE
*CONTENTS DOMESTIC LIFE 312/1-10, ROMANCE OF THE ROSE 312/1-10,
LITERATURE/ ROMANCE OF THE ROSE 312/1-10, BEDROOM WITH
LATTICED WINDOWS AND CANOPIED BEDS 312-1, TILED FLOOR/
WINDOWS/ CHEST/ PEWTER JUG AND PLATES 312-2, HUT/ WOODEN WITH
POVERTY 312-3, POVERTY 312-3, AVARICE 312-2, LARGESSE IN
BEDROOM WITH HANGINGS/ TAPESTRY/ CHAIR 312-4, LOVER AND
FRANCHISE IN ROOM WITH LATTICED WINDOWS/ TAPESTRY 312-5, LOVER
AND FRIEND IN WOOD PANELLED ROOM 312-6, GOD OF LOVE AND
FAUX-SEMBLANT IN ROOM WITH BENCHES 312-7, BEL ACQUEIL AS OLD
WOMAN WITH DISTAFF AND SPINDLE 312-8, NATURE AND GENIUS IN
CHAPEL WITH ALTAR AND BENCH 312-9, NATURE AND GENIUS WITH
BALDACHIN OVER ALTAR 312-10

*$ABSTRACT 313
  *LIBRARY BOD
  *SLIDE SET TITLE BOOK OF HOURS AND PSALTER
  *NEGATIVE REFERENCE ROLL 180A
  *RENTAL FEE SM 313 $2.40
  *COMMENTS HOURS OF THE VIRGIN AND PSALTER EXECUTED FOR
  ELIZABETH DE BOHUN COUNTESS OF NORTHAMPTON PERHAPS AT
  BLACKFRIARS AT LONDON
  *TITLE OF MANUSCRIPT HOURS OF THE VIRGIN AND PSALTER
  *SHELFMARK MS ASTOR A 1
  *PROVENANCE ENGLISH/ BLACKFRIARS AT LONDON
  *DATE EXECUTED 14TH/C1350
  *LANGUAGE LATIN
  *TYPE OF MANUSCRIPT BOOK OF HOURS AND PSALTER
  *CONTENTS VIRGIN/ HOURS OF AND PSALTER 313/1-8, ANNUNCIATION TO
  VIRGIN 313-1, LILY IN POT 313-1, JESSE TREE/ DAVID WITH HARP/
  VIRGIN AND CHILD 313-2, DAVID POINTING TO EYE 313-3, DAVID
  WITH FOOL WHO IS STABBING SELF 313-4, GOD IN CLOUD 313-4,
  DAVID IN WATER/ CHRIST AND ANGELS 313-5, DAVID PLAYING
  CARILLION 313-6, CLERGY CHANTING AT LECTERN 313-7, TRINITY
  313-8

*$ABSTRACT 314
  *LIBRARY BOD
  *SLIDE SET TITLE BOOK OF HOURS
  *NEGATIVE REFERENCE ROLL 180B
  *RENTAL FEE SM 314 $4.60
  *COMMENTS ONCE OWNED BY CARDINAL ALBRECHT OF BRANDENBURG
  *SHELFMARK MS ASTOR A 24
  *PROVENANCE FLEMISH/ BRUGES
  *DATE EXECUTED 16TH/C1525
  *LANGUAGE LATIN
  *ARTIST/ SCHOOL SIMON BENINCK
  *TYPE OF MANUSCRIPT BOOK OF HOURS
  *CONTENTS BOOK OF HOURS/ FLEMISH/ 16TH 314/1-52, DAILY LIFE OF
  16TH CENTURY 314/1-52, COAT OF ARMS/ ALBRECHT OF BRANDENBURG
  314-1, MAN WARMS SELF BY FIRE/ WOMAN PREPARES MEAL 314-2,
  WATER CARRIER 314-3, WOODSMEN/ WOMAN CARRIES WOOD/ MEN
  PLOUGHING 314-4, FISH/ TOWER/ MEN PRUNING/ WOMAN WITH BASKET
  314-5, MEN MAKING BUNDLES OF FAGGOTS 314-6, RAM/ SIGN OF WITH
  GARDENERS/ CASTLE/ LADIES/ GENTLEMEN 314-7, PEASANT DRIVES
  SHEEP AND BLACK RAM FROM BARN 314-8, BULL/ SIGN OF/ MAID MILKS
  COW/ WOMAN MAKES BUTTER 314-9, HAWKING PARTY ENTERS CASTLE
  314-10, TWINS/ SIGN OF/ ROW BOAT AND PEOPLE/ CASTLE 314-11,
  CRAB/ SIGN OF/ SHEEP-SHEARING/ DUCK POND/ DUTCH BARN 314-12,
  SHEEP-SHEARING/ SHEPHERD WITH SPUD 314-13, HAYMAKING/ HAYCOKS/
  WAGON/ WOMAN RAKING 314-14, LION/ SIGN OF/ PEASANT SCYTHING
  HAY/ WOMAN WITH BASKET 314-15, PEASANTS SCYTHING CORN 314-16,

159

VIRGIN/ WOMAN TYING CORN SHEAVES/ HORSES TAKE AWAY CO
314-17, PLOUGHING WITH HORSE-DRAWN PLOUGH 314-18, PEASAI
KNOCKING DOWN ACORNS 314-18, SCORPION/ SIGN OF/ SOWING AI
HARROWING 314-19, GRAPE PICKING/ COURTYARD OF FARMHOUSE/ BUI
314-20, SCALES/ BULL SLAUGHTERING/ FLOWERING PLANTS ON SHEI
314-21, THRESHING CORN IN BARN 314-22, ARCHER/ PIGS FED WI
SWILL/ DOVE-COTE WITH DOVES 314-23, PIG KILLING/ WOMAN CATCHI
BLOOD IN PAN 314-24, GOAT/ PIG CHOPPED BY PEASANTS/ SKATING (
CASTLE MOAT 314-25, SOLAR TABLE 314-26, WREATH MAKING (
FRAME/ BOATING ON LAKE/ DEER 314-26, LUNAR TABLE FOR FINDII
GOLDEN NUMBER 314-27, ASTROLOGER ON SEASHORE 314-2
TOADSTOOLS/ CRESCENT MOON/ STARS 314-27, INITIAL/ DECORATI\
314/28-38 AND 43-49 AND 51-52, MARGINAL ILLUMINATIO
314/28-52, FLOWERS 314-28, FLOWERS/ BUTTERFLIES 314-2
VIOLET/ WILD ROSE/ HEARTSEASE/ CORNFLOWER 314-30, FLOWER:
DECORATIVE 314/28-30 AND 33-34 AND 35 AND 39, FLOWER:
DECORATIVE 314/41 AND 45 AND 49 AND 51, STREET SCENE/ MEN WI'
POTS OF PLANTS/ TOPIARY 314-31, COURTLY SCENE/ MUSICIANS PL
INSTRUMENTS 314-32, VIRGIN AND CHILD MEDALLION 314-3(
SACRIFICE OF ISAAC/ ANGEL HOLDS ABRAHAM'S SWORD 314-35, BEA:
WITH TWO HEADS 314-36, DECORATIVE WRITING 314-37, MAYII
PROCESSION WITH YOUTHS CARRYING BRANCHES 314-38, ADORATION (
SACRED WOUNDS 314-39, MAN OF SORROWS IN MANDORLA/ POPE GREGO\
CELEBRATES MASS 314-40, CRUCIFIXION/ CHRIST NAILED TO CROS
WHEELS FOR EXECUTION 314-41, SACRED FACE/ CHRIST HOLDS O
314-42, CHERUB HOLDING CANDLELABRUM LIKE ORNAMENT 314-4
DIAPERED/ BROCADE PATTERN 314-44, ST LUKE WITH CROZIER
BISHOP 314-45, ST JOHN AS BISHOP WITH EAGLE READING BO(
314-46, GRAPEVINE WITH BUTTERFLIES AND SNAIL 314-47, DIANTHU:
GIANT IN DECORATED POT 314-48, BEGGARS AND RICHLY DRESSED M.
AND WOMAN WITH ANGEL 314-49, TRINITY IN MANDORLA/ CHRIST
MAN OF SORROWS 314-50, ARCHITECTURAL DESIGN 314-52, PASSIOI
SYMBOLS/ CROWN OF THORNS/ CHRIST'S ROBE 314-52

*$ABSTRACT 315
  *LIBRARY BOD
  *SLIDE SET TITLE BOOK OF HOURS
  *NEGATIVE REFERENCE ROLL 180C
  *RENTAL FEE SM 315 $5.60
  *COMMENTS ONCE OWNED BY CARDINAL ALBRECHT OF BRANDENBURG
  *SHELFMARK MS ASTOR A 24
  *PROVENANCE FLEMISH/ BRUGES
  *DATE EXECUTED 16TH/C 1525
  *LANGUAGE LATIN
  *ARTIST/ SCHOOL SIMON BENINCK
  *TYPE OF MANUSCRIPT BOOK OF HOURS
  *CONTENTS BOOK OF HOURS/ FLEMISH/ 16TH 315/1-72, DECORATI
  MARGINS 315/1-72, ST MICHAEL ARCHANGEL WITH SWORD/ SHIEL
  CROSS ABOVE DEVILS 315-1, RIVER WITH BOATING/ BIRDS/ ANIMA
  315-1, TEXT OF TO A GUARDIAN ANGEL 315-2, FLOWERS IN MARGII
  DECORATION 315/2-7 AND 11-15 AND 18, FLOWERS IN MARGII
  DECORATION 315/20-26 AND 28 AND 30-35, FLOWERS IN MARGII
  DECORATION 315/41-51 AND 54-55 AND 57, FLOWERS IN MARGII
  DECORATION 315/61 AND 64 AND 66, FLOWERS IN MARGII
  DECORATION 315/71, DECORATIVE INITIALS 315/1-52, ST JOHN T
  BAPTIST/ TEXT ONLY 315-3, ST MATTHEW WITH AXE 315-4, LANDSCA
  WITH CASTLE 315-4, ST PHILIP WITH CROSS 315-5, LANDSCAPE WI
  CITY 315-5, ST JAMES THE LESS WITH STAFF AND BOOK 315-
  LANDSCAPE OF MEN WITH PACKS REFLECTED IN RIVER 315-6, ST PET
  THE APOSTLE WITH KEYS AND BOOK 315-7, LANDSCAPE WITH ROCKS A
  CAVE 315-7, ST PAUL WITH SWORD AND BOOK 315-8, ST JAMES T
  GREAT WITH STAFF AND SCRIPT 315-9, ST BARTHOLOMEW AND FLAYI
  KNIFE 315-10, LANDSCAPE OF HOUSE WITH MOAT AND SWANS AND BO\
  315-10, ST MATTHEW WITH HALBERD 315-11, ST SIMON WI
  LONG-HANDLED SAW 315-12, LANDSCAPES 315/1-72, ST JUDE T
  APOSTLE WITH WOODEN SQUARE 315-13, ST ANDREW THE APOSTLE WI
  UNDRESSED CROSS 315-14, ST THOMAS THE APOSTLE WITH SPE
  315-15, ST CHRISTOPHER TEXT ONLY 315-16, LANDSCAPE HOUSE WI
  THATCHED ROOF AND HERMIT NEAR SHRINE 315-16, ST LAWREN(
  WEARING DALMATIC WITH BOOK AND GRIDIRON 315-17, ST DEN

DECAPITATED AND HOLDING MITRED HEAD AND CROZIER 315-18, ST
MARK/ TEXT ONLY 315-20, ST JOHN WITH POISONED CHALICE 315-19,
ST LUKE/ TEXT ONLY 315-21, ST SEBASTIAN'S MARTYRDOM WATCHED BY
KING AND ADVISOR 315-22, ST VINCENT WEARING DALMATIC/ BOOK/
FLESH HOOK 315-23, ST BLAZE HOLDING LIGHTED CANDLE AND CROZIER
315-24, ST VALENTINE/ TEXT ONLY 315-25, ST GEORGE/ TEXT ONLY
315-26, ST ERASMUS MARTYRDOM/ MACHINE DISEMBOWELS SAINT AS MEN
WATCH 315-27, LADIES PLUCK BIRD IN GARDEN 315-27, MASSACRE OF
TEN THOUSAND MARTYRS 315-28, ST STEPHEN WEARING DALMATIC/ HEAD
WOUNDED/ CARRIES STONE 315-29, ST ERHARD WITH MITRE AND
CROZIER 315-30, ST ANTHONY WEARING HOODED CLOAK/ ROSARY/ BELL/
BOOK 315-31, ST GREGORY WEARING MITRE WITH OPEN BOOK AND CROSS
315-32, ST BENEDICT/ TEXT ONLY 315-33, ST AMBROSE WITH MITRE
AND CROZIER 315-34, ST DOMINIC AS FRIAR WITH BOOK/ STAFF
315-35, ST ROCHE WITH ANGEL TENDING LEG 315-36, ST BERNARD/
TEXT ONLY 315-37, ST AUGUSTINE/ TEXT ONLY 315-38, ST JEROME IN
GRAY ROBE SEATED WRITING/ STREET SCENE 315-39, CAMEL RIDEN BY
MAN 315-39, ST FRANCIS/ TEXT ONLY 315-40, MEDALLIONS OF ST
CATHERINE AND ST BARBARA 315-40, ST LEONARD WEARING DALMATIC
HOLDING FETTERS AND BOOK 315-42, ST WOLFGANG/ TEXT ONLY
315-41, ST MARTIN DIVIDING CLOAK TO GIVE TO BEGGAR 315-43, ST
NICHOLAS/ TEXT ONLY 315-44, ST AGNES HOLDING LAMB WITH BOOK
315-45, ST BRIDGET/ TEXT ONLY 315-46, ST AGATHA HOLDING BREAST
IN TONGS 315-47, GROTESQUE BEAST RIDEN BY MAN 315-47, ST
DOROTHY HOLDING BOOK AND BASKET OF ROSES 315-48, ANGELS
PICKING ROSES AND PUTTING IN BASKET 315-48, ST APOLLONIA WITH
TOOTH IN TONGS 315-49, ST GERTRUDE/ TEXT ONLY 315-50, ST
MARGARET/ TEXT ONLY 315-51, ST MARY MAGDALENE/ TEXT ONLY
315-52, LANDSCAPE WITH CASTLE BY RIVER 315-52, SHOP/ RICHLY
STOCKED 315-52, ST URSULA AND HER COMPANIONS/ TEXT ONLY
315-54, ST ELIZABETH/ TEXT ONLY 315-55, ST KATHERINE/ TEXT
ONLY 315-56, ST BARBARA WITH WAFER/ CHALICE/ PALM 315-57, ST
OTHILIA/ TEXT ONLY 315-58, GRAPE-PICKING 315-58, FOR EPIPHANY/
TEXT ONLY 315-59, EASTER/ TEXT ONLY 315-60, CHRIST AT TABLE
WITH PILGRIMS AT EMMAUS 315-60, PENTECOST/ TEXT ONLY 315-61,
ALL SAINT'S DAY/ TEXT ONLY 315-63, ASSUMPTION/ TEXT ONLY
315-62, CONFESSION/ MAN KNEELS BEFORE PRIEST/ WOMEN PRAYING
315-64, MASS/ KNEELING MAN RECEIVES COMMUNION 315-65, PRIEST
AND ATTENDANTS BEFORE ALTAR 315-66, ST BERNADINE OF SIENNA IN
HABIT 315-67, TRINITY/ CHRIST CHILD IN MANDORLA/ SAINTS/
DEVILS 315-67, SKULLS IN MARGIN AND MOURNERS AT CHURCH 315-68,
HELL 315-69, ST BRIDGET IN PRAYER 315-70, CREATURES FIGHT ON
LAKE 315-71, SEMI-HUMAN FIGURES IN MARGIN 315-71, MAN OF
SORROWS IN MANDORLA 315-72

*$ABSTRACT 316
  *LIBRARY BOD
  *SLIDE SET TITLE BOOK OF HOURS
  *NEGATIVE REFERENCE ROLL 180D
  *RENTAL FEE SM 316 $2.70
  *SHELFMARK MS ASTOR A 14
  *PROVENANCE FRENCH
  *DATE EXECUTED 15TH/ SECOND HALF
  *LANGUAGE LATIN
  *TYPE OF MANUSCRIPT BOOK OF HOURS
  *CONTENTS BOOK OF HOURS/ FRENCH/ 15TH 316/1-14, ST JOHN ON
PATMOS 316-1, ST JOHN PREACHING TO GROUPS OF PEOPLE 316-1,
ANNUNCIATION TO VIRGIN 316-2, ADAM AND EVE TEMPTED AND GIDEON
PRAYING 316-2, VISITATION 316-3, MARRIAGE OF JOSEPH AND VIRGIN
316-3, HOLY FAMILY WITH ANGELS 316-4, MOSES AND BURNING BUSH
AND PRIEST WITH CENSER 316-4, ANGEL APPEARS TO SHEPHERDS
316-5, SHEPHERDS CROSS BRIDGE 316-5, ADORATION OF MAGI 316-6,
SOLOMON GIVEN GOBLET BY QUEEN OF SHEBA 316-6, PRESENTATION
316-7, ISAAC AND SAMUEL 316-7, FLIGHT INTO EGYPT 316-8, ISAAC
AND JACOB AND RACHEL SENDING JACOB AWAY 316-8, CORONATION OF
VIRGIN 316-9, CRUCIFIXION WITH VIRGIN SWOONING IN ARMS OF ST
JOHN 316-10, SACRIFICE OF ISAAC AND MOSES AND SERPENT 316-10,
PENTECOST 316-11, GOD HANDS MOSES LAW AT MOUNT SINAI 316-11,
ELIJAH'S SACRIFICE/ FIRE CONSUMES 316-11, DAVID SLAYS GOLIATH
BEFORE MASSED HOSTS AND CROWNED 316-12, POPE AND CARDINAL

FOLLOWED BY LAITY IN PROCESSION 316-13, DEAD RIDERS MET BY
LIVING AT WAYSIDE CROSS 316-13, DEATH IN BED ATTENDED BY
PRIEST/ SERVER/ MAID 316-14, FUNERAL 316-14

*$ABSTRACT 317
  *LIBRARY BOD
  *SLIDE SET TITLE BOOK OF HOURS, CALENDAR WITH SIGNS OF ZODIAC
  AND OCCUPATIONS OF MONTHS
  *NEGATIVE REFERENCE ROLL 180E
  *RENTAL FEE SM 317 $4.15
  *COMMENTS ONCE OWNED BY ANTOINE, KING OF NAVARRE
  *SHELFMARK MS ASTOR A 15
  *PROVENANCE FRENCH/ PARIS
  *DATE EXECUTED 15TH/ THIRD QUARTER
  *LANGUAGE LATIN
  *TYPE OF MANUSCRIPT BOOK OF HOURS AND CALENDAR
  *CONTENTS CALENDAR 317/1-24, HOURS OF THE VIRGIN 317/25-43,
  ZODIAC/ SIGNS OF 317/1-24, OCCUPATIONS OF MONTHS 317/1-24,
  FEASTING AT TABLE SET WITH WHITE CLOTH 317-1, WATER CARRIER
  317-2, PEASANT WARMING FEET BY FIRE 317-3, FISH 317-4, PEASANT
  PRUNING 317-5, RAM 317-6, LADY BY ROSE ARBOR 317-7, BULL
  317-8, PEASANTS WITH LEAFY BRANCHES GOING MAYING 317-9, TWINS
  317-10, HAYMAKING 317-11, CRAB 317-12, CORN REAPED BY PEASANT
  317-13, LION 317-14, VIRGIN BETWEEN CORN STOCKS 317-15,
  PEASANT THRESHING CORN 317-16, GRAPES THRESHED IN TUB 317-17,
  SCALES 317-18, SOWING FIELD IN FURROWS 317-19, SCORPION
  317-20, SWINEHERD 317-21, ARCHER 317-22, BUTCHER WITH MALLET
  AND APRON 317-23, GOAT 317-24, ST JOHN EVANGELIST WITH EAGLE
  AND LION 317-25, ST LUKE WITH OX 317-26, ST MATTHEW WITH ANGEL
  AND LECTERN WITH BOOKS 317-27, ST MARK WITH LION 3-7-28,
  CUSTOMS BOOTH 317-28, VIRGIN AND CHILD WITH ANGEL PLAYING
  MANDOLIN 317-29, CHRIST LEARNS TO WALK AND JOSEPH WORKING
  317-29, ANNUNCIATION AND SCENES OF LIFE OF VIRGIN 317-30,
  VISITATION 317-31, ST JOSEPH REPROACHES VIRGIN 317-31, HOLY
  FAMILY 317-32, ANNUNCIATION TO SHEPHERDS WITH SPUDS 317-33,
  ADORATION OF MAGI 317-34, THREE AGES OF MAN 317-34, MAGI'S
  JOURNEY TO BETHLEHEM 317-34, PRESENTATION OF CHRIST IN TEMPLE
  317-35, FLIGHT INTO EGYPT 317-36, LEGEND OF GROWING CORN
  317-36, CORONATION OF VIRGIN 317-37, DAVID BEFORE ALTAR
  PLAYING HARP 317-38, CRUCIFIXION 317-39, PENTECOST 317-40,
  DEATH/ LADY SEWING SHROUD/ BELL-RINGER WITH HANDBELLS 317-41,
  VIRGIN AND CHILD WITH ANGELS AND KNEELING WOMAN 317-42,
  BAPTISM OF CHRIST 317-43, MINISTRY OF ST JOHN BAPTIST 317-43

*$ABSTRACT 318
  *LIBRARY BOD
  *SLIDE SET TITLE BOOK OF HOURS
  *NEGATIVE REFERENCE ROLL 180F
  *RENTAL FEE SM 318 $2.60
  *COMMENTS ONCE OWNED BY THE SEGUIER FAMILY
  *SHELFMARK MS ASTOR A 16
  *PROVENANCE FRENCH
  *DATE EXECUTED 15TH/ SECOND HALF
  *LANGUAGE LATIN
  *TYPE OF MANUSCRIPT BOOK OF HOURS
  *CONTENTS HOURS OF VIRGIN 318/1-12, ANNUNCIATION TO VIRGIN
  318-1, MUSICIANS 318-1, VISITATION WITH MOATED CASTLE IN
  BACKGROUND 318-2, GARDENERS 318-2, SHEPHERDS VISIT VIRGIN AND
  CHILD 318-3, COAT OF ARMS/ AZURE/ AGNUS DEI 318-3,
  ANNUNCIATION TO SHEPHERDS 318-4, PEASANT PLAYS PIPE TO HOUND
  IN MARGIN 318-4, ADORATION OF MAGI/ THREE AGES OF MAN 318-5,
  YOUTH DECLAIMS TO MAIDEN AND POINTS TO FOUNTAIN 318-5,
  PRESENTATION OF CHILD IN TEMPLE 318-6, GROTESQUE WITH
  CROSS-BOW 318-6, FLIGHT INTO EGYPT 318-7, UNICORN APPROACHING
  VIRGIN 318-7, GOD AND VIRGIN ENTHRONED 318-8, PUTTO RIDING
  HOBBY-HORSE IN MARGIN 318-8, ST MARY MAGDALENE WITH JAR OF
  OINTMENT 318-9, SS JOACHIM AND ANN OUTSIDE GOLDEN GATE 318-10,
  MERMAID WITH MIRROR AND ANGEL 318-10, HOLY FAMILY IN STABLE

318-11, COAT OF ARMS/ AZURE/ AGNUS DEI/ STARS IN MARGIN
318-11, ST PETER HOLDING KEY SURROUNDED BY APOSTLES 318-12,
WILD MAN HOLDING CLUB AND LEADING SNAIL BY REINS 318-12

*$ABSTRACT 319
  *LIBRARY BOD
  *SLIDE SET TITLE MISSAL OF POPE JOHN XXIII
  *NEGATIVE REFERENCE ROLL 180I
  *RENTAL FEE SM 319 $6.95
  *COMMENTS CALENDAR WITH OCCUPATIONS OF THE MONTHS AND SIGNS OF
   THE ZODIAC
  *TITLE OF MANUSCRIPT MISSAL OF POPE JOHN XXIII
  *SHELFMARK MS ASTOR A 5
  *PROVENANCE ITALIAN/ BOLOGNESE
  *DATE EXECUTED 15TH/ EARLY
  *LANGUAGE LATIN
  *TYPE OF MANUSCRIPT MISSAL
  *CONTENTS MISSAL 319/1-99, ZODIAC/ SIGNS OF 319/1-99,
   OCCUPATIONS OF THE MONTHS 319/1-99, JANUARY 319-1, MAN WARMING
   FOOT BY FIRE 319-1, WATER POT/ WATER CARRIER 319-2, FEBRUARY
   319-3, FISHERMAN FISHING WITH ROD 319-3, FISH 319-4, MARCH
   319-4, MAN BLOWING TWO HORNS 319-5, RAM 319-6, APRIL 319-7,
   MAN WITH BUNCHES OF FLOWERS 319-7, BULL 319-8, MAY 319-9, MAN
   RIDING WHITE HORSE AND HOUNDS BESIDE 319-9, TWINS 319-10, JUNE
   319-11, REAPING WHEAT 319-11, CRAB 319-12, JULY 319-13, WHEAT
   THRESHED WITH FAIL 319-13, LION 319-14, AUGUST 319-15, COOPER
   HOOPING BARREL 319-15, VIRGIN 319-16, SEPTEMBER 319-17, GRAPE
   HARVEST 319-17, SCALES 319-18, OCTOBER 319-19, PEASANT SEWING
   319-19, SCORPION 319-20, NOVEMBER 319-21, ACORNS KNOCKED DOWN
   FOR SWINE 319-21, ARCHER 319-22, DECEMBER 319-23, PIG
   SLAUGHTERED BY PEASANT 319-23, GOAT PORTRAYED AS UNICORN
   319-24, CHRIST IN MANDORLA SUPPORTED BY ANGELS 319-25, VIRGIN
   PRESENTS POPE 319-25, COAT OF ARMS OF JOHN XXIII 319-25, HOLY
   FAMILY IN STABLE 319-26, INITIALS/ HISTORIATED 319/27-99,
   INNOCENTS WITH PALMS 319-27, ST THOMAS BECKET 319-28, CHRIST
   319-29, HALOED KING 319-30, ADORATION OF MAGI 319-31, ST
   MAURUS WEARING SACKCLOTH 319-32, ST PETER 319-33, ST SABINA
   319-34, ST JOHN EVANGELIST BOILED IN CAULDRON 319-35, ST MARY
   319-36, ST LAURENCE 319-37, VIRGIN 319-38, ST PETER HOLDING
   BOOK AND KEY 319-39, BOYS SINGING AND BEARING PALMS 319-40, ST
   MATTHEW WRITING 319-41, ST MARK WRITING 319-42, ST LUKE WITH
   OX HEAD IN BACKGROUND 319-43, CHRIST AT TABLE WITH THREE
   DISCIPLES 319-44, ST JOHN EVANGELIST WRITING 319-45, BEARDED
   MAN WITH SCROLL 319-46, MASS CELEBRATED IN GOTHIC CHURCH IN
   FULL SPLENDOR 319-47, RESURRECTION AS CHRIST WITH WOUNDS STEPS
   FROM TOMB 319-48, ASCENSION OF CHRIST WITH CROSS AND BANNER
   319-49, PENTECOST 319-50, CHRIST CALLS ST ANDREW AND ST PETER
   BY LAKE 319-51, MEN IN BOAT 319-51, ST PETER AND ST ANDREW
   319-52, ST LUCY WITH HER EYES 319-53, ST LUCY WITH MARTYR'S
   PALM 319-54, ST THOMAS STUDYING BOOKS 319-54, ST THOMAS
   DECLAIMING 319-54, ST FELIX AND ST MARCELLUS CROWNED 319-55,
   MARTYRED VIRGIN 319-56, ST AGNES 319-57, ST PAUL WITH SWORD
   319-58, ST AGNES 319-59, ST AGATHA 319-60, ST VALENTINE
   319-61, ST PETER 319-62, ST GREGORY THE POPE CROWNED 319-63,
   ST BENEDICT IN BLACK COWL 319-64, ANNUNCIATION 319-65, ST
   GEORGE 319-66, ST MARK WITH LION AND SCROLL 319-66, ST PHILIP
   AND ST JAMES 319-67, INVENTION OF THE CROSS 319-68, ST URBAN
   THE POPE CROWNED 319-69, ST ANTHONY OF PADUA IN FRANCISCAN
   HABIT 319-70, NATIVITY OF ST JOHN BAPTIST AND ZACHARIAS WRITES
   NAME 319-71, GROTESQUE BLOWS TRUMPET IN MARGIN 319-72, ST JOHN
   AND ST PAUL/ MARTYRS WITH PALMS 319-73, ST PETER AND ST PAUL/
   WITH KEY AND SWORD 319-74, ST MARY MAGDALENE BAREHEADED WITH
   OINTMENT POT 319-75, ST STEPHEN WITH STONES ON HEAD AND
   MARTYR'S PALM 319-76, ST LAURENCE WITH GRIDIRON/ DALMATIC AND
   PALM 319-77, ASSUMPTION OF VIRGIN WATCHED BY APOSTLES 319-78,
   ST BARTHOLOMEW HOLDING FLAYING KNIFE 319-79, ST AUGUSTINE
   319-80, DECOLLATION OF ST JOHN BAPTIST 319-81, NATIVITY OF
   VIRGIN 319-82, VIGIL OF ST MATTHEW/ HE HAS RED WINGS 319-83,
   ST MATTHEW WITH GREEN WINGS 319-84, ST FRANCIS 319-85, ST LUKE
   WITH OX 319-86, SS SIMON AND JUDE WITH PALM 319-87, ALL

SAINTS/ ST PETER AS POPE 319-88, ST MARTIN MITRED WITH CROZI
319-89, ST CECILIA WITH PALM 319-90, ST CATHERINE WITH WHE
AND PALM 319-91, VIRGIN AMONG DISCIPLES AND ST PETER AND
ANDREW 319-92, ST ANDREW WITH TAU CROSS 319-92, DOVE/ SPIRIT
DESCENDING WITH RED RAYS 319-93, REQUIEM HEAD AND SHOULDERS
SKELETON 319-94, MASS SAID BY TONSURED PRIEST 319-9
VISITATION/ VIRGIN EMBRACES ST ELIZABETH 319-96, INITIA
ORNAMENTED AND MARGIN 319/97-99

*$ABSTRACT 320
  *LIBRARY BOD
  *SLIDE SET TITLE OFFICE OF THE VIRGIN
  *NEGATIVE REFERENCE ROLL 180J
  *RENTAL FEE SM 320 $2.30
  *COMMENTS WRITTEN AND ILLUMINATED FOR GALEAZZO MARIA SFORZA
  *SHELFMARK MS ASTOR A 6
  *PROVENANCE ITALIAN/ MILAN
  *DATE EXECUTED 15TH/C1470
  *LANGUAGE LATIN
  *ARTIST/ SCHOOL MASTER OF THE VITAE IMPERATORUM
  *TYPE OF MANUSCRIPT OFFICE OF THE VIRGIN
  *CONTENTS OFFICE OF THE VIRGIN 320/1-6, INITIALS/ DECORAT
   320/1-6, INITIAL D/ ANNUNCIATION 320-1, INITIAL D ON GO
   GROUND 320-2, INITIAL D 320/1-6, VIRGIN AND CHILD 320-
   CROWNED PORTRAIT HEAD OF MAN 320-5, ANNUNCIATION 320-5, VIRG
   AND CHILD ENTHRONED 320-6, DECORATIVE BORDERS 320/1-6

*$ABSTRACT 321
  *LIBRARY BOD
  *SLIDE SET TITLE BOOK OF HOURS
  *NEGATIVE REFERENCE ROLL 181B
  *RENTAL FEE SM 321 $2.35
  *COMMENTS ONCE OWNED BY THE SEGUIER FAMILY
  *SHELFMARK MS ASTOR A 16
  *PROVENANCE FRENCH
  *DATE EXECUTED 15TH/ SECOND HALF
  *LANGUAGE LATIN
  *TYPE OF MANUSCRIPT BOOK OF HOURS
  *CONTENTS BOOK OF HOURS 321/1-7, ST PETER HOLDING K
   SURROUNDED BY APOSTLES 321-1, WILD MAN WITH CLUB AND SNAIL
   REINS 321-1, DAVID WITH HARP ON FLOOR 321-2, COAT OF ARM
   AZURE/ AGNUS DEI BETWEEN TWO STARS 321-2, PENTECOST 321-
   COAT OF ARMS/ AZURE/ AGNUS DEI BETWEEN TWO STARS 321-3, FO
   PERFORMING BEFORE MAIDEN 321-3, CRUCIFIXION WITH VIRGIN AND
   JOHN EVANGELIST ON RIGHT 321-4, VIGIL OF THE DEAD/ CLER
   READING AT LECTERN 321-5, DEATH POINTS SPEAR AT WOMAN 321-
   BURIAL SCENE 321-6, COAT OF ARMS/ AZURE/ AGNUS DEI BETWE
   STARS 321/6-7, BETRAYAL 321-7, MALCHUS KNEELS ON ONE KNEE A
   PETER DRAWS SWORD 321-7

*$ABSTRACT 322
  *LIBRARY BOD
  *SLIDE SET TITLE BOOK OF HOURS
  *NEGATIVE REFERENCE ROLL 181C
  *RENTAL FEE SM 322 $4.60
  *SHELFMARK MS ASTOR A 13
  *PROVENANCE FRENCH/ PARIS
  *DATE EXECUTED 15TH/C1450
  *LANGUAGE LATIN
  *TYPE OF MANUSCRIPT BOOK OF HOURS
  *CONTENTS BOOK OF HOURS 322/1-16, ST JOHN WRITING ON PATMO
   EAGLE AND DEVIL BESIDE 322-1, ST LUKE WRITING WITH HIS
   322-2, ST MARK WRITING WITH HIS LION 322-3, ST MATTHEW WRITI
   WITH HIS ANGEL 322-4, ANNUNCIATION TO VIRGIN 322-5, MEDALLIO
   WITH SCENES FROM LIFE OF VIRGIN 322-5, HOLY FAMILY IN STABL
   ANGEL/ OX/ ASS 322-6, SHEPHERD WITH BAGPIPES AND SHEPHERDE

164

WITH DISTAFF 322-7, ANNUNCIATION TO SHEPHERDS 322-7, ADORATION
OF MAGI 322-8, PRESENTATION/ MAID WITH DOVES IN BASKET 322-9,
FLIGHT INTO EGYPT/ JOSEPH WITH FIRKIN 322-10, CORONATION OF
VIRGIN 322-11, DAVID PRAYING TO GOD 322-12, SECOND COMING OF
CHRIST/ ANGELS WITH TRUMPETS 322-13, VIRGIN AND CHILD
ENTHRONED OFFERED DISH BY ANGEL 322-14, VIRGIN AND CHILD WITH
ANGELS 322-15, PIETA 322-16

*$ABSTRACT 323
 *LIBRARY BOD
 *SLIDE SET TITLE BOOK OF HOURS
 *NEGATIVE REFERENCE ROLL 181D
 *RENTAL FEE SM 323 $4.60
 *SHELFMARK MS ASTOR A 17
 *PROVENANCE FRENCH
 *DATE EXECUTED 16TH/ FIRST QUARTER
 *LANGUAGE LATIN
 *ARTIST/ SCHOOL SCHOOL OF BOURGES
 *CONTENTS BOOK OF HOURS 323/1-52, COAT OF ARMS/ THREE
 FLEUR-DE-LYS AND MOTTO 323-1, CRUCIFIXION 323-32, ST JOHN
 EVANGELIST AND EAGLE 323-3, ST LUKE AT TABLE AND OX 323-4, ST
 MATTHEW AND ANGEL HOLDING BOX 323-5, ST MARK AND LION 323-6,
 PIETA 323-7, BETRAYAL/ JUDAS EMBRACES CHRIST 323-8,
 ANNUNCIATION/ VIRGIN AT PRIE-DIEU AND GABRIEL WITH SCEPTRE
 323-9, VISITATION/ VIRGIN HOLDS HAND OUT TO ST ELIZABETH
 323-10, HOLY FAMILY IN STABLE 323-11, ADORATION OF MAGI
 323-12, THREE AGES OF MAN 323-12, PRESENTATION/ JOSEPH WITH
 CANDLE AND BASKET OF DOVES 323-13, FLIGHT INTO EGYPT 323-14,
 DORMITION OF VIRGIN 323-15, CRUCIFIXION 323-16, PENTECOST/
 VIRGIN SURROUNDED BY APOSTLES 323-17, LAST SUPPER/ JUDE WITH
 MONEY-BAG GIVEN SOP BY JESUS 323-18, ST JOACHIM AND ST ANN
 MEET AT GOLDEN GATE 323-19, ST BARBARA/ BEHEADING 323-20, JOB
 ON DUNGHILL SURROUNDED BY DEVILS 323-21, MESSENGER IN ARMOR
 KNEELS TO MESSENGER 323-22, LAZARUS RAISED 323-23, TRINITY
 323-24, ST VERONICA WITH CHRIST'S FACE IMPRINTED ON VEIL
 323-25, ST JOACHIM AND ST ANN MEET AT GOLDEN GATE 323-26,
 PRESENTATION 323-27, ANNUNCIATION 323-28, ANNUNCIATION 323-29,
 VISITATION 323-30, ASSUMPTION 323-31, VIRGIN'S BIRTH 323-32,
 PRESENTATION OF VIRGIN AT TEMPLE STEPS 323-33, ST MICHAEL
 ATTACKS DRAGON 323-34, ST MATTHEW AND ANGEL PRESENTING BOOK
 323-35, ST CHRISTOPHER 323-36, ST SEBASTIAN'S MARTRYDOM
 323-37, ST ROCHE WITH DOG AND ANGEL 323-38, ST ADRIAN AND HIS
 ATTRIBUTES 323-39, ST NICHOLAS WITH CHILDREN IN PICKLING TUB
 323-40, ST GOERICUS WITH SCEPTRE BETWEEN TWO DAUGHTERS 323-41,
 ST CLAUDE WITH CROSS ON THRONE 323-42, ST AUGUSTINE WITH
 STATUE OF TRINITY AND CROZIER 323-43, ST JEROME KNEELS BEFORE
 CRUCIFIX AND LION 323-44, ST ANN TEACHING VIRGIN TO READ
 323-45, ST MARY MAGDALENE TAKEN TO HEAVEN BY ANGELS 323-46, ST
 CATHERINE EXECUTED BESIDE HER BROKEN WHEEL 232-47, ST MARGARET
 MIRACULOUSLY SAVED FROM GREEN DRAGON 232-48, DRAGON 323-48, ST
 BARBARA ON THRONE 323-49, ST GOERICUS SEATED ON THRONE BESIDE
 TWO DAUGHTERS 323-50, CHRIST'S WOUNDED SIDE FILLING CHALICE
 HELD BY ANGELS 323-51, VIRGIN WITH CHILD ON CRESCENT MOON
 323-52

*$ABSTRACT 324
 *LIBRARY BOD
 *SLIDE SET TITLE BOOK OF HOURS
 *NEGATIVE REFERENCE ROLL 181E
 *RENTAL FEE SM 324 $2.60
 *SHELFMARK MS ASTOR A 19
 *PROVENANCE FRENCH
 *DATE EXECUTED 16TH/ LATE
 *LANGUAGE LATIN
 *TYPE OF MANUSCRIPT BOOK OF HOURS
 *CONTENTS BOOK OF HOURS 324/1-12, ANNUNCIATION/ GABRIEL WITH
 CROSS ON FOREHEAD 324-1, VISITATION/ ST ELIZABETH KNEELS
 BEFORE VIRGIN 324-2, HOLY FAMILY IN STABLE/ JOSEPH WITH CANDLE

165

324-3, ANNUNCIATION TO SHEPHERDS 324-4, ADORATION OF MA
324-5, THREE AGES OF MAN 324-5, PRESENTATION/ JOSEPH WI
EMPTY BASKET 324-6, FLIGHT INTO EGYPT 324-7, CORONATION
VIRGIN 324-8, CRUCIFIXION 324-9, PENTECOST 324-10, BATHSHE
AND DAVID 324-11, JOB WITH COMFORTERS/ RUINED CASTLE
BACKGROUND 324-12

*$ABSTRACT 325
 *LIBRARY BOD
 *SLIDE SET TITLE OFFICE OF THE VIRGIN
 *NEGATIVE REFERENCE ROLL 181F
 *RENTAL FEE SM 325 $2.95
 *SHELFMARK MS ASTOR A 7
 *PROVENANCE ITALIAN
 *DATE EXECUTED 15TH/ MIDDLE
 *LANGUAGE LATIN
 *TYPE OF MANUSCRIPT OFFICE OF THE VIRGIN
 *CONTENTS OFFICE OF THE VIRGIN 325/1-19, ANNUNCIATION 325-
  ESCTUTCHEON FLANKED BY MUSICIANS 325-1, MUSICIANS 325-
  VISITATION/ JOSEPH WITH BIRDS/ PEACOCK 325-2, PRESENTATI
  325-4, MAGI AND THREE AGES OF MAN 325-5, HOLY FAMILY IN STAB
  325-3, FLIGHT INTO EGYPT 325-6, CHRIST-CHILD PREACHING
  ELDERS IN TEMPLE 325-7, CHRIST-CHILD FOUND BY PARENTS 325-
  DAVID WITH PSALTERY IN LANDSCAPE WITH CROSSES AND CAST
  325-9, HARROWING OF HELL 325-10, BETRAYAL OF CHRIST 325-1
  CHRIST BEFORE PILATE 325-12, MOCKING OF CHRIST 325-1
  FLAGELLATION 325-14, CRUCIFIXION 325-15, PIETA BEFORE CRO
  325-16, GUARDS WITH JEWS AT TOMB 325-17, PENTECOST 325-1
  VIRGIN AND CHILD IN NICHE 325-19, ANIMALS/ ASSORTED LEOPAR
  HARE/ HIND/ DOG/ MONKEY/ DEER/ FOX 325/1-19

*$ABSTRACT 326
 *LIBRARY BOD
 *SLIDE SET TITLE ST ANTHONY THE ABBOT/ ST CHRISTOPHER FROM BOO
  OF HOURS
 *NEGATIVE REFERENCE ROLL 181G
 *RENTAL FEE SM 326 $2.10
 *SHELFMARK MS ASTOR A 18
 *PROVENANCE FRENCH
 *DATE EXECUTED 15TH/ LATE
 *LANGUAGE LATIN
 *ARTIST/ SCHOOL FRENCH PROVINCIAL STYLE
 *TYPE OF MANUSCRIPT BOOK OF HOURS
 *CONTENTS BOOK OF HOURS 326/1-2, ST ANTHONY IN INITIAL V 326-
  ST ANTHONY ADMONISHING WOMAN WITH HORNS 326-1,
  CHRISTOPHER'S HEAD AND SHOULDERS CARRYING INFANT CHRIST 326-
  ST CHRISTOPHER'S LEGS 326-2

*$ABSTRACT 327
 *LIBRARY BOD
 *SLIDE SET TITLE BONIFACE VIII DECRETALS
 *NEGATIVE REFERENCE ROLL 181H
 *RENTAL FEE SM 327 $2.20
 *TITLE OF MANUSCRIPT DECRETALS OF BONIFACE VIII
 *SHELFMARK MS ASTOR A 4
 *PROVENANCE ITALIAN/ BOLOGNESE
 *DATE EXECUTED 14TH
 *LANGUAGE LATIN
 *TYPE OF MANUSCRIPT DECRETALS
 *CONTENTS DECRETALS OF BONIFACE VIII 327/1-4, POPE WIT
  CARDINALS 327-1, BORDERS/ DECORATED 327-1, OFFICE OF LEGA
  WHO PRESENTS RING TO TONSURED FIGURE 327-2, BETROTHAL/ GIFT
  RING 327-3, ACCUSATIONS/ TRIAL OF CLERK 327-4

*$ABSTRACT 328
  *LIBRARY BOD
  *SLIDE SET TITLE PETRARCH/ CICERO/ VALERIUS MAXIMUS
  *NEGATIVE REFERENCE ROLL 181I/1/2/3
  *RENTAL FEE SM 328 $2.80
  *TITLE OF MANUSCRIPT TRIONFI 328/1-3, RHETORICA AD HERENNIUM
  328/4-6, MEMORABILIA 328/7-15
  *SHELFMARK MS HOLKHAM 520 328/1-3, MS HOLKHAM 373 328/4-6, MS
  HOLKHAM 360 328/7-15
  *PROVENANCE ITALIAN
  *DATE EXECUTED 15TH 328/1-3, 14TH 328/4-15
  *LANGUAGE LATIN
  *AUTHOR PETRARCH 328/1-3, CICERO 328/4-6, VALERIUS MAXIMUS
  328/7-15
  *TYPE OF MANUSCRIPT CLASSICAL WRITINGS
  *CONTENTS CLASSICAL WRITINGS 328/1-15, TRIUMPH OF LOVE 328-1,
  TRIUMPH OF CHASTITY 328-2, TRIUMPH OF DEATH 328-3, TEXT WITH
  INITIAL AND BORDER 328-4, MURDER OF CICERO 328-5, CICERO'S
  TOMB 328-6, PREFACE WITH AUTHOR 328-7, DE INSTITUTIS ANTIQUIS/
  THREE WOMEN AT TABLE 328-8, DE INDOLE/ MARCUS CATO THREATENS
  SUICIDE 328-9, DE MODERATIONE/ PUBLIUS VALERIUS PUBLICOLA'S
  HOUSE DEMOLISHED 328-10, DE HUMANITATE AC CLEMENTIA/ SENATE
  MERCIFUL TO CARTHAGINIANS 328-11, DE PUDICITIA/ LUCRETIA
  FALLING ON SWORD 328-12, DE FELICITATE/ QUINTUS METELLUS HAS
  SUCCESSFUL CHILDREN 328-13, INFAMES REI QUIBUS DE CAUSIS
  ABSOLUTI AUT DAMNATI SUNT 328-14, CRATUS KILLS SISTER AND IS
  TRIED 328-14, DE LUXURIA ET LIBIDINE 328-15, SELF-INDULGENT
  ROMAN MATRONS 328-15

*$ABSTRACT 329
  *LIBRARY BOD
  *SLIDE SET TITLE EARLY ENGLISH TRANSLATIONS OF EUCLID FROM TWO
  PRINTED BOOKS
  *NEGATIVE REFERENCE ROLL 182E/1/2
  *RENTAL FEE SM 329 $4.00
  *PROVENANCE ENGLISH
  *LANGUAGE ENGLISH
  *AUTHOR EUCLID
  *CONTENTS EUCLID/ FIRST ENGLISH TRANSLATION 329/1-16, EUCLID/
  FIRST ENGLISH TRANSLATION 329/17-40, TEXT OF ENGLISH
  TRANSLATION OF EUCLID 329/1-40

*$ABSTRACT 330
  *LIBRARY BOD
  *SLIDE SET TITLE EARLY GREEK MATHEMATICS
  *NEGATIVE REFERENCE ROLL 182G
  *RENTAL FEE SM 330 $3.25
  *TITLE OF MANUSCRIPT ELEMENTS OF GEOMETRY 330/1-2, MEASUREMENT
  OF CIRCLE 330/1-2, OPERA 330/6-15, MATHEMATICAL COLLECTION
  330/16-25
  *SHELFMARK MS ARCH SELD B 13 330/1-2, MS AUCT F 5 28 330/3-5,
  MS SAVILLE W 11 330/6-15, E 2 12 ART 330/16-25
  *PROVENANCE ENGLISH 330/1-5, ITALIAN/ VENICE 330/6-15
  *DATE EXECUTED 13TH 330/1-5, 16TH/1558 330/6-15
  *LANGUAGE ENGLISH AND LATIN AND GREEK
  *AUTHOR EUCLID 330/1-5, ARCHIMEDES 330/1-2 AND 6-15, THOMAS
  SALSBURG 330/16-25
  *TYPE OF MANUSCRIPT GREEK MATHEMATICAL TEXTS
  *CONTENTS MATHEMATICAL TEXTS/ GREEK 330/1-25, CIRCLE WITH
  DIAMETER/ TANGENT/ LINES FROM CENTER TO TANGENT 330-1, CIRCLE
  WITH DIAMETER IN SQUARE 330-1, CIRCLE WITH DIAMETER AND
  INSCRIBED RIGHT-ANGLED TRIANGLES 330-2, PYTHAGORAS' THEOREM
  330-3, CIRCLE WITH SQUARE AND OCTAGON INSCRIBED 330-4, CIRCULI
  DIMENSIO/ PROPOSITIO I-III 330/6-9, QUADRATURA PARABOLES/
  PROPOSITIO XX-XXIV 330/10-13, LIBER DE ARENAE NUMERO
  330/14-15, BINDING 330-16, DEDICATION TO SIR JOHN DENHAM
  330/17-18, DEDICATION TO MOST SERENE GRAND DUKE OF TUSCANY
  330/20-21, DIAGRAM OF PLANETS ILLUSTRATING GALILEO'S SYSTEM

330-22, DIAGRAM OF INEQUALITIES OF SUPERIOR PLANETS 330-2:
DIAGRAM OF SUN'S ANNUAL MOTION 330-24, DIAGRAM OF SUN'S ANNU,
MOTION 330-25

*$ABSTRACT 331
  *LIBRARY BOD
  *SLIDE SET TITLE EUCLID/ FURTHER EXAMPLES
  *NEGATIVE REFERENCE ROLL 182H
  *RENTAL FEE SM 331 $3.35
  *COMMENTS 27 SLIDES OF EUCLID'S WORK IN 13TH AND 14TH CENTUR
  MSS AND EARLY PRINTED BOOKS
  *TITLE OF MANUSCRIPT ELEMENTS OF GEOMETRY 331/5-22, LIBR
  ELEMENTORUM 331/23-27
  *SHELFMARK MS D'ORVILLE 301 331/1-4, MS ARCH SELD B 1
  331/5-13, D 5 5 ART 331/14-19, MS AUCT K 3 19 331/23-27
  *PROVENANCE ENGLISH 331/5-19, GREEK 331/1-4, INDIAN/ CALCUTT
  331/20-23, ITALIAN 331/23-27
  *DATE EXECUTED 13TH 331/5-13, 14TH 331/1-4, 15TH/14!
  331/23-27, 16TH/1572 331/14-19, 19TH/1846 331/20-22
  *LANGUAGE LATIN/ GREEK/ BENGALI/ ENGLISH
  *AUTHOR EUCLID
  *TYPE OF MANUSCRIPT MATHEMATICAL TEXTS
  *CONTENTS EUCLID/ EXAMPLES OF WRITINGS 331/1-27, MATHEMATICA
  TEXTS 331/1-27, BOOK I PROPOSITIONS 4-5 331-1, BOOK
  PROPOSITIONS 5-6 331-2, BOOK I PROPOSITIONS 47-48 331-:
  APPENDIX TO BOOK VI 331-4, DEFINITIONS/ POSTULATES/ BEGINNII
  OF CONSTRUCTION 331-5, CONSTRUCTIONS 1-6 CONCERNING STRAIGI
  LINES AND TRIANGLES 331-6, CONSTRUCTIONS 42-46 CONCERNIN
  LINES/ TRIANGLES/ RECTANGLES 331-7, CONSTRUCTIONS 46-4
  CONCERNING LINES 331-8, CONCERNING CIRCLES 331-9, SIDES C
  RECTANGLES IN VARIOUS PROPORTIONS AND SHORT LINES 331-10
  DEFINITIONS 1-13 WITH VARIOUS FIGURES 331-11, BOOK XI/ FIGURE
  INCLUDE TETRAHEDON 331-12, BOOK XIV/ PENTAGONS INSCRIBED 1
  CIRCLES AND SQUARE 331-13, TITLE PAGE 331-14, PUTTO I
  LANDSCAPE 331-15, LINES 331-16, SURFACES 331-17, ANGLE
  331-18, BOOK I PROPOSITIONS 47-48/ PYTHAGORAS' THEOREM AN
  CONVERSE 331-19, TITLE PAGE 331-20, PYTHAGORAS' THEORE
  331-21, PROPOSITION 48 331-22, DEDICATION BY PRINTER TO JOE
  MOCENIGO/ PRINCE OF VENICE 331-23, POSTULATES/ BOOK]
  DEFINTIONS 331-24, PROPOSITIONS 3-7 331-25, PROPOSITIONS 45-4
  331-26, BOOK II/ DEFINTIONS CONCERNING PARALLELOGRAMS 331-27

*$ABSTRACT 332
  *LIBRARY BOD
  *SLIDE SET TITLE TREASURES OF WADHAM COLLEGE
  *NEGATIVE REFERENCE ROLL 184B
  *RENTAL FEE SM 332 $3.35
  *TYPE OF MANUSCRIPT BIBLE 332/1-9, BOOK OF HOURS 332/10-26,
  *TITLE OF MANUSCRIPT COMMISSION FROM DOGE OF VENICE TO GOVERNO
  OF SEBENICO 332-27
  *SHELFMARK MS WADHAM COLLEGE I 332/1-9, MS WADHAM COLLEGE 1
  332/10-16, PRINTED BOOK WADHAM COLLEGE A 1023 332/17-26, M
  WADHAM COLLEGE 15 332-27
  *PROVENANCE FRENCH 332/1-26, ITALIAN/ VENICE 332-27
  *DATE EXECUTED 13TH 332/1-9, 15TH 332/10-16, 16TH/C150
  332/17-26, 16TH 332-27
  *LANGUAGE LATIN
  *ARTIST/ SCHOOL SIMON VERTRE'S PRINTER'S MARK 332/17-26
  *CONTENTS PSALM INITIALS 332/1-9, INITIALS/ PSALM 332/1-9
  BEATUS VIR 332-1, DAVID PLAYING HARP 332-1, DOMINU
  ILLUMINATIO MEA 332-2, DAVID WITH MAN POINTING AT HIS EYE
  332-2, DIXI CUSTODIAM 332-3, DAVID WITH MAN POINTING AT HI
  MOUTH 332-3, SALVUM ME FAC 332-4, CHRIST BLESSES DAVID WHO I
  WAIST-DEEP IN WATER 332-4, QUID GLORIARIS 332-5, ANIMAL MAS
  332-5, DIXIT INSIPIENS 332-6, FOOL WITH SHORN HEAD WEARIN
  ONLY SHIRT 332-6, EXULTATE 332-7, DAVID PLAYING WITH ROW O
  BALLS 332-7, CANTATE 332-8, SINGERS TONSURED WITH BOOK 332-8
  DIXIT DOMINUS 332-9, TRINITY 332-9, MINIATURE 332/10-16

NATIVITY 332-10, ANNUNCIATION TO SHEPHERDS 332-11, ARREST OF
CHRIST 332-12, ROAD TO CALVARY 332-13, CRUCIFIXION WITH
LONGINUS BLINDED 332-14, DEPOSITION 332-15, ENTOMBMENT 332-16,
TITLE PAGE OF BOOK OF HOURS 332-17, ADORATION OF THE TRINITY
332-18, ST JOHN AT THE LATIN GATE 332-19, ARREST OF CHRIST
332-20, ANNUNCIATION TO VIRGIN 332-21, ANNUNCIATION TO
SHEPHERDS 332-22, ADORATION OF THE MAGI 332-23, CIRCUMCISION
OF CHRIST 332-24, HOLY INNOCENTS 332-25, DORMITION OF VIRGIN
332-26, TITLE-PAGE 332-27, COAT OF ARMS OF TAIAPIERA 332-27,
ST MARK/ LION 332-27, ST BERNADINE OF SIENNA 332-27

*$ABSTRACT 333
  *LIBRARY BOD
  *SLIDE SET TITLE WADHAM MISSAL
  *NEGATIVE REFERENCE ROLL 184D
  *RENTAL FEE SM 333 $3.55
  *COMMENTS MADE FOR AMBROSIUS DE ANGELIS, ABBOT OF PARCH, NEAR
  LOUVAIN
  *TITLE OF MANUSCRIPT WADHAM MISSAL
  *SHELFMARK MS WADHAM COLLEGE A 7 8
  *PROVENANCE FLEMISH
  *DATE EXECUTED 16TH/C1521
  *LANGUAGE LATIN
  *ARTIST/ SCHOOL FRANCIS WEERT
  *TYPE OF MANUSCRIPT MISSAL
  *CONTENTS MISSAL 333/1-31, BORDERS/ DECORATED WITH REALISTIC
  FLOWERS/ FRUIT/ INSECTS 333/1-31, INITIAL H/ HODIE 333-1,
  INITIAL D/ DOMINUS 333-2, NATIVITY 333-3, ST JOHN THE
  EVANGELIST 333-4, CIRCUMCISION OF CHRIST 333-5, ADORATION OF
  THE MAGI 333-6, PRESENTATION OF CHRIST 333-7, INITIAL M/
  MISERERIS 333-8, ANNUNCIATION 333-9, ENTRY INTO JERUSALEM
  333-10, LAST SUPPER 333-11, MUSICAL NOTATION AND TEXT OF
  PREFACE 333-12, CRUCIFIXION WITH SAINTS AND BUILDINGS IN
  BACKGROUND 333-13, INITIAL T/ TE IGITUR 333-14, CHRIST AS MAN
  OF SORROWS 333-14, RESURRECTION 333-15, JESUS AND ZACCHAEUS IN
  TREE 333-16, ASCENSION 333-17, PENTECOST 333-18, BLESSED
  SACRAMENT 333-19, TRINITY 333-20, ST JOHN BAPTIST 333-21,
  VISITATION 333-22, ASSUMPTION 333-23, NATIVITY OF VIRGIN MARY
  333-24, ST AUGUSTINE 333-25, VIRGIN AND CHILD WITH ANGELS
  333-26, ALL SAINTS 333-27, ALL SOULS 333-28, INITIAL G/
  GAUDEAMUS 333-29, VIRGIN AND CHILD ON CRESCENT MOON 333-29,
  PRESENTATION OF VIRGIN MARY 333-30, ST CATHERINE 333-31

*$ABSTRACT 334
  *LIBRARY BOD
  *SLIDE SET TITLE ILLUMINATIONS BY THE FASTOLFE MASTER AND
  RELATED MSS
  *NEGATIVE REFERENCE ROLL 185C
  *RENTAL FEE SM 334 $3.15
  *COMMENTS WORK OF MASTER OF SIR JOHN FASTOLFE/ CHRISTINE DE
  PISAN MASTER AND RELATED MSS
  *TITLE OF MANUSCRIPT CHRISTINE DE PISAN/ EPISTOLA OTHEA
  334/1-3, QUADRILOGUE 334/22-23
  *SHELFMARK MS LAUD MISC 570 334/1-3, MS AUCT D INF 2 11
  334/4-8, MS HATTON 45 334/9-11, MS ST JOHN'S COLLEGE 208
  334/12-14, MS TRINITY COLLEGE 46 334/15-16, MS BODLEY 179
  334-17, MS ASHMOLE 764 334/18-21, MS UNIVERSITY COLLEGE 85
  334/22-23
  *PROVENANCE FRENCH/ NORMANDY 334/1-8, FRENCH 334/12-14 AND 17,
  ENGLISH 334/9-11 AND 15-16 AND 18-23
  *DATE EXECUTED 15TH
  *LANGUAGE LATIN 334/1-16, ENGLISH 334/17-23
  *AUTHOR CHRISTINE DE PISAN 334/1-3, ALAIN CHARTIER 334/22-23
  *ARTIST/ SCHOOL MASTER OF SIR JOHN FASTOLFE
  *TYPE OF MANUSCRIPT CALENDAR/ HOURS/ PSALTER 334/4-16, MEDICAL
  TREATISE 334-17, HERALDRIC TRACTS 334/18-21, TRACTS ON
  GOVERNMENT 334/22-23
  *CONTENTS MASTER OF SIR JOHN FASTOLFE/ EXAMPLES OF HIS WORK

334/1-23, CHRISTINE DE-PISAN PRESENTS BOOK TO JEAN DUC
BERRY 334-1, KING MINOS JUDGING TWO MALEFACTORS 334-
CONVICTS EXECUTED IN BACKGROUND 334-2, CALLIGRAPHIC M/ MOT
OF SIR JOHN FASTOLFE 334-3, SEPTEMBER WITH LIBRA A
WINE-PRESSING 334-4, TRINITY 334-5, ST CHRISTOPHER AND PATR
334-6, DAVID KNEELING IN PRAYER WITH HARP ON GROUND 334-
OFFICE OF THE DEAD 334-8, INITIAL/ HISTORIATED 334-9, DAV
PRAYING WITH HARP ON GROUND/ GOD AND ANGEL 334-9, INITIA
DECORATED AND FULL-PAGE BORDER 334-11, OFFICE OF THE DE
334-12, ANGELS BEARING SOUL TO HEAVEN ON CLOTH 334-13, CHRI
WITH INSTRUMENTS OF PASSION 334-14, INITIAL/ DECORATED A
BORDER 334-15, INITIAL AND BORDER 334-16, COAT OF ARMS OF S
JOHN FASTOLFE 334-17, MOTTO/ ME FAULT FAYRE 334-17, KING
ARMS WITH CROWN AND TABARD 334-18, DECORATED PAGE IN FOREI
STYLE 334-19, TOURNAMENT WITH ARMOUR OF PERIOD OF HENRY
334-20, JOUST WITH KNIGHTS WEARING CRESTS ON HELMS 334-2
DEBATE BETWEEN CLERGY/ PEOPLE/ KNIGHT/ AND LAND OF FRAN
334-22, ARISTOTLE AND ALEXANDER 334-23

*$ABSTRACT 335
  *LIBRARY BOD
  *SLIDE SET TITLE FORTUNE-TELLING TRACTS WITH DRAWINGS
  MATTHEW PARIS
  *NEGATIVE REFERENCE ROLL 185D
  *RENTAL FEE SM 335 $4.20
  *TITLE OF MANUSCRIPT EXPERIMENTARIUS 335/1-5, PROGNOSTI
  335/6-22, PROGNOSTICS OF PYTHAGORAS 335/23-44
  *SHELFMARK MS ASHMOLE 304
  *PROVENANCE ENGLISH/ ST ALBANS
  *DATE EXECUTED 13TH
  *LANGUAGE LATIN
  *AUTHOR BERNARD SILVESTRIS OF CHARTRES 335/1-5, SOCRATES T
  KING 335/6-22, PYTHAGORAS 335/23-44
  *ARTIST/ SCHOOL MATTHEW PARIS
  *TYPE OF MANUSCRIPT FORTUNE-TELLING TRACTS
  *CONTENTS FORTUNE-TELLING TRACTS 335/1-44, DRAWINGS OF MATTH
  PARIS 335/1-44, EUCLID WITH HERMAN 335-1, TOWERS OF THE SEV
  PLANETS 335-2, TABLES 335/3-5, SOCRATES AND PLATO 335-
  PROGNOSTICS OF SOCRATES THE KING 335-7, TABLE 335/8-9, SPHE
  OF SPECIES 335-10, SPHERE OF FLOWERS 335-11, SPHERE OF FRU
  335/12-13, SPHERE OF BEASTS 335-14, SPHERE OF BIRDS 335/14-1
  SPHERE OF CITIES 335/18-22, PYTHAGORAS 335-23, TAB
  335/24-25, COLUMBA/ DOVE AND FILIUS COLUMBA 335-26, COCCINU
  SCARLET BIRD AND ANSER/ GOOSE 335-27, GUIZA AND TURTUR/ TURT
  DOVE 335-28, GALLUS/ COCK AND VESPA 335-29, ARQUA/ CRANE A
  PAVO/ PEACOCK 335-30, COTURNIX/ QUAIL AND ARBE/ LARGE BE
  335-31, AIA/ LARGE BEAK AND EFFROA/ FAT TAIL TURNED UP 335-3
  CORVUS/ CROW AND AGAUF/ MAGPIE 335-33, BATHAIANA/ HOOKED BE
  AND VESPERTILIO/ BAT 335-34, ZERZIR AND RAHAHAM/ FAN-TA
  335-35, PERET AND HAZIZA/ RED BIRD WITH GREEN WINGS 335-3
  NISUS/ HAWK AND ZAHAMAT/ LARGE BEAK 335-37, AQUILA/ EAGLE A
  OZINA/ KINGFISHER 335-38, DAA AND SAAF 335-39, COZ AND SAL
  335-40, SESUF AND TINSEMET/ WITH RUFF 335-41, ANAFA A
  DIQUIFA/ WITH EARS 335-42, CAAZ AND ARFARPERET 335-4
  PATRIARCHS AND SONS OF JACOB/ JUDGES WITH NAMES INSCRIB
  335-44

*$ABSTRACT 336
  *LIBRARY BOD
  *SLIDE SET TITLE LESTOIRE DEL SAINT GRAAL
  *NEGATIVE REFERENCE ROLL 185E
  *RENTAL FEE SM 336 $3.40
  *TITLE OF MANUSCRIPT LESTOIRE DEL SAINT GRAAL 336/1-26, QUES
  OF THE HOLY GRAIL 336-27, BOOK OF HOURS 336-28
  *SHELFMARK MS DOUCE 178 336/1-26, MS DOUCE 199 336-27, MS CANC
  LITURG 129 336-28
  *PROVENANCE FRENCH 336-27, ITALIAN/ BOLOGNESE 336/1-26, FLEMIS
  336-28

170

*DATE EXECUTED 14TH 336/1-27, 15TH/C1450-75 336-28
*LANGUAGE FRENCH
*TYPE OF MANUSCRIPT ROMANCE
*CONTENTS MINIATURES FROM LESTOIRE DEL SAINT GRAAL AND RELATED
MSS 336/1-28, LITERATURE/ LESTOIRE DEL SAINT BRAAL 336/1-28,
GOD ADDRESSES JOSEPH OF ARIMETHEA AND HIS BRETHREN 336-1,
MORDRAIN AND MESSENGER 336-2, MORDRAIN'S SENESCHAL IN COMBAT
WITH KING THOLOMER 336-3, MORDRAIN IN BED WEEPING COMFORTED BY
WIFE 336-4, NASCIEN COMFORTED BY MODRAIN'S QUEEN 336-5,
MODRAIN CARRIED 14 DAYS JOURNEY FROM KINGDOM 336-6, MORDRAIN
ON ROCK VISITED BY MAN IN BOAT 336-7, NASCIEN HELD PRISONER BY
CALAFER 336-8, NASCIEN RELEASED FROM PRISON 336-9, NASCIEN
SEES BODILESS HAND/ CARRIES HIM BEYOND CALAFER 336-10, NASCIEN
RETURNED TO TURNING ISLAND 336-11, NASCIEN FINDS SWORD IN SHIP
336-12, NASCIEN IN WATER AND SHIP WITH THREE SPINDLES 336-13,
CELIDEINE/ NASCIEN'S SON CARRIED FROM TOWER 336-14, CELIDEINE
PUT IN SHIP WITH LION 336-15, NASCIEN'S WIFE SENDS MESSENGERS
TO LOOK FOR HIM 336-16, DUCHESS FLAGENTINE BEFORE CASTLE WITH
KNIGHT 336-17, JOSEPH CROSSING EUPHRATES 336-18, NASCIEN IN
BOAT HEARS OF DESCENDANTS FROM OLD MAN 336-19, JOSEPH
INTERPRETS DUKE GANOR'S DREAM 337-20, JOSEPH AND FATHER
LEAVING GALAFORT 336-21, SYMEU CARRIED OFF BY FAIRY MEN
336-22, PETER PERRON CURED BY PRISONER OF KING ORCAN 336-23,
JOSEPH RETURNED TO GALAFORT SHOWS WOUNDED KNEE 336-24, GALAHAD
CROWNED BY JOSEPH 336-25, NASCIEN/ SON/ GRANDSON AT JOSEPH'S
DEATHBED 336-26, QUEEN BIDS FAREWELL TO KNIGHTS OF QUEST
336-27, CHRIST PRAYING IN GETHSEMANE AND GRAIL APPEARS ON HILL
336-28

*$ABSTRACT 337
 *LIBRARY BOD
 *SLIDE SET TITLE CLOCKS
 *NEGATIVE REFERENCE ROLL 186A
 *RENTAL FEE SM 337 $2.35
 *SHELFMARK MS BODLEY 251 337-1, MS RAWL D 939 337-2, MS LAUD
 MISC 570 337-3, MS BODLEY 421 337-4, MS LAUD MISC 570 337-5,
 MS DOUCE 112 337-6, MS DOUCE 256 337-7
 *PROVENANCE FRENCH 337/1 AND 3-5, ENGLISH 337-2, FLEMISH
 337/6-7
 *DATE EXECUTED 14TH 337/1-2, 15TH 337/3-7
 *LANGUAGE LATIN
 *TYPE OF MANUSCRIPT BIBLE COMMENTARY 337-1, CALENDAR 337-2,
 MISCELLANY 337/3-7
 *CONTENTS CLOCKS 337/1-7, SUNDIAL 337-1, CLOCK/ 24 HOUR 337-2,
 TEMPERANCE CARRIES CLOCK ON HEAD 337-3, ATTEMPERANCE/ GODDESS
 GRASPS CLOCK WITH HANGING BELLS 337-4, CLOCK/ INTRICATE ON
 EARTH AND WHEEL-WORK 337-5, ST MARK AND CLOCK WITH WEIGHTS
 337-6, CLOCK PENDULUM/ RED CASE WITH GOLD 337-6

*$ABSTRACT 338
 *LIBRARY BOD
 *SLIDE SET TITLE LES QUATRE VERTUS CARDINAULX, CHRISTINE DE
 PISAN'S L'EPITRE D'OTHEA A HECTOR
 *NEGATIVE REFERENCE ROLL 186G
 *RENTAL FEE SM 338 $2.55
 *TITLE OF MANUSCRIPT LES QUATRE VERTUS CARDINAULX 338/1-4,
 L'EPITRE D'OTHEA A HECTOR 338/5-11
 *SHELFMARK MS LAUD MISC 570
 *PROVENANCE FRENCH
 *DATE EXECUTED 15TH/1454
 *LANGUAGE FRENCH
 *AUTHOR CHRISTINE DE PISAN 338/5-11
 *ARTIST/ SCHOOL MASTER OF SIR JOHN FASTOLFE
 *TYPE OF MANUSCRIPT MISCELLANY
 *CONTENTS MINIATURES OF MASTER OF SIR JOHN FASTOLFE 338/1-11,
 TEXT OF LIVIER DES QUATRE VERTUS CARDINAULX 338-1, PRUDENCE
 STANDS ON WHITE SACK WITH COINS 338-2, INTELLIGENCE IN BLUE
 GOWN 338-2, CIRCUMSPECTION IN GREEN GOWN 338-2, ATTEMPERANCE

171

CARRIES CLOAK ON HEAD 338-3, CONTINENCE AS NUN WITH NAME ON
SCROLL 338-3, CEMENCE IN BLUE GOWN 338-3, MODERANCE IN
VERMILION GOWN 338-3, FORCE AS CENTRAL FIGURE WITH RECTANGULAR
CASKET ON HEAD 338-4, DRAGON/ GREEN AND TWO-LEGGED 338-4,
CONSTANCE IN GREEN 338-4, MAGNIFICENCE IN ROSE 338-4, PACIENCE
IN VERMILION 338-4, PERSEVERANCE IN BLUE HOLDING CROWN 338-4,
CHRISTINE DE PISAN PRESENTS BOOK TO DUC DE BERRY 338-5, DUC DE
BERRY ON CHAIR WITH ATTENDANTS 338-5, HECTOR RECEIVES EPISTLE
FROM GODDESS OTHEA 338-6, LANDSCAPE OF STYLIZED HILLS AND
TREES 338-6, CLOCK IN CENTER OF UNREALISTIC LANDSCAPE 338-7,
SYMBOLS OF GOSPELS/ ANGEL/ EAGLE/ LION/ BULL 338-7, HERCULES
WITH CLUB 338-8, CERBERUS CHAINED AT GATES OF HADES 338-8,
THESEUS AND PIROTHEUS WITH SWORDS FIGHTING BLACK DEVILS 338-8,
KING MINOS BEARDED AND CROWNED ON THRONE 338-9, NAKED/ BOUND
MEN BEFORE MINOS AND GALLOWS IN BACKGROUND 338-10, PERSEUS
WINGED AND RIDING PEGASUS 338-10, ANDROMEDA CROWNED
GESTULATING FROM ISLAND 338-10, CALLIGRAPHIC M WITH MOTTO
338-11

*$ABSTRACT 339
 *LIBRARY BOD
 *SLIDE SET TITLE PORTRAITS OF THE 4 EVANGELISTS IN BYZANTINE
 GOSPEL MSS
 *NEGATIVE REFERENCE ROLL 186I
 *RENTAL FEE SM 339 $3.55
 *SHELFMARK MS AUCT T INF 2 7 339/1-4, MS SELDEN SUPRA 6
 339/5-12, MS LAUD GR 3 339/13-15, MS BAROCCI 29 339/16-19, MS
 E D CLARKE 6 339/20-23, MS CANON GR 38 339/24-27, MS CANON GR
 36 339/28-31
 *PROVENANCE BYZANTINE
 *DATE EXECUTED 12TH 339/1-4, 13TH 339/5-19, 14TH 339/20-31
 *LANGUAGE GREEK
 *TYPE OF MANUSCRIPT GOSPELS
 *CONTENTS GOSPELS/ BYZANTINE 339/1-31, PORTRAITS IN GOSPEL MSS
 339/1-31, FURNITURE AND WRITING MATERIALS 339/1-31, ST JOHN
 339-1, ST MATTHEW 339-2, ST LUKE 339-3, ST MARK 339-4, ST
 MATTHEW 339-5, ST MATTHEW/ ANGEL 339-6, ST MARK WRITING 339-7,
 ST MARK/ LION 339-8, ST LUKE WRITING 339-9, ST LUKE/ OX
 339-10, ST JOHN 339-11, ST JOHN/ EAGLE 339-12, ST MARK 339-13,
 ST LUKE 339-14, ST JOHN 339-15, ST MATTHEW 339-16, ST MARK
 339-17, ST LUKE 339-18, ST JOHN 339-19, ST MATTHEW 339-20, ST
 MARK 339-21, ST LUKE 339-22, ST JOHN 339-23, ST MATTHEW
 WRITING 339-24, ST MARK 339-25, ST LUKE 339-26, ST JOHN
 339-27, ST MATTHEW/ HEADPIECE 339-28, ST MARK/ HEADPIECE
 339-29, ST LUKE/ HEADPIECE 339-30, ST JOHN/ HEADPIECE 339-31

*$ABSTRACT 340
 *LIBRARY BOD
 *SLIDE SET TITLE CATENA ON JOB
 *NEGATIVE REFERENCE ROLL 187A
 *RENTAL FEE SM 340 $3.05
 *COMMENTS SELECTION OF BEST PRESERVED MINIATURES FROM BYZANTINE
 MS
 *TITLE OF MANUSCRIPT CATENA ON JOB
 *SHELFMARK MS BAROCCI 201
 *PROVENANCE BYZANTINE
 *DATE EXECUTED 13TH/ EARLY
 *LANGUAGE GREEK
 *TYPE OF MANUSCRIPT CATENA ON JOB
 *CONTENTS CATENA ON JOB 340/1-21, MINIATURES FROM BYZANTINE MS
 340/1-21, SONS OF GOD PRESENT THEMSELVES BEFORE GOD 340-1,
 SATAN LEAVES GOD'S PRESENCE 340-2, CHALDEAN BANDS KILLING
 JOB'S SERVANTS 340-3, JOB'S CHILDREN KILLED BY GREAT WIND
 340-4, JOB RENDS HIS MANTLE 340-5, SATAN HOLDING JOB BY HAND
 TALKS TO GOD 340-6, JOB COVERED WITH BOILS 340-7, JOB'S WIFE
 REBUKES HIM 340-8, JOB'S WIFE VISITS HIM AGAIN ON THE DUNGHEAP
 340-9, JOB SITTING ON GREEN HILL ARMS RAISED IN PRAYER 340-10,
 JOB'S FRIENDS COME TO MOURN WITH HIM 340-11, JOB CURSES DAY OF

BIRTH AND NIGHT OF CONCEPTION 340-12, JOB'S SIGHING COMES
BEFORE HE EATS 340-13, PLOUGH INQUITY, AND SOW WICKEDNESS
340-14, ROARING OF LION IS BROKEN 340-15, LION/ OLD PERISHES
FOR LACK OF PREY 340-16, ROOTS/ HIS ARE WRAPPED ABOUT THE HEAP
340-17, HE TREADETH ON WAVES AND MAKETH STARS 340-18, THOU
HUNTEST ME AS A LION 340-19, THOU SETTEST PRINT UPON SOULS OF
MY FEET 340-20, HIS HARVEST SHALL PERISH BEFORE THE TIME
340-21

*$ABSTRACT 341
  *LIBRARY BOD
  *SLIDE SET TITLE GIRALDUS CAMBRENSIS/ TOPOGRAPHIA HIBERNIAE
  *NEGATIVE REFERENCE ROLL 187C
  *RENTAL FEE SM 341 $2.50
  *COMMENTS ILLUSTRATIONS OF IRISH LIFE
  *TITLE OF MANUSCRIPT TOPOGRAPHIA HIBERNIAE
  *SHELFMARK MS LAUD MISC 720
  *PROVENANCE ENGLISH
  *DATE EXECUTED 13TH
  *LANGUAGE LATIN
  *AUTHOR GIRALDUS CAMBRENSIS
  *TYPE OF MANUSCRIPT GEOGRAPHY
  *CONTENTS TOPOGRAPHIA HIBERNIAE 341/1-10, IRISH LIFE
  ILLUSTRATED 341/1-10, SEA-EAGLE WITH CLAW ON ONE FOOT/ OTHER
  FOR SWIMMING 341-1, MARTLETS 341-2, WEASEL 341-3, FISH/ GREEN
  AND DEER WITHOUT HORNS 341-4, RATS AND BELL 341-5, IRISHMAN ON
  BACK OF ANOTHER CHOPPING FOREHEAD WITH AXE 341-6, IRISHMAN
  DECAPITATES MARE 341-7, IRISH KING WITH SUBJECTS ALL EATING
  MARE'S FLESH 341-8, CONNAUGHT MEN SITTING IN CORACLE WITH
  PADDLES 341-9, BELL 341-10, WALKING STICK OF JESUS/ ST PATRICK
  USED AGAINST SNAKES 341-10, PRIEST BERNARD WITH ST PATRICK'S
  HORN 341-10

*$ABSTRACT 342
  *LIBRARY BOD
  *SLIDE SET TITLE CHRONICLE OF FRANCE
  *NEGATIVE REFERENCE ROLL 187D
  *RENTAL FEE SM 342 $3.40
  *TITLE OF MANUSCRIPT GRANDES CHRONIQUES DE FRANCE
  *SHELFMARK MS DOUCE 217
  *PROVENANCE FRENCH
  *DATE EXECUTED 14TH
  *LANGUAGE FRENCH
  *ARTIST/ SCHOOL RELATED TO STYLE OF JEHAN DE NIZIERES
  *TYPE OF MANUSCRIPT CHRONICLE
  *CONTENTS CHRONICLE OF FRANCE 342/1-28, HISTORY/ FRANCE
  342/1-28, EXILES LEAVE TROY/ HELENUS WITH SCRIBE/ BATTLE/
  AENEAS CROWNED 342-1, CLOVIS WITH CLOTHILDE AND FOUR SONS
  342-2, KING CHILPERIC STRANGLES WIFE GALSONDE 342-3, BATTLE
  342-4, KING DAGOBERT ORDERING AND SUPERVISING BUILDING 342-5,
  CORONATION OF CHARLEMAGNE 342-6, KINGS MOUNTED 342-7,
  CHARLEMAGNE'S VISION OF ST JAMES 342-8, BATTLE/ ROLAND
  FIGHTING FORNAGU WATCHED BY KINGS 342-9, ROLAND 324-9,
  RONCEVAUX/ BATTLE OF 342-10, KING LOUIS LE DEBONNAIRE GIVING
  UP ROYAL INSIGNIA 342-11, BATTLE OF CHARLES LE CHAUVE/
  FONTENAY 342-12, LOUIS LE BEGUE BEING GIVEN SWORD AND SCEPTRE
  342-13, CORONATION OF LOUIS LE GROS AT ORLEANS 342-14, WEDDING
  OF LOUIS VIII AND ELEANOR OF AQUITAINE 342-15, BIRTH OF
  PHILIPPE DIEU-DONNE 342-16, TAKING OF TOURS BY PHILIPPE
  DIEU-DONNE 342-17, COUNCIL/ PHILIPPE DIEU-DONNE PASSES
  JUDGMENT ON HERETICS 342-18, CONQUEST OF LA ROCHELLE BY LOUIS
  VIII 342-19, ST LOUIS BESEIGING AVIGNON 342-20, KING OF SICILY
  EMBARKING 342-21, BATTLE OF PHILIPPE LE BEL 342-22, WEDDING OF
  LOUIS X OF FRANCE AND CLEMENCE HENGRIE 342-23, CORONATION OF
  CHARLES LE BEL 342-24, PHILIP III DOING HOMAGE TO PHILIPPE DE
  VALOIS 342-25, NOBLES OF NORMANDY BEFORE PHILIPPE DE VALOIS
  342-26, CORONATION OF KING JOHAN BY BISHOPS 342-27, CORONATION
  OF CHARLES V AND HIS QUEEN 342-28

*$ABSTRACT 343
  *LIBRARY BOD
  *SLIDE SET TITLE GARDENS
  *NEGATIVE REFERENCE ROLL 187E
  *RENTAL FEE SM 343 $2.65
  *SHELFMARK MS AUBREY 31 343-1, MS LITURG 98 343-2, MS BODLEY
    850 343-3, MS BUCHANAN E 8 343-4, MS D'ORVILLE 14 343-5, MS
    BUCHANAN E 5 343-6, MS LITURG 58 343-7, MS BODLEY 939 343-8,
    MS RAWL LITURG E 36 343-9, MS DOUCE FF 63 343/10-13
  *PROVENANCE ENGLISH 343/1-3 AND 8, FRENCH 343/4 AND 7 AND 9-13,
    ITALIAN 343-5, FLEMISH 343-6
  *DATE EXECUTED 15TH 343/1-8, 16TH 343/9-13
  *LANGUAGE LATIN
  *AUTHOR JUSTIN 343-5
  *TYPE OF MANUSCRIPT BOOK OF HOURS 343/1-4 AND 6-7 AND 9-13,
    PRIVATE PRAYERS 343-8
  *CONTENTS GARDENS 343/1-13, GETHSEMANE 343/1-3, APRIL SCENE
    WITH GIRL GATHERING FLOWERS 343-4, LADY AND YOUTH TALK
    TOGETHER IN GARDEN 343-5, WALLED GARDEN WITH RED FLOWERS
    343-6, VIRGIN AND CHILD IN GARDEN 343/6-7, CHRIST IN FRONT OF
    TERRACED GARDEN 343-8, LADY AND SERVANT IN GARDEN 343-9, GIRL
    SPINNING AND YOUTH IN ARBORED GARDEN 343-10, LADY PICKING
    FLOWERS IN GARDEN WITH ORNAMENTAL FENCE 343-11, LADY PICKING
    FLOWERS IN GARDEN WITH FENCE/ WALL/ TRELLISES 343-12, LADY
    PICKING FLOWERS IN GARDEN WITH TRELLIS 343-13

*$ABSTRACT 344
  *LIBRARY BOD
  *SLIDE SET TITLE TWO EARLY MSS MADE FOR ENGLISH NUNS
  *NEGATIVE REFERENCE ROLL 187F
  *RENTAL FEE SM 344 $3.15
  *TITLE OF MANUSCRIPT LITTLEMORE ANSELM 344/1-20, GOSPEL LIST
    FROM BENEDICTINE NUNNERY OF ST MARY BARKING 344/21-23
  *SHELFMARK MS AUCT D 2 6 344/1-20, MS BODLEY 155 344/21-23
  *PROVENANCE ENGLISH
  *DATE EXECUTED 12TH/C1150 344/1-20, 10TH 344/21-23
  *LANGUAGE LATIN
  *TYPE OF MANUSCRIPT PRAYERS AND MEDITATIONS 344/1-20, GOSPEL
    LIST 344/21-23
  *CONTENTS MSS MADE FOR ENGLISH NUNS 344/1-23, ST ANSELM 344-1,
    CHRIST IN MANDORLA AND KNEELING LADY 344-2, VIRGIN AND CHILD
    IN MANDORLA AND KNEELING LADY 344-3, VIRGIN HOLDING BOOK
    344/4-6, MARTYRDOM OF ST JOHN BAPTIST 344-7, ST PETER RECEIVES
    KEYS FROM CHRIST 344-8, CONVERSION OF SAUL 344-9, MIRACLE OF
    DRUSIANA FROM LIFE OF SAINT PAUL 344-10, ST NICHOLAS AND THREE
    OFFICERS SAVED FROM EXECUTION 344-11, CLERIC KNEELING BEFORE
    ST PETER 343-12, ST ANSELM GIVES BOOKS TO COUNTESS MATHILDA OF
    TUSCANY 344-13, FEAST IN HOUSE OF SIMON 344-14, CHRIST IN
    HALF-FIGURE IN SYMMETRICAL PATTERN 344-15, CHRIST IN GLORY
    344/16-17, CHRIST ENTHRONED BLESSES KNEELING LADY 344-18,
    PRIEST CELEBRATING MASS 344-19, INITIAL/ ZOOMORPHIC OF TWO
    DRAGONS 344-20, ST MATTHEW 344-21, ST LUKE 344-22, ST JOHN
    344-23

*$ABSTRACT 345
  *LIBRARY BOD
  *SLIDE SET TITLE CONRAD GESNER HISTORIAE ANIMALIUM
  *NEGATIVE REFERENCE ROLL 187G
  *RENTAL FEE SM 345 $2.80
  *TITLE OF MANUSCRIPT HISTORIAE ANIMALIUM
  *SHELFMARK PRINTED BESTIARY ZURICH 1551
  *PROVENANCE SWISS
  *DATE EXECUTED 16TH/1551
  *LANGUAGE LATIN
  *AUTHOR CONRAD GESNER
  *TYPE OF MANUSCRIPT BESTIARY/ PRINTED
  *CONTENTS BESTIARY 345/1-16, AUROCHS 345-1, GIRAFFE 345-2,
    DROMEDARY 345-3, BEAVER 345-4, ELEPHANT 345-5, PORCUPINE

345-6, LION 345-7, LYNX 345-8, OTTER 345-9, SHEEP 345-10,
RHINOCEROS 345-11, MONSTER 345-12, TIGER 345-13, FOX 345-14,
INDIAN GOAT 345-15, BADGER 345-16

*$ABSTRACT 346
 *LIBRARY BOD
 *SLIDE SET TITLE BIBLICAL PICTURES
 *NEGATIVE REFERENCE ROLL 188A
 *RENTAL FEE SM 346 $3.30
 *SHELFMARK MS ASHMOLE 1525
 *PROVENANCE ENGLISH/ ST AUGUSTINE'S CANTERBURY
 *DATE EXECUTED 13TH/ FIRST HALF
 *LANGUAGE LATIN
 *TYPE OF MANUSCRIPT PSALTER/ CHOIR
 *CONTENTS BIBLICAL PICTURES 346/1-26, DAVID ENTHRONED 346-1,
 DAVID STANDING BEFORE ARK 346-2, DAVID ON ONE KNEE HOLDING
 SCROLL 346-3, DAVID ON ONE KNEE 346-4, DAVID HOLDING CHALICE
 AND SCROLL 346-5, CHRIST POINTING TO SCROLL HELD BY MAN AT
 FEET 346-6, ANGEL WITH VIRGIN AND EVE 346-7, CHRIST RISING
 FROM TOMB 346-8, MONK HOLDING SCROLL 346-9, FIGURE WITH GOLD
 CROWN AND CHALICE 346-10, MAN KNEELING BEFORE ALTAR 346-11,
 MAN IN RED CLOAK 346-12, KING WITH BISHOP 346-13, CHRIST
 346-14, MAN KNEELING BEFORE ALTAR 346-15, MAN FEEDING
 MULTITUDES WITH LOAVES 346-16, MEN HOLDING SCROLL OVER HEADS
 OF OTHERS 346-17, PRIESTS HOLDING PALM BRANCHES 346-18, CHRIST
 TEACHING WITHIN CHURCH 346-19, MOSES HOLDING UP TABLETS OF LAW
 346-20, CHRIST CRUCIFIED 346-21, CHRIST HOLDING UP HANDS TO
 GOD 346-22, JUDAS/ KISS 346-23, MOSES HOLDING UP TABLETS OF
 LAW 346-24, CHRIST RISING FROM TOMB 346-25, DAVID PLAYING HARP
 BEFORE ARK ON ALTAR 346-26

*$ABSTRACT 347
 *LIBRARY BOD
 *SLIDE SET TITLE BIRDS
 *NEGATIVE REFERENCE ROLL 188B
 *RENTAL FEE SM 347 $2.75
 *COMMENTS SELECTION FROM BYZANTINE MS IN GREEK
 *SHELFMARK MS AUCT F 4 15
 *PROVENANCE BYZANTINE/ EXECUTED IN PARIS
 *DATE EXECUTED 16TH/1564
 *LANGUAGE GREEK
 *TYPE OF MANUSCRIPT MISCELLANY
 *CONTENTS BIRDS/ BYZANTINE 347/1-15, EAGLE 347-1, HERON 347-2,
 STORK 347-3, PEACOCK 347-4, CRANE 347-5, PARTRIDGE 347-6,
 MALLARD DUCK 347-7, IBIS 347-8, NIGHTINGALE 347-9, SWALLOW
 347-10, WOOD PIGEON 347-11, TURTLE DOVE 347-12, OWL 347-13,
 CUCKOO 347-14, PIED WAGTAIL 347-15

*$ABSTRACT 348
 *LIBRARY BOD
 *SLIDE SET TITLE BOOKS OF HOURS
 *NEGATIVE REFERENCE ROLL 189B
 *RENTAL FEE SM 348 $3.85
 *COMMENTS SELECTED ILLUSTRATIONS FROM FLEMISH BOOK OF HOURS AND
 COMPARATIVE MATERIAL FROM ANOTHER BOOK OF HOURS OF SIMILAR
 DATE AND STYLE
 *SHELFMARK MS DOUCE 8 348/1-50, MS DOUCE 12 348/51-57
 *PROVENANCE FLEMISH
 *DATE EXECUTED 16TH/C1500
 *LANGUAGE LATIN AND ITALIAN
 *TYPE OF MANUSCRIPT OFFICES/ PRAYERS FOR PRIVATE USE
 *CONTENTS OFFICES/ PRAYERS 348/1-57, BOOK OF HOURS 348/1-57,
 BORDERS/ DECORATED WITH REALISTIC FLOWERS/ BIRDS/ INSECTS
 348/1-57, CUR MUNDUS MILITAT 348-1, RICHLY DRESSED MAN READING
 IN TRANSPARENT ORB 348-1, TEXT AND FLORAL BORDER 348-2, TEXT
 ONLY 348-3, SEVEN AGES OF THE WORLD/ AGES 1-4 348-2, AGES OF

WORLD 5-7 348-3, AGES OF WORLD 5-7 348-3, AGES OF WORLD 4-7
348-4, TEXT WITH BORDER 348-5, ST PETER ENTHRONED 348-5, SS
ANDREW/ JAMES/ JOHN/ THOMAS 348-6, SS JAMES LESS/ PHILIP/
BARTHOLOMEW 348-6, SS MATTHEW/ SIMON/ THADDEUS/ MATTHIAS
348-7, TEXT WITH BORDER AND INITIAL 348-7, TEXT WITH BORDER
SHOWING BIRD/ CHAPLET WITH MEDALLION 348-8, PEACOCK IN BORDER/
BUTTERFLIES/ FLOWERS 348-9, DIANTHUS IN POT/ FLY/ ROSES/
STRAWBERRIES/ INSECTS 348-10, PEACOCK FEATHER BORDER/ ARREST
OF CHRIST 348-11, INITIALS IN PANEL/ ROAD TO CALVARY AND
GOTHIC CHAPEL 348-13, INITIALS IN PANEL/ CHRIST BEFORE PILATE
348-12, BORDER OF VIOLETS/ CHRIST NAILED TO CROSS 348-14,
CRUCIFIXION/ TEXT AND SCROLL BORDER 348-15, MERMAID/ FLOWERS/
BIRDS IN BORDERS 348-16, TEXT WITH BORDER 348/1-57,
ENTOMBMENT/ PEACOCK EATING INSECT 348-17, SHEPHERDS AND ANGELS
WITH ALTAR PLATE IN BACKGROUND 348-18, FLOWERS/ FRUIT/ BIRDS/
SNAIL/ STRAWBERRY/ BUTTERFLY 348/19-20, ST JOHN ON PATMOS AND
INSECT BORDER 348-21, ST LUKE WRITING/ INSECTS/ FLOWERS/
PEACOCK 348-22, ST MATTHEW WITH ANGEL 348-23, ST MARK AND
LION/ IRIS 348-24, INITIAL/ ARCHITECTURAL BORDER/ BIRD/
THISTLE 348-25, JESUS AS CHILD/ FLOWER AND SCROLL BORDER
348-26, ST BENEDICT REPELLING DEMON 348-27, ROSE BORDER/
GRASSHOPPER/ SNAIL/ STRAWBERRY/ BUTTERFLY BORDER 348-28, ST
RAPHAEL AND TOBIAS WITH FISH/ FLORAL BORDER 348-29,
ARCHITECTURAL BORDER 348-30, DAVID KNEELING WITH BORDER OF
FLOWERS/ FRUIT/ INSECTS/ BIRDS 348-31, SHEEP/ HE-GOATS/
GRAPES/ SCROLL AND BIRD BORDER 348-32, GOLD AND OTHER VESSELS
IN BORDER 348-33, ST ANNE AND VIRGIN AND CHILD 348-34, ST MARY
MAGDALENE/ FLOWER AND FRUIT BORDER 348-35, ELEVEN THOUSAND
VIRGINS 348-36, ST CATHERINE WITH WHEEL 348-37, BORDER HAS
COLUMBINE/ SNAIL/ CATERPILLAR 348-37, ST BARBARA AND FLORAL
BORDER 348-38, BORDER/ CONVENTIONALIZED 348-39, VIRGIN AND
CHILD AND FLOWER/ INSECT/ BIRD BORDER 348-40, FLOWER AND
SCROLL/ BORDER OF GOLD-SET JEWELS 348-41, CHAPLET IN BORDER/
SCROLL AND BUTTERFLY BORDER 348-42, ST ERASMUS BEING TORTURED/
FLORAL BORDER 348-43, ST BLAISE/ FLORAL AND INSECT BORDER
348-44, ST NICHOLAS AND BOYS IN PICKLING TUB 348-45, ST
CHRISTOPHER CARRYING CHRIST/ PEA BORDER 348-46, ADORATION OF
THE MAGI/ FLOWER AND FRUIT BORDER 348-47, INITIALS/ FLOWER/
FRUIT/ BIRDS BORDER 348-48, BORDER OF JEWELS 348-49, CHAPLET
IN BORDER 348-50, LAST FOUR AGES OF WORLD 348-51, THREE AGES
OF MAN 348-51, MOSES AND TABLETS WITH FLORAL BORDER 348-52,
ARCHITECTURAL BORDER 348-53, CHRIST PRAYING IN GARDEN/
DISCIPLES SLEEPING 348-54, CHRIST LED AWAY BY SOLDIERS 348-54,
ST GREGORY PRAYING AT ALTAR AND FLORAL BORDERS 348-55, ST
AMBROSE WRITING/ FLORAL BORDER 348-56, CRUCIFIXION/ FLORAL
BORDER/ TEXT 348-57

*$ABSTRACT 349
  *LIBRARY BOD
  *SLIDE SET TITLE ROMANCE OF ALEXANDER/ MINIATURES
  *NEGATIVE REFERENCE ROLL 189D
  *RENTAL FEE SM 349 $2.60
  *TITLE OF MANUSCRIPT ROMANCE OF ALEXANDER
  *SHELFMARK MS BODLEY 264
  *PROVENANCE FLEMISH
  *DATE EXECUTED 14TH/1338
  *LANGUAGE FRENCH
  *TYPE OF MANUSCRIPT ROMANCE
  *CONTENTS ROMANCE OF ALEXANDER 349/1-12, LITERATURE/ ROMANCE OF
  ALEXANDER 349/1-12, MINIATURES FROM ROMANCE OFALEXANDER
  349/1-12, DARIUS ON BED/ ALEXANDER AT FOOT WITH MEN 349-1,
  ALEXANDER'S GLASS DIVING-BELL 349-2, BATTLEMENTED ERECTION ON
  EACH END OF BOAT 349-2, ALEXANDER ON GRASSY SLOPE WITH KNIGHTS
  SPEAKING TO MEN 349-3, ALEXANDER AND MEN DEFEND THEMSELVES
  FROM BEASTS 349-4, ALEXANDER AT HEAD OF MEN SPEARS DRAGON
  349-5, ALEXANDER AND KNIGHTS BESIDE PYRE 349-6, PORUS
  ENTHRONED SPEAKS TO ALEXANDER WHO CARRIES PACK 349-7, PORUS
  ATTACKS ALEXANDER 349-8, CASTLES/ ELEPHANTS/ IN ALEXANDER'S
  ARMY 349-8, BATTLE SCENE PORUS'S MEN FIGHTING ALEXANDER 349-9,
  HERALDIC SHIELDS AND BANNERS 349-9, ALEXANDER FIGHTING/ ARMIES

176

OF PORUS WITH BOARS ON SHIELDS 349-10, ALEXANDER FIGHTING
DARK-SKINNED/ TURBANNED INDIANS 349-11, ALEXANDER REFUSES TO
SACRIFICE TO IDOLS MADE BY ARTUS 349-12

*$ABSTRACT 350
  *LIBRARY BOD
  *SLIDE SET TITLE JOSEPH
  *NEGATIVE REFERENCE ROLL 189E
  *RENTAL FEE SM 350 $3.40
  *COMMENTS ILLUSTRATIONS OF GENESIS 37 TO 50
  *SHELFMARK MS DOUCE 48
  *PROVENANCE FRENCH
  *DATE EXECUTED 13TH
  *LANGUAGE LATIN
  *TYPE OF MANUSCRIPT PSALTER
  *CONTENTS GENESIS 37 TO 50 350/1-28, JOSEPH/ LIFE OF 350/1-28,
  JOSEPH DREAMING IN BED 350-1, JOSEPH RECOUNTING DREAM TO
  FATHER 350-1, JOSEPH ASKING WAY TO BRETHREN 350-2, BRETHREN
  CONSPIRING 350-2, BROTHERS/ TEN CAST JOSEPH INTO PIT 350-3,
  BRETHREN/ FOUR KILL A KID 350-3, JOSEPH SOLD TO POTIPHAR
  350-4, BROTHERS BRING JOSEPH'S STAINED COAT TO JACOB 350-4,
  JOSEPH WITH POTIPHAR'S WIFE 350-5, JOSEPH'S MANTLE HELD BY
  POTIPHAR'S WIFE AS HE FLEES 350-5, JOSEPH HUSTLED AWAY BY
  SERVANTS 350-6, POTIPHAR'S WIFE SHOWS HUSBAND MANTLE 350-6,
  POTIPHAR SENDS SERVANT TO ESCORT JOSEPH TO GAOL 350-7, JOSEPH
  TAKEN TO PRISON 350-7, PHARAOH ASLEEP IN BED 350-8, SEVEN FAT
  KINE 350-8, SEVEN LEAN KINE 350-9, BUTLER RESTORED TO PHARAOH
  HANDS HIM CUP 350-9, PHARAOH CONDEMNS BAKER 350-10, BAKER IN
  WHITE AND BLINDFOLDED HANGS FROM GIBBET 350-10, JOSEPH
  KNEELING BEFORE PHARAOH RECEIVING OFFICE 350-11, PHARAOH
  DISMISSES JOSEPH 350-11, JOSEPH AND MILITARY ATTENDANT IN CART
  350-12, HORSES AND RIDER 350-12, JOSEPH INSTRUCTS WORKMAN
  CARRYING SACK OF GRAIN 350-13, WORKERS POURING GRAIN INTO
  GRANARIES 350-14, JOSEPH DROPS WHEAT IN RIVER TO SHOW
  RELATIVES 350-14, WORKERS THROW WHEAT IN RIVER 350-14, JACOB
  SENDS BENJAMIN TO EGYPT 350-15, DEPARTURE OF TWO OF BRETHREN
  350-15, BRETHREN BEFORE SEATED JOSEPH 350-16, JOSEPH SENDS
  SERVANT TO HIDE CUP IN BENJAMIN'S SACK 350-16, SERVANT HIDES
  CUP IN BENJAMIN'S SACK 350-17, BROTHERS DEPARTING ON THEIR
  ASSES 350-17, JOSEPH'S SERVANT FINDS CUP IN BENJAMIN'S SACK
  350-18, BROTHERS BROUGHT BEFORE SEATED JOSEPH 350-18, BROTHERS
  BEFORE JOSEPH 350-19, JOSEPH MAKES HIMSELF KNOWN AND KISSES
  BENJAMIN 350-19, BROTHERS MOUNTED LEAVING EGYPT 350-20,
  BENJAMIN ON HORSE PULLING CART 350-20, BRETHREN WITH CATTLE
  350-21, JACOB SEATED ON WAGON 350-21, BRETHREN ON HORSEBACK
  350-22, JOSEPH REUNITED WITH FATHER IN FRONT OF BRETHREN
  350-22, JOSEPH HOLDING FATHER'S HANDS CONDUCTS HIM TO PHARAOH
  350-23, PHARAOH SEATED 350-23, JOSEPH AND JACOB KNEEL BEFORE
  SEATED PHARAOH 350-24, JOSEPH AND JACOB IN CART 350-24,
  BROTHERS MOUNTED DEPARTING FOR NEW HOME 350-25, BUILDING NEW
  HOME 350-25, JACOB WITH ARMS CROSSED BLESSES MANASSEH AND
  EPHRAIM 350-26, BROTHERS GATHER AROUND JACOB ON BED 350-26,
  BROTHERS ON HORSEBACK ACCOMPANY JACOB'S BODY TO BURIAL 350-27,
  JACOB'S DEAD BODY IN SHROUD ON WAGON 350-28, JOSEPH SEATED
  SPEAKS TO BROTHERS 350-28

*$ABSTRACT 351
  *LIBRARY BOD
  *SLIDE SET TITLE GOSPELS
  *NEGATIVE REFERENCE ROLL 189F
  *RENTAL FEE SM 351 $2.50
  *SHELFMARK MS LAUD LAT 26 351/1-7, MS LAUD MISC 244 351/8-10
  *PROVENANCE FRENCH 351/1-7, FLEMISH 351/8-10
  *DATE EXECUTED 10TH 351/1-7, 12TH 351/8-10
  *LANGUAGE LATIN
  *TYPE OF MANUSCRIPT GOSPELS
  *CONTENTS GOSPELS 351/1-10, CRUCIFIXION 350-1, ST MATTHEW
  351-2, INITIAL L/ LIBER GENERATIONIS 351-3, ST MARK 351-4, ST

LUKE 351-5, ST JOHN 351-6, INITIAL I/ IN PRINCIPIO 351-7
INITIAL L/ LUCAS 351-8, INITIAL Q/ QUONIAM AND ST LUKE'
WINGED OX 351-9, INITIAL F/ FUIT AND SCENE OF ZACHARIAS AN
ANGEL 351-10

*$ABSTRACT 352
    *LIBRARY BOD
    *SLIDE SET TITLE MEDICAL TREATMENT
    *NEGATIVE REFERENCE ROLL 189G
    *RENTAL FEE SM 352 $3.25
    *SHELFMARK MS LAUD MISC 724 352/1-8, MS DIGBY 29 352/9-11, M
     RAWLINSON C 328 352/12-25
    *PROVENANCE ENGLISH 352/1-11, ITALIAN 352/12-25
    *DATE EXECUTED 15TH 352/1-11, 14TH 352/12-25
    *LANGUAGE LATIN
    *TYPE OF MANUSCRIPT MEDICAL TRACTS
    *CONTENTS MEDICAL TREATMENT/ 14TH AND 15TH CENTURIES 352/1-25
     SURGICAL INSTRUMENTS PREPARED AND HEAD OPERATIONS 352-1
     TREPANNING AND CAUTERISATION 352-2, OPERATIONS ON HEAD AN
     OTHER TREATMENTS 352-2, MEDICAL EXAMINATION AND TREATMEN
     352-3, TREATMENTS 352-4, BLEEDING WITH LEECHES AND OTHE
     TREATMENTS 352-6, WOMAN IN LABOR SUPPORTED BY MIDWIFE
     DIAGRAMS OF EMBRYOS 352-7, EMBRYOS IN DIFFICULT BIRT
     POSITIONS 352-8, UROSCOPY DIAGRAMS 352/9-11, CONSTANTINE TH
     AFRICAN LECTURES ON UROSCOPY 352-12, CAUTERY PATIENTS AWAITIN
     TREATMENT 352-13, DOCTOR CAUTERISES PATIENT FOR HEADACHE
     CHOKING 352-14, CAUTERISATION POINTS FOR HEADACHE
     INFLAMMATION OF BREAST 352-15, CAUTERISED PATIENT FOR ASTHM
     AND ANOTHER FOR HERNIA 352-16, CAUTERISATION POINTS FOR SPLEE
     DISEASE AND LIVER DISEASE 352-17, CAUTERISATION POINTS AN
     PATIENT WITH CONSUMPTION 352-18, INFLAMMATION OF GUMS AN
     SCIATICA CAUTERISATION POINTS 352-19, KIDNEY DISEAS
     CAUTERISATION AND STOMACH TROUBLE 352-20, PATIENT'S HAND HEL
     TO RESTRAIN TEARS 352-21, CAUTERISATION POINTS FOR PAINS I
     HIPS/ KIDNEYS/ TOES 352-22, CAUTERISATION POINTS FOR SWELLIN
     KNEES AND JAW/ HEAD ACHES 352-23, PATIENT ABOUT TO B
     CAUTERISED 352-24, PATIENT CAUTERISED FOR ELEPHANTIASIS 352-2

*$ABSTRACT 353
    *LIBRARY BOD
    *SLIDE SET TITLE GREEK SCHOLARSHIP IN THOMAS MORE'S CIRCLE
    *NEGATIVE REFERENCE ROLL 190D
    *RENTAL FEE SM 353 $2.95
    *TITLE OF MANUSCRIPT WORKS OF ST BASIL 353/1-12, MENOLOGIO
     353/15-19
    *SHELFMARK MS BODLEY 439 353/1-7, MS C C C 26 353/8-12, MS C
     C 23 353-13, MS C C C 24 353-14, MS C C C 140 353/15-19
    *PROVENANCE ENGLISH 353/13-14, GREEK 353/15-19
    *DATE EXECUTED 17TH 353/1-7, 16TH 353/13-14
    *LANGUAGE GREEK/ LATIN/ ENGLISH
    *AUTHOR ST BASIL 353/1-12, ST JOHN CHRYSOSTOM 353/13-14
    *TYPE OF MANUSCRIPT MISCELLANY 353/1-14, MENOLOGION 353/15-19
    *CONTENTS GREEK SCHOLARSHIP IN THOMAS MORE'S CIRCLE 353/1-19
     WORKS OF ST BASIL 353-1, LETTER FROM WILLIAM ROPER TO JOH
     MORWEN 353-2, TITLE FOR COMPARISON OF GREEK LETTERS 353/3-5
     GREEK AND LATIN TRANSLITERATION COMPARISON 353-6, MORWEN'
     TRANSLATION OF ST CYRIL OF ALEXANDRIA 353-7, MUTILATED FOLI
     353-8, CAPITAL AND PAGINATION 353-9, PAGES MISSING IN M
     353-10, OPTIMON INSTEAD OF OPTIMUS 353-11, SERBOPULUS O
     CONSTANTINOPLE WRITING ABOUT 1500 353-13, CHRYSOSTOM ON S
     MATTHEW 353-14, BACK COVER WITH CLASP 353-12, FRONT COVER/ EN
     PAPERS AND INDEX 353-16, MEDIEVAL GREEK MS 353-16, MENDE
     PARCHMENT PAGE 353-17, GLOSSES BOTTOM THIRD OF PAGE 353-18,
     WHOLE PAGE WITH GLOSSES WHICH SHOW MORWEN USED VOLUME 353-19

178

*$ABSTRACT 354
 *LIBRARY BOD
 *SLIDE SET TITLE YORKSHIRE HERALDIC GLASS
 *NEGATIVE REFERENCE ROLL 193A
 *RENTAL FEE SM 354 $3.70
 *PROVENANCE ENGLISH/ YORKSHIRE
 *CONTENTS HERALDIC STAINED GLASS 354/1-34, STAINED GLASS/
 YORKSHIRE   354/1-34,   BISHOPSTHORPE/   17TH-19TH   CENTURIES
 354/1-8, PALACE/ CLOAKROOM/ ROYAL ARMS 354/1-2, DINING ROOM
 354/1-8,   ACASTER   MALBIS/   CHURCH   354/9-11,   WEST TANFIELD/
 CHURCH/   15TH CENTURY 354/12-13, WELL CHURCH/ 14TH CENTURY
 354/14-17, COXWOLD/ 1755/ CHURCH 354-18, GILLING/ CASTLE/
 C1585 354/19-34

*$ABSTRACT 355
 *LIBRARY BOD
 *SLIDE SET TITLE STAINED GLASS NORTH AND WEST RIDINGS YORKSHIRE
 *NEGATIVE REFERENCE ROLL 193B
 *RENTAL FEE SM 355 $2.60
 *PROVENANCE ENGLISH
 *DATE EXECUTED 14TH AND 15TH
 *CONTENTS STAINED GLASS/ YORKSHIRE 355/1-12, WEST TANFIELD/
 CHURCH/ 15TH CENTURY 355/1-7, CRUCIFIXION 355-1, ST JOHN
 BAPTIST   355-2,   ST   PETER   355-3,   ST JAMES 355-4, NETHER
 POPLETON/ CHURCH/ 14TH AND 15TH CENTURIES 355/8-12, FIGURES IN
 WINDOWS 355/8-12

*$ABSTRACT 356
 *LIBRARY BOD
 *SLIDE SET TITLE INSECTS/ MAINLY BEES
 *NEGATIVE REFERENCE ROLL 194C
 *RENTAL FEE SM 356 $2.70
 *TITLE OF MANUSCRIPT FONTES MEMORABILES 356-2, MIROUER
 HISTORIAL ABREGIE DE FRANCE 356-3, PROPERTY OF ANIMALS 356-14
 *SHELFMARK MS ST JOHN'S COLL 61 356-1, MS BALLIOL 238E 356-2,
 MS BODLEY 968 356-3, MS DOUCE 31 356/4-6, MS DOUCE 112
 356/7-11, MS LAT LITURG G 5 356-12, MS ASHMOLE 1423 356-13, MS
 AUCT F 4 15 356-14
 *PROVENANCE ENGLISH 356/1 AND 12-13, GERMAN 356-2, FRENCH
 356/3-6 AND 14, FLEMISH 356/7-11
 *DATE EXECUTED 13TH 356-1, 15TH 356/2-11, 16TH 356/12-14
 *LANGUAGE LATIN/ FRENCH/ ENGLISH
 *AUTHOR DOMINICI BANDINI DE ARECIO 356-2, MANUEL PHILES 356-14
 *TYPE OF MANUSCRIPT BESTIARY 356-1, BOOK OF HOURS 356/4-11,
 DEVOTIONAL 356-12, ALCHEMICAL WORKS 356-13, BOOK ON ANIMALS
 356-14
 *CONTENTS BEES AND OTHER INSECTS 356/1-14, BEES FLYING TO SKEPS
 356-1, BEES SWARMING AROUND NEST 356-2, BEE IN DECORATIVE
 BORDER 356-3, BEE IN BORDER 356/4-6, INSECTS AND BEES IN
 BORDER 356/7-13, BEES 356-14

*$ABSTRACT 357
 *LIBRARY BOD
 *SLIDE SET TITLE GOLDEN LEGEND
 *NEGATIVE REFERENCE ROLL 194E
 *RENTAL FEE SM 357 $2.85
 *TITLE OF MANUSCRIPT GOLDEN LEGEND
 *SHELFMARK MS QUEEN'S COLLEGE OXFORD 305
 *PROVENANCE FRENCH
 *DATE EXECUTED 15TH
 *LANGUAGE FRENCH
 *TYPE OF MANUSCRIPT GOLDEN LEGEND
 *CONTENTS GOLDEN LEGEND/ ALL ILLUSTRATIONS FROM MS 357/1-117,
 PASSION 357-1, CHRIST BEFORE PILATE 357-1, FLAGELLATION 357-1,
 CRUCIFIXION 357-1, HARROWING OF HELL 357-1, CONVERSION OF ST
 PAUL 357-2, CONVERSION OF ST PETER 357-3, EXECUTION OF ST PAUL

179

357-4, ST JOHN WRITING 357-5, ST JAMES THE GREAT ATTACKED BY
DEVILS 357-6, ST MATTHEW DISMISSES DRAGONS BROUGHT BY AROES
AND ARFAISSAR 357-7, SS SIMON AND JUDE DISPUTE WITH ZAROES AND
ARPHASSAR 357-8, ST THOMAS WATCHES BUILDERS AT WORK 357-9, ST
PHILIP BAPTIZES KING OF SCYTHIA 357-10, ST JAMES THE LESS
BEATEN TO DEATH 357-11, ST BARTHOLOMEW FLAYED TO DEATH
DIRECTED BY ASTRIARGES 357-12, ST ANDREW TIED TO CROSS/ EGEAS
DIRECTS 357-13, ST BARNABAS 357-14, ST MARK 357-15, ST LUKE
357-16, INVENTION OF HOLY CROSS AND ST HELEN CROWNED 357-17,
LIFE OF ANTICHRIST/ ON THRONE CAST INTO HELL 357-13, HELL
MOUTH 357-13, DAY OF JUDGMENT/ CHRIST SEATED ON RAINBOW
357-19, ST JOHN BAPTIST BAPTISES CHRIST 357-20, ST STEPHEN
357-21, ST CLEMENT/ POPE THROWN INTO SEA/ AMPHIDIANUS
ENTHRONED 357-22, SS CHRYSANTHUS AND DARIA BURIED ALIVE
357-23, ST CLEMENT 357-24, ST SEBASTIAN'S MARTRYDOM/
DIOCLETIAN GIVING ORDERS 357-25, ST VINCENT MARTRY/ DACIAN
DIRECTING TORTURERS 357-26, ST IGNATIUS BEHEADED DIRECTED BY
TRAJAN 357-27, ST VALENTINE BEHEADED DIRECTED BY PLACIDUS
357-28, ST JULIAN MARTYR SHOOTING AT STAG KILLING PARENTS
357-29, ST ALEXANDER/ POPE BEHEADED UNDER DIRECTION OF
AURELIAN 357-30, SS GORDIAN/ JANUIAN/ EPIMACHIAN 357-31,
BROTHERS SPEUSIPPUS/ ELEUSIPPUS/ MELEUSIPPUS BURNED IN FIRE
357-32, ST BABILAS MARTYR PREACHING 357-33, SS MAURUS/
AUDIFAX/ ABACHUM MARTYRED WHILE LUCIAN LOOKS ON 357-34, ST
SIXTUS/ POPE AND MARTYR EXECUTED AT VALERIAN'S ORDER 357-35,
ST LAURENCE ROASTED ON GRIDIRON 357-36, ST HIPPOLYTUS TORN
APART BY TWO HORSES 357-37, ST LAMBERT MARTYR AS DUDO DIRECTS
357-38, SS COSMAS AND DAMIAN MARTYRED AND LYSIAS WATCHES
357-39, ST SAVINIAN/ MARTYR 357-40, ST BLAISE MARTYR TORTURED
WITH IRON COMB 357-41, ST NICASIUS OF RHEIMS MARTYRED AND
BARBARIAN CHIEF WATCHES 357-42, SS GENTIAN/ FUSCIAN/ VICTORIUS
MARTYRED 357-43, ST FABIAN/ POPE MARTYRED AT DECIUS' ORDER
357-44, ST PANCRAS MARTYR KNEELS WHILE VALERIAN DIRECTS
EXECUTION 357-45, ST VICTOR EXECUTED DIRECTED BY COUNT
SEBASTIAN 357-46, ST PETER/ ACOLYTE AND MARTYR KNEELING WITH
ST MARCELLINUS 357-47, SERGIUS DIRECTS EXECUTION 357-47, SS
PRIMUS AND FELICIAN MARTYRED 357-48, ST DENIS AND COMPANIONS
RUSTICUS AND ELEUTHORIUS 357-49, DAGOBERT'S LIFE AND CHRIST
DEDICATES CHURCH OF ST DENIS 357-50, ST CHRISTOPHER BEHEADED
UNDER DIRECTION OF DAFNUS OF SYRIA 357-51, ST HERNOUL'S BODY
TORN APART BY FOUR MEN 357-52, ST CYRIAC ENTERS CAULDRON OF
BOILING OIL 357-53, ST THOMAS OF CANTERBURY MARTRYED 357-54,
ST LONGINUS EXECUTED UNDER DIRECTION OF OCTAVIUS 357-55, ST
GEORGE EXECUTED UNDER DIRECTION OF DOCIAN OF PERSIA 357-56, ST
PANTALEON EXECUTED UNDER DIRECTION OF EMPEROR MAXIMIAN 357-57,
SS PLACIDIUS/ EUTYCHIUS/ AND VICTORINUS MARTYRED 357-58, ST
AYMON EXECUTED AND HYRGAR ON HORSE 357-59, ST NICASIUS AND
COMPANIONS AS SISINIUS DIRECTS EXECUTION 357-60, ST EUSTACE
AND COMPANIONS KNEEL BEFORE STAG WITH CRUCIFIX 357-61, ST
SILVESTER BAPTIZING CONSTANTINE 357-62, ST GREGORY/ POPE
PREACHING 357-63, ST PATRICK'S PURGATORY 357-64, ST ELOI ON
THRONE PERFORMS MIRACLE 357-65, ST NICHOLAS ADDING TO POOR
GIRL'S DOWRY 357-66, ST FELIX COMFORTS GROUP OF SEATED MEN
357-67, ST HILARY OF POITIERS SEATED BETWEEN BISHOPS 357-68,
ST ANTHONY STANDING BY FIRE TEMPTED BY DEVILS 357-69, ST REMY
OF RHEIMS BAPTIZES CLOVIS/ CLOTHILDE WATCHES 357-70, ST FELIX
WITH POPE AND FIGURE BEFORE GOLD IDOL 357-71, ST ARSELIUS
SPEAKING TO FATHERS IN DESERT 357-72, ST PRENDAM AND
COMPANIONS SAILING WESTWARDS 357-73, ST MARTIN DIVIDES CLOAK
WITH BEGGAR 357-74, MIRACLE OF ST MARTIN 357-75, ST BRICE
QUESTIONING INFANT 357-76, ST MAURUS HEALS LAME MAN 357-77, ST
ALEXIS LIES DYING/ EUPHEMIAN AND AGLAIS HIS PARENTS 357-78, ST
BENEDICT PREACHING TO MONKS 357-79, INITIAL A 357-80, ST PAUL
HERMIT VISITED BY ST ANTHONY 357-81, ST JULIAN BAPTIZES
DEFENSOR PRINCE OF LE MANS 357-82, ST SIMEON STYLITES VISITED
BY BASILICUS THE SARACEN KING 357-83, ST JEROME AND WOUNDED
LION 357-84, ST FORSIN OF PERONNE TAKE SOUL AT DEATH 357-85,
ST MARTIAL BAPTIZED BY ST PETER 357-86, ST GILES OF PROVENCE
PROTECTS HUNTED HIND 357-87, ST FRANCIS PREACHES TO BIRDS
357-88, DORMITION OF VIRGIN MARY 357-89, ST MARY MAGDALENE
MEETS RISEN CHRIST 357-90, ST MARY THE EGYPTIAN/ ZOZIMUS
PREPARES HER FOR BURIAL 357-91, ST CATHERINE OF ALEXANDRIA

DISPUTES WITH PAGAN DOCTORS 357-92, ST AGNES AT BROTHEL
WATCHES DEVIL STRUGGLE WITH MAN 357-93, ST AGATHA TORTURED
DIRECTED BY QUINTIAN 357-94, ST JULIANA BEATS DEVIL BELYAN/
HELSEUS AND MEN WATCH 357-95, SS PERPETUA AND FELCIANA
EXECUTED UNDER DIRECTION OF MINUCIUS 357-96, ST DOMITILLA AS
EXECUTION DIRECTED BY AVRELION 357-97, ST PETRONILLA'S
COMPANION ASSAULTED BY MEN 357-98, ST COLUMBA OF SENS BEHEADED
BY AURELIAN 357-99, ST GENEVIEVE OF PARIS DRAWS WATER FROM
WELL 357-100, ST FELICIA'S SONS ALEXANDER/ VITALIS/ MARTIAL
EXECUTED 357-101, ST CHRISTINE PILLORIED AND JUDGE JULIAN
357-102, ST LUCE KNEELS IN FIRE 357-103, ST MARINA AS MONK
DEAD WITH MONKS GATHERED AROUND 357-105, ST EUPHRASIA WITH
GROUP OF KNEELING NUNS 357-104, ST CECILIA STANDING WITH
EXECUTIONER/ ALMACHIUS POINTS 357-106, ST ANASTASIA NAILED TO
CROSS/ LUCILIUS DIRECTS 357-107, ST FENICLE TORTURED/ FLACCUS
DIRECTS 357-108, ST MARGARET PRAYING/ DEVIL IN DRAGON FORM
357/109-110, ST ELIZABETH OF HUNGARY FEEDING POOR 357-111, ST
PELAGIA BAPTIZED BY BISHOP NONNUS 357-112, ST BALTHEUT OF
CHELLES AND QUEEN OF FRANCE 357-113, ST FAITH KNEELS FOR
EXECUTION/ DACIAN DIRECTS 357-114, VIRGINS DIRECTED BY SARACEN
CHIEF TO BE EXECUTED 357-115, ST MARTHA KNEELS BEFORE CHRIST
AND ST MARY MAGDALENE 357-116, ST BERTILLE FIRST ABBESS OF
CHELLES WITH NUNS 357-117

*$ABSTRACT 358
  *LIBRARY BOD
  *SLIDE SET TITLE ABRAHAM AS ILLUSTRATED IN BOOK OF HOURS
  *NEGATIVE REFERENCE ROLL 194G
  *RENTAL FEE SM 358 $2.25
  *SHELFMARK MS DOUCE 135
  *PROVENANCE FRENCH
  *DATE EXECUTED 16TH/ EARLY
  *LANGUAGE LATIN
  *TYPE OF MANUSCRIPT BOOK OF HOURS/ USE OF ROME
  *CONTENTS ABRAHAM 358/1-5, ABRAHAM PRAYS TO GOD 358-1, GOD
  TELLS ABRAHAM TO SACRIFICE ISAAC 358-2, ABRAHAM GOES TO
  SACRIFICE ISAAC/ WHO CARRIES FAGGOTS 358-3, ABRAHAM ABOUT TO
  SLAY ISAAC STOPPED BY ANGEL 358-4, ABRAHAM SACRIFICES RAM/
  ISAAC PRAYS BESIDE HIM 358-5

*$ABSTRACT 359
  *LIBRARY BOD
  *SLIDE SET TITLE CALENDAR/ MONTHS AND OCCUPATIONS/ SIGNS OF
  ZODIAC
  *NEGATIVE REFERENCE ROLL 195A
  *RENTAL FEE SM 359 $3.30
  *TITLE OF MANUSCRIPT DE BRAILLES PSALTER
  *SHELFMARK MS NEW COLLEGE 322
  *PROVENANCE ENGLISH
  *DATE EXECUTED 13TH
  *TYPE OF MANUSCRIPT PSALTER
  *CONTENTS OCCUPATIONS OF THE MONTHS 359/1-26, ZODIAC SIGNS
  359/1-26, JANUARY/ FEASTING 359-1, AQUARIUS 359-2, FEBRUARY/
  MAN DRIES BOOT BEFORE FIRE 359-3, PISCES 359-4, MARCH/ DIGGING
  VINEYARD 359-5, ARIES 359-6, APRIL/ KING WITH FOLIAGE IN HANDS
  359-7, TAURUS 359-8, MAY/ KING HAWKING 359-9, GEMINI 359-10,
  JUNE/ WEEDING CORN 359-11, CANCER 359-12, JULY/ MOWING HAY
  359-13, LEO 359-14, AUGUST/ REAPING 359-15, VIRGO 359-16,
  SEPTEMBER/ GRAPE PICKING 359-17, LIBRA 359-18, OCTOBER/ SOWING
  359-19, SCORPIO 359-20, NOVEMBER/ PIG KILLING 359-21,
  SAGITTARIUS 359-22, DECEMBER/ LOAVES IN OPEN OVEN 359-23,
  CAPRICORNUS 359-24, AUGUST AND SEPTEMBER CALENDAR PAGES
  359-25, NOVEMBER/ CALENDAR PAGE 359-26

*$ABSTRACT 360
  *LIBRARY BOD

181

*SLIDE SET TITLE ILLUMINATIONS BY WILLIAM DE BRAILLES
*NEGATIVE REFERENCE ROLL 195B
*RENTAL FEE SM 360 $2.70
*TITLE OF MANUSCRIPT DE BRAILLES PSALTER
*SHELFMARK MS NEW COLLEGE 322
*PROVENANCE ENGLISH
*DATE EXECUTED 13TH
*LANGUAGE LATIN
*ARTIST/ SCHOOL WILLIAM DE BRAILLES
*TYPE OF MANUSCRIPT PSALTER
*CONTENTS PSALTER ILLUMINATIONS 360/1-14, BEATUS PAGE AND
CALENDAR FOR DECEMBER 360-1, BEATUS VIR/ PSALM I/ JESSE TREE
360-2, JESSE TREE 360-2, DOMINUS ILLUMINATIO MEA/ DAVID FREES
SAUL FROM EVIL SPIRIT 360-3, DIXI CUSTODIAM 360-4, JUDGMENT OF
SOLOMON 360-4, QUID GLORIARIS 360-5, DAVID SLAYS GOLIATH
360-5, DIXIT INSIPIENS 360-6, TEMPTATION OF CHRIST 360-6,
SALVUM ME FAC 360-7, NINEVEH AND JONAH AND THE WHALE 360-7,
EXULTATE DEO 360-8, JACOB DREAMS AND WRESTLES WITH ANGEL
360-8, CANTATE DOMINO 360-9, NATIVITY AND ANNUNCIATION TO
SHEPHERDS 360-9, DOMINE EXAUDI 360-10, GOD ENTHRONED/ DAVID
AND BATHSHEBA/ DAVID AND NATHAN 360-10, DIXIT DOMINUS 360-11,
TRINITY 360-11, BONITATEM FECISTI 360-12, DAVID PLAYING HARP
360-12, MANUS TUAE 360-13, CHRIST LAYS HAND ON DAVID'S HEAD
360-13, DEFECIT IN SALUTARE 360-14, CHRIST BLESSES DAVID
360-14

*$ABSTRACT 361
  *LIBRARY BOD
  *SLIDE SET TITLE GOUGH MAP DETAILS II/ NORTH BRITAIN
  *NEGATIVE REFERENCE ROLL 257B
  *RENTAL FEE SM 361 $2.30
  *COMMENTS 6 SLIDES FROM THE EARLIEST ROAD MAP OF BRITAIN
  *TITLE OF MANUSCRIPT GOUGH MAP
  *SHELFMARK MS GOUGH GEN TOP 16
  *PROVENANCE ENGLISH
  *DATE EXECUTED 14TH/C1360
  *TYPE OF MANUSCRIPT MAP
  *CONTENTS MAP OF NORTHERN SCOTLAND WITH WESTERN ISLES 361-1,
  MAP OF NORTHEAST COAST OF SCOTLAND WITH ORKNEYS 361-2, SHIP/
  WRECKED WITH MAN ON RAFT 361-2, MAP OF CENTRAL SCOTLAND 361-3,
  MAP OF EAST COAST OF SCOTLAND WITH MAY 361-4, MAP OF SOUTHERN
  SCOTLAND AND NORTHERN ENGLAND 361-5, HADRIAN'S WALL ON MAP
  361-5, MAP OF SOUTHEAST CORNER OF SCOTLAND AND DENMARK 361-6

*$ABSTRACT 362
  *LIBRARY BOD
  *SLIDE SET TITLE BROMHOLM PSALTER
  *NEGATIVE REFERENCE ROLL 195E
  *RENTAL FEE SM 362 $3.10
  *TITLE OF MANUSCRIPT BROMHOLM PSALTER
  *SHELFMARK MS ASHMOLE 1523
  *PROVENANCE ENGLISH/ EAST ANGLIA
  *DATE EXECUTED 14TH
  *LANGUAGE LATIN
  *TYPE OF MANUSCRIPT PSALTER
  *CONTENTS PSALTER 362/1-22, INITIALS/ DECORATED   362/1-22,
  CALENDAR PAGE WITH FEASTS IN JUNE 362-1, INITIAL/ DECORATIVE
  362/2-4, INITIAL D/ DIXI CUSTODIAM 362-5, DAVID BLESSED BY
  CHRIST POINTING AT DEVIL 362-5, INITIAL Q/ QUID GLORIARIS
  362-6, MURDERER STABBING HIS VICTIM 362/6-7, INITIAL D/ DIXIT
  INSIPIENS 362-7, DAVID DISPUTING WITH FOOL 362/8-9, INITIAL Q/
  QUI REGIS ISRAEL 362-10, INITIAL E/ EXULTATE DEO 362-11,
  CHRIST ENTHRONED WITH ANGELS AND MUSICIANS 362-11, INITIAL C/
  CANTATE DOMINO 362-12, CREATOR ABOVE AND DAVID AND CHORISTERS
  BELOW 362/12-13, INITIAL A/ AUDITE 362-14, DECORATED
  LINE-ENDINGS ON PAGE OF LITANY 362-15, INITIALS AND PAGE OF
  TEXT 362-16, INITIAL P/ PELLI 362-17, MUSICAL NOTATION 362-17,
  INITIAL V/ VIR 362-18, MAN'S FACE 362-18, INITIAL B/ BEATA

362-19, MUSICAL NOTATION AND INITIALS 362-20, INITIAL X/ XPE
362/21-22, WYVERN DEVOURING MAN 362-22

*$ABSTRACT 363
 *LIBRARY BOD
 *SLIDE SET TITLE FIFTEENTH CENTURY SPANISH AND ITALIAN MSS FROM
 HOLKHAM
 *NEGATIVE REFERENCE ROLL 195F
 *RENTAL FEE SM 363 $5.05
 *TITLE OF MANUSCRIPT ORATIONS 363/32-49, LETTERS OF ST JEROME
 363/50-55, LIBER AEGLOGARUM 363-61
 *SHELFMARK MS HOLKHAM 339 363-1, MS HOLKHAM 391 363/2-7, MS
 HOLKHAM 120 363/8-18, MS HOLKHAM 300 363/19-20, MS HOLKHAM 352
 363/21-31, MS HOLKHAM 389 363/32-49, MS HOLKHAM 125 363/50-55,
 MS HOLKHAM 351 363/56-60, MS HOLKHAM 522 363-61
 *PROVENANCE SPANISH 363-1, ITALIAN 363/2-61
 *DATE EXECUTED 15TH
 *LANGUAGE LATIN
 *AUTHOR SALLUST 363-1, SENECA 363/2-7, LACTANTIUS 363/8-18,
 TERENCE 363/19-20, LIVY 363/21-31, CICERO 363/32-49, ST JEROME
 363/50-55, LIVY 363/56-60, JACOBUS SANNAZARIUS 363-61
 *ARTIST/ SCHOOL FRANCESCO DI ANTONIO/ ASSOCIATED WITH
 *TYPE OF MANUSCRIPT CLASSICAL LITERATURE
 *CONTENTS INITIALS/ ILLUMINATED 363/1-61, BORDERS/ DECORATED
 363/1-61, HOLKHAM MISCELLANY 363/1-61, INITIAL A 363/5 AND 18
 AND 40, INITIAL B 363-17, INITIAL C 363/14 AND 35 AND 39 AND
 45, INITIAL D 363/4 AND 44 AND 55, INITIAL E 363/7 AND 34 AND
 49, INITIAL H 363-46, INITIAL I 363/3 AND 48 AND 59, INITIAL M
 363/11 AND 36 AND 54-55, INITIAL N 363/15 AND 38, INITIAL Q
 363/12 AND 16 AND 41-42, INITIAL S 363/37 AND 43 AND 47,
 INITIAL V 363-13, PAGE WHOLE FROM SENECA 363-2, AUTHOR/ SENECA
 IN HIS STUDY 363-3, SENECA READING 363-7, LACTANTIUS AS MONK
 363-9, ACTANTIUS IN HIS STUDY 363-11, CHRIST BLESSING 363-14,
 PROPHET 363/13-14, KING IN JUDGMENT 363-15, PRIEST
 CONSECRATING HOST 363-16, FRIAR PREACHING 363-17, MAN PRAYING
 363-18, INITIALS/ VINESTEM 363/19-20, LIVY/ BEGINNING OF TEXT
 363/21-22, LIVY/ BOOKS 2-9 363/23-31, ORATIONS OF CICERO
 363/32-49, ST JEROME/ LETTERS 363/50-55, LIVY/ DETAILS OF MS
 PAGES 363/56-60, LIBER AEGLOGARUM 363-61

*$ABSTRACT 364
 *LIBRARY BOD
 *SLIDE SET TITLE HERALDRY
 *NEGATIVE REFERENCE ROLL 195G
 *RENTAL FEE SM 364 $3.40
 *TITLE OF MANUSCRIPT ORMESBY PSALTER
 *SHELFMARK MS DOUCE 366
 *PROVENANCE ENGLISH
 *DATE EXECUTED 13TH/ EARLY 14TH
 *LANGUAGE LATIN
 *TYPE OF MANUSCRIPT PSALTER
 *CONTENTS ORMESBY PSALTER 364/1-28, HERALDRY FROM ORMESBY
 PSALTER 364/1-28, COAT OF ARMS OF FOLIOT OF GREESENHALL 364-1,
 COAT OF ARMS OF BARDOLF OF WORMEGAY 364-1, COATS OF ARMS
 364/1-28, INITIAL D/ DIXIT INSIPIENS 364-2, WAREENEAND
 NEWMARCH OF WORMSELEY 364-2, NEVILL OF ESSEX AND MOWBRAY
 364-3, PERCY 364-4, LAST JUDGMENT 364-5, CORNWALL 364-5, CLARE
 364-6, BALIOL 364-7, FITZLALEN/ EARL OF ARUNDEL 364-8,
 ANOINTING OF DAVID 364-8, LEON AND CASTILLE 364-9, FRANCE/
 ANCIENT 364-10, DREUX 364-11, CLARE/ VARIANT 364-12, DAVID
 KNEELING BEFORE GOD 364-12, CLARE WITH BAUDE AND NAVARRE
 364/13-14, MONHAUT 364-15, EMPIRE/ COUNT OF FLANDERS AND
 TURBERVILLE AND TIPTOFT 364-16, GRENDAN 364/17-18, PIKERING
 AND KERDESTAN 364-19, WARENNE/ DECORATIVE VARIANT 364/21-22,
 WARENNE 364-23, MORTIMER OF ATTLEBOROUGH 364/24-25, LEOPARDS
 OF ENGLAND 364-25, LILIES OF FRANCE 364-27, FOLIOT AND BARDOLF
 364-28

*$ABSTRACT 365
  *LIBRARY BOD
  *SLIDE SET TITLE ENGLISH BIRDS
  *NEGATIVE REFERENCE ROLL 195H
  *RENTAL FEE SM 365 $2.75
  *TITLE OF MANUSCRIPT ORMESBY PSALTER
  *SHELFMARK MS DOUCE 366
  *PROVENANCE ENGLISH
  *DATE EXECUTED 13TH/ LATE
  *LANGUAGE LATIN
  *TYPE OF MANUSCRIPT PSALTER
  *CONTENTS PSALTER 365/1-15, BIRDS/ ENGLISH 365/1-15, PEREGRINE
   FALCON DEVOURING ITS PREY 365-1, OWL/ TAWNY AND MAGPIE 365-2,
   ROBIN AND GOLDFINCH 365-3, JAY 365-4, SHRIKE OR BRAMBLING
   365-5, CRANE 365-6, WHITETHROAT AND SQUIRREL 365-7, FLYCATCHER
   365-8, GREEN WOODPECKER 365-9, WOODCHAT 365-10, COCKS FIGHTING
   365-11, WREN 365-12, FINCH OR BUNTING 365-13, GREENFINCH
   365/14-15

*$ABSTRACT 366
  *LIBRARY BOD
  *SLIDE SET TITLE PSALM INITIALS
  *NEGATIVE REFERENCE ROLL 195I
  *RENTAL FEE SM 366 $3.20
  *TITLE OF MANUSCRIPT ORMESBY PSALTER
  *SHELFMARK MS DOUCE 366
  *PROVENANCE ENGLISH
  *DATE EXECUTED 13TH
  *LANGUAGE LATIN
  *TYPE OF MANUSCRIPT PSALTER
  *CONTENTS PSALM INITIALS 366/1-24, INITIALS/ DECORATED
   366/1-24, INITIAL Q/ QUARE FREMUERUNT 366-1, DAVID SPEAKS TO
   GROUP OF PEOPLE 366-1, INITIAL D/ DOMINE QUID MULTIPLICAT
   366-2, RESURRECTION WITH CHRIST BLESSING KNEELING FIGURE
   366-2, INITIAL C/ CUM INVOCAREM 366-3, INITIAL D/ DOMINE
   DOMINUS NOSTER 366-4, DAVID WITH LARGE GLOBE 366-4, INITIAL C,
   CONFITEBOR TIBI DOMINE 366-5, CHRIST ENTHRONED AND LAST
   JUDGMENT 366-5, INITIAL I/ IN DOMINE CONFIDO 366-6, ASCENSIO
   366-6, INITIAL D/ DIXIT INSIPIENS 366-7, FOOL HOLDING STONE
   AND JESTER'S HAND 366-7, INITIAL D/ DOMINE QUIS HABITABIT
   366-8, MONK OPENING DOOR WITH LARGE KEY 366-8, INITIAL C,
   CONSERVA ME DOMINE 366-9, LAST JUDGMENT 366-9, INITIAL D
   DILIGAM TE DOMINE 366-10, DEATH OF SAUL 366-10, INITIAL C,
   CAELI ENARRANT 366-11, VIRGIN AND CHRIST-CHILD 366-11, INITIA
   E/ EXAUDIAT TE DOMINUS 366-12, ABRAHAM ABOUT TO SACRIFICE
   ISAAC 366-12, INITIAL D/ DOMINE IN VIRTUTE 366-13, DAVI
   KNEELS IN PRAYER 366-13, INITIAL D/ DEUS DEUS MEUS 366-14
   CRUCIFIXION 366-14, INITIAL D/ DOMINI EST TERRA 366-15
   RESURRECTION 366-15, INITIAL A/ AD TE DOMINE 366-16, BETRAYA
   OF CHRIST 366-16, INITIAL A/ AFFERTE DOMINO 366-17, DAVI
   SACRIFICES RAM 366-17, INITIAL E/ EXULTATE TE DOMINE 366-18
   PASSOVER 366-18, INITIAL I/ IN TE DOMINE SPERAVI 366-19
   CHRIST PRAYS AND HOLY SPIRIT DESCENDS AS DOVE 366-19, INITIA
   B/ BEATI QUORUM 366-20, MONK HEARS CHILD'S CONFESSION 366-20
   INITIAL B/ BEATUS QUI INTELLIGIT 366-21, DAVID KNEELS BEFOR
   GOD WHO APPEARS IN SKY 366-21, INITIAL D/ DEUS NOSTER REFUGIU
   366-22, DAVID SPOKEN TO BY GOD AT ALTAR 366-22, INITIAL O
   OMNES GENTES PLAUDITE 366-23, DAVID AND ANOTHER KNEEL BEFOR
   GOD 366-23, INITIAL M/ AGNUS DOMINUS 366-24, CHRIST STANDING
   BESIDE DOMED BUILDING 366-24

*$ABSTRACT 367
  *LIBRARY BOD
  *SLIDE SET TITLE CALENDAR WITH OCCUPATIONS OF THE MONTHS/ SIGN
   OF ZODIAC
  *NEGATIVE REFERENCE ROLL 196A
  *RENTAL FEE SM 367 $2.60
  *SHELFMARK MS ADD A 46

*PROVENANCE FLEMISH/ LIEGE
*DATE EXECUTED 13TH/C1280
*LANGUAGE LATIN
*TYPE OF MANUSCRIPT CALENDAR FROM A PSALTER
*CONTENTS PSALTER 367/1-12, OCCUPATIONS OF THE MONTHS 367/1-12,
ZODIACAL SIGNS 367/1-12, JANUARY/ FEASTING 367-1, AQUARIUS
367-1, MAN WARMING FEET AT FIRE AND DRINKING FROM BOWL 367-1,
FEBRUARY/ HEDGING 367-2, PISCES 367-2, MARCH/ DIGGING 367-3,
ARIES 367-3, APRIL/ PICKING FLOWERS 367-4, TAURUS 367-4, MAY/
HAWKING 367-5, GEMINI 367-5, JUNE FRUIT-PICKING 367-6, CANCER
367-6, JULY/ HAY-MAKING 367-7, LEO 367-7, AUGUST/ HARVESTING
367-8, VIRGO 367-8, SEPTEMBER 367-9, SOWING 367-9, LIBRA
367-9, OCTOBER/ WINE-MAKING 367-10, SCORPIO 367-10, NOVEMBER/
FEEDING HOGS 367-11, SAGITTARIUS 367-11, DECEMBER/
SLAUGHTERING 367-12, CAPRICORN 367-12

*$ABSTRACT 368
 *LIBRARY BOD
 *SLIDE SET TITLE GERARDE/ HERBALL
 *NEGATIVE REFERENCE ROLL 196C
 *RENTAL FEE SM 368 $4.05
 *TITLE OF MANUSCRIPT HERBALL
 *SHELFMARK PRINTED BY JOHN NORTON/ LONDON/ 1597
 *PROVENANCE ENGLISH
 *DATE EXECUTED 16TH/1597
 *LANGUAGE ENGLISH
 *AUTHOR GERARDE
 *ARTIST/ SCHOOL PRINTED BY JOHN NORTON
 *TYPE OF MANUSCRIPT HERBAL
 *CONTENTS HERBAL 368/1-41, TITLE PAGE 368-1, PORTRAIT OF JOHN
GERARDE 368-2, YELLOW TURKIE WHEAT/ GOLDCOLORED/ RED/ BLEW AND
WHITE 368-3, FRENCH CORN FLAG/ ITALIAN 368-4, BLEW ORIENTALL
IACINT/ DOUBLE 368-5, PERSIAN DAFFODILL/ GREAT WINTER/ SMALL
WINTER 368-6, DAFFODILL/ CHECKERED AND CHANGEABLE CHECKERED
368-7, SQUILL OR SEA ONION/ SEA ONION OF VALENTIA 368-8, RED
FLOWERED SEA DAFFODILL/ YELLOW FLOWERED 368-8, DOG'S TOOTH/
WHITE 368-9, GREAT DOG'S STONES/ WHITE 368-10, BIRDES
SATYRION/ SPOTTED BIRDES ORCHIS 368-11, BUTTERFLY ORCHIS/
SOULDIERS SATRYION 368-11, ADONIS RED FLOWER/ YELLOW 368-12,
OUR LADIES SLIPPER 368-13, ROCK SAMPIER/ THORNY/ GOLDEN
368-14, GREAT DOUBLE CARNATION/ DOUBLE CLOVE GILLOFLOWER
368-15, RED VALERIAN/ SPATLING POPPIE 368-16, MATFELLON/
BLACKE AND GREAT 368-17, VIPER'S GRASSE/ COMMON/ DWARFFE/
SPANISH/ DWARFFE SPANISH 368-18, MARIGOLDS 368-19, EINE/ RED
BIRD/ WHITE BIRD 368-20, EARE/ RED BEARES/ SCARLET BEARES
368-21, MARIGOLD/ GREAT MARSH/ SMALL MARSH 368-22, LILLIE/
WHITE WATER/ YELLOW WATER 368-23, SOWBREAD/ ROUND AND IULE
368-24, POMPION/ GREAT LONG/ GREAT ROUND 368-25, POTATUS OR
POTATOES 368-26, POTATOES OF VIRGINIA 368-27, MALLOWE/ VENICE/
THORNEY 368-29, TREE HOLLOHOCKE WITH DOUBLE FLOWERS 368-28,
BATCHELOR'S BUTTONS/ WHITE AND WHITE CROWFOOTE OR TRIPOLIE
368-30, ANGELICA/ GARDEN/ WILDE 368-31, HOLLOW ROOTE/ GREAT
PURPLE/ GREAT WHITE 368-32, SMALL PURPLE/ SMALL WHITE 368-32,
LIVERWOORT/ NOBLE/ NOBLE RED/ WITH DOUBLE FLOWERS 368-33,
GREAT HOLLAND ROSE/ OR GREAT PROVINCE ROSE 368-34, VELVET
ROSE/ YELLOW ROSE 368-35, TAME OR MANURED PINE TREE 368-36,
FILBERD NUT OF CONSTANTINOPLE 368-37, INDIAN FIG TREE AND
FRUIT 368-38, DRAGON TREE AND FRUIT 368-39, LIVERWOORT 368-40,
BREEDE OF BARNACKLE 368-41

*$ABSTRACT 369
 *LIBRARY BOD
 *SLIDE SET TITLE CONRAD GESNER/ DE RERUM FOSSILIUM
 *NEGATIVE REFERENCE ROLL 196D
 *RENTAL FEE SM 369 $2.50
 *TITLE OF MANUSCRIPT DE RERUM FOSSILIUM
 *SHELFMARK G 55 ART SELD
 *PROVENANCE ENGLISH

185

```
*DATE EXECUTED 16TH/1565
*LANGUAGE LATIN
*AUTHOR CONRAD GESNER
*TYPE OF MANUSCRIPT TEXT ON FOSSILS
*CONTENTS FOSSILS 369/1-10, RINGS AND GEMS 369-1, DEICATION/
BEFORE CATALOGUS 369-2, AMIANTH/ SMARAGDUS/ HAMMITES 369-3,
BASALT WITH POINTED APICES 369-4, ROCK SALT AND PUMICE 369-5,
RINGS 369-6, BEADS 369-7, FOSSILS 369-8, FOSSIL TEETH 369-9,
FOSSIL SHELLS 369-10


*$ABSTRACT 370
*LIBRARY BOD
*SLIDE SET TITLE LITURGICAL MSS
*NEGATIVE REFERENCE ROLL 196G
*RENTAL FEE SM 370 $3.05
*TITLE OF MANUSCRIPT MARTYROLOGY OF USUARD 370-8
*SHELFMARK MS LAUD MISC 273 370-1, MS CANON LITURG 352 370-2,
MS LAT LITURG F 26 270/3-4, MS D'ORVILLE 45 370-5, MS LAT
LITURG C 1 370-6, MS LAT LITURG A 5 370-7, MS RAWL D 1225
370-8, MS RAWL B 328 370-9, MS CANON LITURG 379 370-10, MS
DOUCE 245 370-11, MS CANON LITURG 237 370/12-13, MS BODLEY 901
370-14, MS CANON MISC 560 370-15, MS RAWL D 928 370/16-17, MS
RAWL D 939 370-18, MS DIGBY 25 370-19, MS CANON LITURG 333
370-20, MS CANON LITURG 216 370-21
*PROVENANCE FRENCH 370/1 AND 5 AND 11, ITALIAN 370/2 AND 6-7
AND 10 AND 12-15 AND 19-21, ENGLISH 370/3-4 AND 8-9 AND 16-18
*DATE EXECUTED 11TH 370-5, 13TH 370/3-4 AND 6-8 AND 10 AND
12-13, 12TH 370-19, 14TH 370/1-2 AND 9 AND 11 AND 14-15 AND
18, 15TH 370/16-17 AND 20-21
*LANGUAGE LATIN
*TYPE OF MANUSCRIPT LITURGICAL MSS 370/1-21, MISSAL/ NOTED
370-1, MISSAL/ RUBRICATED 370-2, MISSAL/ RUBRICATED PORTABLE
370/3-4, PSALTER/ CHOIR 370-5, ANTIPHONAL 370/6-7, MATRYOLOGY
370-8, OBITUARY 370-9, BREVIARY/ RUBRICATED NOTED CHOIR
370-10, PORTOS/ RUBRICATED 370-11, DIURNAL/ PORTABLE
370/12-13, PONTIFICAL 370-14, CALENDAR 370-15, CALENDAR/
COMPUTISTIC 370/16-17, CALENDAR/ ILLUSTRATED 370-18, TONALE
370-19, COMPUTISTIC HAND 370-20, MUSICAL HAND 370-21
*CONTENTS LITURGICAL MSS FROM 11TH-15TH CENTURIES 370/1-21


*$ABSTRACT 371
*SLIDE SET TITLE EASTERN CHURCH
*NEGATIVE REFERENCE ROLL 196I
*RENTAL FEE SM 371 $2.90
*TITLE OF MANUSCRIPT DAILY MENAION 371-1, LITURGICAL
ANTHOLOGION 371-2, GOSPELS 371/3-7, GREAT RUSSIAN ABECEDARIUM
AND FORMULARY 371-9, WEST RUSSIAN ABECEDARIUM 371/10-13
*SHELFMARK MS CANON GR 58 371-1, MS E D CLARKE 14 371/3-7, MS
BODLEY 945 370-8, MS BODLEY ROLLS 17 370-9, MS RUSS C I
370/10-13
*PROVENANCE GREEK 370/1-2, RUSSIAN 371/3-13
*DATE EXECUTED 11TH 370-1, 16TH 370/2-8, 17TH 371/9-13
*TYPE OF MANUSCRIPT LITURGICAL MSS FROM EASTERN CHURCH
*CONTENTS LITURGICAL MSS FROM EASTERN CHURCH 371/1-13, STICHERA
IDIOMELA FOR FEAST OF ST ANTHIMUS 371-1, SERVIKON MELODY WITH
STICHERON IN GREEK LETTERS 371-2, LIGATURES IN RUSSIAN MS OF
GOSPELS 371/3-7, BALKAN-TYPE WOVEN HEAD-PIECE 371-8, DECORATED
BEGINNING OF RUSSIAN ABECEDARIUM 371-9, CYRILLIC ALPHABET ON
RUSSIAN ABECEDARIUM 371/10-13


*$ABSTRACT 372
*LIBRARY BOD
*SLIDE SET TITLE OXFORDSHIRE DOMESDAY BOOK
*NEGATIVE REFERENCE ROLL 196I
*RENTAL FEE SM 372 $2.75
*TITLE OF MANUSCRIPT OXFORDSHIRE DOMESDAY BOOK
```

*SHELFMARK DOMESDAY BOOK OF GREAT SURVEY OF ENGLAND OF WILLIAM CONQUEROR
*PROVENANCE ENGLISH
*DATE EXECUTED 11TH/ 1086
*LANGUAGE LATIN
*TYPE OF MANUSCRIPT DOMESDAY BOOK
*CONTENTS DOMESDAY BOOK OF OXFORDSHIRE 372/1-15, CONTENTS OF TEXT/ WITHOUT ILLUSTRATIONS 372/1-15, OXFORD/ OXFORD TENANTS 372-1, TERRA REGIS 372-2, ARCHBISHOP AND BISHOPS 372-3, BISHOP OF LINCOLN/ BAYEUX 372-4, BISHOP OF BAYEUX 372-5, BISHOP OF BAYEUX/ LISIEUX/ ABBOT OF ABINGDON 372-6, CHURCHES/ EARLS/ HUGH/ MORTAIN/ EVREUX 372-7, ROBERT DE STATFORD/ ROBERT DE OILGI 372-9, EARL AUBREY/ WALTER GIFARD/ HENRY DE FERRERS/ HUGH D'IVRY 372-8, ROBERT OILGI/ ROBERT DE IVERI 372-10, ROGER DE IVERI/ MILES CRISPIN 372-11, MILES CRISPIN/ GEOFFREY DE MANVILLE 372-12, GEOFFREY DE MANNEVILLE/ ROGER DE IVERI 372-13, WIFE OF ROGER DE IVERI/ MINISTRI REGIS 372-14, MINISTRI REGIS TO END OF BOOK 372-15

*$ABSTRACT 373
 *LIBRARY BOD
 *SLIDE SET TITLE INITIALS FROM A RELIGIOUS MISCELLANY
 *NEGATIVE REFERENCE ROLL 196L
 *RENTAL FEE SM 373 $2.70
 *SHELFMARK MS TRINITY COLLEGE 89
 *PROVENANCE ENGLISH
 *DATE EXECUTED 15TH
 *LANGUAGE LATIN
 *TYPE OF MANUSCRIPT RELIGIOUS MISCELLANY
 *CONTENTS INITIALS FROM A RELIGIOUS MISCELLANY 373/1-14, FIGURE OF A MAN 373-1, INITIAL D/ DULCISSIME 373-2, HEAD OF CHRIST 373-2, INITIAL P/ PARCE 373-3, DRAGON EATING FISH AS LETTER 373-3, INITIAL C/ CUM 373-4, MASK EMERGING FROM GREEN BRANCHES 373-4, INITIAL D/ DILIGAM 373-5, TUDOR ROSE 373-5, INITIAL G/ GAUDIAM 373-6, MILK CHURN FILLED 373-6, INITIAL O/ OTRES 373-7, JANUS IN ROUND HAT 373-7, INITIAL D/ DEUS 373-8, SPECKLED BIRD LIKE SEAGULL/ HOLY GHOST 373-8, INITIAL O/ OMNIS 373-9, VASE OF MADONNA LILIES ON GROUND 373-9, INITIAL O/ OMNIA 373-10, ST PETER IN BLUE MANTLE WITH BOOK AND KEYS 373-10, INITIAL O/ QUIS 373-11, FRIAR IN WHITE TUNIC WITH ROSARY 373-11, INITIAL D/ DICITUR 373-12, FOX AND GOOSE 373-12, INITIAL N/ NOLI 373-13, DOG WITH RABBIT ON BACK 373-13, INITIAL O/ GLORIOSA 373-14, SHIELD WITH FIVE WOUNDS 373-14

*$ABSTRACT 374
 *LIBRARY BOD
 *SLIDE SET TITLE HERALDIC TREATISE
 *NEGATIVE REFERENCE ROLL 196N
 *RENTAL FEE SM 374 $3.10
 *TITLE OF MANUSCRIPT DE OFFICIO MILITARI
 *SHELFMARK MS HOLKHAM MISC 31
 *PROVENANCE ENGLISH
 *DATE EXECUTED 15TH
 *LANGUAGE LATIN
 *AUTHOR NICHOLAS UPTON
 *TYPE OF MANUSCRIPT HERALDIC TREATISE
 *CONTENTS HERALDIC TREATISE 374/1-22, SHIELDS OF ARMS/ COLORED 374/1-22, ARMS 374/1-22

*$ABSTRACT 375
 *LIBRARY BOD
 *SLIDE SET TITLE TRACTATUS DE ARMIS
 *NEGATIVE REFERENCE ROLL 196O
 *RENTAL FEE SM 375 $3.10
 *TITLE OF MANUSCRIPT TRACTATUS DE ARMIS

```
*SHELFMARK MS LAT MISC E 86
*PROVENANCE ENGLISH
*DATE EXECUTED 14TH/C1394
*LANGUAGE LATIN AND ENGLISH
*AUTHOR JOHANNES DE BADO AUREO
*TYPE OF MANUSCRIPT HERALDIC TREATISE
*CONTENTS   HERALDIC   TREATISE   375/1-22,   TRACTATUS   DE   ARMX
 375/1-22,   JOHANNES   DE  BADO  AUREO  375/1-22,  SHIELDS/  HERALDX
 AND COATS OF ARMS 375/1-22
```

*$ABSTRACT 376
```
 *LIBRARY BOD
 *SLIDE SET TITLE HOURS OF ANNE OF BOHEMIA
 *NEGATIVE REFERENCE ROLL 196P
 *RENTAL FEE SM 376 $3.25
 *TITLE OF MANUSCRIPT HOURS OF ANNE OF BOHEMIA
 *SHELFMARK MS LAT LITURG F 3
 *PROVENANCE FLEMISH
 *DATE EXECUTED 14TH/1382-94
 *LANGUAGE LATIN AND DUTCH
 *TYPE OF MANUSCRIPT BOOK OF HOURS/ USE OF ROME
 *CONTENTS HOURS OF ANNE OF  BOHEMIA  376/1-25,  BOOK  OF  HOUF
 376/1-25,   ST   GEORGE   WITH  FEET  ON  DRAGON  376-1,  ANNUNCIATIC
 376-2,  CHRIST  IN  GLORY  376-3,  GROTESQUE  BIRD  AND COAT OF  ARM
 376-4,   HOUND   PURSUED   BY   BIRD   PURSUING  RABBIT  376-5,  CRAM
 DRINKING FROM CHURN AND FOX ALSO TRIES 376-6,  PRESENTATION   X
 THE  TEMPLE   376-7,  ANNE  OF  BOHEMIA  HOLDING HAND OF RICHARD X
 376-8,  ST EDMUND AND ST CUTHBERT 376-8,  BETRAYAL OF CHRIST  X
 GETHSEMANE  376-9,   CHRIST   BEFORE  PILATE  376-10,  FLAGELLATIC
 376-11,  CHRIST  CARRYING  THE CROSS 376-12,  CRUCIFIXION   376-1X
 DEPOSITION   376-14,   ENTOMBMENT   376-15,   NATIVITY   376-1X
 SQUIRREL CHAINED TO DEATH IN GOTHIC KENNEL 376-16,  ANGEL   AN
 THE  SHEPHERDS  376-18,   ADORATION   OF  THE  MAGI  376-19,  FLIGX
 INTO EGYPT 376-20, MASSACRE OF INNOCENTS 376-21, OFFICE OF TX
 DEAD 376-22, ARMS OF HOLY ROMAN EMPIRE 376-23,  PENTECOST   AN
 MARY AND APOSTLES 376-24, VIRGIN AND CHILD ON THRONE WITH ANN
 OF BOHEMIA 376-25
```

*$ABSTRACT 377
```
 *LIBRARY BOD
 *SLIDE SET TITLE MILITARY ORDER OF OUR SAVIOUR'S PASSION
 *NEGATIVE REFERENCE ROLL 196Q
 *RENTAL FEE SM 377 $2.30
 *TITLE OF MANUSCRIPT LA SUSTANCE DE LA PASSION DE JHESUS CRIST
 *SHELFMARK MS ASHMOLE 813
 *PROVENANCE FRENCH
 *DATE EXECUTED 14TH/ LATE
 *LANGUAGE FRENCH
 *AUTHOR PHILIPPE DE MEZIERES
 *TYPE OF MANUSCRIPT RELIGIOUS MISCELLANY
 *CONTENTS   MILITARY   ORDER   OF   OUR  SAVIOUR'S PASSION 377/1-6
 FIGURE WITH BANNER AND ANOTHER WITH SHIELD  AND   SWORD   377-X
 PRINCE  OF  ORDER  IN  CLOAK 377-2,  KNIGHT OF THE ORDER 377-3
 LADY  OF  THE ORDER 377-4,  KNIGHT IN  ARMOR  READY  FOR  BATTLE
 WITH   DAGGER   377-5,   INSIGNIA   OF  THE ORDER/ BANNER AND LANC
 377-6,  SHIELD WITH LAMB/  FLAG  ON  BLACK/  BARBED  QUATREFOX
 377-6
```

*$ABSTRACT 378
```
 *LIBRARY BOD
 *SLIDE SET TITLE ENGLISH HERALDRY
 *NEGATIVE REFERENCE ROLL 196R
 *RENTAL FEE SM 378 $2.50
 *SHELFMARK  MS  ASHMOLE  804  378-1,  POWELL  ROLL C1345-51, M
 BODLEY 316 378-2, MS ASHMOLE 1831 378-3, MS  ASHMOLE  ROLLS
 378/4-6, MS AUCT D 22 378/7-9, MS BODLEY 712 378-10
```

*PROVENANCE ENGLISH
*DATE EXECUTED 14TH
*LANGUAGE ENGLISH
*TYPE OF MANUSCRIPT HERALDIC TEXTS
*CONTENTS HERALDRY/ ENGLISH 378/1-10, COATS OF ARMS 378/1-10,
POWELL ROLL 378-1, ARMS UNIDENTIFIED 378-2, POLYCHRONICON OF
RANULPH HIGDEN 378-2, TWO CHARTERS GRANTED BY RICHARD II TO
CROYLAND ABBEY 378-3, HERALDIC TREATISES ON DORSE OF ASHMOLE
ROLL OF ARMS 378/4-6, BURY ST EDMUNDS/ BENEDICTINE CHOIR
PSALTERS 378-7, WARREN AND BUTLER OR CLETHEROW 378-8, BARDULPH
AND FITZWALTER 378-9, BISHOP WIVILL 378-10

*$ABSTRACT 379
*LIBRARY BOD
*SLIDE SET TITLE ENGLISH HERALDRY
*NEGATIVE REFERENCE ROLL 196S
*RENTAL FEE SM 379 $2.90
*SHELFMARK MS BODLEY 758 379-1, MS BODLEY 693 379-2, MS DOUCE
291 379/3-6, MS RAWL LITURG E 9 379-7, MS LYELL 22 379/8-9,MS
DON D 85 379-10, MS DIGBY 232 379-11, MS AUCT F INF 1 1
379-12, MS RAWL LITURG F 3 379-13, MS JESUS COLL 126 379-14,
MS DOUCE 322 379-15, MS HATTON 10 379/16-18
*PROVENANCE ENGLISH
*DATE EXECUTED 15TH
*LANGUAGE ENGLISH
*TYPE OF MANUSCRIPT HERALDIC TREATISES AND MISCELLANEOUS
*CONTENTS HERALDIC TREATISES 379/1-19, COATS OF ARMS 379/1-19,
STAPLETON/ GOSPEL HARMONY ON PASSION 379-1, DUKE OF SUFFOLK/
CONFESSIO AMANTIS OF JOHN GOWER 379-2, PEDIGREE OF CHALONS
379/3-6, JOHN WAKERING/ BISHOP OF NORWHICH 379-7, KNIGHTS/
HAMMERTON OF HELLIFIELD AND WIGGLESWORTH 379-8, SURCOATS OF
WILLIAM THE CONQUEROR/ ALAIN OF BRITTANY 379-9, NORFOLK
WHETENHALLS 379-10, VINTNER'S COMPANY IN 1442 379-11, ST
ALBAN'S ABBEY/ TYNEMOUTH PRIORY 379-12, ENGLAND/ HYMPHERY DUKE
OF GLOUCESTER 379-12, SHEPARDE FAMILY 379-13, MARGARET OF
ANJOU/ WIFE OF HENRY VI 379-14, ARMS OF KNOLLYS QUARTERING
BARON 379-15, ARMS OF DUNTHORNE 379-16, ARMS OF THOMAS PIGOT
OF WHADDON AND DODDERSHALL 379-17, ARMS OF FRANCE AND ENGLAND
QUARTERED 379-18

*$ABSTRACT 380
*LIBRARY BOD
*SLIDE SET TITLE TREASURES OF BALLIOL COLLEGE
*NEGATIVE REFERENCE ROLL 196V
*RENTAL FEE SM 380 $3.15
*TITLE OF MANUSCRIPT COMMENTARY ON REVELATION 380-2, GLOSS ON
PSALTER 380/3-4, QUESTIONS ON THE SENTENCES OF PETER LOMBARD
380/5-6, GLOSS ON THE EPISTLES OF ST PAUL 380-7, GLOSS ON THE
EPISTLE OF PAUL 380/8-9, SENTENCES 380-10, PHYSICS 380/11-12,
FONTES MEMORABILIUM 380/13-16, NATURAL HISTORY 380/17-18,
LOGICA VETUS ET NOVA 380/19-20, METAPHYSICS 380-21, AUGUSTINE
ON ST JOHN'S GOSPEL 380/22-23
*SHELFMARK MS BALLIOL 2 F 63 380-1, MS BALLIOL F 73 380-2, MS
BALLIOL 35A 380/3-4, MS BALLIOL 56 380/5-6, MS BALLIOL 173B
380-7, MS BALLIOL 183 380/8-9, MS BALLIOL 193 F 152 380-10, MS
BALLIOL 232B 380/11-12, MS BALLIOL 238E 380/13-16, MS BALLIOL
249 380/17-18, MS BALLIOL 253 380/19-20, MS BALLIOL 277 F 43
380-21, MS BALLIOL 6 380/22-23
*PROVENANCE ITALIAN 380/1 AND 8-9 AND 13-18, ENGLISH 380/3-4
AND 7 AND 11-12 AND 21-23, FRENCH 380/5-6 AND 10 AND 19-20,
GERMAN 380-2
*DATE EXECUTED 13TH 380/1 AND 10 AND 19-21, 12TH 380/3-4 AND
7-9 AND 22-23, 14TH 380/5-6 AND 11-12, 15TH 380/2 AND 13-18
*TYPE OF MANUSCRIPT MISCELLANY
*CONTENTS TREASURES OF BALLIOL COLLEGE 380/1-23, MOSES LOOKS UP
TO GOD/ CROWD OF ISRAELITES BELOW 380-1, ST JOHN ON PATMOS
WITH SCROLL ON KNEE 380-2, INITIAL E/ MAN ASTRIDE BEAST 380-3,
INITIAL C/ MAN FIGHTING LION 380-4, FRANCISCUS DE PERUSIO

189

LECTURING TO FRIARS 380-5, GOD ADDRESSES ADAM AND EVE ABO
380-5, ADAM AND EVE 380-5, PETER LOMBARD 380/3-4, NATIVITY A
CRUCIFIXION AND AUTHOR ABOVE 380-6, INITIAL P/ ZOOMORPH
380-7, INITIAL A WITH INTERLACE 380-8, INITIAL H 380-
INITIAL P/ ANNUNCIATION 380-10, WHEEL OF FORTUNE AND ARMS
FAMILY OF MOEL 380-11, INITIAL S/ ARMS OF POMEROY FAMI
380-12, PYTHAGORAS LOOKS THROUGH SIGHTING TUBE 380-1
SOCRATES HOLDS DIVIDERS 380-13, SOCRATES 380-13, SCHOOLMAST
CHASTISES BOY/ NURSE TENDS BABY/ BOY IN TREE 380-14, WOM
ADORNS HERSELF 380-15, JUSTICE APPROACHED BY MESSENGER 380-1
INITIAL M 380-17, INITIAL N 380-18, MASTERS DISPUTING 380-1
TEACHER WITH BIRCH AND NAKED STUDENT 380-20, INITIAL E 380-2
INITIAL S 380-22, INITIAL H 380-23

*$ABSTRACT 381
  *LIBRARY BOD
  *SLIDE SET TITLE FOURTH HOLKHAM MISCELLANY
  *NEGATIVE REFERENCE ROLL 197B
  *RENTAL FEE SM 381 $2.80
  *TITLE OF MANUSCRIPT SEDULIUS 381-1, RAMSEY ABBEY PSALT
   381/2-6
  *SHELFMARK MS HOLKHAM 419 381-1, MS HOLKHAM 26 381/2-6,
   HOLKHAM 647 381-7, MS HOLKHAM 647 381-7, MS HOLKHAM 3
   381/9-12, MS HOLKHAM 451 381-13, MS HOLKHAM 771 381/13-15,
   HOLKHAM 126 381-16
  *PROVENANCE ITALIAN 381/1 AND 7-16, ENGLISH 381/2-6
  *DATE EXECUTED 11TH 381-1, 15TH 381/2-16
  *LANGUAGE LATIN
  *AUTHOR CARMEN PASCHALE 381-1, LIVY 381/8-12, DIOGENES LAERTI
   381-13, JEROME 381-16
  *TYPE OF MANUSCRIPT PSALTER/ AND MISCELLANY
  *CONTENTS HOLKHAM MANUSCRIPTS 381/1-16, SEDULIUS 381-1
   CALENDAR FOR DECEMBER 381-2, DAVID HARPING AND BEATUS V
   381-2, DIXI CUSTODIAM WITH DAVID HOLDING TONGUE 381-3, DAV
   AND GOLIATH 381-4, INITIAL Q/ QUID GLORIARIS 381-4, KING A
   FOOL 381-4, INITIAL D/ DIXIT INSIPIENS 381-4, MONGOL 381-
   COAT OF ARMS WITH GULES AND PHOENIX 381-6, DOGALE GRANTED
   NICCOLO BERNARDO 381-7, COAT OF ARMS 381-8, INITIAL E 381-
   INITIAL C/ CONSUL 381-9, INITIAL I/ INTER 381-10, INITIAL
   PRINCIPIO 381-11, INITIAL L 381-12, BLAZON OF ARMS 381-1
   COAT OF ARMS OF HATTON/ CECILL/ LORD SOWCHE 381-14, COAT
   ARMS RICHARD KNIGHTLEY/ JOHN SPENCER/ JOHN FARNER 381-1
   INITIAL D CONTAINING JEROME 381-16

*$ABSTRACT 382
  *LIBRARY BOD
  *SLIDE SET TITLE ORTELIUS/ ABRAHAM/ THE THEATRE OF THE WHOL
   WORLD
  *NEGATIVE REFERENCE ROLL 198B
  *RENTAL FEE SM 382 $3.50
  *COMMENTS THIS GREAT ATLAS WAS FIRST PUBLISHED IN LATIN I
   1570. THIS IS THE FIRST EDITION IN ENGLISH
  *TITLE OF MANUSCRIPT THEATRE OF THE WHOLE WORLD
  *PROVENANCE ENGLISH
  *DATE EXECUTED 17TH/1606
  *LANGUAGE ENGLISH
  *AUTHOR ABRAHAM ORTELIUS
  *TYPE OF MANUSCRIPT ATLAS
  *CONTENTS THEATRE OF THE WHOLE WORLD 382/1-30, ATLAS OF WORL
   382/1-30, THEATRUM ORBIS TERRARUM 382-1, PORTRAIT 382-2, WORL
   382-3, ASIA 382-4, AFRICA 382-5, AMERICA 382-6, PACIFIC OCEA
   382-7, MEXICO 382-8, WEST INDIES 382-9, PERU 382-10, FLORID
   382-11, WALES 382-12, IRELAND 382-13, AZORES 382-14, GERMAN
   382-15, BOHEMIA 382-16, SILESIA 382-17, MORAVIA 382-18, ITAL
   382-19, ICELAND 382-20, RUSSIA 382-21, TARTARIA 382-22, CHIN
   382-23, JAPAN 382-24, INDIA 382-25, TURKEY 382-26, ETHIOPI
   382-27, BARBARY 382-28, MOROCCO 382-29, IRELAND 382-30

*$ABSTRACT 383
  *LIBRARY BOD
  *SLIDE SET TITLE STORY OF LOT
  *NEGATIVE REFERENCE ROLL 198C
  *RENTAL FEE SM 383 $2.70
  *TITLE OF MANUSCRIPT BIBLE MORALISEE
  *SHELFMARK MS BODLEY 270B
  *PROVENANCE FRENCH
  *DATE EXECUTED 13TH/ MIDDLE
  *LANGUAGE FRENCH
  *TYPE OF MANUSCRIPT ALLEGORICAL BIBLE
  *CONTENTS LOT/ STORY OF IN ALLEGORICAL BIBLE 383/1-14, BIBLE
  MORALISEE 383/1-14, PHARAOH PLAGUED AND BANISHES ABRAHAM AND
  SARAH 383-1, ABRAHAM/ SARAH/ LOT LEAVE EGYPT 383-2, HERDSMEN
  FIGHT AND ABRAHAM AND LOT PART 383-3, ABRAHAM AND LOT SEPARATE
  ONE FROM ANOTHER 383-4, FOUR KINGS DEFEAT FIVE AND LOT
  CAPTURED 383-5, FOUR KINGS FIGHT ABRAHAM WHO RESCUES LOT
  383-6, HAGAR/ HANDMAID TO SARAH HATES HER 383-7, SARAH
  COMPLAINS TO ABRAHAM AND HAGAR AND SON BANISHED 383-8, GOD
  SPEAKS TO ABRAHAM CONCERNING COVENANT AND CIRCUMCISION 383-9,
  ABRAHAM WELCOMES GOD'S MESSENGERS AND WASHES FEET 383-10,
  SARAH PROMISED SON BUT SHE LAUGHS WITHIN 383-11, LOT
  ENTERTAINS ANGELS IN SODOM 383-12, ANGELS GUIDE LOT AND FAMILY
  FROM SODOM 383-13, LOT'S WIFE TURNED TO PILLAR OF SALT 383-14

*$ABSTRACT 384
  *LIBRARY BOD
  *SLIDE SET TITLE HERMITS
  *NEGATIVE REFERENCE ROLL 198E
  *RENTAL FEE SM 384 $3.25
  *TITLE OF MANUSCRIPT SPECULUM HUMANAE SALVATIONIS 384-9, LE
  CHEVALIER DELIBERE 384/19-21
  *SHELFMARK MS ORIEL COLLEGE 75 384-1, MS GOUGH LITURG 15 384-2,
  MS DOUCE 276 384-3, MS LITURG 60 384-4, MS LAUD LAT 15 384-5,
  MS CANON LITURG 92 384-6, MS ADD A 185 384-7, MS LITURG 98
  384-8, MS DOUCE 204 384-9, MS DOUCE 272 384-10, MS RAWL LITURG
  E 4 384-11, MS RAWL LITURG E 12 384-12, MS UNIVERSITY COLLEGE
  8 384-13, MS RAWL LITURG G 7 384-14, MS DOUCE 31 384-16, MS
  LAUD MISC 93 384-17, MS BUCHANAN E 10 384-18, MS DOUCE 168
  384/19-21, MS DOUCE 186 384-22, MS LAT LITURG G 5 384-24, MS
  DOUCE 135 384-23, MS DOUCE 112 383-25
  *PROVENANCE ENGLISH 384/1 AND 5 AND 8, ENGLISH 384/11 AND 13
  AND 24, FRENCH 384/3-4 AND 7 AND 12, FRENCH 384/14-21 AND 23,
  FLEMISH 384/2 AND 25, ITALIAN 384-10, SPANISH 384-9, GERMAN
  384-22
  *DATE EXECUTED 15TH 384/1-18 AND 25, 16TH 384/19-24
  *LANGUAGE LATIN/ FRENCH/ ENGLISH
  *TYPE OF MANUSCRIPT MISSAL 384-1, BOOK OF HOURS 384/2-3 AND 4-8
  AND 11-16 AND 18 AND 23-25, BREVIARY 384-17
  *CONTENTS HERMITS 384/1-25, BEARDED HOODED FIGURE 384-1, HERMIT
  SEES ST CHRISTOPHER WITH CHILD IN RIVER 384-2, ST CHRISTOPHER
  384-2, HERMIT 384/3-4, HERMIT HOLDING LANTERN IN FRONT OF
  CABIN 384/5-7, HERMIT WITH CANDLE AND LANTERN 384-8, HERMIT
  384-9, HERMIT FEEDS RABBIT 384-10, HERMIT 384/11-12, HERMIT IN
  STORY OF ST CHRISTOPHER 384-13, ST CHRISTOPHER 384-13,
  HERMITAGE OF OF ST AVIA 384-14, HERMIT 384-15, HERMIT WITH
  LANTERN LIGHTS WAY OF ST CHRISTOPHER 384-16, HERMIT WATCHES ST
  CHRISTOPHER CARRYING CHRIST 384-17, HERMIT WITH LANTERN
  384-18, HERMIT SPEAKS TO L'ACTEUR IN CHAPEL 384-19, HERMIT
  WELCOMES L'ACTEUR 384-20, HERMIT GIVES LANCE TO L'ACTEUR
  384-21, HERMIT BLESSES SOLDIER 384-23, HERMIT WITH ST
  CHRISTOPHER 384-24, HERMIT WAITS FOR ST CHRISTOPHER ON RIVER
  BANK 384-25

*$ABSTRACT 385
  *LIBRARY BOD
  *SLIDE SET TITLE SS MARY MAGDALENE/ ANTHONY AND PAUL
  *NEGATIVE REFERENCE ROLL 198I

*RENTAL FEE SM 385 $2.25
*SHELFMARK MS LAUD LAT 15 385-1, MS CANON LITURG 327 385-2, M
DOUCE 19 385-3, MS LAT LITURG G 5 385-4, MS DOUCE 112 385-5
*PROVENANCE ENGLISH 385/1 AND 4, ITALIAN 385/2-3, FLEMISH 385-
*DATE EXECUTED 15TH 385/1-2 AND 5, 16TH 385/3-4
*LANGUAGE LATIN
*TYPE OF MANUSCRIPT BOOK OF HOURS 385/1 AND 3-4, BREVIARY 385-
*CONTENTS SS MARY MAGDALENE/ ANTHONY AND PAUL 385/1-5, ST MAR
MAGDALENE PRAYS IN WILDERNESS 385-1, ST MARY MAGDALENE WIT
OINTMENT POT 385-2, ST MARY MAGDALENE HOLDS PALM AND OINTMEN
POT 385-3, ST ANTHONY WITH CROZIER/ BELL AND OPEN BOOK 385-4
ST ANTHONY AND TEMPTRESS BY CHAPEL 385-5, ST PAUL AND S
ANTHONY MEETING 385-5

*$ABSTRACT 386
 *LIBRARY BOD
 *SLIDE SET TITLE ST JEROME
 *NEGATIVE REFERENCE ROLL 198K
 *RENTAL FEE SM 386 $2.75
 *TITLE OF MANUSCRIPT OFFICIUM BEATAE MARIAE VIRGINAE 386/5-6
 *SHELFMARK MS LAT BIB F 3 386-1, MS DOUCE 113 386-2, MS AUBRE
 31 386-3, MS LITURG 401 386-4, MS DOUCE 11 386-5, MS CANO
 LITURG 265 386-6, MS CANON LITURG 168 386-7, MS DOUCE 2
 386-8, MS LITURG 200 386-9, MS AUCT D INF 2 13 386-10, M
 CANON LITURG 229 386-11, MS DOUCE 12 386-12, MS CANON LITU
 197 386-13, MS LAT LITURG G 5 386-14, MS DOUCE 29 386-15
 *PROVENANCE ITALIAN 386/1-2 AND 5-7, ITALIAN 386/11 AND 13 AN
 15, ENGLISH 386/3-4 AND 10 AND 14, FLEMISH 386/8-9 AND 12
 *DATE EXECUTED 13TH 386/1-2, 15TH 386/3-13, 16TH 386/14-15
 *LANGUAGE LATIN
 *TYPE OF MANUSCRIPT BIBLE 386/1-2, BOOK OF HOURS 386/3-4 AN
 8-11 AND 14-15, VOTIVE OFFICE 386-12, MISSAL 386-14, BREVIAR
 386-7, OFFICE OF THE VIRGIN 386/5-6
 *CONTENTS ST JEROME 386/1-15, ST JEROME AT DESK 386-1, S
 JEROME IN GREY HABIT AT DESK 386-2, VISION OF CHRIST ON CROS
 ADORED 386-3, SHAKES HANDS WITH LION 386-4, PRAYING BEFOR
 CAVE 386-5, MINIATURE WITH LION AND OPEN BOOK 386-6, PRAYIN
 BY CROSS/ WITH LION/ WRITING 386-7, SHOWS SORES WHILE PRAYI
 BEFORE CRUCIFIX 386-8, CARDINAL HAT AND ROBE WITH LION I
 STUDY 386-9, SEATED BEFORE DESK 386-10, AS PILGRIM WITH LIO
 386-11, PRAYS BEFORE A CRUCIFIX 386-12, KNEELING WITH LION I
 SIDE 386-13, ST JEROME HOLDS BOOK AND STROKES LION 386-14
 CARDINAL'S HAT/ CROSS/ LION 386-15

*$ABSTRACT 387
 *LIBRARY BOD
 *SLIDE SET TITLE CHRIST'S CHILDHOOD
 *NEGATIVE REFERENCE ROLL 198N
 *RENTAL FEE SM 387 $3.50
 *SHELFMARK MS C C C OXFORD 410
 *PROVENANCE ITALIAN
 *DATE EXECUTED 14TH
 *TYPE OF MANUSCRIPT LIFE OF CHRIST
 *CONTENTS CHRIST'S CHILDHOOD 387/1-19,   ST   FRANCIS   WIT
 STIGMATA/ ST CECILIA 387-1, DISPUTE OF VIRTUES BEFORE GO
 387/2-5, VIRGIN PRAYING IN TEMPLE 387-6, VIRGIN WEAVING WIT
 TWO COMPANIONS AND ANGEL 387-7, PURIFICATION 387-8, SIMEON AN
 ANNA MEET 387-9, HOLY FAMILY AT ALTAR WITH SIMEON AND ANN
 387-10, ANGEL WARNS JOSEPH 387-11, FLIGHT INTO EGYPT/ VIRGI
 RIDES/ JOSEPH WITH CHILD 387-12, ANGEL TELLS JOSEPH TO RETUR
 387-13, DEPARTURE FROM EGYPT/ JESUS RIDES/ TREE BOWS TO VIRGI
 387-14, VISIT TO HOUSE OF ELIZABETH 387-15, VISIT TO TEMPL
 387-16, MARY AND JOSEPH ASK NEIGHBORS WHERE JESUS IS 387-17
 JOSEPH AND MARY SEE CHRIST AMONG DOCTORS 387-18, CHRIS
 OBEDIENT TO HIS PARENTS 387-15

192

*$ABSTRACT 388
  *LIBRARY BOD
  *SLIDE SET TITLE KNIGHTLEY PSALTER
  *NEGATIVE REFERENCE ROLL 1980
  *RENTAL FEE SM 388 $2.55
  *TITLE OF MANUSCRIPT KNIGHTLEY PSALTER
  *SHELFMARK MS HOLKHAM 24
  *PROVENANCE ENGLISH
  *DATE EXECUTED 15TH/ EARLY
  *LANGUAGE LATIN
  *TYPE OF MANUSCRIPT PSALTER
  *CONTENTS KNIGHTLEY PSALTER 388/1-11, CHRIST IN TOMB WITH
  INSTRUMENTS OF PASSION 388-1, INITIALS/ ILLUMINATED 388/2-11
  INITIAL B/ BEATUS VIR 388-2, DAVID PLAYING HARP 388-2, INITIAL
  D/ DOMINUS ILLUMINATIO 388-3, DAVID POINTS TO EYE 388-3,
  INITIAL D/ DIXI CUSTODIAM 388-4, MONTAIN TRAVELLER 388-4,
  INITIAL Q/ QUID GLORIARIS 388-5, KING AND KNIGHT 388-5,
  INITIAL D/ DIXIT INSIPIENS 388-6, FOOL WITH DOG 388-6, INITIAL
  S/ SALVUM ME FAC 388-7, KING SUBMERGED 388-7, INITIAL E/
  EXULTATE DEO 388-8, DAVID WITH BELLS 388-8, INITIAL C/ CANTATE
  DOMINO 388-9, CHOIR 388-9, INITIAL D/ DOMINE EXAUDI 388-10,
  KING AT ALTAR 388-10, INITIAL D/ DIXIT DOMINUS 388-12, FATHER
  AND SON 388-12

*$ABSTRACT 389
  *LIBRARY BOD
  *SLIDE SET TITLE HOLKHAM MISCELLANY V/ HORACE AND PLINY
  *NEGATIVE REFERENCE ROLL 198P
  *RENTAL FEE SM 389 $2.50
  *TITLE OF MANUSCRIPT LECTIONARIUM EVANGELORIUM 389-10
  *SHELFMARK MS HOLKHAM 318 389/1-7, MS HOLKHAM 339 389-9, MS
  HOLKHAM 18 389-10
  *PROVENANCE ITALIAN 389/1-8 AND 10, SPANISH 389-9
  *DATE EXECUTED 15TH
  *LANGUAGE LATIN
  *AUTHOR HORACE 389/1-7, PLINY 389-8
  *TYPE OF MANUSCRIPT CLASSICAL LITERATURE 389/1-9, LECTIONARY
  389-9
  *CONTENTS HOLKHAM MISCELLANY 389/1-10, HORACE AND PLINY
  389/1-10, COAT OF ARMS OF RAPHAEL DE MARCATELLIS 389-1, DETAIL
  389-2, INITIAL AND MINATURE 389-3, HORACE ADDRESSED 389-4,
  JULIUS CAESAR/ BRUTUS AND CASSIUS 389-5, AGRIPPA AND HORACE
  389-6, MOATED CITY WITH TOWERS AND BRIDGE 389-7, PLINY PRINTED
  IN VENICE 1476 389-8, SALLUSTIUS WITH SEMI-HUMANISTIC SCRIPT
  389-9, CORVINUS GOSPEL/ TITLE PAGE 389-10

*$ABSTRACT 390
  *LIBRARY BOD
  *SLIDE SET TITLE RICHARD OF WALLINGFORD'S TREATISE ON
  ASTRONOMICAL CLOCKS
  *NEGATIVE REFERENCE ROLL 200A
  *RENTAL FEE SM 390 $2.20
  *TITLE OF MANUSCRIPT ASTRONOMICAL TREATISE ON CLOCKS
  *SHELFMARK MS ASHMOLE 1796
  *PROVENANCE ENGLISH
  *DATE EXECUTED 14TH/1328-36
  *LANGUAGE LATIN
  *AUTHOR JOHN OF WALLINGFORD
  *TYPE OF MANUSCRIPT ASTRONOMICAL TREATISE
  *CONTENTS ASTRONOMICAL TREATISE ON CLOCKS 390/1-4, DIAL OF
  ELABORATE ASTRONOMICAL CLOCK 390-1, GEARING OF THAT SAME CLOCK
  390-2, EXPLANATIONS 390-3, GEAR WHEEL IN VARIOUS PICTURES
  390-4

*$ABSTRACT 391
  *LIBRARY BOD

193

```
*SLIDE SET TITLE ASTROLOGICAL CALENDAR
*NEGATIVE REFERENCE ROLL 201A
*RENTAL FEE SM 391 $2.75
*SHELFMARK MS BODLEY 614
*PROVENANCE ENGLISH
*DATE EXECUTED 12TH
*LANGUAGE LATIN
*TYPE OF MANUSCRIPT CALENDAR
*CONTENTS ASTROLOGICAL CALENDAR  391/1-15,  CALENDAR  391/1-15
 ZODIACAL SIGNS 391/1-15


*$ABSTRACT 392
 *LIBRARY BOD
 *SLIDE SET TITLE DETAILS OF ZODIACAL SIGNS
 *NEGATIVE REFERENCE ROLL 201B
 *RENTAL FEE SM 392 $2.55
 *SHELFMARK MS LAUD MISC 644
 *PROVENANCE FRENCH/ BAYEUX
 *DATE EXECUTED 13TH/C1268-74
 *LANGUAGE LATIN
 *TYPE OF MANUSCRIPT ASTROLOGICAL TEXT
 *CONTENTS  ASTROLOGICAL  TEXT 392/1-11, ZODIACAL SIGNS/ DETAIL
  OF 392/1-11


*$ABSTRACT 393
 *LIBRARY BOD
 *SLIDE SET TITLE LIBELLUS GEOMANCIE
 *NEGATIVE REFERENCE ROLL 201C
 *RENTAL FEE SM 393 $2.50
 *COMMENTS ASTROLOGICAL TEXT WRITTEN FOR RICHARD II
 *TITLE OF MANUSCRIPT LIBELLUS GEOMANCIE
 *SHELFMARK MS BODLEY 581
 *PROVENANCE ENGLISH
 *DATE EXECUTED 14TH/ AFTER 1391
 *LANGUAGE LATIN
 *ARTIST/ SCHOOL RELATED TO EARLIER STYLE OF CARMELITE MISSAL
 *TYPE OF MANUSCRIPT ASTROLOGICAL TEXT
 *CONTENTS  ASTROLOGICAL  TEXT  393/1-10,   LIBELLUS   GEOMANCY
  393/1-10, ZODIACAL SIGNS 393/1-10


*$ABSTRACT 394
 *LIBRARY BOD
 *SLIDE SET TITLE FIFTEENTH CENTURY ENGLISH ASTROLOGICAL TEXTS
 *NEGATIVE REFERENCE ROLL 201D 1-3
 *RENTAL FEE SM 394 $3.90
 *TITLE OF  MANUSCRIPT  SIGNS  OF THE ZODIAC 394/1-12, BOKE OF
  ASTROLOGY AND OFF PHILOSOPYE 394/13-24, TREATISE OF  PALMISTY
  394/31-38
 *SHELFMARK MS RAWL C 117 394/1-12, MS RAWL D 1220 394/13-24, M
  DOUCE 45 394/25-30, MS DIGBY ROLLS IV 394/31-38
 *PROVENANCE ENGLISH
 *DATE EXECUTED 15TH
 *LANGUAGE LATIN AND ENGLISH
 *TYPE  OF  MANUSCRIPT  ASTROLOGICAL  TEXTS  394/1-30, PALMISTY
  TREATISE 394/13-38
 *CONTENTS   ASTROLOGICAL   TEXTS   394/1-30,   PALMISTRY   TE
  394/31-38, ZODICAL SIGNS 394/1-30


*$ABSTRACT 395
 *LIBRARY BOD
 *SLIDE  SET  TITLE  OCCUPATIONS  OF THE MONTHS AND SIGNS OF TH
  ZODIAC
 *NEGATIVE REFERENCE ROLL 201E
 *RENTAL FEE SM 395 $2.60
```

194

*SHELFMARK MS AUCT D INF 2 11
*PROVENANCE FRENCH
*DATE EXECUTED 15TH/C1440-1450
*LANGUAGE LATIN AND FRENCH
*ARTIST/ SCHOOL MASTER OF SIR JOHN FASTOLF
*TYPE OF MANUSCRIPT BOOK OF HOURS/ USE OF SARUM
*CONTENTS BOOK OF HOURS 395/1-12, OCCUPATIONS OF THE MONTHS
 395/1-12, ZODIACAL SIGNS 395/1-12

*$ABSTRACT 396
 *LIBRARY BOD
 *SLIDE SET TITLE FOURTEENTH AND FIFTEENTH CENTURY ITALIAN TEXTS
 *NEGATIVE REFERENCE ROLL 201F
 *RENTAL FEE SM 396 $4.90
 *TITLE OF MANUSCRIPT LIBER INTRODUCTORIUS 396/13-31,
 ASTRONOMICA 396/32-41, ASTRONOMICA 396/42-46
 *SHELFMARK MS CANON MISC 280 396-1, MS CANON MISC 46 396/2-12,
 MS BODLEY 266 396/13-31, MS BODLEY 646 396/32-41, MS CANON
 CLASS LAT 179 396/42-46, MS CANON MISC 554 396/47-58
 *PROVENANCE ITALIAN
 *DATE EXECUTED 14TH 396/47-58, 15TH 396/1-46
 *LANGUAGE LATIN AND ENGLISH
 *AUTHOR MICHAEL SCOT 396/13-31, BASINI DE TASANI 396/32-41,
 HYGINUS 396/42-46
 *TYPE OF MANUSCRIPT ASTROLOGICAL TEXTS
 *CONTENTS ASTROLOGICAL TEXTS 396/1-58, ZODICAL SIGNS 396/1-58

*$ABSTRACT 397
 *LIBRARY BOD
 *SLIDE SET TITLE JOHN LACY/ SELECTIONS FROM A RELIGIOUS
 MISCELLANY
 *NEGATIVE REFERENCE ROLL 201G
 *RENTAL FEE SM 397 $2.70
 *COMMENTS SELECTIONS FROM A RELIGIOUS MISCELLANY IN HAND OF
 JOHN LACY
 *SHELFMARK MS ST JOHN'S COLLEGE 94
 *PROVENANCE ENGLISH
 *DATE EXECUTED 15TH/1420
 *LANGUAGE LATIN
 *ARTIST/ SCHOOL JOHN LACY
 *TYPE OF MANUSCRIPT RELIGIOUS MISCELLANY
 *CONTENTS RELIGIOUS MISCELLANY 397/1-14, TRINITY/ ANNUNCIATION/
 VIRGIN OF ANNUNCIATION/ CHRIST OF PITY 397-1, ST ANN WITH
 VIRGIN/ VIRGIN WITH ROSE AND CHILD 397-2, ST MICHAEL SLAYING
 DRAGON 397-2, ST PETER 397-2, ST JOHN BAPTIST WITH AGNUS DEI
 397-3, ST JOHN EVANGELIST WITH EAGLE 397-3, ST JAMES LESS WITH
 CLUB 397-3, ST JAMES GREAT WITH STAFF 397-3, ST ANDREW WITH
 CROSS/ ST BARTHOLOMEW 397-4, ST GEORGE SLAYING DRAGON 397-4,
 SS COSMAS AND DAMIAN WITH DOGS AND CRIPPLES 397-5, ST VINCENT
 397-5, ST GILES WITH CROZIER 397-5, ST MARTIN WITH CROSS
 397-5, ST NICHOLAS WITH CHILDREN 397-6, ST ANTHONY WITH PIG
 397-6, ST ALEXIS WITH STAFF 397-6, ST GERMANUS WITH KNEELING
 FIGURES 397-6, ST LEONARD WITH CROZIER 397-7, ST PAUL WITH
 SWORD 397-7, ST CATHERINE WITH WHEEL 397-7, ST MARGARET WITH
 LAMBS 397-7, ST BARBARA WITH TOWER 397-8, ST MARY MAGDALENE
 WITH OINTMENT POT 397-8, ST WENEFREDA WITH SWORD AND BOOK
 397-8, ST SYTHA WITH KEYS 397-8, ST APOLLONIA WITH FORCEPS
 397-9, ST AGNES IN FLAMES 397-9, CALENDAR PAGE/ ORNAMENTATION
 397-9, CALENDAR/ LAST PAGE 397-10, ST IGNATIUS WITH LIONS
 397-10, ST AGATHA WITH KNIFE 397-10, JOHN LACY IN CELL PRAYING
 TO VIRGIN 397-11, LAST JUDGMENT 397-12, OWL AND MONKEY/
 CALLIGRAPHIC INITIALS 397-13, COAT OF ARMS OF JOHN LACY 397-14

*$ABSTRACT 398
 *LIBRARY BOD
 *SLIDE SET TITLE SIXTH HOLKHAM MISCELLANY

195

*NEGATIVE REFERENCE ROLL 201I
*RENTAL FEE SM 398 $2.60
*TITLE OF MANUSCRIPT DOWNES PSALTER 398/1-8, STATUTES 398/9-1
*SHELFMARK MS HOLKHAM 23 398/1-8, MS HOLKHAM 232 398/9-13,
 HOLKHAM 345 398-14, MS HOLKHAM 398-15, MS HOLKHAM 247 398-16
*PROVENANCE ENGLISH 398/1-8, FRENCH 398/9-14 AND 16, ITALI
 398-15
*DATE EXECUTED 15TH
*LANGUAGE LATIN 398/1-8
*AUTHOR LIVY 398/15-16
*ARTIST/ SCHOOL FOUQUET 398-16
*TYPE OF MANUSCRIPT MISCELLANY
*CONTENTS HOLKHAM MISCELLANY 398/1-16, INITIALS/ DECORAT
 398/1-8, APRIL/ CALENDAR PAGE 398-1, BEATUS PAGE 398-2, TE
 398-3, INITIALS WITH LINE DRAWINGS OF FACES 398-4, INITIAL
 DOMINUS ILLUMINATIO MEA 398-5, INITIAL Q/ QUID GLORIAR
 398-6, INITIAL D/ DIXIT INSIPIENS 398-6, INITIAL E/ EXULTA
 DEO 398-7, INITIAL C/ CANTATE DOMINO 398-8, EDWARD II
 ARGENT/ FESSE GULES 398-9, RICHARD II/ SIR THOMAS LATIM
 398-10, HENRY V/ ARMS 398-11, COATS OF ARMS 398/9-14, BAR
 MOUNTJOY/ HENRY VI 398-12, EDWARD IV 398-13, HENRY VII/ JO
 SUTTON 398-14, LIVY/ MASTER OF VITAE IMPERATOR 398-15, LIV
 TITLE PAGE 398-16

*$ABSTRACT 399
 *LIBRARY BOD
 *SLIDE SET TITLE FIFTEEN PEYTON PEDIGREES
 *NEGATIVE REFERENCE ROLL 201J
 *RENTAL FEE SM 399 $2.75
 *TITLE OF MANUSCRIPT PEYTON PEDIGREES
 *SHELFMARK MS TOP GEN A 10
 *PROVENANCE ENGLISH
 *DATE EXECUTED 17TH/ PRE-1629
 *LANGUAGE ENGLISH
 *TYPE OF MANUSCRIPT HERALDIC TEXT
 *CONTENTS PEYTON PEDIGREES 399/1-15, HERALDRY 399/1-15, COAT
 ARMS OF PEYTON 399/1-6, PEYTON PEDIGREE 399/8-10, UFFORD
 UFFORD 399/1-15

*$ABSTRACT 400
 *LIBRARY BOD
 *SLIDE SET TITLE LIFE OF ST MARGARET
 *NEGATIVE REFERENCE ROLL 202A
 *RENTAL FEE SM 400 $3.10
 *TITLE OF MANUSCRIPT LIFE OF ST MARGARET
 *SHELFMARK MS DOUCE 41
 *PROVENANCE ITALIAN/ NORTHERN
 *DATE EXECUTED 14TH/ SECOND HALF
 *LANGUAGE LATIN
 *AUTHOR THEOTIMUS
 *TYPE OF MANUSCRIPT SAINT'S LIFE
 *CONTENTS ST MARGARET/ SCENES FROM HER LIFE 400/1-22, HERDI
 SHEEP 400-1, PREFECT CROWNED RIDING GREY HORSE 400-2, SOLDIE
 TAKE ST MARGARET TO PREFECT 400-3, ST MARGARET CONFESSES H
 CHRISTIANITY TO PREFECT 400-4, ST MARGARET THROWN INTO PRIS
 400-5, PREFECT WORSHIPS HIS GOD 400-6, PREFECT ASKS
 MARGARET TO WORSHIP HIS GOD 400-7, ST MARGARET BEATEN 400-
 ST MARGARET TORTURED 400-9, ST MARGARET TAKEN TO PRIS
 400-10, DRAGON SWALLOWS ST MARGARET 400-11, ST MARGARET COM
 OUT OF DRAGON UNHARMED 400-12, ST MARGARET IN PRISON WI
 DEMON HOLDING HAND 400-13, ST MARGARET OVERCOMES DRAG
 400-14, PRISON AND DEMON FALLS TO EARTH 400-15, ST MARGAR
 BROUGHT TO PREFECT 400-16, ST MARGARET BURNED WITH TORCH
 400-17, ST MARGARET IMMERSED IN BARREL OF WATER 400-1
 CONVERTS BEHEADED BY SOLDIERS 400-19, SOLDIER REFUSES
 BEHEAD ST MARGARET 400-20, ST MARGARET PRAYS 400-21, DEATH
 ST MARGARET 400-22

*$ABSTRACT 401
 *LIBRARY BOD
 *SLIDE SET TITLE HERALDRY EXHIBITION IN THE BODLEIAN I
 *NEGATIVE REFERENCE ROLL 202C
 *RENTAL FEE SM 401 $3.10
 *PROVENANCE ENGLISH
 *TYPE OF MANUSCRIPT HERALDRY 401/1-2, ROLLS OF ARMS 401/3-6,
 ARMORIALS 401/7-18, PEDIGREES 401/19-22
 *CONTENTS HERALDIC TEXTS 401/1-22, COATS OF ARMS 401/1-22,
 JOFFROY D'ASPREMONT AND ISABELLE DE KIEVRAING 401-1, SEAL OF
 WINCHELSEA 401-2, DERING ROLL 401-4, GUILLAM'S ROLL 401-4,
 DUNSTABLE ROLL/ FIRST 401-5, HOLLAND'S ROLL 401-6, COUNCIL OF
 CONSTANCE 401-7, NORMAN FAMILY ARMS FROM BOOK OF MONTJOIE
 401-8, KNIGHTS OF THE BATH 1553 401-91, YORKSHIRE GENTRY 1563
 401-10, ARMES IN CHESHIRE BY W SMITH 1585 401-11, VALE ROYALL
 OF ENGLAND 401-12, LIONS FROM GWILLIM/ HERALDRIE 1610 401-14,
 VALE-ROYAL OF ENGLAND 1656 401-13, GWILLIM WITH RECORD OF
 PAYMENT TO PRINTER 401-15, HERALDIC BIBLIOGRAPHY 401-15,
 CAMDEN'S COPY OF MILLES/ CATALOGUE OF HONOR 401-16, ARGENT TWO
 BARRES GULES 401-17, WILLEMENT/ T ARMORIAL OF BENEFACTORS OF
 WADHAM 401-18, PEDIGREE/ DROP-LINE OF HUNGERFORD 401-19,
 PEDIGREE OF EARLS OF KENDAL BY W CECIL 401-20, FRANCIS
 SANDFORD'S OWN PEDIGREE 401-21, HOWARD PEDIGREE FROM PEYTON
 PEDIGREE 401-22

*$ABSTRACT 402
 *LIBRARY BOD
 *SLIDE SET TITLE MARY'S CHILDHOOD
 *NEGATIVE REFERENCE ROLL 203C
 *RENTAL FEE SM 402 $3.20
 *TITLE OF MANUSCRIPT ACTS OF ST MARY AND JESUS
 *SHELFMARK MS CANON MISC 476
 *PROVENANCE ITALIAN
 *DATE EXECUTED 14TH
 *LANGUAGE LATIN
 *TYPE OF MANUSCRIPT ACTS OF ST MARY AND JESUS
 *CONTENTS ACTS OF ST MARY AND JESUS 402/1-24, ST MARY 402/1-24,
 JESUS 402/1-24, AUTHOR/ MITRED BISHOP WRITING 402-1, ST
 JOACHIM TOLD OF BIRTH OF MARY BY RAPHAEL 402-2, ST ANNE TOLD
 OF BIRTH OF MARY BY RAPHAEL 402-3, ST JOACHIM AND ST ANNE
 EMBRACE AT GARDEN GATE 402-4, ST ANNE CONCEIVES MARY/ GOD
 BLESSING 402-5, ST ANNE GIVES BIRTH/ MIDWIVES 402-5, ST
 JOACHIM REJOICES AT BIRTH OF MARY IN CRIB 402-6, MARY AS
 INFANT BATHED 402-7, MARY'S PARENTS PRESENT HER AT TEMPLE AND
 OFFER SACRIFICE 402-8, MARY/ SEVEN BROUGHT TO TEMPLE AND
 CONSECRATED 402-9, MARY STANDS PRAYING AT TEMPLE 402-10, MARY
 SITS READING 402-11, MARY AND COMPANIONS APPROACH ALTAR AT
 TEMPLE 402-12, MARY HAILED AS QUEEN BY COMPANIONS 402-13, MARY
 ADMIRED BY YOUNG MEN NEAR TEMPLE 402-14, HIGH PRIEST CONFERS
 ABOUT HER MARRIAGE 402-14, SUITORS ASK FOR MARY'S HAND 402-15,
 HIGH PRIEST TELLS MARY TO MARRY 402-15, MARY REFUSES TO MARRY
 402-16, MARY ANSWERS TWO ELDERS/ MARY SUMMONED TO HEAR
 DECISION 402-17, ELDERS AND MAIDENS HEAR VOICE PROPHESYING
 MARY'S FUTURE 402-18, ELDERS SEND FOR ST JOSEPH 402-19, ST
 JOSEPH TOLD TO MARRY MARY 402-20, ANGEL APPEARS TO ST JOSEPH/
 MARY KNEELS IN PRAYER 402-21, ANGEL COMFORTS MARY WHO IS
 DISTRESSED 402-22, BETROTHAL OF MARY AND JOSEPH 402-23, MARY
 RETURNS TO FATHER'S HOME IN NAZARETH 402-24

*$ABSTRACT 403
 *LIBRARY BOD
 *SLIDE SET TITLE HERALDRY EXHIBITION IN THE BODLEIAN II
 *NEGATIVE REFERENCE ROLL 203E
 *RENTAL FEE SM 403 $5.10
 *TITLE OF MANUSCRIPT EVANGELIARY OF MATTHIAS CORVINUS
 *SHELFMARK MS HOLKHAM 18
 *PROVENANCE ENGLISH 403/1-33 AND 40-47, FRENCH 403/34-37,
 ITALIAN 403/48-52, SWISS 403-58, SPANISH AND PORTUGESE

403/59-61, CENTRAL EUROPEAN 403/53-57, HUNGARIAN 403-62
*DATE EXECUTED 15TH/C1490
*TYPE OF MANUSCRIPT HERALDIC TEXTS
*CONTENTS HERALDIC TEXTS 403/1-62, HERALDS AND GRANTS OF AR
403/1-13, ORDER OF CHIVALRY AND VISITATIONS 403/14-18, SUMMO
TO VISITATION OF BERKSHIRE 403/19-20, NOTEBOOK OF NATHANI
GREENWOOD 403-33, FRENCH ARMS 403/34-37, ARMS OF OXFO
UNIVERSITY 403/38-39, ENGLISH ARMORIAL BINDINGS 403/40-4
ENGLISH HERALDIC PLAYING CARDS 403/43-46, FUNERAL ESCUTCHEO
403-47, ITALIAN ARMS 403/48-52, CENTRAL EUROPEAN AR
403/53-57, SWISS ARMS OF JONAS FAMILY 403-58, SPANISH A
PORTUGESE MSS 403/59-61, WHITE EAGLE OF WLADISLAS II/ JAGEL
403-62, EVANGELIARY OF MATTHIAS CORVINUS 403-62

*$ABSTRACT 404
 *LIBRARY BOD
 *SLIDE SET TITLE ARCHERY
 *NEGATIVE REFERENCE ROLL 203J
 *RENTAL FEE SM 404 $2.35
 *TITLE OF MANUSCRIPT ROMANCE OF ALEXANDER
 *SHELFMARK MS BODLEY 264
 *PROVENANCE FLEMISH
 *DATE EXECUTED 14TH/C1338-1344
 *LANGUAGE FRENCH
 *ARTIST/ SCHOOL JEHAN DE GRISE
 *TYPE OF MANUSCRIPT ROMANCE
 *CONTENTS ROMANCE OF ALEXANDER 404/1-7, LITERATURE/ ROMANCE
 ALEXANDER 404/1-7, ARCHERY 404/1-7, ARCHERS WITH LONGBOW A
 CROSSBOW 404-1, HARE WITH CROSSBOW SHOOTS HUNTER 404-
 ARMOURED ARCHERS WITH LONGBOW AND CROSSBOW 404/3-4, ARCHE
 WITH CROSSBOWS/ ONE SHOOTS BIRD 404-5, ARCHERS WITH LONGBO
 404-6, ARCHERS WITH CROSSBOWS 404-7

*$ABSTRACT 405
 *LIBRARY BOD
 *SLIDE SET TITLE ALBUM AMICORUM
 *NEGATIVE REFERENCE ROLL 203K
 *RENTAL FEE SM 405 $3.25
 *TITLE OF MANUSCRIPT ALBUM AMICORUM
 *SHELFMARK MS RAWL B 2
 *PROVENANCE FLEMISH
 *DATE EXECUTED 16TH/AFTER 1592
 *LANGUAGE LATIN
 *AUTHOR JAN VAN DER ECK
 *TYPE OF MANUSCRIPT ALBUM AMICORUM
 *CONTENTS ALBUM AMICORUM 405/1-25, COSTUME/ FINE ILLUSTRATIO
 405/1-25, ARMS OF FRANTZ OF BALEN 405-1, JOANNES A NEUHAUS
 RED/ FUR-LINED ROBE 405-2, RICHLY DRESSED MAN AND WOMAN 405-
 GEORG CHRISTOFF VON WEYTTINGE/ KNIGHT OF MALTA 405-4, GEO
 VON ORSBACH/ KNIGHT OF MALTA 405-5, MAN AND WOMAN IN CARNIV
 DRESS 405-6, WOMAN IN DRESS/ ARMS OF OTTO VON DER GROB
 405-7, WOMAN IN RICH COSTUME WITH FEATHER FAN 405-8, WOMAN
 PINK DRESS WITH FAN 405-10, WOMAN IN PURPLE/ QUILTED COSTU
 WITH FAN 405-11, WOMAN IN SEDAN CHAIR CARRIED BY TWO NEGRO
 405-12, PEASANT WOMAN CARRYING HENS AND OTHER PRODUCE 405-1
 PEASANT MAN CARRYING EMPTY BASKETS ON SHOULDER YOKE 405-1
 WOMAN IN GREEN DRESS WITH MIRROR 405-15, WOMAN IN BLUE DRE
 405-16, EDWARD VON BALEN/ KNIGHT OF MALTA IN ARMOUR 405-1
 VEILED WOMAN HOLDING HANDKERCHIEF 405-18, WOMAN
 BLACK-HOODED DRESS LIKE A MOURNER 405-19, WOMAN IN BLACK DRE
 HOLDING HANDKERCHIEF 405-20, WOMAN IN YELLOW DRESS HOLDING F
 405-21, CARRIAGE CARRYING WOMAN PASSENGERS DRAWN BY TWO HORS
 405-22, STATE BARGE WITH BANNERS 405-23, PEASANT COUP
 DANCING 405-24, HUNTER AND WIFE/ GUN AND DEAD BIRDS 405-25

198

```
*$ABSTRACT 406
  *LIBRARY BOD
  *SLIDE SET TITLE PSALM INITIALS
  *NEGATIVE REFERENCE ROLL 203L
  *RENTAL FEE SM 406 $2.35
  *SHELFMARK MS CANON LITURG 8
  *PROVENANCE ITALIAN/ VENICE
  *DATE EXECUTED 15TH/ THIRD QUARTER
  *LANGUAGE LATIN
  *TYPE OF MANUSCRIPT PSALTER/ PORTABLE FERIAL/ AUGUSTINIAN
  *CONTENTS  PSALTER/  PORTABLE FERIAL AUGUSTINIAN 406/1-7, PSALM
  INITIALS 406/1-7, INITIAL B/ BEATUS VIR 406-1, DAVID  PRAYING/
  ST  JEROME  AND  ST MARK 406-1, INITIAL D/ DOMINUS ILLUMINATIO
  406-2, DAVID POINTS  TO  HIS  EYES  406-2, INITIAL  D/  DIXIT
  CUSTODIAM  406-3, DAVID  IN  PRAYER  406-3, INITIAL D/ DIXIT
  INSIPIENS 406-4, FOOL HOLDING A CLUB 406-4, INITIAL S/  SALVUM
  ME  FAC  406-5, DAVID  IN  PRAYER WAIST DEEP IN WATER/ PARROTS
  406-5, INITIAL E/ EXULTATE 406-6, DAVID  PLAYING  HARP  406-6,
  INITIAL D/ DIXIT DOMINUS 406-7, GOD BLESSING WITH ORB IN RIGHT
  HAND 406-7


*$ABSTRACT 407
  *LIBRARY BOD
  *SLIDE SET TITLE HERALDRY/ FURTHER EXAMPLES
  *NEGATIVE REFERENCE ROLL 204M
  *RENTAL FEE SM 407 $2.60
  *TITLE  OF  MANUSCRIPT  CHRONICLE  OF  JOHN OF WORCESTER 407/1,
  GENEALOGICAL HISTORY FROM BRUTE TO EDWARD I 407/2-3, TRACTATUS
  DE ARMIS 407-4, FEATS OF ARMS AND CHIVELRY  407-6,  BLAZON  OF
  GENTRIE 407-7, ELEMENTS OF ARMORIES 407-8, NOTEBOOK OF MATTHEW
  HUTTON 407-10
  *SHELFMARK MS  C C C  OXFORD  157  407-1,  MS BODLEY ROLLS 3
  407/2-3, MS LAUD MISC 733 407-4, MS DOUCE 278  407-5,  PRINTED
  BOOK  DOUCE  180 407-6, PRINTED BOOK DOUCE F203 407-7, PRINTED
  BOOK WOOD 357 407-8, MS WOOD B 15 407-9, MS RAWL B 397 407-10,
  MS DOUCE 91 407-11, MS CANON LITURG 92 407-12
  *PROVENANCE ENGLISH 407/1-4 AND  6-10,  FRENCH  407/5  AND  11,
  FLEMISH 407-12
  *DATE EXECUTED 12TH/1130-40 407-1, 13TH/1275-1300 407/2-3, 15TH
  407/4-6 AND 12, 16TH 407/7 AND 11, 17TH 407/8-9
  *AUTHOR  JOHN OF WORCESTER 407-1, JOHANNES DE BADO AUREO 407-4,
  CHRISTINE DE PISAN 407-6,  JOHN  FRENE  407-7,  EDMUND  BOLTON
  407-8,
  *TYPE  OF  MANUSCRIPT  HERALDIC  TEXTS  407/1-11, BOOK OF HOURS
  407-12,
  *CONTENTS  HERALDIC  TEXTS  AND  EXAMPLES  OF  FROM  MISC  MSS
  407/1-12,  BARONS  THREATENING  HENRY  I  IN  A  VISION 407-1,
  CAVALRY BATTLE OF HESIONE 407-2, KING EDWY/ EDWYNUS/ HIS  ARMS
  407-3,  HERALD  RECOMMENDS  STUDY  OF  ARMS 407-4, HERALD FROM
  TREATISE ON  HERALDRY  407-5,  ARMORIAL  GLASS  AT  DORCHESTER
  407-9,  ARMS  OF  CASTELNAU DE CLERMONT LODEVE 407-11, ARMS OF
  MARGURITE DE TOUR 407-11, ARMS OF FAMILY LOTTIN 407-12


*$ABSTRACT 408
  *LIBRARY BOD
  *SLIDE SET TITLE SIR WALTER RALEIGH'S BOOK OF HOURS
  *NEGATIVE REFERENCE ROLL 205A
  *RENTAL FEE SM 408 $4.15
  *SHELFMARK MS ADD A 185
  *PROVENANCE FRENCH
  *DATE EXECUTED 15TH/C1440-50
  *LANGUAGE LATIN AND FRENCH
  *ARTIST/ SCHOOL MASTER OF JOUVENEL DES OURSINS AND ASSISTANT
  *TYPE OF MANUSCRIPT BOOK OF HOURS/ USE OF NANTES
  *CONTENTS SIR WALTER RALEIGH'S BOOK OF HOURS 408/1-43, RALEIGH/
  SIR WALTER SIGNATURE 408-1, CALENDAR  FOR  JANUARY  408-1,  ST
  JOHN  EVANGELIST  ON  PATMOS  WRITING  408-2, ST LUKE WRITING
  408-3, ST MATTHEW WITH ANGEL BESIDE 408-4, ST MARK WITH WINGED
```

199

LION BESIDE 408-5, PIETA WITH ST CHRIST MARY MAGDALENE AND ST JOH
408-6, ST CHRISTOPHER AND CHRIST CHILD/ HERMIT IN BACKGROUN
408-7, ST JULIAN THE HOSPITALLER 408-8, ST APOLLONIA HAS TEET
EXTRACTED BY EXECUTIONER 408-9, ST BARBARA STANDS BEFORE HI
TOWER 408-10, ST GREGORY'S MASS/ VISION OF CRUCIFIED CHRIS
408-11, SYMBOLS OF PASSION 408-11, ANNUNCIATION TO VIRGI
408-12, VISITATION/ ST ELIZABETH KNEELS TO VIRGIN 408-13
CRUCIFIXION/ VIRGIN WITH ST JOHN 408-14, PENTECOST 408-15
TRINITY 408-16, ST MICHAEL KILLS DEVIL 408-17, ST JOHN BAPTIS
ABOVE/ ST JOHN EVANGELIST BELOW 408-18, SS PETER AND PAU
408-19, ST JAMES THE GREAT AS PILGRIM 408-20, ST ANDREW WIT
CROSS 408-21, ST SEBASTIAN MARTYRED BY ARCHERS 408-22, S
STEPHEN DRESSED AS DEACON 408-23, ST GEORGE ON WHITE HORS
KILLS DRAGON RESCUES PRINCESS 408-24, ST LAWRENCE AS DEAC
HOLDING GRIDIRON 408-25, ST BLAISE TORTURED WITH IRON COM
408-26, ST MARTIN SHARES CLOAK WITH BEGGAR 408-27, ST GILES I
FRONT OF WATTLE HUT/ DEER 408-28, ST NICHOLAS AND BOYS I
PICKLING TUB 408-29, ST FRANCIS RECEIVES STIGMATA 408-30
CONFESSORS/ SAINTS DOMINIC/ HILARIUS 408-31, ST ANNE TEACHE
VIRGIN TO READ 408-32, ST MARY MAGDALENE IN PANELLED ROO
408-33, ST CATHERINE WITH WHEEL AND SWORD 408-34, ST MARGARE
ESCAPING FROM DRAGON 408-35, ST MARTHA WITH TARASQUE/ DRAGO
TAMED WITH HOLY WATER 408-36, ADORATION OF MAGI 408-37, FLIGH
INTO EGYPT 408-38, CORONATION OF VIRGIN 408-39, LAST JUDGMEN
408-40, BURIAL SCENE OUTSIDE LARGE CHURCH 408-41, VIRGIN AN
CHRIST CHILD IN ROSE GARDEN 408-42, TRINITY 408-43

*$ABSTRACT 409
 *LIBRARY BOD
 *SLIDE SET TITLE MIDWIFE IN BIBLICAL HISTORY AND LEGEND
 *NEGATIVE REFERENCE ROLL 205C
 *RENTAL FEE SM 409 $2.60
 *TITLE OF MANUSCRIPT WILLIAM OF NOTTINGHAM'S COMMENTARIE
 409-10
 *SHELFMARK MS BODLEY 270B 409/1-7, MS CANON MISC 476 409-8, M
 ORIEL COLLEGE 75 409-9, MS LAUD MISC 165 409-10, MS DOUCE 2
 409-11, MS RAWL LITURG E 12 409-12
 *PROVENANCE FRENCH 409/1-7 AND 12, ITALIAN 409/8 AND 11
 ENGLISH 409/9-10
 *DATE EXECUTED 13TH 409/1-7, 14TH 409/8 AND 10, 15TH 409/9 AN
 12, 16TH 409-11
 *AUTHOR WILLIAM OF NOTTINGHAM 409-10
 *TYPE OF MANUSCRIPT BIBLE MORALISEE 409/1-7, ACTS OF ST MAR
 AND JESUS 409-8, MISSAL/ USE OF SARUM 409-9, COMMENTARIES O
 THE GOSPEL 409-10, BOOK OF HOURS 409/11-12
 *CONTENTS MIDWIFE IN BIBLICAL HISTORY AND LEGEND 409/1-12
 MIDWIVES AT TAMAR'S DELIVERY WITH TWINS 409-1, PHARAOH WARN
 HEBREW MIDWIVES TO DESTROY MALE CHILDREN 409-2, MIDWIVE
 FEARED THE LORD AND SPARED HEBREW CHILDREN 409-3, MIDWIFE A
 BIRTH OF MOSES 409-4, MIDWIFE IN TURBAN AT BIRTH OF CHRIS
 409-5, MIDWIFE AT BIRTH OF SAMSON HOLDS UP BABY 409-6, MIDWIF
 WITH MOTHER AND CHILD/ MOTHER LOOKING AT CORPSE 409-7
 MIDWIVES AT BIRTH OF CHRIST 409-8, BIRTH OF MARY/ ST ANN
 RECEIVES BABY FROM MIDWIFE 409-9, BIRTH OF ST JOHN BAPTIST
 MIDWIFE HOLDING BABY 409-10, BIRTH OF ST JOHN BAPTIST WIT
 ZACHARIAH WRITING 409-11, JOSEPH BATHING BABY JESUS 409-12

*$ABSTRACT 410
 *LIBRARY BOD
 *SLIDE SET TITLE VENETIAN MANUSCRIPTS
 *NEGATIVE REFERENCE ROLL 205E
 *RENTAL FEE SM 410 $2.75
 *TITLE OF MANUSCRIPT BREVIARY/ SERVITE 410/1-4, CONSTITUTI
 SUPER COMMISSARIIS DE ULTRA CANALE 410-5, BREVIARY/ CISTERCIA
 410/6-15
 *SHELFMARK MS DOUCE 314 410/1-4, MS ASHMOLE 811 410-5, MS CANO
 LITURG 343 410/6-15
 *PROVENANCE ITALIAN VENICE

*DATE EXECUTED 15TH
*LANGUAGE LATIN
*ARTIST/ SCHOOL LAZARUS DE LARNESA
*TYPE OF MANUSCRIPT BREVIARY/ SERVITE 410/1-4, BREVIARY/
CISTERCIAN 410/6-15
*CONTENTS VENETIAN MANUSCRIPTS 410/1-15, BORDERS/ DECORATED
410/1-15, INITIALS/ HISTORIATED OF ST PAUL AND CHRIST 410-1,
MEDALLION OF CRANE AND SQUIRREL 410-2, INITIAL/ HISTORIATED OF
ADORATION OF THE MAGI 410-2, ADORATION OF THE MAGI 410-2, ST
PETER WITH CROSS 410-3, INITIAL B/ BEATUS WITH DAVID PRAYING
410-3, MEDALLION OF BIRDS 410-4, INITIAL/ HISTORIATED OF ST
PAUL WITH SWORD 410-4, ST PAUL 410-4, ST MARK/ AND WHOLE PAGE
410-5, INITIAL/ HISTORIATED OF ISAIAH 410-6, ISAIAH'S VISION
410-6, INITIALS/ HISTORIATED WITH ST LUKE WRITING AND RISEN
CHRIST 410-7, JUDGMENT OF SOLOMON 410-8, JOB ON DUNGHILL
410-9, TOBIAS AND ARCHANGEL RAPHAEL 410-10, MACCABEUS AS
SOLDIER 410-11, EZEKIEL'S VISION 410-12, INITIAL B/ BEATUS VIR
410-13, DAVID PLAYING ON PSALTERY 410-13, INITIAL D/ DIXIT
DOMINUS WITH DAVID 410-14, ETERNE RERUM CONDITOR/ AMBROSIAN
HYMN 410-15

*$ABSTRACT 411
*LIBRARY BOD
*SLIDE SET TITLE HOLKHAM ITALIAN MSS
*NEGATIVE REFERENCE ROLL 205H
*RENTAL FEE SM 411 $2.40
*SHELFMARK MS HOLKHAM 303 411-1, MS HOLKHAM 367 411-2, MS
HOLKHAM 440 411-3, MS HOLKHAM 350 440-4, MS HOLKHAM 392
411/5-8
*PROVENANCE ITALIAN
*DATE EXECUTED 11TH-12TH 411-1, 15TH 411/2-8
*LANGUAGE LATIN
*AUTHOR VIRGIL 411-1, EUTROPIUS AND FLORUS 411-2, HERODOTUS
411-3, LIVY 411-4, ASCONIUS 411/5-8
*TYPE OF MANUSCRIPT CLASSICAL TEXTS
*CONTENTS HOLKHAM MSS/ ITALIAN 411/1-8, INITIAL AND FULL PAGE
411-1, INITIAL P AND FULL PAGE 411-2, BORDER AND ARMS ON TITLE
PAGE 411-3, INITIAL/ HISTORIATED AND BORDER 411-4, INITIAL H
WITH INTERLACE PATTERN 411-5, INTERLACE 411-5, INITIAL H WITH
JAR 411-6, INITIAL WITH BULL'S MASK 411-7, INITIAL C 411-8

*$ABSTRACT 412
*LIBRARY BOD
*SLIDE SET TITLE NEW TESTAMENT SCENES
*NEGATIVE REFERENCE ROLL 205K
*RENTAL FEE SM 412 $2.20
*SHELFMARK MS RAWL D 939
*PROVENANCE ENGLISH
*DATE EXECUTED 14TH/C1370
*LANGUAGE LATIN
*TYPE OF MANUSCRIPT CALENDAR
*CONTENTS CALENDAR 412/1-4, NEW TESTAMENT SCENES 412/1-4,
ANNUNCIATION 412-1, CASPAR AND MELCHIOR 412-2, BALTHAZAR AND
NATIVITY SCENE 412-3, NATIVITY 412-3, CRUCIFIXION WITH SS MARY
AND JOHN 412-4,

*$ABSTRACT 413
*LIBRARY BOD
*SLIDE SET TITLE NEW TESTAMENT SCENES
*NEGATIVE REFERENCE ROLL 205M
*RENTAL FEE SM 413 $2.50
*SHELFMARK MS CANON LITURG 343
*PROVENANCE ITALIAN VENICE
*DATE EXECUTED 15TH/ LATE
*LANGUAGE LATIN
*TYPE OF MANUSCRIPT BREVIARY/ CISTERCIAN

*CONTENTS BREVIARY 413/1-10, NEW TESTAMENT SCENES 413/1-10,
ANNUNCIATION 413-1, NATIVITY 413-2, CIRCUMCISION OF CHRIST
413-3, CHRIST AND THREE DISCIPLES AT MEAL 413-4,
TRANSFIGURATION OF CHRIST/ WHO STANDS BETWEEN TWO PROPHETS
413-5, LAST SUPPER/ ST PETER SPEAKS TO CHRIST 413-6, CHRIST
MOCKED AND CROWNED WITH THORNS 413-7, CRUCIFIXION 413-8,
CHRIST APPEARS TO ST MARY MAGDALENE IN GARDEN 413-9, TRINITY
413-10

*$ABSTRACT 414
  *LIBRARY BOD
  *SLIDE SET TITLE EARLY SCIENCE/ SCIENTIFIC CALCULATIONS AND
  DRAWINGS
  *NEGATIVE REFERENCE ROLL 205N
  *RENTAL FEE SM 414 $2.70
  *TITLE OF MANUSCRIPT TREATISE ON ASTRONOMY 414-4, MATHEMATICA
  AND CHRONOLOGICA 414-5, LIBER INTORDUCTORIUS 414/8-14
  *SHELFMARK MS RAWL D 939 414/1-3, MS CANON MISC 248 414-4, MS
  DIGBY 88 414-5, MS DIGBY 81 414-6, MS DIGBY 48 414-7, MS
  BODLEY 266 414/8 AND 10-14, MS RAWL B 214 414-9
  *PROVENANCE ENGLISH 414/1-3 AND 5 AND 7 AND 9, FRENCH 414/4 AND
  6, ITALIAN 414/8 AND 10-14
  *DATE EXECUTED 14TH 414/1-4, 15TH 414/5-14
  *LANGUAGE LATIN
  *AUTHOR MICHAEL SCOTUS 414/8-14
  *TYPE OF MANUSCRIPT ASTRONOMICAL AND MATHEMATICAL TEXTS
  414/1-14, CALENDAR 414/1-4
  *CONTENTS ASTRONOMICAL TEXTS 414/1-14, SCIENTIFIC CALCULATIONS
  AND DRAWINGS FROM MSS 414/1-14, HEAVENS IN CHART WITH SYMBOLS
  FOR MONTHS 414-1, ASTROLOGICAL CHART FOR COMPUTING INFLUENCE
  OF PLANETS 414-2, HORLOGIUM CUM SOLE 414-3, ZODIACAL MAN
  414-4, MAN SHOWING VEINS OF BODY 414-5, ZODIACAL MAN 414-6,
  ZODIACAL MAN 414-7, UNIVERSE AS NAKED ZODIACAL MAN 414-8,
  SATURN/ JUPITER/ VENUS/ JUNO/ NEPTUNE/ PLUTO/ OPS GANYMEDE
  414-9, MARS/ APOLLO/ MUSES/ MONSTERS 414-10, MONSTERS 414-10,
  VENUS/ THREE GRACES/ VULCAN/ CUPID/ APOLLO/ MERCURY/ ARGUS
  414-11, DIANA 414-12, JUNO/ CYBELE 414-13, MARS AND VENUS/
  VULCAN/ HERCULES/ AESCULAPIUS 414-14

*$ABSTRACT 415
  *LIBRARY BOD
  *SLIDE SET TITLE BIRDS FROM 13TH CENTURY ENGLISH BESTIARY
  *NEGATIVE REFERENCE ROLL 205P
  *RENTAL FEE SM 415 $3.80
  *SHELFMARK MS BODLEY 764
  *PROVENANCE ENGLISH
  *DATE EXECUTED 13TH
  *LANGUAGE LATIN
  *TYPE OF MANUSCRIPT BESTIARY
  *CONTENTS BESTIARY 415/1-36, EAGLES FISHING 415-1, MARTINS
  FISHING 415-2, FULLICA THE COOT/ HEN COOT GUARDED BY MATE
  415-3, VULTURES DEVOURING SMALL ANIMALS 415-4, GRUS THE CRANE/
  SLEEPING CRANES GUARDED BY ONE 415-5, CICONIA THE STORK EATING
  FROG 415-6, ARDEA THE HERON 415-7, OLOR THE SWAN FISHING
  415-8, IBIS FEEDS ITS YOUNG ON SNAKE'S EGGS 415-9, FULLICA THE
  COOT PREENING ITS FEATHERS 415-10, GRACULUS/ MURMURATION OF
  STARLINGS 415-11, ALCION/ MYTHICAL BIRD 415-12, PHOENIX SEATED
  IN TREE WITH WORM IN BEAK 415-13, CINOMOLGUS IN NEST OF
  CINNAMON ATTACKED 415-14, ERCINEA/ NOCTURNAL BIRD AND HOOPE
  ATTENDED BY YOUNG 415-15, PELICAN PIERCES ITS BREAST AND FEEDS
  BLOOD TO YOUNG 415-16, NOCTUA THE LITTLE OWL 415-17, PERDIX
  THE PARTRIDGE/ WHITE DOG STALKING PARTRIDGES 415-18, PARTRIDGE
  WITH NEST OF EGGS 415-19, PICUS THE MAGPIE 415-20, ACCIPTER/
  HAWK HELD BY WOMAN 415-21, LUCINA THE NIGHTINGALE IN ITS NEST
  415-22, CORVUS THE RAVEN FEEDS ON ITS YOUNG 415-23, CORNIX THE
  CROW 415-24, TURTUR THE TURTLE DOVE 415-25, HIRUNDO THE
  SWALLOW/ SWALLOWS FLY TO NESTS 415-26, COTURNIX THE QUAIL/
  QUAILS CROSS SEA 415-27, ANSER/ GOOSE/ GEESE SCOLD FOX WHO HAS

KILLED GOOSE 415-28, PAVO/ PEACOCK/ ULULA A FICTITIOUS BIRD
WHO WEEPS 415-29, HUPUPA THE HOOPOE 415-30, COCK STANDS ON
BRANCH TO CROW 415-31, HENS AND CHICKS 415-32, ANAS THE DUCK/
DUCKS AND DRAKE 415-33, PASSER/ SPARROW 415-34, MILVUS/ KITE
ATTACKS DOMESTIC FOWL 415-35, PERSINDEUS/ DOVES EAT FRUIT
DRAGONS WAIT TO CATCH 415-36

*$ABSTRACT 416
 *LIBRARY BOD
 *SLIDE SET TITLE MINIATURES AND HISTORIATED INITIALS
 *NEGATIVE REFERENCE ROLL 206B
 *RENTAL FEE SM 416 $2.95
 *SHELFMARK MS AUCT D 4 2
 *PROVENANCE FLEMISH/ GHENT OR BRUGES
 *DATE EXECUTED 13TH/C1276
 *LANGUAGE LATIN
 *ARTIST/ SCHOOL ATELIER OF THE ROYAL GOLD CUP IN BRITISH MUSEUM
 *TYPE OF MANUSCRIPT PSALTER/ PORTABLE
 *CONTENTS MINIATURES 416/1-19, INITIALS/ HISTORIATED 416/1-19,
 PSALTER 416/1-19, ANNUNCIATION 416-1, NATIVITY IN STABLE
 416-2, ADORATION OF THE MAGI 416-3, FLAGELLATION OF CHRIST
 416-4, CRUCIFIXION ON GREEN CROSS 416-5, INITIAL B/ BEATUS VIR
 416-6, DAVID PLAYING HARP/ KILLING GOLIATH/ IN GARDEN WITH
 BATHSHEBA 416-6, HARROWING OF HELL 416-7, INITIAL D/ DOMINUS
 ILLUMINATIO 416-8, SS PETER AND PAUL 416-8, INITIAL D/ DIXI
 CUSTODIAM 416-9, MARTYRDOM OF ST STEPHEN 416-9, INITIAL Q/
 QUID GLORIARIS 416-10, ST LAWRENCE/ MARTYRDOM 416-10, INITIAL
 D/ DIXIT INSIPIENS 416-11, ST BARTHOLOMEW/ MARTYRDOM 416-11,
 INITIAL S/ SALVUM ME FAC 416-12, ST MARGARET ESCAPES FROM
 DRAGON 416-12, DRAGON/ ST MARGARET 416-12, INITIAL E/ EXULTATE
 416-14, ST MARTIN SHARES CLOAK WITH BEGGAR 416-14, ST THOMAS/
 INCREDULITY 416-13, INITIAL C/ CANTATE 416-15, ST JOHN
 BAPTIST/ MARTYRDOM 416-15, PENTECOST 416-16, INITIAL D/ DOMINE
 EXAUDI 416-17, MARTYRDOM OF FEMALE SAINT 416-17, INITIAL D/
 DIXIT DOMINUS 416-18, CORONATION OF VIRGIN 416-18, CHRIST IN
 MAJESTY ON RAINBOW WITH SYMBOLS OF EVANGELISTS 416-19

*$ABSTRACT 417
 *LIBRARY BOD
 *SLIDE SET TITLE MINIATURES AND HISTORIATED INITIALS
 *NEGATIVE REFERENCE ROLL 206D
 *RENTAL FEE SM 417 $2.90
 *SHELFMARK MS LAUD LAT 84
 *PROVENANCE FLEMISH
 *DATE EXECUTED 14TH/ FIRST QUARTER
 *LANGUAGE LATIN
 *TYPE OF MANUSCRIPT PSALTER/ GALLICAN
 *CONTENTS MINIATURES 417/1-18, INITIALS/ HISTORIATED 417/1-18,
 PSALTER 417/1-18, ANNUNCIATION 417-1, NATIVITY 417-2,
 ADORATION OF THE MAGI AND VIRGIN CROWNED 417-3, HOLY INNOCENTS
 SLAUGHTERED AND HEROD WATCHES 417-4, ARREST OF CHRIST/ HE
 HEALS SERVANT'S EAR 417-5, INITIAL B/ BEATUS VIR 417-6, DAVID
 PLAYING HARP/ KILLING GOLIATH 417-6, TRIAL OF CHRIST BEFORE
 PILATE 417-7, INITIAL D/ DOMINUS ILLUMINATIO 417-8, CHRIST
 BLESSES DAVID WHO POINTS TO HIS EYES 417-8, MOCKING OF CHRIST
 417-9, INITIAL D/ DIXI CUSTODIAM 417-10, CHRIST LEANS FROM
 CLOUD AND BLESSES DAVID 417-10, FLAGELLATION OF CHRIST 417-11,
 INITIAL D/ DIXIT INSIPIENS WITH FOOL TEMPTED BY DEVIL 417-11,
 DEVIL 417-11, CHRIST CARRYING CROSS 417-12, INITIAL S/ SALVUM
 ME FAC 417-13, DAVID PRAYS TO GOD TO SAVE HIM FROM WATER
 417-13, CRUCIFIXION ON GREEN CROSS 417-14, INITIAL E/ EXULTATE
 417-15, DAVID PLAYING BELLS 417-15, DEPOSITION OF CHRIST
 417-16, ENTOMBMENT AND RESURRECTION 417-17, INITIAL D/ DIXIT
 DOMINUS 417-18, CORONATION OF VIRGIN 417-18

203

*$ABSTRACT 418
 *LIBRARY BOD
 *SLIDE SET TITLE MINIATURES AND HISTORIATED INITIALS
 *NEGATIVE REFERENCE ROLL 206E
 *RENTAL FEE SM 418 $2.50
 *SHELFMARK MS DOUCE 23
 *PROVENANCE FRENCH/ NORTHWEST
 *DATE EXECUTED 14TH/C1300
 *LANGUAGE LATIN
 *TYPE OF MANUSCRIPT PSALTER/ GALLICAN
 *CONTENTS MINIATURES 418/1-10, INITIALS/ HISTORIATED 418/1-10,
 PSALTER 418/1-10, VIRGIN AND CHILD/ SEPIA DRAWING 418-1,
 CRUCIFIXION/ SEPIA DRAWING 418-2, INITIAL B/ BEATUS VIR 418-3,
 DAVID PLAYING HARP/ KILLING GOLIATH 418-3, INITIAL D/ DOMINUS
 ILLUMINATIO 418-4, DAVID STANDS BESIDE CHRIST AND POINTS TO
 EYES 418-4, INITIAL D/ DIXI CUSTODIAM 418-5, DAVID KNEELS IN
 PRAYER BEFORE SHRINE OF VIRGIN 418-5, INITIAL D/ DIXIT
 INSIPIENS 418-6, DAVID ADMONISHING THE FOOL 418-6, INITIAL S/
 SALVUM ME FAC 418-7, DAVID PRAYING FOR CHRIST TO SAVE HIM FROM
 WATER 418-7, INITIAL E/ EXULTATE 418-8, DAVID PLAYING BELLS
 418-8, INITIAL C/ CANTATE 418-9, CLERICS SINGING AT LECTERN
 418-9, INITIAL D/ DIXIT DOMINUS 418-10, TRINITY 418-10

*$ABSTRACT 419
 *LIBRARY BOD
 *SLIDE SET TITLE HUNTING
 *NEGATIVE REFERENCE ROLL 207B
 *RENTAL FEE SM 419 $2.50
 *SHELFMARK MS RAWL LITURG F 11 419-1, MS DOUCE 276 419/2-4, MS
 DOUCE 135 419/5-8, MS CANON ITAL 38 419/9-10
 *PROVENANCE FRENCH 419/1-8, ITALIAN 419/9-10
 *DATE EXECUTED 15TH 419/1 AND 9-10, 16TH 419/2-8
 *LANGUAGE LATIN
 *TYPE OF MANUSCRIPT BOOK OF HOURS 419/1-8, BESTIARY/ RHYMED
 419/9-10
 *CONTENTS HUNTING SCENES 419/1-10, HUNTER AND HOUND CHASE HARE
 419-1, HOUNDS ATTACK STAG/ HUNTERS BLOWING HORNS 419-2, HUNTER
 SPEARS STAG AT BAY 419-3, BOY WITH LONGBOW SHOOTS BIRD 419-4,
 HUNTER WITH DEAD STAG SLUNG ACROSS HORSE'S SADDLE 419-5,
 HUNTER SPEARS HUGE WILD BOAR 419-6, HUNTER WITH PRIMITIVE GUN
 419-7, HUNTER WITH LONGBOW SHOOTS BIRD 419-8, HUNTER WITH
 MOTHER TIGER AND CUB 419-9, HUNTER WITH BAGPIPES CHARMS STAG
 419-10, BAGPIPES 419-10

*$ABSTRACT 420
 *LIBRARY BOD
 *SLIDE SET TITLE AARON AND MOSES/ EXODUS IV 9-XIV 31
 *NEGATIVE REFERENCE ROLL 207D
 *TITLE OF MANUSCRIPT BIBLE MORALISEE
 *SHELFMARK MS BODLEY 270B
 *RENTAL FEE SM 420 $3.40
 *PROVENANCE FRENCH
 *DATE EXECUTED 13TH/ C1250
 *LANGUAGE FRENCH AND LATIN
 *ARTIST/ SCHOOL FRENCH ROYAL WORKSHOPS
 *TYPE OF MANUSCRIPT BIBLE MORALISEE
 *CONTENTS BIBLE MORALISEE 420/1-28, AARON AND MOSES 420/1-28,
 MOSES TAKES WATER FROM RIVER AND CHANGES TO BLOOD 420-1, AARON
 SENT TO MEET MOSES IN WILDERNESS 420-2, MOSES AND AARON ASK
 PHARAOH TO RELEASE ISRAELITES 420-3, PHARAOH WILL NOT OBEY/
 INCREASES BURDENS 420-4, MIRACLE OF CHANGING ROD INTO SERPENT
 420-5, RODS STRUCK ON WATERS OF EGYPT/ BLOOD IN LAND 420-6,
 PHARAOH DOUBTS POWER OF GOD AS MAGICIANS DO SAME 420-7, PLAGUE
 OF FROGS 402-8, MOSES ASKS PHARAOH IF HE MAY PRAY AGAINST
 FROGS 420-9, PLAGUE OF LICE 420-10, PLAGUE OF SWARMS OF FLIES
 420-11, PLAGUE OF CATTLE 420-12, PLAGUE OF HAIL 420-13, PLAGUE
 OF LOCUSTS 420-14, PLAGUE OF DARKNESS/ EXCEPT IN HOUSES OF
 ISRAEL 420-15, INSTRUCTIONS FOR PASSOVER 420-16, PASCHAL LAMB

ROASTED 420-17, MOSES FORBIDS UNCIRCUMCISED TO KEEP PASSOVER
420-18, ISRAELITES MARK DOORPOSTS WITH HYSSOP AND BLOOD
420-19, ANGEL SMITES FIRST BORN 420-20, CHILDREN OF ISRAEL
SPOIL EGYPTIANS 420-21, PHARAOH LETS JEWS GO 420-22, CHARIOTS
AND HORSEMEN OF PHARAOH PURSUE 420-23, MOSES LISTENS TO HIS
FRIGHTENED PEOPLE 420-24, MOSES CAUSE WATERS TO DIVIDE 420-25,
ISRAELITES FOLLOW MOSES TO DRY LAND 420-26, PHARAOH'S CHARIOTS
AND HORSES FOLLOW THEM INTO SEA 420-27, SEA RETURNS TO BED AND
COVERS PHARAOH'S ARMIES 420-36

*$ABSTRACT 421
  *LIBRARY BOD
  *SLIDE SET TITLE JOSEPHUS
  *NEGATIVE REFERENCE ROLL 207M
  *RENTAL FEE SM 421 $2.95
  *TITLE OF MANUSCRIPT ANTIQUITIES 421/1-8, JEWISH WARS 421-9
  *SHELFMARK MS MERTON COLLEGE M 2 11
  *PROVENANCE FRENCH/ LIEGE
  *DATE EXECUTED 12TH/ THIRD QUARTER
  *LANGUAGE LATIN
  *AUTHOR JOSEPHUS
  *TYPE OF MANUSCRIPT HISTORY
  *CONTENTS JOSEPHUS 421/1-9, INITIAL P/ POST MORTEM ISAAC 421-1,
  PHARAOH GIVES STAFF TO JOSEPH 421-1, MOSES PRAYS TO GOD AND
  EARTH SWALLOWS KORAH AND FOLLOWERS 421-2, TEMPLE OF DAGON/
  PHILISTINES KILL DEFEATED JEWS 421-3, ARK OF COVENANT CARRIED
  OFF BY VICTORS 421-3, DAVID IN BYZANTINE STYLE PORTRAIT 421-4,
  JEHOSAPHAT CROWNED IN ROBE WITH SWORD 421-5, TEMPLE AS
  ROMANESQUE CHURCH 421-6, HEZEKIAH PRAYS BEFORE LAMB ON ALTAR
  421-6, CYRUS CROWNED AND ROBED WITH SCEPTRE AND SCROLL 421-7,
  ALEXANDER OF MACEDON ENTHRONED/ FIGURES MOURN DEATH OF KING
  421-8, INITIAL T FORMING TAU CROSS FROM WHICH MAN HANGS 421-9

*$ABSTRACT 422
  *LIBRARY BOD
  *SLIDE SET TITLE BIBLE INITIALS
  *NEGATIVE REFERENCE ROLL 207N
  *RENTAL FEE SM 422 $2.50
  *SHELFMARK MS MERTON N 2 3
  *PROVENANCE ITALIAN/ NAPLES
  *DATE EXECUTED 13TH/ LATE
  *LANGUAGE LATIN
  *TYPE OF MANUSCRIPT BIBLE
  *CONTENTS INITIALS/ BIBLE 422/1-10, JUDGES/ GOD TELLS JUDAH TO
  FIGHT CAANANITES 422-1, KINGS I/ BATTLE BETWEEN ISRAEL AND
  PHILISTINES 422-2, KINGS III/ ABISHAG BROUGHT TO DAVID TO WARM
  HIM 422-3, KINGS IV/ AHAZIAH FALLS FROM HIS UPPER CHAMBER
  422-4, EZRA I/ MASONS AT WORK BUILDING TEMPLE 422-5, MASONS AT
  WORK 422-5, TOBIT/ TOBIT BLINDED BY SWALLOW 422-6, JUDITH/
  JUDITH BEHEADS HOLOFERNES 422-7, ESTHER/ ESTHER KNEELS BEFORE
  AHASUERUS/ HAMAN 422-8, INITIAL D/ DIXIT INSIPIENS 422-9, FOOL
  WITH CLUB AND BAUBLE 422-9, INITIAL C/ CANTATE 422-10, CLERICS
  SINGING AT LECTERN 422-10

*$ABSTRACT 423
  *LIBRARY BOD
  *SLIDE SET TITLE MIDDLE ENGLISH ROMANCES AND RELATED
  ILLUSTRATIVE MSS
  *NEGATIVE REFERENCE ROLL 208D
  *RENTAL FEE SM 423 $3.75
  *TITLE OF MANUSCRIPT GESTE OF KYNG HOR 423-1, SOUTH-ENGLISH
  LEGENDARY 423-2, VITA ROBERTI REGIS SICILIAE 423-2, PIERS
  PLOWMAN 423-4, SIEGE OF JERUSALEM AND LIFE OF ALEXANDER 423-5,
  STIMULUS CONSCIENCIE AND SIEGE OF JERUSALEM 423-6, LAUD TROY
  BOOK 423-7, SIEGE OF JERUSALEM 423/8-9, APOLLONIUS OF TYRE
  423-11, WARS OF ALEXANDER 423-12, ALEXANDER'S LETTER TO

205

DINDIMUS 423-13, TITUS AND VESPASIAN 423/14-15, BATTLE OF
JERUSALEM 423-18, SIR DEGARE 423-19, KYNG ORFEW 423/21-22,
RICHARD COER DE LYON 423-24, ARTHOUR AND MERLIN 423-25,
AWNTYRE OFF ARTHURE 423-26, WEDDYNG OF SYR GAWEN AND DAME
RAGNELL 423-28, SIR ISUMBRAS 423-30, AMIS AND AMILOUN 423-31,
STORY OF THE ERLE OF TOLOUS 423-32, SIR EGLAMOURE 423-33,
ALEXANDER FRAGMENT/ ALLITERAIVE 423-34
*SHELFMARK MS LAUD MISC F 219 423-1, MS TRINITY COLLEGE OXFORD
D 57 423-2, MS ENGLISH POETRY A 1 423/3-4, MS LAUD MISC 622
423-5, MS DOUCE 126 423-6, MS LAUD MISC 595 423-7, MS LAUD
MISC 656 423/8-9, MS C C C 220 423-10, MS DOUCE 216 423-11, MS
ASHMOLE 44 423-12, MS BODLEY 264 423-13, MS DIGBY 230
423/14-15, MS DOUCE 78 423-16, MS RAWLINSON POETRY 34 423-17,
MS DOUCE 78 423-18, MS RAWL POET E 1 423-20, MS ASHMOLE 61
423/21-22, MS DOUCE 25 423-23, MS DOUCE 228 423-24, MS DOUCE
236 423-25, MS DOUCE 324 423-26, MS RAWL C 86 423/27-28, MS
UNIVERSITY COLLEGE 142 423/29-30, MS DOUCE 326 423-32, MS
ASHMOLE 45 423-32, MS DOUCE 261 423-33, MS GREAVES 60 423-34
*PROVENANCE ENGLISH
*DATE EXECUTED 13TH 423-1, 14TH 423/2-4 AND 13, 15TH 423/5-12
AND 14-33, 16TH 423-34
*LANGUAGE ENGLISH/ MIDDLE
*AUTHOR ROLLE 423-6
*TYPE OF MANUSCRIPT ROMANCES/ MIDDLE ENGLISH AND RELATED
ILLUSTRATIVE
*CONTENTS ROMANCES/ MIDDLE ENGLISH AND RELATED ILLUSTRATIVE MSS
423/1-35, LITERATURE/ MIDDLE ENGLISH ROMANCES 423/1-35,
MANUSCRIPT/ DISPLAY OF REGULAR COMPOSITION 423-7, RELIGIOUS
TRACTS 423-10, ALEXANDER'S LETTER TO DINIMUS 423-13, PROSE
MEDICAL RECEIPT 423-16, MUSICAL NOTATION IN SO-CALLED
MINSTREL'S MANUSCRIPT 423-20, COMMON-PROFIT INSCRIPTION
423-23, ILLUMINATION/ AMATEUR OF PASSION SCENE 423-27, ROMANCE
MSS IN ROW/ BINDINGS ILLUSTRATING FORMATS 423-35

*$ABSTRACT 424
 *LIBRARY BOD
 *SLIDE SET TITLE BEES AND OTHER INSECTS
 *NEGATIVE REFERENCE ROLL 208F
 *RENTAL FEE SM 424 $3.25
 *SHELFMARK MS ASHMOLE 1511 424-1, MS BODLEY 764 424-2, MS DOUCE
 88 424-3, MS UNIVERSITY COLLEGE 120 424-4, MS DOUCE 151-5, MS
 RAWL D 939 424/6-7, MS DOUCE 313 424-9, MS HATTON 10 424-10,
 MS BODLEY 533 424-11, MS ADD A 185 424-12, MS BODLEY 968
 424-13, MS BUCHANAN E 14 424-14, MS RAWL LITURG F 8 424-15, MS
 DOUCE 219-220 424-16, MS NEW COLLEGE 323 424/17-21, MS DOUCE
 241 424-22, MS LAT LITURG G 5 424/23-24, MS DOUCE 205 424-25
 *PROVENANCE ENGLISH 424/1-10 AND 23-24, FRENCH 424/8-9 AND
 11-14, FLEMISH 424/16-21 AND 25, DUTCH 424/15, ITALIAN 424-22
 *DATE EXECUTED 13TH 424-1, 14TH 424/4-9, 15TH 424/10-24, 16TH
 424-25
 *TYPE OF MANUSCRIPT MISCELLANY
 *CONTENTS BEES 424/1-25, INSECTS 424/1-25, BEES FLYING TOWARD
 SKEPS 424-1, BEE HIVE 424/2 AND 6-9, BEES FLYING TO HIVE/ MAN
 AND WOMAN WITH SICKLE 424-3, BEES 424/4-5 AND 10-14 AND 19 AND
 23-25, BUTTERFLY ON ROSES 424-15, DAVID ATTACKS LION WHO
 OVERTURNED BEE SKEP 424-16, BUTTERFLY 424/17-18 AND 20-21,
 BEES ATTACK BEAR 424-22

*$ABSTRACT 425
 *LIBRARY BOD
 *SLIDE SET TITLE VENUS AND OTHER MYTHOLOGICAL CHARACTERS
 *NEGATIVE REFERENCE ROLL 210B
 *RENTAL FEE SM 425 $2.50
 *TITLE OF MANUSCRIPT DICTYS CRETENSIS 425/1-4, COMPLAINT OF
 MARS 425/5-7, ROMAN DE LA ROSE 425-8, CECCO D'ASCOLI:ACERBA
 425-9, PROSDOCIMO DE'BEDOMANDI 425-10
 *SHELFMARK MS RAWL B 214 425/1-4, MS FAIRFAX 16 425/5-7, MS
 SELDEN SUPRA 57 425-8, MS CANON ITAL 38 425-9, MS CANON MISC

554 425-10
*PROVENANCE ENGLISH 425/1-7, FRENCH 425-8, ITALIAN 425/9-10
*DATE EXECUTED 15TH
*LANGUAGE LATIN 425/1-4, ENGLISH 425/5-7, FRENCH 425-8, ITALIAN
 425/9-10
*AUTHOR GUILLAUME DE LORIS AND JEAN DE MEUNG 425-8
*TYPE OF MANUSCRIPT MISCELLANY
*CONTENTS VENUS AND OTHER MYTHOLOGICAL CHARACTERS 425/1-10,
 SATURN AND JUPITER 425-1, MARS AND APOLLO 425-2, VENUS AND
 MERCURY 425-3, DIANA AND MINERVA 425-4, JUPITER/ MARS/ VENUS
 425-5, MARS 425-6, VENUS 425-7, OISEUSE WITH MIRROR AND COMB
 425-8, LUXURIA WITH MIRROR 425-9, VENUS WITH MIRROR AND LOVERS
 425-10

*$ABSTRACT 426
 *LIBRARY BOD
 *SLIDE SET TITLE EXODUS AND THE LAW
 *NEGATIVE REFERENCE ROLL 210C
 *RENTAL FEE SM 426 $3.75
 *TITLE OF MANUSCRIPT BIBLE MORALISEE
 *SHELFMARK MS BODLEY 270B
 *PROVENANCE FRENCH
 *DATE EXECUTED 13TH/C1250
 *LANGUAGE FRENCH
 *TYPE OF MANUSCRIPT BIBLE MORALISEE
 *CONTENTS BIBLE MORALISEE 426/1-35, PHARAOH LETS ISRAELITES GO/
 PILLARS OF CLOUD AND FIRE 426-1, CHRIST GUARDS HIS DISCIPLES
 426-2, CHARIOTS AND HORSEMEN OF PHARAOH PURSUE CHILDREN OF
 ISRAEL 426-3, MOSES LIFTS UP ROD OVER SEA 426-4, MOUNTAINS AND
 SEA 426-5, MOSES PLACES ROD IN SEA AND WIND FORCES BACK SEA
 426-6, MOSES AS GOOD PRELATE 426-7, ISRAELITES FOLLOW MOSES ON
 DRY LAND 426-8, SONS OF ISRAEL LIKE 12 APOSTLES 426-9,
 PHARAOH'S CHARIOTS AND HORSEMEN FOLLOW INTO SEA 426-10, MOSES
 STRETCHES HAND AND SEA RETURNS 426-11, MOSES AND ISRAELITES
 SING PRAISES TO GOD 426-12, ISRAELITES IN WILDERNESS CAN'T
 QUENCH THIRST 426-13, MOSES SWEETENS WATERS WITH TREE 426-14,
 MOSES SWEETENING WATER LIKE CHRIST 426-15, ISRAELITES CAMP BY
 WATERS OF ELIM 426-16, SPRINGS ARE APOSTLES AND PALMS DOCTORS
 OF CHURCH 426-17, GOD SENDS DOWN BREAD FROM HEAVEN 426-18,
 CHRIST SENDS GRACE AND UNDERSTANDING OF DIVINITY 426-19, MOSES
 STRIKES ROCK WITH STAFF 426-20, ROUNDEL WITH GOD/ MOSES/
 AARON/ HUR/ MEN SUPPORTING MOSES 426-21, MOSES ACTS ON COUNSEL
 OF JETHRO 426-23, GOD SPEAKS WITH MOSES ON MOUNT SINAI 426-23,
 HOLY GHOST ON PENTECOST 426-24, GOD IN SMOKE OF FIRE IN CLOUD
 ON SINAI 426-25, GOD COMMUNES WITH MOSES ON MOUNT SINAI
 426-26, CHRIST GIVES LAW AND DOCTRINE TO ST PETER 426-27,
 MOSES INSTRUCTED HOW TO BUILD ARK 426-28, CHRIST TELLS PETER
 TO BUILD CHURCH 426-29, ARK GUARDED BY CHERUBIN OF PURE GOLD
 426-30, ANGELS GUARDING ARK ARE SS PETER AND PAUL 426-31, GOD
 TELLS MOSES HOW TABLE TO BE CONSTRUCTED 426-32, TABLE IS
 DIVINITY/ CROWN OF MARTYRDOM/ RINGS THE EVANGELISTS 426-33,
 CANDLESTICK WROUGHT OUT OF TALENT OF GOLD 426-34, CANDLESTICK
 GOD'S MOTHER/ BRANCHES ARE VIRTUES 426-35

*$ABSTRACT 427
 *LIBRARY BOD
 *SLIDE SET TITLE MUSICAL INSTRUMENTS/ MORE
 *NEGATIVE REFERENCE ROLL 210D
 *RENTAL FEE SM 427 $2.85
 *TITLE OF MANUSCRIPT ORMESBY PSALTER 427/1-3, COMMENTARY ON THE
 PSALMS 427-7, TREATISES OF SS AUGUSTINE AND ISIDORE 427-15
 *SHELFMARK MS DOUCE 366 427/1-3, MS ASHMOLE 1525 427/4-5, MS
 DIGBY 9 427-6, MS AUCT D 2 8 427-7, MS DOUCE 5 427/8-9, MS
 DOUCE 6 427/10-11, MS DOUCE 118 427-12, MS DOUCE 131 427-13,
 MS DOUCE 180 427-14, MS DOUCE 198 427-15, MS DOUCE 198 427-15,
 MS DOUCE 268 427-16, MS EXETER COLL 47 427-17
 *PROVENANCE ENGLISH 427/1-7 AND 13-14 AND 17, FRENCH 427/12 AND
 15-16, FLEMISH 427/8-11

207

*DATE EXECUTED 13TH 427/4-7 AND 14, 12TH 427-15, 14TH 427/1-
AND 8-11 AND 13 AND 17, 15TH 427-16
*LANGUAGE LATIN
*AUTHOR SS AUGUSTINE AND ISIDORE 427-15
*TYPE OF MANUSCRIPT PSALTER 427/1-5 AND 8-13, COMMENTARY O
PSALMS 427-7, APOCALYPSE 427-14, BOOK OF HOURS 427-16, PSALTE
427-17
*CONTENTS MUSICAL INSTRUMENTS 427/1-17, ANGEL WITH FIDDLE AN
FRET 427-1, GITTERN HELD BY ANGEL 427-12, BELLOWS AND TONG:
BEING PLAYED 427-3, HARP AND WIND INSTRUMENT 427-4, INITIAL D
DEUS 427-5, REBEC PLAYED BY MAN 427-5, INITIAL E/ EXULTAT
427-6, DAVID PLAYING BELLS AND PORTATIVE ORGAN 427-6, INITIA
D 427-7, DAVID AND MAN WITH PSALTERY AND CHIMEBELLS 427-7
MUSICIANS WITH FIDDLE AND TRIANGLE 427-8, DEVIL AND ANGEL WIT
HANDBELLS AND HORN 427-9, MUSICIAN WITH JAWBONE AND RAK
427-10, MUSICIAN WITH FIDDLE 427-11, DEVIL/ BLUE WITH HORN AN
TABOR 427-12, MUSICIANS IN GROUP 427-13, HARP/ FIDDLE/ TRUMPE
427-14, INITIAL M/ WITH PIPE/ REBEC/ ORGAN 427-15, FOX PLAYIN
REBEC 427-16, GROTESQUE WITH TABOR AND WIND INSTRUMENT 427-17

*$ABSTRACT 428
*LIBRARY BOD
*SLIDE SET TITLE CHAUCER/ THE PARDONER'S TALE
*NEGATIVE REFERENCE ROLL 210E
*RENTAL FEE SM 428 $2.60
*TITLE OF MANUSCRIPT ROMANCE OF ALEXANDER 428/1-2, L
TORNOIEMENS ANTICHRIST 428-4, 'L'EPITRE D'OTHEA A HECTO
428-8, DOCTRINE OF WISDOM 428-9
*SHELFMARK MS BODLEY 264 428/1-2, MS DOUCE 6 428-3, MS DOUC
308 428-4, MS DOUCE 322 428-5, MS DOUCE 313 428-6, MS DOUCE
428-7, MS BODLEY 421 428-8, MS BODLEY 943 428-9, MS DOUCE
428-10, MS DOUCE 276 428-11, MS CHARTERS OXON A 8 428-12
*PROVENANCE FLEMISH 428/1-3 AND 7, FRENCH 428/4 AND 6 AND 8 AN
11, ENGLISH 428/5 AND 9 AND 12, FLEMISH 428-10
*DATE EXECUTED 14TH 428/1-4 AND 6-7 AND 10, 13TH 428-12, 15T
428/5 AND 8-9, 16TH 428-11
*LANGUAGE FRENCH 428/1-2 AND 4 AND 8 LATIN 428/3 AND 6-7 AN
10-12, ENGLISH 428/4-5
*AUTHOR HUON DE MERI 428-4, CHRISTINE DE PISAN 428-8, STEPHE
SCROPE 428-9
*TYPE OF MANUSCRIPT ROMANCE 428/1-2 AND 8, PSALTER 428/3 AND
AND 10
*CONTENTS PARDONER'S TALE/ ILLUSTRATIONS FROM VARIOUS MS:
428/1-12, LITERATURE/ PARDONER'S TALE 428/1-12, FLEMISH YOUN
FOLK AND MUSICIANS 428-1, DANCING GIRL AND FIDDLER 428-3
GAMBLERS PLAYING AND PAYING DEBTS 428-2, PERSONIFICATION O
DRUNKENESS/ PLAYING DICE AT TAVERN 428-4, DEATH AS SKELETO
WITH BELL AND SPEAR 428-5, PLAGUE/ PRIEST OFFERING MASS FO
VICTIMS 428-6, CHRIST WOUNDED/ BLASPHEMERS WOUNDING CHRIS
428-7, YOUTHS FIND TREASURE/ GIFT OF JUNO 428-8, APOTHECAR
428-9, MAN POURING WINE INTO BOTTLES 428-10, YOUTHS FIGHTIN
WITH DAGGARS 428-11, PAPAL BULL CONFIRMING CONVENTION O
TITHES 428-12

*$ABSTRACT 429
*LIBRARY BOD
*SLIDE SET TITLE OLD TESTAMENT INITIALS
*NEGATIVE REFERENCE ROLL 210F
*RENTAL FEE SM 429 $3.10
*SHELFMARK MS NEW COLLEGE 7
*PROVENANCE FRENCH
*DATE EXECUTED 13TH
*LANGUAGE LATIN
*TYPE OF MANUSCRIPT BIBLE
*CONTENTS INITIALS 429/1-22, OLD TESTAMENT 429/1-22, INITIAL D
DESIDERII 429-1, ST JEROME 429-1, INITIAL V/ VOCAVIT 429-2
LEVITICUS/ GOD POINTS TO LAMB 429-2, INITIAL L/ LOCUTUS 429-3
NUMBERS/ COUNTING THE PEOPLE 429-3, INITIAL E/ ET 429-4

JOSHUA   ADMONISHED/ BATTLE SCENE 429-4, INITIAL P/ POST MORTEM
429-5, JUDGES/ SAMSON KILLING LION 429-5, INITIAL F/ FACTUM
429-6, KING II/ DAVID ORDERS DEATH OF AMELEKITE 429-6, INITIAL
E/ ET 429-7, KINGS III/ ABISHAG AND DAVID 429-7, INITIAL A/
ADAM 429-8, PARALIPOMENON I/ ADAM DELVING AND EVE SPINNING
429-8, ADAM AND EVE AT WORK 429-8, INITIAL I/ IN ANNO 429-9,
ESDRAS I/ CYRUS RELEASES JEWS AND RESTORES HOLY VESSELS 429-9,
INITIAL T/ TOBIAS 429-10, TOBIAS CURES FATHER'S BLINDNESS
429-10, INITIAL A/ ARFAXAT 429-11, JUDITH KILLS HOLOFERNES
429-11, INITIAL I/ IN DIEBUS ASSUERE 429-12, ESTHER/ VASHTI
REFUSES   AHASUERUS   429-12,   ESTHER CROWNED/ HAMAN LEADS
MORDECHAI'S HORSE/ HAMAN HANGED 429-12, INITIAL V/ VIR ERAT IN
TERRA 429-13, JOB/ SHOWN WITH WIFE AND COMFORTERS 429-13,
INITIAL O/ OSCULETUR ME OSCULO 429-14, SONG OF SOLOMON/ CHRIST
CROWNING BRIDE CHURCH 429-14, INITIAL D/ DILIGITE JUSTICIAM
429-15, WISDOM/ SOLOMON ENTHRONED ADDRESSES ARMED MEN 429-15,
INITIAL V/ VERBA 429-16, JEREMIAH/ GOD REBUKES HIM 429-16,
INITIAL E/ ET 429-17, EZEKIEL/ VISION OF APOCALYPTIC BEASTS
429-17, INITIAL A/ ANNO 429-18, HABBAKKUK/ LED BY HAIR BY
ANGEL/ BRINGS DANIEL FOOD 429-18, INITIAL V/ VERBA 429-19,
AMOS/ GOD SPEAKS TO AMOS A SHEPHERD 429-19, INITIAL E/ ET
429-20, INITIAL O/ ONUS 429-21, NAHUM/ GRIEVES OVER COMING
DESTRUCTION OF NINEVEH 429-21, INITIAL E/ ET 429-22, MACCABEES
II/ JUDAS AND BROTHERS EXHORTED BY DYING FATHER 429-22,
KNIGHTS MOUNTED IN SINGLE COMBAT 429-22

*$ABSTRACT 430
  *LIBRARY BOD
  *SLIDE SET TITLE AEGIDIUS DE COLUMNA
  *NEGATIVE REFERENCE ROLL 214D
  *RENTAL FFE SM 430 $2.40
  *TITLE OF MANUSCRIPT DE REGIMINE PRINCIPUM
  *SHELFMARK MS DIGBY 233
  *PROVENANCE ENGLISH
  *DATE EXECUTED 15TH
  *LANGUAGE LATIN TRANSLATED TO ENGLISH BY JOHN OF TREVISA
  *TYPE OF MANUSCRIPT CLASSICAL TEXT
  *CONTENTS AEGIDIUS DE COLUMNA 430/1-8, MINIATURES   AND
  DECORATIONS 430/1-8, BORDER DECORATION AND MINIATURE OF AUTHOR
  PRESENTING BOOK 430-1, AUTHOR PRESENTS BOOK TO PHILIP OF
  FRANCE 430-2, AUTHOR LECTURES KING ON FAMILY DUTIES 430-3,
  DECORATION AND WHOLE FOLIO 430/4-7, DECORATION SHOWING SWAN
  430-8

*$ABSTRACT 431
  *LIBRARY BOD
  *SLIDE SET TITLE FROISSART
  *NEGATIVE REFERENCE ROLL 187B
  *RENTAL FEE SM 431 $2.50
  *COMMENTS FRAGMENTS OF A CHRONICLE OF ENGLAND WRITTEN IN FRENCH
  *TITLE OF MANUSCRIPT ANCIENNES CHRONIQUES D'ANGLETERRE
  *SHELFMARK MS LAUD MISC 653
  *PROVENANCE FLEMISH
  *DATE EXECUTED 15TH
  *LANGUAGE FRENCH
  *AUTHOR JEAN DE WAVRIN
  *ARTIST/ SCHOOL SCHOOL OF LOYSET LIEDET
  *TYPE OF MANUSCRIPT CHRONICLE
  *CONTENTS CHRONICLE OF ENGLAND 431/1-10, KING OF FRANCE 431-1,
  ENGLISH LED BY KNEELING BISHOP BURGHERSH OF LINCOLN 431-1,
  ENGLISH FORCES DRIVE SCOTS FROM CASTLE OF SALISBURY 431-2,
  JOUSTS IN HONOR OF COUNTESS OF SALISBURY 431-3, SIEGE OF
  CALAIS 431-4, DON HENRI MADE KING OF CASTILE 431-5, STREET
  SCENE WITH PETER OF CASTILLE 431-5, BATTLE OF POITIERS 431-6,
  BATTLE 431-7, CAPTURE OF ST LOUEN CONSTANTIN BY EDWARD III
  431-8, TREATY BETWEEN EDWARD III AND LORDS OF FRANCE 431-9,
  BATTLE OF CRECY 431-10

*$ABSTRACT 432
  *LIBRARY BOD
  *SLIDE SET TITLE BOOK OF HOURS
  *NEGATIVE REFERENCE ROLL 211C
  *RENTAL FEE SM 432 $3.90
  *SHELFMARK MS DOUCE 256
  *PROVENANCE FLEMISH
  *DATE EXECUTED 16TH/ EARLY
  *LANGUAGE LATIN
  *ARTIST/ SCHOOL MASTER OF DAVID SCENES IN GRIMANI BREVIARY
  *TYPE OF MANUSCRIPT BOOK OF HOURS/ USE OF ROME
  *CONTENTS   BOOK   OF   HOURS/   FLEMISH/   16TH   432/1-38,   BORDER
  DECORATED   WITH   FLOWERS   AND   BIRDS 432/1-38, ST JOHN WRITIN
  APOCALYPSE ON PATMOS 432-1, ST LUKE PAINTING VIRGIN AND CHIL
  432-2,   ST   MATTHEW   WRITING HIS GOSPEL 432-3, ST MARK WRITIN
  HIS GOSPEL 432-4, CHRIST'S AGONY   ON   GETHSEMANE   432-5,   HOL
  FACE/ PORTRAIT OF CHRIST 432-6, CRUCIFIXION 432-7, HOLY SPIRI
  AS   DOVE   DESCENDS   AT   PENTECOST 432-8, VIRGIN AND CHILD WIT
  ATTENDANT   ANGELS   432-9,   ANNUNCIATION   432-10,   VISITATIO
  432-11,   NATIVITY   432-12,   ANNUNCIATION   TO SHEPHERDS 432-13
  ADORATION OF THE MAGI   432-14, PRESENTATION IN THE TEMPL
  432-15,   FLIGHT   INTO   EGYPT   432-16, MASSACRE OF INNOCENT
  432-17, CORONATION OF VIRGIN 432-18, PRECEDING PENETENTIA
  PSALMS/   DAVID   PRAYS   TO   GOD   432-19, LAZARUS RAISED 432-20
  PIETA/ VIRGIN WITH BODY OF CHRIST 432-21, INITIAL O/
  INTEMERATA   432-22, ST MICHAEL DEFEATING SATAN 432-23, ST JOH
  THE BAPTIST WITH LAMB OF GOD 432-24, SS PETER AND PAUL 432-25
  ST ANDREW 432-26, ST JAMES THE GREATER 432-27, ST JOHN TH
  EVANGELIST   432-28,   ST   THOMAS   432-29,   SS PHILIP AND JAME
  432-30, ST BARTHOLOMEW 432-31, ST MATTHEW 432-32, SS SIMON AN
  JUDE 432-33, ST MATTHIAS 432-34, ST SEBASTIAN 432-35, S
  FRANCIS OF ASSISI 432-36, ST CATHERINE 432-37, ST BARBAR
  432-38

*$ABSTRACT 433
  *LIBRARY BOD
  *SLIDE SET TITLE DOGS
  *NEGATIVE REFERENCE ROLL 211D
  *RENTAL FEE SM 433 $2.70
  *TITLE OF MANUSCRIPT ROMANCE OF ALEXANDER
  *SHELFMARK MS BODLEY 264
  *PROVENANCE FLEMISH
  *DATE EXECUTED 14TH/1338-44
  *LANGUAGE FRENCH
  *TYPE OF MANUSCRIPT ROMANCE
  *CONTENTS ROMANCE OF ALEXANDER 433/1-14, LITERATURE/ ROMANCE O
  ALEXANDER 433/1-14, DOGS 433/1-14, DOG CHASING HARE WHIC
  FACES HIM 433-1, DOG/ COLLARED AND CROUCHING LION 433-2, DO
  WITH LAMB IN MOUTH/ SHEPHERD CHASING IT 433-3, STAG CHASED B
  HOUND 433-4, MAN WITH HAT ON DONKEY WITH DOGS 433-5, LADY WIT
  DOG HOLDING CHAPLET 433-6, DOG/ PERFORMING/ KING CHASE
  WILD-MAN WITH LADY 433-7, MAN IN CHAIR WITH STICK 433-8, BOY
  WITH DOG'S HEADS/ STONE/ SCROLL/ WITH TAILS 433-8, HUNTE
  KILLING STAG/ HOUNDS COME IN FOR KILL 433-9, HOUND CHASIN
  HARE OR RABBIT 433-10, SHAGGY DOG WITH FOUR BOYS 433-11
  SHAGGY DOG LEADS MEN ON HORSEBACK 433-12, LION/ CROWNED AN
  HARES CHASED BY HOUNDS 433-13, PAIRS OF HOODED BOYS/ DOG
  433-14

*$ABSTRACT 434
  *LIBRARY BOD
  *SLIDE SET TITLE PENTATEUCH
  *NEGATIVE REFERENCE ROLL 211E
  *RENTAL FEE SM 434 $2.45
  *TITLE OF MANUSCRIPT BIBLE MORALISEE 434/1-6, BOHUN PSALTE
  434/7-9
  *SHELFMARK MS BODLEY 270B 434/1-6, MS AUCT D 4 4 434/7-9
  *PROVENANCE FRENCH 434/1-6, ENGLISH 434/7-9

*DATE EXECUTED 13TH 434/1-6, 14TH/C1370 434/7-9
*LANGUAGE FRENCH 434/1-6, LATIN 434/7-9
*ARTIST/ SCHOOL FRENCH ROYAL WORKSHOP 434/1-6
*TYPE OF MANUSCRIPT BIBLE MORALISEE 434/1-6, PSALTER 434/7-9
*CONTENTS PENTATEUCH 434/1-9, PHARAOH PLAGUED AND BANISHES
ABRAHAM AND SARAH 434-1, ABRAHAM BANISHED 434-1, ABRAHAM
RESCUES LOT FROM KINGS 434-2, SARAH ASKS ABRAHAM TO EXPEL
HAGAR 434-3, CIRCUMCISION OF ISAAC 434-4, ABRAHAM WELCOMES
ANGELS AT MAMBRE 434-5, LOT'S WIFE TURNED INTO PILLAR OF SALT
434-6, SACRIFICES OF CAIN AND ABEL 434-7, CAIN AND ABEL 437-7,
DEATH OF CAIN 434-8, JACOB AND ESAU 434-9

*$ABSTRACT 435
  *LIBRARY BOD
  *SLIDE SET TITLE ROMANCE OF THE ROSE
  *NEGATIVE REFERENCE ROLL 211G
  *RENTAL FEE SM 435 $3.00
  *TITLE OF MANUSCRIPT ROMANCE OF THE ROSE
  *SHELFMARK MS DOUCE 195
  *PROVENANCE FRENCH
  *DATE EXECUTED 15TH/1487-95
  *LANGUAGE FRENCH
  *ARTIST/ SCHOOL ROBINET TESTARD
  *AUTHOR GUILLAUME DE LORRIS AND JEAN DE MEUNG
  *TYPE OF MANUSCRIPT ROMANCE
  *CONTENTS ROMANCE OF THE ROSE 435/1-20, LITERATURE/ ROMANCE OF
  THE ROSE 435/1-16, LOVER WALKING NEAR CASTLE 435-1, IDLENESS
  OPENS DOOR TO LOVER 435-2, GOD OF LOVE STRIKES LOVER 435-3,
  NERO'S MURDER OF SENECA 435-4, KING CROESUS OF LYDIA AT FEAST
  435-5, IDYLLIC LOVERS OF LONG AGO 435-6, HUSBAND/ SUSPICIOUS
  MALTREATS WIFE 435-7, HOUSE WHERE HUSBAND AND WIFE AGREE
  435-8, WOMAN PLAYING BAGPIPES AT FEAST 435-9, BAGPIPES 435-9,
  FAUX SEMBLANT AND ABSTINENCE/ CONSTRAINTE AS PILGRIMS 435-10,
  VENUS AND ADONIS 435-11, VENUS RIDES IN HER CHARIOT 435-12,
  CASTLE BESIEGED 435-13, NATURE FORGES BIRDS AND ANIMALS
  435-14, WIFE TRIES TO LEARN HER HUSBAND'S SECRETS 435-15,
  GENIUS CHANGES HIS CLOTHES 435-16

*$ABSTRACT 436
  *LIBRARY BOD
  *SLIDE SET TITLE ST ANTHONY ABBOT
  *NEGATIVE REFERENCE ROLL 212I
  *RENTAL FEE SM 436 $2.45
  *SHELFMARK MS RAWL D 939 436-1, MS CANON LITURG 92 436-2, MS
  DOUCE 93 436-3, MS DOUCE 311 436-4, MS CANON LITURG 118 436-5,
  MS CANON LITURG 384 436-6, MS RAWL LITURG E 34 436-7, MS DOUCE
  19 436-8, MS RAWL LITURG E 36 436-9
  *PROVENANCE ENGLISH 436-1, FRENCH 436/7 AND 9, FLEMISH 436/2
  AND 4-5, ITALIAN 436/6 AND 8, DUTCH/ UTRECHT 436-3
  *DATE EXECUTED 14TH 436-1, 15TH 436/2-7, 16TH 436/8-9
  *LANGUAGE LATIN
  *TYPE OF MANUSCRIPT CALENDAR 436-1, BOOK OF HOURS 436/2-5 AND
  7-9, MISSAL 436-6
  *CONTENTS ST ANTHONY ABBOT/ WITH SYMBOLS BELL/ PIG/ STAFF
  436/1-9, ST ANTHONY/ PASTORAL STAFF/ PIG WEARING BELL 436-1,
  ST ANTHONY WITH STAFF/ ROSARY/ PIG WEARING BELL 436-2, ST
  ANTHONY WITH CROZIER/ ROSARY/ BELL 436-3, ST ANTHONY WITH
  STAFF/ BOOK/ BELL/ PIG 436-4, ST ANTHONY WITH BOOK/ BELL/ PIG
  436-5, ST ANTHONY WITH STAFF/ LARGE BELL 436-6, ST ANTHONY
  WITH STAFF/ BELL/ PIG 436-7, ST ANTHONY WITH BOOK/ STAFF/ BELL
  436-8, ST ANTHONY WITH BOOK/ STAFF/ PIG 436-9, CHAPEL WITH
  BELL-COTE IN BACKGROUND 436-9

*$ABSTRACT 437
  *LIBRARY BOD
  *SLIDE SET TITLE DAVID WITH BELLS

*NEGATIVE REFERENCE ROLL 212J
*RENTAL FEE SM 437 $2.75
*COMMENTS COMMON ILLUSTRATION FOR PSALM 80/ EXULTATE DEO
*SHELFMARK MS AUCT D 28 437-1, MS CANON BIBL LAT 47 437-2, MS
 AUCT D 1 17 437-3, MS AUCT D 5 13 437-4, MS CANON BIBL LAT 52
 437-5, MS CANON BIBL LAT 92 437-6, MS LAUD LAT 85 437-7, MS
 NEW COLLEGE 1 437-8, MS C C C 1 437-9, MS E D CLARKE 31
 437-10, MS LAUD LAT 82 437-11, MS JESUS COLL 40 437-12, MS
 DOUCE 245 437-14, MS C C C 18 437-14, MS CANON LITURG 286
 437-14
*PROVENANCE ENGLISH 437/1 AND 4 AND 8 AND 11-12 AND 14, FRENCH
 437/2-3 AND 5-6 AND 9-10 AND 13, FLEMISH 437-7, GERMAN 437-15
*DATE EXECUTED 12TH 437-1, 13TH 437/2-9, 14TH 437/10-14, 15TH
 437-15
*LANGUAGE LATIN
*TYPE OF MANUSCRIPT COMMENTARY ON PSALMS 437-1, BIBLE 437/2-6
 AND 8-10, PSALTER 437/7 AND 11-12 AND 14, BREVIARY 437/13 AND
 15
*CONTENTS DAVID WITH BELLS 437/1-15, BELLS AND KING DAVID
 437/1-15, PSALM 80/ EXULTATE ILLUSTRATED 437/1-15

*$ABSTRACT 438
 *LIBRARY BOD
 *SLIDE SET TITLE BELLS II
 *NEGATIVE REFERENCE ROLL 212K
 *RENTAL FEE SM 438 $2.55
 *SHELFMARK MS DOUCE 185 438/1-2, MS AUCT D 4 14 438-3, MS DOUCE
 272 438-4, MS CANON LITURG 327 438-5, MS DOUCE 80 438-6, MS
 RAWL LITURG G 6 438-7, MS DOUCE F 4 438-8, MS LAT LITURG A 3
 438-9, MS ASTOR A 15 438-15, MS DOUCE 311 438-11
 *PROVENANCE SWISS/ CONSTANCE 438/1-2, ENGLISH 438/3 AND 7-8,
 FRENCH 438/6 AND 10, ITALIAN 438/4-5 AND 9, FLEMISH 438-11
 *DATE EXECUTED 14TH 438/1-3, 15TH 438/4-11
 *LANGUAGE LATIN
 *TYPE OF MANUSCRIPT SERMOLOGIUM 438/1-2, APOCALYPSE 438-3,
 PSALTER 438/4 AND 9, BREVIARY/ CHOIR 438-5, BOOK OF HOURS
 438/6-7 AND 10-11, SPECULUM HUMANAE SALVATIONIS 438-8
 *CONTENTS BELLS 438/1-11, HANDBELLS RUNG BY MAN 438-1,
 HANDBELLS 438-2, BELL/ LARGE HANGING IN CHURCH TOWER 438-3,
 MUSICIANS/ ONE RINGING BELLS HUNG ON BEAMS 438-4, BELL IN
 BELL-COTE RUNG BY MAN 438-5, GROTESQUE RINGING HANDBELLS
 438-6, BELLS IN CHURCH BELL-COTE IN BURIAL SCENE 438-7,
 ISRAELITE WOMAN RINGING HANDBELLS AS SHE GREETS DAVID 438-8,
 ANGEL MUSICIANS/ ONE RINGING BELLS ON BEAM 438-9, DEACON OR
 CLERK RINGING PASSING BELL 438-10, DECORATIVE PATTERN OF
 PEAR-SHAPED BELLS 438-11

*$ABSTRACT 439
 *LIBRARY BOD
 *SLIDE SET TITLE ENGLISH ROMANESQUE SCULPTURE FROM OXFORDSHIRE
 AND GLOUCESTERSHIRE
 *NEGATIVE REFERENCE ROLL 213A
 *RENTAL FEE SM 439 $2.60
 *PROVENANCE ENGLISH
 *CONTENTS ROMANESQUE SCULPTURE FROM OXFORDSHIRE 439/1-12,
 SCULPTURE/ ENGLISH ROMANESQUE 439/1-12, AMPNEY/ ST MARY/ GLOS
 439-1, TYMPANUM/ PRIMITIVE WITH LION AND EAGLE CARVINGS 439-1,
 FRITWELL/ OXON 439-2, TYMPANUM/ CARVING WITH ELEPHANTS EATING
 TREE-LEAVES 439-2, LITTLE BARRINGTON/ GLOS 439-3, TYMPANUM/
 CHRIST CROSS-NIMBED ENTHRONED/ ANGELS 439-3, BLOXHAM/ OXON
 439-4, CHANCEL/ TYMPANUM/ DECORATIVE MOTIFS/ INCISED SCALLOP
 DESIGN 439-4, CHURCH HANDBOROUGH/ OXON 439-5, TYMPANUM/ ST
 PETER WITH KEYS/ AGNUS DEI AND LION 439-5, CHECKENDON/ OXON
 439-6, TYMPANUM/ 19TH CENTURY ADDITION 439-6, WINDRUSH/ GLOS
 439-7, BEAST'S MASKS DECORATION 439-7, WOODSTOCK/ OXON 439-8,
 CHEVRON-PATTERN DECORATION/ REMNANT OF NORMAN BUILDING 439-8,
 ST PETER IN THE EAST/ OXON 439-9, CAPITAL WITH MAN KILLING
 BEAST/ SAMSON OR BELLEROPHON 439-9, LANGFORD/ OXON 439-10,

CRUCIFIXION/ PRE-CONQUEST 439-10, LANGFORD/ OXON 439/11-12,
GREAT ROOD/ CHRIST REIGNING FROM TREE 439-11, FIGURES
ASSOCIATED WITH SUNDIAL/ PERHAPS WITH GREAT ROOD 439-12

*$ABSTRACT 440
 *LIBRARY BOD
 *SLIDE SET TITLE MEDIEVAL WALL-PAINTINGS FROM THE OXFORD REGION
 *NEGATIVE REFERENCE ROLL 213B
 *RENTAL FEE SM 440 $3.60
 *CONTENTS WALL-PAINTINGS MEDIEVAL FROM OXFORD REGION 440/1-32,
 BLOXHAM/ OXON/ SOUTH WALL OF MILCOMBE CHAPEL 440-1, PASSION
 AND MARTYRDOM OF SAINT 440-1, BLOXHAM/ OXON 440-2, ST
 CHRISTOPHER SCENE 440-2, COMBE/ OXON 440/3 AND 7, LAST
 JUDGMENT 440-3, NORTHMOOR/ OXON 440-4, CHRIST IN MAJESTY WITH
 CENSING ANGELS 440-4, CORONATION OF VIRGIN 440-4, NORTH STOKE/
 OXON 440/5-6, PASSION AND RESURRECTION SCENES 440-5, ST
 STEPHEN AND ST CATHERINE MARTYRED 440-6, CRUCIFIXION WITH SS
 MARY AND JOHN 440-7, SOUTH LEIGH/ OXON 440/8-12, ST CLEMENT
 WITH ANCHOR 440-8, SEVEN DEADLY SINS 440-10, VIRGIN HOLDING
 LILY/ REMAINS OF ANNUNCIATION SCENE 440-11, ST MICHAEL
 WEIGHING SOULS/ VIRGIN MARY INTERCEDES 440-12, KINGSTON LISLE/
 BERKS 440-13, SS PETER AND PAUL 440-13, AMPNEY CRUCIS/ GLOS
 440-14, SS PAUL AND JAMES 440-14, BAUNTON/ GLOS 440-15, ST
 CHRISTOPHER WITH HERMIT AND FISHERMAN 440-15, ODDINGTON/ GLOS
 440/16-17, LAST JUDGMENT 440-16, DAMNED CAST INTO HELL'S MOUTH
 440-17, CROUGHTON/ NORTHANTS 440/18-21, LIFE OF VIRGIN/
 INFANCY OF CHRIST/ MAGI SCENES 440-18, INFANCY OF CHRIST/
 MASSACRE OF HOLY INNOCENTS 440-19, FLIGHT INTO EGYPT 440-19,
 PASSION OF CHRIST/ ENTRY INTO JERUSALEM/ LAST SUPPER 440-20,
 HARROWING OF HELL/ DEPOSITION 440-20, PASSION OF CHRIST/
 SCENES FROM 440-21, CHRIST MEETS MOTHER ON WAY TO CALVARY
 440-21, WOMEN SEE ANGEL AT EMPTY TOMB 440-21, BLACK BOURTON/
 OXON 440/23-24, BAPTISM OF CHRIST/ SS PETER AND PAUL 440-23,
 ST STEPHEN/ MARTYRDOM 440-23, ST RICHARD OF CHICHESTER OR ST
 NICHOLAS 440-24, ADORATION AND JOURNEY OF MAGI 440-24, SOUTH
 NEWINGTON/ OXON 440/25-31, ST THOMAS BECKET MARTYRDOM AND ST
 THOMAS OF LANCASTER 440-25, ST MARGARET OF ANTIOCH AND HER
 DRAGON 440-26, DRAGON/ ST MARGARET 440-26, ANNUNCIATION/ ST
 JAMES THE GREAT 440-27, VIRGIN AND CHILD 440-27, LAST JUDGMENT
 440-28, PASSION SCENES 440-29, PASSION SCENES 440-30, PASSION
 EMBLEMS ON SHIELD 440-30, PASSION AND RESURRECTION SCENES/
 DEPOSITION/ ENTOMBMENT 440-31, CHRIST'S APPEARANCE TO ST MARY
 MAGDALENE 440-31, WOOD LATON/ OXON 440-32, ST CHRISTOPHER WITH
 CHRIST CHILD AND SCROLL 440-32

*$ABSTRACT 441
 *LIBRARY BOD
 *SLIDE SET TITLE OLD TESTAMENT SELECTION I
 *NEGATIVE REFERENCE ROLL 214A
 *RENTAL FEE SM 441 $2.85
 *TITLE OF MANUSCRIPT TREATISE ON THE CHURCH TO CHARLES VIII OF
 FRANCE 441/6-8
 *SHELFMARK MS RAWL G 184 441-1, MS AUCT D 4 8 441/2-5, MS RAWL
 A 417 441/6-8, MS CANON BIBL LAT 57 441/9-15, MS CANON BIBL
 LAT 47 441/16-17
 *PROVENANCE FRENCH 441/1 AND 6-8 AND 16-17
 *DATE EXECUTED 13TH 441/1 AND 2-5 AND 16-17, 14TH 441/9-15,
 16TH 441/6-8
 *LANGUAGE LATIN
 *TYPE OF MANUSCRIPT PENTATEUCH 441-1, TREATISE ON CHURCH
 441/2-5, BIBLE 441/6-17
 *CONTENTS OLD TESTAMENT SELECTION 441/1-17, MOSES PUTS TABLETS
 INTO ARK 441-1, MOSES MAKES AN OFFERING 441-2, BALAAM'S ASS
 AND THE ANGEL 441-3, MOSES' DEATH 441-4, ARK BORNE BEFORE
 JERICHO 441-5, JACOB WITH LEAH AND RACHEL 441-6, PHARAOH'S
 DREAM 441-7, JOB'S FAMILY AND HIS SUFFERING 441-8, MOSES/
 ZIPPORAH AND SON RETURN TO EGYPT 441-9, MOSES PRAYING IN
 TABERNACLE 441-10, MOSES' DEATH 441-11, RUTH/ STORY OF

213

441/12-13, MAN FROM SAUL'S CAMP BEFORE DAVID 441-14, AHAZIAH
SICK/ WITH HIS SERVANT 441-15, GOD PRESENTS TABLETS TO MOSES
441-16, PHILISTINE ABOUT TO KILL SON OF ELI 441-17

*$ABSTRACT 442
  *LIBRARY BOD
  *SLIDE SET TITLE ARK OF THE COVENANT
  *NEGATIVE REFERENCE ROLL 214B
  *RENTAL FEE SM 442 $3.00
  *TITLE OF MANUSCRIPT ON EXODUS 442/1-11, BIBLE COMMENTARY
  442/12-20
  *SHELFMARK MS DUKE HUMPHREY 442/1-11, MS BODLEY 251 442/12-20
  *PROVENANCE ENGLISH 442/1-11, FRENCH 442/12-20
  *DATE EXECUTED 14TH 442/12-20, 15TH/C1440 442/1-11
  *LANGUAGE LATIN
  *AUTHOR JOHN CAPGRAVE 442/1-11, NICHOLAS DE LYRA 442/12-20
  *TYPE OF MANUSCRIPT COMMENTARIES ON BIBLE
  *CONTENTS ARK OF THE COVENANT 442/1-20, CHERUBIM HOLDING
  PROPITIATORY OVER ARK 442-1, CHERUBIM STAND ON ARK 442-2,
  RECTANGULAR ARK WITH CHALICES 442-3, ROUND ARK WITH CHALICES/
  EWERS/ CRUETS/ BOWLS 442-4, SEVEN-BRANCHED CANDLESTICKS 442-5,
  BOARD WITH SILVER SOCKETS 442/6-7, JOINED BOARDS WITH SILVER
  SOCKETS/ GOLD BARS/ RINGS 442-8, ALTAR WITH GRILL/ FIRE/
  HORNS/ GOLD CHAIN 442-9, TABERNACLE CURTAIN COLORED WITH GOLD
  TRIMMINGS 442-10, CURTAIN OF BROWN GOAT'S HAIR 442-11, ARK
  WITH RINGS/ CARRYING STAVES/ LID LIFTED BY ANGELS 442-12,
  TABLE WITH KNOBBED LEGS/ BOWLS/ CANDLESTICKS 442-13,
  TABERNACLE CURTAIN WITH BLUE AND RED STRIPES 442-14,
  TABERNACLE/ SECTION OF 442/15-16, ALTAR WITH CARRYING RINGS/
  HORNS/ BRASS 442-17, ALTAR 442-18, AARON/ PRIESTLY ROBES/
  MITRE/ EPHOD/ BREASTPLATE/ GIRDLE 442-19, LEVITE FAMILIES
  PLACED AROUND TABERNACLE 442-20

*$ABSTRACT 443
  *LIBRARY BOD
  *SLIDE SET TITLE GLAGOLITIC MSS
  *NEGATIVE REFERENCE ROLL 214C
  *RENTAL FEE SM 443 $2.35
  *TITLE OF MANUSCRIPT CONFESSIONALE OF ST ANTONIUS OF FLORENCE
  *SHELFMARK MS CANON LITURG 349 443/1-2, MS CANON LITURG 414
  443-3, MS CANON LITURG 412 443-4, MS CANON LITURG 172 443/5-6,
  MS CANON LITURG 373 443-7
  *PROVENANCE DALMATIAN 443/1-6, BYZANTINE/ CROATIA 443-7
  *DATE EXECUTED 15TH
  *LANGUAGE SLAVONIC
  *TYPE OF MANUSCRIPT MISSAL 443/1-2 AND 7, SERMONS 443-3,
  CONFESSIONAL 443-4, BREVIARY 443/5-6
  *CONTENTS GLAGOLITIC MSS 443/1-7, INITIAL 443/1-2, PAGE FILMED
  TO SHOW USE OF COLOR 443-3, PAGE SHOWING CHANGE OF HANDS/
  DATE/ USE OF COLOR 443-4, DATE ENTRY 443-5, INITIAL/ LATIN
  443-6, INITIAL/ LATIN 443-7

*$ABSTRACT 444
  *LIBRARY BOD
  *SLIDE SET TITLE SELDEN APOCALYPSE I
  *NEGATIVE REFERENCE ROLL 217L
  *RENTAL FEE SM 444 $3.15
  *COMMENTS SEE ABSTRACT 468 FOR PART II
  *TITLE OF MANUSCRIPT SELDEN APOCALYPSE
  *SHELFMARK MS SELDEN SUPRA 38
  *PROVENANCE ENGLISH/ FRENCH IN STYLE
  *DATE EXECUTED 14TH/C1320-30
  *LANGUAGE FRENCH
  *TYPE OF MANUSCRIPT APOCALYPSE
  *CONTENTS APOCALYPSE PICTURES 444/1-23, ST JOHN OF PATMOS/ MEN
  LISTEN TO 444-1, ST JOHN OF PATMOS/ HANDS OUTSTRETCHED 444-2,

CHRIST AMID GOLD CANDLESTICKS/ REV 1 VERSES 12-14 444-3, ST
JOHN OF PATMOS/ ANGEL AWAKENS 444-4, ST JOHN OF PATMOS
DIRECTED BY ANGEL TO WRITE 444-5, REV 1 VERSE 19/ JOHN OF
PATMOS WRITING 444-5, ST JOHN OF PATMOS CLIMBS LADDER 444-6,
REV 4 VERSE 1 444-6, CHRIST IN MAJESTY/ TWENTY-FOUR ELDERS
444-7, REV 8 VERSES 12-13/ CHRIST IN MAJESTY 444-7, ST JOHN'S
VISION OF ENTHRONED GOD WITH SEVEN SEALS 444-8, REV 5 VERSES
1-2 444-8, ST JOHN'S VISION OF SEVEN-HORNED LAMB 444-9, REV 5
VERSE 6/ VISION OF LAMB 444-9, LAMB OF GOD 444-9, LAMB OPENS
FIRST SEAL/ WHITE HORSE 444-10, LAMB OPENS SECOND SEAL/ RED
HORSE 444-11, LAMB OPENS THIRD SEAL/ BLACK HORSE 444-12, HUMAN
FIGURES RECEIVE WHITE STOLES 444-13, REV 6 VERSES 9-11 444-13,
LAMB OPENS FIFTH SEAL 444-13, LAMB OPENS SIXTH SEAL/
EARTHQUAKE 444-14, REV 7 VERSE 1/ FOUR WINDS 444-15, REV 7
VERSES 2-3/ ANGEL HOLDS PALM 444-16, REV 7 VERSE 9/ CHRIST IN
MAJESTY 444-17, CHRIST IN MAJESTY 444-17, ST JOHN OF PATMOS/
ELDER SPEAKS TO 444-18, LAMB OPENS SEVENTH SEAL/ CHRIST IN
MAJESTY 444-19, REV 8 VERSES 2-6/ ANGEL WITH TRUMPETS AND
CENSER 444-19, ANGEL/ THIRD SOUNDS TRUMPET/ GOLD STAR FALLS
444-20, REV 8 VERSES 10-11/ THIRD TRUMPET SOUNDS 444-20,
ANGEL/ FOURTH SOUNDS TRUMPET/ SUN/ MOON/ STARS DARKENED
444-21, REV 8 VERSES 12-13/ ONE-THIRD STARS DARKENED 444-21,
ANGEL/ FIFTH SOUNDS TRUMPET/ LOCUST 444-22, REV 9 VERSES 1-6/
LOCUST EMERGE FROM EARTH 444-22, LOCUSTS/ GOLDCROWNED HEADS
444-23

*$ABSTRACT 445
  *LIBRARY BOD
  *SLIDE SET TITLE TUDOR MANUSCRIPTS
  *NEGATIVE REFERENCE ROLL 214E
  *RENTAL FEE SM 445 $2.55
  *TITLE OF MANUSCRIPT TREATISE ON NAVIGATION 445/2-11
  *SHELFMARK MS DOUCE 68 443-1, MS DOUCE 363 445/2-11
  *PROVENANCE ENGLISH
  *DATE EXECUTED 16TH
  *LANGUAGE ENGLISH
  *AUTHOR J DEE/ DR 445/2-11
  *TYPE OF MANUSCRIPT NAVIGATIONAL TREATISE 445/2-11
  *CONTENTS TUDOR MSS 445/1-11, NAVIGATION TREATISE 445/1-11,
  LONDON BRIDGE/ DRAWING 445-1, PLAN OF MILFORD HAVEN AND
  REMARKS OF SPANISH PREPARATIONS 445-3, ILLUSTRATION FROM JURIS
  BOOK OF PRISON CALLED CLYNK 445-4, GEORGE CAVENDISH'S LIFE OF
  WOLSEY 445-5, INITIAL M DECORATED WITH HERMIT-CRAB 445-5,
  WOLSEY RIDES IN PROCESSION TO WESTMINSTER 445-6, WOLSEY
  TRAVELS BY BARGE TO GREENWICH 445-7, WOLSEY'S TRAVEL FROM
  LONDON ON WAY TO FRANCE 445-8, WOLSEY DELIVERS GREAT SEAL TO
  DUKES/ NORFOLK/ SUFFOLK 445-9, KING HENRY VIII SENDS DOCTOR TO
  TREAT WOLSEY 445-10, WOLSEY'S FUNERAL IN ABBEY OF LESTER
  445-11

*$ABSTRACT 446
  *LIBRARY BOD
  *SLIDE SET TITLE LIFE OF WILLIAM OF WYKEHAM
  *NEGATIVE REFERENCE ROLL 214G
  *RENTAL FEE SM 446 $2.20
  *TITLE OF MANUSCRIPT CHAUNDLER MANUSCRIPT
  *SHELFMARK MS NEW COLLEGE 288
  *PROVENANCE ENGLISH
  *DATE EXECUTED 15TH/C1464
  *LANGUAGE ENGLISH
  *TYPE OF MANUSCRIPT BIOGRAPHY
  *CONTENTS LIFE OF WILLIAM OF WYKEHAM 446/1-4, WINCHESTER
  COLLEGE 446-1, WARDEN AND SCHOLARS 446-1, NEW COLLEGE 446-2,
  WARDEN AND SCHOLAR 446-2, PORTRAIT GROUP INCLUDING WILLIAM OF
  WYKEHAM 446-3, WELLS/ SOMERSET/ SHOWING THE CATHEDRAL 446-4

*$ABSTRACT 447
  *LIBRARY BOD
  *SLIDE SET TITLE TEWKESBURY BENEFACTOR'S BOOK
  *TITLE OF MANUSCRIPT TEWKESBURY BENEFACTOR'S BOOK
  *NEGATIVE REFERENCE ROLL 214H
  *RENTAL FEE SM 447 $3.25
  *SHELFMARK MS TOP GLOUC D 2
  *PROVENANCE ENGLISH
  *DATE EXECUTED 16TH/EARLY
  *LANGUAGE ENGLISH
  *TYPE OF MANUSCRIPT BENEFACTOR'S BOOK/ HERALDRY
  *CONTENTS BENEFACTOR'S BOOK   447/1-25,   HERALDRY/   ENGLISH
  447/1-25, WILLIAM EARL OF GLOUCESTER 447-1, ODDO AND DODDO/
  EARLS OF MERCIA 447-2, HUGH/ DUKE OF THE MERCIANS 447-3,
  HAYWARDUS MEAW AND ALGEISA 447-4, ROBERT SON OF HAYMO AND
  SIBILLA 447-5, SHIELDS/ ROBERT CHANDOS WITH MODEL OF
  TEWKESBURY ABBEY 447-6, ROBERT CONSUL AND WIFE MATILDA 447-7,
  JOHN/ SON OF HENRY II/ HERALDIC SHIELDS 447-8, HERALDRY
  447/1-25, RICHARD DE CLARE I/ EARL OF GLOUCESTER AND HERTFORD
  447-9, GILBERT I/ SON OF RICHARD 447-9, RICHARD DE CLARE II
  447-10, GILBERT II AND GILBERT III 447-11, HUGH II LE
  DESPENSER/ EARL OF GLOUCESTER 447-12, SHIELDS 447-13, HUGH III
  LE DESPENSER AND SHIELDS 447-14, EDWARD LE DESPENSER'S
  PORTRAIT/ SHIELDS 447-15, SHIELDS 447-16, THOMAS LE DESPENSER/
  PORTRAIT AND SHIELDS 447-17, SHIELDS/ ISABELLA LE DESPENSER
  BEFORE IMAGE OF VIRGIN 447-18, RICHARD LE BEAUCHAMP/ SHIELDS
  447-19, RICHARD DE BEAUCHAMP/ EARL OF WARWICK/ SHIELDS 447-20,
  ISABELLA DE DESPENSER/ TONSURED MONK HANDING BOOK TO LADY
  447-21, RICHARD NEVILL/ EARL OF WARWICK/ PORTRAIT 447-22,
  EDWARD/ SON OF HENRY VI 447-23, GEORGE/ DUKE OF CLARENCE/ AND
  SON EDWARD 447-24, HERALDIC PANELS WITH NAMES OF BEARERS
  447-25

*$ABSTRACT 448
  *LIBRARY BOD
  *SLIDE SET TITLE ENFANCIE DE NOSTRE SEIGNOUR
  *NEGATIVE REFERENCE ROLL 214L
  *RENTAL FEE SM 448 $5.00
  *TITLE OF MANUSCRIPT GESTA INFANTIAE SALVATORIS
  *COMMENTS ILLUSTRATIONS FROM APOCRYPHAL LIFE OF CHRIST
  *SHELFMARK MS SELDEN SUPRA 38
  *PROVENANCE FRENCH
  *DATE EXECUTED 14TH/C1320-30
  *LANGUAGE FRENCH
  *TYPE OF MANUSCRIPT APOCRYPHAL LIFE OF CHRIST
  *CONTENTS APOCRYPHAL LIFE OF CHRIST 448/1-60, MIRACLES OF
  JESUS/ APOCRYPHAL 448/1-60, ANNUNCIATION 448-1, NATIVITY
  448-2, MAGI SEE STAR GUIDING THEM 448-3, MAGI VISITING HEROD
  448-4, ADORATION OF MAGI AND THEIR DREAM 448-5, SLAUGHTER OF
  THE JEWISH CHILDREN 448-6, FLIGHT INTO EGYPT 448-7, HOLY
  FAMILY RESTING ON THEIR FLIGHT 448-8, TREE TOO HIGH FOR JESUS
  TO REACH 448-9, JESUS COMMANDS TREE TO BECOME STRAIGHT 448-10,
  MARY AND JOSEPH SITTING BESIDE TREE 448-11, ANGEL TAKES AWAY
  BRANCH OF TREE 448-12, ARRIVAL IN EGYPT 448-13, EGYPTIAN RULER
  AND EGYPTIANS KNEEL TO CHRIST 448-14, JESUS AND THE SEVEN
  POOLS 448-15, VIRGIN READING AND JESUS PLAYS 448-16, JESUS AND
  THE SPARROWS 448-17, JESUS SSTRUCK BY JEW WHO FALLS DEAD
  448-18, BOY LEAPING ON JESUS'S BACK 448-19, JESUS STRUGGLING
  WITH BOY 448-20, JESUS ON THE TWO MOUNDS 448-22, PARENTS ARGUE
  WITH JOSEPH/ JESUS RESTORES CHILDREN 448-23, JESUS AND THE
  WATER POTS 448-24, HOT DAY SO JESUS HANGS POT ON SUNBEAM
  448-25, JESUS MENDS WATERPOTS 448-26, BOY IN TOWER 448-27,
  JESUS HELPS BOY LEAVE TOWER 448-28, BOY'S FATHER ON TOWER IN
  FURY 448-29, JESUS AND HIS SECOND TEACHER 448-30, LEVI STRIKES
  JESUS ON FACE 448-31, JESUS HEALS CHILDREN WITH BROKEN LEGS
  448-32, JESUS REVIVES ZENO WHO HAS FALLEN 448-33, JESUS
  REVIVES ZENO WHO DECLARES HIM INNOCENT 448-34, JESUS SENT BY
  MARY TO FETCH WATER 448-35, BOY STRIKES JESUS'S POT/ HE BRINGS
  TO MARY WATER 448-36, JESUS AND HARVEST 448-37, JESUS AND OVEN
  448-38, PEOPLE ASTONISHED WHEN PIGS COME OUT OF OVEN 448-39,

JESUS ON SUNBEAM/ PARENTS COMPLAIN TO JOSEPH 448-40, PARENTS
COMPLAIN TO JOSEPH 448-41, JESUS ENCOURAGING CHILDREN TO
SCHOOL 448-42, JESUS AND TEACHER 448-43, JESUS AND DYER
448-44, JESUS LOWERS CLOTH INTO INDIGO 448-45, DYER IS ANGRY/
JESUS DRAWS OUT TWO-COLORED CLOTH 448-46, JESUS AND LIONS
448-47, JESUS HAS TAMED LIONS 448-48, JESUS AND BEAM OF WOOD
448-49, JESUS AND HIS TEACHERS 448-50, TEACHERS IN TEMPLE
448-51, JESUS HEALS SICK IN CAPERNAUM 448-52, JAMES BITTEN BY
VIPER 448-53, JESUS CURES JAMES/ VIPER DIES 448-54, FEAST
448-55, JESUS IN TEMPLE 448-56, MARRIAGE AT CANA 448-57, JESUS
CHANGES WATER TO WINE 448-58, JESUS TAKES LEAVE OF PARENTS
448-59, DONOR KNEELING HOLDING SCROLL 448-60

*$ABSTRACT 449
   *LIBRARY BOD
   *SLIDE SET TITLE FRANKLIN'S TALE BY GEOFFREY CHAUCER
   *NEGATIVE REFERENCE ROLL 215A
   *RENTAL FEE SM 449 $3.00
   *TITLE OF MANUSCRIPT PIERS PLOWMAN 449-1, ROMANCE OF ALEXANDER
   449/3 AND 9, ROMANCE OF THE ROSE 449/5-6 AND 8 AND 10, ROMANCE
   OF THE ROSE 449/13 AND 18 AND 20, LESTOIRE DE MERLIN 449-16,
   ROMANCE OF THE ROSE 449/11 AND 14 AND 19
   *SHELFMARK MS DOUCE 104 449-1, MS DOUCE 219-220 449-2, MS
   BODLEY 264 449/3 AND 9, MS RAWL LITURG E 36 449-4, MS SELDEN
   SUPRA 57 449/5 AND 10 AND 18, MS DOUCE 195 449/6 AND 8 AND 13
   AND 20, MS DOUCE 219-220 449-7, MS RAWL D 1220 449-12, MS
   BODLEY 270B 449-15, MS DOUCE 178 449-16, MS DOUCE 118 449-17
   *PROVENANCE ENGLISH 449/1 AND 12, FRENCH 449/4-6 AND 8 AND
   10-11 AND 14-15 AND 17-20, FLEMISH 449/2-3 AND 7 AND 9,
   ITALIAN 449-16
   *DATE EXECUTED 15TH 449/1-2 AND 5 AND 7-8 AND 11-14 AND 19-20,
   14TH 449/3 AND 5 AND 9-10 AND 17-18, 13TH 449-15
   *LANGUAGE ENGLISH 449/1 AND 12, FRENCH 449/3-6 AND 8-11 AND
   13-16 AND 18-20, LATIN 449/2 AND 7 AND 17
   *TYPE OF MANUSCRIPT ROMANCE 449/3-6 AND 8-11 AND 13-14 AND 16
   AND 18-20, BOOK OF HOURS 449/2 AND 7, ASTRONOMICAL TEXT
   449-12, PSALTER AND CALENDAR 449-17
   *CONTENTS FRANKLIN'S TALE BY GEOFFREY CHAUCER 449/1-20,
   LITERATURE/ FRANKLIN'S TALE 449/1-20, PILGRIM WITH TYPICAL
   HAT/ STAFF/ BELL/ SCRIP 449-1, DAVID PLAYING HARP BEFORE
   LADIES 449-2, KNIGHT ON HORSEBACK WITH ATTENDANTS 449-3, LADY
   AND SERVANT IN GARDEN 449-4, LOVE AS CROWNED GOD WITH
   COURTIERS 449-5, KNIGHTS AT BATTLE OF BENEVENTO 449-6,
   VISITATION 449-7, CLIFF WITH ROCKS IN SEA 449-8, CHESS PLAYED
   449-9, PEOPLE IN GARDEN 449-10, COURTLY GATHERING/ SINGING
   CAROLS/ DANCING 449-11, VENUS AND HER TYPICAL CHILDREN 449-12,
   LOVER DISTRESSED PRAYS TO GODS 449-13, LOVER IN BED DREAMING
   449-14, VAINGLORY OF ASTRONOMERS BROUGHT TO NAUGHT 449-15,
   MERLIN AS STAG ENTERING EMPEROR'S PALACE 449-16, JANUARY/
   JANUS FEASTING 449-17, SADNESS/ GIRL TEARING HER HAIR 449-18,
   WHEEL OF FORTUNE 449-19, LOVERS UNITED 449-20

*$ABSTRACT 450
   *LIBRARY BOD
   *SLIDE SET TITLE PARDONER'S TALE OF GEOFFREY CHAUCER
   *NEGATIVE REFERENCE ROLL 215B
   *RENTAL FEE SM 450 $2.50
   *TITLE OF MANUSCRIPT PIERS PLOWMAN 450-1, ROMANCE OF ALEXANDER
   450/2 AND 4-5 AND 9-10, MIRACLES DE LA VIERGE MARIE 450-3,
   L'EPITRE D'OTHEA 450-8
   *SHELFMARK MS DOUCE 104 450-1, MS BODLEY 264 450/2 AND 4-5 AND
   9-10, MS DOUCE 374 450-3, MS GOUGH LITURG 15 450-6, MS DOUCE
   135 450-7, MS BODLEY 421-8
   *PROVENANCE ENGLISH 450-1, FLEMISH 450/2-6 AND 9-10, FRENCH
   450/7-8
   *DATE EXECUTED 15TH 450/1 AND 3 AND 6 AND 8, 14TH 450/2 AND 4-5
   AND 9-10, 16TH 450-7
   *LANGUAGE ENGLISH 450-1, FRENCH 450/2-5 AND 8-10, LATIN 450/6-7

217

*TYPE OF MANUSCRIPT ROMANCE 450/2 AND 4-5 AND 8-10, BOOK OF
HOURS 450/6-7, MIRACLES OF THE VIRGIN 450-3
*CONTENTS PARDONER'S TALE OF CHAUCER 450/1-10, LITERATURE/
PARDONER'S TALE 450/1-10, PRIEST HOLDING PARDON 450-1, WEDDING
PROCESSION 450-2, PENITENT SCHOLAR HAS SKIN CHANGED BY VIRGIN
450-3, GAMBLERS 450-3, COOKS AT SALTIRE INN 450-4, INNKEEPER
SERVES CUSTOMER AT SALTIRE INN 450-5, PRIEST IN BURIAL SCENE
450-6, BOYS PLAYING WITH BALL/ DEATH SEIZES ONE 450-7, DEATH
PLAYS BALL WITH BOY 450-7, ATROPOS POINTS SPEAR AT POPE/
EMPEROR/ BISHOP/ KING 450-8, SWORD FIGHTING AS GAME 450-9,
FRIAR PREACHING FROM PULPIT TO FIVE PEOPLE 450-10

*$ABSTRACT 451
  *LIBRARY BOD
  *SLIDE SET TITLE JUSTICE
  *NEGATIVE REFERENCE ROLL 215C
  *RENTAL FEE SM 451 $3.05
  *TITLE OF MANUSCRIPT COMMENTARY ON JUSTINIAN 451-1, MAGNA CARTA
  451-2, LIFE OF ST MARGARET 451/6 AND 9, LETTER FROM OTHEA TO
  HECTOR 451-10, BOKE OF ASTRONOMY 451-11, CHRONICLE OF
  ALEXANDER 451-15, ACTES AND MONUMENTS 451-18, FALL OF PRINCES
  451-19, CAEDMON GENESIS 451-20
  *SHELFMARK MS DOUCE 29 451-1, MS HOLKHAM 206 451-2, MS MERTON
  COLLEGE 297B 451-3, MS ASTOR 4 451-5, MS DOUCE 41 451/6 AND 9,
  MS RAWL LITURG E 12 451-7, MS AUCT D INF 2 11 451-8, MS LAUD
  MISC 570 451-10, MS RAWL D 1220 451-11, MS RAWL E 12 451-12, MS
  C C C OXFORD 410 451-13, MS AUCT D INF 2 11 451-14, MS DOUCE
  313 451-13, MS LAUD MISC 751 451-16, MS LAUD MISC 476 451-17,
  MS DOUCE F 451-18, MS BODLEY 263 451-19, MS JUNIUS 11 451-20,
  MS DOUCE 93 451-21
  *PROVENANCE ITALIAN 451/1-2 AND 5-6 AND 9 AND 13 AND 17,
  ENGLISH 451/3-4 AND 11 AND 18-20, FLEMISH 451-16, DUTCH
  451-21, FRENCH 451/7-8 AND 10 AND 12 AND 14-16
  *DATE EXECUTED 16TH 451/1 AND 18, 15TH 451/4 AND 7-8 AND 10 AND
  12 AND 14 AND 16 AND 19 AND 21, 14TH 451/2 AND 5-6 AND 9, 13TH
  451-3, 11TH 451-20
  *AUTHOR CHRISTINE DE PISAN 451-10, LYDGATE/ JOHN 451-19
  *TYPE OF MANUSCRIPT BOOK OF HOURS 451/1 AND 7-8 AND 12 AND 14
  AND 21, MISSAL 451-15, ROMANCE 451/10 AND 16 AND 19, STATUTES
  451-4, SAINT'S LIFE 451/6 AND 9, DECRETALS 451-5
  *CONTENTS CONTENTS JUSTICE 451-21, LAW OF GOD/ TEN COMMANDMENTS
  GIVEN TO MOSES 451-1, ROMAN LAW 451-2, MAGNA CARTA 451-3,
  HENRY IV/ PORTRAIT 451-4, POPE WITH 4 CARDINALS 451-5, TRIAL/
  ACCUSED PLEADS 451-6, TRIAL/ PROSECUTION GIVING WITNESS 451-7,
  TRIAL OF CHRIST 451-8, TRIAL/ ACCUSED IS CONDEMNED 451-9,
  PRISONERS/ CONDEMNED LED TO BE EXECUTED 451-10, SATURN'S
  CHILDREN INCLUDE CRIMINALS 451-11, TORTURE USED TO EXTRACT
  CONFESSIONS AND AS PUNISHMENT 451-12, CHRIST CONDEMNED TO BE
  SCOURGED BEFORE CRUCIFIXION 451-13, CHRIST SCOURGED 451-14, ST
  THOMAS BECKET/ MARTYRDOM 451-15, CRIMINALS EXECUTED BY
  BEHEADING/ IN PUBLIC 451-16, CAPITAL PUNISHMENT/ SUICIDE OF
  JUDAS 451-17, JUDAS SUICIDE 451-17, CAPITAL PUNISHMENT/
  BURNING OF JOHN HOOPER 451-18, TEMPTATION OF ADAM AND EVE
  451-19, ADAM AND EVE/ TEMPTATION 451-19, CAIN KILLS ABEL
  451-20, LAST JUDGMENT 451-21

*$ABSTRACT 452
  *LIBRARY BOD
  *SLIDE SET TITLE CLERK'S TALE BY GEOFFREY CHAUCER
  *NEGATIVE REFERENCE ROLL 215D
  *RENTAL FEE SM 452 $2.90
  *TITLE OF MANUSCRIPT ROMANCE OF THE ROSE 452/1-2 AND 4, ROMANCE
  OF THE ROSE 452/6 AND 15 AND 17, CAESAR'S COMMENTARIES 452-3,
  BIBLE HISTORIALE 452/5 AND 12 AND 16, LIFE OF THE VIRGIN
  452-9, ROMAN DE LANCELOT DU LAC 452-11, BULL OF HONORIUS III
  452-14, ROMANCE OF ALEXANDER 452-18
  *SHELFMARK MS E MUSAEO 65 452-1, MS DOUCE 195 452/2 AND 4 AND
  15 AND 17, MS DOUCE 208 452-3, MS DOUCE 211 452/5 AND 12 AND

218

16, MS SELDEN SUPRA 57 452-6, MS C C C OXFORD 285 452/7-8, MS
DOUCE 79 452-9, MS BODLEY 764 452-10, MS DOUCE 199 452-11, MS
AUCT D INF 2 11 452-13, MS CHARTERS OXON A 8 452-14, MS BODLEY
264 452-18
*PROVENANCE FRENCH 452/1-2 AND 4-6 AND 11-13 AND 15-17, FLEMISH
452/3 AND 18, ENGLISH 452/7-10 AND 14
*DATE EXECUTED 13TH 452/7-8, 14TH 452/1 AND 5-6 AND 9 AND
11-12, 14TH 452/16 AND 18, 13TH 452/10 AND 14, 15TH 452/2-4
AND 13 AND 17
*LANGUAGE FRENCH AND LATIN
*AUTHOR GUILLAUME DE LORIS 452/1-2 AND 4 AND 15 AND 17
*TYPE OF MANUSCRIPT ROMANCE 452/1-2 AND 4 AND 6 AND 11 AND 15,
ROMANCE 452/17-18, BIBLE HISTORIALE 452/5 AND 12 AND 16,
PSALTER 452/7-8, LIFE OF THE VIRGIN 452-9, BESTIARY 452-10,
BOOK OF HOURS 452-13, PAPAL BULL 452-14
*CONTENTS CHAUCER/ ILLUSTRATIONS OF CLERK'S TALE FROM SEVERAL
MSS 452/1-18, LITERATURE/ CLERK'S TALE 452/1-18, CLERK'S TALE/
FROM SEVERAL MSS 452/1-18, JEAN DE MEUNG DRESSED AS CLERK
452-1, ATROPOS/ RAVAGES OF 452-2, LANDSCAPE 452-3, GERMANS
CROSSING RHINE 452-3, HUNT SCENE 452-4, DARIUS/ KING REMINDED
OF VOW TO REBUILD JERUSALEM 452-5, OLD AGE AS CRIPPLE ON
CRUTCHES 452-6, LABORERS ON LAND SOWING/ OCTOBER 452-7, REAPER
WITH HOOK/ JULY 452-8, NATIVITY 452-9, MILKING OF COW BY WOMAN
452-10, LADY ON WHITE HORSE ARRIVES AT ABBEY 452-11,
NEBUCHADNEZZAR GIVES ORDERS TO HOLOFERNES 452-12, HOLOFERNES
452-12, ST ANNE WITH VIRGIN MARY AS CHILD 452-13, PAPAL BULL
452-14, FORTUNE/ GODDESS AND HER WHEEL 452-15, WHEEL OF
FORTUNE 452-15, JOB TOLD OF DESTRUCTION OF FLOCKS 452-16, LADY
TRAVELLING WITH COURTLY RETINUE 452-17, FEAST 452-18

*$ABSTRACT 453
 *LIBRARY BOD
 *SLIDE SET TITLE TUDOR PRINTED BOOKS
 *NEGATIVE REFERENCE ROLL 214F
 *RENTAL FEE SM 453 $2.55
 *TITLE OF MANUSCRIPT EPISTOLA DE INSULIS NOVITER REPERTIS
 453-1, TRANSLATION OF TWO PLAYS OF EURIPIDES 453-2, FARRAGO
 NOVE EPISTOLARUM ERASMI 453-3, ASSERTIO APUD 7 SACRAMENTEM
 CONTRA M LUTHER 453-4, RULE OF SAYNT AUGUSTYNE 453-5, EIN
 GLAUBWIRDIGE ANZAYGUNG DES TODS HERRN THOME MORI 453-6, DE
 REVOLUTIONIBUS ORBIUM COELESTIUM 453-7, BOOK OF COMMON PRAYER
 453-8, L'ARITHMETIQUE 453-9, FAERIE QUEENE 453-10, TRAGICALL
 HISTORY OF DR FAUSTUS 453-11
 *SHELFMARK MS LAUD MISC 722 453-1, PRINTED BOOK BYW M 8 16
 453-2, PRINTED BOOK ALLEN D 19 453-3, PRINTED BOOK 4 H 6 TH
 SELD 453-4, MS DOUCE A 277 453-5, MS VET D 1 E 60 453-6, MS
 SELD D 40 453-8, PRINTED BOOK 8 521 ART 453-9, LONDON 1590 MAL
 615 453-10, PRINTED BOOK MAL 233 3 453-11
 *PROVENANCE ENGLISH 453/4-5 AND 8 AND 10-11, GERMAN 453/2 AND
 6-7, DUTCH 453-9, FRENCH 453-1
 *DATE EXECUTED 15TH 453-1, 16TH 453/2-10, 17TH 453-11
 *LANGUAGE ENGLISH AND LATIN AND FRENCH
 *AUTHOR CHRISTOPHER COLUMBUS 453-1, ERASMUS 453-2, HENRY VIII
 453-4, RICHARD WHITFORD 453-5, NICOLAUS COPERNICUS 453-7,
 SIMON STEVIN 453-9, EDMUND SPENSER 453-10, CHRISTOPHER MARLOWE
 453-11
 *TYPE OF MANUSCRIPT MISCELLANY
 *CONTENTS TUDOR PRINTED BOOKS 453/1-11, PRINTED BOOKS/ TUDOR
 453/1-11

*$ABSTRACT 454
 *LIBRARY BOD
 *SLIDE SET TITLE BESTIARY/ ENGLISH
 *NEGATIVE REFERENCE ROLL 217A
 *RENTAL FEE SM 454 $2.75
 *SHELFMARK MS DOUCE 88/ FOLS 5-50
 *PROVENANCE ENGLISH
 *DATE EXECUTED 13TH

*LANGUAGE LATIN
*TYPE OF MANUSCRIPT BESTIARY
*CONTENTS BESTIARY/ ENGLISH 454/1-15, LION/ SWEEPING TA}
454-1, LION ASLEEP WITH EYES OPEN 454-2, TIGER WITH GLASS BAI
454-3, PARD 454-4, UNICORN WITH VIRGIN SEATED IN CHAIR STABBI
BY HUNTER 454-5, LYNX 454-6, IBEX/ BREAKING FALL WITH HOF
NEAR TREE 454-7, HYENA DEVOURING CORPSES 454-8, BONNACC
MAKING REARGUARD ACTION AGAINST KNIGHTS 454-9, CAMEL AI
DROMEDARY 454-10, CALADRIUS FACING RECOVERING PATIENT IN BI
454-11, EAGLE 454-12, OWL AND SIREN 454-13, PERINDEUS 454-14
ADAM AND EVE TURNED OUT OF EDEN 454-15

*$ABSTRACT 455
  *LIBRARY BOD
  *SLIDE SET TITLE MONSTERS AND PORTENTS
  *NEGATIVE REFERENCE ROLL 217B
  *RENTAL FEE SM 455 $2.55
  *SHELFMARK MS DOUCE 88
  *PROVENANCE ENGLISH
  *DATE EXECUTED 13TH
  *LANGUAGE LATIN
  *TYPE OF MANUSCRIPT BESTIARY
  *CONTENTS BESTIARY 455/1-11, MONSTERS AND PORTENTS 455/1-11
  GOAT 455-1, ARABIAN CAMEL 455-2, LION FOLLOWED BY HUNTSMA
  WITH HORN 455-3, LION LICKS ANDRONICUS 455-4, BEAR LICKING CU
  INTO SHAPE 455-5, HUNTSMAN GRABBING UNICORN WITH HEAD I
  MAIDEN'S LAP 455-6, GRYPHON 455-7, ELEPHANT AND CASTLE 455-8
  MANTICORA 455-9, MONKEYS WITH YOUNG BEING PURSUED BY HUNTSME
  AND HOUNDS 455-10, BONNACON WITH BULL-LIKE HEAD AND RAM'
  HORNS 455-11

*$ABSTRACT 456
  *LIBRARY BOD
  *SLIDE SET TITLE ILLUSTRATIONS FROM PORTABLE PSALTER II
  *NEGATIVE REFERENCE ROLL 210I
  *RENTAL FEE SM 456 $5.35
  *SHELFMARK MS DOUCE 5
  *PROVENANCE FLEMISH/ GHENT
  *DATE EXECUTED 14TH/C1320-30
  *LANGUAGE LATIN
  *TYPE OF MANUSCRIPT PSALTER/ PORTABLE
  *CONTENTS PSALTER/ PORTABLE 456/1-67, INITIALS/ DECORATIV
  456/1-67, LINE-ENDINGS/ DECORATIVE 456/1-67, GOLDFINCH
  TONSURED HEAD/ BOAR'S HEAD/ SHEPHERD WITH CROOK 456-1, RABBIT
  BLUE TIT/ APE HOLDING POLE 456-2, HUMAN HEAD WEARING CAP
  BEAST'S HEAD/ MAN IN TUNIC 456-3, RABBIT/ BLUE TIT/ APE
  PLAYING INSTRUMENTS 456-4, BAGPIPES PLAYED/ PEACOCK'S HEA
  456-4, BIRD/ HARES/ APE ON GROTESQUE ONE BLOWING TRUMPE
  456-5, CAT WITH RAT IN ITS MOUTH/ KNIGHT WITH SWORD 456-6
  DEVIL-GROTESQUE 456-6, WOMAN IN ROBE WITH CHAPLET/ ANGEL WIT
  POINTED HAT 456-6, FIGURE BLOWING TRUMPET/ DOG'S HEAD
  UNICORN'S HEAD/ PHYSICIAN 456-7, BIRD'S HEAD/ BEAST'S HEADS
  WOMAN'S HEAD/ MAN BLOWING TRUMPET 456-9, HUMAN HEADS
  UNICORN'S HEAD/ STAG'S HEAD/ BEAST'S HEADS 456-10, HUMA
  HEADS/ UNICORN'S HEAD/ BIRD'S HEAD 456-11, HUMAN HEADS/ ANIMA
  HEADS/ WOMAN SPINNING 456-12, HUMAN HEADS/ HOODED AND ONE WIT
  BEARD 456-13, MONK PREACHING/ VEILED WOMAN'S HEAD/ ANIMA
  HEADS 456-14, FIGURE IN RED ROBE/ HEAD OF STAG/ UNICORN
  ANIMALS 456-15, INITIAL WITH ANIMAL'S HEAD/ VEILED LADY/ BLU
  TITS 456-16, HEADS/ UNICORN'S HEAD AND ANIMALS 456-17, HOODE
  MAN'S HEAD/ STAG'S HEAD/ UNICORN HEAD 456-19, INITIAL WIT
  HEAD OF SOLDIER/ ARMORED 456-20, HEADS/ HOODED/ HATLESS
  ANIMAL 456-21, BLANK FOLIOS 456-22, CHRIST OF PITY/ INITIAL D
  DEUS 456-23, MAN WITH SWORD AND SHIELD 456-24, FIGURE POKE
  SPOON AT MONK'S HEAD/ ANIMAL HEAD 456-25, HUMAN HEADS/ DANCER
  UNICORN HEAD 456-26, UNICORN HEADS/ VEILED WOMAN'S HEA
  456-27, INITIAL WITH WOMAN'S HEAD 456-28, INITIAL WITH QUEEN'
  HEAD/ APES/ BIRD/ SICKLE/ HEADS 456-29, MONK/ COWLED/ SHEEP'

HEAD BLOWING TRUMPET/ UNICORN'S HEAD 456-30, INITIAL WITH APE/
BLUE TIT/ RABBITS/ UNICORN/ ANIMALS 456-31, KNIGHT IN ARMOR/
SHIELD/ PENNON 456-32, BISHOP PREACHING TO APE/ BIRD/ RABBIT/
STAG'S HEAD 456-33, HEADS OF UNICORN/ STAG/ BIRD/ ANIMALS
456-34, HUMAN HEADS/ BIRDS' HEADS 456-35, ARREST OF CHRIST/ ST
PETER WITH RAISED SWORD 456-36, HEADS OF UNICORN/ WOMAN IN
WIMPLE/ HUMANS 456-37, HEADS/ MUSICIAN PLAYING GITTERN 456-38,
MUSICIAN WITH GITTERN 456-38, SQUIRREL/ RABBIT/ APES/ ARCHER
SHOOTING AT GREAT TIT 456-39, HUMAN HEADS WITH HEADDRESSES
456-40, INITIAL WITH MAN'S HEAD/ GROTESQUE/ GREAT TIT 456-41,
ANIMALS AND KNIGHT FIGHTING WINGED-LION TYPE MONSTER 456-42,
HEADS OF UNICORN/ WOMAN/ MUSICIAN PLAYING TRUMPET 456-43,
INITIAL WITH TWO HEADS 456-44, MONK BLESSING HUMAN HEADS
456-45, HEADS 456-46, PEACOCK'S HEAD/ ANIMAL'S HEAD WITH SPEAR
IN ITS MOUTH 456-47, MAN WITH SPEAR/ NAKED CHILD/ WOMAN WITH
UNICORN'S HORN 456-48, MAN BLOWING TRUMPET/ UNICORN'S HEAD
456-49, JUGGLER/ RABBIT PLAYING PSALTERY 456-50, PSALTERY
456-50, HEADS/ VARIOUS 456-51, KING'S HEAD/ OTHER HEADS
456-52, PERFORMING BEAR/ HAWK/ MAN BLOWING TRUMPET 456-53,
HEADS 456-54, HEADS/ VARIED 456-55, MAN WITH GOLDEN JAR/
HUMAN-HEADED DOG/ GOLD FINCH/ UNICORN 456-56, FIGURES AND
HEADS 456-57, HEADS/ BEARDED/ HOODED/ WIMPLED/ STAG'S 456-58,
HANDS IN PRAYER/ GOAT'S HEAD 456-59, KNIGHT CARRYING SHIELD/
GROTESQUE/ AMMONITE-LIKE MONSTER 456-61, HEADS 456-62, ANGEL
BLOWING TRUMPET/ DEVIL/ MONSTER/ HEADS 456-63, DEVIL 456-63,
HEADS 456-64, MAN IN ROBE/ WOMAN READING 456-65, MAN HOLDING
HUGE AX/ HEAD OF WOMAN AND GOAT 456-66, HEADS OF WOMAN/ MAN/
GOAT/ ANIMALS AND BIRD 456-67

*$ABSTRACT 457
  *LIBRARY BOD
  *SLIDE SET TITLE NEW TESTAMENT INITIALS
  *NEGATIVE REFERENCE ROLL 210G
  *RENTAL FEE SM 457 $2.60
  *SHELFMARK MS NEW COLLEGE 7
  *PROVENANCE FRENCH
  *DATE EXECUTED 13TH
  *LANGUAGE LATIN
  *TYPE OF MANUSCRIPT BIBLE
  *CONTENTS INITIALS/ NEW TESTAMENT 457/1-12, NEW TESTAMENT
INITIALS 457/1-12, INITIAL M/ MATHEUS 457-1, ST MATTHEW
WRITING GOSPEL 457-1, INITIAL I/ INITIUM 457-2, ST MARK/
WRITING/ THUMB CUT OFF/ LED TO EXECUTION 457-2, INITIAL P/
PAULUS 457-3, PAUL DELIVERS EPISTLE TO ROMANS AS YOUNG MAN
457-3, INITIAL P/ PAULUS 457-4, CHRIST WITH BOOK LISTENED TO
BY MEN 457-4, INITIAL P/ PAULUS 457-5, PAUL HANDS SCROLL TO
TIMOTHY 457-5, SATAN TAKES HYMENEUS AND ALEXANDER 457-5,
INITIAL P/ PAULUS 457-6, PAUL IN PRISON WRITES TO TIMOTHY
457-6, ASIAN MEN TURN AWAY FROM BIBLE 457-6, INITIAL M/
MULTIFARIUM 457-7, PAUL PREACHES TO JEWS 457-7, INITIAL P/
PRIMUM QUIDEM 457-8, ST LUKE WITH OX HEAD/ WRITING TO
THEOPHILUS 457-8, INITIAL I/ IACOBUS JESU CHRISTI SERVUS
457-9, ST JAMES AND TWELVE HEADS OF TRIBES 457-9, INITIAL S/
SIMON PETRUS 457-10, LUCIFER/ FALL OF ANGELS 457-10, FALL OF
ANGELS 457-10, INITIAL A/ APOCALYSIS 457-11, ST JOHN KNEELING
BEFORE CHRIST 457-11, CANON TABLE/ EXAMPLE OF 457-12

*$ABSTRACT 458
  *LIBRARY BOD
  *SLIDE SET TITLE PSALM INITIALS
  *SHELFMARK MS NEW COLLEGE 7
  *NEGATIVE REFERENCE ROLL 210H
  *RENTAL FEE SM 458 $2.95
  *PROVENANCE FRENCH
  *DATE EXECUTED 13TH
  *LANGUAGE LATIN
  *TYPE OF MANUSCRIPT BIBLE
  *CONTENTS BIBLE 458/1-9, INITIALS/ PSALM 458/1-9, INITIAL D/

221

DOMINUS ILLUMINATIO 458-1, GOD STANDING AND DAVID KNEELIN
POINTING TO EYE 458-1, INITIAL D/ DIXIT CUSTODIAM 458-2, GO
STANDING/ DAVID KNEELING POINTING TO MOUTH 458-2, INITIAL D
DIXIT INSIPIENS 458-3, FOOL WEARING MITRE WITH CLUB 458-3
INITIAL Q/ QUID 458-4, DOEG INFORMS SAUL OF DAVID'S CONSPIRAC
458-4, INITIAL S/ SALVUM ME FAC 458-5, GOD REACHING TO DAVI
IN SEA 458-5, INITIAL E/ EXULTATE 458-6, GOD BETWEEN ANGEL
AND MUSICIANS 458-6, INITIAL C/ CANTATE DOMINO 458-7, SHEPHER
WITH SHEEP AND GOATS 458-7, INITIAL D/ DOMINE EXAUDI 458-8
DAVID KNEELING AND GOD ABOVE 458-8, INITIAL D/ DIXIT DOMINU
DOMINO 458-9, GOD AND CHRIST SEATED 458-9

*$ABSTRACT 459
  *LIBRARY BOD
  *SLIDE SET TITLE COMMENTARY ON THE APOCALYSE
  *NEGATIVE REFERENCE ROLL 130B
  *RENTAL FEE SM 459 $3.10
  *TITLE OF MANUSCRIPT COMMENTARY ON THE APOCALYPSE
  *SHELFMARK MS BODLEY 352
  *PROVENANCE GERMAN
  *DATE EXECUTED 12TH/ EARLY
  *LANGUAGE LATIN
  *AUTHOR HAIMO/ BISHOP OF AUXERE
  *TYPE OF MANUSCRIPT COMMENTARY ON APOCALYPSE
  *CONTENTS COMMENTARY ON THE APOCALYPSE 459/1-22, APOCALYPS
  COMMENTARY 459/1-22, PRESENTATION OF MS BY RUDOLPHUS TO S
  BLAISE 459-1, APOSTLES ON FOUNDATION OF WALLS OF JERUSALE
  459-2, ANGELS/ TRUMPETS/ HAND OF GOD 459-2, GOD WITH ANGELS
  JOHN AT FOOT OF CHRIST 459-3, ST JOHN HANDS SCROLL TO ANGEL O
  PERGAMOS 459-4, DEVOUT LISTEN TO JOHN/ SCROLL TO ANGEL O
  LAODICEA 459-4, ST JOHN BEHOLDS VISION OF ENTHRONED GOD
  RAINBOW/ LAMPS 459-4, BEAST WITH MANY EYES/ ELDER AND JOH
  WATCH 459-5, ANGELS WITH VIALS/ ELDERS WITH HARPS/ SEA/ FISHE
  459-5, BEASTS/ LAMBS OF GOD/ ANGEL WITH SCROLL 459-6, HORSES
  RIDERS/ LAMB OF GOD/ DOVE/ DEATH ON HORSE 459-6, STAR AN
  MOON/ EARTHQUAKE/ HEADS OF KINGS IN HIDING 459-6, ANGELS HOL
  WINDS/ TRIBES OF ISRAEL 459-7, ANGEL/ BEASTS/ LAMB OF GOD
  459-7, ELDERS EXPLAIN JOHN'S VISION OF MULTITUDES 459-7
  ANGELS BLOWING TRUMPETS 459-8, ANGEL FILLS CENSER WITH FIRE
  SEA/ FISHES 459-8, ANGEL/ THIRD SOUNDS TRUMPET 459-8, ANGEL
  SIXTH SOUNDS TRUMPET 459-9, HORSES WITH LION'S HEADS DEVOURIN
  MEN 459-9, ANGEL/ JOHN MARVELS 459-9, BEAST MAKING WAR ON ME
  459-10, ANGEL/ SEVENTH SOUNDS TRUMPET 459-10, WOMAN CLOTHE
  WITH SUN AND DRAGON 459-10, ST MICHAEL AND ANGELS FIGHT DRAGO
  459-11, WOMAN GIVEN WINGS TO ESCAPE DRAGON 459-11, BEAST WIT
  HORNS LIKE LAMB BRINGING FIRE FROM HEAVEN 459-11, LAMB O
  MOUNT SION 459-12, ANGEL WITH GOSPEL/ ANGEL POINTING TO FALLE
  BABYLON 459-12, FALL OF BABYLON 459-12, ANGEL WARNS O
  WORSHIPPING BEAST 459-12, VISION OF ANGEL WITH SON OF GOD WIT
  SICKLE 459-13, ANGELS/ SEVEN WITH PLAGUES 459-13, BLESSED WIT
  HARPS ON SEA OF FIRE 459-13, TABERNACLE/ ANGELS WITH GOLDE
  GIRDLES 459-14, ANGELS POUR WRATH OF GOD OVER ENTIRE EART
  459-14, ANGEL SHOWS JOHN GREAT WHORE OF BABYLON 459-14, WHOR
  OF BABYLON 459-14, ANGEL/ BABYLON FALLING/ MERCHANTS LEAVIN
  BABYLON 459-15, ANGELS WITH TRUMPETS/ HARPS/ VIOLS 459-15, GO
  WITH FOUR BEASTS AND ELDERS WORSHIPPING 459-16, FAITHFUL AN
  TRUE ON HIS WHITE HORSE 459-16, ANGEL STANDING IN SUN CALLIN
  FOR FOWLS 459-16, ANGEL BINDING DEVIL AND CASTING HIM INTO PI
  459-17, DEVIL 459-17, ANGELS CLOTHING SOULS OF THE BLESSE
  459-17, DEAD/ SMALL AND GREAT BEING JUDGED 459-17, GO
  SURROUNDED BY ANGELS JUDGING THE BLESSED 459-18, DAMNE
  CARRIED OFF BY DEVILS 459-18, VISION OF HEAVENLY JERUSALE
  459-19, GOD SHOWING VISION TO JOHN WHO INSCRIBES IT 459-20
  LAMB OF GOD/ TREE OF LIFE/ RIVER WITH FISHES 459-20, JOHN A
  FEET OF ANGEL WHO SHOWED HIM VISIONS 459-20, INITIAL L/ JOH
  WITH SCROLL AND MATTHEW WITH BOOK 459-21, INITIAL V 459-22

222

*$ABSTRACT 460
  *LIBRARY BOD
  *SLIDE SET TITLE APOCALYPSE
  *NEGATIVE REFERENCE FILMSTRIPS SERIES 11 NO 15 JACOB'S LADDER
  *RENTAL FEE SM 460 $5.00
  *COMMENTS 60 SLIDES FROM 3 ENGLISH MSS OF THE 13TH CENTURY
  *TITLE OF MANUSCRIPT DOUCE APOCALYPSE 460/1-3 AND 6 AND 10-35
  AND 38-39, DOUCE APOCALYPSE 460/54 AND 57-60
  *SHELFMARK MS DOUCE 180 460/1-3 AND 6 AND 10-35 AND 38-39, MS
  DOUCE 180 460/54 AND 57-60, MS CANON BIBL LAT 62 460/4-5 AND 7
  AND 9, MS AUCT D 17 4 460/8 AND 40 AND 56
  *PROVENANCE ENGLISH
  *DATE EXECUTED 13TH
  *LANGUAGE LATIN
  *TYPE OF MANUSCRIPT APOCALYPSE
  *CONTENTS APOCALYPSE PICTURES 460/1-60, ST JOHN OF PATMOS TOLD
  TO WRITE BY ANGEL 460-1, REV 1 VERSES 10-11/ LETTERS TO SEVEN
  CHURCHES 460-1, CHRIST AMID SEVEN CANDLESTICKS 460-2, REV 1
  VERSES 12-20/ SEVEN CANDLESTICKS 460-2, CHRIST WITH TWO-EDGED
  SWORD IN MOUTH 460-3, REV 2 VERSES 12-17/ CHRIST WITH
  TWO-EDGED SWORD 460-3, SCRIBE/ ST JOHN WITH PEN AND KNIFE AND
  INK-POT 460-3, CHRIST IN MAJESTY/ TWENTY-FOUR ELDERS 460-4,
  REV 4 VERSES 1-11/ VISION OF CHRIST IN MAJESTY 460-4, ST
  JOHN'S VISION OF LAMB 460-5, REV 4 VERSES 1-14/ VISION OF LAMB
  WITH BOOK 460-5, LAMB OPENS FIRST SEAL/ WHITE HORSE 460-6, REV
  6 VERSES 1-2/ OPENING OF FIRST SEAL 460-6, LAMB OPENS SECOND
  SEAL/ RED HORSE 460-7, REV 6 VERSES 3-4/ OPENING OF SECOND
  SEAL 460-7, LAMB OPENS THIRD SEAL/ BLACK HORSE 460-8, REV 6
  VERSES 5-6/ OPENING OF THIRD SEAL 460-8, LAMB OPENS FOURTH
  SEAL/ PALE HORSE 460-9, HELL MOUTH 460-9, DEATH 460-9, DEVIL
  460-9, LAMB OPENS FIFTH SEAL/ SLAIN SOULS RECEIVE WHITE STOLES
  460-10, REV 6 VERSES 9-11/ OPENING OF FIFTH SEAL 460-10, LAMB
  OPENS SIXTH SEAL/ EARTHQUAKE 460-11, REV 6 VERSES 12-17/
  OPENING OF SIXTH SEAL 460-11, REV 7 VERSES 1-3/ FOUR WINDS
  460-12, ST JOHN'S VISION OF THE MULTITUDE WITH PALMS 460-13,
  REV 8 VERSES 9-17/ VISION OF MULTITUDE 460-13, ANGEL CASTS
  CENSER WITH FIRE OVER THE EARTH 460-14, REV 8 VERSES 3-5/ FIRE
  CAST OVER THE EARTH 460-14, ANGEL/ FIRST SOUNDS TRUMPET/ HAIL
  AND FIRE 460-15, REV 8 VERSES 1-7/ FIRST ANGEL SOUNDS TRUMPET
  460-15, ANGEL/ SECOND SOUNDS TRUMPET/ MOUNTAIN CAST INTO SEA
  460-16, SHIPS/ WRECKED 460-16, REV 8 VERSES 8-9/ SECOND ANGEL
  SOUNDS TRUMPET 460-16, ANGEL/ THIRD SOUNDS TRUMPET/ STAR FALLS
  ON WATERS 460-17, REV 8 VERSES 10-11/ STAR FALLS ON WATERS
  460-17, ANGEL/ FOURTH SOUNDS TRUMPET/ SUN/ MOON/   STARS
  DARKENED 460-18, REV 8 VERSE 12/ FOURTH ANGEL SOUNDS TRUMPET
  460-18, ST JOHN HEARS VOICE OF GREAT EAGLE 460-19, REV 8 VERSE
  13/ JOHN HEARS EAGLE 460-19, ANGEL/ FIFTH SOUNDS TRUMPET/
  LOCUSTS EMERGE FROM PIT 460-20, APOLLYON/ KING OF THE PIT
  460-20, REV 9 VERSES 1-11/ LOCUSTS 460-20, ANGEL/ SIXTH SOUNDS
  TRUMPET/ ANGELS RELEASED FROM EUPHRATES 460-21, HORSEMEN OF
  APOCALYPSE KILLS A THIRD PART OF MEN 460-21, REV 9 VERSES
  14-16/ ANGELS RELEASED FROM EUPHRATES 460-21, ST JOHN OF
  PATMOS AND ANGELS 460-22, REV 10 VERSES 1-11/ JOHN AND ANGELS
  460-22, APOCALYPSE/ TWO WITNESSES KILL ENEMIES 460-23, REV 11
  VERSES 3-6/ TWO WITNESSES 460-23, WITNESSES KILL PEOPLE
  460-23, BEAST/ APOCALYPTIC KILLS WITNESSES 460-24, REV 11
  VERSES 7-10/ BEAST KILLS WITNESSES 460-24, WITNESSES ASCEND
  INTO HEAVEN 460-25, EARTHQUAKE 460-25, REV 11 VERSES 11-13/
  WITNESSES ASCEND INTO HEAVEN 460-25, ANGEL/ SEVENTH SOUNDS
  TRUMPET 460-26, REV 11 VERSES 15-18/ SEVENTH ANGEL SOUNDS
  TRUMPET 460-26, ST JOHN'S VISION OF TEMPLE 460-27, REV 11
  VERSE 19/ VISION OF TEMPLE 460-27, WOMAN CLOTHED IN THE SUN
  460-28, DRAGON AND WOMAN/ MAN-CHILD DELIVERED 460-28, REV 12
  VERSES 1-6/ DRAGON AND WOMAN 460-28, ST MICHAEL FIGHTS DRAGON
  460-29, DRAGON AND ST MICHAEL 460-29, REV 12 VERSES 7-9/ ST
  MICHAEL AND DRAGON 460-29, ST MICHAEL AND DRAGON 460-29,
  DRAGON TRIES TO CAPTURE WOMAN 460-30, REV 12 VERSES 13-18/
  DRAGON AND WOMAN 460-30, BEAST/ APOCALYPTIC RISES FROM SEA
  460-31, REV 13 VERSES 1-4/ BEAST RISES FROM SEA 460-31, BEAST/
  APOCALYPTIC KILLS SAINTS WITH SWORD 460-32, REV 13 VERSES 7-9/
  BEAST KILLS SAINTS 460-32, BEAST MARKS FOREHEADS OF BELIEVERS
  460-33, REV 13 VERSES 11-18/ BEAST MARKS BELIEVERS 460-33,

LAMB WORSHIPED BY BELIEVERS DEPICTED AS LAMBS 460-34, REV 1
VERSES 1-5/ LAMB AND BELIEVERS 460-34, CHRIST IN MAJEST
460-35, REV 14 VERSE 3/ CHRIST IN MAJESTY 460-35, ANGEL WARN
THOSE WHO ADORE BEAST 460-36, REV 14 VERSES 9-11/ ANGEL WARN
FOLLOWERS OF BEAST 460-36, SOULS OF FAITHFUL LEAVING BODIE
460-37, REV 14 VERSE 13/ THE FAITHFUL 460-37, CHRIST WIT
SICKLE 460-38, REV 14 VERSES 14-16/ CHRIST REAPS CORN 460-38
ANGEL GATHERS GRAPES WITH SICKLE 460-39, WINEPRESS OF GC
460-39, REV 14 VERSES 17-20/ WINEPRESS 460-39, FAITHFUL ON SE
OF GLASS WITH HARPS 460-40, REV 15 VERSES 2-4/ FAITHFUL ON SE
OF GLASS 460-40, ANGELS/ APOCALYPTIC EMPTY THREE FLASK
460-41, REV 16 VERSES 1-7/ ANGELS EMPTY FLASKS ON EART
460-41, ANGEL/ FOURTH EMPTIES FLASK/ MEN BLASPHEME 460-42, RE
16 VERSES 8-9/ FOURTH ANGEL EMPTIES FLASK 460-42, ANGELS
FIFTH AND SIXTH EMPTY FLASKS 460-43, REV 16 VERSES 10-12
5TH-AND-6TH ANGELS EMPTY FLASKS 460-43, ANGEL/ SEVENTH EMPTIE
FLASK/ EARTHQUAKE 460-44, REV 16 VERSES 17-21/ SEVENTH ANGE
EMPTIES FLASK 460-44, WHORE OF BABYLON 460-45, REV 17 VERSE
1-2/ WHORE OF BABYLON 460-45, WHORE OF BABYLON RIDING BEAS
460-46, REV 17 VERSES 3-18/ WHORE OF BABYLON ON BEAST 460-46
FALL OF BABYLON 460-47, DEVIL AND UNCLEAN BIRDS 460-47, REV 1
VERSES 1-3/ FALL OF BABYLON 460-47, ANGEL/ APOCALYPTIC THROW
MILLSTONE INTO SEA 460-48, REV 18 VERSES 21-24/ MILLSTON
THROWN INTO SEA 460-48, ST JOHN HEARS VOICES OF FAITHFU
460-49, REV 19 VERSES 1-6/ DEFEAT OF GREAT WHORE 460-49, LAME
MARRIAGE 460-50, REV 19 VERSES 7-9/ MARRIAGE OF LAMB 460-50
ANGEL CALLS FAITHFUL TO MARRIAGE OF LAMB 460-51, REV 19 VERS
9/ MARRIAGE OF LAMB 460-51, ST JOHN OF PATMOS/ VISION OF WHIT
HORSE 460-52, CHRIST IN WINEPRESS 460-52, REV 19 VERSES 11-16
CHRIST IN WINEPRESS 460-52, WINEPRESS/ CHRIST IN 460-52
BEAST/ APOCALYPTIC AND KINGS OF EARTH 460-53, ANGEL LOCK
DRAGON IN BOTTOMLESS PIT 460-54, DRAGON IN BOTTOMLESS PI
460-54, REV 20 VERSES 1-3/ DRAGON LOCKED IN PIT 460-54, DEVI
EMERGES FROM PIT 460-55, GOG AND MAGOG 460-55, REV 20 VERSE
7-9/ DEVIL/ GOG AND MAGOG 460-55, BEAST/ DEVIL/ FALSE PROPHE
CAST INTO HELL 460-56, DEVIL CAST INTO HELL 460-56, REV 2
VERSES 9-10/ CAST INTO HELL 460-56, LAST JUDGMENT/ BLESSED AN
DAMNED 460-57, DAMNED AS MURDERERS AND IDOLATERS 460-57, RE
20 VERSES 11-15/ LAST JUDGMENT 460-57, ST JOHN OF PATMOS
VISION OF NEW JERUSALEM 460-58, REV 21 VERSES 9-27/ VISION C
NEW JERUSALEM 460-58, CHRIST IN MAJESTY/ RIVER OF LIFE 460-59
REV 22 VERSES 1-2/ RIVER OF LIFE 460-59, CHRIST AND ST JOH
460-60, REV 22 VERSES 16-21/ ST JOHN AND CHRIST 460-60

*$ABSTRACT 461
  *LIBRARY BOD
  *SLIDE SET TITLE APOCALYPSE
  *NEGATIVE REFERENCE ROLL 139C
  *RENTAL FEE SM 461 $3.05
  *TITLE OF MANUSCRIPT DOUCE APOCALYPSE
  *SHELFMARK MS DOUCE 180
  *PROVENANCE ENGLISH
  *DATE EXECUTED 13TH/ BEFORE 1272
  *LANGUAGE LATIN AND FRENCH
  *TYPE OF MANUSCRIPT APOCALYPSE WITH COMMENTARY
  *CONTENTS APOCALYPSE/ DOUCE 461/1-21, SEVEN CHURCHES 461-1
  LETTER TO CHURCH AT SMYRNA 461-2, LION OF JUDAH LIES AMON
  TREE ROOTS WITH BOOK 461-3, LAMB 461-4, OPENING OF FOURTH SEA
  461-5, ANGEL OF THE WINDS 469-6, OPENING OF SEVENTH SEA
  461-7, LOCUSTS 461-8, MEASURING THE TEMPLE 461-9, JUDGMEN
  461-10, WOMAN CLOTHED WITH THE SUN 461-11, DRAGON AND SEED C
  WOMAN 461-12, BEAST FROM SEA AND BEAST FROM EARTH 461-13, LAM
  ON MOUNT SION 461-14, VINEYARD OF THE EARTH 461-15, MERCHAN
  AND KINGS LAMENT OVER BABYLON 461-16, ANGEL WITH THE MILLSTON
  461-17, MARRIAGE IN HEAVEN 461-18, SIEGE OF HOLY CITY 461-1
  JUDGMENT 461-20, NEW JERUSALEM 461-21

*$ABSTRACT 462
 *LIBRARY BOD
 *SLIDE SET TITLE HORSES AND HARNESS
 *NEGATIVE REFERENCE ROLL 166J
 *RENTAL FEE SM 462 $2.30
 *TITLE OF MANUSCRIPT DOUCE APOCALYPSE
 *SHELFMARK MS DOUCE 180
 *PROVENANCE ENGLISH
 *DATE EXECUTED 13TH/ BEFORE 1272
 *LANGUAGE LATIN AND FRENCH
 *TYPE OF MANUSCRIPT APOCALYPSE WITH COMMENTARY
 *CONTENTS HORSES AND HARNESS 462/1-6, APOCALYPSE/ DOUCE
 462/1-6, RIDER ON WHITE HORSE/ FIRST SEAL 462-1, RED HORSE
 GALLOPING WITH RIDER 462-2, SEAL/ SECOND 462-2, RIDER ON BLACK
 HORSE/ THIRD SEAL 462-3, HORSEMEN ON LION-HEADED HORSES 462-4,
 TROOP OF MEN ON WHITE HORSES/ LEADER IS CHRIST 462-5, BATTLE
 WITH THE BEAST/ CHRIST AND ARMY ON HORSEBACK 462-6

*$ABSTRACT 463
 *LIBRARY BOD
 *SLIDE SET TITLE ARTIST AT WORK
 *NEGATIVE REFERENCE ROLL 166L
 *RENTAL FEE SM 463 $2.80
 *TITLE OF MANUSCRIPT DOUCE APOCALYPSE
 *SHELFMARK MS DOUCE 180
 *PROVENANCE ENGLISH
 *DATE EXECUTED 13TH/ BEFORE 1272
 *LANGUAGE LATIN AND FRENCH
 *TYPE OF MANUSCRIPT APOCALYPSE WITH COMMENTARY
 *CONTENTS   ARTIST   AT   WORK/ UNFINISHED ILLUMINATIONS 463/1-16,
 APOCALYPSE/ DOUCE 463/1-16, ANGEL POURS CONTENTS OF SIXTH VIAL
 INTO EUPHRATES 463-1, LAMENT/ MEN TEARING HAIR/ AND WOMAN IN
 BABYLON 463-2, ANGEL SUMMONS BIRDS OF PREY TO DEVOUR FLESH
 463-3, CHRIST'S ARMY VICTORIUS/ BEAST IN HOLE BENEATH GROUND
 463-4, DEVIL, FEET CHAINED GATHERS ARMY 463-5, CHRIST ON
 RAINBOW JUDGING SOULS/ HELL MOUTHS 463-6, HELL MOUTH 463-6,
 CHRIST   ON   RAINBOW ADDRESSING ST JOHN 463-7, HEADS OF
 463-8, CHRIST'S WORDS/ RECEIVED BY JUST/ WITH SORROW BY
 UNRIGHTEOUS 463-9, CHRIST WITH SAINTS/ LAMB/ BEAST SLAYING
 SAINTS 463-10, MARK OF THE BEAST/ FALSE PROPHET APPEARS TWICE
 463-11, NEW SONG/ ST JOHN/ ELDERS SEATED/ LAMB 463-12, WOE TO
 WORSHIPPERS OF THE BEAST/ LAMB AND CHALICE 463-13, BLESSED ARE
 JUST/ ST JOHN WITH PEN AND BOOK 463-14, HARVEST OF THE EARTH/
 ST JOHN 463-15, VINTAGE OF THE EARTH/ ANGEL IN HEAVEN WITH
 SICKLE 463-16

*$ABSTRACT 464
 *LIBRARY BOD
 *SLIDE SET TITLE APOCALYPSE
 *NEGATIVE REFERENCE ROLL 167I
 *RENTAL FEE SM 464 $3.80
 *TITLE OF MANUSCRIPT DOUCE/ APOCALYPSE
 *SHELFMARK MS DOUCE 180
 *PROVENANCE ENGLISH
 *DATE EXECUTED 13TH/ BEFORE 1272
 *LANGUAGE LATIN AND FRENCH
 *TYPE OF MANUSCRIPT APOCALYPSE WITH COMMENTARY
 *CONTENTS APOCALYPSE/ DOUCE 464/1-36, ST JOHN DISPUTING WITH
 IDOLATORS 464-1, DRUSIANA'S BAPTISM 464/1-2, ST JOHN BROUGHT
 BEFORE EMPEROR 464-3, ST JOHN IN BOILING OIL/ DELIVERED
 UNSCATHED 464-3, ST JOHN BROUGHT BEFORE EMPEROR 464-4, OPENING
 OF FIRST SEAL/ SECOND SEAL 464-5, OPENING OF FIRST SEAL 464-6,
 OPENING OF SECOND SEAL 464-7, OPENING OF THIRD AND FOURTH
 SEALS 464-8, OPENING OF THIRD SEAL 464-9, OPENING OF FOURTH
 SEAL 464-10, ANGEL/ FOURTH AND FIFTH SOUNDS TRUMPET 464-11,
 ANGEL/ FOURTH 464-12, LOCUSTS WITH BRIDLES AND BITS FOLLOW
 ABADDON/ ANGEL SIXTH 464-13, LOCUSTS FOLLOW ABADDON 464-14,

225

ANGELS ON HORSES GO TO DESTROY/ ST JOHN AT DESK 464-15, ANGEL
ON HORSEBACK GO TO WORK OF DESTRUCTION 464-16, ST JOHN SEATE
AT DESK 464-17, ST JOHN AND ANGEL 464-18, ANGEL/ MIGHTY AN
ENOCH AND ELIAS 464-19, ANGEL/ MIGHTY 464-20, ANGEL 464-21
DEATH OF ENOCH AND ELIAS/ ANTICHRIST UPROOTING TREE 464-22
DEATH OF ENOCH AND ELIAS 464-23, WOMAN WITH CHILD IN SUN/ MOO
AT FEET 464/24-26, DRAGON/ SEVEN-HEADED WAITS TO DEVOUR CHILD
ST MICHAEL SLAYS 464-24, ANGELS HOLDING SCROLL 464-27, DRAGO
FIGHTING WITH SEED OF WOMAN/ JOHN WATCHING BEAST 464/28-30, S
JOHN SEES SEVEN ANGELS IN CLOUD 464/31-32, BEAST/ FALS
PROPHET/ MARKED MEN CAST INTO BRIMSTONE 464/33-34, HELL MOUT
OPEN 464-35, ST JOHN DELIVERS DEAD TO JUDGMENT 464-35, HEI
MOUTH 464-36

*$ABSTRACT 465
  *LIBRARY BOD
  *SLIDE SET TITLE APOCALYPSE/ MIDDLE SECTION OF DOUCE APOCALYPS
  *NEGATIVE REFERENCE ROLL 167J
  *RENTAL FEE SM 465 $3.30
  *TITLE OF MANUSCRIPT DOUCE APOCALYPSE
  *SHELFMARK MS DOUCE 180
  *PROVENANCE ENGLISH
  *DATE EXECUTED 13TH/ BEFORE 1272
  *LANGUAGE LATIN AND ENGLISH
  *TYPE OF MANUSCRIPT APOCALYPSE WITH COMMENTARY
  *CONTENTS APOCALYPSE 465/1-24, VISION OF CHRIST AND TEX
  465/1-2, LETTER TO PHILADELPHIA/ CHRIST/ ST JOHN/ ANGEL 465-3
  CHRIST AND ST JOHN 465-4, LETTER TO LAODICEA/ CHRIST/ ST JOHN
  ANGEL 465-5, OPENING OF FOURTH SEAL/ HORSE/ RIDER WITH ST JOH
  465-6, TRUMPET/ FOURTH SOUNDED BY ANGEL 465-6, TRUMPET/ FIFTH
  CHRIST/ BEES/ DEVILS 465-7, DRAGON 465-8, VIRGIN AND CHILD AN
  ANGEL 465-9, TRIUMPH IN HEAVEN/ ST JOHN/ LAMB AND DRAGO
  465-10, DRAGON PERSECUTES WOMAN/ ANGEL COMES TO AID 465-11
  BEAST ASCENDING OUT OF EARTH 465-12, VINTAGE OF EARTH/ ANGE
  PICKING GRAPES 465-13, ANGELS IN HEAVEN 465-13, ANGEL PICKIN
  GRAPES 465-14, ENTRY OF ANGELS AND TEXT 465/15-16, VIALS GIVE
  UP/ EAGLE GIVES VIALS TO ANGELS 465-17, VIAL/ FIRST POURED C
  GROUND 465-18, VIAL/ SECOND POURED INTO SEA 465-19, HARLOT C
  BEAST 465-20, HEADS OF KINGS 465-21, DRAGON IMPRISONED FO
  THOUSAND YEARS 465-22, APOCALYPSE/ CONCLUSION/ CHRIST/ ANGEL
  ST JOHN 465-23, CHRIST HOLDING BOOK 465-24

*$ABSTRACT 466
  *LIBRARY BOD
  *SLIDE SET TITLE APOCALYPSE
  *NEGATIVE REFERENCE ROLL 196U
  *RENTAL FEE SM 466 $4.25
  *SHELFMARK MS NEW COLLEGE 65
  *PROVENANCE ENGLISH
  *DATE EXECUTED 14TH
  *LANGUAGE LATIN
  *TYPE OF MANUSCRIPT APOCALYPSE
  *CONTENTS APOCALYPSE 466/1-45, CHRIST HOLDING KEY FROM WHIC
  HANGS SCROLL 466-1, ST JOHN KNEELING 466-1, ST JOHN WRITES
  CHRIST WITH SWORD IN MOUTH 466-2, SEVEN CANDLESTICKS/ SEVE
  CHURCHES 466-2, ANGEL IN CLOUDS/ DOOR BELOW/ ST JOHN ON LADDE
  466-3, CHRIST ON THRONE/ BEASTS/ ELDERS 466-4, CHRIST WIT
  PIERCED LAMB/ ELDERS/ BEASTS 466-5, GOD ENTHRONED WITH BOOK
  ST JOHN/ WHITE HORSE 466-6, LAMB OPENS SECOND SEAL/ RED HORS
  466-7, LAMB OPENS THIRD SEAL/ BLACK HORSE 466-8, LAMB OPEN
  FOURTH SEAL/ PALE HORSE WITH DEATH 466-9, GOD ENTHRONED
  SOULS OF SLAIN RECEIVE WHITE ROBES 466-10, STARS FALL FRO
  HEAVEN/ KING AND FIGURES IN HOLES 466-11, GOD SEATED WIT
  LAMB/ ANGELS AND SAVES PRAISING HIM 466-12, GOD WITH LAMB
  ANGELS WITH TRUMPETS/ CENSER 466-13, ANGEL/ SECOND/ SEA WIT
  MAN/ BOAT/ ROWER STRUGGLING 466-14, ANGEL/ THIRD AND GREA
  FALLING STAR 466-15, ANGEL/ FOURTH/ SUN/ MOON/ STARS DARKENE
  466-16, ANGEL/ FIFTH/ STAR FALLS/ KEY IN BOTTOMLESS PIT

LOCUSTS 466-17, BOTTOMLESS PIT 466-17, ANGEL/ SIXTH/ ANGELS
OUT OF EUPHRATES WITH SWORDS 466-18, HORSES WITH RIDERS LOOSED
TO SLAY 466-19, ST JOHN BY SEA/ GREAT ANGEL COMES DOWN 466-20,
FIGURES/ TWO WITH BOOKS AND ONE WITH SCROLL 466-21, WITNESSES/
PRAYING PEOPLE/ LOCUST HORSES ATTACK 466-22, WOMAN IN BED
CLOTHED WITH THE SUN 466-23, DRAGON WAITS TO DEVOUR NEW-BORN
CHILD 466-24, WAR IN HEAVEN/ ST MICHAEL AND ANGELS FIGHT
DRAGON 466-26, ST MICHAEL AND DRAGON 466-26, ANGELS DRIVE
DEVIL OUT OF EARTH 466-27, BEAST AND DRAGON ARE WORSHIPPED
466-28, BEAST MAKES WAR ON SAINTS AND OVERCOMES THEM 466-29,
LAMB STANDING ON MOUNT SION 466-30, FALL OF BABYLON 466-31,
CHRIST ON THRONE ON CLOUD 466-32, TEMPLE AND ALTAR/ ANGELS
CUTTING VINES 466-33, ANGELS EMPTY VIALS ON EARTH 466-34,
UNCLEAN SPIRITS FROM MOUTHS OF DRAGON/ BEAST/ FALSE PROPHET
466-35, GOD ENTHRONED IN FRONT OF TEMPLE 466-36, ST JOHN AND
GREAT WHORE 466-37, WHORE OF BABYLON 466-37, BABYLON IN FLAMES
466-38, CHRIST AND 24 ELDERS AND 4 BEASTS 466-39, WHITE HORSE
AND CROWNES RIDER 466-40, WHITE HORSE WITH RIDER AND ARMY/
ATTACKED BY BEAST 466-41, NEW HEAVEN AND EARTH 466-42,
FOUNDATIONS AND WALLS OF NEW JERUSALEM 466-43, ANGEL SHOWS
JOHN GOD AND LAMB ON THRONE 466-44, JESUS HOLDING SCROLL AND
BLESSING 466-45

*$ABSTRACT 467
  *LIBRARY BOD
  *SLIDE SET TITLE APOCALYPSE PICTURES
  *NEGATIVE REFERENCE ROLL 198M
  *RENTAL FEE SM 467 $4.10
  *SHELFMARK MS CANON BIBL LAT 62 467/1-8, MS TANNER 184
  467/9-11, MS LINCOLN COLLEGE LAT 16 467/12-14, MS NEW COLLEGE
  65 467-15, MS UNIVERSITY COLLEGE 100 467/16, MS AUCT D 4 14
  467/17-23, MS ASHMOLE 753 467-24
  *PROVENANCE ENGLISH
  *DATE EXECUTED 13TH 467/1-14 AND 24, 14TH 467/15-23
  *LANGUAGE LATIN
  *TYPE OF MANUSCRIPT APOCALYPSE
  *CONTENTS APOCALYPSE PICTURES 467/1-24, VISION OF CHRIST 467-1,
  VISION OF THRONE OF GOD 467-2, LAMB OF GOD 467-3, LAMB TAKING
  BOOK 467-4, WITNESSES TWO 467-5, DRAGON PERSECUTES WOMAN
  467-6, DRAGON AND SEED OF WOMAN 467-7, BATTLE WITH THE BEAST
  467-8, ST MICHAEL AND DRAGON 467-8, LAMB OPENS ONE OF SEALS
  467-9, HARVEST OF WINE 467-10, HELL MOUTH 467-11, HEAVEN'S
  DOORS OPEN/ ANGEL IN WHITE/ LADDER 467-12, LAMB OPENS FIRST
  SEAL 467-13, LAMB OPENS SECOND SEAL/ RED HORSE 467-14, DRAGON
  GIVES POWER TO BEAST WITH WHITE WAND 467-15, DRAGON/ WINGED
  KILLING MEN 467-16, WITNESSES TESTIFYING TO POPULACE 467-17,
  BEAST KILLING TWO WITNESSES 467-18, WOMAN WAITING TO BE
  DELIVERED OF CHILD 467-19, DRAGON AND WOMAN 467-20, BEAST
  BEING WORSHIPPED 467-21, MARKING OF BELIEVERS 467-22, DEVIL
  CAST BACK TO HELL 467-23, BEAST/ SECOND PUTS MARK ON MEN'S
  FOREHEADS 467-24

*$ABSTRACT 468
  *LIBRARY BOD
  *SLIDE SET TITLE SELDEN APOCALYPSE II
  *NEGATIVE REFERENCE ROLL 219B
  *RENTAL FEE SM 468 $3.95
  *COMMENTS SEE ABSTRACT 444 FOR PART I
  *TITLE OF MANUSCRIPT SELDEN APOCALYPSE
  *SHELFMARK MS SELDEN SUPRA 38
  *PROVENANCE ENGLISH/ FRENCH IN STYLE
  *DATE EXECUTED 14TH/C 1320-30
  *LANGUAGE FRENCH
  *TYPE OF MANUSCRIPT APOCALYPSE
  *CONTENTS APOCALYPSE PICTURES 468/1-39, ANGEL/ SIXTH SOUNDS
  TRUMPET 468-1, REV 9 VERSES 13-14/ ANGELS RELEASED FROM
  EUPHRATES 468-1, APOCALYPSE/ FOUR HORSEMEN 468-2, HORSEMEN OF
  APOCALYPSE 468-2, REV 9 VERSES 17-19/ FOUR HORSEMEN 468-2,

227

APOCALYPSE/ SEVEN THUNDERS 468-3, REV 10 VERSES 1-4/ SEV
THUNDERS 468-3, ST JOHN OF PATMOS RECEIVES BOOK 468-4, REV
VERSES 8-9/ ST JOHN RECEIVES BOOK 468-4, ST JOHN OF PATM
RECEIVES MEASURING ROD 468-5, REV 11 VERSE 1/ ST JOHN MEASUR
TEMPLE 468-5, APOCALYPSE/ TWO WITNESSES KILL ENEMIES 468-
REV 11 VERSES 3-5/ WITNESSES KILL ENEMIES 468-6, APOCALYPT
BEAST ARISES FROM BOTTOMLESS PIT 468-7, BEAST/ APOCALYPTI
BOTTOMLESS PIT 468-7, SODOM TOPPLED BY EARTHQUAKE 468-7, R
11 VERSES 7-13/ BEAST/ SODOM 468-7, ANGEL/ SEVENTH SOUN
TRUMPET 468-8, CHRIST IN MAJESTY 468-8, REV 11 VERSES 15-1
SEVENTH TRUMPET 468-8, WOMAN CLOTHED IN SUN 468-9, REV
VERSE 19/ WOMAN CLOTHED IN SUN/ EARTHQUAKE 468-9, DRAGON A
WOMAN/ CHILD DELIVERED 468-10, REV 12 VERSES 3-5/ DELIVERAN
OF CHILD OF WOMAN 468-10, ST MICHAEL AND TWO ANGELS FIG
THREE DRAGONS 468-11, REV 12 VERSE 7/ MICHAEL FIGHTS DRAG
468-11, ST MICHAEL CASTS DRAGON HEADFIRST INTO EARTH 468-1
REV 12 VERSE 9/ DRAGON CAST DOWN 468-12, DRAGON TRIES TO TR
WOMAN WITH GOLD WINGS 468-13, BEAST/ APOCALYPTIC 468-14, R
13 VERSES 1-2/ JOHN WATCHES BEAST ON SEA 468-14, BEAST A
DRAGON/ APOCALYPTIC 468-15, REV 13 VERSE 4/ PEOPLE WORSH
DRAGON 468-15, LAMB/ SEVEN ANGELS HARPING 468-16, REV
VERSES 1-2/ ANGELS HARPING 468-16, APOCALYPSE/ RIVER WI
SEVEN PATCHES OF FLAME 468-17, ANGELS/ EAGLE BRINGS GO
FLASKS 468-18, REV 15 VERSES 5-8/ SEVEN ANGELS WITH FLAS
468-18, ANGELS EMPTY SEVEN FLASKS 468-19, REV 16 VERSES 1-
SEVEN ANGELS EMPTY FLASKS 468-19, BEAST/ APOCALYPTIC WORSHIP
BY PEOPLE 468-20, REV 13 VERSES 11-16/ BEAST ADORED/ BELIEVE
MARKED 468-20, LAMB WORSHIPED 468-21, REV 14 VERSE 1/ LA
WORSHIPED 468-21, ANGEL EXTENDS BOOK TO PEOPLE 468-22, REV
VERSE 6/ BOOK GIVEN TO PEOPLE 468-22, FALL OF BABYLON 468-2
REV 14 VERSE 8/ FALL OF BABYLON 468-23, ANGEL/ GRAY WI
SICKLE 468-24, REV 14 VERSES 14-16/ ANGEL HARVESTS WHE
468-24, HARVEST OF WHEAT AND GRAPES/ APOCALYPTIC 468-25, R
14 VERSES 17-20/ HARVEST/ RIVER OF BLOOD 468-25, FAL
PROPHET/ DRAGON/ BEAST/ FROGS ISSUE FORTH 468-26, ANGE
APOCALYPTIC EMPTIES FLASK OVER DESTROYED CITY 468-27, REV
VERSES 17-21/ ANGEL WITH FLASK DESTROYS CITY 468-27, ST JO
OF PATMOS/ WOMAN WITH URN 468-28, ANGEL/ APOCALYPTIC THRO
MILLSTONE INTO SEA 468-29, REV 18 VERSE 21/ MILLSTONE THRO
INTO SEA 468-29, ST JOHN OF PATMOS/ VISION OF WHITE HOR
468-30, CHRIST IN WINEPRESS 468-30, WINEPRESS/ CHRIST
468-30, KNIGHTS IN CHAINMAIL/ APOCALYPTIC 468-30, REV
VERSES 11-15/ WHITE HORSE/ WINEPRESS 468-30, BIRDS OF PR
468-31, REV 19 VERSES 17-18/ ANGEL SUMMONS BIRDS OF PR
468-31, BEAST WITH CRUSADER'S SHIELD ATTACKS BEAST 468-3
BEAST/ APOCALYPTIC ATTACKED BY ARMED CHRIST 468-32, REV
VERSE 19/ CHRIST ATTACKS BEAST 468-32, ANGEL/ APOCALYPT
LOCKS DRAGON IN BOTTOMLESS PIT 468-33, BOTTOMLESS PIT/ DRAG
468-33, REV 20 VERSES 1-2/ ANGEL LOCKS DRAGON IN PIT 468-3
ST JOHN OF PATMOS BEHOLDS NEW HEAVEN AND EARTH 468-34, REV
VERSE 1/ JOHN BEHOLDS NEW HEAVEN 468-34, ST JOHN OF PATMO
VISION OF NEW JERUSALEM 468-35, REV 21 VERSES 10-14/ N
JERUSALEM 468-35, ST JOHN OF PATMOS/ ANGEL/ LAMB 468-37
CHRIST IN MAJESTY/ LAMB ON LAP 468-37, ST JOHN OF PATM
RECEIVES BOOK FROM ANGEL 468-38, ST JOHN OF PATMOS INSTRUCT
BY CHRIST 468-39

*$ABSTRACT 469
 *LIBRARY BOD
 *SLIDE SET TITLE SAXON LIFE
 *COMMENTS DETAILS FROM ANGLO-SAXON OUTLINE DRAWINGS
 *NEGATIVE REFERENCE ROLL 172D
 *RENTAL FEE SM 469 $4.05
 *SHELFMARK MS JUNIUS II
 *PROVENANCE ENGLISH/ WINCHESTER OR CANTERBURY
 *DATE EXECUTED 11TH/C1000
 *LANGUAGE OLD ENGLISH
 *ARTIST/ SCHOOL WINCHESTER OR CANTERBURY
 *TYPE OF MANUSCRIPT LITERATURE/ ANGLO-SAXON
 *CONTENTS LITERATURE/ CAEDMON GENESIS 469/1-41, GENESI

PARAPHRASE IN OLD ENGLISH 469/1-41, LUCIFER/ REBELLION IN
HEAVEN 469-1, THRONE OF LUCIFER 469-1, CREATION OF EVE 469-2,
EVE CREATED 469-2, EDEN/ LADDER REACHES HEAVEN 469-2, ST
MICHAEL IN CREATION SCENE 469-2, SATAN AS MONARCH OF HELL
469-3, HELL/ SATAN/ DEVILS 469-3, CHRIST ENTHRONED 469-3,
SERPENT/ CURSED BY GOD 469-4, ADAM AND EVE/ GOD CALLING TO
469-4, VIKING ORNAMENT 469-4, ADAM AND EVE/ EXPULSION 469-5,
TOOLS/ SPINDLE AND SPACE 469-5, ADAM AND EVE/ EXPULSION/ ANGEL
GUARDS GATE 469-6, GATE OF EDEN WITH HINGES 469-6, ABEL/ BIRTH
SCENE 469-7, ADAM ON CUSHIONED CHAIR 469-7, ADAM AND EVE
TOILING 469-8, ABEL TENDS GOATS 469-9, CAIN KILLS ABEL WITH
CLUB 469-10, CAIN AS WANDERER 469-11, ENOCH WITH WIFE AND
CHILD 469-12, ZODIAC SIGN/ ARIES 469-12, IRAD AS GREAT
CHIEFTAN 469-13, IRAD'S WIFE AND MIDWIFE 469-14, MIDWIFE
469-14, MAHALALEL'S WIFE AND SON 469-15, LAMECH WITH TWO WIVES
469-16, JUBAL/ FATHER OF MUSIC 469-17, HARP 469-17, TUBAL-CAIN
AS SMITH 469-18, SMITH/ TUBAL-CAIN 469-18, TUBAL-CAIN PLOWING
469-19, PLOWING 469-19, ADAM AND EVE WITH INFANT SETH 469-20,
SETH AS INFANT 469-20, SETH WITH WIFE AND SON ENOS 469-21,
CAINAN ENTHRONED 469-22, VIKING ORNAMENT IN ANGLO-SAXON
DRAWING 469-22, CAINAN'S WIFE WITH SON 469-23, MALALEHEL/
DEATH 469-24, BURIAL RITES/ CENSER 469-24, METHUSELAH
ENTHRONED 469-25, INITIAL L/ LAMECH/ UNUSUAL COLUMN 469-25,
LAMECH/ BIRTH 469-26, NOAH/ THREE SCENES 469-27, NOAH WITH
ADZE BUILDS ARK 469-28, TOOLS/ SHIPBUILDING WITH ADZE 469-28,
NOAH'S ARK/ THREE TIERED VIKING SHIP 469-29, NOAH'S WIFE/
CONTRARY 469-29, TYPOLOGY AND SYMBOLISM/ NOAH'S ARK 469-29,
ARK AS VIKING SHIP ON WATER 469-30, ARK AS VIKING SHIP/ WINDOW
WITH BOLT 469-31, NOAH'S SACRIFICE TO GOD 469-32, GOD WITH
UNUSUAL RINGED SCROLL/ APOCALYPTIC SYMBOL 469-32, SYMBOLISM/
STAG IN GENESIS SCENE 469-32, NOAH PLOWING 469-33, PLOWING
469-33, ARTIST AT WORK/ TEXT RUNS THROUGH OLD ENGLISH TEXT
469-33, NOAH/ NAKEDNESS 469-34, NIMROD SENDS OUT PRINCES WITH
MALLETS 469-35, NIMROD AS MIGHTY HUNTER 469-36, TOWER OF
BABEL/ WORKMEN BUILD 469-37, BUILDING OF TOWER OF BABEL
469-37, ABRAHAM'S HOUSE/ SARAH AND LOT WITHIN 469-38, ABRAHAM
WITH AXE BETWEEN BETHEL AND HAI 469-39, ABRAHAM OFFERS POT OF
INCENSE 469-40, ABRAHAM APPROACHES EGYPT 469-41

*$ABSTRACT 470
  *LIBRARY BOD
  *SLIDE SET TITLE GENESIS
  *NEGATIVE REFERENCE ROLL 172E
  *RENTAL FEE SM 470 $3.85
  *COMMENTS ANGLO-SAXON OUTLINE DRAWINGS
  *SHELFMARK MS JUNIUS 11
  *PROVENANCE ENGLISH/ WINCHESTER OR CANTERBURY
  *DATE EXECUTED 11TH/C1000
  *LANGUAGE OLD ENGLISH
  *ARTIST/ SCHOOL WINCHESTER OR CANTERBURY
  *TYPE OF MANUSCRIPT LITERATURE/ ANGLO-SAXON/ GENESIS
  *CONTENTS LITERATURE/ CAEDMON GENESIS 470/1-37, GENESIS/
PARAPHRASE IN OLD ENGLISH 470/1-37, CHRIST ENTHRONED ABOVE
CHAOS 470-1, CHERUBIM/ SIX WINGS 470-1, CHRIST ENTHRONED WITH
CHERUBIM 470-2, LUCIFER/ REBELLION 470-2, ST MICHAEL IN
GENESIS SCENE 470-2, LUCIFER/ POINTS TO RIVAL THRONE IN HEAVEN
470-3, LUCIFER RECEIVES PALMS OF VICTORY FROM VASSAL ANGELS
470-3, FALL OF REBEL ANGELS 470-4, ANGELS/ FALL 470-4, HELL
MOUTH AS LEVIATHAN 470-4, SATAN CHAINED IN HELL MOUTH 470-4,
DEVILS 470-4, CREATION/ SEPARATION OF LIGHT FROM DARK 470-5,
SPIRIT OF GOD UPON DEEP 470-5, PERSONIFICATION OF NIGHT FROM
OCTATEUCH 470-5, CREATION/ CONFLATION OF 3RD-6TH DAYS 470-6,
ROOD TREE LEGEND 470-6, CREATION OF EVE 470-7, EVE CREATED
470-7, EDEN/ LADDER REACHES HEAVEN 470-7, ST MICHAEL IN
CREATION SCENE 470-7, PROHIBITION 470-8, ADAM AND EVE/
PROHIBITION 470-8, TYPOLOGY/ EVE STANDS ON CREATURE 470-8,
CREATION/ GOD BEHOLDING EXCELLENCE OF HIS WORK 470-9, ADAM AND
EVE/ GIVE THANKS TO CREATOR 470-9, ADAM AND EVE POINT TO TREES
OF LIFE/DEATH 470-10, ROOD TREE LEGEND 470-10, LUCIFER/
REBELLION AND FALL 470-11, HELL MOUTH 470-11, SATAN CHAINED IN

229

HELL 470-11, ANGELS/ FALL 470-11, SATAN AS MONARCH OF HE
470-12, HELL/ SATAN/ DEVILS 470-12, HEAVEN AND HELL 470-1
SATAN ENCHAINED SENDS EMISSARY DEVIL TO EDEN 470-13, HEL
DEVILS 470-13, EVE/ TEMPTATION BY SERPENT 470-13, E
RESTRAINS ARM FROM TOUCHING TREE 470-13, DEVIL DISGUISED
ANGEL TEMPTS EVE 470-14, EVE/ TEMPTATION BY DEVIL DISGUISED
ANGEL 470-14, ADAM AND EVE/ UNUSUAL CONFLATION OF TEMPTATIO
470-15, DEVIL DISGUISED AS ANGEL TEMPTS ADAM AND EVE 470-1
EVE TEMPTS ADAM/ DISGUISED DEVIL URGES EVE 470-16, ADAM A
EVE/ REMORSE 470-16, DEVIL TRIUMPHS OVER FALLEN ADAM AND E
470-16, ADAM AND EVE/ KNOWING NAKEDNESS 470-17, ADAM AND EV
HIDE IN WOODS 470-17, DEVIL RETURNS TO HELL IN TRIUMPH 470-1
SATAN CHAINED IN HELL 470-18, ADAM AND EVE/ REMORSE 470-1
ADAM AND EVE/ GOD CALLING TO 470-20, SERPENT/ CURSED BY G
470-20, ADAM AND EVE/ SENTENCED BY GOD 470-21, ADAM AND EV
EXPULSION 470-22, ADAM AND EVE/ EXPULSION 470-23, ABEL/ BIR
SCENE 470-24, ADAM AND EVE/ TOILING 470-25, ABEL TENDS GOA
470-25, CAIN KILLS ABEL WITH CLUB 470-25, ABEL'S BLOOD CRI
TO LORD 470-25, CAIN AND ABEL/ OFFERINGS TO LORD 470-25, CAI
GOD'S JUDGMENT UPON 470-26, CAIN AS WANDERER 470-26, ENOCH A
WIFE 470-26, JUBAL/ FATHER OF MUSIC 470-27, TUBAL-CAIN
SMITH 470-27, TUBAL-CAIN PLOWING 470-27, ADAM AND EVE WI
INFANT SETH 470-27, SETH WITH WIFE AND SON ENOS 470-28, NOA
BIRTH 470-29, NOAH RECEIVES DIVINE WARNING 470-30, NOAH WI
ADZE BUILDS ARK 470-30, SHIPBUILDING/ NOAH 470-30, NOAH'S AR
3 TIERED VIKING SHIP 470-31, ARK AS VIKING SHIP 470-32, NOAH
ARK/ ARTIST FUSES RAINBOW TO ARK 470-33, NOAH OFFERI
SACRIFICE TO GOD 470-34, NOAH/ BLESSED BY GOD 470-35, NO
PLOWING 470-36, PLOWING 470-36, NOAH/ NAKEDNESS 470-37

*$ABSTRACT 471
   *LIBRARY BOD
   *SLIDE SET TITLE PORTABLE PSALTER/ GHENT
   *NEGATIVE REFERENCE ROLL 218K
   *RENTAL FEE SM 471 $3.60
   *COMMENTS ILLUSTRATIONS FROM MS DOUCE 5/ VOL 1
   *TITLE OF MANUSCRIPT GHENT PORTABLE PSALTER
   *SHELFMARK MS DOUCE 5
   *PROVENANCE GHENT
   *DATE EXECUTED 14TH/ C1320-30
   *LANGUAGE LATIN
   *TYPE OF MANUSCRIPT PSALTER
   *CONTENTS PSALM 37/ ILLUMINATED D/ DOMINE 471-1, GROTESQU
PRODDING FIGURE 471-1, GROTESQUE WEARING RED HOOD/ UNICO
HEADS 471-2, BEASTS/ UNICORN/ MEN 471-3, UNICORN HEAD
HOOKED-BEAKED BIRD 471-4, CHRIST BLINDFOLDED AND MOCKED 471-
PSALM 38/ ILLUMINATED D DIXI 471-5, DAVID KNEELING BEFORE G(
471-5, GROTESQUES AND MONSTERS/ MARGINAL 471-5, UNICORN/ BIR
BEASTS 471-6, LION CLUBBED BY HUMAN FIGURE 471-7, MAN HOL
DOG'S HEAD/ APE WITH BOOTS 471-7, STAG/ ANIMALS/ HUMAN HEA
471-8, UNICORNS/ BEAST/ HUMAN HEADS 471-9, HUMAN HEAD/ ANIMA
471-10, MAN AND WOMAN CONVERSING/ APES/ GROTESQUE 471-1
UNICORN/ HUMAN HEADS/ ANIMALS 471-12, PSALM 41/ ILLUMINATED
QUEMADMODUM 471-13, BISHOP PREACHING TO APE 471-13, DEVI
GROTESQUE/ UNICORN 471-13, BAGPIPES/ UNICORNS/ STAG 471-1
APE AND STAG/ BEASTS 471-15, PSALM 43/ ILLUMINATED D DE
471-16, APE CLUBS KNIGHT 471-16, MEN/ HOODED 471-17, GAME
HANDBALL 471-18, HUMAN FIGURE HOLDS TAPER/ HEADS 471-1
BAGPIPES/ MAN PLAYING 471-20, UNICORN/ HARE/ BIRDS 471-2(
BEAST/ STAGS/ HEADS 471-21, UNICORN HEADS/ STAGS/ HUMAN HEA
471-22, PSALM 45/ ILLUMINATED D DEUS 471-23, MAN WITH HOOP A
STICK/ MONK/ BIRDS 471-23, PSALM 46/ ILLUMINATED O OMN
471-24, CLERIC AS APE FEEDING HORNED ANIMAL 471-24, PSALM 4
ILLUMINATED M MAGNUS 471-25, FALCONER/ GROTESQUE WITH SWO
AND SHIELD FIGHTING DRAGON 471-25, HUMAN HALF FIGURES A
HEADS 471-26, GAME OF MUMBLETY PEG/ APES PLAY 471-27, BISH(
WITH MITRE AND CROZIER 471-27, BIRD WITH FROG IN BEAK/ UNICO
471-28, STAG/ BEAST/ HUMAN HEADS 471-29, PSALM 49/ ILLUMINAT
D DEUS 471-30, HARE CHASING DOD/ APE WITH TROLLEY 471-3
BISHOP BLESSING HUMANS AND ANIMALS 471-31, HEADS/ HUMAN A
ANIMAL 471-32

*$ABSTRACT 472
  *LIBRARY BOD
  *SLIDE SET TITLE ARTILLERY
  *NEGATIVE REFERENCE ROLL 177E
  *RENTAL FEE SM 472 $2.70
  *COMMENTS WATERCOLOR DRAWINGS OF ARTILLERY
  *TITLE OF MANUSCRIPT MACHINES ET UTENSILS DE GUERRE
  *SHELFMARK MS DOUCE B 2
  *PROVENANCE PORTUGESE
  *DATE EXECUTED 16TH/ 1582
  *LANGUAGE FRENCH
  *TYPE OF MANUSCRIPT MILITARY TEXT
  *CONTENTS   ARTILLERY/   WATERCOLOR   DRAWINGS   472/1-14, MILITARY
  TEXT 472/1-14, CANNON HOISTED BY PULLEY 472-1, CANNON ON
  FOUR-WHEELED CARRIAGE 472-2, GUN-CARRIAGE HOLDING LONG METAL
  TUBES 472-3, RIBAUDE OR ORGAN GUN 472-3, GUN CARRIAGE WITH
  FOUR WHEELS 472-4, MORTAR IN UPRIGHT POSITION 472-5, CANNON ON
  WAGON WITH SUPPORT 472-6, GAUGE/ FOR MEASURING CANNON BALLS
  472-7, PINCERS FOR CASTING MOULD FOR CANNON BALLS 472-8,
  CANNON   ON   TWO-WHEELED   GUN   CARRIAGE   472-9, RAM ROD/
  LONG-HANDLED 472-10, SPOON WITH LONG HANDLE/ SWABBER 472-11,
  CAULDRON/ IRON FOR MOLTEN LEAD 472-12, PINCERS WITH CASTING
  MOULD 472-12, MUSKET/ PART WITH STRIKING PIN 472-13, POWDER
  FLASK 472-13, CANNON IN ACTION 472-14

*$ABSTRACT 473
  *LIBRARY BOD
  *SLIDE SET TITLE MECHANISMS
  *NEGATIVE REFERENCE ROLL 177F
  *RENTAL FEE SM 473 $2.30
  *COMMENTS WATERCOLOR DRAWINGS OF MECHANISMS
  *TITLE OF MANUSCRIPT MACHINES ET UTENSILS DE GUERRE
  *SHELFMARK MS DOUCE B 2
  *PROVENANCE PORTUGESE
  *DATE EXECUTED 16TH/ 1582
  *LANGUAGE FRENCH
  *TYPE OF MANUSCRIPT MILITARY TEXT
  *CONTENTS   MECHANISMS/   WATERCOLOR   DRAWINGS   473/1-6, MILITARY
  TEXT 473/1-6, LADDER/ EXTENDING IN THREE PARTS 473-1, JACK
  WITH TURNING HANDLE 473-2, JACK WITH SPIKES AT BASE OF BOX
  473-3, SCALES/ PORTABLE SUSPENDED FROM POLES 473-4, BELLOWS
  CONTROLLED BY LEVER FROM SUPPORT 473-5, MOULD/ BULLET 473-6

*$ABSTRACT 474
  *LIBRARY BOD
  *SLIDE SET TITLE TOOLS
  *NEGATIVE REFERENCE ROLL 177G
  *RENTAL FEE SM 474 $3.15
  *COMMENTS WATERCOLOR DRAWINGS OF TOOLS
  *TITLE OF MANUSCRIPT MACHINES ET UTENSILS DE GUERRE
  *SHELFMARK MS DOUCE B 2
  *PROVENANCE PORTUGESE
  *DATE EXECUTED 16TH/ 1582
  *LANGUAGE FRENCH
  *TYPE OF MANUSCRIPT MILITARY TEXT
  *CONTENTS TOOLS/ WATERCOLOR DRAWINGS 474/1-23, MILITARY TEXT
  474/1-23, SPADE/ SQUARE ENDED WITH BADGE ON BLADE 474-1,
  SPADE/   SHIELD-SHAPED WITH BADGE 474-2, ADZE WITH BADGE ON
  LOWER SIDE 474-3, ADZE/ SMALL BLADE 474-4, TOOL/ TRENCHING
  WITH LEAF SHAPED BLADE 474-5, BILLHOOKS 474-6, BILLHOOK/
  CURVED BLADE AND MARK 474-7, PICK/ MINER'S WITH POINTED BLADE
  AND MARK 474-8, PICK-AX/ POINTED AND SPADE 474-9, PICK-AXES
  474-10, SPADE WITH WOODEN SHOULDERS HOLDING BLADE 474-11,
  WHEELBARROW   PUSHED   BY   MAN 474-12, BASKETS/ ONE WITH HANDLES
  AND ONE WITH STRAPS 474-13, AXE/ MARK 474/14-15, HORSE-SHOES
  AND NAILS 474-16, SICKLE WITH SAW-EDGE 474-17, LANTERN/ CANDLE
  FOR HANGING 474-18, PUMP/ CYLINDRICAL 474-19, BASKET WORK
  COVER/ PERHAPS FIELD KITCHEN 474-20, CALLIPER/ METAL GRADED
  FOR PRECISION 474/21-22, MOULD/ BULLET 474-23

*$ABSTRACT 475
  *LIBRARY BOD
  *SLIDE SET TITLE EARLY ARITHMETIC AND ALGEBRA
  *NEGATIVE REFERENCE ROLL 182D
  *RENTAL FEE SM 475 $3.35
  *COMMENTS ILLUSTRATIONS FROM ONE MS AND FIVE PRINTED BOOKS (
   EARLY ARITHMETIC AND ALGEBRA
  *TITLE OF MANUSCRIPT GEOGRAPHISCHE ASTRONOMISCHE U'
   ASTROLOGISCHE TAFELN 475/3-9, KEY OF MATHEMATICKS 475/10-1
   ARITHMETICAE IN NUMERIS INSTITUTIO QUAE-MATHEMATICAE CLAV
   EST 475/14-15, DE LATITUDINIBUS 475/16-21, DISCOURS DE .
   METHODE 475/22-27
  *SHELFMARK MS BODLEY 309 475/1-2
  *PROVENANCE FRENCH/ VENDOME 475/1-2, GERMAN 475/3-9, ENGLIS
   475/10-20, DUTCH 475/22-27
  *DATE EXECUTED 11TH/ C1075 475/1-2, 17TH/ 1637 475/22-27
  *LANGUAGE LATIN 475/1-9 AND 14-27, ENGLISH 475/10-13
  *AUTHOR BOETHIUS 475/1-2, DURER/ ALBRECHT 475/3-9, OUGHTRED/
   475/10-15, HOREN/ N 475/16-21, DESCARTES 475/22-27
  *TYPE OF MANUSCRIPT MATHEMATICAL TEXTS
  *CONTENTS ARITHMETIC AND ALGEBRA 475/1-27, MATHEMATICAL TEX'
   475/1-27, ARITHMETICA/ DE 475/1-2, IMAGINES COE'
   SEPTENTRIONALES IMAGINES COELI MERIDIONALES 475-4, HOROSCOPI(
   UNIVERSALE BY JOANNES STABIUS 475-5, HOROSCOPES/ PROBLE
   RELATING TO 475/6-7, HOROSCOPE 475-8, MERIDIES 475-9

*$ABSTRACT 476
  *LIBRARY BOD
  *SLIDE SET TITLE NUREMBURG SCHEMBART CARNIVAL
  *NEGATIVE REFERENCE ROLL 184H
  *RENTAL FEE SM 476 $3.70
  *COMMENTS ILLUSTRATIONS OF MEDIEVAL FESTIVAL OF MASKED BUTCHE
  *TITLE OF MANUSCRIPT RATHS UND GESCHLECHTBUCH DER STAT NURNBE
  *SHELFMARK MS DOUCE 346
  *PROVENANCE GERMAN/ NUREMBERG
  *DATE EXECUTED 17TH/ C1640
  *LANGUAGE GERMAN
  *ARTIST/ SCHOOL HANNS AMMON/ PERHAPS
  *TYPE OF MANUSCRIPT CARNIVAL ILLUSTRATED
  *CONTENTS SCHEMBART CARNIVAL ILLUSTRATED 476/1-34, SHROVETID
   CARNIVAL 476/1-34, COATS OF ARMS/ GERMAN 476/1-34, RING DANC
   OF BUTCHERS 476-1, BUTCHERS IN MASKS 476/1-34, PIPERS 476-'
   MUMMERY 476-2, CUNTZ ESCHENLOHER 476-3, ENDERES WAGNER 476-4
   ANDONI DALLER 476-5, HANNS ELWANGER 476-6, FRITZ HOLFELD
   476-7, HEINRICH RUMMEL 476-8, NICKLES ZENNER 476-9, HAN
   GRABNER 476-10, HAINZT HEYDT 476-11, HANS FLOCKS 476-1
   SEBALDT HALBWACHS AND MICHAEL BAUMGARTNER 476-13, HANNS KRE
   ALIAS DAUBER 476-14, HANNS KRESS 476-15, SABALDT BAUMGARTN
   476-16, HANNS REITER ALIAS SCHELHAMER 476-17, HOLFELDER AN
   HANNS KRESS 476-18, FRANZ HEGNER AND MICHAEL GRUBER 476-1'
   SEBALDT KRENNER 476-20, HANS SCHISSEL-FELDER 476-21, HEINRIC
   SCHERB 476-22, MASTER VEIT ARMOURER 476-23, CUNTZ LOFFLE
   476-24, HANS FREY/ BENADICKS FREY 476-25, DRAGON ON SLED(
   476-26, HANS WERNER 476-27, HANS STORR 476-28, SEBALDT GEUDE
   LIENHART TETZEL 476-29, GOTZ GEUDER AND JEORG CUNRADT 476-3(
   ULERICH MAGER 476-31, HANNS BAUMHAUER AND MAGER/ SADDLE
   476-32, HANS SCHRAINLEIN/ GIRDLER 476-33, ULERICH MAGER 476-

*$ABSTRACT 477
  *LIBRARY BOD
  *SLIDE SET TITLE PARLIAMENT ROLL
  *NEGATIVE REFERENCE ROLL 196M
  *RENTAL FEE SM 477 $2.65
  *COMMENTS 17TH CENTURY COPY OF ROLL SHOWING PROCESSION C
   ABBOTS/ BISHOPS/ TEMPORAL PEERS PRESENT AT THE PARLEAMEN
   HOLDON AT WESTM THE IIIITH DAY OF FEBRUARY THE TRID YERE OF
   OURE SOU'AIGNE LORD KING HENRY THE VIIITH
  *TITLE OF MANUSCRIPT PARLIAMENT ROLL

*SHELFMARK MS ASHMOLE ROLLS 45
*PROVENANCE ENGLISH
*DATE EXECUTED 17TH
*LANGUAGE ENGLISH
*TYPE OF MANUSCRIPT PARLIAMENT ROLL
*CONTENTS PARLIAMENT ROLL 477/1-13, ABBOTS/ BISHOPS/ TEMPORAL
PEERS IN PROCESSION 477/1-13, ABBOTS OF TEWKESBURY/ WALTHAM/
CIRENCESTER/ COLCESTER/ CROYLAND 477-1, PRIOR OF COVENTRY
477-1, ABBOTS OF SHREWSBURY/ SELBY/ BARDNEY/ ST BENET OF HULME
477-2, ABBOTS OF THORNEY/ HYDE BY WINCHESTER/ WINCHCOMB/
BATTLE 477-2, ABBOTS OF READING/ YORK/ RAMSEY/ PETERBOROUGH/
GLOUCESTER 477-3, ABBOTS OF GLASTONBURY/ BURY ST EDMUNDS/
CANTERBURY/ ST ALBANS 477-4, ABBOTS OF CARLISLE AND CHICHESTER
477-4, BISHOPS OF ELY/ LLANDAFF/ ROCHESTER 477-4, BISHOPS OF
ROCHESTER/ HEREFORD/ EXETER/ BATH AND WELLS 477-5, BISHOPS OF
ST ASAPH/ COVENTRY AND LICHFIELD/ SALISBURY/ DURHAM 477-5,
BISHOP OF NORWICH 477-5, BISHOP OF WORCESTER/ LINCOLN/ DURHAM/
WINCHESTER/ LONDON 477-6, ARCHBISHOP OF CANTERBURY/ HERALD/
DUKE OF BUCKINGHAM 477-7, HERALD/ DUKE OF BUCKINGHAM 477-8,
KING HENRY VIII 477-8, MARQUIS OF DORSET 477-9, EARLS OF
NORTHUMBERLAND/ SURREY/ SHREWSBURY/ ESSEX 477-9, EARLS OF
SHREWSBURY/ ESSEX/ KENT/ DERBY/ WILTSHIRE 477-10, LORD PRIOR
OF ST JOHN OF JERUSALEM 477/10-11, LORDS IN PROCESSION WITH
HENRY VIII 477/11-13, KING HENRY VIII 477/11-13

*$ABSTRACT 478
*LIBRARY BOD
*SLIDE SET TITLE ST CHRISTOPHER CARRYING CHRIST ACROSS STREAM
*NEGATIVE REFERENCE ROLL 198 F AND G AND H
*RENTAL FEE SM 478 $4.15
*COMMENTS ILLUSTRATIONS OF ST CHRISTOPHER
*SHELFMARK MS DOUCE 231 478-1, MS AUCT D 4 4 478-2, MS RAWL D
939 478-3, MS RAWL LIT F 28 478-4, MS BODLEY 851 478-5, MS LAT
LITURG F 2 478-6, MS JESUS COLLEGE 72 478-7, MS LITURG 401
478-8, MS LITURG 98 478-9, MS ASHMOLE 1291 478-10, MS RAWL
LITURG E 12 478-11, MS RAWL LITURG E 4 478-12, MS ADD A 185
478-13, MS UNIVERSITY COLLEGE 8 478-14, MS RAWL LITURG G 7
478-15, MS DON D 85 478-16, MS AUCT D INF 2 13 478-17, MS RAWL
LITURG D 1 478-18, MS GOUGH LITURG 15 478-19, MS DOUCE 8
478-20, MS RAWL LITURG G 3 478-21, MS RAWL LITURG E 34 478-22,
MS LITURG 404 478-23, MS BUCHANAN E 4 478-24, MS DOUCE 8
478-25, MS BODLEY 939 478-26, MS LITURG 41 478-27, MS RAWL
LITURG F 30 478-28, MS RAWL LITURG F 10 478-29, MS LAUD MISC
93 478-30, MS DOUCE 31 478-31, MS DOUCE 311 478-32, MS DOUCE
112 478-33, MS BUCHANAN E 10 478-34, MS LAUD LAT 15 478-35, MS
LAUD MISC 7 478-36, MS DOUCE 19 478-37, MS RAWL LITURG E 36
478-38, DOUCE FF 63/ PRINTED BOOK 478-39, MS RAWL LITURG F 38
478-40, MS RAWL LITURG F 36 478-41, MS LAT LITURG G 5 478-42,
MS DOUCE 8 478-43
*PROVENANCE ENGLISH 478/1-3 AND 5-6 AND 8-9 AND 12 AND 14,
ENGLISH 478/16-18 AND 21 AND 26 AND 35 AND 41-42, FRENCH 478/4
AND 11 AND 13 AND 15 AND 22-24, FRENCH 478/28-31 AND 34 AND
38-39 AND 43, FLEMISH 478/7 AND 10 AND 19-20 AND 25 AND 32-33,
FLEMISH 478/36, ITALIAN 478-37, DUTCH 478-40
*DATE EXECUTED 14TH 478/1-5, 15TH 478/6-35, 16TH-18TH 478/36-43
*LANGUAGE LATIN
*TYPE OF MANUSCRIPT BOOK OF HOURS 478/1 AND 4 AND 6-14 AND
17-19, BOOK OF HOURS 478/21-24 AND 27-29 AND 31-40, PSALTER
478/2 AND 16, CALENDAR 478-3, VOTIVE OFFICES 478/20 AND 25,
BREVIARY 478-30, MYSTERY/ FRENCH 478-43, PRAYERS 478/26 AND 41
*CONTENTS ST CHRISTOPHER CARRYING CHRIST ACROSS STREAM
478/1-43, CHRIST CARRIED ACROSS STREAM BY ST CHRISTOPHER
478/1-43, CHRIST CHILD HANGS TO HALO OF ST CHRISTOPHER 478-3,
STAFF ABOUT TO BUD 478-8, ST CHRISTOPHER AS GIANT 478-11,
STAFF ENDING IN BUNCH OF OAK LEAVES 478-16, RIVERS AND STREAMS
478/1-43

233

*$ABSTRACT 479
  *LIBRARY BOD
  *SLIDE SET TITLE FIFTEENTH CENTURY ASTROLOGICAL TEXTS
  *NEGATIVE REFERENCE ROLL 201D 1-5
  *RENTAL FEE SM 479 $3.90
  *COMMENTS FIVE MSS OF ASTROLOGICAL TEXTS
  *TITLE OF MANUSCRIPT SIGNS OF THE ZODIAC 479/1-12, BOKE O
    ASTRONOMY AND OFF PHYLOSOPHYE 479/13-24, DRAWINGS OF HAN
    479/25-30, TREATISE OF PALMISTRY 479-31, HANDS AND FACES F
    CHARACTER READING 479/32-38
  *SHELFMARK MS RAWL C 117 479/1-12, MS RAWL D 1220 479/13-24,
    DOUCE 45 479/25-30, MS DIGBY ROLLS IV 479-31, MS DIGBY
    479/32-38
  *PROVENANCE ENGLISH
  *LANGUAGE LATIN AND ENGLISH
  *TYPE OF MANUSCRIPT ASTROLOGICAL TEXTS
  *CONTENTS ASTROLOGICAL TEXTS 479/1-38, ZODIAC/ SIGNS OF
    DETAIL 479/1-12, DRAWINGS OF HANDS 479/25-30, HANDS 479/25-30
    MEDICAL AND ASTRONOMICAL PIECES 479/25-30, ZODIAC/ SIGNS
    479/13-24, PALMISTRY/ TREATISE 479-31, HANDS AND FACES F
    CHARACTER READING 479/32-38, CHARACTER READING 479/32-38

*$ABSTRACT 480
  *LIBRARY BOD
  *SLIDE SET TITLE PETER THE LOMBARD SENTENCES AND ROBE
    KILWARDBY CONCORDANCE
  *NEGATIVE REFERENCE ROLL 207L
  *RENTAL FEE SM 480 $2.25
  *TITLE OF MANUSCRIPT SENTENCES WITH CONCORDANCE
  *SHELFMARK MS MERTON L 2 5
  *PROVENANCE ENGLISH
  *DATE EXECUTED 14TH/ C1300
  *LANGUAGE LATIN AND ENGLISH
  *AUTHOR LOMBARD/ PETER AND ROBERT KILWARDBY
  *TYPE OF MANUSCRIPT RELIGIOUS TEXT
  *CONTENTS SENTENCES OF PETER LOMBARD 480/1-5, KILWARDBY
    CONCORDANCE 480/1-5, PETER LOMBARD LECTURING GROUP OF MONN
    480-1, SENTENCES/ BOOK 1/ BEGINNING 480-2, TRINITY/ GNADESTUN
    REPRESENTATION 480-2, SENTENCES/ BOOK 2/ BEGINNING 480-
    CREATION OF EVE 480-3, EVE CREATED 480-3, SENTENCES/ BOOK
    BEGINNING 480-4, NATIVITY OF CHRIST 480-4, CHRIST/ NATIVI
    480-4, SENTENCES/ BOOK 4/ BEGINNING 480-5, GOOD SAMARIT
    480-5, GOD ABOVE BLESSING GOOD SAMARITAN 480-5

*$ABSTRACT 481
  *LIBRARY BOD
  *SLIDE SET TITLE BODLEIAN EXHIBITION
  *NEGATIVE REFERENCE ROLL 212H
  *RENTAL FEE SM 481 $2.35
  *COMMENTS ILLUSTRATIONS FROM ANGLO-SAXON CHRONICLE/ MAGN
    CARTA/ LETTERS
  *TITLE OF MANUSCRIPT ANGLO-SAXON CHRONICLE 481/1-3, MAGNA CAR
    481-4, LETTER FROM GEORGE WASHINGTON 481-5, LETTER FROM NELSO
    481-6, LETTER FROM ARTHUR WELLESLEY/ DUKE OF WELLINGTON 481-
  *SHELFMARK MS LAUD MISC 636 481/1-3, MS CH GLOUCS 481-4,
    MONTAGUE D 18 481/5-6, MS ENG LETT C139 481-7
  *PROVENANCE ENGLISH 481/1-4 AND 6-7, AMERICAN 481-5
  *DATE EXECUTED 12TH/1-3, 13TH 481-4, 18TH 481/5-6, 19TH 481-7
  *AUTHOR WASHINGTON/ GEORGE 481-5, NELSON 481-6, WELLESLEY
    ARTHUR 481-7
  *TYPE OF MANUSCRIPT HISTORICAL DOCUMENTS AND LETTERS
  *CONTENTS HISTORICAL DOCUMENTS AND LETTERS 481/1-7, ANGLO-SAXO
    CHRONICLE/ COPY FROM PETERBOROUGH 481/1-3, MAGNA CARTA/ 12
    REISSUE WITH SEALS 481-4, LETTER FROM GEORGE WASHINGTON
    BIRTHDAY 1788 481-5, LETTER FROM NELSON AT TOULON/ OCTOB
    11/1793 481-6, LETTER FROM ARTHUR WELLESLEY/ MARCH 20/ 182
    481-7

234

*$ABSTRACT 482
  *LIBRARY BOD
  *SLIDE SET TITLE BESTIARY/ ENGLISH
  *NEGATIVE REFERENCE ROLL 217C
  *RENTAL FEE SM 482 $2.50
  *TITLE OF MANUSCRIPT BESTIARY
  *SHELFMARK MS ASHMOLE 1511
  *PROVENANCE ENGLISH/ PETERBOROUGH
  *DATE EXECUTED 13TH/ C1200
  *LANGUAGE LATIN
  *TYPE OF MANUSCRIPT BESTIARY
  *CONTENTS BESTIARY/ ENGLISH 482/1-10, PANTHER FOLLOWED BY OTHER
  ANIMALS ATTACKS DRAGON 482-1, UNICORN KILLED IN VIRGIN'S LAP
  BY HUNTSMEN 482-2, HUNTER/ BLACK WIELDS AX 482-2, HYENA
  DEVOURING CORPSE 482-3, BONNACON SOILS KNIGHT 482-4, MANTICORA
  482-5, VULPIS FEIGNING DEATH TO ATTACK BIRDS 482-6, FOXES LOOK
  ON 482-6, WOLF PREYING ON SHEEP IN FOLD 482-7, GARAMANTES AND
  HIS RESCUE BY FAITHFUL DOGS 482-8, DOGS/ FAITHFULNESS AND
  MURDERER IDENTIFIED 482-9, PELICAN CARING FOR YOUNG/ KILLING
  AND REVIVING 482-10

*$ABSTRACT 483
  *LIBRARY BOD
  *SLIDE SET TITLE BESTIARY/ NETHERLANDS 13TH CENTURY
  *NEGATIVE REFERENCE ROLL 217D
  *RENTAL FEE SM 483 $2.65
  *TITLE OF MANUSCRIPT DE BESTIIS
  *SHELFMARK MS E MUS 136
  *PROVENANCE DUTCH/ LISTED AS ENGLISH IN PACHT AND ALEXANDER
  *DATE EXECUTED 13TH
  *LANGUAGE LATIN
  *TYPE OF MANUSCRIPT BESTIARY
  *CONTENTS BESTIARY 483/1-13, ADAM NAMING ANIMALS 483-1,
  SHEPHERD WITH THREE WETHERS 483-2, PANTHER 483-3, BEAR 483-4,
  UNICORN WITH HEAD IN VIRGIN'S LAP 483-5, UNICORN 483-6, TIGER
  LOOKING AT SELF IN MIRROR 483-7, GRIFFIN EATING MAN'S HEAD
  483-8, ANTELOPE WITH HORNS CAUGHT ON SHRUB 483-9, ELEPHANT AND
  CASTLE 483-10, MANTICORA 483-11, FOX LYING ON BACK WITH BIRDS
  483-12, BONNACON 483-13

*$ABSTRACT 484
  *LIBRARY BOD
  *SLIDE SET TITLE BESTIARY
  *NEGATIVE REFERENCE ROLL 217E
  *RENTAL FEE SM 484 $2.60
  *SHELFMARK MS BODLEY 533
  *PROVENANCE ENGLISH
  *DATE EXECUTED 13TH/ MIDDLE
  *LANGUAGE LATIN
  *TYPE OF MANUSCRIPT BESTIARY
  *CONTENTS BESTIARY 484/1-12, LION WITH EYES OPEN WHILE ASLEEP
  484-1, TIGER 484-2, BONNACON 484-3, MONOCEROS AND BEAR 484-4,
  LEOCROTA/ CROCODRILLUS/ MANTACORA WITH MAN'S HEAD 484-5,
  PARANDRUS AND FOX 484-6, DOGS 484-7, ADAM GIVES NAMES TO
  CAMELS AND STAG 484-8, PARROT/ CALADRIUS ON BED OF SICK MAN
  484-9, PHOENIX 484-10, CINNAMOLGUS/ ERCINEE BIRD WITH
  PHOSPHORECENT FOLIAGE 484-11, HOOPOE AND PELICAN 484-11,
  PEREDIXION AND ANGUIS THE SNAKE 484-12

*$ABSTRACT 485
  *LIBRARY BOD
  *SLIDE SET TITLE BESTIARY
  *NEGATIVE REFERENCE ROLL 217F
  *RENTAL FEE SM 485 $2.70
  *SHELFMARK MS DOUCE 151
  *PROVENANCE ENGLISH

*DATE EXECUTED 14TH/C1300
*LANGUAGE LATIN
*TYPE OF MANUSCRIPT BESTIARY
*CONTENTS BESTIARY 485/1-14, ADAM NAMING BEASTS 485-1, LION/
LIONESS AND CUBS 485-2, LIONS DEVOURING MAN 485-3, COCK 485-3,
TIGER CUB AND TIGERESS LOOKING AT REFLECTION 485-4, GRIFFIN
485-5, ELEPHANT WITH HOWDAH AND WARRIORS 485-5, HYENA EATING
CORPSE BY TOMB 485-6, MONKEY WITH YOUNG ESCAPING FROM WARRIOR
485-7, MANTICORA 485-8, GARAMANTES AND HIS DOGS 485/9-10,
HEDGEHOG 485-11, PELICAN 485-12, OSTRICH 485-13, CALADRIUS
485-14

*$ABSTRACT 486
  *LIBRARY BOD
  *SLIDE SET TITLE BESTIARY/ ENGLISH
  *NEGATIVE REFERENCE ROLL 217G
  *RENTAL FEE SM 486 $2.60
  *SHELFMARK MS UNIVERSITY COLLEGE 120
  *PROVENANCE ENGLISH
  *DATE EXECUTED 14TH/ C1300
  *LANGUAGE LATIN
  *TYPE OF MANUSCRIPT BESTIARY
  *CONTENTS BESTIARY 486/1-12, LION 486-1, TIGER 486-2, PARD AND
  PANTHER 486-3, ANTELOPE AND UNICORN 486-4, MONKEYS/ SATYR/
  STAG 486-5, SATYR 486-5, MANTICORA/ RED WITH TAIL AND WHITE
  CREST 486-6, DOGS AND KING GERAMANTES 486-7, DOGS 486-8,
  PELICANS 486-9, SIRENS 486-10, EAGLES 486-11, PERINDEUS TREE
  486-12

*$ABSTRACT 487
  *LIBRARY BOD
  *SLIDE SET TITLE ANGLO-SAXON ILLUMINATION
  *NEGATIVE REFERENCE ROLL 217H
  *RENTAL FEE SM 487 $2.75
  *COMMENTS A PICTORIAL COMPANION TO BODLEIAN LIBRARY PICTURE
  BOOK SPECIAL SERIES 1, ANGLO-SAXON ILLUMINATION IN OXFORD
  LIBRARIES
  *TITLE OF MANUSCRIPT PASTORAL CARE 487/1-2, HISTORIA
  ECCLESIASTICA 487/3 AND 5-7, ST DUNSTAN'S CLASSBOOK 487-8,
  PENITENTIAL OF ARCHBISHOP EGBERT OF YORK 487-9, HISTORIA
  APOSTOLICA 487-10, DE CONSOLATIONE PHILOSOPHIAE AND SATIRES
  487-11, CAEDMON MANUSCRIPT 487/12-15
  *SHELFMARK MS HATTON 20 487/1-2, MS TANNER 10 487/3 AND 5-7, MS
  BODLEY 579 487-4, MS AUCT F 4 32 487-8, MS BODLEY 718 487-9,
  MS RAWL C 570 487-10, MS AUCT F 1 15 487-11, MS JUNIUS 11
  487/12-15
  *PROVENANCE ENGLISH
  *DATE EXECUTED 09TH/890-897 487/1-2, 10TH 487/3-8, 11TH
  487/9-15
  *LANGUAGE OLD ENGLISH AND LATIN
  *AUTHOR GREGORY THE GREAT 487/1-2, BEDE 487/3 AND 5-7, ST
  DUNSTAN 487-8
  *TYPE OF MANUSCRIPT MISCELLANY OF ANGLO-SAXON MSS
  *CONTENTS ANGLO-SAXON ILLUMINATION 487/1-15, ILLUMINATION/
  ANGLO-SAXON 487/1-15, INITIAL B 487-1, INITIAL A 487-2,
  INITIAL P 487-3, INITIAL E 487-4, INITIAL P 487/5-6, INITIAL O
  487-7, INITIAL I 487-9, INITIAL M 487-10, INITIAL P 487-11,
  ENOCH/ TRANSLATION OF 487-12, TOWER OF BABEL 487-13,
  DISPERSION OF CHILDREN OF MAN 487-13, DESIGN FOR METALWORK/
  EMBROIDERY OR BINDING 487-14, VIKING RINGERRIJKE DESIGN IN
  ANGLO-SAXON MS 487-15

*$ABSTRACT 488
  *LIBRARY BOD
  *SLIDE SET TITLE PEDIGREE OF KINGS OF ENGLAND/ ARMORIAL PATRONS
  OF TEWKESBURY ABBEY

236

*NEGATIVE REFERENCE ROLL 217I
*RENTAL FEE SM 488 $3.25
*SHELFMARK MS LAT MISC B 2 ROLL
*PROVENANCE ENGLISH
*DATE EXECUTED 15TH/ C1435 AND ADDITION C1475-8
*LANGUAGE ENGLISH AND LATIN
*TYPE OF MANUSCRIPT PEDIGREE AND ARMORIAL
*CONTENTS PEDIGREE/ KINGS OF ENGLAND 488/1-16, ARMORIAL/
PATRONS OF TEWKESBURY ABBEY 488/1-16, COATS OF ARMS 488/1-16,
MEDALLION WITH SEATED GOD BLESSING 488-1, ROUNDELS WITH
KINGDOMS OF NATURE 488-1, ADAM AND EVE AND DESCENDANTS OF NOAH
488-1, JABAL/ INVENTOR OF TOOLS 488-1, JUBAL/ FATHER OF MUSIC
488-1, BRUTUS AND TROJAN'S DESCENT FROM NOAH AND JAPETH 488-2,
BRUTUS IN MEDALLION 488-2, BRUTUS'S DESCENT TO CONSTANTINE AND
HELENA 488-3, VIRGIN AND CHILD 488-3, WELSH PRINCES/
CASSIVELLAUNUS AND LUD 488-3, ARTHUR AND WELSH PRINCES/ FAMILY
OF 488-4, WODEN AND ROYAL LINES OF DESCENT 488-5, AUGUSTINE
AND LINE OF ARCHBISHOPS OF CANTERBURY 488-5, ARCHBISHOPS OF
CANTERBURY 488-5, EGBERT IN MEDALLION 488-6, MONARCHS FROM
EGBERT TO EDWARD THE CONFESSOR 488-7, KINGS FROM EDWARD
CONFESSOR TO EDWARD I 488-8, KINGS FROM HENRY III TO HENRY IV
488-9, KINGS EDWARD III TO HENRY IV 488-10, ARMORIAL PEDIGREE/
PATRONS OF TEWKESBURY ABBEY 488-10, ODDO AND DODDO WITH ARMS
OF CROSS OF TEWKESBURY 488-11, ALGAR TO WILLIAM/ EARL OF
GLOUCESTER 488-12, WILLIAM/ EARL OF GLOUCESTER TO GILBERT DE
CLARE 488-13, GILBERT DE CLARE TO THOMAS LE DESPENCER 488-14,
EDWARD LE DESPENCER TO GEORGE/ DUKE OF CLARENCE 488-15,
RICHARD/ DUKE OF GLOUCESTER 488-15, COATS OF ARMS/ KEY TO
THIRTY 488-16

*$ABSTRACT 489
*LIBRARY BOD
*SLIDE SET TITLE SELECTION/ MAINLY VIRGIN MARY
*NEGATIVE REFERENCE ROLL 217J
*RENTAL FEE SM 489 $2.50
*COMMENTS FROM MENOLOGION MADE FOR DEMETRIUS I PALAIOLOGOS
*SHELFMARK MS GR TH F 1
*PROVENANCE GREEK/ THESSALONIKA
*DATE EXECUTED 14TH/ 1ST HALF
*TYPE OF MANUSCRIPT MENOLOGION
*CONTENTS MENOLOGION/ GREEK 489/1-10, VIRGIN MARY AND SOME
SAINTS OF EASTERN CHURCH 489/1-10, SAINTS OF EASTERN CHURCH
489/1-10, ANNUNCIATION/ VIRGIN STANDING AS GABRIEL GREETS HER
489-1, NATIVITY/ SCENES OF MAGI AND WASHING INFANT 489-2,
PRESENTATION OF CHRIST IN TEMPLE 489-3, SS SIMEON AND ANNA
489-3, DORMITION OF VIRGIN 489-4, CHRIST HOLDS MOTHER'S SOUL
489-4, BIRTH OF VIRGIN 489-5, ST ANNE ATTENDED BY FOUR MAIDS
489-5, PRESENTATION OF VIRGIN IN TEMPLE 489-6, SS JOACHIM AND
ANNA AT THE GOLDEN GATE 489-7, SS JUSTINIUS/ NICEPHORUS/
LUCILLIANUS/ METROPHANES 489-8, VIRGIN BEING CLOTHED 489-9, SS
ADRIANUS POEMEN/ MOSES AETHIOP/ PRODROMUS 489-10

*$ABSTRACT 490
*LIBRARY BOD
*SLIDE SET TITLE PRIVATE PRAYER BOOK WRITTEN FOR WLATISLAUS/
KING OF BOHEMIA
*NEGATIVE REFERENCE ROLL 217K
*RENTAL FEE SM 490 $2.70
*COMMENTS PRIVATE PRAYER BOOK OF WLATISLAUS/ PROBABLY CROWN
PRINCE OF POLAND WHO BECAME KING OF BOHEMIA IN 1471 AND OF
HUNGARY IN 1490
*SHELFMARK MS RAWL LITURG D 6
*PROVENANCE POLISH/ CRACOW
*DATE EXECUTED 15TH/ C1470-80
*LANGUAGE LATIN
*TYPE OF MANUSCRIPT PRAYER BOOK
*CONTENTS PRAYER BOOK/ PRIVATE 490/1-14, VIRGIN AND CHILD
ENTHRONED/ KNEELING OWNER 490-1, PATRON KNEELING BEFORE VIRGIN

237

AND CHILD 490-1, GOD SUPPORTING CHRIST ON CROSS 490-2, VIRGIN
KNEELING AND OWNER OF MS 490-2, FIGURE CROWNED WITH SCEPTER
AND SWORD 490-3, ALTAR TABLE WITH TREFOIL-SHAPED DISH 490-3,
VIRGIN AND CHILD ON CRESCENT MOON ADORED BY OWNER 490-4,
INITIAL O 490-5, VIRGIN OF SORROWS WITH HEART PIERCED BY SWORD
490-5, INITIAL D 490-6, ST JOHN THE EVANGELIST 490-6, INITIAL
P 490-7, SS PETER AND PAUL 490-7, INITIAL O 490-8, CHRIST
STANDING IN TOMB DISPLAYS WOUNDS TO OWNER 490-9, CRUCIFIXION
WITH VIRGIN/ ST JOHN AND OWNER 490-9, INITIAL D 490-10, CHRIST
WOUNDED AND CROWNED WITH THORNS 490-10, OWNER/ KNEELING
CATCHES WINE IN CHALICE 490-11, INITIAL O 490-11, ARCHANGELS
MICHAEL/ GABRIEL/ RAPHAEL/ URIEL APPEAR TO OWNER 490-11,
INITIAL O 490-12, ANGEL/ PERHAPS ST MICHAEL AND OWNER 490-12,
ANGELS APPEAR TO OWNER AS HE PRAYS BEFORE ALTAR 490-13,
INITIAL O 493-14, GOD STANDING GIVING ORDERS TO ANGEL AND
OWNER 490-14

*$ABSTRACT 491
 *LIBRARY BOD
 *SLIDE SET TITLE GARDEN OF LOVE
 *NEGATIVE REFERENCE ROLL 218A
 *RENTAL FEE SM 491 $2.70
 *COMMENTS SELECTION FROM 6 FRENCH MSS
 *TITLE OF MANUSCRIPT ROMANCE OF THE ROSE 491/12-13, DECAMERON
 491-14
 *SHELFMARK MS DOUCE 72 491/1-3, MS DOUCE 276 491/4-6, MS LITURG
 60 491-7, MS GOUGH DRAWINGS GAIGNIERES 16 491/8-11, MS DOUCE
 188 491/12-13, MS DOUCE 213 491-14
 *PROVENANCE FRENCH
 *DATE EXECUTED 16TH 491/1-6, 15TH 491/7 AND 12-14, 18TH/C1700
 491/8-11
 *LANGUAGE FRENCH AND LATIN
 *AUTHOR GUILLAUME DE LORRIS AND JEAN DE MEUNG 491/12-13,
 BOCCACCIO 491-14
 *TYPE OF MANUSCRIPT BOOK OF HOURS 491/1-6, PSALTER 491-7,
 ARMORIAL 491/8-11, ROMANCE 491/12-13
 *CONTENTS GARDEN OF LOVE 491/1-14, LOVE/ GARDEN OF 491/1-14,
 APRIL/ TAURUS 491-1, MAN PICKS FLOWERS AND LADY MAKES MAJES
 CHAPLET 491-1, MAY/ HAWKING AND GEMINI 491-2, MAN AND WOMAN
 RIDE IN FOREST 491-2, GEMINI ILLUSTRATED BY LOVERS 491-2,
 ZACARIAS EMBRACES ELIZABETH IN WALLED GARDEN 491-3, GEMINI AS
 TWO LOVERS 491-4, LOVERS WITH FLOWER 491-5, YOUTHS DROP FRUIT
 IN LAP OF WOMAN 491-5, CHANDLERS/ TALLOWER DIPS AND OTHERS
 PREPARE WICKS 491-6, GEMINI/ NAKED COUPLE IN FOREST CLEARING
 491-7, LADIES IN ENCLOSED SUMMER GARDEN WEAVING AND
 EMBROIDERING 491-8, GARDEN/ LADIES WITH TAME SONGBIRDS 491-9,
 OWL TIED BY JESSES TO LOG 491-9, HAWKING PARTY BY STREAM
 491-10, HAWKING PARTY 491-11, CAROLE IN GARDEN 491-12, GOD OF
 LOVE LEADS DANCERS AROUND HILLOCK 491-12, MUSICIANS WITH
 TRUMPETS 491-12, DANCERS/ INCLUDING NUN IN BROWN 491-13,
 GARDEN WITH PEOPLE LISTENING TO POET 491-14, BOCCACCIO SITS
 OUTSIDE GARDEN LISTENING AND WRITING 491-14

*$ABSTRACT 492
 *LIBRARY BOD
 *SLIDE SET TITLE GEOMANTIC TEXTS
 *NEGATIVE REFERENCE ROLL 218B
 *RENTAL FEE SM 492 $3.90
 *COMMENTS 14TH CENTURY COLLECTION OF WRITINGS ON GEOMANCY, A
 QUASI-ASTROLOGICAL FORM OF DIVINATION AND FORTUNE TELLING
 *TITLE OF MANUSCRIPT LIBER FORTUNAE
 *SHELFMARK MS DIGBY 46
 *PROVENANCE ENGLISH
 *DATE EXECUTED 14TH
 *LANGUAGE LATIN
 *AUTHOR BERNARDUS SILVESTER
 *TYPE OF MANUSCRIPT GEOMANTIC TEXTS
 *CONTENTS GEOMANTIC TEXTS 492/1-40, LIBER FORTUNAE 492/1-40,

FORTUNE/ BOOK OF 492/1-40, DIVINATION AND FORTUNE TELLING
TEXTS 492/1-40, COGWHEELS/ EACH WITH POINTING FIGURES 492-1,
BERNARD SILVESTER/ PORTRAIT 492-2, AUTHOR PORTRAIT 492-2,
TREATISE I/ ASSIGNED TO PHYSICIAN OF KING AMALRICUS 492-3,
PROLOGUE/ END TO LIBER EXPERIMENTARIUS 492-4, EUCLID/ PICTURE
WITH SPHERE SQUINTING THROUGH DIOPTRON 492-5, TABLES TO WHICH
GEOMANTIC PATTERN OR QUESTIONS LED 492-6, BERNARD SILVESTER/
PORTRAIT 492-7, PLATO AND SOCRATES 492-8, BOXES/ LETTERED WITH
POSSIBLE QUESTIONS 492-9, TABLES OF SPHERES OF SPICES 492-10,
SPHERES OF FLOWERS 492-11, SPHERES OF FRUITS 492-12, SPHERES
OF BEASTS 492-13, SPHERES OF BIRDS 492-14, SPHERES OF CITIES
492-15, KINGS/ ANSWERS OF 492-15, PYTHAGORAS 492-16, TABLE OF
POSSIBLE QUESTIONS AND BIRD GOVERNING EACH 492-17, BIRDS
ILLUSTRATED 492/18-26, JUDGES/ TWELVE SONS OF JACOB 492/27-28,
JACOB/ SONS 492/27-28, ANAXAGORAS 492-29, CICERO FOLLOWED BY
DIVINATIO CICERONALIS 492-30, JUDGES/ TWENTY 492/31-34,
PLANETS/ SEVEN 492/31-34, DRAGON 492/31-34, ZODIAC/ SIGNS OF
492/31-34, LION AND UNICORN 492-35, DRAGON AND CROCODILE EATEN
BY IOHNEUMON MEN 492-35, SPHERE OF LIFE AND DEATH 492-36,
PLANETARY INFLUENCE TOLD BY TABLES OF NUMBERS 492-37,
GEOMANTIC CIRCLE 492-38, RUBEUS AND PRUELLA 492-38, GEOMANTIC
PATTERNS 492/39-40

*$ABSTRACT 493
    *LIBRARY BOD
    *SLIDE SET TITLE FEASTS OF THE EASTERN CHURCH
    *NEGATIVE REFERENCE ROLL 218C
    *RENTAL FEE SM 493 $2.25
    *COMMENTS ILLUSTRATIONS FROM MENOLOGION MADE FOR DEMETRIUS 1
    PALAIOLOGUS
    *TITLE OF MANUSCRIPT MENOLOGION
    *SHELFMARK MS GR TH F 1
    *PROVENANCE GREEK/ THESSALONIKA
    *DATE EXECUTED 14TH
    *LANGUAGE GREEK
    *TYPE OF MANUSCRIPT MENOLOGION
    *CONTENTS MENOLOGION 493/1-5, FEASTS OF VIRGIN MARY AND
    FESTIVALS OF EASTERN CHURCH 493/1-5, VIRGIN MARY/ FEASTS
    493/1-5, LAMENTATION AT BURIAL OF CHRIST 493-1, ANASTASIS /
    RISEN CHRIST RESCUES ADAM AND EVE FROM HELL 493-2, HARROWING
    OF HELL 493-2, ASCENSION/ CHRIST IN MANDORLA SUPPORTED BY
    ANGELS 493-3, PENTECOST/ CROWNED FIGURE OF KOSMOS 493-4,
    ELEVATION OF CROSS 493-5, SS NICHOLAS/ EUPHEMIA/ SOPHIA 493-5

*$ABSTRACT 494
    *LIBRARY BOD
    *SLIDE SET TITLE MARGUERITE DE NAVARRE
    *NEGATIVE REFERENCE ROLL 218D
    *RENTAL FEE SM 494 $2.55
    *COMMENTS A LATE EXAMPLE OF THE MEDIEVAL DEBAT D'AMOUR, A GENRE
    IN WHICH TWO OR MORE ARGUMENTS ARE PRESENTED FOR JUDGMENT
    BEFORE AN ARBITOR. IN LA COCHE, THREE LADIES ASK MARGUERITE
    TO DECIDE WHICH OF THEM IS THE MOST UNFORTUNATE IN LOVE
    *TITLE OF MANUSCRIPT LA COCHE OU LE DEBAT DE L'AMOUR
    *SHELFMARK MS DOUCE 91
    *PROVENANCE FRENCH
    *DATE EXECUTED 16TH/ 1541
    *LANGUAGE FRENCH
    *AUTHOR MARGUERITE QUEEN OF NAVARRE
    *TYPE OF MANUSCRIPT DEBAT D'AMOUR
    *CONTENTS DEBATE OF LOVE 494/1-11, LITERATURE/ DEBAT D'AMOUR
    494/1-11, FRENCH LITERATURE/ DEBAT D'AMOUR 494/1-11, LA COCHE
    494/1-11, MARGUERITE DE NAVARRE ENCOUNTERS MUSICIANS AND
    PEASANT 494-1, SPRINGLIKE AND BUCOLIC SCENES 494/1-9,
    MARGUERITE INTERRUPTED BY THREE LADIES IN BLACK 494-2,
    MARGUERITE OFFERS TO HEAR SAD TALES 494-3, MARGUERITE'S
    INTEREST CONVINCES LADIES TO TELL STORIES 494-4, LADY LOSES
    LOVE AND FAINTS 494-5, LOVER LEAVES LADY 494-6, LADY LOVED BUT

SHARES FRIENDS' GRIEF 494-7, LADIES ARGUE THEIR CASES 494-8,
LADIES SEEK SHELTER FROM STORM 494-9, MARGUERITE SEEKS JUDGE
OF STORIES 494-10, MARGUERITE LEAVES TO WRITE STORY 494-10,
MARGUERITE PRESENTS BOOK TO DUCHESSE D' ETAMPS 494-11

*$ABSTRACT 495
  *LIBRARY BOD
  *SLIDE SET TITLE HERALDRY FROM DOUCE APOCALYPSE
  *NEGATIVE REFERENCE ROLL 196T
  *RENTAL FEE SM 495 $2.15
  *TITLE OF MANUSCRIPT DOUCE APOCALYPSE
  *SHELFMARK MS DOUCE 180
  *PROVENANCE ENGLISH
  *DATE EXECUTED 13TH/ BEFORE 1272
  *LANGUAGE LATIN AND FRENCH
  *TYPE OF MANUSCRIPT APOCALYPSE WITH COMMENTARY
  *CONTENTS APOCALYPSE/ DOUCE 495/1-7, HERALDRY 495/1-7, INITIAL
  S/ TRINITY BETWEEN KNEELING FIGURES 495-1, COAT OF ARMS OF
  EDWARD AND ELEANOR OF CASTILE 495-1, TRUMPET/ SECOND 495-2,
  SEA WITH SINKING SHIPS 495-2, TRUMPET/ SIXTH 495-3, ARMY OF
  HORSEMEN WITH HERALDIC DEVICES ON LANCES 495-3, LION RAMPANT
  WITH FORKED TAIL ON FIELD OF YELLOW 495-4, COAT OF ARMS OF
  SIMON DE MONTFORT 495-4, ST MICHAEL WITH CROSS-SHIELD
  APPROACHES DRAGON 495-5, DRAGON 495-5, SATAN'S HOST WITH FLAGS
  495-6, FLAGS OF HOST OF SATAN 495-6, FLAG OF GILBERT DE CLARE
  WHO OPPOSED HENRY 111 495-6, SIEGE OF HOLY CITY AND DEFEAT OF
  ENEMY 495-7, SOLDIERS WITH HERALDIC SHIELDS 495-7

*$ABSTRACT 496
  *LIBRARY BOD
  *SLIDE SET TITLE ANTICHRIST
  *NEGATIVE REFERENCE ROLL 218F
  *RENTAL FEE SM 496 $2.20
  *TITLE OF MANUSCRIPT LIVRE DE LA VIGNE NOSTRE SEIGNEUR
  *SHELFMARK MS DOUCE 134
  *PROVENANCE FRENCH
  *DATE EXECUTED 15TH/C1450-70
  *LANGUAGE FRENCH
  *TYPE OF MANUSCRIPT LIFE OF CHRIST
  *CONTENTS LIFE OF CHRIST 496/1-4, ANTICHRIST 496/1-4,
  ANTICHRIST'S TWOFOLD NATURE 496-1, ANTICHRIST ARRIVES AT
  JERUSALEM AS POPE 496-2, CHRISTIANS PERSECUTED BY ANTICHRIST
  496-3, TORTURE SCENES 496-3, DEATH OF ANTICHRIST ON MOUNT OF
  OLIVES 496-4

*$ABSTRACT 497
  *LIBRARY BOD
  *SLIDE SET TITLE LAST JUDGMENT
  *NEGATIVE REFERENCE ROLL 218G
  *RENTAL FEE SM 497 $2.35
  *TITLE OF MANUSCRIPT LIVRE DE LA VIGNE NOSTRE SEIGNEUR
  *SHELFMARK MS DOUCE 134
  *PROVENANCE FRENCH
  *DATE EXECUTED 15TH/C1450-70
  *LANGUAGE FRENCH
  *TYPE OF MANUSCRIPT LIFE OF CHRIST
  *CONTENTS LAST JUDGMENT 497/1-7, BLESSED AND DAMNED 497-1,
  CHRIST APPEARS AT JUDGMENT 497-2, CHRIST JUDGES THE DAMNED
  497-3, ST MICHAEL WITH SCALES FOR WEIGHING DAMNED 497-4,
  CHRIST ACCUSES THE WICKED OF THEIR SINS 497-5, CHRIST AND
  APOSTLES SIT IN JUDGMENT OVER SINNERS 497-6, DEVILS 497-6,
  CHRIST PRONOUNCES SENTENCE OF DAMNATION 497-7

*$ABSTRACT 498
  *LIBRARY BOD
  *SLIDE SET TITLE HEAVEN
  *NEGATIVE REFERENCE ROLL 218H
  *RENTAL FEE SM 498 $2.55
  *TITLE OF MANUSCRIPT LIVRE DE LA VIGNE NOSTRE SEIGNEUR
  *SHELFMARK MS DOUCE 134
  *PROVENANCE FRENCH
  *DATE EXECUTED 15TH/C1450-70
  *LANGUAGE FRENCH
  *TYPE OF MANUSCRIPT LIFE OF CHRIST
  *CONTENTS HEAVEN 498/1-11, MARTYRS AND ANGELS 498-1, SAINTS/
  FIVE MALE 498-2, SAINTS/ FIVE MALE AND FIVE FEMALE 498-3,
  SAINTS/ MALE AND FEMALE 498-4, KING/ BISHOP/ EMPEROR 498-4,
  CHRIST WITH FEMALE SAINTS 498-5, SAINTS/ MALE AND FEMALE
  498-5, SAINTS 498/6-8, PALMS CARRIED BY SAINTS 498-8, HEAVENLY
  COURT ADORING GOD 498-9, MUSICIANS/ ANGELIC PRAISE GOD 498-10,
  HEAVEN AS GREEN WOOD FULL OF ANIMALS 498-11

*$ABSTRACT 499
  *LIBRARY BOD
  *SLIDE SET TITLE HELL
  *NEGATIVE REFERENCE ROLL 218I
  *RENTAL FEE SM 499 $2.80
  *TITLE OF MANUSCRIPT LIVRE DE LA VIGNE NOSTRE SEIGNEUR
  *SHELFMARK MS DOUCE 134
  *PROVENANCE FRENCH
  *DATE EXECUTED 15TH/C1450-70
  *LANGUAGE FRENCH
  *TYPE OF MANUSCRIPT LIFE OF CHRIST
  *CONTENTS HELL 499/1-16, SOULS OF SINNERS BURN IN FURNACE
  499-1, FIRE AND BRIMSTONE 499-2, DAMNED WRITHING IN HELL
  499-3, DAMNED TORMENTED BY BEAST AND SERPENT 499-4, DAMNED
  ENCASED IN ICE 499-5, DEVILS TORTURE THE DAMNED/ POUR METAL
  INTO MOUTHES 499-6, DEVILS/ TWELVE WITH FORKS 499-7, DAMNED/
  CLAWED AND EMBRACED BY DEVILS 499-8, DEVILS BITE AND SCRATCH
  THE DAMNED 499-9, DEVILS ATTACK THE DAMNED WITH WEAPONS
  499-10, DEVILS SCOURGE AND BEAT THE DAMNED 499-11, FIRESTONES
  AND HAIL RAIN ON DAMNED 499-12, DAMNED/ BURNING BODIES 499-13,
  USURERS PUNISHED BY PLUNGING INTO BOILING WELLS 499-14, WATER
  IN WELLS DEPTH OF WICKEDNESS 499-14, THIEVES HUNG OVER FIRES
  499-15, MURDERERS AND TYRANTS ATTACKED BY DEVILS WITH SPEARS
  499-16,

*$ABSTRACT 500
  *LIBRARY BOD
  *SLIDE SET TITLE PROPHECIES OF THE POPE AND ORACLES OF LEO THE
  WISE
  *NEGATIVE REFERENCE ROLL 218J
  *RENTAL FEE SM 500 $3.95
  *TITLE OF MANUSCRIPT PROPHECIES OF THE POPE 500/1-14 AND 19-27,
  ORACLES OF LEO THE WISE 500/15-18 AND 28-39
  *SHELFMARK MS DOUCE 88 500/1-14, MS BAROCCI 170 500/15-18, MS
  LAUD MISC 588 500/19-21, MS ITAL C 73 500/22-27, ASHMOLE/
  PRINTED 1597 500/28-31
  *PROVENANCE ENGLISH 500/1-14, ITALIAN 500/15-39
  *DATE EXECUTED 14TH 500/1-14, 16TH 500/ 15-21 AND 28-31, 17TH
  500/ 22-27 AND 32-39
  *LANGUAGE LATIN 500/1-14 AND 19-39, GREEK WITH LATIN
  TRANSLATION 500/15-18
  *TYPE OF MANUSCRIPT PROPHECIES
  *CONTENTS PROPHECIES OF THE POPES 500/1-39, ORACLES OF LEO THE
  WISE 500/1-39, POPE NICHOLAS III AND BEAR WITH CUBS 500-1,
  POPE MARTIN IV 500-2, SERPENT WITH DOG'S FACE PECKED BY CROWS
  500-2, POPE HONORIUS IV 500-3, UNICORN WITH CROSS AND EAGLE
  500-3, POPE NICHOLAS IV WITH SICKLE AND KNEELING ANGEL 500-4,
  POPE CELESTINE V 500-5, COW 500-5, POPE BONIFACE VIII 500-6,
  CITY REPRESENTED AS GABLED BUILDING 500-7, POPE BENEDICT XI

241

500-7, BEAR SUCKLING CUBS 500-6, PROPHETIC FIGURES/ POPE AND FOX WITH STANDARDS 500-8, THRONE/ EMPTY WITH HAND BELOW 500-9, HERMIT ON TOMB SUMMONED TO BE POPE 500-10, POPE SUMMONED FROM DEAD BY ANGEL 500-11, BIRD OF DEATH FLIES AWAY 500-11, POPE MITRED BY ANGEL 500-12, POPE FLANKED BY TWO ANGELS 500-13, POPE HOLDING MITRE 500-14, BEAR SUCKLING CUBS 500-15, SERPENT/ BETWEEN HOVERING COWS 500-16, UNICORN AND EAGLE WITH CROSS 500-17, RULER WITH SICKLE AND ROSE 500-18, POPE SIXTUS V MITRED BY ANGELS 500-19, ANIMAL WITH HUMAN FACE AND SUPPORTING ANGELS 500-19, PROPHECIES OF POPES 500-20, POPE CROWNED BY ANGELS 500-20, POPE/ ANGELIC 500-20, WHEEL/ PROPHETIC WITH SEQUENCE OF POPES 500-21, POPES SIXTUS IV TO CLEMENT V REPRESENTED BY EMBLEMS 500-21, POPE SIXTUS IV 500-22, BEARS 500-22, EMPEROR AND MONK'S BUSTS 500-23, POPE AND COW 500-24, CROWNED HEADS 533-24, POPE HOLDS MITRE OVER FLOCK OF SHEEP 500-25, POPE HOLDS MITRE OVER BEARDED/ HORNED ANIMAL 500-26, PROPHETIC TREE REPRESENTING POPES 500-27, POPES NAMED PAUL III TO GREGORY XIV 500-27, EMPEROR HOLDING SICKLE AND ROSE CROWNED BY ANGEL 500-28, HERMIT ON TOMB SUMMONED TO BECOME EMPEROR 500-29, SUN AND MOON ABOVE 500-29, ANGEL OFFERS THE CROWN 500-30, EMPEROR AND PATRIARCH 500-31, EMPEROR WITH SICKLE AND ROSE CROWNED BY ANGEL 500-32, COW/ BULL AND TWO HEADS 500-33, HEAD BELOW WALLED CITY 500-34, FOX WITH THREE STANDARDS 500-35, THRONE/EMPTY AND HAND 500-36, UNICORN WITH CRESCENT 500-37, HERMIT ON TOMB SUMMONED TO BECOME EMPEROR 500-38, SUN AND MOON ABOVE 500-38, ANGEL HOLDS CROWN OVER DEAD EMPEROR 500-39, BIRD OF DEATH FLIES AWAY 500-39, DOGS BELOW 500-39

a

b

c

d

Plate III

(SLIDE SET TITLE)

251

a

b

c

d

Plate IV

```
(NEGATIVE REFERENCE)
    FILMSTRIPS SERIES 11 NO 15 JACOB/S LADDER..............460.
    ROLL 79.................................................1.
    ROLL 89.................................................2.
    ROLL 93...............................................254.
    ROLL 108................................................9.
    ROLL 115...............................................10.
    ROLL 116...............................................11.
    ROLL 117...............................................12.
    ROLL 120...............................................16.
    ROLL 123..............................................256.
    ROLL 126...............................................18.
    ROLL 129...............................................19.
    ROLL 132...............................................22.
    ROLL 137...............................................27.
    ROLL 142...............................................33.
    ROLL 144...............................................34.
    ROLL 155...............................................47.
    ROLL 160...............................................54.
    ROLL 161..............................................265.
    ROLL 178..............................................145.
    ROLL 181 I 1..........................................150.
    ROLL 183..............................................155.
    ROLL 198 F AND G AND H................................478.
    ROLL 209..............................................239.
    ROLL 101A...............................................3.
    ROLL 101B...............................................4.
    ROLL 101C...............................................5.
    ROLL 101D...............................................6.
    ROLL 102A.............................................247.
    ROLL 103A...............................................7.
    ROLL 103B...............................................8.
    ROLL 119A..............................................13.
    ROLL 119B..............................................14.
    ROLL 119C..............................................15.
    ROLL 121A.............................................255.
    ROLL 121B..............................................17.
    ROLL 130A.............................................244.
    ROLL 130B.............................................459.
    ROLL 130C..............................................20.
    ROLL 131A..............................................21.
    ROLL 131B.............................................253.
    ROLL 135A..............................................23.
    ROLL 135B..............................................24.
    ROLL 136A..............................................25.
    ROLL 136C..............................................26.
    ROLL 138A.............................................248.
    ROLL 138B..............................................28.
    ROLL 139A..............................................29.
    ROLL 139B..............................................30.
    ROLL 139C.............................................461.
    ROLL 139D.............................................257.
    ROLL 140A..............................................31.
    ROLL 140B.............................................258.
    ROLL 140C.............................................259.
```

252

253

EGATIVE REFERENCE)

a

b

c

d

Plate V

264

266

a

estoient et chauer de
he et iolant de la uie
neut que dieu li auo
donnee.

roi leodagan ⁊ auce
iusques a tant que i
des plaies ⁊ des bleceu
uoir receues en la ba

b

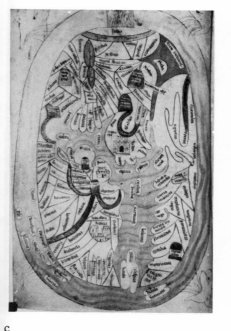

c

d

Plate VI

(SHELFMARK)
```
MS AUCT D 2 2 66-1.....................................66.
MS AUCT D 2 2 68-7.....................................68.
MS AUCT D 2 4 32-11....................................32.
MS AUCT D 2 6 296/14 AND 20 AND 26....................296.
MS AUCT D 2 6 3-12......................................3.
MS AUCT D 2 6 344/1-20................................344.
MS AUCT D 2 6 42/15-19.................................42.
MS AUCT D 2 6 49/1-10..................................49.
MS AUCT D 2 6 5/17-18...................................5.
MS AUCT D 2 6 63-21....................................63.
MS AUCT D 2 6 65-1.....................................65.
MS AUCT D 2 8 427-7...................................427.
MS AUCT D 2 8 5-15......................................5.
MS AUCT D 2 15 234/10-12..............................234.
MS AUCT D 2 15 5-16.....................................5.
MS AUCT D 2 16.........................................16.
MS AUCT D 2 19.........................................87.
MS AUCT D 2 19 23/1-7..................................23.
MS AUCT D 2 19 79/29-44................................79.
MS AUCT D 3 2 296-1...................................296.
MS AUCT D 3 2 4/12-14...................................4.
MS AUCT D 3 2 4-19......................................4.
MS AUCT D 3 2 4-41......................................4.
MS AUCT D 3 2 65-3.....................................65.
MS AUCT D 3 4 4-15......................................4.
MS AUCT D 3 4 59-42....................................59.
MS AUCT D 3 5........................................283.
MS AUCT D 3 5 59-43....................................59.
MS AUCT D 4 2.....................................225,416.
MS AUCT D 4 2 26/5-6...................................26.
MS AUCT D 4 3 63-20....................................63.
MS AUCT D 4 3 65-2.....................................65.
MS AUCT D 4 4.........................................30.
MS AUCT D 4 4 194-11..................................194.
MS AUCT D 4 4 200-10..................................200.
MS AUCT D 4 4 3-13......................................3.
MS AUCT D 4 4 4/31-32...................................4.
MS AUCT D 4 4 434/7-9.................................434.
MS AUCT D 4 4 478-2...................................478.
MS AUCT D 4 4 53-17....................................53.
MS AUCT D 4 4 73-8.....................................73.
MS AUCT D 4 8 113-1...................................113.
MS AUCT D 4 8 177-3...................................177.
MS AUCT D 4 8 213-3...................................213.
MS AUCT D 4 8 4/16-17...................................4.
MS AUCT D 4 8 441/2-5.................................441.
MS AUCT D 4 8 59-44....................................59.
MS AUCT D 4 14 438-3..................................438.
MS AUCT D 4 14 467/17-23..............................467.
MS AUCT D 4 17 170-22.................................170.
MS AUCT D 4 17 266-67.................................266.
MS AUCT D 4 17 4-5......................................4.
MS AUCT D 4 17 69-2....................................69.
MS AUCT D 4 17 70-4....................................70.
```

281

282

283

288

289

297

303

305

306

307

311

313

a

b

c

d

Plate VII

319

324

325

a

b

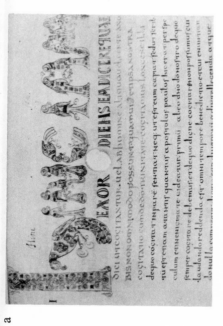

c

d

Plate VIII

331

332

333

334

335

341

a

b

c

d

Plate IX

345

a

b

c

d

Plate X

a

b

c

d

Plate XI

349

352

354

355

a

b

c

d

Plate XII

357

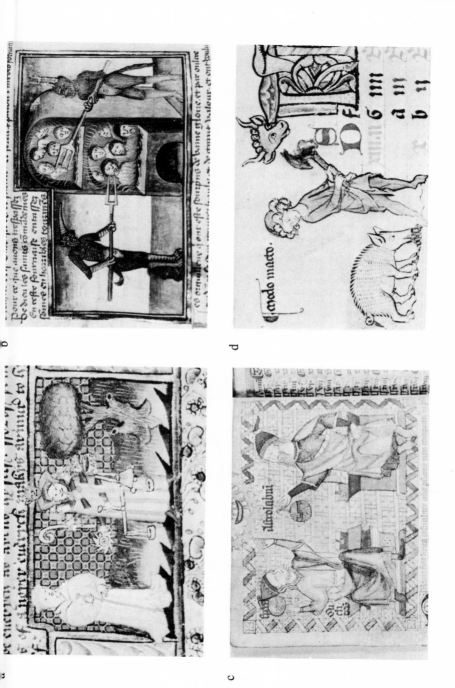

Plate XIII

(CONTENTS)

369

(CONTENTS)

(CONTENTS)

371

(CONTENTS)

373

(CONTENTS)

(CONTENTS)

375

(CONTENTS)

377

(CONTENTS)

378

(CONTENTS)

379

(CONTENTS)

380

(CONTENTS)

(CONTENTS)

(CONTENTS)

383

(CONTENTS)

(CONTENTS)

(CONTENTS)

(CONTENTS)

(CONTENTS)

(CONTENTS)

391

(CONTENTS)

393

(CONTENTS)

395

(CONTENTS)

(CONTENTS)

397

399

(CONTENTS)

(CONTENTS)

(CONTENTS)

402

(CONTENTS)

(CONTENTS)

(CONTENTS)

(CONTENTS)

(CONTENTS)

408

(CONTENTS)

411

(CONTENTS)

412

(CONTENTS)

(CONTENTS)

415

(CONTENTS)

(CONTENTS)

417

(CONTENTS)

(CONTENTS)

(CONTENTS)

(CONTENTS)

(CONTENTS)

423

(CONTENTS)

(CONTENTS)

(CONTENTS)

426

(CONTENTS)

427

(CONTENTS)

429

(CONTENTS)

(CONTENTS)

431

(CONTENTS)

432

(CONTENTS)

(CONTENTS)

(CONTENTS)

435

(CONTENTS)

(CONTENTS)

(CONTENTS)

(CONTENTS)

(CONTENTS)

441

(CONTENTS)

442

(CONTENTS)

443

(CONTENTS)

445

446

(CONTENTS)

447

(CONTENTS)

448

(CONTENTS)

449

(CONTENTS)

451

(CONTENTS)

(CONTENTS)

453

(CONTENTS)

455

(CONTENTS)

(CONTENTS)

457

458

(CONTENTS)

459

(CONTENTS)

(CONTENTS)

(CONTENTS)

(CONTENTS)

(CONTENTS)

471

(CONTENTS)

(CONTENTS)

(CONTENTS)

476

(CONTENTS)

478

(CONTENTS)

(CONTENTS)

(CONTENTS)

481

(CONTENTS)

(CONTENTS)

483

(CONTENTS)

484

(CONTENTS)

(CONTENTS)

(CONTENTS)

487

(CONTENTS)

(CONTENTS)

(CONTENTS)

490

(CONTENTS)

(CONTENTS)

(CONTENTS)

(CONTENTS)

496

(CONTENTS)

(CONTENTS)

502

(CONTENTS)

(CONTENTS)

(CONTENTS)

505

(CONTENTS)

506

(CONTENTS)

(CONTENTS)

(CONTENTS)

511

(CONTENTS)

513

(CONTENTS)

514

(CONTENTS)

515

(CONTENTS)

(CONTENTS)

518

(CONTENTS)

520

(CONTENTS)

(CONTENTS)

(CONTENTS)

CONTENTS)

(CONTENTS)

(CONTENTS)

527

(CONTENTS)

528

(CONTENTS)
529

(CONTENTS)

(CONTENTS)

(CONTENTS)

(CONTENTS)

(CONTENTS)

(CONTENTS)

(CONTENTS)

(CONTENTS)

541

(CONTENTS)

(CONTENTS)

(CONTENTS)

(CONTENTS)

(CONTENTS)

(CONTENTS)

551

(CONTENTS)

554

555

(CONTENTS)

CONTENTS)

557

(CONTENTS)

CONTENTS)

(CONTENTS)

565

(CONTENTS)

566

(CONTENTS)

(CONTENTS)

(CONTENTS)

(CONTENTS)

574

(CONTENTS)

575

(CONTENTS)

577

(CONTENTS)

(CONTENTS)

(CONTENTS)

(CONTENTS)

582

583

(CONTENTS)

(CONTENTS)

(CONTENTS)

(CONTENTS)

(CONTENTS)

(CONTENTS)

(CONTENTS)

592

(CONTENTS)

(CONTENTS)

(CONTENTS)

595

(CONTENTS)

(CONTENTS)

597

(CONTENTS)

(CONTENTS)

(CONTENTS)

600

(CONTENTS)

601

(CONTENTS)

(CONTENTS)

(CONTENTS)

604

(CONTENTS)

605

(CONTENTS)

607

(CONTENTS)

(CONTENTS)

(CONTENTS)

610

(CONTENTS)

612

(CONTENTS)

613

(CONTENTS)

(CONTENTS)

(CONTENTS)

(CONTENTS)

617

(CONTENTS)

(CONTENTS)

619

(CONTENTS)

(CONTENTS)

624

(CONTENTS)

628

(CONTENTS)

630

(CONTENTS)

(CONTENTS)

(CONTENTS)

634

(CONTENTS)

(CONTENTS)

636

(CONTENTS)

637

638

639

641

(CONTENTS)

(CONTENTS)

(CONTENTS)

(CONTENTS)

(CONTENTS)